THE
MIDDLE EAST
AND THE
UNITED STATES

UPDATED 2013 EDITION

Fifth Edition

THE
MIDDLE EAST
AND THE
UNITED STATES

History, Politics, and Ideologies

edited by

David W. Lesch
Trinity University

Mark L. Haas
Duquesne University

WESTVIEW
PRESS

A MEMBER OF THE PERSEUS BOOKS GROUP

Westview Press was founded in 1975 in Boulder, Colorado, by notable publisher and intellectual Fred Praeger. Westview Press continues to publish scholarly titles and high-quality undergraduate- and graduate-level textbooks in core social science disciplines. With books developed, written, and edited with the needs of serious nonfiction readers, professors, and students in mind, Westview Press honors its long history of publishing books that matter.

Westview Press books are available at special discounts for bulk purchases in the United States by corporations, institutions, and other organizations. For more information, please contact the Special Markets Department at the Perseus Books Group, 2300 Chestnut Street, Suite 200, Philadelphia, PA 19103, or call (800) 810-4145, ext. 5000, or e-mail special.markets@perseusbooks.com.

The Library of Congress has cataloged the fifth edition as follows:

Library of Congress Cataloging-in-Publication Data
The Middle East and the United States : history, politics, and ideologies / edited by David W. Lesch, Mark L. Haas. — 5th ed.
    xiii, 540 p. : map ; 23 cm.
    Includes bibliographical references and index.
    ISBN 978-0-8133-4529-1 (pbk.) — ISBN 978-0-8133-4530-7 (e-book) 1. Middle East—Foreign relations—United States. 2.United States—Foreign relations—Middle East.

DS63.2.U5 M43 2012
327.56073

                                                                                            2011924776
PB ISBN: 978-0-8133-4914-5 (fifth edition, updated)
E-book ISBN: 978-0-8133-4915-2 (fifth edition, updated)
ISBN: 978-0-8133-5021-9 (economy edition)

TO OUR CHILDREN,

Katie, Abby, and Will (MLH)
and Michael (DWL).

MAY THEY KNOW A WORLD AT PEACE.

CONTENTS

PART TWO

Arab-Israeli War and Peace

PART THREE

Allies and Enemies in the Gulf and Beyond

PREFACE TO THE FIFTH EDITION

As typically occurs between editions of this volume, a lot happens in the Middle East—and for this edition in the United States as well—that has significantly affected the US–Middle Eastern dynamic and thus warrants the publication of a new edition. The last edition, the fourth, was published in 2007; therefore, with the lead time necessary for the publication process, the contributors to that edition could only comment on and analyze events that occurred through the first half of 2006. A slew of important events have occurred in the interim, such as the summer 2006 Hizbollah-Israeli war in Lebanon, the 2007 Annapolis meeting convened by the George W. Bush administration aimed at jump-starting Arab-Israeli peace negotiations, the heightening of tensions between Iran and the United States over Iran's nuclear program, the US military surges in both Iraq and Afghanistan, the rise to power of a far-right-wing government in Israel in early 2009, the election of President Barack Obama in the United States, and in 2011 the ouster due to popular pressure of presidents Zine al-Abidine Ben Ali and Hosni Mubarak of Tunisia and Egypt, respectively (which took place as the book was going to print). In addition, the distance in time from the seminal events early in the last decade, 9/11 and its aftermath, including the US-led invasion of Afghanistan in 2001 and Iraq in 2003, has afforded contributors more perspective and historical context.

One notable change in content from earlier additions is the de-emphasis on the 1990–1991 Gulf crisis and war, when a US-led United Nations coalition gathered and then expelled Iraq from Kuwait after the former had invaded and taken over the latter in August 1990. The first edition of this volume was in large measure a response to the new circumstances for the United States in the Middle East following the Gulf War. However, with so much history occurring since that time, it has been determined to significantly reduce the previous focus on the 1990–1991 Gulf crisis and war and concentrate more on various important aspects of US–Middle Eastern relations that have appeared in the last decade. Unfortunately, constraints on space compelled us to remove some excellent chapters. For instance, Amatzia Baram's chapter on the influence of US actions on Iraqi decision making prior to Iraq's invasion of Kuwait in 1990, which appeared in each of the first four editions, continues to be considered a seminal work on the subject. With much less emphasis on this war in the current edition, we were unable to include it; however, we strongly encourage the reader who is interested in this subject to read Amatzia's chapter in a previous edition. This is but one example of worthy chapters having been elided due to this reorganization process.

In terms of the shape of this fifth edition, perhaps the most important change from previous editions is the fact that there is now a coeditor—Dr. Mark Haas, a professor at Duquesne University. He has contributed an excellent chapter to this edition, and, with his training in international relations, he has provided a fresh new perspective, resulting in the reorganization of this fifth edition, as well as new content. Even the title of the volume, which was the same in the first four editions, has been tweaked for this edition to better reflect the changes. He is a most welcome addition.

Mark thanks his wife, Margaret, and his three children, Katie, Abby, and Will, and David thanks his wife, Judy, and his son, Michael, for all their love and support. Their presence is a constant reminder of what is most important, and for that we are eternally grateful.

NOTE ON THE TEXT

One of the challenges of compiling an edited volume written by different individuals is ensuring stylistic consistency among chapters. In particular, many authors have used their own system of transliteration. We generally retained each author's style except for names and terms that appear throughout the text. In these cases, we selected one variation of spelling, which is often the more recognizable version rather than a strict transliteration: for example, "Hussein" rather than "Husayn" or "Hussain"; "Faisal" rather than "Faysal" or "Feisal"; "Nasser" rather than "Nasir"; and "Mussadiq" rather than "Mossadeq," "Mossadegh," or "Musaddiq." Many of the chapters include a diacritic mark (') for the important Arabic consonant 'ayn; however, we have eliminated the diacritic mark for the Arabic hamza (ˀ). One hopes few exceptions have slipped through.

The war in the Middle East in 1990–1991 is generally known in the United States as the Persian Gulf crisis and Persian Gulf War, a conflict that was precipitated by the surprise Iraqi invasion of Kuwait. In the Gulf itself, this event is generally referred to as the Second Gulf War (the first being the Iran-Iraq war of 1980–1988), the Kuwaiti crisis, the War to Liberate Kuwait, the Iraqi crisis, or simply the Gulf crisis and war, the latter being employed by most contributors in this book. Some references to other conflicts have also been standardized. For instance, two major conflicts involving Israel are generally referred to as the 1967 Arab-Israeli war and the 1973 Arab-Israeli war; however, the first is also known as the June War or Six Day War, the second as the October War, the Yom Kippur War, or the Ramadan War. In certain instances, individual contributors employ these terms.

Since the international community, including the United States, still recognizes Tel Aviv as the official capital of Israel, some of the contributors use Tel Aviv rather than Jerusalem in some references to Israeli policy even though the seat of government in Israel is clearly located in Jerusalem. Generally, we let the authors decide.

D.W.L. AND M.L.H.

xiii

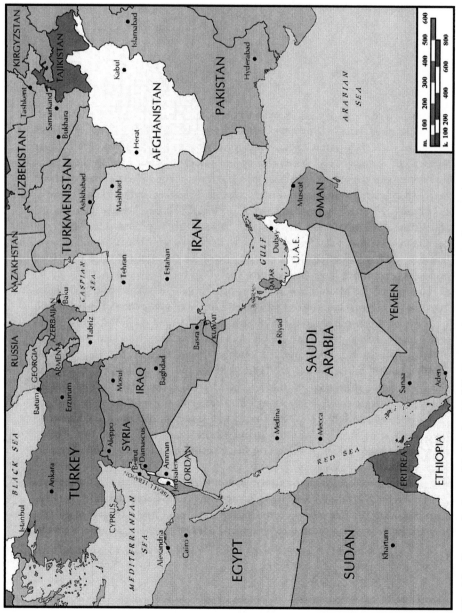

The Map Project by Justin McCarthy, Middle East Studies Association of North America, Inc. 2003

INTRODUCTION

David W. Lesch and Mark L. Haas

US involvement in the Middle East has spanned the breadth of this country's existence, beginning most dramatically with the administration of President Thomas Jefferson, which tried to stop pirating by the North African (or Barbary) provinces of the Ottoman Empire in the early 1800s. This was a war to ensure freedom of navigation on the high seas, which was essential for US trade, as the new republic no longer enjoyed the benefits of British naval protection. Aside from this early encounter, US interaction with and interest in the Middle East during the nineteenth century was limited to the private activities of missionaries and merchants. In the following century, however, World War I propelled the United States onto the world stage—and into European politics—in a role it had neither sought nor experienced before. As the war was winding down, the United States quickly developed an interest in the disposition of the Middle East provinces of the defeated Ottoman Empire. The result was the first significant official foray by Washington into the region in the twentieth century: the King-Crane Commission was sent to Syria, Palestine, Lebanon, and Anatolia to inform American policy on the future of the region. Nonetheless, no US administration gave the region a high priority during the interwar years (1918–1939), although there was some interest in the growing involvement of multinational oil companies in the Middle East.

The strategic value of the region became clear in World War II, when, in 1942 and 1943, Anglo-American forces attacked and defeated German-Italian forces in the North African campaign. Soon the realization that the reconstruction of Europe and Japan—as well as the postwar economic boom in the United States—would become more and more dependent on Middle East oil (which makes up more than two-thirds of the world's known reserves) boosted the policy significance of the region in the eyes of Washington's policymakers. Moreover, the strategic value of the Middle East became linked to the emerging cold war between the United States and the Soviet Union. Washington dutifully grasped a global foreign policy and came to believe that it was the only nation that could successfully prevent Moscow from extending its influence in the region in the wake of the weakened British and French imperial positions. As a result, the Middle East became a policy priority for post–World War II administrations. The emergence of the state of Israel in 1948 reinforced US interest in the Middle East, but this event also complicated Washington's relations with and objectives toward the Arab world, as Arabs increasingly perceived US and Israeli interests as being one and the same. Complication and complexity came to define the US–Middle East relationship during the forty or so years of the cold war, intertwined as it was with the decolonization process, Arab nationalism and state building, the Arab-Israeli conflict, the "Arab cold war," the growing strength of OPEC (the Organization of Petroleum Exporting Countries), and Islamist movements. The end of the US-Soviet cold war in 1989 resolved some tensions and mitigated others in the Middle East. However, the regional environment produced by the termination of the cold war was soon altered by the 1990–1991 Gulf War, which created new tensions and problems.

The Madrid peace process, which was launched after the Gulf War in 1991, and the Israeli-Palestinian Oslo Accords, which followed in 1993, engendered a great deal of hope that a comprehensive Arab-Israeli peace could be achieved. The process proceeded in fits and starts but made significant progress; the 1994 Israeli-Jordanian peace treaty, the Israeli-Syrian negotiations, and the regional multilateral talks that for a time paralleled the Madrid process nurtured hopes for peace. Unfortunately, the overall goals set forth in the 1990s were not achieved, and the Oslo and Madrid peace processes came to an end with the eruption of the al-Aqsa intifada in 2000 that followed the failed last-gasp attempt by the Bill Clinton administration to settle the Israeli-Palestinian final status issues.

In the wake of the failure to conclude the Madrid and Oslo processes, combined with continued economic problems in the Muslim world amid the general prosperity of Americanized globalization, a virulently anti-American form of Islamism arose that increasingly found violent expression through such groups as Osama bin Laden's al-Qa'ida, the culmination of which led to the tragedy of September 11, 2001. The United States, under the leadership of President George W. Bush, reacted to 9/11 in a dramatic manner. The distance traveled from the secure, if not invincible, feeling Americans enjoyed prior to 9/11 to the sense of vulnerability in the aftermath of the attacks was enormous. It was this feeling that in large measure produced a consensus in the United States in support of President Bush's more assertive foreign policy. This became manifest in the US-led invasion of Afghanistan in October 2001 that successfully evicted the ruling Taliban regime by the end of the year. It became even more apparent in the enunciation of the administration's national security strategy in September 2002, otherwise known as the Bush Doctrine, which, among other things, advocated the application of preventive war through preemptive action in order to deal with rising threats before they could injure the United States and its interests. In March 2003, the Bush Doctrine became the rationale for the US-led invasion of Iraq, which toppled the regime of Saddam Hussein. The Iraq war also became a centerpiece of the Bush administration's strategy of spreading democracy—including by force—as a key means of reducing security threats to the United States. Amid the global war on terror spearheaded by the Bush administration after 9/11, the United States became caught in a quagmire in Iraq generated by a lethal insurgency composed of Iraqi elements and a small number of foreign jihadists. Although violence and political stalemate continue in Iraq today, the situation is improved from the darkest days in the mid-2000s, when the state appeared to be on the verge of full-fledged civil war and possibly partition.

The Barack Obama administration has reversed course on many of the hallmark policies of its predecessor—renouncing both preventive war to deal with emerging threats and the use of force to spread democracy and increasing the role of diplomacy over force in dealing with enemy states. Although the Obama administration's stated intentions are to engage actively in Middle Eastern politics, these efforts will take place within the context of high political partisanship and dissent, as well as tight budgetary constraints as the United States confronts the effects of recession, high national debt, and looming massive costs associated with its aging population. As the 2011 political upheavals in Tunisia and Egypt demonstrate, however, constraints from the American side will by no means stop Middle Eastern politics from changing, sometimes in dramatic and unpredicted ways.

As many questions surround US foreign policy in the Middle East now as in the immediate aftermath of 9/11. What are the root sources of various Middle Eastern groups' enmity toward America? How can the United States repair its sullied image in the region? Should the United States push for the empowerment of liberalizing parties and leaders as a means of alleviating security threats? If so, by what means? Relatedly, does the ouster of authoritarian rulers due to large-scale popular protests—as was the case in 2011 for presidents Zine al-Abidine Ben Ali in Tunisia and Hosni Mubarak in Egypt—threaten more than bolster US interests by potentially empowering Islamist parties, making terrorist attacks easier to carry out, and undermining other authoritarian allies of the United States? Or are the gains created by the spread of more liberal regimes so significant that they will likely offset these and other potential security costs? Should America's leaders consider waging another preventive war as Iran moves closer to developing nuclear weapons? Can Arab/Palestinian-Israeli negotiations be successfully concluded as traditional security, terrorist, and demographic challenges in the region increase? In answering these questions, it is clear that the Middle East continues to be a region where old and new problems meet, where history and politics meld together, where power and ideology interact for both good and ill, and where conflict and hope for peace exist side by side.

This volume endeavors to cover these issues. Part 1, "From Idealism to Realism: Wilsonian Intent to Cold War Practice," begins with an examination of the King-Crane Commission, which emanated from the idealistic intentions of President Woodrow Wilson's Fourteen Points enunciated near the end of World War I—particularly that of self-determination for subject peoples—and was ostensibly created to assess the wishes of the native population in Syria regarding postwar independence. The commission did not quite fit the reality of European politics or, for that matter, American politics, and as James Gelvin points out in Chapter 1, it was not as idealistic as it seemed, since it simply reflected and transferred democratic elitism. After examining the King-Crane Commission from the Syrian perspective, Gelvin concludes that the commission actually established a pattern for subsequent US encounters with nationalism and state building in the Middle East that had unforeseen and often deleterious results for both the United States and the region.

The incipient nature of US policy in the Middle East evident in the immediate post–World War I period became more pronounced following what has been called the great divide of World War II, which awakened policymakers to the necessity of a more active and goal-oriented foreign policy commensurate with the onset of the cold war and related regional issues.[1] Yet there was a strong desire rooted in the American heritage to portray the United States as anything but a second-generation imperialist trying to trade places with the Europeans. This schizophrenia made itself apparent in US development diplomacy toward the Third World in the immediate post–World War II period and was evident in President Harry S Truman's Point Four program, which was intended to be something like a Marshall Plan for the Third World. The inherent difficulties of this policy framework in light of the new global and regional realities in the Middle East were exemplified by the short but dramatic mission of Truman's special assistant to the Middle East, Edwin Locke Jr., whose story is examined by Paul Kingston in Chapter 2.

The manifest great divide in the Middle East, where a cold war–based, realpolitik foreign policy supplanted any pretense of a developmentally based one, can arguably be seen in the Muhammad Mussadiq crisis of 1953, when covert efforts primarily engineered by the United States succeeded in overthrowing the popularly elected Iranian prime minister. At the time, Washington and London thought Mussadiq would tilt Iran toward the Soviet Union, which was viewed as an unacceptable strategic setback that could lead to a potentially disastrous superpower confrontation. The Mussadiq crisis reveals how the United States began almost instinctively to follow in the footsteps of British imperialism, demonstrating a preference for the status quo rather than the forces of change. This episode and surrounding events are examined by Mark Gasiorowski, who details—and is critical of—US policy in the matter (Chapter 3) and by Sir Sam Falle, who provides the on-the-ground viewpoint (Chapter 4). Falle was a high-level official in the British embassy in Tehran at the time of the crisis and maintains that US and British actions were correct—not only then but also in retrospect.

The perceived success of the Iranian coup reinforced the Dwight D. Eisenhower administration's emphasis on a more interventionist policy, which was characterized by covert activities designed to fight the Soviets in the cold war in the Third World through tactics short of nuclear confrontation. The Mussadiq crisis seemed to be repeated in various ways in the Middle East throughout the remainder of the decade, some with perceived equally positive results, some with more negative results.

Peter Hahn (Chapter 5) offers a description of this transitional stage in US diplomacy toward the Middle East as strategic necessities of the cold war became the paramount consideration by studying Washington's relationship with Egypt from the last stage of the King Farouk regime to the early Nasserist period ending with the Suez crisis in 1956. Elie Podeh (Chapter 6) further covers US strategic policy in the Middle East by focusing on the creation of a regional pro-West defense pact, specifically the seminal 1955 Baghdad Pact, the role of the United States in its formation, and the repercussions of its consummation. David Lesch (Chapter 7) examines the Syrian crisis of 1957 and the associated complex political environment of the Middle East in the 1950s, when the international cold war in the region was at its height and was superimposed on the Arab-Israeli conflict, Arab state building, and the emerging Arab cold war.

In Chapter 8, Malik Mufti discusses the relationship of the United States with pan-Arabism, specifically that proffered by Egyptian President Gamal 'Abd al-Nasser versus that espoused by the Ba'thists in Iraq and Syria following the 1956 Suez crisis and bridging the Arab cold war to the seminal 1967 Arab-Israeli war. Mufti concludes that US policies under Eisenhower and his secretary of state, John Foster Dulles, as well as those under the John F. Kennedy and Lyndon B. Johnson administrations, which have been "roundly criticized" in the past (as in this volume), have been to a large extent misinterpreted and were actually much more prescient and successful than is popularly perceived, especially as the United States began to see Arab nationalism as an antidote to communism. As others have observed, however, the objectives may have been achieved despite US policy, especially as the dynamics of Malcolm Kerr's "Arab cold war" tended to define the political and diplomatic parameters in the Middle East during this period.[2]

The section concludes with two chapters that examine Middle Eastern politics largely through the lens of the cold war rivalry between the United States and the Soviet Union. In Chapter 9, Georgiy Mirsky, writing from scholarly examination and personal experience, discusses the motivations, ideological commitment, and interests of Soviet policy toward the Middle East during the cold war era and the transformation of this policy in the post–cold war world. Noting that the Kremlin historically preferred to undermine the West through support of national liberation movements (many of which were thoroughly un-Marxist/Leninist), Mirsky observes that the ideological baggage associated with substantiating such policies quickly disappeared following Gorbachev's glasnost (or what Mirsky calls the "de-ideologization" of Soviet foreign policy), clearing the way for a more cooperative relationship with the United States in the Middle East.

In a new chapter, Rashid Khalidi (Chapter 10) analyzes America's Middle Eastern policies through the lens of its cold war rivalry with the Soviet Union. Khalidi pays particular attention to US leaders' support of conservative Islam, such as that practiced in Saudi Arabia, as an ideological counter to communism and Arab nationalism, and thus as a key barrier to Soviet penetration in the region. This approach, though, had important costs for US interests. Not only did it cause US leaders to downplay their support of human rights and democracy advancement in the Middle East, but it helped to empower some of the radical Islamic groups that threaten the United States today. Khalidi also examines at length America's and the Soviet Union's evolving relations with Israel as a component of their cold war hostilities. The nature and effects of this rivalry not only made peace in Middle East a relatively low priority for the two superpowers, but repeatedly undermined the peace process, such as it was.

Since the emergence of the state of Israel in 1948 and the subsequent Arab-Israeli conflict, there seems to have been a recurrent cycle of conflict followed by missed opportunities for peace or the establishment of something less than a comprehensive peace, which in turn has created an environment in which tensions continue and issues remain unresolved, which then leads to the resumption of some form of conflict—and so forth and so on. The role of the United States in this process has varied considerably, from pacifier to antagonist, from mediator to peacemaker, from belligerent to bystander. Part 2, "Arab-Israeli War and Peace," examines the role the United States has played in this seemingly never-ending cycle. At the close of the cold war, there was a widely held perception that this cycle could be terminated with a sustainable comprehensive peace in the Arab-Israeli arena, and a number of important steps were made to facilitate the achievement of this. However, as the breakdown of the Oslo and Madrid peace processes and the current situation in the region demonstrate, there remain significant obstacles to a complete resolution of the Arab-Israeli dispute.

Fawaz Gerges begins this section (Chapter 11) with a discussion of the 1967 Arab-Israeli war, which initiated the peace process as we know it today and effectively brought the superpower cold war together with the Arab-Israeli issue. In the 1969–1970 war of attrition and the 1973 Arab-Israeli war, the Soviets became intimately involved, the result being a near superpower confrontation during the latter stages of the 1973 hostilities. In examining the impact of the 1967 war on Arab nationalist perceptions of the United States, Gerges argues that the war had a "devastating negative impact" on Arab views of the US role in the peace process. Nevertheless, the "indispensable and preponderant" role of Washington in this process was made abundantly clear: the United States "held most of the cards."

Janice Stein (Chapter 12) discusses the intricate, tension-filled, and dramatic superpower negotiations during the latter stages of the 1973 Arab-Israeli war, the results of which altered the international and regional configuration in the Middle East and contributed to a "second cold war" between the Soviet Union and the United States that lasted until the early 1980s. In an updated chapter, Bernard Reich and Shannon Powers (Chapter 13) then analyze the "special relationship" that developed between Israel and the United States, especially from the Jimmy Carter through the Obama presidencies. The authors examine the factors that work for the continuation of this relationship, despite at times some important frictions.

Jeremy Pressman contributes a chapter (Chapter 14) that outlines the Oslo and Madrid peace processes through the failed Camp David meeting in July 2000 and critically examines the roles played by each of the principal players, including the United States. In the process, Pressman offers some cogent reasons why both the Oslo and Madrid Accords broke down.

In a new contribution, Robert O. Freedman (Chapter 15) covers in intricate detail the policies of the George W. Bush and Obama administrations toward the Arab-Israeli arena. In doing so, Freedman reveals the complexities of the Arab-Israeli dynamic and the challenges to reaching comprehensive, lasting peace agreements.

The years spanned in Part 3 mark the most intimate involvement of the United States in the Middle East. The Gulf wars climaxed more than a half century of US vital interest in the Persian Gulf area. US policy has been based primarily on maintaining stability in the area to ensure easy access to and the safe transport of oil—and during the cold war, to keep the Soviets from fishing in troubled waters.

Balance-of-power politics played an important part in US calculations toward achieving these objectives. First, the United States initiated a relationship with Iran through the Mussadiq coup, and then it enhanced this relationship by supporting the shah of Iran as the US "policeman" in the Gulf as part of the Vietnam-induced 1969 Nixon Doctrine, which sought to secure US surrogates for its global strategic interests. (The United States envisioned Israel playing a similar role in the heartland of the Middle East.) With the fall of the shah in the 1979 Iranian revolution and with the ensuing Iran-Iraq war, Washington began to see Iraq's Saddam Hussein as its new gendarme in the region, keeping Khomeinism at bay, restoring Gulf stability, and possibly playing the role that Egyptian President Anwar Sadat never filled—leading a moderate Arab consensus toward peace with Israel. US and British support backfired, however, a turn of events that became readily apparent when Iraq invaded Kuwait in 1990, eliciting the decision by the administration of George H. W. Bush to intervene militarily. The 1991 Gulf War, along with the end of the cold war, contributed to a new regional configuration full of prospects for peace and stability as well as conflict and instability. Importantly, this resulted in an enhanced role for the United States in a part of the Middle East that had traditionally been wary of US influence.

US involvement reached a pinnacle with America's preventive war against Iraq in 2003. This conflict was fueled by accusations from the Bush administration that the regime of Saddam Hussein was manufacturing and stockpiling weapons of mass destruction (WMD) and had links with al-Qa'ida. According to the prescription of the Bush Doctrine, the supposed threat from Iraq needed to be dealt with before it developed into a direct threat to the United States—no one wanted to see another 9/11. Bush administration officials, while assiduously maintaining a commitment to a satisfactory resolution of the Iraqi situation, have admitted that things did not go entirely according to plan. No WMD were found in Iraq, and no serious Iraqi links to al-Qa'ida were proven. Moreover, a growing insurgency against what was perceived to be an American occupation and a dysfunctional Iraqi government led to tremendous instability in the country. Neither US forces nor Iraqi forces were prepared to deal with an insurgency, and reconstruction of the country's basic infrastructure was impeded by constant violence. A combination of factors in 2007—led by the "awakening" in al-Anbar province (when many Sunni nationalist insurgents abandoned their alliance with al-Qa'ida in Iraq and instead joined with US forces against their former partners) and the "surge" in American troops deployed to the country—resulted in significant improvements in Iraq's domestic stability, though domestic violence and political paralysis continue. The United States is currently on track to remove all combat forces from Iraq by the end of 2011.

Robert Allison (Chapter 16) opens this section with a look back at America's views and interactions with the Middle East during the earliest years of the Republic. He shows how many Americans in this period held a distorted image of the region and Islam, and these misperceptions contributed to the Tripolitan War.

Gary Sick, who served on the National Security Council staff during the Carter administration, examines in Chapter 17 US policy in the Gulf in the post–World War II era through the period of "dual containment" in the 1990s, particularly focusing on the enhanced role of the United States in the region following the 1979 Iranian revolution. In addition to providing context for this section in the book, Sick also critically analyzes the changing role of the United States in the area, as the interests defined and the subsequent policies enacted by Washington have been adjusted and readjusted in reaction to the frequent shifts in the regional balance of power in the Gulf.

F. Gregory Gause (Chapter 18) follows with an updated examination of the Saudi view of its relationship with the United States before the period of the Gulf wars to the present day. He concludes that although the dilemma that has traditionally faced Saudi rulers (keeping the United States as its "over-the-horizon" defense while maintaining its distance from Washington for domestic and regional purposes) was smashed with the open reception of US troops during the 1991 Gulf War, a quandary still exists because of domestic public opinion weighted against too close an attachment. Of course, the tensions between the two countries have only been exacerbated in the aftermath of 9/11, as the majority of the terrorists who carried out the attacks, as well as Osama bin Laden himself, were Saudi. Common threats—most notably mutual enmity toward al-Qa'ida (which engineered a series of attacks in the kingdom beginning in 2003) and an increasingly powerful Iran—have, however, tightened the alliance despite the two states' differences and frictions in other areas.

Steve Yetiv and Ali Abootalebi contribute two updated chapters (Chapters 19 and 20, respectively) examining the US-led invasion of Iraq in 2003 and its aftermath. Yetiv first outlines the rationale of the Bush administration in making the decision to go to war in Iraq. In doing so, he analyzes the popular perceptions—and misperceptions—of why the Bush administration went against the wishes of most of the international community and invaded Iraq. In the process of his examination, he outlines what appear to be the real reasons. Abootalebi offers a stinging critique of the Bush administration's decision to go to war and the series of missteps it made during and after the initial military phase of the conflict. While outlining these issues, he also examines the important and related US-Iranian dynamic. To Abootalebi, sectarianism in Iraq continues to create huge difficulties to the realization of America's objectives well into Barack Obama's presidency.

In another revised chapter, Henri Barkey (Chapter 21) analyzes the increasingly important relationship between the United States and Turkey, which comprises strategic as well as economic elements. After surveying the post–World War II history of the US-Turkey relationship, which reveals the waxing and waning of relations between the two countries based on a variety of circumstances, Barkey describes the close strategic cooperation that developed between Washington and Ankara by necessity as a result of the Gulf War and the sanctions regime implemented thereafter against Iraq. This strategic cooperation was strengthened after the events of 9/11, when Turkey became vitally important to US strategic interests in Central Asia and the Middle East, but then suffered a setback in 2003 when Istanbul, fearing domestic backlash, would not allow the United States to use its territory to launch the invasion of Iraq. Many Western analysts even fear that Turkey, led by the moderate Islam-oriented Justice and Development Party, is abandoning Western-oriented foreign policies as the party has both pushed for more engagement of Muslim-majority countries (including Iran and Syria) and become increasingly critical of Israel. Barkey argues that the party, while distancing itself from the United States, will not break with it, as close relations with the West remain indispensable.

Marvin Weinbaum (Chapter 22) provides another updated chapter that examines the US-Afghani dynamic. After detailing the development of the Soviet-Afghani and US-Afghani relationships in the post–World War II era, he then comments on the seminal period surrounding the Soviet invasion of Afghanistan in 1979 and the changes that it wrought in and outside of the region. Weinbaum goes on to analyze the breakdown of the Afghani state following the Soviet withdrawal in 1989, which led to the Taliban takeover by 1996 and the establishment of the al-Qa'ida terrorist infrastructure shortly thereafter. He follows with a discussion of how Afghanistan again arose from "marginality" and acquired a prominent foreign policy position in Washington following the September 2001 attacks. Weinbaum closes with a recapitulation of the potential benefits, challenges, successes, and, above all, the missed opportunities that have characterized America's nation-building efforts during the Bush and Obama administrations since the ouster of the Taliban by American forces in 2001.

In a new chapter, Mark Haas (Chapter 23) discusses how ideological variables were critical to Iranian leaders' views and policies toward the United States during the Clinton and George W. Bush presidencies. Iranian reformers/liberalizers were consistently much less threatened and more supportive of the United States than were Iranian ideological hard-liners. These differences were exhibited in key issues, including views on developing nuclear weapons and the US-led wars in Afghanistan and Iraq. These variations occurred despite the constancy from Iranian leaders' perspective of US power and policies. The major policy differences among various ideological factions created significant opportunities for the advancement of American interests, though US leaders, Haas argues, frequently have not taken advantage of these openings.

Jon Alterman's chapter in this volume (Chapter 24) critically examines the Bush administration's attempts to promote democracy in the Middle East. The object of this strategy was to help drain the facilitating swamp of Islamic extremism created by the lack of political space imposed by authoritarian regimes and associated corruption and socioeconomic deprivation. While applauding the promotion of democracy in the region, Alterman criticizes the methodology employed by the United States over the years, which tended to focus on the so-called Arab liberals to the exclusion of other important elements of Arab societies. The efforts at democratization have therefore produced decidedly mixed results and contributed to the rising influence and power of Islamist groups that Washington has been trying to marginalize. While pointing out the mistakes of US policy in this area—and their consequences—Alterman concludes by offering some ideas for American administrations to consider that might produce a more desirable outcome for US and indigenous interests alike.

Yvonne Haddad's updated analysis in Chapter 25 also examines the threat posed by Islamist groups to US interests. The rise of Islamist movements in the Middle East has obviously created a good deal of consternation among policymakers in Washington, and the foreign policy and security establishments have been mobilized in a heretofore unparalleled way in an attempt to deal with this issue following the events of 9/11 and the 2003 war in Iraq. Many see this phenomenon as inherently inimical and dangerous to US and Western interests in the region. In an attempt to understand the Islamist perspective toward US foreign policy in the Middle East, Haddad analyzes the root causes of Islamism in general as well as its specific views toward the role that the United States and the West have played in the area. She does not paint a very optimistic picture. Haddad offers a glimpse at the potential of continuing conflict in the Middle East unless certain long-standing grievances held by many groups in the region are addressed in what they perceive to be a satisfactory manner.

Heather Gregg offers the final new contribution to this volume (Chapter 26). In it, she analyzes the al-Qa'ida phenomenon and US strategies that have attempted to defeat it. Gregg argues that al-Qa'ida is an organization, an ideology, and an aspiring social movement. The problem for US counterterrorism efforts is that tactics designed to defeat one of these dimensions may bolster the other two. The United States has paid considerable attention to fighting al-Qa'ida as an organization through targeting its leadership, freezing its assets, and attempting to deny it sanctuary in Afghanistan and Pakistan. However, these actions taken to defeat al-Qa'ida as an organization may actually be fulfilling its ideological prophecies and increasing its popularity. The chapter concludes with thoughts on how to better fight al-Qa'ida in a comprehensive way, including defeating it as an organization, undermining its ideology, and diminishing its appeal.

William Quandt's updated chapter (Chapter 27) offers a retrospective examination of US foreign policy toward the Middle East and looks at what opportunities and problems in the region lie ahead for policymakers. Although acknowledging that many people, particularly those in the region itself, have had good reason to be highly critical of US actions in the Middle East, he asserts that the objectives as traditionally defined by US policymakers have been for the most part achieved, and at least until 9/11, with relatively little cost in human and economic terms, especially when compared to US policy in Southeast Asia. While this relative success may be on the wane in recent years, US administrations nonetheless must define objectives commensurate with the changes that have occurred in the international and regional environment, while remaining sensitive to the fact that many of the problems in the region are intrinsic to the area and cannot be solved in Washington.

This updated fifth edition ends with a wholly new essay exploring the changes in US relations with the region following the Arab Spring protests and other developments in 2011 and 2012. The chapter covers three areas: a summary of the major political effects of the protests and conflicts in North Africa and the Middle East; an analysis of how and why US leaders responded to these uprisings, paying special attention to the threats and opportunities they have created for US interests; and suggestions on what policies the US can pursue to best advance US security in the region in a post–Arab Spring world. All of these have had a major influence on how Obama has responded to the region since the middle of his first term.

As will become apparent throughout this book, involvement in the Middle East has been an adventurous and, at times, tumultuous experience for the United States, one that has not been without its successes. But it is also one that has had numerous failures; even what the United States typically considers successes, moreover, are not always viewed as such by those in the region itself. The United States is by far the most influential outside power in the Middle East, but it is also far from the most popular. The two do not always, and sometimes should not, go together. Is this the dilemma of a superpower with global interests working through a regional environment, or could US policy have been much more discerning and prescient? The answer probably lies somewhere in between. By analyzing the successes and failures of America's Middle Eastern policies, the chapters in this volume provide key insights into how US leaders can build on their strengths while minimizing weaknesses in a region that remains critical to America's security interests.

Notes

1. Raymond Hare, "The Great Divide: World War II," *Annals*, May 1972, pp. 23–30.

2. Malcolm H. Kerr, *The Arab Cold War: Gamal 'Abd al-Nasir and His Rivals, 1958–1970* (New York: Oxford University Press, 1971).

PART ONE

From Idealism to Realism

Wilsonian Intent to Cold War Practice

CHAPTER I

THE IRONIC LEGACY OF THE KING-CRANE COMMISSION

James Gelvin

In the immediate aftermath of World War I, a US observer in Syria wrote:

> Without visiting the Near East, it is not possible for an American to realize
> even faintly, the respect, faith and affection with which our Country is re-
> garded throughout that region. Whether it is the world-wide reputation
> which we enjoy for fair dealing, a tribute perhaps to the crusading spirit
> which carried us into the Great War, not untinged with the hope that the
> same spirit may urge us into the solution of great problems growing out
> of that conflict, or whether due to unselfish or impartial missionary and
> educational influence exerted for a century, it is the one faith which is held
> alike by Christian and Moslem, by Jew and Gentile, by prince and peasant
> in the Near East.[1]

If, during the three-quarters of a century that have passed since these words
were written, those who have chronicled the relations between the United States
and the nations of the Middle East have had few, if any, opportunities to repeat
our observer's findings, they can at least take solace from the fact that the goodwill
that may have existed seventy-five years ago has been dissipated precisely because
of US intervention in the "great problems" engendered by the destruction of the
Ottoman Empire.

The first official US foray into the politics of the post-Ottoman Middle East came about as the result of a suggestion made by President Woodrow Wilson to the Council of Four entente powers (France, Great Britain, the United States, and Italy) assembled in Paris to determine the terms of peace. In an attempt to resolve an acrimonious dispute between Britain and France over the future disposition of the Arab provinces of the Ottoman Empire, Wilson suggested the formation of an interallied commission on Syria. The commission would travel to the Middle East "to elucidate the state of opinion and the soil to be worked on by any mandatory. They should be asked to come back and tell the Conference what they found with regard to these matters. . . . If we were to send a Commission of men with no previous contact with Syria, it would, at any rate, convince the world that the Conference had tried to do all it could to find the most scientific basis possible for a settlement."[2] Although both France and Britain acquiesced to the idea of the commission, neither power appointed delegates to participate in its activities. As a result, the commission became a US commission and thus has been commonly referred to by the names of its two commissioners, Henry Churchill King, president of Oberlin College in Ohio, and Chicago businessman and Democratic Party activist Charles R. Crane. King and Crane traveled to Palestine, Syria, Lebanon, and Anatolia in the summer of 1919 to meet with local representatives. Their findings, filed with the US delegation at Paris, were subsequently ignored by the peace negotiators.

Diplomatic historians have usually cited the King-Crane Commission as either an example of US naïveté in the face of European realpolitik or as a representation of the principles that differentiate the "new diplomacy" from the old. In reality, the legacy of the commission is far more complex. Although the commission's impact on entente policy was doomed from the beginning by a variety of factors—a confusion of secret agreements, historic claims, and postwar realities; the Parti Colonial in France and the Republican Party in the United States; and the British realization that "the friendship of France is worth ten Syrias"[3]—contemporary students of US foreign policy can draw two lessons from the story of the commission. The first lesson is that in diplomacy, as in physics, neutral observers do not exist; rather, a world power necessarily influences the object of its interest simply by turning its attention to it, by defining it as a problem to be solved and then framing the possible terms for its solution. Second, a review of the effects of the visit of the King-Crane Commission on the Syrian population[4] underscores the need for US policymakers to reassess the preconceptions and misapprehensions that have guided them, often with disastrous results, when formulating policies that deal with "nation building" and nationalism.

THE DOCTRINE OF SELF-DETERMINATION AND ITS APPLICATION IN THE MIDDLE EAST

During World War I and the subsequent peace negotiations, the French, British, and US governments all made declarations that indicated support for self-determination for the peoples of the Ottoman Empire. At the same time, however, all three governments committed themselves to policies that made true self-determination impossible.

For Woodrow Wilson, the liberation of peoples and postwar self-determination were sine qua nons for US participation in the war. From December 1917 through September 1918, Wilson delivered a series of addresses, enunciating US principles in Fourteen Points (January 8, 1918), Four Supplementary Points (February 11, 1918), Four Additional Points (July 4, 1918), and Five Additional Points (September, 27 1918). "Self-determination," Wilson warned, "is not a mere phrase. It is an imperative principle of action which statesmen will henceforth ignore at their peril."[5] In Point Twelve of the original Fourteen Points, Wilson directly addressed the status of Turks and non-Turks in the Ottoman Empire, promising the latter "an absolutely unmolested opportunity of autonomous development."[6]

Stung by the revelation of secret agreements reached during the war for a colonial-style division of the Ottoman Empire, and wishing to allay the doubts of Arab nationalists who suspected entente perfidy, France and Britain adopted Wilson's call for self-determination for the inhabitants of the Middle East. On November 9, 1918, they issued the following joint declaration, which they distributed throughout liberated Syria: "The object aimed at by France and Great Britain in prosecuting in the East the War let loose by the ambition of Germany is the complete and definite emancipation of the peoples so long oppressed by the Turks and the establishment of national governments and administrations deriving their authority from the initiative and free choice of the indigenous populations."[7]

In the same statement, however, the two powers displayed their ambivalence to the principle of self-determination by making their support for the doctrine conditional on the acceptance by the indigenes of guidance from "advanced nations":

> In order to carry out these intentions France and Great Britain are at one in encouraging and assisting the establishment of indigenous Governments and administrations in Syria and Mesopotamia, now liberated by the Allies, and in the territories the liberation of which they are engaged in securing and recognising these as soon as they are actually established.
>
> Far from wishing to impose on the populations of these regions any particular institutions they are only concerned to ensure by their support and by adequate assistance the regular working of Governments and administrations freely chosen by the populations themselves. To secure impartial and equal justice for all, to facilitate the economic development of the country by inspiring and encouraging local initiative, to favour the diffusion of education, to put an end to dissensions that have too long been taken advantage of by Turkish policy, such is the policy which the two Allied Governments uphold in the liberated territories.

For many Arab nationalists, particularly those who had preferred sitting out the war in Egypt to joining the British-inspired Arab Revolt of Sharif Hussein and his sons, the Anglo-French statement appeared to be little more than a rationalization for a thinly veiled colonialism.[8] As if to confirm their suspicions, French President Georges Clemenceau visited London in December 1918, where, in the words of British Prime Minister Lloyd George, it was "agreed that Syria should go to France [as a mandate] and Mesopotamia to Great Britain."[9] To mollify the French further, the British (as well as the United States) disavowed any interest in Syria in a meeting of the Council of Four held three days before the peace conference authorized the assignment of mandates in the region.

Whereas the French and British attitude toward both self-determination for the inhabitants of the region and the King-Crane Commission was thus clear, US support for both was surprisingly ambiguous. Its European allies might easily have argued that the United States had, on several occasions, already placed its imprimatur on their wartime and postwar arrangements for the region. After all, not only had Woodrow Wilson issued a statement of support for the Balfour Declaration[10] in September 1918 without bothering to ascertain the attitude of the inhabitants of Palestine toward the establishment of a Jewish homeland in their midst, but one month later he approved the official US Department of State commentary on the Fourteen Points, which recognized the preeminent position of France in Syria and affirmed that Britain was "clearly the best mandatory for Palestine, Mesopotamia, and Arabia."[11] Little wonder, then, that Henry King and Charles Crane, in a memorandum written to the US president before their tour of the Middle East, argued that the mandate for Syria should go to France "frankly based, not on the primary desires of the people, but on the international need of preserving friendly relations between France and Great Britain,"[12] or that, within a week of proposing the commission, Wilson had, according to Ray Stannard Baker, a close associate and head of the US press bureau in Paris, "clean forgotten" about it.[13]

Support among the entente powers for the activities of the commission thus ranged from lackluster to dismissive. The commission's recommendations were nonbinding, and even if the commission were to find, as it did, that Syrian public opinion supported a united Syria and (in ranked order) no mandate, a US mandate, and a British mandate,[14] all three options had already been foreclosed. It was in this context that Lloyd George, like the proverbial Western sheriff who remarked, "First we give him a fair trial, then we hang him," urged his French colleague to support the activities of the commission, but "first let us agree [about the disposition of territory] between ourselves."[15]

THE US PERSPECTIVE ON SELF-DETERMINATION
AND PUBLIC OPINION

Not only did decisions made in Paris preclude the possibility that the King-Crane Commission would influence entente policy, but preconceptions held by both the commissioners and their president—preconceptions about democracy, progress, public opinion, and nationalism that both underlay the commission's flawed procedure and circumscribed the range of its possible findings—impeded the commission's ability truly to "elucidate the state of opinion and the soil to be worked on by any mandatory" in Syria.

The extent to which his father's Calvinism shaped Woodrow Wilson's worldview and principles of his foreign policy is a well-worn cliché.[16] But because Wilson was a historian as well as the son of a Presbyterian minister, he tempered his belief in a mankind tainted by original sin with the optimism implicit in the Whiggism common to the academic milieu from which he emerged. History, for Wilson, was the chronicle of liberty—"the enlargement of the sphere of independent action at the expense of dictatorial authority."[17] From the Greek polis and the confrontation at Runnymede through the ratification of the US Constitution, human progress could thus be measured in two ways: by the multiplication of the personal freedoms available to the (Anglo-Saxon) heirs of this tradition, and by the spread of democracy—the political correlate to this tradition—throughout the world.

In his writings, Wilson argued that the expansion of international trade, print media, and, most important, public education during the previous century had created an autonomous realm of public opinion in most nations that facilitated the global diffusion of democratic ideals and structures.[18] Wilson's definition of public opinion thus differed dramatically from the definition used by his German idealist contemporaries: Rather than being the repository of common sense ("all-pervasive fundamental ethical principles disguised as prejudices"),[19] Wilson's public opinion was an *informed* public opinion shaped by the most enlightened strata of society.[20] This was the public opinion upon which the doctrine of self-determination rested, the public opinion that Wilson charged the King-Crane Commission to elucidate.

The members of the King-Crane Commission shared Wilson's understanding about the nature of public opinion. Their fact-finding consisted of holding audiences with, and receiving petitions drafted by, those whom they considered to be the most important and most representative Middle East opinion makers: thirty-four mayors and municipal councils, fifteen administrative councils, sixty-five councils of village chiefs, thirty Arab shaykhs, seventeen professional and trade organizations, and so on. It should not be surprising, therefore, that in its final report the commission advocated strengthening Syrian nationalism through an expansion of education "in clear recognition of the imperative necessity of education for the citizens of a democratic state and the development of a sound national spirit."[21]

Although members of the King-Crane Commission disagreed about the extent to which the Syrian population was prepared for self-determination and how long "the systematic cultivation of national spirit" in Syria would take, all agreed on the liberal and secular foundations on which Syrians had to base their nationalism. In the conclusion to its final report, the commission recommended imposing a mandate on Syria but optimistically predicted that the period during which a mandatory power would have to oversee Syrian affairs might be brief. According to the report, mandatory control could be relinquished as soon as the leaders of the Syrian

nationalist movement demonstrated their sincerity in midwifing a modern democratic nation-state that protected the rights of minorities:

> The western world is already committed to the attempt to live in peace
> and friendship with the Moslem peoples, and to manage governments in
> such a way as to separate politics from religion. Syria offers an excellent
> opportunity to establish a state where members of the three great
> monotheistic religions can live together in harmony; because it is a country
> of one language, which has long had freedom of movement and of business
> relations through being unified under the Turkish rule. Since now the ma-
> jority declare for nationalism, independent of religion, it is necessary only
> to hold them to this view through mandatory control until they shall have
> established the method and practice of it. Dangers may readily arise from
> unwise and unfaithful dealings with this people, but there is great hope
> of peace and progress if they be handled frankly and loyally.[22]

In contrast to the findings of the commissioners, the reports filed by William
Yale, one of two technical advisers attached to the King-Crane Commission, cast
doubt on the short-term "possibility of developing among the people of Syria a
national spirit upon the community of language which exists, the similarity of race,
the sense of economic dependence, and the germ of nationalism." Yale predicted
disaster without a long-term and energetic mandatory presence in Syria:

> There is a liberal movement among the Syrian Moslems, a movement
> which under proper guidance and with proper assistance may be able to
> awaken a new spirit in the younger generation, might have been able to
> lessen the fanaticism not only of the effendi class but of the lower classes.
> At the present time this liberal movement was too feeble, too weak in
> numbers and conviction . . . to rally to their support the ignorant fanatical
> masses which are swayed by the Ulemas and the Young Arab Party.[23]

Ironically, the very search by members of the King-Crane Commission for their
counterparts in Syrian society directly (and adversely) affected the latter's ability
to shape Syrian public opinion. Those whom Yale entrusted to nurture "liberal nationalism" naturally believed, like the commissioners, that educational achievement
or professional status entitled them to play a special role in nation building. While
actively courting the commissioners, this grouping simultaneously sought to convince the Syrian population that, having achieved the approbation of the commission, it would secure Syrian independence through negotiation and
compromise—if not absolute independence, then at least independence under the
benevolent guidance of the Americans or British. The refusal by the entente powers
to accept the recommendations of the King-Crane Commission destroyed the credibility of this sodality within the nationalist movement and thus assured the emergence of a new and very different kind of nationalist leadership.

THE "LIBERAL MOVEMENT"

The thin strata of society behind what William Yale (ingenuously) identified as the "liberal movement" had emerged in Syria as the result of two processes that had, over the course of the half-century that preceded the dissolution of the Ottoman Empire, increasingly determined institutions and social relationships in the Arab Middle East. Both the accelerating rate of integration of the region into the world economy and attempts made by the Ottoman government to rationalize and strengthen central control increased the salience of capitalist relations and encouraged their diffusion (albeit unevenly) throughout the empire. These effects, in turn, not only induced the reconstruction and/or enlargement of certain previously existing social classes, but they prompted the emergence of new social classes as well. Members of two of these classes, often intertwined through reciprocal ties of interest and/or consanguinity, formed the core of Yale's "liberal movement": the so-called middle strata, comprising intellectuals, trained military officers, professionals, and so on, who were necessary to implement Ottoman "modernization" and state-building policies, and a reconstituted urban notability whose economic and political status was increasingly based on a combination of land ownership and good relations with Istanbul.[24]

Two types of bonds united these groups with their counterparts in the West. Because both the formation of the middle strata and the post-1860 transformation of the urban notability depended upon the spread of peripheral capitalism and modern institutions of governance in the Middle East, the categories used by these groups to organize the world and their society were coherent with the categories used by analogous groups—both in the metropole and in other peripheral areas— who benefited from, or whose origins can be traced to, the worldwide expansion of capitalism. In addition, elective ties of affinity, nurtured, for example, through education, religious affiliation, and/or wartime experiences, often linked members of these groups to their European counterparts. These natural and emulative bonds not only account for the strategies used by these newly empowered groups to craft state institutions in post-Ottoman Syria, but also explain why, during the same period, an influential bloc readily worked within the parameters set by the Paris Peace Conference in an attempt to win Syrian independence.

The Arab government that was established in Damascus at the close of World War I depended upon individuals from these groups to administer the territory of inland Syria and to mobilize the support of the indigenous population. Working both within the government and through allied political and cultural organizations (the most important of which were al-Fatat, the Arab Club *[al-nadi al-'arabi]*, and the Literary Society *[al-muntada al-adabi]*),[25] the self-proclaimed elite within the nationalist movement (labeled in their own writings the *mutanawwirun, mustanirun,* or *mufakkirun*) designed governmental and extragovernmental institutions to expand the authority of the state, reorganize traditional structures within civil society, introduce mores and values compatible with or derived from those of Europe, and inculcate new national myths and symbols among the population. In a report written in November 1919, for example, British traveler Gertrude Bell described her visit to one such institution, the "School for the Daughters of Martyrs" *(madrasat banat al-shuhada)*, which was established in Damascus to educate orphans whose fathers had died during the Arab Revolt. The school, according to Bell,

> is run on private subscriptions by a committee of ladies presided over by Naziq bint al 'Abid, a girl of 21 belonging to one of the best families of Damascus. She is a niece of 'Izzat Pasha, who was the all-powerful Secretary of Abdul Hamid for a period of years, during which he earned great wealth and the bitter recriminations of the C.U.P. [Committee of Union and Progress] when it came into the saddle. In spite of their threats Izzat managed to escape to Europe, where he had already lodged a respectable part of his fortune. Sitt Naziq was educated in a mission school at Beyrut, speaks English, and is the most advanced lady in Damascus. She and her mother sat unveiled among a company of men, a select company, but none of them related to the 'Abid family. Another Mohammadan lady of the committee was present, and she also was unveiled. . . . The mistresses were mostly Christians educated in Beyrut and speaking fairly good English. Besides the orphans there were an equal number of girls of good Damascene families who pay for the education they receive. These girls 16 to 18 years old, were not seen by the men of the party. Girls and children were brought out into the large garden which surrounds the house to sing patriotic songs. In one of them a chorus of the elder girls addressed the orphans, reminding each one that her father died in the cause of liberty and bidding her never to forget that she was "bint ul 'Arabi," while the children replied that they would never forget their birth, nor King Husain who fought for their race, nor finally (this stanza was specially prepared for the US Commission) President Wilson who laid down—save the mark—the principles of freedom.[26]

A more comprehensive picture of the attitudes and activities of like-minded *mutanawwirun* during the period preceding the visit of the King-Crane Commission to Damascus is displayed in an unusual parable, entitled "The True Vision," that was published on the front page of the official gazette of the Arab government in May 1919.[27] The fantasy begins with a description of the author at his desk, contemplating the news of demonstrations held in Egypt to show popular support for Egyptian independence: "We hardly see such good order in the demonstrations of the most advanced Western nations. I said to myself, 'By God! They unjustly accuse the East and its people of savagery, immaturity, and an inability to imitate the civilization of the West. What is more indicative of their readiness [for independence] than this admirably ordered and perfect demonstration?'" Troubled by his meditations and by concerns about the upcoming visit of the King-Crane

Commission to Damascus, the author falls asleep. His dreams transport him to an unfamiliar Middle East location where the inhabitants speak classical Arabic and dress in traditional attire. In the tent of their chieftain lies a strange mechanism and two mirrors: one mirror reflects the past, the other forecasts the future. The author, having begged the apparition for a glimpse of the future, spends the remainder of the dream watching upcoming events unfold, "like in a movie."

The author's first vision is of the near future. On the eve of the arrival of the King-Crane Commission, "the people of distinction and their intellectuals" *('ilyat al-qawm wa mufakkiruhum),* assembled in a general congress, make preparations to convince the commission that the Syrian population is mature (the words "*madani,*" "*umrani,*" and "*adabi*" are used throughout the article) and therefore merits independence. To accomplish this, as the parable continues, the delegates plan to use locally based artisan guilds and patriotic clubs to organize demonstrations similar to those of Egypt and to distribute placards among the population calling for complete independence:

> In conformity with this plan each citizen placed a sign on his forearm and on his breast on which was printed "We demand complete independence." Shop owners placed signs with this slogan written in English and Arabic on their shops. Hardly had these plans been made when all inhabitants— regardless of religion, sect, and nationality—showed these placards . . . and one could not walk down the street without seeing the signs on every building and wall. As the size of demonstrations swelled, the people daubed this slogan on the tarbooshes of small boys and embroidered it on the frontlets of small girls. I laughed when I saw a bald man with the slogan written on his head. I saw the owners of carriages and horses who placed this slogan on the faces of their horses and the sweets-sellers put the slogan on the lids of containers of sweets and milk. I was truly amazed when I saw the work of the residents of Salhiyye—they spelled out this slogan with lanterns on Mt. Qasiun by night in letters that could be read for seven miles. The people kept up this sort of activity until the delegation left Damascus.

Impressed by the "intelligence, advancement, and worthiness for independence" of Syrians, the King-Crane Commission returns to Paris and convinces the peace conference to offer the Syrians independence. Under the benevolent leadership of Faisal, now king of Syria, and guided by a new congress, presumably composed of the same notables and intellectuals who had convened in the previous congress, the nation can now enjoy the fruits of its independence:

> I saw . . . the people now turning their attention to the founding of schools and colleges until no village remained without an excellent primary school. I saw prosperity spreading throughout the country and railroads

connecting populous villages and farms. I saw farmers using the most modern agricultural techniques, extensive trade, and flourishing industry. Damascus appeared to me to be the most advanced of cities in terms of its construction. Its streets and lanes were paved with asphalt and the Barada River was like the Seine, traversing the city from east to west. On its banks was a corniche on which towering buildings stood. I saw Aleppo: its water, brought by canals from the Euphrates, sustained its gardens and parks and anointed its waterless desert. . . . Factories were founded throughout the kingdom so that the country had no need for manufactured goods from the West, but instead exported its products to China, India, and Africa. Its people grew rich, its power increased, and it moved to the forefront of advanced nations.

As is common with prophetic narratives, the accuracy of the dreamer's vision increasingly fades the further it advances into the future. Much of what the author wrote about imminent events did transpire as foretold. The Syrian General Congress, composed primarily of representatives whose backgrounds placed them among the "people of distinction," met in early June 1919 to formulate a consentient list of demands to be presented to the US commission.[28] The Arab government distributed *khutab* (sermons) to be read at Friday prayers and, in conjunction with political and cultural associations and government-sanctioned guilds, sponsored petition campaigns and mobilized demonstrations in support of the "Damascus Program" promulgated by the congress.[29] Local political activists and *makhatir* (government officials assigned to quarters within cities) ensured that shopkeepers throughout Syria placarded their storefronts with the slogan "We demand complete independence."[30] However, the long-term vision for Syria espoused by the author—a vision suffused with Eurogenic ideals and expressed through an alien discourse—not only failed to materialize but proved to be far removed from the concerns of the vast majority of the Syrian population.

With adequate resources, it might have been possible for the Arab government and its allies gradually to enlist the support of the Syrian population for its "true vision": The *mutanawwirun* not only enjoyed the requisite social prestige to attract the spontaneous consent of nonelites, but because of their access to institutions of governance, they possessed potentially formidable coercive powers as well. However, on September 13, 1919, the British government decided to reduce its substantial subsidy to the Arab government by half and to withdraw its forces from Syria. This decision undercut both the economic and the political positions of the Arab government and its allies and generated a crisis from which they never recovered.[31] Widely interpreted as portending French rule in Syria ("protection and mandate are synonyms, and are the precursors to annexation"),[32] the action seemed to confirm the bankruptcy of the plan to achieve the complete independence of Syria through negotiation. Almost overnight, the slogan "Complete independence for Syria within its natural boundaries, no protection, tutelage, or mandate *(la himaya, la wisaya, wa la intidab)*" replaced its shorter but obviously inadequate predecessor on placards posted throughout Syria.[33]

THE RESPONSE OF NONELITES TO THE FAILURE OF THE COMMISSION

> *The enemy have cloaked themselves in hypocrisy, and*
> *enfolded it in rancor and hatred.*
> *They took an oath of loyalty and they were disloyal,*
> *and from among them you have trusted some as*
> *allies who were treacherous. . . .*
> *What is amiss with those who have carried the scales of*
> *guidance on their arms, that they have failed to*
> *discern the truth?*
> *If they do not help those who need help and bring*
> *success to those who deserve it, then let the*
> *scales be broken.*
>
> **—KHAYR AL-DIN AL-ZIRIKLI[34]**

For many in the Arab Middle East, the expansion of capitalist relations and the reorganization of imperial institutions that had taken place during the seventy years preceding the dissolution of the Ottoman Empire induced social changes that ranged from disorienting to calamitous. Not only did the status of those local elites who lacked landed wealth and/or bureaucratic connections decline, but rivalry intensified among established and emergent elites for highly coveted posts in the reinvigorated state bureaucracy. The spread of capitalism frequently transformed peasant life: Peasants often found themselves at the mercy of usurers, planted cash crops for export, and supplemented family incomes by participating, sometimes seasonally, sometimes permanently, in the urban labor force. Coastal cities and extramural urban areas expanded, and newcomers to cities frequently settled in neighborhoods (such as the Maydan in Damascus and al-Kallasa in Aleppo) that lacked homogeneity and established social structures. New demands made by the state (such as the universally loathed conscription), agricultural crises, alterations in patterns of land tenure, conflicts on the periphery of the empire and World War I, and postwar inflation and rural insecurity further disrupted the lives of nonelites.

The social and economic shocks experienced by both nonelites and former elites had two relevant effects. First, because the expansion of market relations and the intrusion of a uniform apparatus of power into previously unregulated or underregulated domains increasingly determined the nature and extended the scope of ties among Syrians, the significance of horizontal, associational, and national linkages among the population grew at the expense of vertical, communal, and parochial bonds—a necessary precondition for "proactive" collective activity and what historian George Mosse calls the "nationalization of the masses."[35] Second, the social and economic shocks engendered an ideological backlash among the self-described "aggrieved" *(mankubun)*,[36] who frequently expressed their disaffection through a populist discourse that extolled the historic ties and common interests that united Syrians into an egalitarian national community, celebrated the central role played by nonelites in preserving "traditional" values, and affirmed the integrity of community boundaries.

Starting in September 1919, populist activists—disempowered notables, merchants, *qabadayat* (local toughs), *ulama,* petit-bourgeois merchant/*ulama,* and so on[37]—took advantage of the opportunities for mobilization that both the prolonged social transformations and the immediate economic and political crises provided to create the structures necessary for a sustainable populist movement. Over the course of the next nine months, these activists founded an array of interconnected organizations (the most important of which were the Higher National Committee *[al-lajna al-wataniyya al-'ulya],* based in Damascus, and local committees of national defense *[lijan al-difa' al-watani]*) that challenged the authority of the crippled Arab government, the discredited *mutanawwirun,* and the representatives of the entente powers meeting in Paris.

The populist organizations attracted widespread support, particularly among the Sunni Muslim population of inland Syria, for several reasons. As described earlier, in anticipation of the arrival of the King-Crane Commission in Syria, the Arab government and its extragovernmental allies applied modern techniques for mass mobilization that had, even before the founding of the populist organizations, acclimated much of the population to participation in national politics. But where the Arab government attempted to reach a settlement with the entente powers through negotiation and compromise, the populist organizations preached the more popular doctrine of militant anti-imperialism and marshaled and/or supplied local volunteer militias and guerrilla bands to resist mandatory authority. The organizations connected individuals to a national political machine through neighborhood and village branch organizations and supervisory committees *(al-lijan al-far'iyya, al-lijan al-taftishiyya)* and promoted participation by sponsoring electoral campaigns, demonstrations, military exercises, and charitable activities. Finally, the populist organizations assumed responsibility for services—protecting and provisioning urban quarters, assessing taxes, licensing monopolies, ensuring a "fair price" for grain, providing relief for the indigent and families of soldiers—which the local notability and the Arab government could no longer provide.

In contrast to the anonymous dreamer and his colleagues—who were willing to accept a temporary mandate in exchange for technological assistance and the accouterments of civilization—populist spokesmen articulated a vision for Syria that met the concerns of "the great mass of the nation [that] is not confined to the educated, the notables, and the merchants of the cities who read the daily newspapers, follow international and domestic politics, and are concerned with scientific discoveries and technological innovation."[38] Scornful of the aspirations of the Westernized elites ("[The French] only want to possess the sources of wealth and turn the free population into slaves in the name of progress, and only the Syrians [will] feel the effects"),[39] populist spokesmen eschewed the dichotomization of Syrian society inherent in "A True Vision"—a dichotomization that stigmatized and alienated a vast majority of the population by pitting the cultured and educated formulators of public opinion against the passive nonelites—and expounded a vision of Syria that was both comprehensive and inclusive. Populist organizers thus counterpoised their own definition of public opinion to the definition used by Woodrow Wilson and his epigones in Syria:

> The people possess a spirit which transcends the inclinations of individuals . . . and the nation possesses an independent personality stronger than the personalities of its members. . . .Those who would penetrate the heart of the Syrian people . . . know that public opinion is made from two sources: the first is its historical traditions in which there is strong faith and fidelity. This is fixed and immutable at its core, and even though it changes form it is imperishable and indestructible. The old illiterate, the religious 'alim, the cultured youth all equally respect historical traditions and aspire to the general goal. . . . [T]he people compel outside influences to be compatible with their traditions, and they desire to harmonize the elements of public opinion by making the second element compatible with the first, that is, with historic tradition.[40]

The aggressive posture assumed by the leaders of the populist movement and the potential empowerment of their constituents alarmed both foreign observers and the *mutanawwirun*. Populist rhetoric, suffused with Islamic and apocalyptic images and embellished with anecdotes that described the treachery of "those who would sell the nation like merchandise," foreign conspiracies, French and Zionist atrocities, the defilement of Muslim innocents, and exculpatory vengeance, aroused their apprehensions as well. "Over 90% of the Moslems of Syria are ignorant and fanatical, and can be swayed by their religious leaders," reported William Yale. "They are profoundly anti-Christian and anti-foreign and can be easily led to excesses by the recognized leaders, the clergy, land owners, and tribal chiefs."[41] Similarly, in a letter addressed to a former finance minister, a physician working in the foreign ministry of the Arab government depicted the populist movement as a form of mass pathology: "Individual dementia is among the greatest afflictions I know, but worse still is the complete dementia of a nation. . . . I am not a prophet, yet I see the end result very clearly if the transgressors do not return to their senses."[42]

The transgressors did not, of course, "come to their senses." To the contrary, worsening economic conditions, widening border warfare, the demands made by an apparently incompetent yet increasingly rapacious Arab government, and the announcement of the decision made by the entente powers at San Remo in April 1920 (to divide Syria and impose mandates) boosted support for the populist movement and the organizations it spawned while further undermining the authority of the Arab government and the counsel of the *mutanawwirun*. When the

Arab government finally acquiesced to a French ultimatum that threatened unspecified "acts" unless the government accepted a French mandate, antigovernment
rioting—which left scores dead in Damascus and hundreds dead in Aleppo—
erupted throughout Syria. In the aftermath of this final display of the "state of
opinion and the soil to be worked on by any mandatory," the French army marched
on Damascus and France began its quarter-century occupation of inland Syria—
one year to the day after the departure of the King-Crane Commission from the
Middle East.

THE KING-CRANE COMMISSION AND THE
CONSTRUCTION OF SYRIAN NATIONALISM

In truth, the politics which followed in Syria were very strange, inasmuch
as the intellectuals—the men of public opinion—and the men of the government themselves stirred up, by all means possible, the excitement of
the people and pushed it to the extreme. Then, all of a sudden, they re-
treated before the slightest obstacle which blocked their way, and they
abandoned the people who were perplexed, not knowing how to explain
their position. . . . This created a situation of enormous emotional turmoil
and squandered the trust which the people had placed in their leaders.
They openly accused their leaders of treachery to the point that, gradually,
that trust was dissolved, and the leaders to whom the people had entrusted
the reins of government were not able to lead and they were scoffed at.

—AS'AD DAGHIR[43]

Following World War I, revolutionary violence convulsed much of the non-Western
world, from Turkey through India to China and Korea. The situation in the Arab
Middle East was no different, with conflagrations erupting in Egypt (1919), Syria
(1919–1920), and Iraq (1920). Despite the fact all the affected areas could sustain
complex, programmatic political movements (as opposed to movements that might
be characterized as temporary, defensive, and prepolitical)[44] because all had been subjected to analogous processes—the uneven and asymmetric spread of dependent capitalism and the introduction of modern institutions of governance—a unique interplay
of local, regional, and international determinants ignited and shaped each uprising.

Although Woodrow Wilson had originally proposed an interallied commission
merely to ascertain and convey the wishes of the Syrian population, the King-Crane
Commission had the unintended effect of catalyzing and, in many ways, defining
the political movement that arose to resist the imposition of a mandate on Syria.
Gulled by the promise implicit in the commission's tour of Syria, the *mutanawwirun* constructed structures that expedited the mobilization of the population. Because these elites were oriented toward Europe and the peace conference,
however, they designed institutions, demonstrations, and propaganda campaigns
for the purpose of presenting to an outside audience an image of a sophisticated
nation eager and prepared for independence. They thus deferred the task of inte-

grating the majority of the population into their framework of legitimacy. As a result, during the period that preceded the French mandate, the *mutanawwirun* never truly involved nonelites in their nationalist project: They never dickered with the population over questions of ideology and program, they never synthesized a political discourse that was compelling to nonelites, and they never established connections with the population comparable to those that the Wafdist leadership had established with the population of Egypt, for example. In short, the announcement of the formation of the King-Crane Commission and its subsequent visit to Syria initiated an unintended chain of events that culminated in the strengthening of a populist nationalism dissociated from the guidance of the more Westernized nationalist elites.

Notes

1. *Editor and Publisher*, 2 December 1922, iii.

2. Notes by Sir Maurice Pascal Alers from the 20 March 1919 meeting of the Council of Four, in Arthur S. Link, ed., *The Papers of Woodrow Wilson*, vol. 56 (Princeton, 1987), p. 116.

3. British Prime Minister David Lloyd George to French President Georges Clemenceau, 25 April 1919, in ibid., 58:134.

4. Unless otherwise indicated, the term "Syria" is meant to designate the territory of the Middle East that comprises present-day Syria, Lebanon, Jordan, Israel and the Occupied Territories, and western Iraq.

5. Ray Stannard Baker and William E. Dodd, eds., *Public Papers of Woodrow Wilson*, vols. 5–6: *War and Peace: Presidential Messages, Addresses, and Public Papers (1917–1925)* (New York: Harper & Brothers, 1927), 5:180.

6. Ibid., 5:160–161.

7. J. C. Hurewitz, ed., *The Middle East and North Africa in World Politics: A Documentary Record*, vol. 2: *British-French Supremacy, 1914–1945* (New Haven, 1979), 112.

8. For the position of the Syrian nationalists in the Egyptian exile community, see James L. Gelvin, "Popular Mobilization and the Origins of Mass Politics in Syria, 1918–1920," Ph.D. diss., Harvard University, 1992, 209–211. See also Muhibb al-Din al-Khatib, autobiographical manuscript stored in the Dar al-Watha'iq al-Tarikhiyya, Damascus.

9. Link, *The Papers of Woodrow Wilson*, 58:328.

10. The Balfour Declaration (named after British Foreign Secretary Arthur Balfour and issued on November 2, 1917) was in the form of a letter from Balfour to a leading British Zionist, Lord Walter Rothschild; it promised British support for the creation of "a national home for the Jewish people" in Palestine. The declaration provided a much-needed boost to the Zionist movement by providing the legal framework for continued Jewish immigration and land purchases in Palestine, the twin pillar of the Zionists' policy to make Palestine their national home. The British issued the declaration for a number of reasons: to preempt what was expected to be a similar announcement by Germany; to win the support of worldwide Jewry, especially in the United States and USSR, that would aid the war effort; and to have a group beholden to British interests in Palestine in order to protect the right flank of the Suez Canal, act as a buffer between the anticipated French position in Syria and the British position in Egypt,

and provide a land bridge from the Mediterranean Sea to the Persian Gulf (from Palestine across Transjordan and Iraq to the Gulf).

11. Charles Seymour, ed., *The Intimate Papers of Colonel House: The Ending of the War* (Boston, 1928), 153, 199.

12. Link, *The Papers of Woodrow Wilson*, 58:322–326.

13. Ray Stannard Baker in ibid., 56:442. Baker also wrote the following entry in his diary (21 May 1919; see ibid., 58:368) about the circumstances that led to the commission's departure: "[Wilson] told me with a kind of amused satisfaction—he gets very little fun out of his conferences, but he had it today—of the discussion this morning of the Syrian question and of a red-hot conflict of view between Lloyd George and Clemenceau. It seems that Lloyd George calmly proposed to give to Italy (to induce a settlement of the Fiume question) a slice of Syria which Clemenceau had already decided to gobble down. This perfectly frank scramble for territory, which in a moment of anger was fought with all guards down, seemed to amuse the President very much. It also had the effect of once more reviving the plan for the Syrian Commission (King and Crane). The President told the Four, positively, that our commissioners were leaving for Syria on Monday! It has given him his chance."

14. According to the report of the King-Crane Commission, "It is certain from the oral statements that accompanied the petitions that the term, 'Absolute independence,' was seldom used in the sense of an entire freedom from only foreign guidance such as that of a mandatory under the League of Nations, inasmuch as the request was frequently combined with a choice of mandate or a request for foreign 'assistance.' While a few of the Young Arab clubs certainly desired freedom from all foreign control, the great majority asked for independence and defined a mandate to mean only economic and technical assistance." "Report of the American Section of the International Commission on Mandates in Turkey (28 August 1919)," in U.S. Department of State, *Papers Relating to the Foreign Relations of the United States*, vol. 12: *The Paris Peace Conference: 1919* (Washington, DC, 1947), 767.

15. Link, *The Papers of Woodrow Wilson*, 58:133–134.

16. See Arthur S. Link, *Wilson the Diplomatist: A Look at His Major Foreign Policies* (Baltimore, 1957), 12.

17. Woodrow Wilson, "Political Sovereignty," in *Selected Literary and Political Papers and Addresses of Woodrow Wilson* (New York, n.d.), 91–92.

18. See, for example, Woodrow Wilson, "The Character of Democracy in the United States," in ibid., 89–93.

19. G. W. F. Hegel, *Philosophy of Right*, trans. T. M. Knox (New York, 1952), 204.

20. In an interview with Ida M. Tarbell, Wilson quoted the following lines from "The Princess," by Alfred Lord Tennyson: "A nation yet, the rulers and the ruled— / Some sense of duty, something of a faith, / Some reverence for the laws ourselves have made, / Some patient force to change them when we will, / Some civic manhood firm against the crowd." *Collier's*, 28 October 1916, 37.

21. For the strategy of the King-Crane Commission, a complete listing of the groups it received, and its conclusions, see "Report of the American Section of the International Commission," cited in note 13 above.

22. Ibid., 863.

23. William Yale, "A Report on Syria, Palestine, and Mount Lebanon for the American Commissioners," Yale Papers, Boston University, Box X/Folder 8/22–23.

24. For details about the "middle strata" and its role in nationalist movements, see E. J. Hobsbawm, *Nations and Nationalism Since 1780: Programme, Myth, Reality* (Cambridge, 1990), 90–94, 117–122; Miroslav Hroch, *Social Preconditions of National Revival in Europe: A Comparative Analysis of the Social Composition of Patriotic Groups Among the Smaller European Nations,* trans. Ben Fowkes (Cambridge, 1985), particularly 129–155. For a discussion of the changing nature of the urban notability during the nineteenth century, see Philip Khoury, *Urban Notables and Arab Nationalism: The Politics of Damascus, 1860–1920* (Cambridge, 1983).

25. It is important to note that, contrary to the assumptions of William Yale and other Western observers, neither the Arab government nor any of the allied organizations were monolithic; moreover, the government and the political and cultural clubs included members who espoused a variety of ideologies and practices. For example, as late as the autumn of 1919, al-Fatat included three factions: the "dissenters" (*rafidun*) who refused to support any mandate; a "pro-British/anti-French" faction allied with Emir Faisal; and a faction that still held out hope for a US mandate. See 'Izzat Darwaza, *Mudhakkirat wa Tasjilat* (Damascus, 1984), 2:76–77, 81–82; Gelvin, "Popular Mobilization," 55–63, 74–85. In this essay, the term "Arab government" refers to the faction of the government that included Emir Faisal, his entourage, and his allies.

26. India Office, London: L/PS/10/802. Gertrude Bell, "Syria in October 1919," 15 November 1919, 11.

27. *al-'Asima,* 7 May 1919, 1–2.

28. See Khoury, *Urban Notables,* 86–88; Yusuf al-Hakim, *Dhikrayat,* vol. 3: *Suriya wa al-'ahd al-Faysali* (Beirut, 1966), 90–97; Safiuddin Joarder, *Syria Under the French Mandate: The Early Phase, 1920–1927* (Dacca, 1977), 209–211.

29. Archives Diplomatiques, Nantes (hereinafter AD): 2430/no no. Cousse to Dame, 18 April 1919; Ministère des Affaires Etrangères, Paris (hereinafter MAE): L:AH vol. 4/237–238; Picot to Pichon, 22 May 1919; MAE L:SL vol. 14/#897; Picot to MAE, 17 June 1919; MAE L:SL vol. 44/3D; Minault (Latakia) to Administrateur du Vilayet de Beyrouth, 18 July 1919; Ministère de la Defense, Vincennes (hereafter MD) 7N4182/Dossier 4/340; Picot to MAE 21 July 1919; MAE L:SL vol. 43/39–41. "Renseignements d'Agent," 10–20 July 1919; AD 2430 Dossier Confidential-Départ/#240, 11 August 1919. For texts of sermons distributed 11 and 18 April 1919, see AD 2343/286, Cousse to Haut Commissionaire, 24 April 1919.

30. MD L:SL vol. 12/32–38. Cousse to Haut Commissionaire, 6 April 1919; Gelvin, "Popular Mobilization," 321–322.

31. See Malcolm Russell, *The First Modern Arab State: Syria Under Faysal, 1918–1920* (Minneapolis, 1985), 93–131.

32. See leaflet entitled, "Independence or Death!" in MAE L:SL vol. 43/72–73, 21 July 1919 (in Arabic with French translation).

33. See Gelvin, "Popular Mobilization," 240.

34. Khayr al-Din al-Zirikli, *Diwan Zirikli: al-a'mal al-shi'riyya al-kamila* (Amman[?], n.d.), 24–25 (translation by author).

35. See Charles Tilly, Louise Tilly, and Richard Tilly, *The Rebellious Century, 1830–1930* (Cambridge, Mass., 1975), 51–53; George L. Mosse, *The Nationalization of the Masses: Political Symbolism and Mass Movements in Germany from the Napoleanic Wars Through the Third Reich* (New York, 1977).

36. For copies of leaflets signed "mankub," see: MAE L:SL vol. 43/62, 64. n.d.; MD 7N4182/Dossier 4/340. Picot to MAE, 21 July 1920.

37. For a listing of the backgrounds of the primary and secondary leadership of the Higher National Committee of Damascus, see Gelvin, "Popular Mobilization," 125–130, 457–458.

38. Muhibb al-Din al-Khatib, "The Job of Guidance," al-'Asima, 16 October 1919, 1–2.

39. Foreign Office, London: FO371/5188/E7808/#42. "Arabic Press Abstracts for Week ending June 14, 1920," 26 May 1920.

40. al-'Asima, 23 October 1919, 1–2. It is interesting to contrast this statement with one made by Woodrow Wilson: "When I try to disentangle the ideas of the people and endeavor to express them if at first there is disaccord I am not astonished. I have firm confidence that their ideas will rally to mine." Quoted by Daniel Halevy, President Wilson, trans. Hugh Stokes (New York, 1919), 244.

41. Yale, "A Report on Syria," 24.

42. Sudan Archives, University of Durham: SA/493/6/51. Amin M'aluf to Ahmad Shuqayr, 1 June 1920.

43. As'ad Daghir, Mudhakirrati 'ala hamish al-qadiya al-'arabiyya (Cairo, 1956), 122.

44. See Tilly, Tilly, and Tilly, The Rebellious Century, 50–54; E. J. Hobsbawm, Primitive Rebels: Studies in Archaic Forms of Social Movement in the 19th and 20th Centuries (New York, 1959), 1–2, 110.

CHAPTER 2

THE "AMBASSADOR FOR THE ARABS"

The Locke Mission and the Unmaking of US Development Diplomacy in the Near East, 1952–1953

Paul W. T. Kingston

This chapter examines President Harry S Truman's policy toward the Near East[1] during the last years of his administration.[2] It focuses on the creation, in late 1951, of a regional office based in Beirut. Its mandate was to coordinate US economic policy in the region including capital assistance from the Mutual Security Program (MSP), refugee assistance channeled through the United Nations Relief and Works Administration (UNRWA; the United Nations alone will be referred to as the UN), and technical assistance from the Technical Cooperation Administration (TCA), commonly known as Point Four. Truman appointed Edwin Locke Jr., a young banker, to head the office. His official title was special assistant to the secretary of state, and he was given the rank of ambassador with direct lines of communication to the president.[3]

The "Locke mission" is interesting from several perspectives. First, it has become a forgotten episode in the history of US policy in the Near East that reflects a more general scholarly neglect of US policy in the region in the last years of the Truman administration. The prevailing perception is one of drift and frustration caused both by the failure to reach any political settlement to the Arab-Israeli conflict and

by the parallel difficulties in pursuing an economic approach to peacemaking, symbolized by the cautious recommendations of the Economic Survey Mission (ESM)
in 1949. This chapter suggests, however, that the Truman administration attempted
to reinvigorate the economic approach to peacemaking in the early 1950s. As such,
the Locke mission emerges as a link between the initial launching of the ESM in
1949 and the later attempts by Eric Johnston under the Eisenhower administration
to resurrect the same kind of approach. Finally, the dispatching of the Locke mission also represents a concerted, if failed, attempt to promote a more regional US
approach to the Near East, a break from past US emphases on bilateralism.

The main issue at stake here is whether an economic approach to pursuing US
objectives in the region was realistic. Certainly, the creation of the regional economic
office and the appointment of Locke was greeted in many circles with much fanfare.
The *New York Times* carried the story on its front pages;[4] the British, in part influenced by Locke's appointment, transferred their own regional economic office, the
Development Division of the British Middle East Office (BMEO), to Beirut;[5] the
Arab states were clearly buoyed by the prospects of a stronger US economic presence
in the region; and, as we shall see, the announcement won praise—and indeed had
been the result of pressure—from those within the US State Department who had
persistently called for the application of a Marshall Plan–type policy to the region.

However, despite the promising beginning, the Locke mission ended in ig-
nominy and, ultimately, oblivion: Locke resigned within a year of his appointment
without having effected any appreciable shift in US economic policy in the region,
and the Beirut-based regional economic office was disbanded. After briefly examining the origins of US economic diplomacy in the Near East, I set out to examine
why Truman's economic approach to the Near East faltered so badly. This entails
examining the relationship of the Locke mission to the three pillars of US development policy in the region: technical assistance under the Point Four program,
capital assistance under the Mutual Security Program, and refugee assistance channeled through UNRWA. Part of the explanation revolves around the person of
Locke himself, who, in persistently advocating a more pro-Arab line, emerged as
an early if unlikely example of that much-maligned group of State Department
officials known as the "Arabists."[6] Equally important are the vague terms of reference given to Locke that merely masked fundamental conflicts in objectives among
the various bureaucratic parties concerned and that served to sap the "collective
will" of the Truman administration. Ultimately, however, the question must be examined not at the level of personalities nor of policy implementation but at the
level of philosophical approach. Locke represents that generation of Americans
who believed that the injection of US finance and expertise into troubled parts of
the underdeveloped world could help to create a more empathetic political environment in the short run while laying the foundations for self-sustained growth
and, thus, political stability in the long run. The assumptions behind this optimistic
approach have now been openly questioned. Capital and technology by themselves
rarely promote development; development does not necessarily promote political
stability. Nevertheless, these were the assumptions that governed policy in the early

cold war and it is worth reminding ourselves how strong their hold was on policy-makers and development planners.

THE ORIGINS OF TRUMAN'S ECONOMIC
APPROACH TO THE NEAR EAST

The roots of postwar US economic diplomacy in the Near East are found in the wartime participation of the United States in the Middle East Supply Centre (MESC). Originally created to regulate the flow of imports and exports in and out of the region so as to conserve shipping space for military purposes, the MESC ultimately became involved in promoting regional economic production. It did such a good job at this latter task that some began to consider the idea of continuing the development functions of the MESC after the war. Despite some initial and favorable consideration, the idea was ultimately rejected by the US government and, at the close of the war, the MESC was immediately disbanded. The reasons were threefold. First, there was a strong desire not to continue to underwrite the British Empire in the region (which, it was felt, a regional economic approach would do). Second, there was an equally strong sense that a bilateral approach to the Near East would better serve US commercial interests by allowing for the unfettered expansion of private trade and investment in the region. Finally, economic orthodoxy in the United States dictated that private investment would best promote economic development in the "undeveloped" parts of the world. Hence, initial US economic policy in the Near East would be based on bilateralism with an emphasis on the private sector.

Three factors forced US Near East policymakers to change these calculations: the Arab-Israeli conflict, the emerging cold war, and the rise of anti-Western Arab nationalism. The Palestine War of 1948 and the subsequent upheavals in the Arab world as a whole, for example, forced US Near East policymakers to think more in regional terms. This led to the initiation of a series of Chief of Mission meetings, the first being held in Istanbul in November 1949. It also resulted in the emergence of a more favorable attitude toward Britain's regional presence, particularly the string of British military bases across the region symbolized by that at Suez and, as W. R. Louis has noted, led US Near East policymakers to defer to, if not underwrite, Britain's regional security system.[7] This ultimately led to the (stillborn) joint Anglo-American proposal to create a Middle East Command (MEC) in October 1951. Finally, this new interest in regionalism was extended to the economic realm, symbolized by the dispatching of the ESM under the auspices of the UN and headed by Gordon Clapp, the former director of the Tennessee Valley Authority (TVA).

Clapp assumed his task enthusiastically and initially considered creating two organizations—one to deal exclusively with refugee relief and the other to deal more directly with economic development. The latter was, in effect, the reemergence of an earlier British proposal to create a Middle East Development Board. He was strongly supported in these views by George C. McGhee, assistant secretary of state for Near Eastern affairs; both believed in the potential of economic development to erase intractable political problems. However, the initial foray into regionalism produced few dividends. The Chief of Mission conferences did not produce a coherent regional approach but merely acted as forums for exchanging information. Moreover, Clapp dramatically scaled down his originally ambitious ideas. Instead of two organizations, the UN amalgamated relief and resettlement functions into one organization, the UNRWA. Such cautiousness was dictated by a number of factors. Clapp himself concluded in his final report that "the region is not ready, the projects are not ready [and] the people and the governments are not ready for large scale development."[8] Moreover, the British changed their tune and raised strong objections to the idea of creating a regional development organization for fear of arousing the indignation of Arab nationalists. Instead, they advocated the creation of a development board in each country.[9] Thus, we witness an interesting shift with Britain, the dying imperial power moving away from a regional policy, and the United States, an emerging imperial power looking at the potential of a regional policy in a more favorable light. The launching of the Point Four program in 1950, however, seemed to offer some consolation, and in its initial years, it became active in the independent states of the Middle East, notably Iran, Lebanon, and Jordan, where the first general agreement under Point Four was signed.

However, in 1951, there was a significant polarization of both the global and regional climate. Driven by the outbreak of the Korean War and sparked by the nationalization of the Anglo-Iranian Oil Company by Iranian Prime Minister Muhammad Mussadiq in March, the assassination of King Abdullah of Jordan in July, and the unilateral abrogation of the 1936 Anglo-Egyptian treaty by the Wafdist government in October, there was a revival of discussions about the utility of economic approaches to diplomacy. Globally, this culminated in the establishment of the MSP, the main task of which was to coordinate all overseas economic, technical, and military assistance programs. Regionally, this led first to an allocation of $160 million for the Near East from the MSP. It then resulted in a US-backed decision by the UN General Assembly to strengthen the ability of UNRWA to promote refugee resettlement as well as relief by giving it an expanded budget of $250 million over three years. Finally, on the strong recommendation of McGhee, President Truman created the regional economic office in Beirut as a mechanism for coordinating all regional economic activity. With the appointment of Locke to head the office on November 13, 1951, it seemed that the regional economic approach to securing peace and stability in the Near East would finally be given a chance to work.[10]

LOCKE, POINT FOUR, AND LEBANON

A youthful forty-one years, Locke seemed an inspired choice to head the new regional economic office, combining both a successful career in the private and public sectors with an interest in the Middle East. His public-sector experience, acquired during and immediately after World War II, was impressive and included such positions as executive assistant to Donald Nelson, head of the War Productions Board

(1943–1944), Truman's personal representative to Chiang Kai-shek in China (1945), and Truman's special assistant in the White House (1946). Locke's natural environment, however, was the private sector, where his demonstrated instinct and friendly charm eventually led to his appointment in 1946 as vice president of Chase Manhattan Bank. He used his position to generate various business opportunities in the Middle East, principally Saudi Arabia, where he entered into negotiations to build both a cement plant and, later, a Coca-Cola plant. His growing involvement in the region eventually earned him a seat on the board of governors of the American University of Beirut. Locke, therefore, was seen as exactly the kind of person who could activate an economic approach to achieving peace and security in the Near East.[11]

Locke arrived in Beirut in early December 1951. It seemed an opportune moment. After protracted negotiations over the terms of US involvement in development activities,[12] the Lebanese government agreed to ratify the Point Four General Agreement in November 1951 and, with the subsequent announcement of Locke's appointment, was looking forward to a significant infusion of US aid into the country. Therefore, Locke, upon his arrival, was given a very friendly and high-profile welcome, the kind befitting a potential new patron. Harold Minor, the US minister in Lebanon, was clearly surprised at the receptivity of the Lebanese to the arrival of Locke—or "Saint Locke," as one leftist Lebanese paper sarcastically noted. In reaction to one of the many receptions in Locke's honor, Minor reported, "I have never in my many years in the Foreign Service attended a function more jovial and friendly. The Lebanese were simply bubbling over with enthusiasm. . . . It was something like a football rally." He went on to suggest that the Lebanese government seemed willing to cooperate with Locke to a degree that "we had hardly dared hope for."[13] Certainly, Locke would turn out to be a darling of Beirut society, hosting numerous dinner parties and, on several occasions, being the personal guest of President Faris al-Khuri at his mountain home. This was the kind of access to the top echelons of power in Lebanon that US representatives had hitherto not known.

From the outset, Locke seemed determined to take advantage of this favorable atmosphere. Having arrived in Beirut only the day before, Locke immediately wrote to his contact in the State Department, Arthur Gardiner, suggesting that a significant expansion of the development program for the Arab states would be needed if his mission was to be a success.[14] Within a week, Locke was also transmitting these ideas directly to Truman, bypassing the State Department and TCA. This was to become a feature of the Locke mission and it revealed the degree to which he perceived (and, as it turned out, misperceived) that he could count on Truman's personal support. Nevertheless, this letter is important, for it sets the tone for his entire mission. The main thing, wrote Locke, is that "a lot more life needs to be put into our aid programs here and in the other Middle Eastern countries." Not only were there "too many plans and too little action" (a complaint heard universally among the recipient governments in the region), but those plans that were being made operational under the Point Four program were making no significant impact economically or psychologically. This, above all, was Locke's self-appointed agenda, "to get these people [the Arabs] thinking in positives rather than negatives." In a classic espousal of the economic approach to peacemaking, Locke emphasized that "if we can get them started in an important way on developing the very attractive natural resources that they have, I believe that the political problems will suddenly become much less difficult to solve."[15]

Locke was looking for impact projects to fulfill his Near East mandate and, in Lebanon, there seemed one ready at hand: the Litani River project. Lebanon had been one of the first countries to receive assistance from Point Four even before a general agreement had been signed. It was in the form of a survey mission for the Litani River basin and was initiated by the first director of Point Four, Dr. Henry Bennett, upon his inaugural tour of the Middle East as a way of getting activity off the ground for the newly established TCA. Six months later, however, rumblings were surfacing in the Lebanese press about the lack of immediate, concrete results, and there was further fear that the project would be geared to the interests of private Lebanese citizens and, perhaps, Israel. The result was what one report referred to as "a vigorous campaign" in the Lebanese press against Point Four's association with the Litani River project.[16] Although one of Locke's first public actions was to issue a statement deflecting such criticisms, in fact he looked upon them as valid.[17] According to Locke, US involvement in the Litani River project, based as it was on technical assistance, was ill-designed to obtain quick results. Nor was it likely to solicit anything more than "polite unenthusiastic foot-dragging cooperation from [the] Lebanese."[18] Needed was a more significant infusion of development capital, and this was precisely what Lebanon could not provide. Its public finances were insufficient to keep up with the demands for development projects and, even where capital was available, it was tremendously difficult to achieve any kind of political consensus over its use. Nor did the kind of private investment needed for large projects seem to be forthcoming, as demonstrated by the failure of the Syrian government to raise capital for the development of the port at Latakia through the sale of public bonds. In Locke's opinion, an infusion of US development capital would solve both of these problems; it would provide a "take-off" point for sustained economic growth and improve the climate for private investment. All of this would, in turn, lay the psychological foundations for a more solid political alliance.

However, not all US representatives in Lebanon were delighted with the rather spectacular arrival of Locke in Beirut and his promise of a dramatic expansion of US aid to the Middle East. The bulk of this opposition emanated from Lebanon's Point Four team, whose program Locke was pledging to aggrandize. Part of the problem stemmed from confusion over the exact nature of Locke's mandate. When the regional economic office was first created, the local field offices of Point Four were assured that Locke's mandate would not allow him to interfere in the specific work of country programs or to supersede the authority of local country directors. Whether such a distinction could work in practice was problematic; the British certainly had had their share of administrative problems in launching the regionally based BMEO in 1945.[19] By choosing Beirut as Locke's headquarters and by sending him out at a time when the local Point Four office was without Country Director Hollis Peter, Washington seemed to be asking for problems.[20]

They did not take long to appear. Less than a month after Locke's arrival, one member of Lebanon's Point Four staff, Richard Farnsworth, complained in a personal letter to Peter that their operations in Lebanon had been taken over "Locke, stock, and barrel," so much so that the Lebanese government was beginning to submit project requests to Locke's office directly.[21] Well over a month later, Point Four's staff in Lebanon continued to complain about "the Locke concept": "[He] is still 'Mr. TCA' in Lebanon," wrote US official William Crockett, "and I am afraid will remain so as long as he stays in Lebanon."[22] When Peter finally arrived in Beirut at the end of March, he was forced to spend much of his time clarifying the actual extent of Locke's authority to the rather confused Lebanese—and to Locke himself.[23]

Had the confusion been merely administrative, little harm would have been done to basic US policy in the country. However, the real conflict in Beirut revolved around fundamental policy issues—issues that had never been satisfactorily resolved as a result of the amalgamation of Point Four with the MSP in May 1951. Point Four's approach, epitomized by the views of its founding administrator, Dr. Bennett, and shared by most in the field, was based on the idea that development would come only by building up human capital at the grassroots level. This required a long-range development policy based on the provision of technical assistance in such areas as education, health, and agriculture. Moreover, those results had to be part of a cooperative effort, one in which the local government made significant contributions of both finance and manpower. The concern here, of course, was with the long-term sustainability of projects. Those more politically minded in the State Department, however, had little time for an approach to development policy that ignored short-term political imperatives. George McGhee, who in many ways had masterminded the economic approach to peacemaking between the Arabs and the Israelis by first suggesting the formation of the ESM, was clearly unimpressed with the scope and philosophy of the Point Four program as it emerged in its severely reduced form in 1950;[24] Dean Acheson, secretary of state at the time, referred to Point Four in retrospect as "the Cinderella of the foreign aid family."[25]

The emergence of Locke, ostensibly an ambassador for the Point Four program yet an emissary whose ideas turned out to be much at odds with its philosophy, brought this latent conflict over US development policy to the surface. At a meeting in Washington, DC, between representatives of Point Four and those from the Near East Division of the State Department to discuss Locke's request for an infusion of financial aid into the Litani River project, the two parties found themselves unable to reach any consensus. Whereas the latter argued strongly for Locke's proposal on the basis that the overriding need was to get some large and visible project under way in one of the Arab states, Point Four staff continued to object on the basis that "the principle of picking up the check on partially completed projects was a basic departure from TCA philosophy and policy."[26] After several conversations with Locke upon his return to Beirut, Peter revealed much the same story: "It is quite clear that Ed Locke and I do not see eye to eye on the points of major importance in the Aid Program to Lebanon. I believe he listened politely at my expounding the Point Four philosophy which we feel must be an integral part of each project . . . while he believes there is a real distinction to be made between pure technical assistance on the one hand and economic or financial grant aid on the other."[27]

Peter was further concerned by Locke's propensity to project his ideas about US development policy in the region in an official manner in meetings with Lebanese officials. Fouad Ammoun, Lebanese director-general of foreign affairs, even suggested that Locke had virtually promised them increased amounts of aid, $5 million in fiscal year 1952 and $10 million in fiscal year 1953.[28] This was not only a break in diplomatic protocol, not to speak of constitutional procedure, but it also threatened the viability of the existing Point Four program in the country. The basic dilemma, of course, was that if the Lebanese were led to believe that a large infusion of US capital was imminent, they would be less interested in making the kind of small-scale commitments of local finance that were so important to all Point Four projects. Indeed, this seemed to be the case: At one point in the protracted negotiations over the terms of a Point Four agreement for the almost completed fiscal year 1952, Fouad Ammoun admitted that the Lebanese had not acted more quickly because they were waiting to see what Locke could produce.[29] This also explained, in Peter's opinion, the rather cavalier attitude taken by the Lebanese toward the visit of the World Bank's regional representative, Dorsey Stephens.[30] The dilemma, as US official Victor Skiles stated, was that "[if] U.S. aid is to be accepted not as a cooperative endeavor but as a substitute for local financing . . . we will have failed miserably in the total effort."[31]

Not all disagreed with Locke's ideas, notably Afif Tannous, an agriculturalist of Lebanese origin based with the Point Four team in Beirut. He was understandably delighted to be part of an expanded development assistance program for his mother country. This, however, made the matter potentially more dangerous by creating divisions within the US diplomatic community in the country. For the time being, Minor and Peter worked to maintain a facade of diplomatic unity in order to avoid unduly embarrassing Locke or damaging the prestige of his newly established position. Peter stressed, however, that this was being done at the cost of giving the impression of Point Four staff support for Locke's ideas, which was not always the case.[32] Peter, therefore, warned Washington that Locke's presence in Beirut could jeopardize his own ability to fulfill Point Four's mandate in the country. He wrote: "I do not believe it is too late to obtain the cooperation and enthusiastic support of the Lebanese Government officials for a real Point Four program, but it is hard for them to concentrate on this aspect which requires considerable understanding and foresightedness with the promise of large sums dangling in front of their noses."[33]

LOCKE AND REGIONAL DEVELOPMENT
IN THE NEAR EAST

Locke's actions in Lebanon during the early stages of his mission cannot be understood without placing them in the broader context of the Near East as a whole. Locke's mandate, after all, was a regional one and would require a regional solution. Here, Locke's diagnosis was similar to that made in Lebanon. What he found was an economic assistance program badly structured to meet the needs of the Near East. US assistance under the Point Four program was judged to be slow and insufficient by Arab governments—a "broken reed" as one Jordanian official remarked. This was particularly so in contrast to the large sums of capital assistance being provided by the United States to Israel, a point that Locke was constantly reminded of during travels to various Arab capitals. Moreover, though the United States was providing capital assistance to UNRWA, the funds were going largely unused due to the reluctance of Arab states to accept anything that smacked of the principle of reintegration. Acceptance of UNRWA assistance for refugee resettlement was looked upon as tantamount to abandoning the rights of the refugees to return to their homes. The result was an aid program ill-equipped to solve the kind of political problems in the region for which it was ultimately designed. It was these political problems that underlay all of Locke's thinking on the matter. As he wrote in a memorandum to Truman: "I feel that I must say frankly to you that our entire economic effort to help the Near East achieve a more secure freedom, a lasting peace and a rising standard of living is in danger of being overwhelmed by political turmoil."[34]

Locke's sense of urgency was further accentuated by the tight legislative schedule in Washington. Before Locke scarcely had his feet on the ground in Beirut, the State Department was already drawing up its proposed budget for the MSP for fiscal year 1953. By mid-February, it had released its initial estimates, which showed little change in the size or distribution of aid to the Near East. Having staked the success of his mission on the need for an increased allocation to the region, Locke once again bypassed the State Department and cabled directly to Truman, expressing his utmost concern at what he saw as the continued drift of US policy in the region: "If we do not (rpt [repeat] not) now (rpt now) make it clear to the Arab states that we mean what we have been saying these past three years about wanting to help them develop their countries, I am mortally afraid we will have lost our last chance and that the reaction to this . . . program will be bitter and sharp, and the inclination to look for other friends greatly increased."[35]

Locke's recommendation to Truman was the establishment of a $100 million Arab development fund designed to provide capital assistance to the Arab states, especially the non-oil states of Lebanon, Syria, Jordan, and Egypt. This would, in effect, add a fourth stream to US development policy in the region, separate and distinct from already existing programs to Israel, UNRWA, and Point Four. The purpose of the fund was to finance the completion of several impact projects in the fields of transportation and/or river development, placing special emphasis on the former as a result of Locke's experiences in China.[36] In all, he presented nine possible projects.[37] In an attempt to make his proposal more palatable to Congress, Locke presented it up as a "one-shot" deal that would pave the way for the greater involvement of the World Bank and private capital.

There had been numerous criticisms made of US development policy in the region, but never had a call for change come so explicitly and forcefully and never from such high levels of government. In effect, Locke was calling for not only a break with the traditional approach to development as advocated by Point Four, but also a significant shift in US policy toward the Arab world. Aid was to be raised to a level on par with that given to Israel, and it was to be given on an unconditional basis, free from linkages with the Arab refugee issue. On this last point, Locke was especially insistent: "If we try bargain for pol[itical] and military advantages as direct quid pro quo, believe results w[ou]ld be nil and our whole position considerably weakened. . . . Realize this entails certain risks but consider it infinitely less than contains as at present."[38] In short, Locke's proposal was a genuine attempt at instituting an economic approach to peacemaking in the Arab world. It advocated a separation of the economic from the political in a way that US contributions to UNRWA could not.

Locke faced serious obstacles in effecting such a significant shift in US policy in the region. The dissenting views of many Point Four officials have already been mentioned; no doubt, these were joined by opposition from those wary of undermining US support for Israel. However, the most immediate obstacle was time—a problem not helped by Locke's sudden illness in Beirut in mid-February, which forced him to delay a trip to Washington designed to allow him to make his case before the State Department and, if necessary, Congress. By the time Locke returned to Washington at the end of March, the bill to extend the MSP, which made no provision for the kind of program advocated by Locke, had reached an advanced stage in its presentation to Congress.[39]

To compensate for his absence, Locke tried several methods to build support for his proposal. In mid-March, Donald Bergus, then second secretary in the Lebanese legation, was sent to Washington to lobby the State Department. This was accompanied by a flurry of supportive telegrams from US officials in Lebanon and Syria, the latter seeing in Locke's plan an opportunity to break the impasse over the introduction of Point Four into the country.[40] As was mentioned earlier, Locke also took the unorthodox step of building up an Arab constituency for his ideas by officially informing the president and prime minister of Lebanon of his proposal to increase US assistance to the Arab world, much to the horror of Peter.[41] It seems apparent, however, that Locke was really counting on the personal support of Truman. "I beg of you," wrote Locke after falling ill in Beirut, "to give this every consideration. I stake on this proposal such reputation as I may have and feel that it is the only way to get the results I know you want me to get out here."[42]

Truman did not provide the kind of hands-on support Locke was looking for. Although he expressed appreciation for Locke's imaginative approach, Truman passed the buck, so to speak, by referring Locke's request back to the State Department, where it ran aground over conflicting policy interests.[43] In Bergus's initial meeting with officials from the MSP, for example, objections were raised on the grounds that unconditional aid would set dangerous precedents and would probably militate against promoting the kinds of reforms that the United States felt were needed.[44] Averell Harriman, the director for mutual security under the auspices of the MSP, later raised these same issues in a memo to Secretary of State Acheson.[45] In short, the kinds of objections raised by the Point Four team in Beirut seem to have carried much weight in Washington.

Neither did there seem to be a great deal of respect for Locke's political analysis. Crucial to Locke's argument was his oft-repeated view that the political situation in the Near East was "precarious" and "threatening," requiring immediate action. But, to paraphrase Harriman's query, was it so serious as to require amendments to the mutual security bill in such a way that might jeopardize the entire program put forward?[46] There were similar questions raised about whether increased aid to the Arab states would, in fact, improve matters. One memo described Locke's aim of winning the friendship of the Arab world as "an endless task" that did not provide a basis for formulating programs of an extraordinary character.[47] There was particularly strong objection to his idea of divorcing development from the Palestinian refugee issue. In response to one compromise suggestion that Locke's program of capital assistance be confined to Syria as a way of breaking the impasse in relations with that country, Reeseman Fryer, a Point Four official, responded that: "To offer Syria an unconditional development program much greater in magnitude, different in organizational structure and purpose from the programs now getting underway in Lebanon, Jordan, Egypt and Iraq would tend to undermine Point 4 programs in the latter countries by appearing to pay a premium for non-cooperation—'It pays to hold out.'"[48] The only way a program of expanded assistance could be justified, wrote Fryer, was if it was paralleled by an appropriate concession on the part of the Syrian government—one that would have to revolve around the issue of refugee settlement.[49] In short, unconditional economic assistance to the Arab world was out of the question.

Thus, Locke's proposal never did see the light of day. Ostensibly it was rejected on the grounds that its passage through Congress would prove an impossibility;[50] in reality, the Truman administration was not inclined to consider any dramatic changes in its policy toward the Near East. Truman may have wanted "action" in the Near East, but he was not willing to become actively involved himself in promoting such changes. With Locke's proposal also threatening the viability of Point Four's operations in the Near East—it had already shown signs of doing just that in Lebanon—without offering any immediate solution to the Palestinian refugee issue, he was also unable to muster much support within the appropriate bureaucratic circles in Washington. Locke, in short, must have been a rather isolated figure upon his return to Washington, a far cry from his more heady days as Truman's special representative to China and, subsequently, the White House itself. It is this sense of isolation and inertia in Washington policy circles that would eventually lead to Locke's unmaking as a representative of US policy in the Near East.

LOCKE, THE ARAB REFUGEES, AND UNRWA

After the proposal to create an Arab Development Fund was shelved, Locke was kept in Washington for an additional month. Part of the reason for Locke's delayed return was to ensure that he did not go back to Beirut completely empty-handed. Due to his own indiscretions, there was a high sense of expectation in such Arab states as Syria and Lebanon of a possible shift in US development policy. This led to the creation of a smaller $25 million fund aimed at financing more moderately demanding projects, which Locke was to draw up in cooperation with the local Point Four country directors. However, the principal reason for delaying Locke in Washington was to brief him more thoroughly on the goals and procedures of both the State Department and his mission. This meant clarifying Locke's role within the Point Four program, a task that met with some success, if Peter's subsequent comments are any guide.[51] Even more fundamental to US interests in the region, however, was the need to make UNRWA more effective. Locke had been appointed as the US representative on the Advisory Commission of UNRWA in late February but had been unable to take up his duties with any seriousness due to his illness and subsequent return to Washington. Since State Department policy now held that a capital aid program for the Arab states be considered only if and when the considerable resources of UNRWA, of which 70 percent came from the United States, were fully utilized, Locke was now instructed to help make that US contribution an effective one.[52] Thus, upon returning to Beirut, Locke's mandate had been clarified: much reduced involvement in the Point Four program and much enhanced involvement in UNRWA.

Locke's appointment to the Advisory Commission of UNRWA came at a propitious moment in its history. In January, the UN General Assembly, including its Arab members, had approved a three-year, $250 million reintegration program designed to remove the refugees from their dependence on international relief. The agreement of the Arab states to this program had been obtained on the theory that settlement and integration would not interfere with the legal rights of the refugees to repatriation and compensation. In the Arab world, it became known as the "Blandford Plan," after John Blandford, the US director of UNRWA, who was a former manager of the TVA. Following the vote, Blandford became involved in a series of bilateral negotiations on specific refugee settlement projects with the Arab states.

Despite Locke's fundamental objection to using UNRWA as a channel for US development (as opposed to relief assistance to the Arab world), he did take an active part in its affairs. Upon his return from Washington, Locke began a series of visits to refugee camps in order to get a firsthand view of actual camp conditions. He would often visit the camps unannounced, meet with refugee leaders, listen to their grievances, and receive their petitions. What he found appalled him: inadequate health and educational facilities, a lack of employment opportunities, complaints about reductions in rations, and particularly vitriolic rhetoric reserved for the West in general and for the "dictator" of UNRWA, Blandford.[53] What was interesting about these trips was Locke's tendency to distance himself from past US policy in the region and to set himself up more as a spokesman for the refugees. After a meeting with refugee leaders in Beirut during early autumn, for example, Locke held a news conference and declared the refugee situation "more serious now than it has ever been" and intimated that he would push for a change in US policy toward these "forgotten people."[54] So delighted were the refugees with this new-found and high-level US advocate that one refugee leader described him as the "Ambassador for the Arabs."[55] It was this image—the public champion of the refugees—that Locke brought to the meetings of the Advisory Commission of UNRWA.

One of the most immediate and acute problems facing UNRWA upon Locke's return was the widening disparity between the growing number of refugees, on the one hand, and the shrinking resources available for relief on the other. Although the Blandford Plan had pledged $50 million for relief, much of that had been ear-marked for the first year of the program with the hope that the reintegration pro-gram, for which there was $200 million, would increasingly be able to pay the bills in subsequent years. In the absence of any concrete agreements on reintegration projects, however, UNRWA very quickly began to face a financial crisis. Less than eight months after the passage of the program, the estimates for the relief budget for fiscal year 1953 had already been raised from $18 million to $23 million, a fig-ure even Locke felt was optimistic.[56]

In Locke's opinion, one of the reasons for this budgetary crisis was the undisci-plined and profligate manner in which UNRWA spent money. To correct the sit-uation, Locke launched within the Advisory Commission a campaign for greater fiscal austerity. Initially, Locke raised the idea of cutting refugee rations, though he avoided making any personal or governmental commitments and eventually backed away from the suggestion for political reasons.[57] A more concerted effort was made to improve the administrative efficiency of the agency. Locke was as-tounded, for example, that at a time when UNRWA was trying to reduce the fi-nancial allocations for relief, the number of staff on its payroll was increasing out of all proportions.[58] There were similar problems with the procurement operations, which Locke described as amateurish and amazingly soft, particularly when it came to the negotiation of prices for wheat purchases from local governments.[59] There was also talk of corruption within UNRWA itself—of supplies like wheat and med-icine being sold privately on the open market.[60] To investigate these problems, Locke successfully put pressure on Blandford to hire an outside auditing firm to examine UNRWA's supply division. Although no corruption was actually uncov-ered, the report revealed, in Locke's words, a situation "even less satisfactory than I had imagined."[61]

The real issue facing UNRWA, however, was how to push forward with the reintegration program, so crucial in solving UNRWA's budgetary problems let alone in improving the plight of the growing number of refugees. Here, the signals were mixed. Jordan had proved reasonably cooperative over plans to finance dam construction and irrigation development on the Yarmuk River. Originally drawn up by a Point Four engineer, Miles Bunger, the Yarmuk–Jordan River scheme was subsequently adopted by UNRWA, which allocated an initial $10 million from the reintegration fund. Negotiations with the Syrian government were slower, but in the beginning of October, they, too, had resulted in a $30 million reintegration agreement.

However, the difficulty of implementing these agreements was quickly apparent, the Syrian agreement being a case in point. Despite his numerous trips to Damascus to meet with Syrian President Adib al-Shishakli—a "stalky little guy" with whom he professed to get on "beautifully"[62]—Locke was never very optimistic about the prospect of significant progress in refugee settlement there. Even after the initial talks between the Syrian chief of state, Colonel Fawzi Selu, and Blandford in February 1952—which some thought was an encouraging start—Locke's summary of the discussions led him to a much different conclusion: "1. [Selu] didn't think the amount of aid in Blandford's Plan was sufficient and moreover felt the Agency should pay for any land it wanted; 2. He was more interested in industrial than agricultural development—he feels the West is turning the Middle East into a great farm; 3. He is worried about competition for jobs between Syrian nationals and Palestinian refugees . . . If that's progress, I'm the son of a donkey."[63] The substance of the $30 million agreement with Syria in October bore out this initial skepticism. By the end of November, only one project was actually under way—the conversion of a rundown army barracks southwest of Homs into an orphanage; it was expected, at a cost of $100,000, to remove, at most, 200 refugees from the relief rolls. All of the additional agricultural projects under consideration were hampered by the marginality of the land being offered.[64] Debates over the technical and political feasibility of the proposed Yarmuk scheme were causing similar delays in Jordan.

The frustrations over this halting progress spilled over into meetings of the Advisory Commission and were symbolized by the deteriorating relations between Locke and Blandford, the two most prominent Americans involved in UNRWA. There were a variety of issues over which the two locked horns. The conflict over budgetary practices within UNRWA has already been mentioned. This was accompanied by a series of backstabbing exchanges over Blandford's decision to replace UNRWA's US representative in Amman with a former British military officer. Locke, who was somewhat suspicious of British policy in the region, wanted to see Americans in key positions in UNRWA, both to improve its efficiency and to take advantage of any good press, particularly in Jordan, where the most promising program existed.[65] Locke and Blandford also squared off over whether Arab members should be accepted on the Advisory Commission; Blandford eventually succumbed to Locke's strong advocacy of this issue when it received the support of the State Department.[66]

The most substantial dispute between the two concerned UNRWA's approach to the resettlement issue. Locke was critical of Blandford's desire for political agreement before planning the specifics of any resettlement program, an approach that had led to delays in building up the technical arm of UNRWA. In Locke's opinion, this had left UNRWA an "empty shell" and unable to draw up, let alone execute, the kind of reintegration projects that would ultimately attract the cooperation of Arab governments. The result was "a lot of talk and a lot of running around," but no action.[67] Locke felt that by strengthening UNRWA's technical side Blandford would be able to negotiate on a much more compelling, project-by-project basis. It was a position often forwarded by Syrian officials in their negotiations with UNRWA.[68] Thus, he pushed Blandford repeatedly in meetings of the Advisory Commission to hire more technicians who could proceed with the immediate job at hand. Faced with Blandford's persistent opposition, however, Locke reverted to his initial lack of optimism about the prospects for UNRWA's success. The extent of his disillusionment was revealed by comments made in a letter to Truman at the end of September:

> UNRWA . . . is doing a pretty awful job and getting practically nowhere. What meat it would be for a new Truman committee—inefficiency on a broad scale, overstaffing and complete lack of results. The frame of mind of the refugees, now in their fifth year of homelessness, is becoming increasingly desperate. I have come to the firm conclusion that UNRWA is not the answer. No one believes in it anymore, especially in the Near East and least of all the refugees themselves.[69]

"LOCKE HITS OUT AT US AID POLICY"

Where was Locke to go from here? (The headline that serves as the title for this section portends his fate.) Although he had been sent to the Near East to activate policy, he had no confidence in the tools at his disposal. He had discarded UNRWA as a viable mechanism for US development policy in the Near East. Neither was he impressed with the potential of the Point Four program to make a noticeable political impact. It was true that the State Department had agreed to the establishment of a $25 million capital investment program for the Near East. However, when Locke convened a meeting of regional TCA country directors in late August to draw up a plan of action, he was extremely unimpressed with the nature and quality of the project proposals, especially those from the Lebanese group, whom Locke described as less than cooperative.[70] Moreover, as the following remarks to Truman indicate, Locke had become increasingly impatient with the "indecisive" State Department: "That organization, as I found out by personal experience last spring, has fallen into the way of doing things by committee and by unanimous vote which means that new ideas are under severe and sometimes almost insuperable handicap."[71] No doubt, this growing antagonism was fueled by rumors that the State Department's recall of Locke was imminent.[72]

These growing frustrations coincided with the marked deterioration of the Near East political climate in the autumn of 1952. Revolution in Egypt, a change of government in Lebanon, continued drift in Jordan, and the uncertainty of the political situation in Syria: All were factors pushing local Arab leaders into championing a more radical anti-Western stance, particularly in regard to the Arab-Israeli conflict and the refugee problem. The opening of the UN General Assembly in the autumn of 1952 provided the Arab states with a diplomatic forum where they could voice their criticisms. The net result was, in Locke's words, an "explosive situation," with the Arab states "feeling their oats," the Israelis becoming more "restive," and the Russians making continuous and discreet advances.[73]

Locke's response to this growing sense of crisis was to revive his old proposal for the creation of an Arab development fund. It was his hope that the deteriorating political situation might now induce Truman to give it personal endorsement.[74] However, with Eisenhower's victory in November and the emergence of a new sense of expectancy in the Arab world about an impending realignment of US policy in the region, Locke changed his tactics. Eisenhower was looked upon as having fewer ties with Israel and as being more conscious of the benefits of closer ties to the Arab states. In order to create some bureaucratic momentum for a policy shift, some diplomats began to advocate a formal reevaluation of US policy in the region.[75] Locke approved of this campaign but saw little hope of its success using normal diplomatic channels. Having first come out to the Near East with the hope of making a psychological impact on Arab public opinion, Locke now reversed his target and sought to make an impact on US public opinion. At the beginning of December, he gave three interviews with a US reporter, all of which appeared in the Beirut newspaper, the *Daily Star,* the second under the byline, "Locke Hits Out at U.S. Aid Policy."[76] He then gave a talk at the influential Lebanese policy institute, le Cenacle Libanais, on December 6, calling for the formulation of a "new and hard-hitting policy" in the Near East based on the creation of a US-financed Arab development fund that could push ahead with such vital projects as the development of the Euphrates River and the Yarmuk Plan. In effect, it was a rehashed version of the proposal that he had presented to Truman six months earlier.[77]

The reactions to Locke's outbursts were swift and predictable. In Amman, Green, a US official who on the whole was supportive of the kind of approach being suggested by Locke, was taken aback by his public attacks on US policy;[78] in Beirut, Minor was equally shocked at Locke's public policymaking and warned that "I can only see harm in this";[79] and in Washington, those who had become increasingly concerned about the adverse effects that Locke's appointment was having on US policy in the region finally had their excuse for action. One day after his talk at le Cenacle Libanais, Locke was called back, "for consultations" in Washington; one week later he resigned. Thus, less than one year after his high-profile return to public service, Locke was on his way back to the private sector.

What is interesting about "the Locke affair," as it was called for a short time in Beirut, was the reaction it received in parts of the Arab world. When Locke took his criticisms of US development policy public, the Lebanese press responded with support and praise: "The Arab world can only be grateful for such men as Locke who have . . . seen the flow of American policy and have spoken out," read one editorial in the *Daily Star*;[80] "wise and righteous," read another, containing an added hope that Locke would now be free to continue his campaign unshackled by diplomatic protocol.[81] Moreover, when Locke returned to Beirut at the end of December to finalize his affairs, he was given a hero's welcome. The Syrian government hosted a dinner in his honor in Damascus, and the Lebanese government awarded him the Order of the Cedars, the highest honor of state. Clearly, by publicly championing the Arab cause within the Truman administration, Locke had won himself a secure if fleeting spot in Arab history texts. As Peter summed it up, "There can be no question now . . . that he is the man of the hour—the white hope of the Arabs who is assumed to have spoken out on the basis of his convictions."[82]

The affair has since become a forgotten episode in the history of US policy in the region. This may seem somewhat surprising, given Locke's penchant for publicity even after his return to the United States.[83] Moreover, Locke's recommendations were not without support in US policy circles; their roots went back to George McGhee, Gordon Clapp, and the ESM. Nevertheless, history has probably been an accurate judge of the significance of the Locke mission. To start with, even if Locke's ideas did strike a sensitive vein within the State Department, his tactics left much to be desired and lost him the respect of all those who might have lent him support. Moreover, his call for unconditional aid to the Arab states, friend or foe, would never have carried much weight, especially in the context of an intensifying cold war that stressed the importance of helping one's allies. Perhaps the most important reason for the disappearance of the Locke mission from history was its complete overshadowing by the incoming Eisenhower administration, rumored to be interested in pursuing a more evenhanded regional policy. In that sense, Locke found himself all of a sudden swimming with the tide rather than against it.

However, though the Eisenhower administration did make efforts to improve relations between the United States and the Arab world, it never considered the kind of changes to US development policy in the Near East that Locke had hoped to see. The United States did continue to channel its assistance through UNRWA, though with the resignation of Blandford in early 1953 the grandiose settlement plans gradually gave way to the reality of day-to-day relief operations. Moreover, though Point Four did begin to consolidate its presence in the region, it never did receive the kind of capital resources that Locke felt were needed. Finally, by insisting on regional linkages and prior political agreements, the Eisenhower administration, despite the diplomatic efforts of Eric Johnston, was never able to activate the kind of "impact project" approach to development advocated by Locke. In short, what was labeled as "an economic approach" to peacemaking in the Near East has always been burdened with explicit political baggage.

This raises a more general question, one that is ultimately relevant to an evaluation of the Locke mission. Would the kind of more strictly economic approach advocated by Locke have been any more effective? Certainly, the Arab states were calling for it, and in that sense, Locke was really acting as a conduit for Arab views. However, whereas what was called the "TCA approach" may have worked in the context of the developed states of Europe (a debatable point at best), its application in the developing world has proven more problematic. It has taken theorists and practitioners of development many years to realize that modernization was not simply a linear process dependent on the infusion of technology and capital. The development process has been complicated by a whole series of structural and cultural factors, ones that are consistently ignored in the context of aid policies such as those suggested by Locke. These complicating factors have been particularly salient in the Middle East, plagued as it has been by the Arab-Israeli conflict, the extraordinarily high degree of regional interaction, and the superimposition upon them of the cold war. Locke, by so exclusively placing his hopes for an improved relationship between the Arab world and the United States on the provision of more US finance and technology, essentially ignored all of these factors. Thus, although more pro-Arab on the surface, his proposal can in fact be criticized for its insensitivity to the details of Arab politics—a common criticism of US policy in general in the Middle East in the 1950s. Whether linked or unconditional, greater amounts of capital assistance would not have been the decisive factor in winning Arab friendship, nor would they have effected any dramatic and broad-based economic take-off. It might have improved the lives of a few peasants, provided work for a few Arab bureaucrats and technicians, and even settled a few Palestinian refugees—all very laudable on human grounds. However, it could not have effected the kind of broad structural changes in the region that were at the root of its instability. These were simply beyond the scope of US power.

Notes

I would like to thank Myriam Noisette and David Wesl for commenting on earlier drafts of this chapter. Needless to say, all errors of judgment and interpretation are my responsibility. I would also like to thank the Connaught Fund at the University of Toronto for generously funding this research and the National Archives in Washington, DC, and the Truman Library in Independence, Missouri, for facilitating it.

1. For definition's sake, the term "Near East" is used to refer to the Levant states of Syria, Lebanon, Jordan, Israel, and also Egypt.

2. Truman succeeded the presidency upon Franklin D. Roosevelt's death in April 1945. Elected outright in 1948, Truman served out one full term; Republican Dwight D. Eisenhower took office in 1953 by defeating Adlai Stevenson in the 1952 presidential election.

3. For background on Truman's policy toward the Middle East in the last years of his administration, see H. Fields, "Pawns of Empire: A Study of United States Middle East Policy, 1945–53," Ph.D. diss., Rutgers University, 1975; J. Hurewitz, *Middle East Dilemmas* (New York: 1953); M. Kolinsky, "The Efforts of the Truman Administration to Resolve the Arab-Israeli Conflict," *Middle East Studies* 20(1) (January 1984); and I. Pappe, *Britain and the Arab-Israeli Conflict, 1948–51* (Basingstoke: 1988).

4. *New York Times,* 14 November 1951.

5. Cf. Parker to Hare, "Transfer of the British Middle East Office from Cairo," 29 December 1951, Lot 57D/298, Near East (hereinafter NE) Files, National Archives (hereinafter NA). In fact, Bill Crawford, the head of the Development Division, responded enthusiastically to Locke's appointment, describing him as "one of the brightest guys to hit this part of the world." Crawford to Evans, 23 January 1952, Foreign Office (hereinafter FO) 371/98276/E11345/5.

6. Cf. R. Kaplan, *The Arabists: The Romance of an American Elite* (New York: 1993), for a recent journalistic account.

7. Cf. W. R. L. Louis, *The British Empire in the Middle East: Arab Nationalism, the United States, and Postwar Imperialism* (Oxford: 1984).

8. Cf. United Nations Conciliation Commission for Palestine, *Final Report of the United Nations Economic Survey Mission for the Middle East* (Lake Success, N.Y.: 1949).

9. Cf. Laborne to Clapp, 6 October 1949, Morton to Clapp, 8 November 1949, Clapp to Morton, 11 November 1949, Morton to Clapp, 2 December 1949, and Keeley to Clapp, 17 March 1950, all contained in Papers of Gordon Clapp, Box 3, United Nations Economic Survey Mission (hereinafter UNESM), Harry S Truman Library (hereinafter HSTL).

10. For details on the events leading up to Locke's appointment, see "Oral History Interview with Edwin Locke Jr." and "Oral History Interview with George McGhee," HSTL.

11. Edwin Locke Jr., interview by author, 7 February 1994.

12. In 1951, Syria and Yemen had still not signed Point Four agreements. Cf. Pinkerton to US Department of State, "Point IV Agreement with Lebanon," 883A.00-TA/2–2851, and Geren to US Department of State, "Why a Point IV Agreement has not been concluded with Syria," NA 883.00TA/5/28/51.

13. Minor memo, 9 January 1952, Papers of Edwin Locke Jr., Box 4, HSTL.

14. Locke to Gardiner, 21 December 1951, ibid.

15. Locke to Truman, 26 December 1951, ibid.

16. Cf. "Campaign Against Point IV Litani River Project," Beirut to US Department of State, 883A.00-TA/1–752.

17. Cf. "Statement by Ambassador Edwin Locke Jr.," 23 December 1951, Papers of Edwin Locke Jr., Box 4, HSTL.

18. Locke to US Secretary of State, 883A.00-TA/1–3152.

19. Cf. P. Kingston, "Pioneers in Development: The British Middle East Development Division and the Politics of Technical Assistance, 1945–1960," D.Phil. diss., Oxford University, 1991.

20. Cf. Staff Memorandum, US Department of State, "Responsibilities of Ambassador Locke in the Near East," 12 May 1952, Lot 57D/298, NE Files, for details on the policy discussions surrounding the creation of the regional office.

21. Farnsworth to Peter, 16 January 1952, Record Group (hereinafter RG) 84, Lebanon, Classified General Records, Box 28, NA Records Administration (NARA).

22. Crockett to Skiles, 29 February 1952, RG 84, Lebanon, Classified General Records, Box 28, NARA.

23. Peter to Reeseman Fryer, 1 April 1952, RG 84, Lebanon, Classified General Records, Box 28, NARA.

24. Cf. Oral History Interview with George McGhee, p. 44, HSTL.

25. Cf. D. Acheson, *Present at the Creation: My Years in the State Department* (New York: 1969).

26. Cf. Memo of Conversation, "Telegrams from Amb. Locke Proposing the U.S. Complete the Markabi, Kasmie, and Taibe Projects for Lebanon," 883A.00-TA/2–1352.

27. Peter to Reeseman Fryer, 1 April 1952, RG 84 Lebanon, Classified General Records, Box 28, NARA.

28. Cf. "Negotiation of Point 4 Program Agreement in Lebanon," 883A.00-TA/4–2452.

29. Cf. ibid.

30. Peter to Reeseman Fryer, 7 June 1952, RG 84 Lebanon, Classified General Records, Box 28, NARA.

31. Skiles to Tannous, 28 February 1952, ibid.

32. Peter to Reeseman Fryer, 1 April 1952, ibid.

33. Ibid.

34. Locke to Truman, "Action Program for the Near East," 25 April 1952, Presidential Secretary's Files, Papers of Harry S Truman, HSTL.

35. Locke to Truman, 19 February 1952, Papers of Edwin Locke Jr., Box 5, HSTL.

36. Locke, for example, justified these priorities by citing the "remarkable success" of the Japanese in developing Manchuria during World War II based on the modernization of infrastructure in the areas of transportation, fuel, and power. Cf. Locke to US Secretary of State, 880.00-TA/3/24/52.

37. These were: improvement to the port of Beirut, improvement to the port of Tripoli, the construction of a port at Latakia, the construction of a natural gas pipeline from Kirkuk to the Levant region, the development of the Litani River, the development of the Tigris and Euphrates Rivers in Syria, the development of the Orontes River, the development of the Yarmouk-Jordan area, and the implementation of the equatorial Nile plan.

38. Locke to US Secretary of State, 880.00-TA/3/24/52.

39. Cf. Harriman to Acheson, 880.00-TA/4/9/52 for background on the legislative obstacles concerning Locke's proposal.

40. Cf. Cannon to US Secretary of State, 880.00-TA/3/15/52, Tannous to US Secretary of State, 883A.00-TA/3/5/52, and Tannous to US Secretary of State, 883A.00-TA/3/17/52.

41. Peter to Reeseman Fryer, 1 April 1952, RG 84, Lebanon, Classified General Records, Box 28, NARA.

42. Locke to Truman, 19 February 1952, Presidential Secretary's Files, HSTL.

43. Cf. Berry memo, "Grant Aid for Arab States for Fiscal Year 1953," 880.00-TA/2/29/52.

44. Cf. Memo of Conversation, "Arab States Development Programs" 880.00-TA/3/17/52.

45. Harriman to Acheson, 880.00-TA/4/9/52.

46. Ibid.

47. Cf. Thorp to Acheson, "Near East Aid Program," 880.00-TA/2/25/52.

48. Reesemen Fryer to Andrews, 9 May 1952, Lot 57D/298, NA.

49. Ibid.

50. Memorandum of Conversation with the President, "The Locke Proposal," 1 May 1952, Dean Acheson Papers, Box 67, HSTL.

51. Cf. US Department of State, Staff Memorandum, "Responsibilities of Ambassador Locke in the Near East," 12 May 1952, and Gardiner to Locke, 15 May 1952, Lot 57D/298, NE Files, NA. See also Peter to Reeseman Fryer, 7 June 1952, RG 84, Lebanon, Classified General Records, Box 28, NARA; and Gardiner to Locke, 15 May 1952, Lot 57 D/298, Records of the Office of Near Eastern Affairs, NA.

52. Cf. Thorp to Secretary of State, "Near East Aid Program," 880.00-TA/5/2/52.

53. Cf. Locke to Gardiner, 4 September 1952, Papers of Edwin Locke Jr., Box 5, HSTL, and Fidler to Locke, "Discussion with Palestine Arab Refugee Leaders," 15 September 1952, Papers of Edwin Locke Jr., Box 5, HSTL.

54. Cf. *Le Soir* (Beirut), 15 September 1952.

55. Cf. "Notes on Locke's Visits to Refugee Camps," Notebooks 1 and 2, Papers of Edwin Locke Jr., Box 4, HSTL.

56. Locke to Gardiner, 4 September 1952, Papers of Edwin Locke Jr., Box 5, HSTL.

57. Ibid.

58. Ibid.

59. Ibid.

60. Cf. Amawi to Locke, 3 October 1952, Papers of Edwin Locke Jr., Box 5, HSTL, for a discussion of possible corruption within the United Nations Relief and Works Administration.

61. Locke to Gardiner, 30 July 1952, and Locke to Gardiner, 24 September 1952, Papers of Edwin Locke Jr., Box 5, HSTL.

62. Edwin Locke Jr., interview by author, 7 February 1994.

63. Locke to Gardiner, 23 February 1952, Papers of Edwin Locke Jr., Box 5, HSTL.

64. Cf. Locke to Gardiner, 29 November 1952, ibid.

65. Cf. Green to US Secretary of State, 320.2AA/9–2752, and Lobenstine to Byroade, 320.2AA/10/4/52.

66. Cf. Funkhouser to Hart, "Arab Membership on ADCOM," 320.2AA/9/12/52, Memorandum of Conversation, "UNRWA Relief Budget and Syrian Membership on the Advisory Commission," 320.2AA/9/17/52, and Lobenstine to Byroade, 320.2AA/10/4/52.

67. Locke to Gardiner, 23 February 1952, Papers of Edwin Locke Jr., Box 5, HSTL.

68. Cf. Geren to US Department of State, "Selo Gives Opinion on U.S. Aid," 883.00/10/16/52.

69. Locke to Truman, 24 September 1952, Papers of Edwin Locke Jr., Box 5, HSTL.

70. Cf. Locke and Peter to TCA Country Directors, Near East, 880.00-TA/8/4/52, and Locke to Gardiner, 6 September 1952, Papers of Edwin Locke Jr., Box 5, HSTL.

71. Locke to Truman, 24 September 1952, Papers of Edwin Locke Jr., Box 5, HSTL.

72. Fidler memo, 9 October 1952, ibid.

73. Locke to Truman, 24 September 1952, ibid.

74. Ibid.

75. Minor to US Secretary of State, 880.00-TA/11/24/52.

76. Cf. *Daily Star* (Beirut), 28 November, 30 November, and 2 December 1952, all found in the papers of Edwin Locke Jr., Box 4, HSTL.

77. Edwin Locke, "The Arab Economy: The Truth and the Challenge," 5 December 1952, Papers of Edwin Locke Jr., Box 4, HSTL.

78. Green to Minor, 3 December 1952, RG 84, Lebanon, Box 28, NARA.

79. Minor to Green, 9 December 1952, ibid.

80. Cf. *Daily Star* (Beirut), 13 December 1952.

81. *Daily Star* (Beirut), 27 December 1952.

82. Peter to Young, 19 December 1952, RG 84 Lebanon, Classified General Records, Box 28, NARA.

83. At the end of January, Locke spoke at a meeting of the American Friends of the Middle East in which he repeated his criticisms of US development policy in the Near East, this time directing some added invective at officials of the State Department, whom he described as "scrubs." Cf. *Daily Star* (Beirut), 10 February and 21 March 1953. For a rather unabashedly vicious response from one of the "scrubs," see Bruins to Hart, 320.2-AA/3/23/53.

CHAPTER 3

US FOREIGN POLICY TOWARD IRAN DURING THE MUSSADIQ ERA

Mark Gasiorowski

Muhammad Mussadiq, who served as the Iranian prime minister from April 1951 until August 1953, is revered by almost all secular democratic Iranians and admired even by many supporters of the regimes of the shah and Ayatollah Khomeini. He ended a long period of British hegemony in Iran by nationalizing the British-controlled oil industry, instilling a strong sense of national pride in most Iranians, and setting the stage for several decades of rapid economic growth fueled by oil revenues. He also tried to democratize Iran's political system by reducing the powers of the shah and the traditional upper class and by mobilizing the urban middle and lower classes. Although he ultimately failed in this latter endeavor, his efforts made him a hero in the eyes of those Iranians who have dreamed of establishing a democratic regime in their country.

At the start of the Mussadiq era the United States had a very positive image in Iran, created by the small group of US teachers, missionaries, archaeologists, and administrators who had ventured there and by the commitment to freedom, democracy, and independence espoused by the US government and most Americans. The United States initially supported Mussadiq, upholding Iran's right to nationalize the oil industry, trying to mediate an agreement with the British, giving Iran a small amount of economic aid, and generally praising Mussadiq and his democratic aspirations. However, US support for Mussadiq gradually declined, and under the administration of President Dwight D. Eisenhower the United States engineered a coup d'état that drove Mussadiq from office and ended the movement toward democracy he had been leading. The United States thereafter strongly backed the shah, greatly facilitating his efforts to create an authoritarian regime in the decade after the coup. Consequently, the Mussadiq era also marked a period in which the popular image of the United States in Iran began to change from that of benevolent outsider to malevolent supporter of the shah's despotic regime.

This chapter examines US policy toward Iran during the Mussadiq era. It focuses particularly on the strategic considerations that led US officials to change from a policy of supporting Mussadiq to one of opposing and eventually overthrowing him, thus engendering the malevolent image many Iranians still have of the United States. The chapter does not provide a detailed account of the August 1953 coup or the events leading up to it, which are examined at length elsewhere.

PROLOGUE: US POLICY TOWARD IRAN
BEFORE THE MUSSADIQ ERA

Before World War II the United States had little strategic or economic interest in Iran, and relations between the two countries were cordial but distant. The United States had established diplomatic relations with Iran in 1856 but did not send a diplomat of ambassadorial rank there until 1944. During the late 1800s and early 1900s contact between the two countries was very limited, consisting mainly of missionary activity with a handful of US missionaries, teachers, and archaeologists; these Americans created a very positive image of the United States in Iran. Nevertheless, relations between the two countries were evidently of such little importance by the late 1930s that Iran's monarch, Reza Shah Pahlavi, recalled his ambassador to Washington for several years after derogatory comments about him appeared in the US press.[1]

With World War II raging in Europe, Britain and the Soviet Union jointly invaded Iran in September 1941 to establish a supply route to the Soviet army. The invading forces quickly overpowered the hapless Iranian army and forced Reza Shah, who was seen as a German sympathizer, to abdicate in favor of his twenty-one-year-old son, Muhammad Reza Pahlavi, the late shah. Following US entry into the war the United States sent troops to Iran in conjunction with the supply operation, initiating a period in which US-Iranian relations grew rapidly. By early 1944 some 30,000 US soldiers were stationed in Iran, guarding the supply route against bandits and German agents, expanding and improving Iran's transportation system and oil production facilities, and building plants to assemble aircraft, trucks, and oil drums. The United States sent military missions to Iran to reorganize and train the Iranian army and gendarmerie and gave Iran some $8.5 million in lend-lease aid during the war. Unlike Britain and the Soviet Union, the United States did not meddle in Iran's domestic affairs during the war, reinforcing its image as a champion of freedom and independence.[2]

As the German threat eased in 1944, the Soviet Union began to expand its influence and demand oil concessions in the northwestern Iranian provinces of Azerbaijan and Kurdistan, which it had been occupying since 1941. Constrained by its need to maintain the wartime alliance, the United States initially made no effort to block these activities. However, as World War II drew to a close in 1945, the Soviet posture toward Iran grew more menacing and was paralleled by similar activities elsewhere in the world. As US officials grew increasingly concerned about Soviet expansionism, and after Harry S Truman replaced the more diplomatic Franklin D. Roosevelt as president, the United States began to pressure the Soviet Union to withdraw its forces from Iran. Soviet officials demurred, and in December 1945 and January 1946 Soviet-backed rebels established the Autonomous Republic of Azerbaijan and the Kurdish People's Republic in northwestern Iran. Powerless to stop these activities, the Iranian government sought backing from the United States and Britain and petitioned the United Nations (UN) to demand a Soviet withdrawal. US officials issued protests to the Soviet government and strongly supported Iran's position at the UN. Backed by the United States, Iranian Prime Minister Ahmad Qavam traveled to Moscow in March 1946 and negotiated an agreement under which Soviet troops would be withdrawn from Iran. The Iranian army reoccupied Azerbaijan and Kurdistan in December 1946, crushing the autonomy movements and ending one of the first chapters in the cold war.[3]

As the crisis in Azerbaijan and Kurdistan was drawing to a close, the US Department of State and other US government agencies conducted a thorough review of US interests in Iran. Reflecting the considerable effort US officials had made earlier to eject Soviet forces from northwestern Iran, US officials concluded that Iran was "of vital strategic interest" because Persian Gulf oil would be critical in the event of a war with the Soviet Union.[4] However, despite this finding, no major changes occurred in US policy toward Iran during the late 1940s. US policymakers at this time were pursuing a strategy of "strongpoint defense" in their efforts to contain Soviet expansionism. This strategy called for a concentration of US defense efforts in Western Europe and Japan—on the western and eastern borders of the Soviet Union—and accorded a much lower priority to other regions, including the area south of the Soviet Union where Iran lay. Consequently, though the shah and the various Iranian prime ministers of this period made repeated requests for US military and economic aid, Iran was not given a large aid package under the Truman Doctrine, as were Greece and Turkey, and it received less US aid in the late 1940s than countries like Ireland, Portugal, and Sweden, despite its larger size and poorer economic conditions.[5]

The United States did slowly increase its involvement in Iran in other ways during this period, however. The military training missions begun during World War II were renegotiated and extended in 1947 and 1948. The US embassy staff grew considerably in size, enhancing diplomatic, commercial, and cultural interactions between the two countries. More important, the Office of Strategic Services, the predecessor to the Central Intelligence Agency (CIA), established a station in the Tehran embassy in early 1947 to take over covert operations then being conducted by US military attachés and embassy political officers. These covert operations included intelligence-gathering and propaganda operations aimed at the Soviet Union and its allies in Iran, cross-border espionage and subversion raids into Soviet territory, and efforts to map out escape and evasion routes and organize "stay-behind" guerrilla networks for use in the event of a Soviet invasion. Although these operations were all aimed ultimately at the Soviet Union, they did have the effect of strengthening or weakening various Iranian political actors in minor ways during this period.[6]

In the late 1940s unrest grew steadily among politically active Iranians, due mainly to the absence of meaningful opportunities for political participation and to growing resentment toward the Anglo-Iranian Oil Company (AIOC), a British-owned firm that was earning large profits from its monopoly over Iran's oil industry. Much of this unrest was mobilized and articulated by the Tudeh (Masses) Party, a pro-Soviet Communist Party established in 1941 that had become Iran's largest political party before falling into disfavor after the Azerbaijani crisis. In October 1949 a group of prominent political figures established an organization known as the National Front to press for political reforms and nationalization of the AIOC's assets in Iran. The National Front quickly became extremely popular and managed to elect eight of its members to the Majlis (the Iranian parliament) in late 1949. It was led by Muhammad Mussadiq, a charismatic Majlis deputy from a wealthy landowning family who had established a reputation as an ardent nationalist and democrat and one of Iran's few honest politicians.[7]

By early 1950 US officials had become alarmed about political conditions in Iran, with one describing Iran as "dangerous and explosive" and another warning that it might become a "second China."[8] Simultaneously, the National Security Council was undertaking a major reevaluation of US global strategy, which was codified in the April 1950 document known as NSC–68. The new strategy called for a "renewed initiative in the cold war" involving large increases in military and economic aid to countries located all along the Sino-Soviet periphery—not just those on the western and eastern borders of the Soviet Union.[9] The growing unrest in Iran and this new global strategy together led US officials to undertake a thorough review of US policy toward Iran, which concluded that a major effort had to be made to prevent the Tudeh Party from coming to power and delivering Iran into Soviet hands. As a result, during the following year US officials agreed to provide Iran with $23 million per year in military aid and a modest amount of economic aid; they approved a $25 million Export-Import Bank loan to Iran (which was never actually provided); and they supported Iran's request for a $10 million World Bank loan. They also sharply increased the number of US Foreign Service and CIA officers working in the Tehran embassy and named Henry Grady, a highly respected diplomat, to be the new US ambassador.[10] By early 1951 the United States had positioned itself to play a major role in Iranian politics.

THE TRUMAN ADMINISTRATION AND THE FIRST MUSSADIQ GOVERNMENT

Throughout 1950 unrest continued to grow in Iran, with political reform and oil nationalization remaining the most contentious issues. Prime Minister Ali Razmara initiated a program of political and socioeconomic reforms but also attempted to implement an agreement with the AIOC negotiated under his predecessors that fell far short of popular demands. In response, Mussadiq and the National Front began to call for outright nationalization of the oil industry, and a member of the Islamist group Fedayan-e Islam (Devotees of Islam) assassinated Razmara in March 1951. The shah then appointed Hussein Ala, a loyal ally, to replace Razmara. The country was swept with a new wave of unrest, leading the Majlis to nominate Mussadiq for the premiership and pass a bill nationalizing the oil industry. Bowing to popular sentiment, the shah appointed Mussadiq prime minister on April 29 and signed the oil nationalization bill into law on May 2.[11]

Nationalization of the AIOC posed a serious threat to Britain's weak economy and dwindling prestige, so the nationalization decree initiated a period of growing confrontation between Britain and Iran. In the following months British officials adopted a three-track strategy aimed at reestablishing Britain's control over Iran's oil industry either by pressuring Mussadiq into a favorable settlement or removing him from office. The first track was a halfhearted effort to negotiate a new oil agreement that would recognize the principle of nationalization but retain de facto British control over Iran's oil. This effort collapsed in August 1951, and the British thereafter refused to negotiate directly with Mussadiq. The second track consisted of a series of hostile measures aimed at undermining popular support for Mussadiq. The most important of these was a successful effort to persuade the major world oil companies to boycott Iranian oil exports. The British also imposed a series of bilateral economic sanctions on Iran and began an ominous military buildup in the region. The third element of the British strategy was a series of covert efforts to overthrow Mussadiq. These efforts continued throughout Mussadiq's tenure as prime minister and were carried out primarily through a network of politicians, businessmen, military officers, and clerical leaders that had been cultivated by British intelligence officers during their long years of intrigue in Iran.[12]

After Mussadiq assumed office the Truman administration publicly expressed strong support for him, recognizing that he was very popular and therefore could serve as an effective alternative to the Tudeh Party. Officials in Washington again undertook a review of US policy toward Iran, concluding that Iran must be kept in the Western camp at all costs because of its strategic location and that a protracted oil crisis might weaken the US economy and threaten US and Western security. Accordingly, for the remainder of Truman's term in office the administration pursued a policy of supporting Mussadiq, opposing British efforts to overthrow him, and attempting to mediate an agreement that would satisfy both parties to the oil dispute and minimize disruption of the world oil market.[13]

Soon after the oil nationalization law was enacted, US officials began to implement a plan to ease the effect of the British oil blockade on the world oil market. Under this plan US oil companies were asked to provide oil to US allies that had been adversely affected by the blockade. Some 46 million barrels of oil were delivered under this plan in the first year of the blockade, amounting to roughly 20 percent of Iran's 1950 production. Although this effort was intended to help stabilize the world oil market, it also reinforced the oil blockade and therefore inadvertently helped to weaken the Iranian economy and undermine Mussadiq's popular support.[14]

At the same time, US officials began a concerted effort to facilitate a negotiated settlement of the oil dispute. They privately advised the British to accept nationalization of the AIOC and agree to a 50–50 division of profits with Iran—an arrangement that had become common throughout the industry by that time. In July 1951 Secretary of State Dean Acheson asked special envoy Averell Harriman to lead a mission to Tehran and London to mediate the dispute. Harriman worked assiduously to bring the British and Iranian positions closer together, inducing the British to send a negotiating team to Iran under the leadership of Sir Richard Stokes. The Stokes mission made little headway, and negotiations between Britain and Iran collapsed in August.[15]

Throughout this period the British had been working strenuously to replace Mussadiq with their close ally, Sayyid Zia al-Din Tabatabai. This had involved direct pressures on the shah to dismiss Mussadiq and appoint Sayyid Zia as prime minister as well as efforts to build support in the Majlis through the British intelligence network for Sayyid Zia's candidacy. British officials even went so far as to work out a set of guidelines for settling the oil dispute with Sayyid Zia. US officials were generally aware of these activities and neither supported nor opposed them. The British effort to install Sayyid Zia had not made much headway by the time the Stokes mission collapsed. Accordingly, in September 1951 British officials began to implement a plan to invade southwestern Iran and seize the oil fields. When US officials were told about this plan, President Truman notified British Prime Minister Clement Attlee that the United States would not support an invasion and urged him to resume negotiations. As a result, Attlee was forced to abandon the invasion plan, telling his cabinet that "in view of the attitude of the United States Government, [he did not] think it would be expedient to use force" in Iran.[16]

Mussadiq traveled to New York in October to address the UN Security Council about the oil dispute. US officials invited him to Washington, hosting him warmly and making another concerted effort to mediate the dispute. These efforts again failed to bring about a settlement. During the following year US officials made a series of additional proposals that called for Iranian oil to be marketed by a consortium of US and other oil companies. When antitrust concerns led the major US oil companies to reject this plan, US officials first tried to persuade US independents to accept it and then, in the fall of 1952, decided to waive antitrust laws to persuade the majors to participate. Despite these efforts, US officials were unable to settle the oil dispute.[17]

Having failed to reverse the nationalization law, to install Sayyid Zia as prime minister, or to seize the oil fields forcibly, the British began to search for other options in their efforts to regain control over Iran's oil. Another option soon materialized. Ahmad Qavam, who had been prime minister during the 1945–1946 Azerbaijani crisis, approached the British seeking support in his bid to replace Mussadiq as prime minister. British officials sent an emissary to meet with Qavam in

Paris in March 1952. Qavam told the emissary that he would settle the oil dispute on terms acceptable to the British, and he produced a list of potential cabinet ministers for their approval. The British supported Qavam by accepting his plan to end the oil dispute and having their network of Iranian allies help him. Qavam spent the next several months trying to build support in Iran for his candidacy.[18]

Mussadiq evidently learned about Qavam's activities and suddenly resigned on July 16. The shah then appointed Qavam prime minister. During the next several days the National Front organized a series of massive demonstrations calling for Mussadiq's return to office. Army and police units attacked the demonstrators, killing at least sixty-nine and injuring over 750. Since Qavam had no popular backing, Mussadiq's supporters dominated the streets of Tehran. On July 21 the shah bowed to the popular will and appointed Mussadiq to a second term as prime minister. Qavam slipped quietly into exile.[19]

THE TRUMAN ADMINISTRATION AND THE SECOND MUSSADIQ GOVERNMENT

The Qavam episode initiated a period of growing political instability in Iran. Morale in the armed forces dropped sharply. The Tudeh Party became much more active. Mussadiq filled his new cabinet with close supporters and persuaded the Majlis to grant him emergency powers, angering National Front leaders such as Ayatollah Abul Qassem Kashani, Hussein Makki, and Muzaffar Baqai. More ominously, a group of military officers led by General Fazlollah Zahedi began to plot against Mussadiq with the Rashidian brothers, who were the central figures in the British intelligence network. Zahedi had briefly served as interior minister in Mussadiq's first government and had supported the National Front until the July 1952 uprisings, when the resurgence of Tudeh activity and plummeting morale in the armed forces apparently drove him into the opposition.[20]

Kashani, Makki, and Baqai soon approached Zahedi, expressing their dissatisfaction with Mussadiq and thereafter collaborating loosely with him in his plot. Zahedi also obtained the support of Abul Qassem Bakhtiari, a leader of the Bakhtiari tribe who had worked with him in collaboration with German agents during World War II. He then met with the British chargé d'affaires, asking for assurance that the British would not oppose him, would agree to a settlement of the oil dispute on terms similar to those worked out with Qavam, and would obtain US acquiescence in his activities. The chargé reported this to London and was told to help Zahedi. British intelligence officers then provided arms to the Bakhtiari. The chargé described Zahedi's activities to US Ambassador Loy Henderson. Either Zahedi or a close lieutenant also met with Henderson in early September, telling him that a government would soon come to power that would halt the growth of Tudeh influence. Henderson reported these conversations back to Washington but remained noncommittal.[21]

US policy toward Iran during this period was ambiguous. Ambassador Henderson was alarmed about the resurgence of the Tudeh Party and the generally

chaotic situation in Iran in the aftermath of the Qavam episode, and he recommended that Washington prop up the Mussadiq government with a large aid package. Although this did not occur, US officials renewed their efforts to resolve the
oil dispute and continued to support Mussadiq, both publicly and in private conversations with the British. However, at the same time, CIA officers in Tehran
began to turn some of their anti-Soviet covert operations in directions that undermined Mussadiq's base of support. Under a propaganda operation code-named
BEDAMN, they distributed newspaper articles and cartoons that depicted Mussadiq as corrupt and immoral and portrayed him as exploiting Kashani. They provided financial assistance to certain clergymen to drive them away from Mussadiq
and create a clerical alternative to Kashani. CIA officers with long-standing ties to
the Pan-Iranist Party and the Toilers' Party—both had strongly supported Mussadiq—made efforts to turn these organizations against Mussadiq. In a particularly
noteworthy case, two CIA officers in the fall of 1952 approached Baqai, who had
headed the Toilers' Party, encouraging him to break with Mussadiq and giving him
money. Similar approaches may have been made to Kashani, Makki, and other
prominent figures.[22]

By November 1952 both the Pan-Iranists and the Toilers' Party had split into
pro- and anti-Mussadiq factions; Kashani, Makki, Baqai, and other National Front
leaders had openly turned against Mussadiq, seriously weakening him. These three
men, like most other Iranian politicians at the time, were extremely opportunistic
and may well have had other reasons for breaking with Mussadiq. Moreover, the
British were carrying out very similar—and probably much more extensive—covert
activities against Mussadiq at this time. Therefore, although these CIA activities
may well have helped to undermine Mussadiq's base of support, they were not the
only forces operating against him in this period, and it is impossible to say with
any certainty how much of a role they actually played in weakening him.

Mussadiq evidently learned about Zahedi's plot and moved to stop him before it
could be implemented. As a member of the Iranian senate, Zahedi enjoyed parliamentary immunity and therefore could not be arrested. However, Mussadiq issued
arrest warrants on October 13 for the Rashidians and for General Abdul Hussein He-
jazi, a close ally of Zahedi. A General Aryana was dismissed from the army in connection with the plot. More important, on October 16 Mussadiq broke diplomatic
relations with Britain, claiming British officials had supported Zahedi. This act
alarmed US officials and persuaded some of them that the situation in Iran had gotten
out of hand.[23]

No longer able to operate from the safety of their Tehran embassy, the British decided to seek US help in their efforts to oust Mussadiq. Christopher Montague Woodhouse, who had been heading British intelligence operations in Iran, was sent to
Washington in November to present US officials with a plan to oust Mussadiq. The
plan called for a coordinated uprising to be engineered by the Rashidians and certain
Bakhtiari tribal elements, with or without the shah's approval. Although the British
believed Zahedi was well suited to lead the coup, they proposed several possible coup
leaders. Woodhouse met with CIA and State Department officials. Most high-ranking

CIA officials favored a coup by this time, although some lower-ranking Iran specialists and the CIA station chief in Tehran were opposed to the idea. State Department officials told Woodhouse that Truman would not support a coup but that president-elect Dwight Eisenhower and his foreign policy advisers probably would.[24]

THE EISENHOWER ADMINISTRATION AND MUSSADIQ

Dwight Eisenhower entered office in January 1953, and the administration harbored bold plans to restructure US foreign policy in ways that would more effectively contain the Soviet Union. Its new global strategy, which was eventually set out in the October 1953 National Security Council study NSC–162, called for a broad effort to enhance containment while reducing US defense expenditures. An important element of this effort was a decision to strengthen pro-Western countries located along the Sino-Soviet periphery—a project that the Truman administration had begun but set aside as the Korean War and European reconstruction distracted its attention. These countries were to be strengthened with large military and economic aid programs, defense alliances, and, where necessary, covert political operations conducted by the CIA.[25] As a result of this new global strategy, the Eisenhower administration redirected the US military and economic aid programs away from Europe toward the Third World; it constructed a ring of defense alliances around the Soviet Union and China; and it greatly increased the CIA's use of covert operations. With its proximity to the Soviet Union, and Mussadiq's failure to resolve the oil crisis, Iran was a crucial pawn in this new strategy and quickly became a major preoccupation for the Eisenhower administration.

Secretary of State designate John Foster Dulles and his brother, Allen Dulles, who was deputy head of the CIA's covert operations division under Truman and was to become CIA director under Eisenhower, had been following the situation in Iran with growing alarm. Although they did not regard Mussadiq as a Communist, they believed conditions in Iran would probably continue to deteriorate as long as he remained in office, strengthening the Tudeh Party and perhaps enabling it to seize power. In light of Iran's crucial role in the US strategy for containing the Soviet Union, they viewed this possibility with grave concern. The Dulles brothers therefore concluded that Mussadiq had to be removed from office—a conclusion that was not shared at this time by Assistant Secretary of State for Near Eastern and South Asian Affairs Henry Byroade, Ambassador Henderson, the CIA station chief in Tehran, or several lower-ranking State Department and CIA officials. Allen Dulles had met with Woodhouse in November 1952 and expressed his support for a coup to overthrow Mussadiq. The Dulles brothers were ready to begin preparations for a coup by the time Eisenhower was inaugurated.[26]

On February 3, 1953, two weeks after the inauguration, top US and British officials met in Washington to discuss the situation in Iran. At this meeting a decision was made to develop and carry out a plan to overthrow Mussadiq and install Zahedi as prime minister. The operation was to be led by Kermit Roosevelt, who headed the CIA's Middle East operations division. Roosevelt traveled to Iran several times during the following months to prepare for the coup, meeting with Zahedi, the Rashidians, members of the Tehran CIA station, and two Iranians code-named Nerren and Cilley, who were the main operatives in the BEDAMN propaganda operation. A US specialist on Iran working under contract for the CIA was assigned to develop an operation plan for the coup with a British intelligence officer. Roosevelt presented the coup plan to the Dulles brothers and other top US officials in a June 25 State Department meeting. He was directed to implement it immediately.[27]

Zahedi had continued to intrigue against Mussadiq after the exposure of his plot in October 1952. He remained in contact with Bakhtiari tribal leaders, who were given arms and money by the British during this period. His allies in the Majlis undertook a series of parliamentary maneuvers to try to oust Mussadiq. In February 1953 a group of retired military officers loyal to Zahedi and Bakhtiari tribesmen led by Abul Qassem attacked an army column, apparently trying to spark a coup. Mussadiq responded by issuing an arrest warrant for Zahedi, who had lost his parliamentary immunity. Zahedi's allies then organized a series of violent disturbances in Tehran that nearly toppled the Mussadiq government. A similar incident occurred in late April, when several Zahedi associates apparently kidnapped and murdered the commander of the national police, a staunch Mussadiq supporter. Rumors of coup plots circulated throughout the winter and spring of 1953.[28]

Following the June 25 State Department meeting, Roosevelt and his CIA team began to work in loose coordination with Zahedi. They used the BEDAMN network to launch an extensive propaganda barrage against Mussadiq and organize antigovernment and anti-Tudeh demonstrations, adding considerably to the turmoil that was engulfing Tehran. They sought the support of top military officers, arranging to have certain army units participate in the coup. In late July and early August they sent two emissaries to see the shah and obtain his support. When these approaches proved unsuccessful, Roosevelt arranged through the Rashidians to meet personally with the shah. After direct US and British involvement were confirmed through special radio broadcasts, the shah agreed to support the plot.[29]

Having obtained the shah's backing, Roosevelt was ready to proceed with the coup. The shah signed decrees dismissing Mussadiq and appointing Zahedi prime minister. The commander of the shah's Imperial Guard delivered the first of these decrees to Mussadiq on the night of August 15 and was promptly arrested. Army and police units loyal to Mussadiq then set up roadblocks throughout the city, began a massive search for Zahedi, and arrested several of his associates. An armored column that had been assigned to move into Tehran in conjunction with Mussadiq's dismissal failed to arrive. As the coup plot unraveled the shah fled the country in panic, first to Baghdad and then to Rome. Zahedi was brought to a CIA safe house, where he remained for the next several days. Roosevelt made contingency plans to evacuate himself, Zahedi, and a few other participants.[30]

Despite these setbacks, Roosevelt and his colleagues began to improvise a new plan. They distributed copies of the decrees dismissing Mussadiq and appointing

Zahedi throughout Tehran in order to publicize the shah's actions. They brought two US newspaper reporters to meet with Ardeshir Zahedi, who told them about the shah's decrees and characterized Mussadiq's rejection of them as a coup, since the decrees were in accord with the constitution. This information was quickly published in the *New York Times*. Ardeshir Zahedi and one of the CIA officers were sent to Kermanshah and Isfahan to persuade the garrison commanders in those cities to send troops to Tehran. The US military advisory group distributed military supplies to pro-Zahedi forces to encourage them to support the plot.[31]

On August 17 Nerren and Cilley used $50,000 given to them by Roosevelt's team to hire a large crowd that marched into central Tehran shouting Tudeh slogans, carrying signs denouncing the shah, tearing down statues of the shah and his father, and attacking Reza Shah's mausoleum. This crowd played the role of an agent provocateur: It generated fear of a Tudeh takeover among Tehran residents and was even joined by many real Tudeh members, who assumed it had been organized by the party's leadership. These disturbances continued on the following day. Mussadiq therefore ordered the police to disperse the crowds, even though the Tudeh was tacitly supporting him against Zahedi and the shah. The Tudeh responded by ordering its members off the streets, removing an important obstacle to Mussadiq's opponents.[32]

By the evening of August 18 the police were closing in on the CIA safe house where Zahedi was hiding. Roosevelt therefore began to look for a new way to spark a coup. Knowing that Ayatollah Kashani was strongly opposed to Mussadiq and had considerable influence over lower- and middle-class Iranians, he decided to seek Kashani's help in organizing another crowd to agitate against Mussadiq. Following the Rashidians' advice, he had two CIA officers meet with Ahmad Aramesh, an influence peddler who apparently had connections with Kashani. They asked Aramesh to ask Kashani to organize an anti-Mussadiq crowd and gave him $10,000 to finance the effort. At the same time, the Rashidians and Nerren and Cilley probably made independent efforts to organize such a crowd.[33]

Although it is not clear whether Kashani or these figures were involved, a large crowd suddenly emerged near the Tehran bazaar in the late morning of August 19. The crowd attacked government office buildings and the offices of newspapers and political parties that supported Mussadiq. It was joined by army and police units and by onlookers who had become alarmed by the "Tudeh" demonstrations of the previous days. Realizing that events had turned decisively against him, Mussadiq refused to order his security forces to disperse the crowd. At the same time, an army unit seized the Tehran radio station and began to broadcast bulletins condemning Mussadiq and supporting Zahedi. An air force general led a column of tanks to the safe house where Zahedi was hiding and rescued him from the police units closing in around him. Military units and large groups of demonstrators then seized the army headquarters and marched on Mussadiq's home, where a nine-hour tank battle ensued. The walls around Mussadiq's house were destroyed and the house itself was stormed; some 300 people were killed. Mussadiq escaped into a neighbor's yard but surrendered to Zahedi's forces the next day. Several days later the shah returned to Iran and personally thanked Roosevelt, telling him, "I owe my throne to God, my people, my army—and to you."[34]

The shah's comment to Roosevelt seems to have been appropriate, for the United States did indeed play a key role in overthrowing Mussadiq and ending the threat he had posed to Iran's autocratic monarchical system. Roosevelt and his colleagues had planned, financed, and led the coup, taking decisive action after the attempt to arrest Mussadiq had failed that later made the coup successful. Zahedi, its nominal leader, hid in a CIA safe house almost until the coup had been completed. The shah was not consulted about the decision to undertake the coup, the manner of its execution, or the candidate chosen to replace Mussadiq, and he had been reluctant to support the coup and had fled the country at the first sign of failure. The British had played only a minor role in the coup, helping develop the initial plan for it—which failed— and directing the Rashidians to work with Roosevelt. Although the AIOC's oil boy-cott had weakened Iran's economy and thus helped undermine popular support for Mussadiq, many other outcomes could have resulted from Mussadiq's declining pop-ularity. Zahedi and his allies had failed repeatedly to overthrow Mussadiq during the previous year. Although they might possibly have engineered a coup without US help, outstanding arrest warrants greatly hindered Zahedi's activities, and he had no real popular support. No other Iranian appears to have had the popularity of military connections necessary to carry out a coup without external backing. It therefore seems safe to conclude that the United States played a decisive role in overthrowing Mus-sadiq and severely weakening the political movement he led.

CONCLUSION

This chapter has emphasized that US security interests—as conceived by the Tru-man and Eisenhower administrations—required that Iran be kept in the Western camp during the cold war, and therefore it has implied that domestic political con-ditions in Iran could not be permitted to move beyond certain boundaries in the eyes of US policymakers. Under the Truman administration these boundaries ini-tially were drawn rather broadly: Mussadiq did not seem to pose a threat to US interests, and US policymakers believed he could serve as an effective counterbal-ance to the Tudeh Party. However, these perceptions slowly changed as Mussadiq remained in power and unrest grew in Iran. When Eisenhower entered office, the more stridently anti-Communist views of his foreign policy advisers and the chang-ing perceptions of Mussadiq among some holdovers from the Truman administra-tion together led the United States to drop its support for Mussadiq and take steps to overthrow him. Consequently, US security interests associated with the cold war and changing views in Washington about how Mussadiq's regime affected these interests were responsible for the fateful US decision to undertake the August 1953 coup.

During the following decade these same considerations led US policymakers to provide extensive support to the shah, building up his autocratic regime as a bul-wark against Soviet expansionism. Immediately after the coup they provided him with $68 million in emergency aid, amounting to roughly one third of the total revenue Iran had lost as a result of the British oil embargo. Over $300 million in additional US economic aid was given to Iran during the next ten years. After the coup US officials renewed their efforts to settle the oil dispute, fostering an agreement that permitted Iran to begin exporting oil again in late 1954. Iran's oil income grew quickly as a result of this agreement, exceeding total US aid receipts by 1958 and thereafter serving as the shah's main source of revenue. The United States also began a major effort to strengthen the shah's security forces soon after the coup, reorganizing and training his domestic intelligence apparatus and giving him almost $600 million in military assistance during the next decade.[35]

With the threat from Mussadiq and the National Front effectively contained, the economy growing rapidly, and an increasingly effective security apparatus in place, the shah consolidated his grip on power in the late 1950s and early 1960s. By late 1963 this process had been completed: The shah presided over an authoritarian regime under which organized opposition to his authority was not tolerated, and there seemed little chance that he would fall from power. However, many politicians were aware that Iranians deeply resented the shah's regime; they increasingly blamed the United States for restoring him to power in 1953 and then helping him to consolidate the new regime. This resentment generated a new challenge to the shah in the 1970s that differs from the one posed by Mussadiq: nondemocratic, violent, and deeply anti-American. This new challenge brought the shah's regime crashing down in the late 1970s and created a series of crises for the United States during the following decade that only recently have begun to subside.

The strategic considerations that led US policymakers to undertake the 1953 coup and then build up the shah's regime therefore helped set in motion a chain of events that later destroyed his regime and created severe problems for US interests. One can only hope that the end of the cold war will make it possible for the United States and other major powers to think more clearly about domestic political effects of their actions and thus avoid the kind of outcome that resulted from US policy toward Iran during this era.

Notes

1. Abraham Yeselson, *United States–Persian Diplomatic Relations, 1883–1921* (New Brunswick, N.J.: Rutgers University Press, 1956); John A. Denovo, *American Interests and Policies in the Middle East, 1900–1939* (Minneapolis: University of Minnesota Press, 1963), ch. 9.

2. T. Vail Motter, *United States Army in World War II: The Middle East Theater, the Persian Corridor, and Aid to Russia* (Washington, DC: Department of the Army, Office of the Chief of Military History, 1952); Mark Hamilton Lytle, *The Origins of the Iranian-American Alliance, 1941–1953* (New York: Holmes and Meier, 1987), chs. 2–4.

3. Bruce Robellet Kuniholm, *The Origins of the Cold War in the Near East* (Princeton: Princeton University Press, 1980), chs. 5–6.

4. US Joint Chiefs of Staff (hereinafter JCS), *United States Strategic Interests in Iran* (Washington, DC), JCS 1714/1, October 4, 1946, p. 6.

5. John Lewis Gaddis, *Strategies of Containment* (New York: Oxford University Press, 1982), chs. 2–3; US Department of State, *Foreign Relations of the United States, 1947,* vol. 5 (Washington, DC: US Government Printing Office, 1970), pp. 905ff.; ibid., 1948, vol. 5, pp. 170ff.; ibid., 1949, vol. 6, pp. 528ff.; US Agency for International Development, *U.S. Overseas Loans and Grants: Series of Yearly Data,* vols. 1–5 (Washington, DC: US Agency for International Development, 1984).

6. Rouhollah K. Ramazani, *Iran's Foreign Policy, 1941–1973: A Study of Foreign Policy in Modernizing Nations* (Charlottesville: University Press of Virginia, 1975), pp. 159–162; confidential interviews conducted by the author with several CIA officers stationed in Iran during this period.

7. Ervand Abrahamian, *Iran Between Two Revolutions* (Princeton: Princeton University Press, 1982), ch. 5. On Mussadiq's background and beliefs, see Farhad Diba, *Mohammad Mossadegh: A Political Biography* (London: Croom Helm, 1986); James A. Bill and Wm. Roger Louis, eds., *Mussadiq, Iranian Nationalism, and Oil* (Austin: University of Texas Press, 1988); and Homa Katouzian, ed., *Musaddiq's Memoirs* (London: JEBHE, National Movement of Iran, 1988).

8. US Department of State, *Foreign Relations of the United States, 1950,* vol. 5 (Washington, DC: US Government Printing Office, 1976), pp. 510, 523.

9. US National Security Council (hereinafter NSC), *United States Objectives and Programs for National Security,* NSC–68, April 14, 1950, reprinted in Thomas H. Etzold and John Lewis Gaddis, eds., *Containment: Documents on American Policy and Strategy* (New York: Columbia University Press, 1980), p. 434; Gaddis, *Strategies of Containment,* ch. 4.

10. US Department of State, *Foreign Relations of the United States, 1950,* vol. 5, pp. 509–529, 551, 604; confidential interviews conducted by the author with several retired CIA officers.

11. Mostafa Elm, *Oil, Power, and Principle: Iran's Oil Nationalization and Its Aftermath* (Syracuse, N.Y.: Syracuse University Press, 1992), chs. 4–5.

12. For a fuller examination of these activities, see Mark J. Gasiorowski, *U.S. Foreign Policy and the Shah: Building a Client State in Iran* (Ithaca: Cornell University Press, 1991), pp. 62–67.

13. NSC, *The Position of the United States with Respect to Iran,* NSC 107/2, June 27, 1951.

14. NSC, *National Security Problems Concerning Free World Petroleum Demand and Potential Supplies,* NSC 138, December 8, 1952, pp. 9–10.

15. Elm, *Oil, Power, and Principle,* ch. 8.

16. Henry Byroade, interview by author, Potomac, Maryland, August 7, 1984; "Record of Interdepartmental Meeting," March 20, 1951, Foreign Office (hereinafter FO) 371/91525; "View that HMG Should Refrain from Any Statement," August 26, 1951, FO/371/91582; "Approach to a New Persian Government," September 8, 1951, FO/371/91590; "Text of Reply from President Truman," September 26, 1951, FO/371/91591; CAB 128/20, pp. 231–234. All of these documents are from the British Public Records Office, London (hereinafter cited as PRO).

17. Elm, *Oil, Power, and Principle,* chs. 11–12; "American Proposal that the Royal Dutch/Shell Group Should Take Over and Operate the Abadan Refinery Considered Impractical," November 6, 1951, FO/371/91610 (PRO); Paul Nitze, interview by author, Washington, DC, July 5, 1984.

18. "Qavam's Proposals," January 7, 1952, FO/371/98683 (PRO); "Intervention of Mr. Julian Amery," February 7, 1952, FO/371/98683 (PRO); "Qavam's Proposals," March 25, 1952, FO/371/98683 (PRO); "Internal Situation," n.d., FO/248/1531 (PRO); Sir George Middleton, interview by author, London, January 16, 1985.

19. Elm, *Oil, Power, and Principle,* ch. 16.

20. "Annual Report on Persian Army for 1952," September 12, 1952, FO/371/98638 (PRO); "Internal Situation," cited in note 18; *New York Times,* August 15, 1952, p. 2, and August 20, 1952, p. 1; Fitzroy Maclean, *Eastern Approaches* (London: Cape, 1950), p. 266; Henderson to Acheson, July 7 and 21, August 3, 4, and 15, and October 17, 1952, Record Group 84, Box 29. The latter documents are from the US National Archives, Washington (hereinafter cited as USNA).

21. "Internal Situation," cited in note 18; "Tribal Affairs and Tribal Policy," n.d., FO/248/1521 (PRO); "Intrigues Among the Bakhtiari Tribes," November 28, 1952, Record Group 84, Box 28 (USNA); Middleton interview by author; Henderson to Acheson, September 9, 1952, Record Group 84, Box 29 (USNA).

22. Elm, *Oil, Power, and Principle,* pp. 244–246; confidential interviews conducted by the author with several retired CIA officers.

23. *New York Times,* October 13, 1952, p. 4, and October 16, 1952, p. 6; "Annual Report on Persian Army for 1952," December 9, 1952, FO/371/98638 (PRO).

24. Christopher Montague Woodhouse, *Something Ventured* (London: Granada, 1982), pp. 116–119; Kermit Roosevelt, interview by author, Washington, DC, June 5, 1985; Henry Byroade, interview by author, Potomac, Md., August 7, 1984; and CIA officer who was working in Iran at the time, interview by author.

25. Gaddis, *Strategies of Containment,* ch. 5.

26. Interviews conducted by author with Henry Byroade and Gordon Mattison, Bethesda, Md., June 30, 1984, Roy Melbourne, Chapel Hill, N.C., February 1, 1984, and several CIA officers who worked in Iran at this time.

27. Kermit Roosevelt, *Countercoup: The Struggle for the Control of Iran* (New York: McGraw-Hill, 1979), pp. 120–124; Roosevelt interview; confidential interview with the Iran specialist, August 5, 1984.

28. Henderson to Acheson, January 19, 1953, Record Group 59, Box 4117; "Internal Affairs," February 18, 1953, FO/371/104562 (PRO); "Internal Affairs," February 24, 1953, FO/371/104562 (PRO); "Internal Affairs," February 28, 1953, FO/371/104563 (PRO); "Dr. Musaddiq's Quarrel with the Shah," February 23, 1953, FO/371/104563 (PRO); "The Murder of Chief of Police Afshartus," May 8, 1953, FO/371/104566 (PRO); "Internal Situation," n.d., FO/371/104563 (PRO).

29. Confidential interviews with several retired CIA officers; Princess Ashraf Pahlavi, *Faces in a Mirror* (Englewood Cliffs, N.J.: Prentice Hall, 1980), pp. 134–140; Roosevelt, *Countercoup,* pp. 147–157.

30. Confidential interviews with several retired CIA officers.

31. Confidential interviews with several retired CIA officers. See also articles published in the *New York Times* during this period.

32. Ibid.

33. Ibid.

34. *New York Times,* August 20, 1953, p. 1, and August 21, 1953, p. 1; Roosevelt, *Countercoup,* p. 199.

35. Gasiorowski, *U.S. Foreign Policy and the Shah,* ch. 4.

CHAPTER 4

THE MUSSADIQ ERA IN IRAN, 1951–1953

A Contemporary Diplomat's View

Sir Sam Falle

In the 1950s, I served Great Britain in Iran, Lebanon, and Iraq and at the Foreign Office in London on the Middle East oil desk. These postings gave me a worm's-eye view of a period of unprecedented change in the Middle East. There were revolutions in three countries: Iran, Iraq, and Egypt; I was present at the first two. The causes were intrinsically the same: resurgent nationalism against the British, who were, in any event, beginning to dismantle their empire and to dissociate themselves from their so-called stooges or puppets. In the midst of this change, the British and Americans shared the fundamental policy of denying the region to the Soviet Union while preserving oil supplies for the West, though sometimes they differed on the details. Both countries eventually came to agree on policy and methodology during the Muhammad Mussadiq crisis in Iran, a seminal event not only in Iran but also in the entire Middle East, especially in terms of the development of US foreign policy. In now turning to this episode, I take a different perspective from most who have commented on and written about the Mussadiq period.

When I arrived in Iran in 1949, the cold war was gathering impetus. The British had left India, and Prime Minister Clement Attlee's Labour government hoped for a steady and orderly transfer of power throughout the old empire. The United States had already become, by far, the most powerful country in the free world.

The Middle East was disproportionately important, considering its relatively small population, because of its vast oil reserves and strategic position between the cold war adversaries. Arab nationalism, suppressed for many centuries by the Ottoman Empire and briefly by the British and French, was awakening. The Arabs, angry, wounded, and humiliated by the creation of Israel, still felt that they were not yet free from "imperialism." Iran had just emerged from World War II, during which it had in practice been partitioned between Britain and the Soviet Union. The British oil company then known as the Anglo-Persian Oil Company (later Anglo-Iranian Oil Company, or AIOC, and then British Petroleum) continued to take the major share of the profits of Iran's oil for itself and the British government.

Thus, the Iran to which I came in 1949 was uneasy. The Soviet threat remained in the north, and the British and their oil company in the south were regarded as imperialist oppressors, even though Anglo-Iranian official relations were correct. The British and also the Russians had deposed Iran's ruthless modernizing ruler, Reza Shah Pahlavi, in 1941 for his pro-Nazi sympathies. His thirty-year-old son, Muhammad Reza Pahlavi, sat uneasily on the peacock throne. He had little of his father's courage or ruthlessness, and I suspect he was a reluctant tyrant in his later years. In 1952 he was summed up by one of my Iranian acquaintances: "His Majesty is very, very, weak."[1] At that time he was certainly vacillating and indecisive. Furthermore, he disliked the British for deposing his father; I wrote in an official minute, "The Shah hates our guts." However, on the positive side, it is worth noting that he reacted courageously and not vindictively to an attempt on his life by the Tudeh Party in February 1949. He neither lost his nerve nor ordered reprisals.

The AIOC had been exploiting Iranian oil since the beginning of the century. This cheap oil was of immense importance to the Royal Navy, which had converted from coal just before World War I. "Anglo-Persian" built a great refinery at Abadan on the Gulf and dominated the economic life of Iran. To be fair, it was a remarkable commercial enterprise, providing a living as well as tolerable working conditions for its Iranian employees and investing huge sums of money in Iran. Sadly, however, the leadership of the AIOC failed to understand the nationalist spirit of postwar Iran. More foresight on their part could have saved the United States, Britain, and Iran from a sea of troubles, certainly from Mussadiq and perhaps even from Ayatollah Khomeini. Here I pay tribute to the United States for the famous "golden gimmick," the ARAMCO (Arab-American Oil Company) 50–50 profit-sharing agreement with Saudi Arabia in December 1950, which recognized the fact that the host country would want at least an equal share of the profits; in Iran, the AIOC had actually been paying more taxes to the British government off its profits than it did royalties to the Iranian government. If only AIOC had been equally wise. In international terms it might have made sense for ARAMCO and the US government to have warned the AIOC and the British government in advance of the imminent deal with the Saudis, but this does not excuse us. It should have been obvious which way the wind was blowing. The AIOC had already signed the "supplemental agreement" with the Iranian government in July 1949 (supplemental because it affirmed and augmented the concession of 1933). Although this was an improvement over previous terms, it lacked the apparent clear-cut simplicity and fairness of 50–50 profit-sharing. The fact that the US tax system ensured that ARAMCO did better than AIOC would have under a similar agreement does not affect the main issue. Sir William Fraser, AIOC's boss, saw the danger and tried to dress up the supplemental agreement, but it was too late.

Ali Razmara, chief of staff of the army, was appointed prime minister by the shah in June 1950. He tried to get the supplemental agreement through the Majlis, the Iranian parliament, but the Majlis forced its withdrawal in December 1950. Nationalism and strong feelings against the company were too strong, even for Razmara to combat, and in any event the ARAMCO 50–50 agreement finally scuppered the supplemental agreement. Razmara had been the best hope, indeed the last hope, for a settlement of the oil crisis anywhere near the AIOC's terms— or perhaps for any settlement at all. He was strong and capable, fully supported by the shah. He was a practical liberal nationalist, to use the jargon of the time. He was prepared to work with the British toward a solution, for which he has, of course, been condemned as an imperialist stooge. On the surface this was a time of relative calm in which a reasonably competent cabinet tried to move forward with a seven-year development plan. The cabinet ministers raised expectations of far-reaching reforms at all levels of Iranian society, and this was, of course, the moment for the AIOC to make an unequivocal 50–50 offer, although Razmara seemed to accept the supplemental agreement.

Razmara was assassinated in March 1951, presumably because of his efforts on behalf of the supplemental agreement. Dr. Muhammad Mussadiq became prime minister in April 1951 with tremendous popular support. His appeal was simple and straightforward: unequivocal nationalism, the nationalization of the oil industry, and the elimination of the AIOC's influence, indeed of all British influence, from Iran. His first act was oil nationalization, on May 2, 1951. This was a heady moment for Iran, and the rejoicing crowds cried, "Oil has been nationalized: Long Live Dr. Muhammad Mussadiq, Iran's beloved prime minister!" And they really meant it, because, at last, they could walk tall, the imperialists had been defeated, and the streets of Tehran would soon be paved with the gold that the AIOC had been stealing from them.

The AIOC was badly shaken but still hoped that the crisis could be solved by negotiation. They sent a representative, Basil Jackson, with a 50–50 offer, which was not accepted, perhaps partly because of its presentation but more so because of Mussadiq's aversion to the British and the company. His position, power, and popularity were based on his nationalization of the AIOC, and it was probably politically impossible for him to allow them to return, certainly not openly, perhaps not even in disguise. This is one of the most important factors in this story.

The United States viewed the crisis with alarm, not out of sympathy for the AIOC but out of fear that chaos and economic collapse in Iran could lead to a Tudeh takeover. This was a dominant theme. In July President Harry S Truman sent a most distinguished and able diplomat, Averell Harriman, as his special envoy to mediate. Mussadiq was better disposed toward the Americans than the British, and Harriman persuaded him to accept a British ministerial mission led by Cabinet Minister Sir Richard Stokes. This again failed; not so much because of its substance but partly on account of its presentation, and mostly because it was British. Indeed, the distinguished historian Professor Wm. Roger Louis writes: "It is debatable whether any Englishman, even of the stature of Mountbatten, could have success-fully negotiated with Mussadiq."[2] Yet it was not as straightforward as that; the next offer after Stokes was from the World Bank, and it was also turned down on the grounds that it would infringe upon Iranian sovereignty. If we assume that Mus-sadiq, in his own very theatrical way, had the interests of Iran at heart, this was his first serious mistake. He had been entirely consistent in his opposition to the British for reasons that are easy to understand. But it was foolish to antagonize the Amer-icans, who were fundamentally most sympathetic to him personally and to his ideas. But his rejection of the World Bank offer gave the Americans food for thought and made them understand how intensely different (and difficult) it was to negotiate with him.

On September 25, 1951, the British staff in Abadan were given notice to quit the country. The British government had considered the use of force to protect their great asset, but Prime Minister Attlee was opposed to this. The arguments against intervention were powerful and, if there were any doubt, certainly clinched by US opposition. The next occurrence was an international boycott of Iranian oil, which caused a shutdown of the Abadan refinery and the cessation of the flow of oil. I visited the refinery while it was shut down; nobody bothered me but it was an uncanny experience, seeing that vast complex, all silent and dead.

Early in 1952 I left Shiraz, from where I had followed the above events with in-creasing disquiet, to take up the post of Oriental Secretary in the British Embassy in Tehran. Things looked bleak but not completely hopeless. We were fortunate in having a brilliant chargé d'affaires, George Middleton, and a first-class, very wise, and experienced US ambassador, Loy Henderson. They worked well together. My job was political adviser and, when necessary, interpreter for Middleton. We were all three in sympathy with Iranian nationalism and recognized that, at that period in time, its personification was Mussadiq, although more and more rational and responsible Iranians were increasingly beginning to doubt his competence and to fear that he was leading the country to economic ruin. Middleton, like Mus-sadiq, was bilingual in French, and the personal relations between the two were excellent. They had many meetings, often exasperating for Middleton but person-ally agreeable. Middleton really liked "Mossy" and tried with immense perseverance to reach a settlement with him. I vividly recall one occasion when he returned from a marathon session almost elated: "I think we have done it at last, Sam." He sent his telegram to London describing the proposed settlement. I expressed some skep-ticism, to his annoyance, but two days later Mussadiq turned the whole idea on its head. This was typical and happened time and time again, but Middleton persisted until even he realized that Mussadiq was not prepared to make any deal. Even though Middleton was British, Mossy liked him back, for he was modern-minded and saw the Iranian point of view. Mussadiq would have been wise to use this able and sympathetic interlocutor in order to move toward agreement, but he always balked at the last moment.

The next significant episode during this period was the Ahmad Qavam interlude in July 1952, when this elder statesman briefly took Mussadiq's place as prime minister. This tends to be represented as a last, desperate attempt by the British to replace Mussadiq with their own man. I was in the thick of all this and can attest that the facts were very different. We were in no position either to depose Mussadiq or impose Qavam, although it was clearly in our interest that he should take over. He was as much of a nationalist as Mussadiq but more restrained, and he regarded the Soviet Union rather than Britain as the principal threat to Iran. Mussadiq's resignation on July 16 was precipitated by the shah's refusal to agree to his prime minister's request for control of the armed forces, which constituted the shah's principal source of influence. Qavam's five-day stay as prime minister is a story in itself. Briefly, however, he fell because the shah lost his nerve, failed to support him, and succumbed to a Tudeh-controlled mob. Both Henderson and Middleton believed Qavam could have held if the shah had backed him. He had considerable support among thinking Iranians. Middleton wrote: "The Shah was in the grip of fear: fear of taking a decision that might expose him to the fury of the populace, should Qavam not, in the event, remain in control. This attitude of the Shah is one of the central features of this crisis; we had long known that he was indecisive and timid, but we had not thought that his fear would so overcome his reason as to make him blind to the consequences of *not* supporting Qavam" (emphasis added). There is more in the same vein and I do not want to belabor the point, but it is important because popular mythology holds that Qavam was doomed from the beginning and his prime ministership was one more example of British stupidity and failure to move with the times. Middleton also wrote:

> The Shah defended his prerogatives against Mussadiq to the point of the latter's resignation and then he began to get cold feet at once and very nearly discouraged the Opposition from voting for Qavam. When the Opposition [in the Majlis] proved encouragingly firm and voted for Qavam, he refused him the support he required to stabilize the situation. When, despite his hesitancy, his troops remained loyal and effective, in the face of physical attacks and powerful propaganda, [contrary to the mythology] he withdrew his backing from them and exposed their commanders to the risks of savage reprisals. He hates taking decisions and cannot be relied upon to stick to them when taken; he has no moral courage and easily succumbs to fear; he is pre-occupied with his personal position on the Throne and thinks to retain it by a policy of appeasement; and, I am now convinced, we must see in him a deep-rooted dislike and distrust of the British. He has constantly ignored all sound advice given to him by responsible Persian statesmen and by the United States Ambassador and myself, and is swayed by the advice of his Minister of Court who, I suspect, echoes His Majesty's doubts and fears.

Even Middleton, who had been prepared to give Mussadiq the benefit of every possible doubt, had reached the end of the road, although he was always prepared to go on talking. He wrote:

> If we look beyond this crisis and take a wider view it is clear that the responsibility for Persia's present ills lies principally with Mussadiq and his entourage. His strength lies in his power of demagogy, and he has so flattered the mob as the source of his power that he has, [I fear,] made it impossible for a successor to oust him by normal constitutional methods. His followers, and principally Ayatollah Kashani, have probably gone further than he intended on enlisting the support of the Tudeh for Monday's trial of strength. The chief question now facing us is whether Mussadiq's government or any other (short of a military dictatorship) can avoid the "kiss of death" which is the well-known consequence of flirting with communists.

So Mussadiq returned in triumph on the shoulders of the mob and with the backing of the Tudeh Party. The shah acceded to all of Mussadiq's demands, which he had previously refused, and he became steadily more helpless and terrified. Although Middleton had more or less given up hope for Mussadiq, this was not yet the US position, although Loy Henderson and George Middleton were generally pretty close in their assessments.

When I came to Tehran at the beginning of that year (1952), support for Mussadiq was by no means monolithic. He had, of course, touched the nationalist chord, which was full of resentment against imperialism and the desire of a once great nation to be respected again. But he had delivered nothing positive; he had destroyed but he had not built up, and he had cut off almost all of Iran's revenues. He had not known when to close a deal and had constantly asked for more. He must have understood that, although the US government was sympathetic to him personally and to his nationalist aspirations, there were limits to even its generosity. It could not afford to conclude an agreement that would start a vast series of renegotiations with the world's oil producers. At the same time, he was well aware of US concern that Iran might turn to communism. So he decided to go on bargaining and came with an unacceptable counterbid to the Truman-Churchill proposal of September 1952. This proposal stated that the amount of compensation should be subject to arbitration, that the Iranian government and the AIOC should negotiate on the resumption of oil production, and that the United States would grant $10 million in budgetary aid. Mussadiq demanded £50 million as an advance against oil. The proposal ultimately failed and certainly reinforced a negative view of Mussadiq.

Another major player in all this was General Fazlollah Zahedi. He seemed like a possible focus of opposition to Mussadiq and possibly even a successor. He had been imprisoned by the British during World War II for pro-Nazi activities, a strong point in his favor, from the point of view of most Iranians, for having been on record as opposing the British. Both Middleton and I met him and were favorably impressed. He was tough, clearheaded, and rational. October 1952 was a tense time and ended in the severance of diplomatic relations between Iran and Britain. (It is worth mentioning that, throughout this difficult time for Anglo-Iranian relations, we were never personally harassed and I did not feel any danger or threat.)

I next went to Washington, DC, as a member of a small delegation to discuss Iran. Many in Washington still thought that Mussadiq was the last, best hope; we disagreed, believing that his remaining in power would lead to a Communist takeover.

What happened in 1953 is now well known: the overthrow of Mussadiq; the restoration of the shah, who had fled for a brief period; and the establishment of a pro-Western government in Tehran under General Zahedi. This was followed by the remarkable consortium oil agreement, which reflects the greatest credit on all concerned and even enabled AIOC to obtain 40 percent of the consortium with handsome compensation.

It is a widely held view among those interested in the history of the Middle East that it was a grave mistake to depose Mussadiq. It is interesting to speculate what would have happened if the Democrats had won in the United States in 1952. Democrat Adlai Stevenson, as president, would presumably have retained Dean Acheson as secretary of state and George C. McGhee as assistant secretary of state for Near East and South Asian affairs and continued to negotiate with Mussadiq. It is impossible to predict whether they would have succeeded, bearing in mind that there were limits to what the United States could concede. Mussadiq did indeed reject the "final offer" by the Republicans on March 10, 1953. With hindsight it could conceivably have been better to continue until some sort of agreement was reached with Mussadiq, but we shall never know. I very much doubt it, even today.

Let us go back forty years. The Korean War had just ended; World War III had been avoided. It was thought at the time that a Communist takeover of Iran would have been a disaster of appalling magnitude and might indeed have led to global conflict. It is questionable whether the United States could have tolerated the Soviet Union on the Gulf. One cannot in any way compare this scenario with what actually happened: a pro-Western government until 1979 and, thereafter, the irritant of Khomeini, who was impartial in his hatred of the superpowers. It was impossible to predict in 1953 that the shah, who was in a relatively strong position at the time of his restoration, could have developed into such a disagreeable tyrant, nor could we have foreseen Khomeini. We saw the immediate danger, and I remain completely convinced that it was right and, indeed, vital, *given the circumstances of the time,* to topple Mussadiq.

While we are considering "what ifs," there is another, intriguing possibility. Let us imagine that the AIOC and the British government had listened to their wisest advisers. A 50–50 oil agreement would have been concluded between the AIOC and the Iranian government no later than 1950. It seems highly probable that Mussadiq would never have come to power. Iran would have become prosperous some five years earlier, and the poverty, misery, and political instability of the Mussadiq years would have been avoided. The shah's throne would not have been threatened, and there would have been far less reason for a passionate, xenophobic nationalist movement. In spite of Iran's endemic corruption, some of the oil wealth would have gone toward development and even filtered down to the people years earlier. It is possible that the weak shah, not having been threatened and terrified to the extent he was during the Mussadiq period, might have developed into a capable and benevolent ruler. He seemed genuinely to want to help his people, and his tyranny was probably motivated by fear as much as anything. So perhaps there would have been less opposition to him, and perhaps he would have survived. Nevertheless, he would still have tried to Westernize too fast, angering the *mullahs,* and his family would have been no less corrupt. Then we can ask whether tough US support could have saved him at the end of the 1970s.

Many scholars have criticized US and British policy vis-à-vis Mussadiq. Their arguments, in summary, are as follows: Mussadiq was a rare phenomenon in Iran in that he was both honest and a democrat. He represented resurgent Iranian nationalism and was both beloved and respected by the Iranian people. He was not a Communist—far from it—and he came from the landed ruling class, although he differed in his humanity and caring approach. Consequently, he was exactly the sort of leader whom the West should have supported, since he stood for nonviolent, progressive change. This was precisely what was needed to combat communism and lead Iran to true freedom and prosperity. Such an Iran would have been friendly to the United States. For the wrong reasons, however, the US government deposed Mussadiq, supported the increasingly tyrannical shah, and thereby helped to bring about the Khomeini revolution, with all its unfortunate consequences for US-Iranian relations. The corollary to this argument is that an oil deal should have been made with Mussadiq, whatever the cost; or, even if this had proved impossible in the medium term, he should have been supported as our last, best hope in Iran and a bulwark against communism.

This chapter spells out the case that favored the deposing of Mussadiq. Clearly it would have been more desirable and in the interests of the United States, Iran, and, indeed, Britain if we could have made a reasonably satisfactory deal with Mussadiq. It might even, with the benefit of hindsight, have been better to make a poor deal than no deal at all. There were, however, limits beyond which it would have been impossible to go without upsetting the global oil business. Maybe it would have been worth it, and the cost to the United States might have been less than that of the Khomeini revolution. It is difficult to say, but, in my opinion, Mussadiq turned down some good offers that might have prevented the crisis.

In 1952 we were very worried about the Soviet, Chinese, and world Communist threats, with extremely good reason: Tensions were high and real. There was the Korean War and Stalin was still alive in all his psychopathic and dangerous malevolence. At the time, the prospect of a communist Iran was alarming and, we thought, could have led to World War III.

The US government was anxious to see, at least up to our visit to Washington in November 1952, that Mussadiq remain in office. It was with reluctance, and after the rejection of its final offer in March 1953, that it decided to support the coup. As for Mussadiq himself, he was probably an honest, sincere Iranian nationalist. He was certainly a brilliant demagogue. It is questionable, to say the least, whether he was capable of running Iran. Many Iranians—by no means all "lackeys of the imperialists"—to whom we spoke at the time were convinced of the contrary. There was a sort of mob rule. To this day, I remain utterly convinced that the Communist danger was too great to ignore and would have produced knee-jerk reactions that could have led to global catastrophe. Not only our intelligence services but an enlightened liberal of the caliber of George Middleton, who tried desperately to reach agreement with Mussadiq, were in no doubt that the lovable old man had to go.

To conclude on a personal note: In the British Foreign Service I was known as "Red Sam." This was because I believed in liberal causes, resurgent nationalism, and the like. Later I was a fervent supporter of both Egyptian president Gamal 'Abd al-Nasser and the Iraqi nationalists. Thus, Dr. Mussadiq was initially a man after my own heart, and I am on record as a remorseless critic of the AIOC. The fact that even I eventually became convinced that he had to be replaced says something; all my beliefs, or, if you like, prejudices, were in the other direction—on his side. Sadly, he could not control the Communists, and they would have removed him from power and replaced him with one of their own.

The Mussadiq crisis of 1951–1953, and, as I see it, the first Iranian revolution, led to two contradictory and consequently misleading conclusions. First, the strength of nationalism and the need for foreign governments and commercial enterprises to come to terms with it were clearly demonstrated. The second point, however, is that foreign powers were nevertheless able to depose at will uncooperative governments in Third World countries. The latter was highly dangerous and led to grievous miscalculation in the 1956 Suez crisis when, as in Iraq in 1958, the former was ignored.

Notes

1. These and other quotes contained in this chapter are gleaned from the personal records of the author.

2. Wm. Roger Louis, *The British Empire in the Middle East, 1945–1951* (Oxford: Clarendon, 1984), p. 652.

CHAPTER 5

NATIONAL SECURITY CONCERNS IN US POLICY TOWARD EGYPT, 1949–1956

Peter Hahn

From the late 1940s through the Suez crisis of 1956, US officials faced a bewildering variety of security problems with regard to Egypt. In the late 1940s, a bitter dispute raged between Great Britain, a cold war partner that wished to remain in possession of its military base facilities in the Suez Canal Zone, and Egypt, a nationalistic state that sought to escape British military occupation. Each side sought US endorsement of its position in this dispute, which remained unsolved into the early 1950s. After the Egyptian revolution of 1952, President Gamal 'Abd al-Nasser negotiated the departure of British forces from his country and challenged the remnants of Western imperialism elsewhere in the region. US officials found it impossible to reconcile Nasser's nationalism to their security interests in the Middle East and therefore sought to undermine his prestige and influence in the region. When Britain decided to wage war on Egypt in late 1956, however, US officials took steps to halt the attack on the grounds of US national security. From the late 1940s to 1956, Washington consistently made policy toward Egypt on the basis of its security interests.

During the decades preceding World War II, Egypt emerged as a region of strategic importance to the British Empire. Britain militarily occupied Egypt in 1882 in order to protect the Suez Canal and lines of communication to India, and it gained enormous advantages during World War I by closing the canal to the

79

Central Powers and by staging troops in Egypt for the Gallipoli and Jerusalem campaigns. Having legally secured the right to occupy Egypt through the 1936 Anglo-Egyptian treaty, the British used the Suez Canal Zone during World War II to deny Axis forces in North Africa easy access to oil fields in the Middle East, to ensure vital communications and transit between the Indian Ocean and the Mediterranean, and to develop a major base that boasted airfields, supply dumps, repair shops, and personnel facilities. At war's end, nearly 200,000 British troops were stationed in the Canal Zone base.[1]

US officials who examined the security situation in the Middle East during the early years of the cold war recognized the immense potential strategic importance of Egypt. As international tensions escalated during 1945 and 1946, defense officials identified the British base in the Suez Canal Zone as a facility of vital importance. In the event of war against the Soviet Union, they reasoned, Western access to the base would prove essential to victory. To promote national security, in other words, US officials would support London's quest to maintain its base in Egypt.

The US-Soviet confrontation over Turkey in 1946 first attracted the attention of Pentagon officials to Egypt. "Any action which threatens Britain's control of the Suez Canal and deprives her of a sizable portion of the Middle East oil fields," the Joint War Plans Committee (JWPC) observed, "threatens her position as a world power." Soviet conquest of the Suez Canal "would have serious adverse effects upon British capabilities in a major war."[2]

Contingency war plans devised in the Pentagon in 1946 also stressed the importance of maintaining access to British air bases in Egypt. In the event of hostilities, according to a war plan code-named PINCHER, US bombers would attack the Soviet Union's oil industry in order to cripple its war-making capability. Bombers would need air bases in Egypt in order to reach a sufficient number of vulnerable targets in the southern Soviet Union. Bombers dispatched from England, Pakistan, or Japan would lack the range to strike such targets. From airfields in the Suez Canal Zone, Western bombers could reach Moscow, the "nerve center" of Soviet power, and a host of other valuable targets. "Early availability of secure V[ery] H[eavy] B[omber] operating bases in the Cairo area," the war plan MAKEFAST added in late 1946, "is essential to the attainment of the strategic air offensive objectives."[3]

Military bases in Egypt also possessed other attractive features. Pentagon planners were confident that bases in the Canal Zone could be defended against the southward Soviet thrust anticipated in the opening stages of war. Egypt's proximity to the Soviet Union qualified it as a staging area for offensive operations into south-central Russia. The Suez Canal corridor enabled provision of the country from the Indian Ocean should the enemy close the Mediterranean. Egypt would likely emerge as a base for psychological warfare measures targeted especially at secessionists in southern Russia. As the JWPC stressed, the importance of possessing bases in Egypt "can hardly be over-emphasized."[4]

Pentagon planners confirmed the importance of British bases in Egypt as the cold war escalated in 1948 and 1949. In June 1948, during the Berlin crisis, the

Joint Strategic Planning Group (JSPG) observed that facilities in Egypt needed to defeat the Soviet Union in war "far exceed[ed] those envisaged" in earlier plans. In July, the Joint Chiefs of Staff (JCS) stressed that Egypt remained essential "as a base from which to initiate an air offensive against vital elements of the Soviet war-making capacity." In December, army officers recognized Egypt's "important role" in any military engagement in the Middle East. In March 1949, US Secretary of Defense James Forrestal confirmed Egypt's abiding importance to US national security. "In the event of global war," the National Security Council (NSC) resolved in late 1949, after the Chinese Communist revolution and the Soviet detonation of an atomic bomb, "the United States would probably wish to use facilities in the Cairo-Suez area in conjunction with the British." Indeed, army planners presumed, "should emergency dictate, the U.S. will avail itself of any facilities held by the British."[5]

From 1950 to 1953, the strategic value of British facilities in Egypt diminished slightly but remained significant. The development of long-range aircraft reduced the importance of Egypt as a launching point for any strategic air offensive against Soviet targets, but the country remained vital as a poststrike landing-and-refueling point for heavy bombers launched from Britain and as a defensive barrier, supply depot, and staging area. Renovations at Abu Sueir, Canal Zone (started in 1949 and completed in 1952), made it the only air base in the Middle East capable of handling heavy bombers. US military officials secretly stockpiled supplies at Abu Sueir and Cairo International Airport. In the eyes of US strategists, national security dictated that British military facilities in Egypt remain accessible to Western powers in the event of war.[6]

US interest in maintaining British military facilities in Egypt for national security reasons conflicted with US interest in mollifying Egyptian nationalism for political reasons. In the late 1940s, Egyptian nationalists began to challenge Britain's presence in their country. Specifically, they demanded revision or abrogation of the 1936 Anglo-Egyptian treaty that authorized the British base in the Canal Zone. Extensive Anglo-Egyptian negotiations in the late 1940s failed to reach a settlement, and nationalists turned to other tactics, including work stoppages, boycotts, and terrorist attacks, to compel the British to leave. Until the early 1950s, Britain resisted the Egyptian demands, and a deadlock ensued.[7]

The Anglo-Egyptian conflict confronted the United States with a thorny dilemma. Some officials of the US Department of State wanted to recognize Egyptian national aspirations in order to ensure the loyalty of the Egyptian people and other Third World nations in the cold war as well as to honor the US ideal of self-determination. To Pentagon officials, however, a British departure from Egypt, in the absence of satisfactory promises by Egypt to allow access to its bases, would imperil national security.[8]

US officials considered access to military bases in Egypt so vital that they repeatedly subsumed their conflicting political interests in Egypt. In May 1946, for example, US officials interceded on London's behalf in Anglo-Egyptian negotiations that had stalemated over the question of Britain's right to return to bases in

Egypt after it departed the country. US Secretary of State James Byrnes told King Farouk that he hoped Egypt would avoid "running the risk of undermining the security of the Middle East" in its quest for "full sovereignty." Egypt's hostile reaction to that message made US officials reluctant to intercede again, but they quietly encouraged the British to remain firm in negotiations with Cairo.[9]

In preparation for the Anglo-American "Pentagon talks" of October 1947, US Department of Defense officials insisted that the United States endorse Britain's position in Egypt for reasons of national security. Despite their fears that angering Egyptian nationalists might undermine the very Western interests that the Pentagon wished to preserve, officials at Foggy Bottom agreed. At the talks, State Department officials suggested that Britain appease Egyptian nationalism by agreeing in principle to withdraw eventually from Egypt, but they relented easily when British officials protested that this step would signal weakness. US and British officials agreed that "the British should have the right to maintain [in Egypt] . . . certain strategic facilities . . . during peacetime in such a condition that they could be effectively and speedily used in case of an immediate threat to the security of the Middle East." It would be "dangerous in the present world situation for the British Government to abandon such strategic facilities to which it is entitled by treaty in Egypt." In these Anglo-American talks—conducted as the cold war was intensifying—US officials sacrificed their interest in appeasing nationalism to national security considerations.[10]

US officials showed slightly more concern for Egyptian nationalism in 1949. Because Egypt blamed the United States for the creation of Israel, the war in Palestine had embittered Cairo against Washington. To avoid further alienation, US officials refused a British request to participate in talks between British and Egyptian military officers about the future of the British bases in the Canal Zone. By early 1950, however, State Department officials again interceded in Anglo-Egyptian negotiations to urge the government of Egyptian Prime Minister Mustapha Nahas to recognize that Western defense rights in Egypt were consonant with Egyptian sovereignty. "If Egypt insists that Britain withdraw her troops from the Suez zone," Assistant Secretary of State George C. McGhee told the Egyptian ambassador, "it would result in a weakening of Egypt's military strength at precisely a time when Egypt desires to increase her powers of resistance." In July, following the eruption of the Korean War, McGhee refused an Egyptian appeal for support in negotiations with London, instead warning that "Russian aggression in the Near Eastern area" loomed possible, in which case "it would be essential to our common strategic plans to have the British on the spot."[11]

In late 1950 and early 1951, however, US officials came to fear that unmollified Egyptian nationalism might abet the rise of neutralism in that state and throughout the Middle East. "The Near Eastern nations are at a point of decision," Samuel K.C. Kopper, deputy director of the Division of Near Eastern Affairs, noted in December 1950, "as to whether to cast their lot irrevocably with the West, to remain neutral, or to drift into the Soviet orbit." Pressuring Egyptian leaders to align with the West, McGhee concluded in early 1951, was bound to fail. A compromise solution to the base dispute, McGhee realized, "would outweigh the present advantages of the British position."[12]

In 1951, therefore, US officials devised the Middle East Command (MEC) concept to bridge the gap between strategic and political interests in Egypt. The MEC idea envisioned a multilateral, anti-Soviet defense arrangement that would include Egyptian military officers with headquarters in Cairo. Unfortunately, the chance that Egypt would approve MEC diminished in the summer of 1951, when the United Nations (UN) Security Council, at the behest of Britain and France, passed a resolution censuring Egyptian restrictions on canal shipping destined for Israel. Before Western powers found the time to propose MEC to the government in Cairo, Prime Minister Nahas had commenced parliamentary procedures to nullify the 1936 Anglo-Egyptian treaty. Egypt summarily rejected MEC.[13]

State Department officials were deeply troubled by Egypt's rejection of MEC, by its abrogation of the treaty, and by a wave of violence between British troops and Egyptian guerrillas in late 1951 and early 1952. The turmoil helped trigger the revolution of July 1952, in which a clique of military officers led by Gamal 'Abd al-Nasser ousted King Farouk. Alarmed by the parallel rise of revolutionary nationalism in Egypt and Iran, Secretary of State Dean G. Acheson feared that the entire Middle East might turn hostile to the West unless Britain made concessions to end its impasse with Egypt. Pentagon officials, on the other hand, favored fully endorsing Britain's stubborn position. The NSC reconciled these positions by resolving in April 1952 "to induce the U.K. to modify its position in ways which, while maintaining basic Western interests, might make possible an early negotiated settlement." But Britain would not be induced to make any concessions, and the Anglo-Egyptian impasse persisted into 1953. In light of national security requirements, US officials refrained from strongly pressuring the British to make those concessions that might have served the US political interest of mollifying Egyptian nationalism.[14]

In 1952 and 1953, changing circumstances in the Middle East and elsewhere rendered the Canal Zone military base less essential to US and British security. British officials concluded in late 1952 that Soviet development of atomic weapons made it dangerous to concentrate 80,000 soldiers in a single base site within Soviet bomber range. Attacks by Egyptian guerrilla fighters, moreover, inflicted severe human, psychological, and financial costs. The Canal Zone base, though still important, seemed to the British no longer indispensable. They decided to move their headquarters to Cyprus, relocate troops to the home isles, and rely on rapid air transit in the event of an emergency.[15]

Similar ideas developed on the western shore of the Atlantic. When Turkey joined the North Atlantic Treaty Organization (NATO) in 1952, the Pentagon began thinking about shifting its Middle East security focus from Egypt to the northern tier of the region. After Pakistan joined the Southeast Asia Treaty Organization (SEATO) in 1954, a northern tier pact offered to complete a chain of anti-Soviet pacts from East Asia to northern Europe. The governments of the northern tier seemed more ready than Arab states such as Egypt to cooperate with

Western defense plans. More secure than the lone, gigantic base at Suez, a series of smaller facilities scattered along the Soviet perimeter also provided advantages in intelligence collection and offensive capabilities. For example, Thor and Jupiter missiles, developed in the mid-1950s, could carry nuclear payloads but for only short distances.[16]

In 1953, President Dwight D. Eisenhower and Secretary of State John Foster Dulles approved a shift in US strategic focus from Egypt to the northern tier. Conversations during a tour of the Middle East in the spring of 1953 convinced Dulles that Egypt, beset by rampant forces of nationalism, would not serve as a reliable security partner but that northern tier states would. Turkey and Pakistan, he observed, would serve as cornerstones of a defense pact of states that "are most conscious of the Soviet threat and most disposed to cooperate with western powers." Dulles declared the original MEC idea to be "on the shelf." In 1954, US Air Force officials canceled planned improvements at the Abu Sueir airfield. The northern tier idea came to fruition with the signing of a Turkish-Iraqi pact in Baghdad on February 24, 1955. Britain joined the Baghdad Pact in April 1955; Pakistan joined in September and Iran in October.[17]

In light of Egypt's diminished strategic importance, US officials pressed the British to make concessions needed to break their deadlock with Egypt. With strong US urging, a reluctant Churchill government approved a base treaty in July 1954 (signed in October 1954). The accord terminated the 1936 treaty, provided for withdrawal of British forces over twenty months, permitted British civilian technicians to maintain the base, and authorized the British military to return in the event of a Soviet attack on Turkey or any Arab state. British forces completed their departure in June 1956.[18]

US officials hoped that Nasser, with his independence secured, would cooperate with Western security plans, endorse the northern tier pact, and eventually join it. "We are counting on Egypt," Deputy Assistant Secretary of State John D. Jernegan noted on August 16, 1954, "to play an important leadership role . . . in the achievement of United States policy objectives in the Middle East." Nasser talked about forming an Arab League collective security pact and Dulles suggested linking this pact to the northern tier arrangement via an Egyptian-Turkish mutual defense treaty. Nasser's initial reaction and his acceptance of $40 million in US economic aid in late 1954 encouraged US hopes that Nasser would become a security partner.[19]

By early 1955, however, such US optimism seemed unfounded. Nasser refused to accept US military aid because of the standard condition that a US military mission would administer it, a condition that to him smacked of colonialism. He also rejected a secret US plan, which would have violated congressional rules for administering aid, to divert $5 million of the $40 million in economic aid to military hardware purchases.[20]

As negotiations on military aid stalemated, Nasser emerged as a thorn in America's side in the Middle East. He reversed himself on the northern tier idea and became a chief critic of the Baghdad Pact. He claimed as Egypt's mission the riddance

of Western imperialism from the Middle East. He reacted strongly to Israeli provocations and responded coolly to the Anglo-American "Alpha" peace plan. In the
absence of US military aid grants, Nasser purchased a massive quantity of arms
from the Soviet Union in September 1955.[21]

Eisenhower and Dulles at first tried to appeal to Nasser by offering to finance
construction of the Aswan Dam, and they tried to pacify the Egyptian-Israeli situation by sending special emissary Robert Anderson to broker a deal in early 1956.
But Nasser would neither accept the conditions of the dam aid offer nor cooperate
fully with the Anderson mission. Worse, in early 1956, he encouraged anti-British
rioters in Jordan and Bahrain, continued to criticize the Baghdad Pact, bought
weapons from Poland, and recognized the People's Republic of China. NSC officials concluded that Nasser's "positive neutralism actually works in favor of the Soviet bloc since it is directed against established western positions."[22]

US officials had concluded by March 1956 that, despite their efforts to woo
Nasser, he had emerged as a threat to their national security interests in the Middle
East. With the British, therefore, they concocted the Omega policy, a series of steps
designed to undercut Nasser's prestige among Arab peoples and possibly to remove
him from power. Omega would "let Colonel Nasser realize," Dulles noted, "that
he cannot cooperate as he is doing with the Soviet Union and at the same time
enjoy most-favored-nation treatment from the United States." Omega planned for
the gradual withdrawal of the Aswan aid offer, but in July, under strong congressional pressure, Dulles canceled the deal abruptly. Nasser retaliated against the
Aswan renege by nationalizing the Suez Canal Company and announcing that its
revenues would finance the dam.[23]

Nasser's seizure of the canal company provoked the Suez Crisis of late 1956.
The British at once resolved to use force to recover control of the waterway and
knock Nasser from power, and they eventually conspired with the French and the
Israelis to launch a tripartite attack against Egypt that began October 29. President
Eisenhower, by contrast, decided early in the crisis that force would threaten US
national security interests. A British attack on Egypt would foment Anglophobia
around the world, inflame Arab nationalism (and thus imperil oil supplies to the
West), and result in a long and costly British occupation of the Suez Canal Zone.
For the United States to allow London to wage war on Egypt, Eisenhower told the
NSC on July 31, "might well array the world from Dakar to the Philippine Islands
against us." A breach with London would "be extremely serious, but not as serious
as letting a war start and not trying to stop it."[24]

Accordingly, Eisenhower sought to use diplomacy to delay a British attack, on
the calculation that time would cool British tempers and avert war. In late July he
dispatched Deputy Under Secretary of State for Political Affairs Robert Murphy
and Dulles to London to soothe British anger. In August, Eisenhower and Dulles
arranged the London Conference to devise a diplomatic solution to the question
of control of the canal, in September they proposed establishment of a Suez Canal
Users Association to govern the waterway, and in October they encouraged Britain
and Egypt to resolve their differences through negotiations sponsored by the United

Nations. Eisenhower also publicly and privately appealed to British Prime Minister Anthony Eden to practice restraint. "The use of force," he cabled Eden on September 3, "would . . . vastly increase the area of jeopardy." The developing world "would be consolidated against the West to a degree which, I fear, could not be overcome in a generation and, perhaps, not even in a century."[25]

Once hostilities began on October 29, Eisenhower moved to end the fighting promptly for three national security reasons. First, he regretted that the attack on Egypt diverted global attention from Moscow's brutal crushing of the rebellion in Hungary. Second, he feared that the Soviets would politically support Egypt and thereby win favor among developing nations. Unless the United States ended the fighting, Dulles observed, "all of these newly independent countries will turn from us to the USSR. We will be looked upon as forever tied to British and French colonialist policies." "How can we possibly support Britain and France," Eisenhower added, "if in so doing we lose the entire Arab world." US inaction would enable the Soviet Union to seize "a mantle of world leadership through a false but convincing exhibition of concern for smaller nations."[26]

Third, Eisenhower gravely worried about Soviet threats to intervene militarily to defend Egypt. On November 5, one day after crushing the rebellion in Budapest, Moscow threatened to send troops to Egypt and to fire rockets on London and Paris. The JCS interpreted this statement as "serious intent on the part of the Soviets." Eisenhower observed that Soviet leaders were "scared and furious" over Hungary, "and there is nothing more dangerous than a dictatorship in this frame of mind." The president warned Moscow that the United States would defend its allies, but he also tightened his diplomatic and financial squeezes to convince Britain and France to halt the fighting. Both powers accepted a UN cease-fire on November 6.[27]

From the mid-1940s to the mid-1950s, US officials consistently made policy toward Egypt on grounds of national security. From 1946 to 1953, the overriding strategic importance of British military facilities in Egypt compelled them actively and passively to endorse Britain's determination to remain in the Suez Canal Zone over Egypt's strong opposition. Such security concerns, in light of the cold war and the Korean War, convinced officials in Washington to subsume their conflicting political interest in befriending Egyptian nationalism. Only when the move to the northern tier diminished the strategic importance of Egypt did US officials find it safe to pressure Britain to reach a settlement providing for withdrawal of British forces from the Suez Canal Zone.

After the 1954 Anglo-Egyptian treaty, US officials hoped to win Nasser's cooperation with their plans for securing the Middle East against Soviet expansion. But Nasser refused US overtures and emerged as a leading critic of Western influence in the region. Therefore, again for reasons of national security, US officials together with the British initiated the Omega policy to undermine Nasser's prestige in the Middle East and, perhaps, even his power in Cairo.

National security concerns also determined US behavior during the Suez crisis of late 1956. Fear that the Soviet Union would gain politically or intervene militarily compelled Eisenhower to oppose British plans for war against Nasser and then to use his power to halt the attack once it began. Contrary to its political concerns, the United States censured its British ally and rescued Nasser from aggression during the Suez conflict. Such actions were entirely consistent with Washington's national security imperatives, which prevailed, as before, over its competing political interests.

Notes

1. D. A. Farnie, *East and West of Suez: The Suez Canal in History* (Oxford: Clarendon, 1969), pp. 32–93; and Peter Mansfield, *The British in Egypt* (London: Weidenfeld and Nicolson, 1971), pp. 201–219, 265–275.

2. JWPC 450/3, 10 March 1946, Record Group (RG) 218, Records of the Joint Chiefs of Staff, CCS 092 USSR (3–27–45), section 6 (hereinafter RG 218 with appropriate filing designations), National Archives, Washington, DC (hereinafter National Archives).

3. "PINCHER," JPS 789, 2 March 1946, US Department of Defense, Joint Chiefs of Staff, Records of the Joint Chiefs of Staff: Soviet Union (Washington, DC: University Publications Microfilm, 1978), reel 1; and "Air Plan for MAKEFAST," n.d. [autumn 1946], RG 165, Records of the Army Staff, ABC 381 USSR (2 March 1946), section 3, National Archives.

4. JWPC 450/3, 10 March 1946, RG 218, CCS 092 USSR (3–27–45), section 7. See also JIS 226/3, 4 March 1946, RG 218, CCS 092 USSR (3–27–45), section 5.

5. JSPC 684/40, 2 June 1948, RG 319, Records of the Army Staff, P&O 686 TS, case 1, National Archives (hereafter RG 319 with appropriate filing designations); JCS 1887/1, 28 July 1948, RG 218, CCS 381 EMMEA (11–19–47); unsigned report on Egyptian airfields, 1 December 1948, RG 319, P&O 686, case 273; NSC 47/2, 17 October 1949, Harry S Truman Papers, President's Secretary's Files, Subject File: NSC Series, box 193, Harry S Truman Library, Independence, Missouri (hereinafter Truman Library); and memorandum by Maddocks, 4 February 1949, RG 319, P&O 686 TS, case 9. See also NSC 45, 17 March 1949, RG 273, Records of the National Security Council, National Archives (hereafter RG 273 with appropriate filing designations).

6. NSC 68, 14 April 1950, US Department of State, Foreign Relations of the United States, 1950 (Washington, DC: US Government Printing Office, 1959–1990), 1:261–262 (hereinafter FRUS with volume and page citations); Walter S. Poole, *The History of the Joint Chiefs of Staff*, vol. 4: The Joint Chiefs of Staff and National Policy, 1950–1952 (Wilmington, Del.: Glazier, 1980), pp. 161–172; Bradley to Lovett, 25 June 1952, RG 330, Records of the Office of the Secretary of Defense, CD 092 (Egypt) 1952, National Archives (hereafter RG 330 with appropriate filing designations); NSC 129/1, 24 April 1952, RG 273; and JSPC 684/130, 1 November 1952, US Department of Defense, Joint Chiefs of Staff, Records of the Joint Chiefs of Staff: The Middle East (Washington, DC: University Publications Microfilm, 1978), reel 1.

7. Peter L. Hahn, *The United States, Great Britain, and Egypt, 1945–1956: Strategy and Diplomacy in the Early Cold War* (Chapel Hill: University of North Carolina Press, 1991), pp. 94–109, 132–139.

8. See, for example, memorandum of conversation by Battle, 27 January 1952, RG 59, General Records of the US Department of State, 774.00, National Archives

(hereafter RG 59 with appropriate filing designations); report by Hendershot, 4 April 1952, RG 59, 611.80; Summary of Discussion, 23 April 1952, and NSC 129/1, 24 April 1952, RG 273; and Bradley to Lovett, 25 June 1952, RG 330, CD 092 (Egypt) 1952.

9. Byrnes to Tuck, 24 May 1946, RG 59, 741.83. See also Tuck to Byrnes, 27 May and 11 June 1946, and Clark to Byrnes, 27 June 1946, ibid.

10. US-U.K. Agreed Minute, n.d. [16 October 1947], Foreign Office (hereinafter FO) 800/476, Records of the Foreign Secretary's Office, ME/47/17, Public Record Office (hereinafter PRO), Kew Gardens, London. See also Memorandum of Conversation by Hare, 9 October 1947, FRUS 5 (1947):561–562; State Department Policy Memoranda, n.d. [c. early October 1947], ibid., pp. 521–522, 543–544; and Royall to Marshall, 29 September 1947, and Unsigned Memorandum for the Record, 23 September 1947, RG 319, P&O 091.7 (section 2), case 50.

11. Memorandum of Conversation by Acheson, 13 April 1950, Dean G. Acheson Papers, US Secretary of State Series, box 64, Truman Library; and Memorandum of Conversation by Stabler, 17 July 1950, RG 59, 641.74. See also Acheson to Holmes, 17 February 1949, FRUS 6 (1949):194–195.

12. Paper by Kopper, 27 December 1950, FRUS 5 (1950):11–14; and Minutes of Meeting, 2 May 1951, FRUS 5 (1951):113–120.

13. Peter L. Hahn, "Containment and Egyptian Nationalism: The Unsuccessful Effort to Establish the Middle East Command, 1950–1953," *Diplomatic History* 11(1) (Winter 1987):23–40.

14. NSC 129/1, 24 April 1952, RG 273.

15. Memorandum by Eden, 27 October 1952, Records of the Cabinet Office, CAB 129/56, C(52)369, PRO; Minutes of Meeting, 29 October 1952, Cabinet Meetings Minutes, CAB 128/25, CC 91(52)7, PRO; and Minutes of Meeting, 11 December 1952, Records of the British Defence Committee, CAB 131/12, D(52)12/4, PRO.

16. JCS to Lovett, 17 October 1952, RG 330, CD 092 (Middle East 1952); NSC 155/1, 14 July 1953, NSC 5428, 23 July 1954, and progress report on NSC 5428, 7 April 1955, RG 273; and unsigned Memorandum by State Department, 17 May 1954, RG 59, 611.41.

17. Circular Telegram by Dulles, 30 July 1953, RG 59, 780.5. See also Washbourne to Division of Operations, 28 September 1954, and Memorandum for the Record by Logan, 8 December 1954, RG 341, Records of the Headquarters of the US Air Force, National Archives.

18. Shuckburgh diary, 27 July 1954, Evelyn Shuckburgh, *Descent to Suez: Diaries, 1951–1956* (New York: Norton, 1987), p. 233; and Murray to Eden, 3 November 1954, PREM 11/702, Records of the Prime Minister's Office, PRO (hereinafter PREM with appropriate filing designations).

19. Jernegan to Murphy, 16 August 1954, RG 59, 774.13. See also Hart to Byroade, 26 October 1954, and Caffery to Dulles, 6 November 1954, RG 59, 774.5MSP.

20. Caffery to Dulles, 16 September and 27 November 1954, RG 59, 774.5MSP; Memorandum by Operations Coordinating Board (hereinafter OCB) working group, 21 December 1954, OCB.091, Egypt folder, OCB Central File Series, NSC Staff Papers, Dwight D. Eisenhower Library, Abilene, Kansas (hereinafter Eisenhower Library); and Stevenson to Eden, 17 January 1955, Political Correspondence of the Foreign Office, FO 371/113608, JE1057/1, PRO.

21. Byroade to Dulles, 20 May and 9 June 1955, FRUS 14 (1955–1957):192, 234; Powers to Radford, 18 August 1955, RG 218, CJCS (Radford) 091 Egypt; State Department Report, 12 September 1955, IR 7042, Records of the Research and Analysis Branch, RG 59; and progress report on NSC 5428, 2 November 1955, RG 273.

22. Progress Report on NSC 5428, 17 May 1956, RG 273. See also Progress Report on NSC 5428, 2 November 1955, RG 273; Dulles to Macmillan, 5 December 1955, FRUS 14 (1955):820–821; Memorandum of Conversation, [30 January 1956], Dwight D. Eisenhower Papers (Ann Whitman File): International Series, box 20, Eisenhower Library (hereafter Whitman File with appropriate filing designations); Hoover to Dulles, 16 March 1956, John Foster Dulles Papers, White House Memoranda Series, box 4, Princeton University, Princeton, N.J. (hereinafter Dulles Papers with appropriate filing designations); and Eisenhower diary entry, 8 March 1956, Whitman File: Diary Series, box 9.

23. Dulles to Eisenhower, 28 March 1956, Whitman File: Diary Series, box 13. See also Memorandum of Conversation, 19 July 1956, and Byroade to Dulles, 26 July 1956, FRUS 15 (1955–1957):867–873, 906–908.

24. Memorandum of Conversation by Goodpaster, 31 July 1956, Whitman File: Diary Series, box 16. See also Eden to Eisenhower, 27 July 1956, PREM 11/1098; Minutes of Meeting, 27 July 1956, Whitman File: Cabinet Series, box 7; Memorandum of Conversation by Goodpaster, 28 July 1956, Whitman File: Diary Series, box 16; and Memorandum of Conversation by Dulles, 30 July 1956, Dulles Papers, Telephone Conversation Series, box 5.

25. Eisenhower to Eden, 3 September 1956, PREM 11/1100. See also Dulles to Murphy, 30 July 1956, and Dulles to Eisenhower, 2 August 1956, Whitman File: Dulles-Herter Series, box 5; Minutes of Meeting with Dulles, 1 August 1956, PREM 11/1098; Memorandum for the Record, 12 August 1956, Whitman File: Diary Series, box 17; Position Paper, 11 September 1956, Dulles Papers, Subject Series, box 7; and Lloyd to Eden, 8–12 October 1956, PREM 11/1102.

26. Summary of Discussion, 1 November 1956, Whitman File: NSC Series, box 8; and Eisenhower to Dulles, 1 November 1956, Whitman File: International Series, box 19.

27. Circular Telegrams by JCS, 6 November 1956, RG 218, CCS 381 EMMEA (11–19–47), section 47; Memorandum of Conversation by Goodpaster, 6 November 1956, FRUS 16 (1955–1957):1014; and Memorandum of Conversation by Goodpaster, 7 November 1956, Dulles Papers, White House Memoranda Series, box 4.

CHAPTER 6

THE PERILS OF AMBIGUITY

The United States and the Baghdad Pact

Elie Podeh

On February 24, 1955, Iraq and Turkey signed a military pact, which would later develop into a wider organization, encompassing Britain, Pakistan, and Iran. The Baghdad Pact (BP), as it came to be known, was devised to interlock with a chain of alliances already surrounding the Soviet Union, such as NATO, SEATO, and ANZUS. From a Western perspective, the role of the BP was to defend the Middle East from the Soviet "menace." In many respects, the formation of the BP was a consummation of Secretary of State John Foster Dulles' Northern Tier concept, devised following his Middle East tour as US secretary of state in May 1953. Though supporting it behind the scenes and joining some of its committees, the United States never formally joined the BP. Instead, in early 1957 it launched the Eisenhower Doctrine, which largely superseded the pact.

The BP episode had been considered marginal in American historiography.[1] Recent studies, however, based on declassified archival material, have somewhat corrected this perception. Largely focusing on the role played by the United States and Britain in establishing the pact, these studies offer three interpretations: The first sees it as a US initiative;[2] the second views it as a US initiative "hijacked" by Britain;[3] and the third sees it as a British initiative.[4] These studies, as shown elsewhere, underestimate the role of the regional powers—particularly Iraq and Turkey—in the formation of the pact.[5] Moreover, in analyzing the BP within the framework of US-British relations, most studies do not delve into global and internal constraints that hampered US accession.[6] More specifically, they largely neglect several important questions that would be the focus of this chapter: Why did the United States allow the initiative to be taken over by the British? What was the purpose of US ambiguous policy toward the pact, and how successful was it? How did interdepartmental controversies shape US policy toward the pact? And, finally, what does this episode tell us about the nature of Eisenhower-Dulles relations?

EARLY MIDDLE EASTERN DEFENSE PLANS

Until the advent of the Republican administration headed by President Dwight D. Eisenhower and Dulles in January 1953, US interest in the Middle East was limited. This partial aloofness was caused by US extensive involvement in cold war crises and its efforts to contain Soviet expansion in Western Europe, leading to the launching of the Truman Doctrine (1947) and the formation of NATO (1949). But US interest in the Middle East was far from negligible. Strategically, the region was seen as a source of oil; a center of communications; a shield to Africa and the Indian Ocean; and no less important, an irreplaceable offensive base against the Soviet Union. Yet the Middle East was considered a British and Commonwealth responsibility due to Britain's historical role and its control of military bases there.

With the formation of NATO, the United States considered establishing a regional defense organization in the Middle East, but all the available options seemed premature or irrelevant. In the meantime, the bilateral treaties between Britain and several Arab countries remained the basis of Western security.[7] The outbreak of the Korean War in 1950, followed by the Iranian oil crisis in March 1951, led to a change in American thinking. The United States became convinced that the cold war was not confined to the European theater and that remote areas such as the Far East, and by implication the Middle East, were exposed to Soviet penetration. In the long run, the cold war led to the adoption of a new policy called the "New Look." In the short run, both the United States and Britain thought that a more aggressive policy for the defense of the Middle East was required. In September 1951, they launched the Middle East Command (MEC), an allied anti-Soviet pact comprising the United States, Great Britain, France, Turkey, Australia, New Zealand, and South Africa. Egypt was the only regional state to be offered the status of a founding member—a decision determined by the strategic value of the Suez area as well as British desire to overcome the deadlock in the negotiations over the Anglo-Egyptian treaty. Unable to join what was regarded as "perpetuation of British occupation" and suffering from a variety of domestic problems, the Egyptian government rejected the offer and simultaneously abrogated the 1936 treaty. Without Egypt, the MEC idea simply withered away.[8]

The revision of MEC, which took place during the first half of 1952, resulted in a joint US-British project to establish a planning organization located in Cyprus, called the Middle East Defense Organization (MEDO).[9] The July 1952 military coup in Egypt suspended its execution, although it rekindled Western hopes that the new Egyptian regime would be willing to discuss the original MEC plan, especially in light of the contacts held between the CIA and the rebelling officers prior to the takeover. However, Muhammad Naguib and Gamal 'Abd al-Nasser, the two leading officers, refused to commit themselves to any Western defense plans subjecting Egypt to foreign control.[10] It was thus evident that Egypt—the cornerstone of Western strategic planning—had become a stumbling block in the way of establishing a Middle Eastern defense organization. A new line of thinking was needed, and that is exactly what Dulles offered with his Northern Tier concept.

In 1953, Eisenhower's administration devised the "New Look." It derived mainly from the need to reduce military spending. The new strategy came also as a response to the Berlin crisis and the Korean War, which—according to the critical view—left the enemy the freedom to choose the time, place, and conditions of any confrontation. Thus, the policy was designed to protect America's global interests without risking new "Koreas." In addition, it constituted a kind of response to the successful hydrogen bomb tests by the Soviet Union in August 1953, which ended the Western monopoly on this kind of weaponry. The New Look meant that the United States would meet any Communist aggression "with massive retaliation by means and at places of its own choosing."[11] This resulted in a drastic cut of the army and navy budgets; in contrast, the budget of the air force, which was trained to carry out atomic strikes, was substantially increased. The credibility of America's second-strike capacity, however, depended on encircling the Soviet Union with airbases from which US bombers could attack. This necessitated bases in Europe, South Asia, and the Middle East.[12] Because NATO had already been established in Europe and some form of organization in Asia was beginning to take shape (the Southeast Asia Treaty Organization, SEATO, would be formed in September 1954), the Middle East was seen as the remaining vacuum in the strategic belt being constructed around the two communist "behemoths"—the Soviet Union and the People's Republic of China.

Dulles' tour in the Middle East and Southeast Asia in May 1953 proved to be a turning point in the formulation of US Middle East policy. Following his mission, Dulles realized that the Anglo-Egyptian dispute, the Arab-Israeli conflict, and the question of local legitimacy were of more concern to the revolutionary Egyptian regime than were the Soviets. In contrast, the Northern Tier countries—Turkey, Pakistan, Iran, Iraq, and possibly Syria—were thought to be more concerned with this menace and thus constituted a more realistic basis for the creation of a regional organization.[13] In July 1953, Dulles' conclusions were drawn into a National Security Council (NSC) memorandum, which set out the objectives and policies of US policy in the Middle East. In general, the paper urged the development of secret plans for the defense of the area with Britain, Turkey, and other "northern" countries.[14]

The US Joint Chiefs of Staff kept up the momentum by advising the US Department of Defense in November 1953 to encourage Turkey, Pakistan, Iran, and possibly Iraq to create a regional defense organization, thus skirting the thorny issues of the Anglo-Egyptian dispute and the Arab-Israeli conflict.[15] Indeed, the United States was instrumental in bringing about a treaty of friendship and collective security between Turkey and Pakistan, the two most ardent supporters of collaboration with the West, in April 1954. Despite US attempts to portray the agreement as a "local" initiative, it was clear that the United States orchestrated it. The treaty was intended to serve as a nucleus of a wider defense organization subsequently including other Muslim-Arab members, with the formal or tacit endorsement of Washington. When Iraq agreed to sign a military agreement with the United States in April, it seemed that it was to become the first Arab state joining the Turco-Pakistani pact.[16] At that point, Dulles' Northern Tier concept seemed not only innovative but also successful.

The centrality of the Turco-Pakistani agreement in US thinking was reflected in an NSC policy statement in July 1954. After reiterating US interests in the Middle East, and acknowledging receding British influence, it noted that this pact was the first step in the direction of creating an indigenous regional defense arrangement including also Iran and Iraq. It was acknowledged that as long as the Anglo-Egyptian dispute and the Arab-Israeli conflict remained unresolved, the chances for enlisting other Arab states to the organization were slim. Still, the document advised to "associate Egypt with the defense arrangements should she so request, and make clear to her that the 'northern tier' concept does not derogate from the importance the US attaches to strengthening Egypt." The paper also attached importance to the British position in determining the success of the Northern Tier concept, advising the policymakers to invest efforts to "overcome the doubts now held by the UK."[17]

While the Arab world began feeling the first reverberations of the Turco-Pakistani agreement, Dulles was preoccupied with interlocking the chain of pacts surrounding the Soviet Union in Southeast Asia. Following the Korean War, the region remained highly unstable, culminating in the French loss of Dien Bien Phu to the Vietminh forces on May 7, 1954. This was followed by the Geneva conference in July, where it was decided to grant independence to Cambodia and Laos, while Vietnam was temporarily divided into two entities. Western desire to bring stability to the region, as well as to check the spread of communism, led to the establishment of SEATO, comprising the United States, France, Britain, Australia, New Zealand, Pakistan, and the Philippines. The signatories pledged to consult in the event of common danger. A separate protocol extended the protection of SEATO to the territory of Laos, Cambodia, and South Vietnam.[18]

The signing of SEATO enabled Dulles to concentrate on the last vacuum in the chain of pacts—the Middle East. The signing of the Anglo-Egyptian agreement in October 1954 raised US hopes that both Great Britain and Egypt would be more forthcoming in their attitude toward the Turco-Pakistani pact. Soon, however, it became evident that the pact would not serve as a basis for a wider defense organization. Apparently, the United States had misjudged the behavior of three key players: Britain, Iraq, and Egypt. Although the British were considered—and rightly so—a cold war partner, they were keen to maintain an effective political and military presence in the Middle East. The Northern Tier concept, however, threatened to shift the focus of regional defense from Egypt to the countries located on the southern border of the Soviet Union, thus further eroding Britain's influence. The Hashemites in Iraq, for their part, hoped to use the idea of regional defense as a mechanism that enabled them to revise the Anglo-Iraqi treaty and to pose a credible claim for Arab hegemony. Evidently, they realized that even if they joined a US-sponsored pact, it would not constitute a vehicle to revise the Anglo-Iraqi treaty, and by joining an existing non-Arab pact, Iraq had negligible chances for leading this enterprise. The third key player—Egypt—was determined to defend its perceived leading role in the Arab world, which seemed to be challenged by Iraq's moves. As a result of these conflicting interests, the Turco-Pakistani pact was rejected as a basis for regional defense; instead, Iraq and Turkey—with the active support of British and US knowledge—devised a somewhat different formula, which culminated in the establishment of the Baghdad Pact.

THE FORMATION OF THE TURCO-IRAQI PACT

Western defense plans coincided with the aspirations of Nuri al-Sa'id, the Iraqi prime minister, who faithfully served the Hashemite monarchy. Since the early 1950s, Nuri attempted to find a defense mechanism enabling Iraq to improve its standing in the Arab world and to modify the Anglo-Iraqi treaty, which was to expire in 1957 under heavy domestic criticism. Nuri was disappointed that initial Western plans treated Iraq as a minor player. Yet, Egypt's rejection of these plans and the consequent shift in the strategic thinking toward the Northern Tier concept improved Iraq's bargaining position. Nuri was intent on exploiting this opportunity to elevate Iraq to its "deserved" position in the Arab world. It would make up for what Iraq viewed as the regrettable British decision to place the Arab League in Cairo in 1945.

Since Iraq's adherence to the Turco-Pakistani pact did not meet its interests, and as a result of Egyptian-led Arab opposition to the pact, Nuri began searching for another mechanism. His search commenced in London in September 1954, where he raised several ingenious ideas about regional defense, envisaging a central role for Iraq. Although Nuri was convinced that a regional pact without Western participation would be worthless, he came to the conclusion that the first step should be a pact between Iraq and a Muslim-Asian country—a step that the Iraqi parliament would unconditionally approve. An agreement between two equal "oriental" countries would, he thought, help camouflage the subsequent adherence of Great Britain and perhaps the United States as well. Although the visit did not produce any tangible results, it became the starting point for the new defense project. Interestingly, however, Nuri did not disclose all the details of the London visit to the US ambassador in Baghdad, in spite of Iraq's good relations with the United States.[19]

In October, while the British were reviewing their defense plans in light of Nuri's ideas, the latter went to Ankara to promote the possibility of an Iraqi-Turkish pact. Although the talks were tough and inconclusive, Turkish prime minister 'Adnan Menderes assured Washington that within six months a "pattern of Middle East defense in [a] manner particularly satisfactory to [the] US and UK" would be established.[20] At that point, it seems that Great Britain and the United States began moving in opposite directions. While the Foreign Office realized that an Iraqi-Turkish pact allowing for subsequent British adherence was a desirable solution, the State Department still thought that the Turco-Pakistani pact was the most appropriate basis from which a "full-fledged defense organization could grow."[21] Moreover, it complained that British thinking on the Northern Tier concept "is not so positive as it was last autumn."[22]

The Iraqi-Turkish initiative gained further momentum during Menderes' visit to Baghdad in early January 1955. On January 13, the two prime ministers published a joint communiqué, pledging to sign a pact aimed at cooperation in the event of external or internal aggression, open to other states "eligible by virtue of their geographical location or their potential contributions."[23] The terms of the statement surprised both Great Britain and the United States, but they were quick to respond favorably.[24] On January 18, Dulles publicly endorsed the Iraqi-Turkish statement, describing it a "very constructive development" in the direction of "building up the so-called 'Northern Tier' of which Turkey and Pakistan are already pioneers," adding that every step closing the gap between Turkey and Pakistan improved the security of the area.[25]

Two possible explanations may be offered for the quick US endorsement of the statement. First, Dulles realized that Nuri and the British Foreign Office would not be induced to join the Turco-Pakistani pact, which did not serve their interests. On the other hand, he could not oppose an anti-Soviet regional defense pact, which served overall US global interests. By encouraging Iraq, the United States was at risk of alienating Egypt. Yet it seems that the force of circumstances made any debate in the State Department or the White House between "Egypt-firsters" and "Iraq-firsters" superfluous. Unaware of the deep Egyptian-Iraqi animosity, Dulles still entertained the notion of holding the rope on both ends.[26] He hoped that the fact that the United States was not directly involved in planning the new venture would enable it to maintain friendly relations with Nasser's Egypt at the same time.[27]

The second reason for the quick endorsement was connected with US world affairs. In mid-January 1955, the United States was deeply embroiled in an East Asian crisis, which threatened to deteriorate into World War III. The previous September, a military and political crisis had ensued between Communist China and the Nationalist Chinese led by Chiang Kai-shek in Taiwan, when the former made a move that was interpreted as an attempt to capture the islands of Quemoy and Matsu, near the Chinese shore. Although the military significance of the islands was doubtful, their conquest by Chou En-Lai's forces was perceived as the beginning of Taiwan's fall. The United States was resolved to face this challenge, even if it meant the use of force. Subsequently, a security treaty was signed with Taiwan in December 1954. In mid-January, however, communist forces made some military moves that propelled the United States to make a stronger commitment. On January 24, Congress approved the Formosa Resolution, which authorized "to use force if, in Eisenhower's sole judgment, an attack on the offshore islands was a part of, or a definite preliminary to, an attack against Taiwan and the Pescadores."[28] Seemingly no direct connection existed between the crisis and the question of Middle East defense, but it is probable that Dulles' preoccupation with the Chinese affair (which would end only in April) prevented him from delving too deeply into the relatively tranquil Middle East situation.

Following the Turco-Iraqi statement, the United States attempted to advance a two-pronged policy: supporting the build-up of a realistic defense organization, including Turkey, Pakistan, Iraq, and Iran and advancing an Arab-Israeli settlement through Operation Alpha.[29] This was a code name for a secret US-British project to bring about an Egyptian-Israeli settlement. Early versions of the plan were drafted already in the second half of 1954, but the actual details were worked out in Washington in January–February 1955. After being endorsed by Dulles and Anthony Eden, the plan was waiting to be presented to Nasser and Ben-Gurion at the earliest possible opportunity.[30] Because Nasser's consent for the project seemed crucial, the United States made efforts not to alienate him over the issue of regional defense. Pursuing these two goals successfully, therefore, necessitated limiting the pact to the Northern Tier countries and preventing Arab states other than Iraq from joining it. In retrospect, these two aims seem irreconcilable, but at that time the State Department thought otherwise.[31]

Egypt, for its part, exerted considerable efforts to frustrate the Iraqi-Turkish move. On January 22, Nasser convened a conference of Arab prime ministers aiming to elicit a resolution forbidding Iraq to sign a military pact outside the framework of the Arab League. After debilitating discussions, the conferees were unable to reach an acceptable formula.[32] Perceiving this outcome a triumph, Nuri continued his negotiations with the Turks. Both the United States and Great Britain closely followed the contacts and, in certain cases, even Dulles and Eden were personally involved. While the Foreign Office's main concern was the appearance of the "umbrella" clause, enabling Great Britain to join the pact at a later stage, the State Department's main concern was the formulation of a document that would not antagonize either Egypt or Israel. The US involvement during the consultations assumed particular importance whenever Nuri showed signs of crumbling under Turkish pressure.[33]

When the nucleus of the future Middle East regional defense organization—the Turco-Iraqi pact—was finally concluded on February 24, both Dulles and Eden were attending the first annual meeting of SEATO in Bangkok. Publicly, they expressed satisfaction, but in private they were concerned that Nasser's anti-pact policy would jeopardize it. Having met Nasser on his way to Bangkok, Eden was convinced that his objection stemmed from jealousy and a frustrated desire to lead the Arab world. Concurring with Eden's assessment, Dulles expressed willingness to support Nasser's claim for Arab leadership once the Arab-Israeli problem was settled.[34] For Dulles, therefore, there existed an inevitable linkage between the future success of the pact and the progress of Alpha. Undoubtedly, Dulles viewed US formal abstention from the pact as an advantage. Moreover, because the United

States had special ties with Turkey (through NATO) and Pakistan and Iraq (through military agreements), as well as ongoing secret military talks with the British, Dulles did not feel any urgent need to formally commit the United States to this new project.

THE US POSITION: TO JOIN OR NOT TO JOIN? STAGE I

Following the conclusion of the pact, US policy toward Middle East regional defense straddled a thin line: Although it refused to join the pact, it was encouraging—but not pressing—Pakistan and Iran to join. On the other hand, the United States maintained a posture of neither encouraging nor discouraging the adherence of other Arab states, fearing that such a move would jeopardize Nasser's cooperation with Washington on Alpha. This was a continuation of US policy as outlined in NSC-5428 of July 1954 with one difference: relying on the Turco-Iraqi pact rather than the Turco-Pakistani pact as a major instrument of policy. This change stemmed from the corrected assessment that the provisions of the former provided a better foundation for regional defense than the latter.[35] Unaware of all these complex US interests, its allies considered this policy to be ambiguous.

In early April, when Great Britain was about to join the pact, Dulles was considering a conciliatory approach to Nasser. It aimed at enhancing his prestige and confidence, following his loss of face over the pact and his humiliating defeat to Israel in Gaza on February 28, 1955.[36] Dulles was prepared to grant Egypt political, economic, or military support if it contributed to the consolidation of the Northern Tier or to the progress of Alpha. Dulles thought that the United States would commit itself not to seek new Arab members whereas Egypt would participate in the defense of the Middle East—possibly through the Turco-Pakistani pact, which was less binding than the Turco-Iraqi pact. It is unclear why Dulles thought Nasser would suddenly be willing to participate in any Western-led organization. Perhaps, as indicated above, he did not attach enough importance to the Nasser-Nuri (or the Egyptian-Iraqi) rivalry, hoping that some mechanism appeasing them both would eventually be found. The idea withered away quickly, and the American ambassador in Cairo assured Nasser that the United States had no intention of joining the pact nor pressing other Arab states to do so.[37]

Internally, frustration at US policy toward regional defense came from the State Department. On April 22, Deputy Under-Secretary of State for Political Affairs Robert Murphy submitted a memorandum to Dulles, in which he criticized US policy with regard to regional defense:

> We are not reaping the full benefit of these developments because we lack a comprehensive political-military strategy for the defense of the Middle East. On the one hand, the "Northern Tier" countries do not know what is required of them; on the other, we are undecided as to our own role and have inadequate criteria against which to measure the effectiveness of our country programs of military aid in terms of regional defense.[38]

Murphy recommended adopting the proposal of the Joint Chiefs of Staff (JCS) for a review of US military-political policy by the National Security Council and to set up a State-Defense working group to formulate policy recommendations. Dulles reacted promptly, and the subject was raised at the NSC meeting on May 5. Although the president was unwilling to revise present policy on the Middle East, it was decided to set up a joint State-Defense committee at the assistant secretary level to study defense problems.[39] These discussions were intended also to prepare for British-US military talks that were scheduled for June–August 1955. A month later, the joint working group submitted clear-cut recommendations:[40]

> It will be politically necessary for the US to adhere, probably within a year at most, to a Middle East defense organization. It will be also militarily necessary, so that we may be in a position to influence defense planning and preparations. The best procedure is to adhere to the existing Turk-Iraqi Pact. The timing of US adherence depends upon political developments, primarily in connection with the Arab-Israeli dispute. It should, in any case, follow that of Pakistan and Iran. If there were prospects of a real relaxation of Arab-Israel tensions, our adherence should be delayed until that had been achieved. . . . If there were no such prospects, we should adhere without too much delay, in order to maintain momentum in the regional defense build-up.

A convincing argument on why the United States should join this pact was raised:

> Politically, it would be most damaging to our position in the area and our hopes for regional defense if we declined to associate ourselves with these arrangements. At the least, it would dampen the enthusiasm of the countries concerned for a further development of their own defensive arrangements and would greatly reduce the influence we could bring to bear on the direction those arrangements might take. At the worst, it could be interpreted as a reversal of policy and decision that the Middle East could not or would not be defended, thus precipitating a move by the area toward a neutral or pro-Soviet position. In view of our strong advocacy of the principle of collective security in Europe, the Far East and Latin America, it is hard to see how we could justify a refusal to join a collective security organization in the Middle East, the only area directly exposed to communist aggression where we do not now participate in an organization of that kind.

The working group also presented the question of military expenditure ingeniously. It was assessed that $4 billion was the probable cost over a five-year period, which meant that the gross annual amount for all forms of US aid would be $800 million. But since $500 million would be required even if no regional defense plan were undertaken, the net cost of the plan would be only about $300 million annually.

These recommendations were somewhat mollified by a JCS report. But the JCS, too, thought that "the US should decide now, in principle, to adhere to the Northern Tier pact after such a pact is consummated [that is, the accession of Pakistan and Iran]." The timing of US adherence, the JCS concluded, "should not be too dependent upon developments in the Arab-Israeli controversy."[41] The notion that it would be necessary for the United States to adhere, within a year, to a regional organization was also supported by the CIA.[42] These positions gave Dulles the "green light" to defer the decision at least until the "consummation" of the pact. When the British inquired whether the United States would become a full-fledged member or at least associated with military planning, Dulles explained that until the relaxation of the Arab-Israeli conflict, the United States would not accede.[43] A State Department paper confirmed that "the position of close collaboration but non-adherence can in all probability be sustained for 6 to 12 months."[44] Still, to substantiate US commitment, Dulles was willing to establish an informal liaison with the pact organization once it was formed.[45]

The final composition of the pact was sealed with the adherence of Pakistan in September and Iran in the following month. With this, it became a five-member pact, known as the Baghdad Pact, as the organization headquarters were located at the Iraqi capital. With the formation of the BP, the United States established a liaison aimed at coordinating plans and channeling aid. The US ambassador in Baghdad was assigned as a permanent political liaison and the army attaché as a military liaison. The two participated as observers at the opening session of the BP Council, held in Baghdad, on November 21.[46] In this way, the United States thought it was enjoying the benefits of a member without being exposed to the criticism of anti-pact states.

Following the Baghdad meeting, British Foreign Minister Harold Macmillan urged Dulles to reconsider US adherence to the pact. He also attempted to receive US blessing for Arab adherence, but Dulles remained opposed: "An immediate move to expand the BP," he said, "would deny us Nasser's cooperation. If we failed with Egypt, we should then secure the immediate adherence of both Jordan and Lebanon." Once again Dulles rejected US adherence because such a move "would probably have to be coupled with a security guarantee to Israel."[47] In contrast to Dulles' advice, however, Britain and Iraq exerted pressure on Jordan to join the BP in December 1955. This move unleashed a vehement Egyptian-Saudi response that almost toppled King Hussein.[48] Both Eisenhower and Dulles saw the episode as a confirmation that no Arab state having common borders with Israel should join the BP.[49]

The dissatisfaction from what was considered ambiguous US policy toward the BP came from different angles. The first kind of criticism came from members of the pact, pressing for US adherence or for another US commitment. This pressure would intensify whenever a crisis engulfed the region. A typical approach was a letter from Eden to Eisenhower, on March 4, 1956, in which he urged the United States to take "urgent and effective measures to shore up the BP and Iraq in particular." In his opinion, US accession would impress Nasser "more than our attempts

to cajole him have yet done." Evoking historical analogies, Eden concluded: "a policy of appeasement will bring us nothing in Egypt. Our best chance is to show it
pays to be our friends."[50] Eden's immediate reason for sending this alarming letter
was the dismissal of Glubb Pasha, commander of the Arab Legion in Jordan. The
urgency was also dictated by British desire to augment the BP before the pact's annual meeting in Tehran. Apparently, the British and Pakistani pressure on Dulles
was heavy because it was the first—and only—time he tentatively entertained the
notion of joining the BP.[51]

The second kind of criticism came from the US embassy in Baghdad. Ac-
quainted with Iraq's domestic difficulties, Ambassador Gallman thought US refusal
to join the BP jeopardized the cooperation of regional states and consequently the
general security of the Middle East. In a typical letter to Dulles sent in early January
1956, Gallman wrote that because the United States did not adhere to the BP, "we
get all the blame from critic-countries for supporting it, and none of the credit
which our friends in the Pact accord only to fellow members."[52] Certain officials
at the State Department occasionally shared this kind of criticism.

The third kind of criticism, and perhaps the most important, came from the Department of Defense and the JCS. On February 10, 1956, Admiral Arthur Radford,
chairman of the JCS, claimed that the United States was pursuing a confusing policy
with regard to regional defense. In order to become more involved in military planning, he recommended joining the pact. Otherwise, he concluded, the BP "will fall
apart."[53] Following the Tehran meeting, where all members once more urged the
United States to adhere, Secretary of Defense Wilson notified Dulles that early adherence, or an indication of intent, would be necessary in order to avoid the disintegration of the pact.[54] In light of Dulles' continued refusal to join the BP, Wilson
asked to place this question on the NSC agenda to determine the desirability of announcing this step during the 1957 BP meeting in Karachi, Pakistan.[55]

Clearly, an interdepartmental controversy emerged concerning the policy the
United States should adopt regarding the BP. The military establishment thought
US adherence would augment the pact, enhance the US position in the Middle
East, and strengthen its security. In contrast, the State Department, and particularly
Dulles, objected for a variety of political reasons. It seems that during April 1956,
following his return from the SEATO conference in Karachi, he made up his mind
against the BP. He particularly resented the British role; they "have taken it over,"
he told Eisenhower, "and run it as their instrument."[56] Dulles also disliked the fact
that the pact had become "a forum for Arab politics and intrigue."[57] Since he assessed that the Senate would not sanction adherence to the pact, the effect of such
a failure on the pact, he reasoned, would be far more serious than non-adherence.
Such a defeat could also adversely affect an incumbent president in an election
year. Finally, he assessed that such a move would elicit pressures to give Israel a security guarantee, resulting in the alienation of the Arab states and perhaps even
pushing them in the Soviet direction.[58] In the ensuing controversy between the
military and political wings, Eisenhower sided with Dulles.

As a sop to pact members, Dulles informed them that the United States would
join the BP Economic Committee, retain an observer status in both the military

and countersubversive committees, and request an increase in military assistance to all members in fiscal year 1957.[59] These measures, of course, did not satisfy the members or the US military establishment. Yet the Suez war gave them another opportunity to raise their case, and this time with more vigor.

THE US POSITION: TO JOIN OR NOT TO JOIN? STAGE II

Great Britain's participation in the war had a devastating effect on the BP. In their despair, the Muslim members decided to temporarily suspend Britain from the pact's activities, thus turning it into an Islamic pact. Because there was a fear that the war's reverberations would lead to the fall of the Hashemite regime, it was no surprise that a meeting of the four Islamic members called for the United States to join the BP, especially considering Washington's opposition to and actions taken toward stopping the British-French-Israeli tripartite invasion of Egypt.[60]

At the same time, the severe repercussions of the war brought the Department of Defense and the JCS to raise again—this time more forcefully—their demand for US adherence to the BP. The military establishment presented four arguments in support of this demand. First, the events created a convenient atmosphere for passing such a resolution in Congress. Second, Israel would be now more inclined to accept this development without the United States having to pay the price of a security guarantee. Third, it was the only effective way to counter Nasser's growing popularity in the Arab world on the one hand and to bolster Iraq's shaky situation on the other. Fourth, it would enable more US involvement in military planning, give more control of pact activities, and lead to the establishment of US bases in member states. A strong sense of urgency accompanied the presentation of these arguments; Admiral Radford estimated that if the United States would not act by December 1, the chances would be lost.[61] In the same vein, Ambassador Gallman sent a lengthy report to Dulles, persuasively arguing that should the United States stay out of the BP, it "will slowly die."[62]

All these arguments, however, did not impress Dulles, who was convinced that the war did not change his arguments against accession. A State Department paper enumerated all the pros and cons of such a step but its conclusions were clear: "The disadvantages of US adherence to the Pact are of such a nature that it is concluded that our joining now would not serve the US national interest." The paper listed twelve arguments against and only five in favor of adherence to the BP. Some of the arguments could not be easily dismissed: the possibility that the Soviets would exploit the opportunity and react; the doubt about the effectiveness of the BP in preventing Soviet penetration; the greater involvement in Arab conflicts; and the idea of being associated with Great Britain in local public opinion.[63] It seems, however, that the main goal of the paper was to convince the president not to succumb to the military pressure.

The contrasting views of the military establishment and the State Department were presented to the president on November 21, 1956. Eisenhower was most impressed by the argument that if the British got the United States into the pact—as the matter would certainly appear to the Arabs—Washington would lose its influence with the latter. He also entertained the idea of "building" the leadership of the Saudi monarch as a substitute to Nasser and, with Saudi support, declaring US support of the pact.[64] Eventually, this interdepartmental "battle" resulted in a tepid statement, issued on November 29, to the effect that the United States reaffirms its support for the BP and for the "collective efforts of these nations to maintain their independence."[65] Although important, this declaration was a far cry from the wishes of the BP members.

The inconclusive nature of the discussions with the president led the military establishment to initiate another round in the struggle over the BP. In late November, the JCS prepared a paper listing all the reasons compelling the United States to join the BP.[66] Secretary Wilson incorporated these ideas in a letter to the president on December 4. In this unusual communication, which exposed some of the passions behind its formulation, Wilson indicated that because "we feel so strongly about the need to join the BP," he allowed himself to attach some supporting data. In contrast to Dulles' twelve-point letter, Wilson listed ten advantages gained by adhering to the BP, first and foremost allowing the United States "to fill the political and military vacuum created by the decline of British position." Failure to take this step, the letter concluded, would result in general lack of confidence in US resolve, greater Soviet penetration, and the collapse of the pact.[67] Clearly, in his determination to persuade the president to join the BP, Wilson highlighted not only military but purely political interests as well.

In early December 1956, it became evident that a new—or at least clear—policy for the United States in the Middle East was needed in order to pacify US allies and to resolve the simmering interdepartmental controversy. The important decisions in this respect were taken following several phone consultations between Eisenhower and Dulles. On December 6, Dulles told the president that the Defense Department and the JCS were anxious to join the BP but that he had "considerable reservations" about such a move, which should be a political decision.[68] In their second talk, Dulles listed three possible alternatives open for the United States: adhering to the BP; organizing a new Middle East grouping; or devising a congressional resolution authorizing the president to use the armed forces and to spend certain sums to bolster military cooperation with US allies. Dulles favored the last option, which would give the United States "maneuverability in the area, which would not exist through the BP or a new Pact."[69] As Eisenhower immediately concurred, it was clear that the die had been cast. On the same day, Dulles discussed the idea with William Knowland, an influential senator and an enthusiastic supporter of the administration. In the following days, the details of what would become known as "the Eisenhower Doctrine" were worked out. Interestingly, Dulles' idea was not novel; Congress had already authorized a similar plea—the Formosa Resolution—during the 1955 crisis over the islands of Quemoy and Matsu.

To ensure the safe inauguration of the resolution, Dulles prepared the ground with the British.[70] His most important task, however, was to convince the military establishment that the resolution indeed offered a better framework for US policy than the BP. On December 20, both the secretary of defense and the JCS chairman expressed satisfaction with the new plan. Admiral Radford stated somewhat apologetically that the JCS supported adherence to the BP "simply to take some major action quickly."[71] After overcoming this major hurdle, the president met a bipartisan congressional leadership on January 1, 1957, which paved the way for the approval of the Eisenhower Doctrine by Congress a few days later.[72]

The Eisenhower Doctrine sealed the fate of the BP. If there had been a chance that the United States would join it, the doctrine made this step superfluous. In late January, Dulles briefed all diplomatic missions to the effect that US adherence was unlikely because joining a pact in which Britain was a member might prove "embarrassing." Moreover, the BP had become a liability because nonmembers perceived it as a Western organization, thus rendering the US concept of an indigenous organization meaningless. As a result, Dulles concluded, the United States would strengthen its allies through bilateral channels and through the Eisenhower Doctrine.[73] The BP Islamic members soon realized that despite the advantages that might accrue from the Eisenhower Doctrine, it adversely affected the fate of their pact. Consequently, they kept pressing the United States, claiming that "we are four zeros and those only add up to zero."[74]

Once more, the United States adopted an ambiguous position: Eisenhower's envoy to the area, James Richards, was instructed to tell member states that the doctrine "in no way supplant[s] the BP."[75] In fact, until the very last moment, Washington kept insisting that "there has been no final decision taken not to join the BP."[76] In addition, on March 22 the United States decided to join the BP Military Committee during the Karachi Council meeting in June. Thus, an anomalous situation emerged: The United States was a full member in several important committees of the BP, yet it was not a member of the pact itself. Another sign of US commitment to the pact was shown when Dulles, for the first time, attended the Ankara annual council meeting in January 1958. But when the members asked the United States to head the command of the BP military forces, the JCS politely declined.[77] All these mixed signals created the impression that Washington did not consider the BP as a major instrument of policy.

On July 14, 1958, a group of army officers headed by Colonel 'Abd al-Karim Qasim overthrew the Hashemite regime in Iraq, leading to its suspension from the BP. Great Britain and the United States discussed the possibility of changing its name, reorganizing it, or even setting up an alternative organization, yet Britain resisted any change because so long as Iraq remained a member, the "umbrella" clause concerning the use of Iraqi installations in wartime was legally binding.[78] This situation had changed, however, when Qasim announced Iraq's formal withdrawal from the BP on March 24, 1959. The remaining members renamed the pact "Central Treaty Organization" (CENTO), with Ankara replacing Baghdad as its headquarters. Iran's withdrawal in February 1979, following the Ayatollah Khomeini's revolution, signaled CENTO's death knell.

CONCLUSION

US policy toward the BP demonstrated the perils of ambiguity. In terms of success, it was not one of America's finest hours. Ambiguity could well serve US policy,

which attempted to satisfy its allies while simultaneously not alienating other potential partners. It ended up, however, disappointing all. In theory, some of Dulles'
moves were logical, even ingenious, particularly the Northern Tier concept, which
skirted the Anglo-Egyptian impasse over Suez, and the Eisenhower Doctrine, which
thwarted the military intention of joining the BP following the Suez debacle. In
reality, however, the results amounted to a blunder: First, this policy alienated US
allies, as well as potential allies. The main lesson to be drawn from the Baghdad
Pact episode from a US point of view is that an ambiguous policy does not necessarily pay off; perhaps it is better to satisfy a limited group of allies than to forge a
broad, yet inconclusive, front. Eventually, when the United States came up with a
more definite policy—the Eisenhower Doctrine—it was viewed with disdain in
the Arab world: Indeed, what goodwill the administration received following its
positive stance in the Suez war was lost with the enunciation of the doctrine. Second, the Baghdad Pact episode accelerated the penetration of the Soviet Union,
which leapfrogged into the heart of the Arab Middle East with the September 1955
arms deal with Egypt, exactly the opposite of what the BP was intended to accomplish. Even though recent studies show that the entrance of the USSR to the region,
particularly in Egypt, preceded the pact, undoubtedly the formation of an anti-
Soviet pact in the Middle East deepened Soviet involvement.[79]

The British did not "hijack" the Northern Tier concept from Dulles. Although
he somewhat resented their "bossy" attitude regarding the BP, it seems clear that
this perceived behavior of the British cannot solely explain US refusal to join the
pact. Moreover, because he believed that US accession would antagonize both
Egypt and Israel, Dulles preferred adopting an ambiguous position. Such a policy
was meant to allow the United States to enjoy the fruits of association without
being subjected to the constraints of a formal member.

The greatest mistake of the United States was its failure to comprehend Arab
psychology in the postcolonial era and the depth of Arab rivalries. The belief that
Nasser could be enticed to join a Western-led pact if only the price was right or
that it would be possible to "build" King Sa'ud as an alternative Arab leader to
Nasser attested to the shortsightedness of US thinking. Unwittingly, the Eisenhower administration was caught up in a dual Arab struggle: that between Egypt
and Iraq for Arab hegemony, and that between Nasser and the Iraqi Hashemites
(represented by Nuri al-Sa'id) for Arab leadership. The United States should have
reasoned that between these two contenders there was no middle path. Since decolonization in the Third World constituted one of the hallmarks of the 1950s,
Nasser-type leaders could promise a better reward for the United States than the
Nuri-type, which was largely detested as a result of its long collaboration with the
West. Although a policy oriented solely toward Nasser would have not necessarily
paid off (as was the case during the Kennedy administration), it could still offer
more dividends for the United States than an ambiguous policy alienating all.

Dulles, however, was more successful in his struggle with the military establishment as the political interests eventually prevailed over the military-strategic considerations. It was a classic example of the interplay between domestic and foreign

policies, in which the former did *not* affect the latter because of Dulles' central position in the foreign decision making.

Finally, what does the Baghdad Pact tell us about the US decision-making process? Was Dulles a "foreign policy czar," as some scholars have claimed?[80] A close scrutiny of US conduct in this episode substantiates Richard Immerman's thesis that in spite of Dulles' impressive hold over foreign affairs, Eisenhower also played an important role in the decision-making process.[81] Indeed, Dulles enjoyed a large amount of respect and confidence from Eisenhower. For example, in the controversy between the State and Defense Departments, he supported Dulles even though his personal background made him prone to accept the military view. True, Dulles "invented" the Northern Tier concept and the Eisenhower Doctrine, but the president was intimate with the details and active in the decision-making process. Thus, it seems that Chester Pach and Elmo Richardson rightly concluded that the two "forged an extraordinary partnership in the making of foreign affairs."[82] Moreover, the BP episode demonstrates that the analogy of Dulles as an international lawyer who advises and counsels his client-president is not far-fetched. Steven Spiegel claimed that Dulles "always understood that he was the president's lawyer in foreign affairs and that he must maintain his client's confidence in order to retain his portfolio."[83] After all, whereas the lawyer has to show ingenuity, it is left to the client to make the final decision after carefully evaluating the alternatives presented by the lawyer. The fact that the lawyer lost the BP case does not exempt the client from responsibility—at least in this case. Hence, one must conclude that it is the lawyer-client pattern of behavior that typified the Eisenhower-Dulles relations in this episode.

Notes

1. A recent dictionary by David Shavit, *The United States in the Middle East: A Historical Dictionary* (Westport, Conn.: Greenwood, 1996), did not mention the Baghdad Pact at all. Many books dealing with the Eisenhower administration, cited below, hardly discussed this episode. Only one single Ph.D. dissertation has been written on the subject, but it is not based on archival material: Donald James Decker, "The U.S. Policy Regarding the Baghdad Pact" (The American University, Washington, DC, 1975).

2. Ayesha Jalal, "Towards the Baghdad Pact: South Asia and Middle East Defence in the Cold War, 1945–1957," *International History Review* 11 (1989), pp. 409–433.

3. Nigel Ashton, "The Hijacking of a Pact: The Baghdad Pact and Anglo-American Tensions in the Middle East, 1955–1958," *Review of International Studies* 19 (1993), pp. 123–137.

4. Brian Ried, "The 'Northern Tier' and the Baghdad Pact," in John W. Young (ed.), *The Foreign Policy of Churchill's Peacetime Administration, 1951–1955* (Worchester: Leicester University Press, 1988), pp. 159–181; Richard L. Jasse, "The Baghdad Pact: Cold War or Colonialism?" *Middle Eastern Studies* 27 (1991), pp. 140–156. For an older version of this attitude, see Elie Kedourie, "Britain, France and the Last Phase of the Eastern Question," in J. C. Hurewitz (ed.), *Soviet-American Rivalry in the Middle East* (New York: Praeger, 1969), pp. 189–197.

5. For an analysis of Iraq's role in the formation of the Baghdad Pact, see Elie Podeh, *The Quest for Hegemony in the Arab World: The Struggle over the Baghdad Pact* (Leiden: E. J. Brill, 1995). For an emphasis on the Turkish role, see Ismail Sosyal, "The 1955 Baghdad Pact," *Studies on Turkish-Arab Relations* 5 (1991), pp. 43–116; Ara Sanjian, "The Formulation of the Baghdad Pact," *Middle Eastern Studies* 33 (1997), pp. 226–266.

6. For a study that referred to domestic interdepartmental controversies, although still within the framework of U.S.-British relations, see Magnus Persson, *Great Britain, the United States, and the Security of the Middle East: The Formation of the Baghdad Pact* (Lund: Lund University Press, 1998).

7. Elie Podeh, "The Cold War in the Middle East: The Western Quest for a Regional Defense Organization, 1945–1953," *Orient* 33 (1992), pp. 265–268. On early western Middle Eastern plans, see Persson, *Great Britain*, pp. 66–80.

8. On the consultations leading to the formulation of the MEC, see *Foreign Relations of the United States, 1951* (Washington: 1977), Vol. V, pp. 144–267. For the Egyptian response, see ibid., pp. 209–210. See also Peter L. Hahn, *The United States, Great Britain, and Egypt, 1945–1956: Strategy and Diplomacy in the Early Cold War* (Chapel Hill: University of North Carolina Press, 1991), pp. 109–116: Persson, *Great Britain*, pp. 80–85.

9. On MEDO, see FRUS, 1952–1954, Vol. IX (Washington: 1986), pp. 178–183, 188–191, 198–199, 213–218, 226–234, 249–252, 271–274, 301–305; Hahn, "National Security Concerns," p. 95; Podeh, "The Cold War in the Middle East," pp. 273–274; Hahn, *The United States*, pp. 144–145, 149–154, 156–159, 162; Persson, *Great Britain*, pp. 90–98, 114–116, 119–124.

10. Geoffrey Aronson, *From Sideline to Center Stage: U.S. Policy Towards Egypt, 1946–1956* (Boulder: Westview, 1986), p. 51; Podeh, "The Cold War in the Middle East," p. 274.

11. Nadav Safran, *From War to War: The Arab-Israeli Confrontation, 1948–1967* (New York: Pegasus, 1969), p. 104.

12. For more on the New Look, see Townsend Hoopes, *The Devil and John Foster Dulles* (Boston: Little, Brown, 1973), pp. 191–201; Richard A. Melanson, "The Foundations of Eisenhower's Foreign Policy: Continuity, Community, and Consensus," in R. A. Melanson and D. Mayers, *Reevaluating Eisenhower: American Foreign Policy in the 1950s* (Urbana: University of Illinois Press, 1987), pp. 54–55; Dwight D. Eisenhower, *Mandate for Change, 1953–1956* (New York: Doubleday, 1963), pp. 446–447, 451–454; Chester J. Pach Jr. and Elmo Richardson, *The Presidency of Dwight D. Eisenhower*, rev. ed. (Lawrence: University Press of Kansas, 1991), pp. 81–82.

13. FRUS, 1952–1954, Vol. IX, pp. 379–386; Podeh, "The Cold War in the Middle East," p. 275; Persson, *Great Britain*, pp. 113–158.

14. Steven Z. Freiberger, *Dawn over Suez: The Rise of American Power in the Middle East, 1953–1957* (Chicago: Ivan R. Dee, 1992), pp. 53–54.

15. Aronson, *From Sideline to Center Stage*, p. 80.

16. Meyer, *Egypt and the United States*, pp. 89–90; Aronson, *From Sideshow to Center Stage*, pp. 84–87; Podeh, *The Quest for Hegemony*, pp. 64–76.

17. FRUS, 1952–1954, Vol. IX, pp. 525–531.

18. On SEATO, see Pach and Richardson, *The Presidency of Eisenhower*, pp. 95–96; Hoopes, *The Devil and John Foster Dulles*, pp. 202–261.

19. For further details, see Podeh, *The Quest for Hegemony*, pp. 91–92.

20. FRUS, 1952–1954, Vol. IX, pp. 554–555. On Nuri's discussions in Turkey, see Podeh, *The Quest for Hegemony,* pp. 93–95.

21. FRUS, 1952–1954, Vol. IX, pp. 2402–2404.

22. FO-371, Shuckburgh's Minute, 11 January 1955, V1073/26, 115484; USNA, RG-59, London to Secretary of State, Dispatch 1945, 10 January 1955, 780.5/1–1055. On 10 January 1955, Dulles again expressed concern over the British coolness toward the Northern Tier concept. See USNA, RG-59, Dulles to London, Tel. 3574, 780.5/1– 755. Evelyn Shuckburgh, Under-Secretary in the Foreign Office in charge of Middle East policy, admitted that "there does appear to be a difference of emphasis between US and UK." See RG-59, Butterworth to Secretary of State, Tel. 3053, 11 January 1955, 780.5/1–1155.

23. FO 371, Hooper to FO, Tel. 31, 13 January 1955, V1073/12, 115484; USNA, RG-59, Baghdad to Department of State, Dispatch 319, 13 January 1955, 682.87/1– 1355.

24. USNA, RG-59, Dulles to Baghdad, Tel. 406, 14 January 1955, 682.87/1–1455. A similar note was sent to Ankara. After hurried consultations with the State Department, the British Foreign Office also gave its blessing to the statement; see FO 371, FO to Baghdad, Tel. 45, 14 January 1955, V1073/33, 115484.

25. Podeh, *The Quest for Hegemony,* p. 103. See also Dulles's congratulatory messages to both Nuri and Menderes, USNA, RG-59, Tel. 406, 14 January 1955, 682.87/1– 1455. For more on US reaction, see Persson, *Great Britain,* pp. 202–203.

26. See, for example, USNA, RG-59, Dulles to Ankara, Tel. 853, 28 January 1955, 780.5/1–2255.

27. On the development of US-Egyptian relations during that period, there is ample material. See, for example, Hahn, *The United States;* Muhammad Abd el-Wahab Sayed-Ahmed, *Nasser and American Foreign Policy 1952–1956* (London: LAAM, 1989); Meyer, *Egypt and the U.S.;* Aronson, *From Sideline to Center Stage;* Matthew F. Holland, *America and Egypt: From Roosevelt to Eisenhower* (Westport, Conn.: Praeger, 1996).

28. Hoopes, *The Devil and John Foster Dulles,* p. 274. On the whole crisis, see pp. 264–283; Pach and Richardson, *The Presidency of Eisenhower,* pp. 98–102.

29. USNA, RG-59, Memo from Burdett to Hart, 3 February 1955, 682.87/2–355; FRUS, 1955–1957, Vol. XII (Washington: 1991), p. 14.

30. On the Alpha plan, see Shimon Shamir, "The Collapse of Project Alpha," in Roger R. Louis and Roger Owen (eds.), *The Suez 1956: The Crisis and Its Consequences* (Oxford: Oxford University Press, 1989), pp. 81–100.

31. See, in particular, USNA, RG-59, memo from Burdett to Hart, 3 February 1955, 682.87/2–355. On the Alpha project and the Baghdad Pact, see Persson, *Great Britain,* pp. 186–224.

32. On the Cairo conference, see Podeh, *The Quest for Hegemony,* pp. 107–112.

33. For the last round of negotiations in February, see ibid., pp. 118–125.

34. For a report on Dulles-Eden meeting, see USNA, RG-59, Dulles to Washington, DULTE 4, 24 February 1955, 684A.86/2–2455; FRUS, 1955–1957, Vol. XIV (Washington: 1989), pp. 71–72. On Eden's meeting with Nasser, see FO-371, Stevenson to FO, Tel. 269, 21 February 1955, V1073/289, 115492; Enclosure to Dispatch 31, 21 February 1955, V1073/323, 115493.

35. See George Allen's memo, 1 April, in FRUS, 1955–1957, Vol. XII, p. 49. Generally on US policy, see the memo by Allen approved by Hoover, USNA, RG-59, 11 March 1955, 780.5/3–1155. On the attitude toward Pakistan, see Hoover to Karachi,

Tel. 1368, 18 March 1955, 780.5/3–755. On the attitude toward Iran, see Dulles to Ankara, Tel. 1206, 25 March 1955, 780.5/3–2155. On the attitude toward Arab states, see Dulles to Damascus, Tel. 515, 26 March 1955, 682.87/3–2455. The US policy toward the Arab states was cabled to London, see Tel. 5107, 6 April, 780.5/4–455.

36. Israel launched the attack—the biggest since the 1948 war—as a response to Egyptian *fidayeen* infiltration. The attack, which resulted in heavy Egyptian losses, had far-reaching consequences for Egyptian-Israeli relations (and by implication Egyptian-Western relations).

37. USNA, RG-59, Dulles to Damascus, Tel. 515, 26 March 1955, 682.87/3–2455; FRUS, 1955–1957, Vol. XII, pp. 45–47, 50–51.

38. FRUS, 1955–1957, Vol. XII, p. 51.

39. Ibid., p. 55; Persson, *Great Britain*, pp. 246–247.

40. For a short summary, see FRUS, 1955–1957, Vol. XII, pp. 63–70. For the full report, see USNA, attachment from Jernegen to Cyr, Baxter, and Jones, 6 June 1955, 780.5/6–655. It was a top secret report with limited distribution. All the quotations cited below were taken from this report.

41. Memo from the JCS to Secretary of Defense Wilson, 16 June 1955, FRUS, 1955–1957, Vol. XII, pp. 70–74. For a comparison between the report of the working group and the JCS report, see ibid., pp. 98–102. For more on the position of the military, see USNA, Scott's memo, 22 June 1955, 780.5/6–2255.

42. USNA, RG-59, Allen Dulles to Jernegen, undated, 780.5/7–2755.

43. The issue came up during US-British military talks held in June 1955; see memo of conversation, 11 August 1955, 780.5/8–1155.

44. The paper was presented to the president on July 11; see FRUS, 1955–1957, Vol. XII, pp. 129–132. For a summary of the US position as approved by the president, see USNA, RG-59, Dulles' memo entitled "US Views on Middle East Defense," 17 September 1955, 780.5/9–1755.

45. FRUS, 1955–1957, Vol. XII, p. 141.

46. The US mission to the council included also Admiral Cassady, the Commander-in-Chief of US Naval Forces, Eastern Atlantic and Mediterranean. See USNA, RG-59, Memo by Russell to Dulles, 18 October 1955, 780.5/10–1855; Gray to Secretary of State, 30 January 1956, 780.5/1–3056; FRUS, 1955–1957, Vol. XII, p. 198.

47. For the exchange of letters, see ibid., pp. 206–207; USNA, RG-59, Dulles to London, Tel. 3132, 5 December 1955, 780.5/11–2555.

48. The Jordanian episode was highly critical from an Arab point of view because it made it clear that if Jordan, a Hashemite ally of both Great Britain and Iraq, could not join the BP, then the chances that other Arab states would take this step were slim. For details, see Podeh, *The Quest for Hegemony*, chap. 8; Persson, *Great Britain*, pp. 274–280.

49. See the discussion at the NSC, 22 December 1955, FRUS, 1955–1957, Vol. XII, p. 214.

50. Ibid., p. 249. For Eisenhower's reply, see PRO, FO-371, 10 March 1955, V1075/71, 121272. The same argument was posed by Lloyd to Dulles at the Karachi SEATO conference on 6 March, FRUS, 1955–1957, Vol. XII, p. 250.

51. USNA, RG-59, Dulles (from Karachi) to Hoover, DULTE 14, 780.5/3–856. Dulles sent a four-point program for the U.S. adherence. It was written that the tel. was a "speculative exercise" transmitted without any recommendation because there

was no time to seriously discuss it. Concomitantly, Dulles entertained the idea of reaching some truce with Nasser, including a promise not to recruit Arab members to the BP for certain Egyptian undertakings. See Podeh, *The Quest for Hegemony*, p. 198.

52. Ibid., p. 215; Persson, *Great Britain*, p. 246.

53. FRUS, 1955–1957, Vol. XII, p. 248.

54. Letter from Wilson to Dulles, 5 April 1956, ibid., p. 267.

55. Memo from Wilson to the executive secretary of the NSC, 15 May 1956, ibid., p. 298. The issue also came up during a State-JCS meeting on 23 May 1956, see ibid., pp. 299–302.

56. Ibid., p. 270.

57. See Dulles' conversation with the JCS, 9 April 1956, ibid., p. 275.

58. Ibid.; Dulles' letter to Wilson, 23 April 1956, ibid., p. 294.

59. On these measures, see ibid., pp. 269, 282, 285; USNA, RG-59, Hoover to Baghdad, Tel. 908, 4 May 1956, 780.5/5–456.

60. FRUS, 1955–1957, Vol. XII, pp. 319–321.

61. For papers and statements of the military establishment, see ibid., pp. 325, 327–329; USNA, RG-59, Wilson to Dulles, 14 November 1956, 780.5/11–1456.

62. USNA, RG-59, Gallman to Department of State, Dispatch 307, 15 November 1955, 780.5/11–1556.

63. FRUS, 1955–1957, Vol. XII, pp. 331–337. See also Dulles' memo sent to Radford, USNA, RG-59, 17 November 1956, 780.5/11–1756.

64. FRUS, 1955–1957, Vol. XII, p. 341.

65. Ibid., p. 360.

66. Memo by the JCS to Wilson, 30 November 1956, ibid., pp. 361–363.

67. Ibid., pp. 373–376; USNA, RG-59, Wilson to Dulles, 4 December 1956, 780.5/12–456.

68. FRUS, 1955–1957, Vol. XII, p. 390.

69. Ibid., pp. 395–396. In fact, the new grouping was also a new idea. It envisaged incorporating the BP into a new and larger grouping to be called the Middle East Charter, which would also include Saudi Arabia and Lebanon. The idea was soon dropped. See Podeh, *The Quest for Hegemony*, p. 224.

70. FRUS, 1955–1957, Vol. XII, pp. 399–400.

71. Ibid., p. 416.

72. On the meeting, see ibid., pp. 432–437. On the congressional approval and the doctrine, see ibid., pp. 437–439; Spiegel, *The Other Arab-Israeli Conflict* (Chicago: University of Chicago Press, 1985), pp. 83–91.

73. USNA, RG-59, Dulles to all diplomatic missions, 28 January 1957, 780.5/1–2857.

74. See a memo of a conversation between Dulles and Prince 'Abd al-Ilah, the Iraqi Crown Prince, USNA, RG-59, 5 February 1957, 780.5/2–557; 787.11/2–557.

75. FRUS, 1955–1957, Vol. XII, p. 451.

76. See ibid., memo from Rountree to Dulles, 20 June 1957, 780.5/6–2057.

77. USNA, RG-59, the JCS to Murphy, 27 May 1957, 780.5/5–2757. This was a main issue on the agenda of the Karachi council meeting, Henderson to Dulles, Tel. 3331, 6 June 1957, 780.5/6–657; Dulles to Henderson, Tel. 3201, 5 June 1957, 780.5/6–557.

78. PRO, FO-371, FO to Washington, Tel. 236, 13 January 1959, EB10345/54, 132921.

79. That was also the US view at the time. See David Lesch, *Syria and the United States: Eisenhower's Cold War in the Middle East* (Boulder: Westview, 1992), p. 85. It should be noted that the Czech arms deal of September 1955 is often mentioned as a direct consequence of the pact. Recent studies, however, show that the origins of the deal lay in the years before the conclusion of the pact. See Rami Ginat, "Origins of the Czech-Egyptian Arms Deal: A Reappraisal," in David Tal (ed.), *The 1956 War: Collusion and Rivalry in the Middle East* (London: Frank Cass, 2001), pp. 145–168.

80. The term "czar" is taken from Spiegel, *The Other Arab-Israeli Conflict*, p. 59. In connection with the Eisenhower-Dulles controversy, see Pach and Richardson, *The Presidency of Dwight D. Eisenhower*, p. 84.

81. Richard H. Immerman, "Eisenhower and Dulles: Who Made the Decisions?" *Political Psychology* 1 (1979), pp. 21–38.

82. Pach and Richardson, *The Presidency of Dwight D. Eisenhower*, p. 85.

83. Spiegel, *The Other Arab-Israeli Conflict*, p. 59. See also Pach and Richardson, *The Presidency of Dwight D. Eisenhower*.

CHAPTER 7

THE 1957
AMERICAN-SYRIAN CRISIS
Globalist Policy in a Regional Reality

David W. Lesch

The Syrian crisis of 1957 (I will refer to it as the American-Syrian crisis) is one of those occasions where the flaws of applying a globalist analytical methodology to the Middle East—in lieu of a serious appreciation of the regional dynamics in the area—are, in retrospect, dramatically revealed. Indeed, the parameters of the crisis itself were determined as much by regional forces as they were by international actors. It was a telling irony, an indication of the policy misconceptions and misapplications surrounding the approach to the Middle East taken by the administration of President Dwight D. Eisenhower in 1957. What started out as a policy designed to isolate and reduce the power of Egyptian President Gamal 'Abd al-Nasser, that is, the Eisenhower Doctrine, was effectively abandoned during the US-Syrian crisis; thus, a modus vivendi was reached with Egypt, whose help Washington sought during the latter stages of the crisis in order to salvage the situation in Syria. Because of this rather embarrassing experience, the Eisenhower administration began to thoroughly realize that the Middle East was much more complex, not simply an area of East-West ingress.

THE NEW US ALLY IN THE MIDDLE EAST

The American-Syrian crisis officially began on August 12, 1957, when the Syrian government announced the discovery of a US-engineered attempt to overthrow

the regime, which the Eisenhower administration believed was close to becoming
a Soviet "outpost" in the region.[1] The next day the Syrian government expelled
three US diplomats; the United States responded in kind on August 14, declaring
the Syrian ambassador to Washington and his second secretary personas non gratas.

The Eisenhower administration, during the height of the cold war, steadfastly
held this incident out as a sign of unacceptable growth in Soviet influence in Syria
(especially since the leadership in Syria was generally pro-Ba'thist, the new army
chief of staff, 'Afif al-Bizri, was thought to be a Communist, and Syria and the Soviet Union had agreed to sign a wide-ranging economic accord a week earlier), with
possible calamitous repercussions for the US position in the entire Middle East.
With the Suez debacle so fresh in their minds, Eisenhower and his secretary of state,
John Foster Dulles, were careful not to appear to be second-generation imperialists
and therefore preferred an Arab-led response to "correct" the situation in Syria,
either through diplomatic or military pressure. None would be forthcoming.

The administration was confident that it could count on the support of Saudi
Arabia to arrange the Arab response, since King Sa'ud, upon his visit to Washington
earlier in the year, had been officially touted as an ally of the United States in the
Middle East as a counterpoise to Nasser. Winning over Sa'ud had been an unofficial
corollary to the Eisenhower Doctrine (announced in January 1957 and passed in
March), a rather hastily formulated policy intended to fill the perceived vacuum
of power in the Middle East following British and French humiliations at Suez.[2]
One of the objectives of the Eisenhower Doctrine was to subvert the alliance Nasser
had built to isolate Iraq, then the only pro-Western and Arab Baghdad Pact member. To do this, Washington sought to isolate Nasser—then at his zenith of popularity in the Arab world due to his successes in the Suez crisis—and to halt any
further increase in Soviet influence in the Middle East. Thus, Washington had to
find an Arab leader who could rival Nasser in prestige and convince other Arab
states to turn pro-Western, if not join the Baghdad Pact outright. Because of Saudi
Arabia's growing oil wealth and its central position in the Islamic world, Eisenhower
and Dulles chose Sa'ud, despite his putative limitations, to rival Nasser and they
systematically set about augmenting his stature in the region.

Sa'ud, however, had his own set of objectives that he wanted to achieve through
this anointment.[3] The Saudi monarch (or those within the Saudi ruling circles who
were guiding him) saw US support as his stepladder to a leadership position in the
Arab world. But by choosing this route, he (or they) also invited an inherent contradiction, one that left the king vulnerable and ultimately led to his failure: In
order to challenge and possibly assume Nasser's mantle, Sa'ud had to distance himself from Washington's policies. However, this was a given, for Nasser had long set
the standard for Arab nationalist leadership, and any pretender to this position had
to sufficiently detach himself from the West. Thus, there ensued a schizophrenic
Saudi foreign policy, supporting Washington's interests vis-à-vis a four-power conference meeting (between Saudi Arabia, Egypt, Syria, and Iraq) in Cairo in February 1957 and the Jordanian crisis in April 1957 (among other things), yet opposing
the Eisenhower administration's policies related to the right of Israeli shipping

through the Gulf of Aqaba (Sa'ud was against it, Washington for it) and the Buraimi Oasis dispute (which actually caught the United States between two allies since the dispute pitted Great Britain against Saudi Arabia).

King Sa'ud became the Arab spokesman for the Israeli shipping question following Nasser's convenient abdication of that role in the wake of the Suez crisis and the establishment of United Nations (UN) emergency forces in the Sinai Peninsula. That was a brilliant move by Nasser because he took advantage of Sa'ud's strong desire to build up his own Arab nationalist credentials and simultaneously hid his own inability to prevent Israeli ships from passing through the gulf by shifting the blame onto Sa'ud, thereby promoting a rift in US-Saudi relations in the process.

There were those, however, who had serious doubts about Sa'ud's usefulness to the United States in the inter-Arab arena. In Cairo, following the four-power conference, a US diplomat remarked, "If after this meeting [the] United States doesn't fulfill what Saud thinks are its promises, the King could react very dangerously. He has staked his reputation and honor on [the] United States and could switch completely if he feels betrayed."[4] The king, as stated earlier, had his own reasons for cooperating with Washington: He wanted US pressure on Israel to withdraw from the Sinai Peninsula (portions of which it occupied during the Suez crisis), as well as solutions to the Suez Canal sovereignty question, the shipping dispute, and the Palestinian refugee problem. Success on any one of these issues would have significantly heightened Sa'ud's standing in the Arab world. Although the United States managed to arrange an Israeli withdrawal from the Sinai (and only after Eisenhower personally intervened with a nationally televised speech designed to pressure Israel), it came through on little else.

Events at the conference also demonstrated that Sa'ud remained ultimately subordinate to Nasser or, more to the point, to Nasser's popular slogans of Arab nationalism and his ability to cause problems for the king within Saudi Arabia. The communiqué emerging from the four-power meeting, despite Sa'ud's attempts to revise it, said nothing about the threat of communism in the Middle East but instead reflected Nasser's stand on foreign policy and inter-Arab issues. This fact was not lost upon US embassy officials in Jeddah, who began to see the chinks in the armor of the US-Saudi partnership and warned the US Department of State in April 1957 that "it was clear [that the] Palestine question, Aqaba, Buraimi and in general, old issues of Zionism and imperialism loom large in Saudi thinking and could easily affect our relations quite seriously."[5] The British, for their part, had been very skeptical of the US plan to build up Sa'ud as a rival to Nasser. As one British official noted, "The Americans may have been deceived both about the area of real agreement between Saudi and American policy and the degree of influence which Saud exercises over his Arab colleagues. Saud must know that Egypt is able to make serious trouble for him in his own country."[6] In retrospect, this observation seems to have been correct on all counts. As a result, by the time the American-Syrian crisis developed, Saudi Arabia and the United States were essentially on different wavelengths regarding Middle East policy.

Saudi Arabia as well as other presumed pro-West Arab states, particularly Iraq, were unwilling to take the leadership role in response to the situation in Syria in August–September 1957. This compelled the Eisenhower administration to adopt an alternative and, as it turned out, much more dangerous path toward "correcting" the situation in Syria.

WASHINGTON'S RESPONSE TO THE CRISIS

Both Eisenhower and Dulles felt that the course of events in Syria in August 1957 was "unacceptable." Both believed the United States "could not afford to have exist a Soviet satellite not contiguous to the Soviet border and in the midst of the already delicate Middle East situation."[7] And both were also anxious to take advantage of the initial trepidation expressed by Syria's neighbors, which would subside, it was thought, if the United States did nothing. The administration also knew their friends in the Middle East were looking to it to lead the way, but Eisenhower and Dulles were looking in the opposite direction for a regional response to the crisis, hamstrung as they were by the specter of Suez and Soviet actions in Hungary.

It is clear that the United States was seriously contemplating direct military action against Syria. In a telephone conversation with Chief of Staff General Nathan Twining on August 21, Dulles stated that "we are thinking of the possibility of fairly drastic action."[8] Also on August 21, Dulles wrote to British Foreign Minister Selwyn Lloyd that "it seems to us that there is now little hope of correction from within and that we must think in terms of the external assets reflected by the deep concern of the Moslem states. . . . We must perhaps be prepared to take some serious risks to avoid even greater risks and dangers later on."[9] British Prime Minister Harold Macmillan commented on August 27 that "this question is going to be of tremendous importance. The Americans are taking it very seriously, and talking about the most drastic measures—Suez in reverse. If it were not serious . . . it would be rather comic."[10]

The desire for a regional response supported by Saudi Arabia, however, was most clearly demonstrated in a letter from Eisenhower to Sa'ud dated August 21, 1957: "We believe that it is highly preferable that Syria's neighbors should be able to deal with this problem without the necessity for any outside intervention. In view of the special position of Your Majesty as Keeper of the Holy Places of Islam, I trust that you will exert your great influence to the end that the atheistic creed of Communism will not become entrenched at a key position in the Moslem world."[11]

The constraints upon the willingness and ability of Sa'ud to play this role and the misperception by the administration that the king had significant influence in the Middle East eliminated any hope for a regional response. Macmillan wrote Dulles on August 23 that the "essential point is that the other Arabs should expose the pretensions of the present Syrian regime to be good Arab nationalists and should denounce them for what they are, namely, Communists and Communist stooges."[12] The problem was that Syria's neighbors did not agree with Macmillan's assessment. Instead, the White House received two notes from Sa'ud on August

25, one that dealt with the shipping question and the other with Syria. Although their contents are unknown, they were described as being "couched in extremely tough language," suggesting that Sa'ud was placing the blame for the events in Syria squarely on the United States and/or was presenting the administration with a quid pro quo of his own connected with the shipping dispute.[13] In response, the State Department wrote to its embassy in Jeddah: "We find it very disappointing indications you have received of King's attitude toward developments in Syria. . . . In interests [of] Saudi Arabia and in those of all NE [Near East] states we are anxious that [the] King use his political and moral authority to rally opposition in area to present Syrian regime and to facilitate generating of pressures designed to isolate Syria and to work toward an improvement of situation in that country."[14] The US ambassador in Jeddah also emphasized to the king the danger of communism and Soviet influence in the Middle East while trying to play down the relationship with Israel. He was unable to persuade Sa'ud.

POLICY TRANSFORMATION IN WASHINGTON

Eisenhower faced two major problems with military intervention in Syria. First, during the Suez crisis and the Soviet invasion of Hungary, he had supported the principle that "military force was not a justifiable means for settling disputes."[15] But he was also convinced that Syria was on the road to becoming a Soviet satellite, and he was determined not to let this happen; he was not going to be accused of "losing" any country to communism, much as the Republicans had rhetorically bashed the Truman administration for "losing" China. Thus, the president had to find a way to rationalize this dilemma, first to himself, then to the outside world. He did this by viewing the Syrian situation as inherently different from the Suez crisis. The Arabs, he postulated, were "convinced" that Syria had been clandestinely invaded through infiltration and subversion, whereas during Suez they believed Nasser had acted well within his rights in nationalizing the Suez Canal Company. Eisenhower decided that Arab action against Syria "would be *basically* defensive in nature, particularly because they intended to react to *anticipated aggression,* rather than to commit a naked aggression" (emphasis added).[16] The sticky question of how to deal with subversion, one that critics of the Eisenhower Doctrine had asked when it was announced, had again come to the forefront; the administration was forced to answer it. Now, however, instead of the pretext being an open attack of one country against another, the administration was preparing the way for possible military intervention on the grounds of *anticipated aggression.* All the United States needed was an arbitrary finding that Syria was controlled by international communism.

The second problem facing Eisenhower revolved around the fact that no Arab state was willing to assume a leadership role in response to the crisis. This was apparent when the White House sent an experienced and respected diplomat, Loy Henderson, who was then deputy undersecretary for administration, to the Middle East to sound out Washington's allies in the region regarding the Syrian situation.

Unexpectedly, he did not have a solid proposal to put forth to the conferees when he arrived in Istanbul on August 24. In fact, the British ambassador to Turkey described Henderson as having been "inadequately briefed and rather devoid of ideas."[17] The conferees had obviously expected Henderson to arrive with a proposal, but none was forthcoming, and all they could agree upon was that something had to be done soon. Crown Prince 'Abd al-Ilah of Iraq admitted there was no trust between Jordan's King Hussein and himself; the United States had counted on Iraqi-Jordanian cooperation against Syria.[18] The Jordanians insisted that Saudi support was the key to the whole situation; without it Hussein could only leave Turkey to vacation in Italy and Spain, a move that led Eisenhower to conclude that "contrary to what we had been led to believe . . . [Jordan] did not want to join in any move against Syria."[19]

Within the ruling circles in the Arab world, differences of opinion could also be found as to the seriousness of the Syrian situation. They had to be wary of the sentiments of the populace, who were largely sympathetic with the Syrian regime. Henderson was reported to have been "shocked" by the negative reaction of the Lebanese press to his visit to Beirut, a reaction that was typical below the government level in most Arab states at the time. Nowhere was this more evident than in Iraq; the Iraqi government's refusal to lead an all-Arab response against Syria was as important to the disruption of the Eisenhower administration's plans vis-à-vis Syria as Saudi Arabia's decision not to follow the US lead, for if the administration was depending on Saudi political and economic support, it was also depending on Iraq to provide the muscle needed to intimidate or take direct action against Syria.

Henderson's findings left the White House confused. Referring to Henderson's trip to the Middle East, the president would write in his memoirs that "whereas early information had indicated the possibility of prompt Iraqi military action with the Turks abstaining, there were now hints of a reversal of this arrangement."[20] The United States at first wanted Turkey to play a secondary role, conscious of the fact that many Arabs still had a strong distaste for the Turks rooted in the days of Ottoman rule in addition to the fact that action by a North Atlantic Treaty Organization member might enlarge the dispute to the international level with possible Soviet involvement. However, the Turkish government, already bordering the Soviet Union to the north, was very concerned about a possible Soviet satellite coming into being to the south.

With the failure of the Henderson mission, the administration, especially John Foster Dulles, reverted to standard cold war thinking. From this point on, it viewed the US-Syrian crisis as it related to the Soviet Union, with all the trappings befitting the "Munich mentality," something that would have a particularly telling impact on the Turks. In a letter to Harold Macmillan discussing Henderson's findings, Dulles wrote the following:

> There is nothing that looks particularly attractive and the choice of policy will be hard. We are not completely satisfied with any of the alternatives which have thus far been suggested. There are risks involved in and objection

found to all of them. We are continuing to explore other possibilities. . . . I do not suggest that we have reached any conclusion in favor of encouraging positive action. However, Loy Henderson has the impression that the Turks are desperately serious about this situation, and I do not think either of our governments wants to try to impose what could be another Munich.[21]

How Dulles concluded that the Turks should be given the green light to proceed militarily against Syria if they chose to do so, thereby contradicting the rationale of an all-Arab response, is not the question that should be addressed at this time.[22] Suffice it to say that, having failed to acquire the support of Saudi Arabia and Iraq, the administration looked elsewhere to "correct" the situation in Syria. However, this move transformed the crisis, already elevated from the bilateral level to the regional level, then from the regional level to the international level, as the Soviet Union felt compelled to intervene in order to protect its potential client state and enhance its standing in the Third World. The Kremlin directly warned Turkey, and by implication the United States, to stay out of Syria. And, contrary to many previous studies of this incident that conclude the Soviet Union purposefully exaggerated the crisis after the climax had already passed in order to gain propaganda points, Moscow quite probably saved Syria from external intervention. Outside Turkey, the players in the region itself were more than ready to end the crisis, but Dulles insisted on some kind of "victory" over Syria, and thus the Soviet Union, and this raised the level of international tension.

SA'UD TAKES THE INITIATIVE

As the United States and the Soviet Union were indulging in their superpower standoff, diplomacy shifted back to the regional level as Saudi Arabia entered the scene. Sa'ud saw the incident as an opportune moment to assert himself in the inter-Arab arena by mediating a percolating crisis. On the more practical side, he also wanted to salvage his assets in Syria and pull it again toward the Saudi orbit and away from Nasser's influence. Iraq was unable to do this because its government was unredeemably regarded as a lackey of imperialism—in addition to the fact that it had lost most of its "assets" in Syria as a result of the exiles and trial verdicts following the exposure of the failed British-Iraqi plot (Operation Straggle) to overthrow the Syrian regime in late 1956; but Sa'ud had distanced himself from Washington sufficiently to act the part of an Arab nationalist leader, and he was totally at odds with the British.[23] It was important that he also maintained valuable leverage over other Arab states, namely, the knowledge that Saudi Arabia was one of the linchpins to the Arab coalition the Eisenhower administration had hoped to form (i.e., if Syria and Egypt did not support his mediatory efforts he would throw his weight behind the US initiative). As expected, the Syrian regime, which had repeatedly branded Sa'ud an imperialist tool and a US lackey earlier in the year, started praising the Saudi monarch for his farsightedness, compassion, and commitment to Arab causes. The government began to vociferously support Saudi

Arabia's position on the shipping and Buraimi questions and initiated a back-and-forth stream of diplomatic visits between Damascus and Riyadh.

En route to receive "medical treatment" in West Germany, Sa'ud made a twenty-four-hour stopover in Beirut on September 7 to consult with various Lebanese officials and, almost assuredly, with Syrian officials as well (an especially likely event in light of the somewhat coordinated sequence of events that transpired soon thereafter). The Syrians, who earlier in the year would have viewed Sa'ud's mediatory efforts as unwarranted interference in Syrian affairs, now publicly welcomed this visit. Almost overnight, the Lebanese, Jordanian, and Iraqi governments started to back away from their earlier condemnation of Syria and began to make noises in support of the Syrian regime. The Saudi ambassador to Syria stated on September 10 that his country would "spare no effort to support, back, and aid" Syria should it be the object of outside aggression.[24] On September 12, a Saudi official was quoted as saying that "Saudi Arabia will not stand with hands folded in the event of any aggression against Syria."[25] Also on September 12, Sa'ud reportedly sent a note to Eisenhower urging patience and forbearance in dealing with the Syrian situation, and he claimed that reports of the Syrian threat had been exaggerated.[26] As the climax to his diplomatic efforts, Sa'ud appeared at the airport in Damascus on September 25, 1957, to "consult" with Syrian officials. (Iraqi Premier 'Ali Jawdat arrived the following day.) Arab newspapers across the Middle East, including Egyptian ones, hailed Sa'ud's efforts.

NASSER'S RIPOSTE

This course of events was something Nasser was unwilling to accept, for he had worked extremely hard to keep Syria out of the West's sphere of influence (as well as that of Iraq) and to place pro-Nasserist Ba'thist and army elements in the Syrian hierarchy. Now he was in danger of "losing" Syria to Saudi Arabia or even the Soviet Union.[27] As early as September 11, 1957, Nasser was scheming with Syrian officials to counter Sa'ud. Nasser, along with his commander in chief, 'Abd al-Hakim 'Amr, and the chief of staff of the joint Egyptian-Syrian command, Hafiz Isma'il, met in Cairo with the Syrian chief of staff, 'Afif al-Bizri, and Colonel 'Abd al-Hamid Sarraj, who was the head of Syrian intelligence and the real power in Syria. In retrospect it is clear that at this meeting plans were drawn up for a dramatic move to reestablish Nasser's preeminence in the Arab world. He also intended to build up the pro-Nasser army/Ba'thist faction in Syria (through Bizri and Sarraj) in order to check Saudi advances through President Shukri al-Quwatli and Prime Minister Sabri al-'Asali, as well as Soviet influence through Khalid al-'Azm and Communist deputy Khalid Baqdash. Nasser thus began a diplomatic offensive that was at first subtle so as not to appear to be in conflict with Sa'ud's popular mediation efforts. In addition, Nasser was well aware of the Saudi monarch's relationship with the Americans and probably realized that he too would benefit from Sa'ud's mediation, for the Egyptian president did not want to be in a position where he would be forced to come to Syria's aid against fellow Arab states, least of all Turkey or the United States, or play second fiddle to the only country really capable of protecting Syria—the Soviet Union. Nasser would cleverly allow Sa'ud to commit himself to a peaceful resolution before he made his move.

That move was to send troops to the Syrian coastal city of Latakia on October 13, ostensibly to defend Syria against Turkish "aggression" (the Turks, with encouragement from Washington, had been steadily massing forces along the border). This was done while Sa'ud was in Beirut attending a soccer match. The contrast of Sa'ud at a sports event and Nasser sending Egyptian troops to the aid of a sister state threatened by outside forces did not go unnoticed, as was, most certainly, Nasser's intent. Helped by a massive propaganda campaign, Egypt became the Arab state that matched words with deeds and honored its defense commitments. *Al-Ahram* (Egypt's government-controlled newspaper) printed on October 14 that the action showed that the defense agreement between Egypt and Syria (entered November 1955) was not "merely ink on paper . . . it is a reality." The Syrian press hailed the arrival of Egyptian troops, and Damascus Radio simultaneously intensified its charges against Turkey for its "provocations" and "aggressions" on the border. On October 17, Syria placed the army on alert and arms were distributed to civilian groups (the Popular Resistance Organization); it would have seemed even more awkward than it already was to have Syrian troops in a state of unreadiness at the exact moment that Egyptian troops were supposedly helping Syria face the imminent threat from Turkey. Had the threat been real, of course, Nasser would not have sent his troops. The Soviet Union had already explicitly warned Turkey and the United States against any action vis-à-vis Syria, so in a sense Nasser was operating under a Soviet defense umbrella. That it was more of a political than a military move is borne out by the fact that only about 2,000 Egyptian troops landed at Latakia, which was a woefully inadequate number for the supposed task. Nasser had effectively turned the tables on Sa'ud and won a tremendous propaganda victory.

In addition to upstaging Sa'ud and regaining the diplomatic initiative in the Arab world, Nasser had other reasons for sending Egyptian troops to Syria at this particular moment. With Egyptian troops on the ground in Syria, Nasser was in a position to regain his influence in the country, manipulate the political process, and protect his Ba'thist/army assets. It also prevented Bizri's advancement in the Syrian power structure through the vehicle of the joint command (Nasser reportedly did not trust Bizri and shared the US view that he was a Communist).[28] The move was also designed to solidify support for Akram al-Hawrani, who was up for election on October 14, 1957, as speaker of the Chamber of Deputies against incumbent Nazim al-Qudsi, a leading member of the traditionally pro-Iraqi Populist Party. Nasser preferred to see Hawrani win election, and the timing of the Egyptian troop landing was intended to help his chances. In view of the fact that Hawrani won by only a slim margin, Nasser's timely assistance could have been a decisive factor in the outcome. It was important to Nasser to have Hawrani in the position of the speaker of the chamber, for it was, ex officio, the vice presidency of the Syrian Republic, and if the president became ill or was away, the speaker would undertake his functions.[29] With Quwatli in his seventies and often ill (in a real or diplomatic sense), this position assumed added significance. Hawrani, as a leader of the Ba'th Party and the key to its link with the military, had essentially become the number two figure in Syria, and he was therefore in the catbird seat for the next presidential election. In this way, Nasser and his Syrian supporters could continue to keep the "Russian millionaire," Khalid al-'Azm, from his longtime ambition.

As mentioned, Nasser was intent on securing the Ba'th Party's position in Syria. In this fashion, he could enhance the ability of the Ba'thists to withstand and reverse growing Soviet influence in Syria and solidify the country's attachment to Egypt. The fact that the Egyptian troops immediately moved inland toward Aleppo only supports this assertion. Nasser and his Ba'thist allies believed that they could help their cause in elections scheduled to be held soon in Aleppo by staging a dramatic "rescue," with the possibility of changing the view of most Aleppans toward Egypt and thus providing more votes for Ba'thist candidates. It is not surprising that the Egyptians and Ba'thists exaggerated the Turkish threat, giving plenty of air time to the purported Turkish battle cry "On to Aleppo!" Nasser and the Ba'thists, as well as the conservatives, were clearly concerned about Communist advances in Syria (particularly prevalent in northern Syria, including Aleppo) and the concomitant increase in Soviet influence.[30] The Ba'th Party had allied itself with the Communists to combat imperialism and the old guard Syrian politicians; when they succeeded, with proportionately more power accruing to the Communists as Syria's relationship with the Soviet Union tightened during the crisis, the Ba'thists decided to unofficially split from the Communists and utilize Nasser's own willingness to prevent Syria from falling under the influence of the Kremlin. All of this maneuvering proved unnecessary, however, as al-'Asali, bowing to pressure from all sides, indefinitely postponed the elections, thus buying more time for the Ba'thists to figure out a way to prevent their onetime allies from leapfrogging them. The landing of Egyptian troops returned Nasser to prominence in Syria, which made Ba'thist control and union with Egypt more palatable to many and inevitable to all.

The Egyptian troop landing at Latakia took Sa'ud totally by surprise. At a loss, he could only offer to put his armed forces at Syria's disposal, but this was hopelessly outshone by Nasser's initiative, and it was clear to all that the latter was now dictating the pace and direction of the regional diplomatic game. Evidence of this came on October 16, 1957, when King Hussein informed the ambassadors of Turkey, the United States, and Britain that Jordan would fully support Syria in the event of an attack and that Syria's independence should be maintained. Iraq publicly restated its support for Syria; even the Lebanese government reportedly gave Syrian officials assurances that they would offer assistance in case of an attack.[31]

The information disseminated from Cairo also focused at this time on linking Israel and Turkey (with US support) to an alleged plot against Syria, with reports that Israeli chief of staff Moshe Dayan of the Israeli Defense Forces had paid a visit to Turkey to discuss such plans. Not only did Nasser effectively portray Egypt as the savior of Syria and Arabism against Turkey and the "imperialists," but also against Public Enemy No. 1, Israel, which compelled other Arab states to follow his lead. In addition, a Turkish delegation visited Saudi Arabia on October 24 as part of Turkey's support for Sa'ud's mediation; however, it cast the king in a negative light in the Arab world since he was personally negotiating with the country that Egypt had effectively portrayed as an aggressor and imperialist tool. Sa'ud had various constraints upon his diplomatic maneuvering; namely, he did not and could not detach himself completely from the United States, and his efforts therefore seemed to be slow and plodding, especially in comparison to Nasser's actions from October 13 on. The king had to walk a tightrope to maintain a balance between Arab nationalist forces, on the one hand, and the West and pro-West elements in the Arab world on the other. Nasser, however, did not have this constraint, which allowed him to take the bold and decisive step of sending his forces into Syria. Nasser also had the military wherewithal to do so; Sa'ud did not, and the only role the king could play was that of mediator. Sa'ud's fatal mistake was that he could accomplish his objectives only at Nasser's expense. This compelled Nasser to respond to the challenge in a way that Sa'ud could not, and, for all intents and purposes, the "Arab cold war" had already begun.

US-EGYPTIAN MODUS VIVENDI?

The American-Syrian crisis showed on several occasions how similar objectives can sometimes make strange bedfellows. Both Egypt and the United States were very interested in keeping Syria from becoming Communist and from falling too deeply into the Soviet orbit. In fact, a confidant of Nasser informed US officials on December 11, 1957, that the Egyptian president

> had investigated recent information we [United States] had given him relative to the communist connections of [Syrian Chief of Staff Afif al-] Bizri and is now convinced Bizri [is] a communist and that something must be done about it. . . . He [Nasser] asks of us only that we keep hands off Syria for a maximum period of three months and particularly that we do nothing which could have unintentional effect of making heroes out of Bizri, [Communist Deputy] Bakdash and [pro-Soviet] Khalid Al Azm.[32]

The Egyptian official suggested that there were "several ways of attacking the Syrian problem," but the "only country with capability [to] succeed, and which can do so with minimal repercussions is Egypt. Of [the] countries primarily concerned with [the] Syrian situation, US and Egypt have greatest interest in ensuring that country [has] stable, anti-communist government."[33] On December 10, the US ambassador to Egypt, Raymond Hare, had had a conversation with a member of the inner circle of the Revolutionary Command Council (the ruling group within Egypt), 'Ali Sabri, in which the latter stated that Egypt had more reason to worry than the United States regarding the prospect of Arab nationalism taking too much of a left-hand turn, since Egypt "had to live in the area and could not escape the consequences."[34] The State Department reacted by stating that "we wish [to] avoid impeding any Egyptian efforts to bring about change and in particular appreciate considerations re[garding] Bizri, Bakdash and Azm."[35]

The three months Nasser had asked for was one more than he actually needed. The long courtship over union between Egypt and Syria was finally consummated on February 1, 1958, producing the United Arab Republic. The regional solution to the Syrian problem that Eisenhower and Dulles so desperately wanted had occurred, albeit from an unexpected source. The Eisenhower administration calculated that if it could not keep the Soviets out of Syria, it might as well trust the job to someone who could. The United States had tried just about everything short of committing US forces to keep Syria from becoming a Soviet base in the Middle East. Dulles turned to a policy of "containment-plus," keeping the "virus" from spreading out from Syria. Nasser had successfully kept the Soviets at arm's length in Egypt; maybe his stature and power in the Arab world was enough to do the same in Syria.

The US-Egyptian rapprochement did not occur overnight and, at least from the US perspective, was by default bred more out of necessity than prescience. There had been signs during the crisis that their coinciding interests vis-à-vis Syria might produce some sort of a working relationship. In early October, the State Department publicly expressed its desire for closer relations with Egypt. Egyptian press and radio comment reacted favorably to this and generally welcomed US friendship. A piece in *Al-Sha'b* stated on October 12 that Egypt "is anxious to have good relations with the United States and other states." The next day, *al-Jumhuriya* printed that "we antagonize those who antagonize us and pacify those who pacify us."

This budding cooperation was clearly evident early on at the UN debate over the Syrian situation. The Egyptian representative to the UN, Mahmoud Fawzi, apparently told UN Secretary-General Dag Hammarskjold that the Egyptians were doing their best to keep the Syrians from proceeding with their complaint in the UN General Assembly, including trying to dissuade them from insisting that an investigatory commission be sent to the Turkish border.[36] They felt the debate would not be confined to the relatively narrow Syrian-Turkish item but would expand to cover broader issues in the Middle East that could place Nasser in some rather uncomfortable diplomatic positions, especially on the Arab-Israeli front. Fawzi also told the secretary-general that he was "bitter" over how the Soviets were forcing the hand of the Syrians in the UN.[37] Indeed, Soviet guidance of Syrian actions at the UN seemed to have awakened the US and Egyptian delegations to the possibility of limited cooperation.

From the point of view of the Eisenhower administration, cooperation with Egypt became more desirable after Sa'ud's mediation had failed and Nasser had regained his paramount position in the Arab world after the landing of Egyptian troops at Latakia on October 13. Evidence of this is found in a summary record of conversations US officials had had with Fawzi. One of these stated:

> We told Fawzi in our opinion his statement . . . was restrained and we appreciated [the] tone he had struck in it. We said we believed objectives which had outlined to us for handling this item [Syrian complaint in the UN] . . . were shared by U.S. Fawzi said Egypt and U.S. share desire to see in Middle East peaceful, constructive, independent states, free from outside interference of any kind. . . . Fawzi said he appreciated our initiative and our approach which, as far as he was concerned, represented a clean slate from which to start.[38]

The Eisenhower administration began to realize what the Egyptians already knew, that is, the latter were the only ones capable of preventing an increase of Soviet influence in Syria. Fawzi's actions at the UN (and other indications from Cairo) convinced Dulles that Nasser was sincere in his desire to "save" Syria. Having exhausted all other reasonable avenues, Dulles had no choice.

Recognizing the new political balance in the Middle East, *al-Ahram* stated on November 6, 1957, that the Soviet Union "may be on its way to the conquest of space but America can certainly conquer people's hearts." For Nasser, however, he had just traded in one headache for another with his reluctant acquiescence to the union with Syria. Most Syrians saw union with Egypt as a necessary step to avoid more internal turmoil and external interference. But for Egypt and Nasser, it was a political disaster that directly contributed to the heightening tension of the Arab cold war and the environment for the outbreak of the 1967 Arab-Israeli war. Nasser's diplomatic acumen in this particular episode certainly enabled him to achieve his immediate objectives, and it had short-term positive results. But the long-term implications were ultimately negative, as it contributed to a level of responsibility and popularity that Nasser spent the rest of his tenure in power trying to live up to—and never quite reaching.

CONCLUSION

With Nasser's fait accompli, and lacking any alternative, Sa'ud continued to pursue his mediation policy, but its effects were much more keenly felt in the UN than in the Middle East. Blocked at the domestic level by the disclosure of the coup attempt in Syria, at the regional level by the actions of Sa'ud and Nasser, among other persons, and at the international level by the threats emanating from the Kremlin, the Eisenhower administration opted to pursue "victory" in the UN. In doing this, however, the United States had unwittingly reignited at the international level what was a diminishing crisis by early to mid-October. Sa'ud's official offer to mediate the Syrian-Turkish crisis (as it was termed at the time) actually had the effect of lessening tensions at the UN, as other Arab delegates began to support his efforts. On October 22, 1957, the UN General Assembly officially suspended debate on the Syrian-Turkish dispute pending the outcome of Sa'ud's mediation. It would come to absolutely nothing, as Syria politely rejected his intervention, but it did provide a respite in the UN that allowed the United States and the Soviet Union to reassess their positions and separately agree to just let the crisis peter out.[39] Soviet General Secretary Nikita Khrushchev realized the untenable situation in the UN in the wake of Sa'ud's efforts. His objective of deterring the Turks and the Americans from intervening in Syria had been successful, with the concomitant rise in Soviet prestige in the Arab world and influence in Syria. It was time to end the crisis before the Soviets lost at the UN much of what they had won in the Middle East. With this in mind, Khrushchev unexpectedly appeared at a reception at the Turkish Embassy in Moscow on October 29, unofficially ending the American-Syrian crisis.

Regional players had largely dictated the pace and scope of the crisis, whereas the global superpowers, especially the United States, initiated policies in a reactionary fashion that only escalated tensions to higher and more dangerous levels. The Eisenhower Doctrine signified a globalist application of foreign policy to the Middle East, focusing on the Soviet threat, something that most Arabs thought was absolutely incongruous considering the fact that Egypt had just been attacked by Britain, France, and Israel and not by the Soviet bloc or Communist forces. By remaining at, and constantly retreating to, this analytical level, US policymakers failed to appreciate the agendas of regional actors that, in many cases, had nothing to do with the East-West conflict yet set the parameters of the political dynamics of the Middle East.

In Iran, the Eisenhower administration was successful in blunting a nationalist movement that was deemed susceptible to Communist takeover; however, this did not prevent Iranian disillusionment with, and ultimately anger toward, the United States for betraying its stated principles with democracy and self-determination, a hostility that poured forth in 1979 with the added venom of twenty-six years of repression. In Syria, the United States was unable to curb the rise of leftist Arab nationalist forces and ironically found itself ultimately, and indirectly, through Nasser's sangfroid, relying on a nationalist movement to prevent the Soviet Union from expanding its position in the Middle East; the hostility engendered by a feeling of imperialist victimization nonetheless was created, severely hampering US-Syrian relations for more than a generation. The circumstances surrounding Syria during this turbulent period compelled its leaders to think in terms of national survival rather than national development, preordaining choices and options that invariably sent it down a path trodden by many other Third World nations caught in the vice of the cold war: stunted economic growth, regional conflict and hostility, and superpower confrontation.

Notes

1. For a detailed examination of this subject and the events that led up to it, see David W. Lesch, *Syria and the United States: Eisenhower's Cold War in the Middle East* (Boulder: Westview, 1992).

2. The Eisenhower Doctrine essentially offered American military and economic aid to those nations in the Middle East that requested it in order to resist the advances of other states who were, in the official opinion of the administration, dominated by "international communism."

3. On Sa'ud's relationship with the United States and his role in the American-Syrian crisis, see David W. Lesch, "The Role of Saudi Arabia in the 1957 American-Syrian Crisis," *Middle East Policy* 1, no. 3, 1992.

4. Foreign Reports, letter to John Foster Dulles from Harry Kern, February 28, 1957, John Foster Dulles Papers, Box 118, John Foster Dulles Collection, Seeley G. Mudd Library, Princeton University, Princeton, N.J.

5. Telegram from the Embassy in Saudi Arabia to the Department of State, April 11, 1957, *Foreign Relations of the United States*, vol. 8 (1955–1957) (hereinafter FRUS), at 492.

6. British Foreign Office (FO) Report, "Middle East: The Nature of the Threat and Means of Countering It" (in preparation for the Bermuda Conference with the United States in March 1957), March 8, 1957, FO 371/127755, Public Record Office, Kew Gardens, London (hereinafter PRO); Foreign Office Reports in preparation for Anglo-American talks on June 12–14, 1957, "Measures to Ensure Continued Access to Middle East Petroleum Resources," FO 371/127756, PRO; and, "Saudi Arabia and Buraimi and Their Relations to Kuwait," FO 371/127756, PRO.

7. Memorandum of a Conversation, Department of State, Washington, DC, August 19, 1957, 3:45 p.m., FRUS 8 (1955–1957):340–341.

8. Dulles telephone call to General Twining, August 21, 1957, John Foster Dulles Papers, Telephone Calls Series, Box 7, Dwight D. Eisenhower Library, Abilene, Kans. (hereinafter DDEL).

9. Dulles to Selwyn Lloyd, August 21, 1957, Ann Whitman File, Dulles-Herter Series, Box 7, DDEL.

10. Harold Macmillan, *Riding the Storm, 1956–1959* (New York: Harper and Row, 1971), pp. 279–280.

11. Eisenhower to King Sa'ud, August 21, 1957, Ann Whitman File, International Series, Box 42, DDEL.

12. British Foreign Office, August 23, 1957, FO 371/128224, PRO; also, Macmillan, *Riding the Storm,* 279.

13. Memorandum of a Conversation with the President, White House, Washington, DC, August 28, 1957, FRUS 8 (1955–1957):659–660.

14. Telegram from the Department of State to the Embassy in Saudi Arabia, August 27, 1957, FRUS 8 (1955–1957):500–502.

15. Dwight D. Eisenhower, *Waging Peace, 1956–1961* (Garden City, N.Y.: Doubleday, 1965), p. 198.

16. Ibid.

17. British Consulate-Istanbul, August 25, 1957, FO 371/128224, PRO.

18. As a US official pointed out, Iraqi troops would have a much easier time penetrating Syria through Jordan than to traverse the vast desert and roadless space directly across the Syrian-Iraqi border. Memorandum of a Conversation Between the President and the Secretary of State, White House, Washington, DC, September 2, 1957, FRUS 8 (1955–1957): 669–670.

19. British Embassy-Amman, August 28, 1957, FO 371/128225, PRO, and Eisenhower, *Waging Peace,* 200–201.

20. Eisenhower, *Waging Peace,* 200.

21. Letter from Secretary of State Dulles to Prime Minister Macmillan, September 5, 1957, FRUS 8 (1955–1957):681–682.

22. For a detailed analysis of this policy transformation, see Lesch, *Syria and the United States*. There are no "smoking-gun" documents to prove that the United States gave or was prepared to give the Turks the "green light," but there is enough circumstantial evidence as well as confirmations acquired from players who were intimately involved in the process at the time (who wish to remain anonymous), that I am convinced that the Eisenhower administration did so and that it was only Soviet threats against Turkey that prevented what could have been a very dangerous situation from developing. For a particularly revealing document on the subject, see Telegram from the Department of State to the Embassy in Turkey, September 10, 1957, FRUS 8 (1955–1957):691–693.

23. On October 6, 1957, the Saudi government officially denied its acceptance of the Eisenhower Doctrine, countering what had been taken for granted in diplomatic circles since Sa'ud's visit to Washington in February, even though the king never publicly announced his country's adherence to it.

24. Foreign Broadcast Information Service (FBIS), September 11, 1957, A2.

25. FBIS, September 16, 1957, A1.

26. *New York Times*, September 15, 1957.

27. If Syria was "lost" to Saudi Arabia, it is likely that pro-West elements would have gained in strength and possibly even assumed power (with the issues of union with Iraq and membership in the Baghdad Pact resurfacing), but there is nothing to suggest that Saudi Arabia and the United States were working together toward this goal, that is, Washington was not supportive of Sa'ud's mediation until it became useful to do so to escape from a United Nations dilemma later during the US–Syrian crisis; indeed, there exists much evidence that Riyadh and Washington were at odds with each other during most of the crisis period. See Lesch, *Syria and the United States*, 190–209.

28. Telegram from the Embassy in Egypt to the Department of State, December 11, 1957, FRUS 8 (1955–1957):744–746.

29. "Syria's Egyptian Visitors," *Economist*, October 19, 1957, 230–231.

30. Elias Murqus, a former Syrian Communist, offers an interesting criticism of the Communist Party's activities at this time. He felt its overaggressiveness vis-à-vis the Ba'th seriously damaged its chances to gain power. *Tarikh al-ahzab al-shuyu'iyya fi al-watan al-'arabi (History of the Communist Parties in the Arab World)* (Beirut: al-Jam'a al-Lubaniya, 1964), 91–92.

31. FBIS, October 17, 1957, A2.

32. Telegram from the Embassy in Egypt to the Department of State, December 11, 1957, FRUS 8 (1955–1957):744–746.

33. Ibid.

34. Ibid.

35. Telegram from the Department of State to the Embassy in Egypt, December 12, 1957, FRUS 8 (1955–1957): 746–747.

36. British United Nations (UN) Delegation-New York, October 16, 1957, FO 371/128242, PRO.

37. British UN Delegation-New York, October 18, 1957, FO 371/128242, PRO. The US delegate at the UN, Henry Cabot Lodge, told Dulles that "Bitar is here and is lonely and overwhelmed by Soviet overtures and would like to talk with someone from

the West." Telephone Call from Lodge to Dulles, October 2, 1957, 5:40 p.m., John Foster Dulles Papers, Telephone Calls Series, Box 7, DDEL.

38. Telegram from the Mission at the United Nations to the Department of State, October 24, 1957, FRUS 8 (1955–1957):728–729.

39. British UN Delegation-New York, October 28, 1957, FO 371/128244, PRO.

CHAPTER 8

THE UNITED STATES AND NASSERIST PAN-ARABISM

Malik Mufti

In this chapter I shall argue that US Middle East policy from the mid-1950s to the early 1960s consisted primarily of safeguarding US interests by accommodating the populist pan-Arabism of Egyptian President Gamal 'Abd al-Nasser. After its initial attempt (1955–1956) to bring together all regional actors in a grand pro-US alliance collapsed, Washington watched with dismay as Soviet influence appeared to advance, first in Syria and then in Iraq. Nasser successfully played on these fears to enlist US support for his regional ambitions from 1958 to 1962. Around 1963, however, when Nasser himself became a threat to its interests, the United States started building up his pro-Western rivals in Israel, Jordan, and Saudi Arabia while entrusting the campaign of liquidating the remnants of Arab communism to the Ba'th Party in Syria and Iraq.

WASHINGTON'S INITIAL FOUR-PRONGED POLICY

US interests in the Middle East can be boiled down to two strategic objectives, both of which emerged after World War II. First, the United States was intent on keeping Saudi Arabia and its smaller oil-rich neighbors securely under the US umbrella; and second, it wanted to prevent the expansion of Soviet influence in the Arab world. Initially—during the period roughly from 1947 to 1955—Washington relied on a four-pronged policy approach to accomplish those objectives. First, it sought to maintain the regional status quo by opposing the pan-Arab ambitions of the Hashemites in Baghdad and Amman—particularly given their Hijazi roots. As a 1950 US Department of State paper on Syrian-Iraqi union put it at the time: "There would thus be no contribution to United States interests in giving encouragement to the movement, and any suggestion of intervention by this Government in favor of [a] union [of Arab states] would undoubtedly incur deep resentment among peoples of the Near East, particularly in Saudi Arabia where U.S. strategic interests are of vital importance."[1]

Second, Washington decided instead to support, wherever possible, leaders whose populist nationalism gave them credibility in their peoples' eyes but whose visions did not extend beyond modern reforms within their countries. In other words, US support went to anti-Communists whose pan-Arab rhetoric remained just that. In Syria, this policy resulted in US support first for Colonel Husni Za'im when he seized power in March 1949, then for Colonel Adib al-Shishakli, who succeeded in his coup in December of the same year. Shishakli turned out to be a relatively competent dictator who seemed to fit the US bill well.

In Egypt, the Americans pinned even greater hopes on Colonel Gamal 'Abd al-Nasser and his fellow officers who overthrew the monarchy in 1952. Contacts between the two sides predated the coup and intensified significantly during the years immediately following it. During this time, Nasser enlisted Washington's support for his fledgling regime and for its struggle to free Egypt from lingering British influence by convincing the Americans that his interests and theirs coincided on most issues. In the fall of 1954, for example, "Colonel Nasser declared that Egypt was basically inclined toward the West and that Russia and communism represented the only conceivable danger to Egypt's security."[2] For its part, Washington forced Israel to suspend its diversion of Jordan River waters, by temporarily suspending aid in October 1953, brokering a final Anglo-Egyptian agreement signed on October 19, 1954, and concluding an economic assistance agreement with Egypt on November 6, 1954. A State Department paper, prepared in 1966, recalled nostalgically: "U.S. economic assistance during the sunny early years of the Nasser regime, 1952–1956, amounted to $86 million."[3]

US support continued even after Nasser—having consolidated his hold on power—delivered his famous speech of July 23, 1954, which outlined Cairo's new foreign policy orientation: Henceforth, his government would abandon its isolationist outlook and strive for Arab solidarity under Egyptian leadership. Thus, Wilbur Crane Eveland, a US intelligence operative in the region at the time, remembers that US Central Intelligence Agency (CIA) propaganda experts were kept busy during late 1954 "dreaming up ways to popularize Nasser's government in Egypt and the Arab world."[4] They apparently went to unusual lengths to maintain Nasser's nationalist credibility. According to another operative involved in those events:

> While the "straights" in Washington were increasingly displeased with the anti-American content of Nasser's public utterances and the anti-American

propaganda that poured out of Radio Cairo . . . can you guess who was
writing a goodly portion of the material? We were. . . . We took pains to
make it subtly counter-productive, of course, and we included a lot of
patent nonsense, but we kept virtually in control of its production. We
even had Paul Linebarger, perhaps the greatest "black" propagandist who
ever lived, come to Egypt to coach the Egyptian-American team that
turned out the stuff.[5]

The third element of US policy during this period envisaged bringing all the
"progressive" but pro-Western Arab regimes that could be sustained into a regional
anti-Soviet alliance modeled on the North Atlantic Treaty Organization (NATO).
The fourth and final element was a logical extension of this third objective: Avoid
regional conflicts that would weaken the alliance, such as those that would pit
members against one another and force Washington to choose sides, thereby creating opportunities for Moscow to gain influence.

COLLAPSE OF THE FOUR-PRONGED STRATEGY

Unfortunately for the United States, its four-pronged strategy soon fell victim to
the conflicting objectives of other regional actors. Nasser, for one, realized that the
optimal strategy for him would be to play the two superpowers off one another
and to extend Egyptian influence abroad, even if that brought him into conflict
with other US allies. Iraq's Hashemites still harbored dreams of ruling a greater
Arab homeland, dreams that of course conflicted with Nasser's hegemonic dream.
In this they received limited backing from the British, who viewed Iraq as the linchpin to their own regional ambitions and were therefore willing to support the extension of Hashemite influence—primarily through the Baghdad Pact—so long
as it did not result in actual border changes (for example, with Kuwait). The Saudis,
who initially welcomed Nasser's foray into Arab politics as a counterweight to their
nemeses, the Hashemites, gradually began to fear Egyptian expansionism as well.

Most decisively, Israel's concern about the close relationship between Washington and Cairo led it to pursue an aggressive policy culminating in the Gaza raid of
February 28, 1955, its first major engagement with Egypt since 1948 and a humiliating blow to Nasser's prestige. The raid scuttled Washington's attempts to
focus regional attention on the Soviet threat, brought the Arab-Israeli conflict to
the fore, and initiated an arms race that forced Washington to choose sides among
friends in the Middle East. Thus, Israel succeeded in its primary objective of driving
a wedge between Cairo and Washington. When Nasser's subsequent request for
US weapons received a negative response, he announced six months later that he
would be purchasing arms from the Soviet bloc instead. Further setbacks, such as
the Aswan Dam financing dispute and the failure (despite private lip service by
both sides)[6] of a secret US attempt to mediate the dispute between Egypt and Israel
in early 1956, led US Secretary of State John Foster Dulles to conclude:

In view of the negative outcome of our efforts to bring Colonel Nasser to adopt a policy of conciliation toward Israel, we should, I believe, now adjust certain of our Near Eastern policies, as indicated below. The primary purpose would be to let Colonel Nasser realize that he cannot cooperate as he is doing with the Soviet Union and at the same time enjoy most-favored-nation treatment from the United States. We would want for the time being to avoid any open break which would throw Nasser irrevocably into a Soviet satellite status and we would want to leave Nasser a bridge back to good relations with the West if he so desires.[7]

ESTRANGEMENT, 1956–1958

The adjustments that Secretary of State Dulles eventually specified for President Dwight D. Eisenhower established a pattern that would be repeated whenever the United States sought to discipline Nasser: freeze economic aid to Egypt, extend support to Nasser's Arab rivals, and draw closer to Israel. Thus, in addition to withdrawing its offer to finance the Aswan High Dam, Washington halted PL–480 food shipments and other assistance in 1956. It also expressed greater public support for the Baghdad Pact (without actually joining it), as well as the pro-Western governments of Sudan, Libya, Lebanon, and Jordan. Finally, although the United States continued to refrain from providing arms to Israel directly, it now encouraged other Western governments to do so.[8] As Dulles indicated, however, US officials did not want to back Nasser too far into a corner because they still held hope that he would become a cooperative ally. Hence they rejected repeated British invitations to join the Baghdad Pact. More significantly, of course, hence also they refused to back Britain and France in their ill-conceived collusion with Israel during the 1956 Suez crisis.

Eisenhower had begun musing about the need for an Arab counterweight to Nasser even before Suez. Now—with Nasserist radicalism developing into an irresistible force that destabilized the governments of Syria, Lebanon, Jordan, and Iraq itself—he referred to him as "an evil influence" and argued the need "to build up an Arab rival . . . to capture the imagination of the Arab world."[9] After an early candidate, Saudi Arabia's King Sa'ud, proved deficient in the personal and ideological attributes necessary for such a role, however, US officials decided to take things into their own hands. In accordance with the Eisenhower Doctrine (enunciated in January 1957, the doctrine was a policy generally designed to halt Communist expansion in the Middle East, specifically to isolate and reduce Nasser's power), the new approach envisaged a series of bilateral security arrangements with individual states rather than relying on one key ally to act as regional policeman. Saudi Arabia, Jordan, and Iraq responded positively, and US officials concluded the next (and last) step was to bring Syria into line, thereby isolating Nasser and dashing his hopes of parlaying his influence into a negotiating chip with which to play Moscow and Washington off one another. Then, or so the rosy scenario continued, the ensuing network of moderate Arab states would make peace with Israel and come together in an anti-Communist alliance under US leadership.

But bringing Syria into line turned out to be problematic. A power struggle that pitted the pro-Egyptian Ba'th Party against an increasingly pro-Soviet faction headed by Khalid al-'Azm caused the US National Security Council (NSC) to place Syria "in the dangerous category"[10] and to initiate a series of covert operations aimed at reversing Syria's leftward lurch. As is well known, the failure of those plots only strengthened pro-Communist elements in the Syrian military, led by new Chief of Staff 'Afif al-Bizri. The mood in Washington now shifted from concern to panic. Dulles in particular became convinced that a Communist takeover of Syria was imminent. Four days after Bizri's appointment, he concluded that "there is now little hope of correction from within and . . . we must think in terms of . . . external assets."[11]

Accordingly, Dulles sent his deputy, Loy Henderson, to Ankara on August 24, 1957, for talks with Turkish, Iraqi, and Jordanian leaders. Henderson expressed his government's support for unspecified Iraqi or Jordanian "action" against Syria and promised that it would block any interference by the Soviet Union, Egypt, or Israel. He did set one condition however: In order to allay the concerns of the Saudis and others, it had to be clear that the proposed action "[did] not aim at the unification of Syria and Iraq" and that the goal was only "the return to power in Syria of a truly independent leadership." Iraq's rulers had to agree to the stipulation.[12] This point is worth underlining: Even though Washington was extremely fearful of a Communist takeover in Syria, it remained unwilling to countenance any Hashemite action that aimed at revising the regional status quo. As Dulles once reiterated to his underlings, "No success achieved in Syria could possibly compensate for the loss of Saudi Arabia."[13]

As described in more detail elsewhere in this book (see especially Chapter 7, by David Lesch), Iraq and Jordan felt unable to mount an unprovoked military attack on a fellow Arab state, so soon after Suez anyway. Turkey therefore took the lead, massing troops on the Syrian border and carrying out threatening maneuvers all through September.[14] This, however, unleashed a storm of indignation in the Arab world, further tarnishing Washington's image and providing Moscow with a new opportunity to portray itself as the champion of Arab nationalism—and the Third World. Soviet Premier Nikolay Bulganin warned Ankara on September 13 that armed conflict in Syria "would not be limited to that area alone."[15] One week later, two Soviet warships arrived at the Syrian port of Latakia amid great popular fanfare, and Turkey was forced to back off. Suddenly, just as the crisis was winding down into a Soviet propaganda coup, Nasser stepped into the breach. Units of the Egyptian army arrived in Latakia on October 13 and took up positions to "defend" Syria in case of an attack. It was a brilliant stroke. On the one hand, his prestige and popularity as the nemesis of imperialism soared to new heights in Syria and throughout the Arab world. On the other hand, the Soviet Union had gained so much sympathy in Syria during the preceding weeks that Nasser could credibly justify his intervention to the United States as the only way of dampening pro-Communist fervor there.[16]

Sure enough, a report prepared by the commander of US naval forces in the Mediterranean welcomed the Egyptian military landing in Latakia, viewing it as likely "to bolster Pan-Arabism and check Syrian drift into Soviet orbit." The report went on: "'If you can't lick them join them' and Nasser probably better than any prospective replacement anyway."[17] There would be many more twists and turns in the US-Egyptian relationship, but the convergence of interests in Latakia set a precedent and strengthened those officials in Washington who wanted to abandon the attempt to find alternatives to Nasser.

THE UAR AND THE IRAQI COUP

Still, not everyone was convinced—certainly not John Foster Dulles. When Syria and Egypt announced their unification under the flag of the United Arab Republic (UAR) in January 1958, for example, he interpreted it as a plot masterminded by Moscow, telling an emergency session of the Baghdad Pact Council held in Ankara on January 28 and 29 that the "union between Syria and Egypt would be dangerous to all our interests and if we remained passive it would expand and would shortly take in Jordan and Lebanon and ultimately Saudi Arabia and Iraq leaving us with a single Arab State ostensibly under Nasser but ultimately under Soviet control. It was clear that we ought to oppose such a union."[18]

It is instructive, however, that when Iraq's Hashemites—acutely aware of the mortal peril posed to them by the UAR—agitated for effective countermeasures, neither Britain nor the United States would hear of it. Thus, Iraqi Crown Prince 'Abd al-Ilah insisted to the British ambassador in late February that to save the monarchy it would be necessary to incorporate Kuwait into the hastily arranged "Arab Federation" of Iraq and Jordan—"both on economic grounds and because of the moral effect"—and "to bring over Syria, by the use of force if there was no other way."[19] Later, Iraqi Prime Minister Nuri Sa'id caused considerable alarm in London by drawing up a memorandum threatening to annex half of Kuwait's territory unless it joined the Arab Federation at once,[20] but to no avail. Britain's ambassador assured his government that he was doing all he could to prevent the Iraqis "from taking any rash step over Syria or Kuwait,"[21] and John Foster Dulles fretted about "Nuri's recent intemperate statements."[22] The matter became moot on July 14, 1958, when Iraqi military leaders overthrew the Iraqi government in a coup and slaughtered its Hashemite leadership.

In the final analysis, both Britain and the United States continued to view Hashemite pan-Arabism as a threat to their interests in the oil-producing shaykhdoms of the Arabian Peninsula. Even John Foster Dulles, paranoid as he was about the Communist "threat" in Syria and elsewhere, never allowed this concern to overshadow the greater strategic objective of maintaining US hegemony over the oil lanes. He put it to the National Security Council this way, in response to an earlier proposal that the United States might discretely encourage the "ultimate union of Arab countries in the Arabian peninsula": "If the policy on the supply of oil from the Arab states to Western Europe were made uniform as a result of the unification of the Arab states, [the intervening portion of the quote is censored] the threat to the vital oil supply of Western Europe from the Near East would become critical."[23] Dulles added that he "was not saying that the State Department opposed moves in the direction of Arab unity; but the State Department wanted to be very careful that we did not end up by uniting the Arab states against the United States and the West."[24] Although Washington might have liked to see the Hashemites in Iraq and Jordan thwart Nasser's newly formed UAR, in short, it would not allow them to do so at the cost of creating a new political entity that could potentially threaten the US protectorates in the Arabian Peninsula.

Nevertheless, 'Abd al-Karim Qasim's sudden Iraqi coup took Washington aback. CIA Director Allen Dulles (the secretary's brother) told Eisenhower that "the hand of Nasser in these developments is very evident" and added that if the coup "succeeds, it seems almost inevitable that a chain reaction will set in which will doom the governments of Iraq, Jordan, Saudi Arabia, Turkey and Iran."[25] Accordingly, US troops were landed in Lebanon to prop up the Christian Maronite government already besieged by pro-UAR rebels, and British forces arrived in Jordan to stabilize the situation there. Ten days after the Iraqi coup, John Foster Dulles was still arguing that "the real authority behind the Government of Iraq was being exercised by Nasser, and behind Nasser by the USSR."[26]

In fact, Qasim initially went out of his way to project a moderate stance: refusing to join the UAR; adopting a hostile stance toward Nasser; dropping all claims on Kuwait (whose emir was one of the first to congratulate him); and abiding by the 50–50 profit-sharing arrangement with foreign oil companies that the Hashemites had long been trying to overturn. As a result, when the new dictator managed to foil two Egyptian-backed plots to overthrow him in late 1958, he apparently did so with some assistance from Britain, which continued to view Nasser as the greater threat to its regional interests.[27] Qasim certainly appreciated the helping hand. According to Britain's ambassador: "He said he wanted to assure me that he wished friendship with Britain to stand fast and continued, with some emphasis, 'I will even say that not even friendship with any Arab country shall interfere with it.'"[28]

But the Americans reached a different conclusion than the British: Qasim's growing reliance on the Iraqi Communist Party (ICP) in his struggle against his domestic opponents induced Washington to replace its hostility toward Nasser with a new phase of close cooperation.

ANTI-COMMUNIST COOPERATION
AND NSC 5820/1, 1958–1963

Evidence of Washington's renewed tilt toward Nasser could be found even before the Iraqi coup. Egypt's union with Syria and the ensuing wave of pan-Arab enthusiasm that swept the region greatly impressed US officials, prompting them to conclude that "Western interests will be served by placing US-UAR relations on a more normal basis" and to resume limited economic assistance to Egypt.[29] After Qasim's coup and his growing association with the ICP, however, the pro-Nasser chorus became deafening. US Information Agency Director George Allen, for example, argued for a renewed alliance with Nasser even if it meant abandoning allies such as King Hussein: "We must adjust to the tide of Arab nationalism, and must do so before the hotheads get control in every country."[30] Eisenhower balked at Allen's more extreme suggestions, but even he could be heard musing, "Since we are about to get thrown out of the area, we might as well believe in Arab nationalism."[31]

A split developed within the Eisenhower administration regarding the extent to which it should accommodate Nasser. The Department of Defense and Department of Treasury argued that Washington should merely "accept pan-Arab nationalism, of which Nasser is the symbol" and seek to normalize relations with him only as head of the UAR. But the State Department and CIA—representing the majority opinion—wanted to go further, suggesting that the United States actively "accept and seek to work with radical pan-Arab nationalism," even to the extent of cooperating with Nasser on "certain area-wide problems."[32]

In the end their arguments prevailed, and the result was NSC 5820/1, a watershed National Security Council report dated November 4, 1958, that formed the basis of US Middle East policy for the next three years. It began by acknowledging that "the prevention of further Soviet penetration of the Near East and progress in solving Near Eastern problems depends on the degree to which the United States is able to work more closely with Arab nationalism."[33] Securing Washington's "primary objectives" in the region—foremost the "denial of the area to Soviet domination" and secondarily the "continued availability of sufficient Near Eastern oil to meet vital Western European requirements on reasonable terms"[34]—required the United States to "deal with Nasser as head of the UAR on specific problems and issues, area-wide as well as local, affecting the UAR's legitimate interests."[35] And though NSC 5820/1 warned against accepting Nasser's hegemony over the entire Arab world, it also recognized that "too direct efforts on our part to stimulate developments lessening the predominant position of Nasser might be counter-productive."[36]

Nasser's regional rivals received short shrift in NSC 5820/1. US support for Saudi Arabia would remain intact, of course, but even there the report acknowledged the "reduced influence of King Saud" and called for strengthening "United States influence and understanding among groups in Saudi Arabia from which elements of leadership may emerge, particularly in the armed forces and the middle level Saudi Arabian Government officials."[37] As to Jordan, NSC 5820/1 had more drastic recommendations: "Recognizing that the indefinite continuance of Jordan's present political status has been rendered unrealistic by recent developments [seek] to bring about peaceful evolution of Jordan's political status . . . including partition, absorption, or internal political realignment."[38] And though Washington continued to support the preservation of Israel "in its essentials, we believe that Israel's continued existence as a sovereign state depends on its willingness to become a finite and accepted part of the Near East nation-state system."[39]

NSC 5820/1 remained a controversial document, and both Defense and Treasury felt obliged to put their dissenting opinions on record. John Foster Dulles also continued to argue—against his own department—that it went too far in appeasing Nasser at the expense of more important allies such as Britain. But the secretary of state was dying of cancer and would soon leave office. As Qasim increasingly tied his fate to that of the Communists, fewer and fewer voices would be heard opposing the tilt toward the UAR.

EGYPTIAN OPPORTUNISM

Nasser's case was greatly helped by the reception accorded in Baghdad to William Rountree, the US assistant secretary of state who visited the region in December 1958. Rountree endured volleys of rotten vegetables and trash thrown at his motorcade by angry Iraqi crowds only to receive a cool and perfunctory reception from Qasim himself. The shrewd Egyptians gave him a warmer welcome, and when he returned to Washington, Rountree reported that they were "showing a real concern over Communist penetration of the Middle East" and that "we can work with Nasser on the Iraqi situation."[40] The desk officer for Iraq at the State Department told Britain's ambassador after Rountree's trip that the "only hope for retrieving the situation now [seems?] to lie in the army acting under the inspiration of Arab nationalism of a pro-United Arab Republic and anti-Communist kind. This need not mean a takeover by the United Arab Republic."[41]

In fact, Nasser had been preparing the ground for a rapprochement with the United States for some time. He had already purged Bizri and his pro-Communist officers within weeks of the UAR's creation in an effort to earn the Syrian business community's trust as well as to defuse the ideological challenge posed by communism to his brand of radicalism—a challenge that grew particularly acute after the coup in Iraq and the subsequent rise of ICP influence there. It was partly in order to nip this threat in the bud and partly to curry US favor that Nasser launched his anti-Communist campaign in earnest with a vitriolic speech in Port Sa'id on December 23, 1958. Many party members lost their lives during the days that followed, and hundreds more were thrown into prison. A second wave of arrests in March liquidated the Communists as a political force in the UAR altogether.

In Iraq, by contrast, the Communist advance seemed inexorable. The crushing of an Egyptian-backed revolt in Mosul in March 1959, followed by extensive purges of Arab nationalists, strengthened the ICP still further. As the party gained control of one professional association after another, as its armed militia grew to 25,000 members by May 1959, and as it began to infiltrate the army itself, even Qasim started to worry. Every time he tried to rein in the Communists, however, a resurgence of Nasserist and Ba'thist opposition would force him to turn to them once again. Thus, a crackdown on the ICP after a particularly grisly outbreak of class warfare in Kirkuk in July 1959 ended in October after a Ba'thist attempt on the president's life.

British officials continued to insist that Qasim represented the best hope of preventing an all-out Communist takeover in Iraq and pointed to the strongly anti-

Communist sentiments of senior military officers,[42] but the Americans remained far less sanguine. Mosul and the ICP's subsequent gains dispelled any remaining doubts about the reorientation outlined in NSC 5820/1 and led CIA Director Allen Dulles to describe the Iraqi situation as "the most dangerous in the world today."[43] Another US official captured the mood of helpless frustration that gripped Washington during this period by observing that "we sit and watch unfolding events which seem to point inevitably to Soviet domination of Iraq, acknowledging, I am afraid, an inability to do anything about it. It is almost like watching a movie whose end we will not like but which we are committed to see."[44]

Nasser astutely fueled Washington's anxiety. He told reporters, for example, that he had "reliable information" of a Soviet master plot to create a "red fertile crescent"— a Communist federation encompassing Iraq, Syria, Jordan, Lebanon, and Kuwait. Only Egypt, he implied, blocked the path of this fiendish plan. Not surprisingly, relations with Moscow deteriorated. Three days after the collapse of the Mosul revolt, Soviet General Secretary Nikita Khrushchev declared, "Nasser wants to annex Iraq. As I see it he is a hot-headed young man who has taken on more than he can manage." Nasser retaliated on March 20 by denouncing communism and accusing Khrushchev of "intervention in our affairs."[45]

Nasser's strategy paid off: The loss of Soviet support was more than offset by the advantages of a renewed alliance with Washington, where the initial trepidation concerning Nasser's role in Iraq gave way—much as it had in Syria in 1957—to a sense of enormous relief. An NSC report listed some of those advantages: $125 million in special assistance and surplus commodity sales in 1959; additional export guarantees and loans; US backing for a $56 million Egyptian loan request to the International Bank for Redevelopment and Development (the IBRD, or World Bank); and in "support of the UAR's anti-communist propaganda offensive . . . grant aid for the purchase of newsprint and . . . basic anti-communist material for use by UAR press and radio." Perhaps most important for Nasser, the report added: "Consistent with our recognition of the lack of any desirable alternatives for Syria's future and our understanding that continuance of the present trend in US-UAR relations will depend, in part, on our willingness to assist Nasser in his Syrian economic objectives, we have given special attention to DLF loan applications for the Syrian region."[46]

Both sides clearly understood the quid pro quo involved: It was spelled out by a State Department paper in mid-April 1959: "While we have not directly linked with Nasser's present campaign against communism the steps we have recently taken to aid Egypt, there is no doubt that Nasser knows that we have taken these steps as a sign of approval of his current campaign and that they have emboldened him in his anti-communist efforts."[47]

US RESERVATIONS

Washington's renewed affinity with Nasser alarmed those who resented the spread of his influence. Britain, Turkey, Saudi Arabia, Jordan, and Israel all felt that US support for Nasser's subversive campaign against Iraq was tilting the regional balance of power too far in his favor. Turkey had warned from the beginning that it would take military action if the Egyptians tried to bring Iraq into the UAR and made threatening moves along its southern borders both after the Mosul revolt in March 1959 and following the failed attempt on Qasim's life in October. In December, Foreign Minister Fatin Rustu Zorlu confided his fears to the British ambassador: "He believed that the C.I.A. were dickering with the idea that the situation in Iraq was so precarious that Egypt ought to be ready to do something about it in case things went completely wrong. He even thought it possible that some hint of this thinking might be available to the Egyptians."[48]

Saudi Arabia, already embarrassed by the revelation in March 1958 that King Sa'ud had financed an assassination plot against Nasser, also kept up steady pressure on Washington to do something about Nasser's growing influence in Arab politics. King Hussein of Jordan, for his part, tried to put himself forward as a viable alternative to Nasserism and communism in both Syria and Iraq. A skirmish involving armored vehicles on the Jordanian-Syrian border occurred in late April 1959, and in August the British embassy in Amman got wind of a coup plot in Syria that the Jordanians were at least aware of.[49] On the Iraqi side, Hussein was just as assertive. Asked by an interviewer in October whether he would consider invading Iraq, he responded by saying "we would do everything we could to save Iraq from Communism" and that the "showdown" was now imminent.[50] There were reports of tension on the Jordanian-Iraqi border as well later in the month.

But US officials, believing that King Hussein could not hope to compete with either Nasser or the Communists for the allegiance of the Arab masses, categorically refused to support his initiatives. As a State Department official told one of his British counterparts, "There could be no question of a Hashemite restoration either in Iraq or Syria."[51] Quite the contrary: The British embassy in Amman reported on April 24, 1959, that the US military attaché and his assistant had been "touting pro-Nasser views round the various offices" much to the consternation of the Jordanian government.[52] This at a time of ongoing clashes along the Jordanian-Syrian border—and just five months after UAR jets tried to shoot down Hussein's plane. In a conversation with a Canadian diplomat, Nasser once again evoked the Communist bogeyman: "Nasser said categorically that King Hussein's idea of intervening militarily with Arab Legion in Iraq was profoundly unwise. Quote it could ruin everything unquote. It might have some effect in the short term and locally, but the implication that there might be a Hashemite restoration would inevitably play into the hands of the Communists, who would be quick to exploit it."[53] Washington concurred. Not only did US officials oppose Hussein's revisionist pan-Arab ambitions, they even "cautioned" him against "provocative acts" directed at the UAR.[54] Hussein abandoned his efforts in August 1960 after a bomb placed by UAR operatives killed Prime Minister Hazza' al-Majali and ten other Jordanians in Amman.

US officials tried to allay the concerns of their other allies by assuring them that the UAR had no further expansionist ambitions and by pointing out that "Nasser's recent attacks on Communism had done more to stay the advance of Communism in the Middle East than anything the Western Powers could have achieved in years of work."[55] Still, it became evident even to Washington that the excessive reliance on Nasser was growing increasingly problematic: Freed of almost all restraints, he was antagonizing his neighbors to the point where any one of them—Turkey, Jordan, Israel, Saudi Arabia, or Iraq itself—might lash out in a dangerously unpredictable fashion.

The dilemma confronting Washington was the same one it had faced since 1955: to find a credible anti-Communist movement that was not a mere vehicle for Egyptian expansionism. Some other version of radical pan-Arabism seemed the only answer, reflected in a conclusion suggested by Eisenhower in the aftermath of the Iraqi coup: "If we could somehow bring about a separation of Syria from Egypt and thereafter a union of Syria with Iraq, this might prove very useful."[56] Qasim, with his narrow popular base and his dependence on the ICP, would clearly not do. Neither would Hussein's Hashemite alternative, since Washington doubted it could work and feared the consequences for its hegemony in Saudi Arabia and the Persian Gulf if it did.

THE SYRIAN SECESSION

Deliverance came on September 28, 1961, when a group of Syrian officers mounted a coup d'état and effected Syria's secession from the UAR. The implications of this devastating blow to Nasser's prestige for US-Egyptian relations were not lost on the foreign policy team of the newly elected president, John F. Kennedy. Robert Komer of the NSC observed just five days after the secession: "I am convinced that recent events may present us with the best opportunity since 1954 for a limited marriage of convenience with the guy who I think is still, and will remain, the Mister Big of the Arab World."[57] Kennedy's special envoy, Chester Bowles, fleshed out Komer's observation in a telegram from Cairo in early 1962:

> I believe the time has come for a change of emphasis in our dealings with the UAR in general and with Nasser in particular. If Nasser were now riding high he might view any effort by us to establish a new relationship as an act of weakness. However, Nasser is deeply conscious of the serious problems which now face him and his regime. . . . Under these circumstances I believe that a skillful, sophisticated, sensitive effort to establish a more affirmative relationship is called for. Furthermore, I believe that Nasser is likely to meet us more than half way.[58]

During the winter of 1961–1962, then, Nasser's stock in Washington rose still further, bolstered largely by his diminished ability to provoke other US allies in the Middle East after Syria's secession, but also in part by the Kennedy administration's generally more tolerant attitude toward Third World radicalism. In practical terms this meant increased assistance for Egypt's now seriously ailing economy, including a three-year PL–480 agreement signed in 1962 for the sale of about

$430 million worth of surplus foods. In return, Nasser agreed to maintain his anti-Communist stance and—as he put it in 1961 to the new US ambassador, John S. Badeau—to cooperate with the United States in keeping "the Israeli-Arab question 'in the icebox' while devoting themselves to the development of mutual interests."[59] As a result, Badeau could report at the onset of 1964 that "the United States now wields more influence in the Near East than it has at any time since 1955."[60] Yet even before Badeau penned those words, the US-Egyptian relationship had already begun the inexorable process of disintegration that would culminate when Nasser, in his desperation and folly, took a final, fatal step in 1967, which brought his world crashing down around him.

BREAKDOWN, 1963–1967

Exactly two months after Badeau's rosy assessment, Nasser complained to visiting US Assistant Secretary of State Phillip Talbot that "he could not accept . . . Talbot's presentation that U.S. Middle East policy had not changed since the death of President Kennedy."[61] One year later Nasser's envoy in Washington, Mustafa Kamel, also dated the downturn in bilateral relations to the transition from the Kennedy to the Lyndon B. Johnson administrations: "In late 1963, primarily as result of Yemen problem but possibly also as effect of US-Soviet détente, Kamel said Egyptians had sensed slow-down in US aid."[62]

The Egyptians were not imagining things, although the change in fact predated Kennedy's assassination. Its roots lay in the weakening of Nasser's regional influence following the Syrian secession. Whereas the events of 1958 convinced US officials that even the appearance of opposing Nasser would harm their fundamental interests, by 1962 the picture had changed dramatically. In Saudi Arabia, Crown Prince Faisal—now the effective ruler—coupled domestic reform with a foreign policy that did not shrink as readily from confrontations with Nasser. Syria's secessionist regime, wobbly as it was, enjoyed good relations with the United States while trading bitter public invectives with Egypt. Qasim of Iraq, his economy in ruins, found himself bogged down in a Kurdish revolt that conveniently broke out just weeks after his ill-considered bid for Kuwait in June 1961 (which may have received some US backing). His relations with Nasser were, if anything, worse than those of the Saudis and Syrians. Even King Hussein of Jordan proved more resilient and durable than NSC 5820/1 had predicted, and now he too engaged in a spirited propaganda battle with the Egyptian leader. Nasser's isolation gave Washington leverage to diversify its regional assets by strengthening its ties with countries such as Saudi Arabia, Jordan, and, above all, Israel—all of which began receiving significantly increased levels of US military aid during the early 1960s. As Secretary of State Dean Rusk observed on August 7, 1962: "An extensive and intensive review of our policy toward Israel has been conducted in recent months. . . . The relatively high standing of the United States among the Arabs, while still fragile, provides us with a minor degree of maneuvering room in terms of adjustments in policy with respect to Israel."[63]

Twelve days later a presidential envoy informed Israeli leaders that Kennedy had approved Hawk missile sales to their country, initiating a process that would see US military assistance to Israel soar from $44.2 million in 1963 to $995.3 million by 1968.[64] Domestic political considerations undoubtedly played a role in this shift—both Kennedy and Johnson were far more sensitive to the pro-Israeli feelings of the US Jewish community than Eisenhower had been—but they cannot be understood in isolation from the strategic imperative: "to reinforce Israel as a counterweight to Nasser in case he misused or abused American assistance to him."[65] No wonder Nasser's high expectations in late 1961 regarding his new rapprochement with the United States gave way so quickly to disappointment.

As 1963 rolled by, moreover, Washington's "minor degree of maneuvering room" expanded considerably. Ba'thist coups in Iraq (February 8) and Syria (March 8) at last brought to power regimes that fit the US bill exactly: Although radical and nationalist, they could be counted on to slaughter Communists efficiently while maintaining a hostile stance toward Nasser. There are indications that the United States played a role both in the overthrow of Qasim and in the subsequent hostility between the two Ba'thist regimes and Egypt. Jamal Atasi, one of the new cabinet ministers in Damascus, recalled what happened when the Syrian Ba'thists received reports about clandestine meetings between their Iraqi counterparts and CIA operatives in Kuwait:[66]

> When we discovered this thing we began to argue with them. They would assert that their cooperation with the CIA and the US to overthrow 'Abd al-Karim Qasim and take over power—they would compare this to how Lenin arrived in a German train to carry out his revolution, saying they had arrived in a US train. But in reality—and even in the case of the takeover in Syria—there was a push from the West and in particular from the United States for the Ba'th to seize power and monopolize it and push away all the other elements and forces [i.e., both the Communists and the Nasserists].

By mid-1963, then, Nasser had lost his indispensable status in US eyes. Even as the onset of détente and the development of intercontinental ballistic missiles reduced US fears about Soviet penetration of the Middle East generally, the rise of the Ba'th Party to power in Iraq and Syria liquidated any remaining danger of Communist takeovers in those countries. Nevertheless, Nasser remained leader of the most powerful state in the Arab world—still "Mr. Big," as Komer put it—and had he resigned himself to his diminished status, he might have continued to enjoy a constructive relationship with Washington. But Nasser could not do that. From the beginning his "statesmanship" had consisted of appealing to the vulgar enthusiasms of the mob by pulling off one spectacular public relations coup after another, each time by exploiting the blunders and misperceptions of others: Suez in 1956; Latakia in 1957; the UAR in 1958. Incapable of formulating more serious long-term policies for his country, Nasser now cast about for yet another quick fix to restore him to past glory.

ENDGAME

The years between 1963 and 1967 witnessed a series of foreign policy gambits by Nasser aimed at showing the United States that it could not take him for granted. All of them failed when US counterpressure forced him to retreat, but not before undermining his standing in Washington still further. Nasser's most fateful adventure was in Yemen, where his intervention in the civil war ultimately sucked in a third of his entire army and occasionally spilled over both into the British-controlled South Arabian Federation to the south and—more dangerously—north into Saudi Arabia in the form of bombing raids on royalist bases. These raids provoked extreme alarm in Riyadh and forced the US Air Force to carry out demonstration flights over Saudi towns in July 1963 as a show of support for the oil-rich kingdom's territorial integrity. Nasser had come perilously close to crossing the reddest of all US redlines in the Middle East. In addition, Nasser responded to Washington's arms sales to Israel by signing a military agreement of his own with Moscow in June 1963; by exerting pressure on Libya to expel US and British forces from Wheelus Air Base in early 1964; and by indulging in violent tirades against the United States. After a visit to Egypt by Soviet leader Khrushchev in May 1964, the pipeline from Washington shut down as US officials "simply allowed the Egyptian request for aid renewal to get lost in a maze of formalities without ever saying no to it."[67] Nasser's initial response was defiant. In a fiery speech on December 23, 1964, he praised the Soviet Union, announced his intention to continue arming rebels fighting US-Belgian "aggression" in the Congo, and concluded: "Whoever does not like our conduct can go drink up the sea. If the Mediterranean is not sufficient, there is the Red Sea, too."[68]

But as Egypt's deteriorating economy sparked protest demonstrations, illegal strikes, and even coup plots in late 1964 and 1965, Nasser realized he could not do without US aid. He therefore took steps to appease the United States, terminating his support for the Congo rebels, urging moderation in the Arab-Israeli dispute over the Jordan River waters, and toning down his anti-American rhetoric. Most important, he signed an agreement with King Faisal on August 24, 1965, that envisaged a total withdrawal of Egyptian troops from Yemen within thirteen months. PL–480 food shipments were resumed forthwith, albeit in reduced amounts and for shorter periods.

By mid-1966, however, Nasser—convinced now that the Americans were conspiring with the British and Saudis to bring him down—changed tacks yet again, drawing still closer to Moscow, hunkering down in Yemen, and resuming his propaganda offensive against the United States and its regional allies. Was he right? Probably as far as Britain and Saudi Arabia were concerned; the Saudis certainly seemed determined not to permit him an honorable exit from Yemen. But were the Americans also plotting his downfall? One background paper prepared for President Johnson in August 1966 suggests not:

There are those—certainly the British and probably the Saudis—who think that any successor regime in Egypt would be better than the present one. This is dubious. Egypt's aspirations to lead the entire area go back many decades, if not centuries. They antedate Nasser and will not disappear with him. . . . If the Egyptians should decide to depose him that is their business. But there is no American interest in becoming a party to a plot or in letting the situation in Egypt degenerate into total instability in the hope that something better will turn up.[69]

In other words, Nasser could be contained successfully through a policy of calculated sanctions and rewards. Others were not so sanguine. David Nes of the US embassy in Cairo warned that "we are moving inexorably toward a showdown in the area arising from this current attempt of our 'friends' to bring Nasser down and his largely defensive reactions. I agree with Bob Strong that even if we do no more than stand by and watch we shall be inextricably involved."[70]

In any case, US aid to Egypt dried up once again and Nasser retaliated in characteristic style—lambasting the United States as "leader of the imperialist camp" and vowing to remain in Yemen "until the British-American-Saudi danger is completely removed" and threatening to resume bombing of Saudi border towns.[71] Nes in Cairo mused gloomily on May 11, 1967: "We seem to have driven Nasser to a degree of irrationality bordering on madness, fed, of course, by the frustrations and fears generated by his failures domestic and foreign. Our debate here revolves around where he will strike next—Libya, Lebanon?"[72] But Nasser, woefully underestimating the ferocity of Israel's determination to crush him and deluding himself that Washington still cared enough to rescue him from disaster, chose instead to roll the dice in Sinai.

CONCLUSION

John Foster Dulles once summarized Washington's attitude toward Arab nationalism by likening it to "an overflowing stream—you cannot stand in front of it and oppose it frontally, but you must try to keep it in bounds. We must try to prevent lasting damage to our interests in the Near East until events deflate the great Nasser hero myth."[73] And that is precisely what the Americans did. Despite some false steps, they ultimately succeeded in keeping Arab nationalism in bounds, and in doing so they achieved their two fundamental strategic objectives: maintaining control over the oil fields and denying the region to the Soviets. When Hashemite pan-Arabism threatened Saudi Arabia or Kuwait, Washington helped build up a counterweight in Cairo. When Nasser in turn got too big for his britches, Washington neutralized him by sanctioning the rise of the Ba'thists in Syria and Iraq and by letting Israel out of the icebox (where it had moved neither toward resolution of Arab issues nor toward war).

The competence of US Middle East policy during the period in question is often faulted. Eisenhower and Dulles in particular have been roundly criticized (including in this volume) for their clumsy covert operations and for their tendency to see Soviet plots everywhere. Some of this criticism is fair. But in most really crucial respects they were right: They were correct that a "Hashemite solution" in Syria in 1956–1958 would have been—from the standpoint of US hegemonic interests—a cure worse than the disease. Despite a little initial confusion, they did finally recognize that Nasser was a useful ally against the 'Azm-Bizri-Bakdash bloc in Syria; there was a real Communist threat in Iraq after 1958; and given the popular mood of the time, Nasser was in fact the only viable counterweight.

Similarly, there is a long tradition of criticism that blames the breakdown in US-Egyptian relations during the early 1960s on the receptivity of Presidents Kennedy and (especially) Johnson to lobbying by domestic supporters of Israel. But this criticism erroneously assumes that the rationale for close US ties to Nasser—which existed under Eisenhower—continued to exist after 1961. This chapter has tried to show that it did not. Kennedy and Johnson were more responsive to their Jewish electorates largely because they could afford to be.

It made sense for the Americans to use Nasser so long as he was useful to them, just as it made sense for them to drop him when he outlived his usefulness. If there is blame to be assigned, it must fall squarely on Nasser's shoulders: It was he who failed to comprehend the magnitude of the change in his strategic relationship with the United States during the early 1960s; it was he who indulged in demagoguery and reckless foreign adventures rather than addressing the pressing problems confronting Egypt's society and economy; and it was he who chose to give the Israelis the excuse they needed to destroy him in 1967.

At the end of the day the Arab world remained divided, Saudi Arabia and the other oil-rich protectorates huddled safely under the US umbrella, and the Soviets were no closer to breaking Washington's regional hegemony. This may not have been the optimum solution for advocates of Arab nationalism, but by the standard of US national interests, it must be reckoned a great foreign policy success.

Notes

1. "The Political Union of Syria and Iraq," 25 April 1960. US Declassified Documents Reference System (Washington, DC: Carrollton Press, 1975), microfiche (hereinafter USDD) 1975:26H.

2. George Lenczowski, *The Middle East in World Affairs* (Ithaca: Cornell University Press, 1980), p. 527.

3. Department of State Paper: "US-U.A.R. Relations," 20 [?] February 1966. USDD–1982:000982.

4. Wilbur Crane Eveland, *Ropes of Sand: America's Failure in the Middle East* (London: W. W. Norton, 1980), p. 103.

5. Miles Copeland, *The Game Player: Memoirs of the CIA's Original Political Operative* (London: Aurum Press, 1989), p. 167.

6. Nasser wrote to Eisenhower on 6 February 1956 that "in the interest of peace Egypt recognizes the desirability of seeking to eliminate the tensions between the Arab States and Israel." USDD–1981:192C.

7. Memorandum from Dulles to Eisenhower, 28 March 1956. USDD–1989:001511.

8. Washington allowed France to divert NATO military equipment to Israel in the spring of 1956. Dulles also asked Canada to supply Israel with F–86 aircraft. Dulles Telegram from Paris, 3 May 1956; USDD–1987:000714.

9. Eisenhower Message to Dulles, 12 December 1956. USDD–1989:003548.

10. National Security Council (NSC) Progress Report: "United States Objectives and Policies with Respect to the Near East," 2 November 1955. USDD–1988:001022, p. 3.

11. Dulles Telegram to Selwyn Lloyd, 21 August 1957. USDD–1987:002090.

12. See the notes of Rafiq 'Aref, the Iraqi chief of staff who attended the talks, in *Mahkamat al-Sha'b, Al-Muhadarat al-Rasmiyya li-Jalasat al-Mahkama al-'Askariyya al-'Ulya al-Khassa (The People's Court: Official Proceedings of the Sessions of the Special Higher Military Court)* (Baghdad: Mudiriyyat Matba'at al-Hukuma, 1959–1962), vol. 4, pp. 1516–1519.

13. Quoted in Eveland, *Ropes of Sand,* p. 181.

14. For a detailed analysis of this episode, see Chapter 7 by David Lesch in this volume. See also his *Syria and the United States: Eisenhower's Cold War in the Middle East* (Boulder: Westview Press, 1992).

15. Quoted in Patrick Seale, *The Struggle for Syria: A Study of Post-War Arab Politics, 1945–1958* (New Haven: Yale University Press, 1965), p. 300.

16. For more on Nasser's actions during the American-Syrian crisis, see David W. Lesch, "Gamal 'Abd al-Nasser and an Example of Diplomatic Acumen," *Middle Eastern Studies* 31(2) (April 1995), pp. 384–396.

17. Appendix to a Memorandum by the Chief of Naval Operations for the Joint Chiefs of Staff on "Middle East Policy," dated 7 November 1957. USDD–1984: 000135, pp. 3096–3097.

18. Summary of Dulles's comments reported by Secretary of State Sir J. Bowker in Ankara to the Foreign Office on 28 January 1958. British Foreign Office Documents (hereinafter BFOD) FO371/134386/VY10316/10.

19. Report from Michael Wright in Baghdad on his conversation with Crown Prince 'Abd al-Ilah on 25 February 1958. BFOD:FO371/134198/VQ1015/18.

20. See F. Hoyer Millar's Foreign Office Minute of 25 June 1958 on the talks with Nuri in London. BFOD:FO371/134219/VQ1051/19.

21. Letter from Wright to London, 23 June 1958. BFOD:FO371/134198/VQ1015/49.

22. US Department of State, "Memorandum of Conversation," dated 15 June 1958. USDD–1981:371B.

23. Briefing Note dated 21 January 1958 on the suggestions of the Planning Board of the National Security Council. USDD–1985:000640, p. 2.

24. Summary of the discussion at the 353rd meeting of the NSC, 30 January 1958. USDD–1990:000328, p. 8.

25. "Memorandum of Conference with the President," 14 July 1958. USDD–1993:002371.

26. Memorandum of the discussion at the 373rd meeting of the NSC, 25 July 1958. USDD–1990:000330, p. 3.

27. See, for example, the observation by Britain's ambassador in Ankara in early January 1959 that "we took certain action in favour of Qasim in regard to the recent plot in Iraq." BFOD:FO371/140956/EQ1071/1.

28. Cable from Ambassador Wright in Baghdad to the British Foreign Office, 24 November 1958. BFOD:FO371/133090/EQ1051/69.

29. "Background Paper" dated 9 June 1958 for Eisenhower's meeting with British Prime Minister Harold Macmillan. USDD–1988:001568. Among the steps taken to

146   MALIK MUFTI

"normalize" US-UAR relations between January and July 1958: removal of export restrictions on civilian items such as aircraft spare parts; reinstitution of an "Exchange of Persons" program; and release of $400,000 (frozen since 1956) road-building and communications equipment.

30. Summary of the 373rd NSC meeting on 24 July 1958. USDD–1990:000330, p. 6.

31. Summary of the 374th NSC meeting on 31 July 1958. USDD–1990:000331, p. 11.

32. "Briefing Notes" for the NSC meeting of 21 August 1958. USDD–1990:000352, p. 3; and 16 October 1958. USDD–990:000332, p. 2.

33. "NSC 5820/1: U.S. Policy Toward the Near East," 4 November 1958. USDD–1980:386B, p. 2.

34. Ibid., p. 3.

35. Ibid., p. 10.

36. Ibid.

37. Ibid., p. 11. Two years later, Sa'ud would be effectively overthrown by his more reformist brother, Faisal.

38. Ibid., pp. 11–12.

39. Ibid., p. 9.

40. "Memorandum of Conference" dated 23 December 1958. USDD–1983:001435.

41. Cable from Ambassador H. Caccia in Washington to the Foreign Office, 18 December 1958. BFOD:FO371/133086/EQ10345/7.

42. See, for example, Humphrey Trevelyan's report of 19 January 1960 to Selwyn Lloyd on the political situation in Iraq. BFOD:FO371/149841/EQ1015/10.

43. Interview in the *New York Times*, 29 April 1959, quoted in Hanna Batatu, *The Old Social Classes and the Revolutionary Movements of Iraq: A Study of Iraq's Old Landed and Commercial Classes and of Its Communists, Ba'thists, and Free Officers* (Princeton: Princeton University Press, 1978), p. 899.

44. Note by Gordon Gray, special assistant to the president for national security affairs, 1 April 1959. USDD–1984:000586.

45. See Mohamed Hassanein Heikal, *Sphinx and Commissar: The Rise and Fall of Soviet Influence in the Arab World* (New York: Harper and Row, 1978), p. 107.

46. Operations Coordinating Board (OCB) Report on the Near East, 3 February 1960, pp. 6–7. USDD–1984:002567.

47. "The Situation in Iraq: Policy the United States Should Follow to Prevent Communism from Establishing Control of the Country," 15 [?] April 1959. USDD–1992:002638.

48. Cable from Ambassador Burrows in Ankara to the Foreign Office, 12 December 1959. BFOD:FO371/140959/EQ1071/70.

49. See the Cable dated 5 August 1959 from Amman to the Foreign Office (BFOD: FO371/ 141900/VG1017/9), as well as a later dispatch from the Canadian Embassy in Cairo reporting the arrest of fourteen officers in Syria on conspiracy charges. 22 September 1959, BFOD:FO371/141900/VG1017/12.

50. Quoted in a dispatch from the British Embassy in Baghdad on 3 November 1959. BFOD:FO371/140958/EQ1071/52(D).

51. Letter from Burrows to London, 23 May 1959. BFOD:FO371/140957/EQ 1071/31.

52. Ibid., BFOD:FO371/140957/EQ1071/28.

53. Report dated 20 October 1959 from Arnold Smith in Cairo to the Canadian Foreign Ministry. BFOD:FO371/141903/VG10110/36.

54. At least that is what Deputy Undersecretary of State Raymond Hare told Nasser in New York on 30 September 1960. USDD–1984:002451.

55. Ambassador Burrows's account of remarks made by a US State Department official to Turkish Foreign Minister Zorlu. Cable from Ankara to the Foreign Office on 23 May 1959. BFOD:FO371/140957/EQ1071/31. Stuart Rockwell, director of the State Department's Office of Near Eastern Affairs, explained his government's position to the British envoy by saying, "He did not think there was any serious danger of overt military intervention by the U.A.R. This being so he thought that it would be unwise to urge moderation on Nasser," since the United States did not wish to be seen as supporting communism against Arab nationalism. Cable from Ambassador Caccia in Washington to the Foreign Office, 19 March 1959. BFOD:FO371/140937/EQ10316/96.

56. Memorandum of the discussion at the 383rd meeting of the NSC, dated 17 October 1958. USDD–1990:000332, p. 8.

57. Memorandum from Komer to McGeorge Bundy and Walt Rostow. USDD–1991:001643.

58. Bowles Telegram dated 21 February 1962. USDD-I:454A.

59. Badeau Letter to President Johnson, 3 January 1964. USDD–1976:274C, p. 4.

60. Ibid., p. 3.

61. "Nasir's Comments on His Meeting with Assistant Secretary Talbot," CIA cable, 3 March 1964. USDD–1976:12B.

62. Outgoing State Department telegram dated 12 January 1965 summarizing a meeting between Kamel and Secretary of State Dean Rusk four days before. USDD–1982:002580.

63. "Review of United States Policy Toward Israel," State Department memorandum to the President, 7 August 1962. USDD–1992:003242.

64. Steven L. Spiegel, *The Other Arab-Israeli Conflict: Making America's Middle East Policy, from Truman to Reagan* (Chicago: University of Chicago Press, 1985), p. 135.

65. Nadav Safran, *Israel: The Embattled Ally* (Cambridge: Belknap Press of Harvard University Press, 1981), p. 374.

66. Interviews conducted by author in Damascus, 22 July 1991.

67. Nadav Safran, *From War to War: The Arab-Israeli Confrontation, 1948–1967* (New York: Pegasus, 1969), p. 135.

68. Quoted in Spiegel, *The Other Arab-Israeli Conflict*, p. 122.

69. "Current Status of U.S.-U.A.R. Relations," 12 August 1966. USDD–1980:323B.

70. Letter from Nes to Rodger P. Davies at the State Department, 17 October 1966. USDD–1985:001635.

71. "Nasser's May 2 Speech," State Department memorandum dated 4 May 1967. USDD–1993:001379.

72. Letter from Nes to Rodger P. Davies at the State Department, 11 May 1967. USDD–1985:002605.

73. Memorandum summarizing the discussion at the 374th National Security Council meeting on 31 July 1958. USDD–1990:000331, p. 7.

CHAPTER 9

THE SOVIET PERCEPTION
OF THE US THREAT

Georgiy Mirsky

Throughout history, the official Soviet mentality was chronically one of a besieged fortress. "Capitalistic encirclement" was the key word, the implacable struggle of the two world systems was an axiom, the famous expression *kto kovo* (who will beat whom) both motto and leitmotif. And the imperialist monsters biding their time to attack and destroy the first country of the victorious proletariat changed names: First it was Britain and France, then Nazi Germany and Japan, then the United States. But the essence of the external imperialist threat remained the same, the mortal danger was always there, and the options facing the beleaguered Soviet people never varied: Tough it out or perish.

Soviet citizens always felt they were unique, in more than one way. Even those who knew that life in the West was incomparably better and that the party propaganda praising the advantages of socialism was a huge fraud still believed that, given half a chance, the United States and its allies would attempt to crush the Soviet Union. Why? Because everybody was convinced that the Soviet Union—our country—was the biggest pain in the neck for world capitalism, the source of constant anger, fear, and irritation. By and large people did not question the necessity to maintain our armaments on the same level as the United States or to have allies and military footholds in diverse areas to counteract the US encirclement policy. This was why Moscow's activist policy in the Middle East never met with disapproval, inasmuch as it was regarded as a counterbalance to dangerous US expansion in that sensitive region. Discontent and irritation emerged later when one Arab-Israeli war after another demonstrated the incapacity of Soviet clients to effectively use the weaponry they had received from the USSR.

At this point, a question may be asked: Was it really so important for Kremlin rulers to take into account public opinion, considering the totalitarian nature of the regime? Certainly, political actions used to be taken without anybody in the Kremlin even thinking about the possible reaction of the people. Anything was certain to be approved. However, a protracted pattern of political activity, as distinct from a single action, in a specific area had better be popular and easy to swallow by the masses. The point is that, unlike during Stalin's rule, successor Kremlin regimes were based not so much on the *fuehrerprinzip* (principle of a single leader) as on the principle of collective leadership. It was an oligarchy ruling by consensus that was not confined solely to the Politburo but had to exist in lower party echelons as well. Signals that the "apparatchik aristocracy," the party, and management bosses were constantly sending to the very top might be vague, but still they could give a clue as to the prevailing opinion on specific issues inside the dominant class as a whole. And this opinion largely reflected views and beliefs of much broader sections of the population, even of the masses, it may be said. For, contrary to the concepts of some Sovietologists, the Soviet state, inhuman and antihuman as it was, could still be called the "people's state" in the sense that there was a close affinity between ideas, views, and cultural and social tastes of the rulers and the ruled. Soviet propagandists were not far from the truth when they claimed that they were representatives of the people who were in charge in the Soviet Union. Sure, they were exploiting and humiliating the people, depriving them of human rights and liberties, condemning them to a miserable and beastly life. However, all of this was being done not on behalf of some closed and privileged strata, as had been the case in prerevolutionary Russia, but on behalf of those sons of peasants and workers who had made it to the top. Thus, the Soviet elite was never socially and culturally alienated or even differentiated from the bulk of the population. The big shots and the masses basically shared the same mentality.

This helps to explain why it was important for any long-term political strategy to meet with the approval, if not the actual backing, of the people. Popular tastes, traditions, and prejudices, in their turn, could be used by policymakers for the rationalization of their line. The Middle East was a perfect example of convergence of popular beliefs—crude and false but mostly genuine—and the Kremlin's realpolitik. A widespread apprehension of US aggressive designs coupled with anti-Semitism (since the US ally, partner, and "vanguard striking force" in the Middle East happened to be a Jewish state, distasteful almost by definition to quite a few Russians, Ukrainians, and others) helped to ensure solid popular backing for an activist and militant anti-American line of Soviet policy in the Middle East. In practice, of course, it was translated into a strategic alliance with left-wing Arab regimes against the US-Israel axis.

What were the motives of the Soviet leadership in the confrontation with the United States in the Middle East? Here, too, we must take as a starting point the overall Soviet concept of the global struggle between socialism and capitalism.

Some Western authors seemed to have overestimated the degree of the ideological component of Soviet foreign policy. They believed that ideology was paramount in determining the Kremlin's actions. Others, on the contrary, tended to focus almost exclusively on geopolitics. In fact it was a combination of both. There is no doubt that such people as Nikita Khrushchev, Leonid Brezhnev, Andrei Gromyko, Mikhail Suslov, and the rest sincerely believed in the inherent superiority of socialism and its ultimate victory over capitalism on the global scale; but at the same time they could not but realize that it was highly improbable for them to actually see the great triumph of Marxism-Leninism in their lifetimes. It was necessary for them to create conditions for this triumph, that is, to strengthen by all means the forces of world socialism and to weaken the imperialist enemy. To achieve this, it was imperative for the Kremlin leaders to change the global balance of forces, foremost in the political and military spheres, since they already lost faith in socialism's ability to achieve greater productivity of labor (in accordance with Lenin's concept). It was, of course, Lenin who predicted that it would be precisely in the sphere of productivity that socialism would eventually prove superior to capitalism. As early as the 1960s it was already impossible to seriously believe in such an eventuality given the obvious and growing gap between the economies of the two world systems. Thus, stress had to be placed on the undermining and sapping of the imperialist forces in the noneconomic sphere since the economy increasingly looked like the Achilles' heel of socialism. The adversary had to be defeated on a different battlefield, and it was clear that it was first in the sphere of military power and second in the ability to appeal to anticolonial, anti-Western sentiments of Third World nations that socialism could really have an edge over capitalism.

As to the first factor—military power—the Kremlin had to be very cautious about using it, especially after the Cuban missile crisis demonstrated the limits of brinkmanship. A world war was tacitly acknowledged to be suicidal, although the top military brass was reluctant to admit it. The awesome military might of the Soviet Union was to be used in three dimensions: First, as a reminder to Western Europe that tens of thousands of Soviet tanks were ready to roll in should the imperialists try to stage a counterrevolution in the socialist camp; second, as a counterbalance to US sea power (this was why so much emphasis was laid on the expansion of the Soviet Navy); third, as a means of arming Soviet allies in the Third World.

The second factor—spreading Soviet influence in the Third World—was more promising, and the prospects seemed bright indeed of transforming the national liberation movement into a strategic ally against the West. Broadly speaking, this was the picture: To strike a military blow at the citadel of world capitalism was too dangerous due to the inevitable nuclear disaster it would entail; internal contradictions of capitalism were growing but the results were too slow in coming; the situation in Europe was frozen, forces on both sides engaged in trench warfare with no prospect of a breakthrough in either direction; the developing countries seething with discontent and driven by the dynamics of anticolonial inertia presented an excellent opportunity of undermining the imperialist system from within rather than engaging it in a frontal clash.

Finally, it must be said that if this kind of global thinking existed in the minds of the top leaders, this was not the case with the people down the road, with those who were planning and implementing the actual policy. For them, it was a given: The cold war was on, the United States was the enemy, everything had to be done to weaken it. It was a zero-sum game not necessarily motivated by ideological hatred and intransigence. The Communist commitment of the diplomats and the scholars in think tanks was actually skin-deep, as evidenced by the subsequent transformation of many of those people in the post–Mikhail Gorbachev era: They have quietly forgotten their Marxism and perfectly adapted to the new situation.

THE SOVIET UNION AND THE MIDDLE EAST IN THE ERAS OF KHRUSHCHEV AND BREZHNEV

If, during the Khrushchev and Brezhnev eras (1953 to 1982), you asked any young Soviet diplomat just out of the Institute of International Relations (MGIMO) about the significance of the Middle East for the USSR, he would answer matter-of-factly: Too vital to yield even an inch to the Americans. If you had pressed him for specifications, he would have mentioned the geostrategic dimension first, oil second, and the necessity to back our allies, the Arab anti-imperialist forces, third.

Upon a closer look, however, all three dimensions would prove to be not so terribly vital to the interests of the Soviet Union. From the geopolitical and strategic point of view, nobody in his right mind could imagine US tanks rolling across the Arab deserts to the Caucasus in a new world war. In the "ICBM era" the value of any piece of territory was greatly reduced anyway. As to oil, the USSR had plenty of it to begin with; any attempt to deprive the US allies of Middle East oil would have been extremely dangerous since it was clear that the West would not hesitate to protect its access to that commodity with military force. The only thing left, therefore, was the USSR's strategic alliance with the left-wing Arab regimes.

This alliance was born under Nikita Khrushchev, who, in 1955, struck the famous arms deal with Egyptian President Gamal 'Abd al-Nasser. At the time, Khrushchev overruled the objections of the Soviet ambassador to Egypt, who was dismayed by the very idea of dealing with such a patently non-Communist and politically doubtful character as Nasser. Khrushchev was not inhibited by Marxist dogmatic puritanism. He regarded Nasser and his like as valuable partners in the anti-imperialist struggle. It was a bold and imaginative pattern; fabulous opportunities seemed to be in the offing.

From then on, the new alliance rapidly gained momentum. It expanded to involve Syria, Iraq, and Algeria, and, later, the Palestine Liberation Organization (PLO) and South Yemen. For a brief moment it seemed that Sudan, too, joined the "progressive camp"; Libya always was an embarrassing partner, but Mu'ammar al-Qaddafi's anti-imperialism appeared on balance to be more important than his bizarre theories, which were clearly incompatible not only with Marxism but also with the "revolutionary-democratic ideology" shared by Nasserists and Ba'thists. Typical of our attitude toward Qaddafi was a curious fact: Sometime in the 1970s, after one of his particularly vicious anti-Communist outbursts, it was decided to publish a reply to Qaddafi—not in *Pravda*, of course, but in the *Literary Gazette*, and a high-ranking official in the Central Committee's International Department was entrusted with this job. At the last moment, however, the article, which sounded very lucid and convincing to me, was taken out of the newspaper; apparently somebody higher up in the hierarchy decided that it was not worthwhile annoying the erratic colonel.

Pertaining to ideology, two observations might not be out of place. First, Khrushchev's new course of aligning Moscow with Nasser-type leadership was, of course, a purely pragmatic matter devoid of any ideological overtones. But in a socialist state it had to be rationalized and explained in terms of Marxist theory. This is when academic scholars, myself included, were called upon to work out a plausible theory aimed at proving in a convincing manner exactly why it was not only possible but necessary and highly helpful for the Great Cause to establish an alliance with such people as Nasser. The concept we elaborated was that of "Revolutionary Democracy," a non-Marxist, nonproletarian set of ideas and politics founded first on anticolonialism and second on the alleged impossibility of resolving the urgent problems of the developing countries on the basis of capitalism. The idea was that, although anti-imperialist nationalists were not ready to acknowledge and adopt Marxism's eternal truth, the logic of life would sooner or later teach them that only by following the socialist path could they hope to overcome their countries' backwardness and dependence on imperialism. Thus, the anticolonial, anti-imperialist revolution would inevitably grow into a social one, directed against both foreign and domestic oppressors. The national liberation movement would be transformed into a national-democratic revolution with a clear anticapitalist content and, later, into a popular-democratic revolution of a distinct socialist orientation.

The key terms in this concept were "noncapitalist development" and "socialist orientation." It was assumed that someday Nasser and his ilk would realize the futility of their hopes to modernize their countries and to build an industrial society within the framework of the world capitalist system with the help of the domestic bourgeoisie. Then, socialism would come naturally to them as the only way out of the horrible mess left behind by the imperialist exploiters.

Moreover, these theoretical constructions had very little to do with a genuine desire to build a happy socialist society in the dirt-poor and miserably backward Third World countries. I am not referring now to beliefs and motivations of the scholars who were busy writing memos, papers, and monographs on the issue: To the contrary, actual policymakers were indifferent to the results of "noncapitalist development" in Asia and Africa. What mattered, for them, was the involvement of the states ruled by the "revolutionary democrats" into a worldwide anti-Western coalition. Ideology for them was secondary; it was just instrumental in bringing about decisive change in the correlation of world forces. The Third World leaders who proclaimed their allegiance to socialism, even if only of a homemade and not Marxist variety, were ipso facto committed to the Soviet Union and the socialist community in the international arena. Just how successful they were in regard to the socialist transformation of their states was largely irrelevant. The main thing was to get into the "soft underbelly" of the capitalist system—Asia, Africa, and Latin America—so as to eventually besiege imperialism in its citadel. The more Third World countries proclaimed socialism as their goal, and thus became hostage to Soviet political support, arms deliveries, and so on, the better. Each of these countries could, from that moment on, be regarded as a loss to the United States and its allies: It was a zero-sum game. The propaganda aspect was important, too. Certainly what mattered for Brezhnev was being able to say in his report at the next party congress: "Comrades, the period under review has demonstrated once more that ideas of socialism are on the march throughout the globe; more countries now stand under the banner of socialism."

In regard to practical politics in the Middle East, the Kremlin's strategy aimed at ensuring a position of strength for the Arab allies in their confrontation with Israel, which was viewed as America's stooge. Disappointment and bitterness set in each time the Arab forces were defeated by Israel; over and over again, an escalation in arms deliveries followed. The more the USSR became committed to the protection of its Arab allies, the more it had to up the ante or else prepare to lose face.

At the same time, there is no evidence that Moscow ever wanted to escalate the Arab-Israeli confrontation to the point of large-scale war. First, Soviet leaders feared that Arab armies would be soundly beaten; second, they were apprehensive about the war spilling over into a US-Soviet armed conflict signaling the outbreak of a nuclear world war. I happened to witness twice the worry and upset of high-ranking Soviet officials as Israeli forces seemed on the verge of closing in on Cairo and Damascus in 1967 and 1973. The PLO, too, was to be supported only inasmuch as it represented a nuisance in harassing Israel, but it was never regarded as a liberation army built up to recapture Palestine or even a part of it.

The official Soviet position, of course, was in accordance with UN Resolution 242. In the International Department of the Soviet Communist Party Central Committee, which was the place where policy guidelines were usually outlined (this also occurred in various academic institutions), debates took place from time to time over goals in the Middle East. The main issue was whether it would serve our interests if Resolution 242 was implemented and a Palestinian entity created. Opinions differed sharply, some people feeling that the Arabs would no longer need our military backing and that Moscow would lose its leverage.

GORBACHEV, PERESTROIKA, AND NEW POLITICAL THINKING

At first, Gorbachev's foreign policy course was quite traditional, which is not surprising given his background as a career Soviet apparatchik. Even when he embarked on a course of far-reaching domestic reforms, the habitually tough anti-imperialist line showed no signs of slackening. The perestroika leaders, breaking new ground at home, were anxious to cover their flank in the forum of foreign policy. They felt they could not advance on two fronts simultaneously and they were afraid of being perceived as soft on imperialism. So Gorbachev and Shevardnadze preferred to be seen as strong and tough vis-à-vis the West; accordingly, Soviet Middle East policy remained for a time basically unchanged.[1]

Things began to move with the advent of the "new political thinking," particularly when "de-ideologization" of foreign policy was announced. This entailed a decline of ideological priorities and "socialist" commitments abroad. I remember speaking at a conference convened by Shevardnadze in 1987, with all of the Soviet ambassadors abroad participating. When I professed my disillusionment with the practical results of the "socialist orientation" in the Third World, it was a shock to many. However, a group of our ambassadors in the African states approached me after my talk and hastened to thank me for my outspokenness. "At last, somebody has told the truth," they said. "We knew all along that this socialist orientation was a fraud and a failure but, of course, in our official reports things just had to look quite different."

Inevitably, reappraisal of our long-standing line in the Middle East was due to come. More and more, scholars and journalists began questioning the very foundations of our policy in the Arab-Israeli conflict. Doubts were expressed as to the wisdom of our 1967 decision to break off diplomatic relations with Israel. A new approach was shaping up with regard to the Camp David Accords.

It is well known that opposition to Camp David and bitter denunciation of Egyptian President Anwar Sadat's political line were the cornerstones of Soviet policy in the Middle East in the 1980s.[2] Much later, in the days of perestroika, I ventured an opinion that it was high time Egypt was readmitted into the family of Arab states. Immediately, a prominent party official with an Arabist background retorted: "Well, and how about the slogan, 'Bury Camp David'?" In spite of the utter absurdity of this position, the official stand on Camp David remained steadfast during the first perestroika years. But this, too, began to change as glasnost gained strength.

Some authors, Western as well as Russian, seemed to underestimate the role of the ideological factor and, correspondingly, of glasnost in the demise of Communist rule. As the ideological barriers were crumbling, suddenly it became possible to question the Soviet past as a whole. When Gorbachev finally, albeit reluctantly, gave the green light to de-Stalinization, little did he think that very soon it would turn into de-Leninization and de-bolshevization. Then, an end to the cold war and to the confrontation era was announced. Almost overnight, the United States ceased to be an enemy; the very word "imperialism" disappeared from the newspapers. The party apparatus suddenly realized that the bottom line was not there anymore, the cornerstone fell out, the raison d'être of the system having vanished. This partly explains why the resistance to the overthrow of the Communist regime in the aftermath of the August coup was so feeble: The heart was no longer there; the ideological commitment was gone.

Even before the final collapse, there was a sea change in foreign policy. Anti-imperialism as a guideline disappeared; promoting socialism worldwide became a futile task. Diplomatic relations with Israel had to be restored. De-ideologization meant that our relations with the Arab world were no longer dictated by the commitment to leftist Arab regimes and the need to deny the United States the dominant role in the area. Since the United States was not an enemy anymore, why bother about Israel as an enemy foothold?

When the Gulf crisis erupted with the Iraqi invasion of Kuwait, the Soviet Union for the first time sided with the United States in a confrontation with a Third World country—and a socialist-oriented country at that. Some took it very hard. When I spoke at the Academy of the Warsaw Treaty Organization in Moscow at the height of the crisis, I bluntly told my audience that, in my opinion, Saddam Hussein was a gangster and a butcher. There was an uproar, angry exclamations, and some colonels even walked out. These were the kind of people who had arrived by the hundreds to attend the recent reception at the Iraqi Embassy in Moscow to celebrate the 1958 Iraqi revolution. For them, Saddam is a hero, an anti-American, anti-Jewish, anti-democratic, tough, no-nonsense leader. In short, he is their kind of man.

Faced by strong opposition to his allegedly pro-US policy, Gorbachev tried, for the last time, to play a relatively autonomous role. Middle East adviser Yevgeny Primakov was sent to Baghdad to lobby for a compromise solution. Had he succeeded, it would have been a serious boost to Gorbachev's prestige. First, it would have placated the Russian "patriots" unhappy with what they perceived as Gorbachev's subservience to Bush. Second, it could have assuaged the Arabs, who by that time were mad at Gorbachev over the issue of Jewish immigration to Israel. Soviet ambassadors in Arab capitals were reporting to the Kremlin that Soviet prestige in the Arab world was at an all-time low. Arabs felt that Gorbachev (much loved by Bush) could, if he wished, have persuaded the US president to channel the bulk of the Soviet Jews to the United States rather than to Israel. If Gorbachev was not even trying to do this, it could only mean that he did not care about Arabs at all.

Gorbachev, of course, knew that he could not do any such thing. The only way to restore, if only partially, Soviet prestige in the Arab world was to save Iraq from imminent disaster. But Primakov's mission was doomed from the beginning. Later Primakov told me that, given three more days, he would have persuaded Tariq 'Aziz and thus Saddam Hussein to make concessions that would have prevented the US ground offensive. The question arises: Just who did Primakov think he was that the US president would give him three days when everything was already decided and D-Day had already been fixed?

At the subsequent Madrid conference the Soviet Union tried to posture as an independent actor, but nobody took it seriously; the USSR was no longer a superpower. Paradoxically, it was Bush who tried to place the Soviet Union on a superpower basis for the last time. In fact, his "new world order" envisaged a situation in which both superpowers were to continue playing a dominant role in world affairs, but in cooperation and not in confrontation. Gorbachev would undoubtedly have gone along with that, but it was too late. The hands on the clock were nearing midnight.

POST-COMMUNIST RUSSIA AND THE MIDDLE EAST

Currently Moscow has little foreign policy to speak of. The main trend is to maintain good relations with the West, although the rising tide of Russian nationalism can already be seen as threatening the seemingly well-established pattern. Anti-Western and anti-American backlash in particular is evident in Russian public opinion.

In the foreseeable future, only the Middle East offers Russia the chance to play a role in world affairs. Europe is lost to Russian influence, cut off as it is by Poland and Ukraine both geographically and politically. Even if it were not so, the united Germany effectively prevents Russia from playing any major role in European affairs. The Balkans are a powder keg. In the Far East and Southeast Asia more powerful players are flexing their muscles: Japan, China, the United States. Tropical Africa and Latin America are largely irrelevant to Moscow at this point. The only region left is the Middle East.

In that region Russia has commitments, political and military investments, allies, and leverage of sorts. As a successor state to the Soviet Union, Russia is cochair, along with the United States, of the Geneva Conference. Like the United States, Russia can now wield some influence, although to a far lesser degree, in both the Arab world and in Israel. Russian diplomats can sit at international conferences on the Middle East, pretending to be on equal footing with the United States. Thus, Russia can be perceived (by the Russians themselves, of course, and in Russian public opinion) as not having been pushed out of the picture altogether in world affairs.

Perception is what matters, not substance. As former US Speaker of the House Tip O'Neill once said, all politics is local. For any government in Moscow, it is vital to be seen by the people as not neglecting Russian national interests abroad, as pursuing an independent foreign policy worthy of a great power. The Russians like to think of their country as a great power, no longer as a superpower. An honorable role in the Middle East will be good for their self-esteem. And it is in the Middle East alone that Russia has a tradition of diplomatic success. The Middle East is where its foreign policy future lies.

Notes

1. Information for this point was obtained in conversations the author conducted with Alexander Yakovlev, a top adviser for Gorbachev.

2. Probably the best scholarly expression of Soviet anger and frustration is Yevgeny Primakov's book on Sadat, entitled *Story of Betrayal.*

CHAPTER 10

THE SUPERPOWERS AND THE COLD WAR IN THE MIDDLE EAST

Rashid Khalidi

I

Precisely when the cold war began is subject to some dispute.[1] Winston Churchill's March 5, 1946, speech at Westminster College in Fulton, Missouri, declaring that "from Stettin in the Baltic to Trieste in the Adriatic an *iron curtain* has descended across the Continent," is often seen as indicating that the cold war was already under way by that point.[2] We now know that even earlier, at the height of the colossal joint effort against Nazi Germany during World War II, the cold war rivalry was already presaged by deep suspicions among the wartime allies. This was especially the case with those old adversaries, Churchill and Stalin, whose antagonism to each other's system was of very long standing.[3] From a very early stage in the cold war, the rivalry of the Soviets and the Western powers was notable in the Middle East and the adjacent regions south of the Union of Soviet Socialist Republics (USSR), whence Britain had launched its repeated interventions to crush the Bolshevik regime during the four-year Russian civil war after the 1917 revolution. It is unlikely that either Churchill or Stalin, who were central figures in this earliest phase of the East-West rivalry, ever fully forgot the impact of this deadly struggle. Churchill's entire career shows that he was always profoundly concerned about communism in the Middle East, while Stalin's long-standing obsession with Britain as an imperialist power in the Middle East at times seemed to eclipse his concerns about the growing US role there. American policymakers, less experienced internationally than their British counterparts, often tended to be influenced by the latter's concerns about the spread of communism in the Middle East.

Not surprisingly, therefore, the first non-European confrontations between the USSR and the United States and its allies transpired in the Middle East. Much historical work has been done in recent years on the origins of the cold war.[4] However, there has been relatively little new research about the central role of this great international rivalry in a number of regional conflicts.[5] This is as true of the Middle East as it is of other areas that felt the impact of the cold war rivalry from the 1940s until the 1990s.[6] These regions have been haunted since then by the "ghosts" of the cold war. The most striking example is the blowback from US involvement in the Afghan war against the Soviet occupation of that country in the 1980s.[7]

Immediately after its Soviet rival disappeared in 1990–1991, the United States confidently asserted its unrivaled power in the Middle East by leading a coalition against Iraq's invasion of Kuwait in the first Gulf War, and in convening the 1991 Madrid Arab-Israeli Peace Conference. The former was the first American land war in Asia since Vietnam. Madrid constituted the only serious and sustained American (or international) effort in over half a century at a comprehensive resolution of the Arab-Israeli conflict. In light of these apparently radical departures in American Middle Eastern policy immediately after the collapse of the Soviet Union, it would be useful to revise our understanding of the cold war as simply a prolegomena to the current era of unfettered American dominance over the region. Such a revision would help us to answer a number of questions: Was the United States previously as constrained by the presence of its Soviet rival as sometimes seemed to be the case—and as these two novel departures immediately after the demise of the USSR seemed to indicate? Alternatively, was America in fact more dominant in the Middle East throughout the cold war era than may have been evident at the time?

These are important questions, since for the United States the cold war was the ostensible reason for a vastly expanded American post–World War II global presence. Similarly, the perceived Soviet threat was the pretext for the establishment of US military bases spanning the globe and for the development of a vastly enhanced American international intelligence, economic, and diplomatic profile compared to America's relatively modest world role before December 7, 1941. In many regions, this expansion of America's global reach meant that the wartime arrival of US troops—in the case of the Middle East this occurred in North Africa and Iran in 1942—was not followed after the end of the war by their disappearance back over the horizon. These initial wartime deployments of American forces, and the later establishment and postwar maintenance of major US air bases at Dhahran in Saudi Arabia, Libya, Morocco, and Turkey, marked the beginning of an ongoing US military presence in different locales that continues to this day. These early wartime and postwar moves constituted the beginning of an American role as *the* major Middle Eastern power, a reality that was masked for a time by the power and regional proximity of the USSR.

Although overshadowed at times by other cold war arenas, the Middle East was not just a secondary region where the United States and the USSR contended. Already during World War II, the crucial strategic importance of the Middle East had been amply demonstrated in terms of its central geographic location on the southern flank of Europe astride vital sea and air lanes and the vast energy reserves it was known to contain. The region's importance in terms of strategy and oil was further established during the cold war. This importance has been demonstrated again since the cold war ended, as evidenced by a series of major recent American initiatives in the region, including the 1991 Gulf War, the 1991–1993 Madrid-Oslo Middle East peace process, the Iraq sanctions regime from 1991 until 2003, and the invasion of that country in 2003 and its subsequent occupation. These initiatives in the Middle East have been among the most dramatic actions taken by the United States in the world arena since the end of the cold war.

<h2 style="text-align:center">II</h2>

It is useful to start with the meeting between President Franklin D. Roosevelt and Saudi King 'Abd al-'Aziz Ibn Sa'ud in Egypt on February 12, 1945. Roosevelt, infirm and only two months away from his death, was on his way home from the Yalta conference. Why did the weary president of the most powerful country on earth spend the better part of a day meeting with this apparently minor Middle Eastern potentate? The answer is that this meeting was arranged because of Saudi Arabia's importance in the eyes of those who were already planning for the postwar era. The account of Colonel William Eddy, the head of the American legation at Jedda who organized and translated at the meeting, provides much valuable detail.[8] We know that by this point the vast extent of Saudi oil reserves was familiar to American strategic planners and oil executives.[9] Saudi oil had just begun flowing to support the Allied war effort, which was simultaneously strangling both German and Japanese oil supplies, measurably shortening the war. Finally, in 1945 the United States was already planning to acquire a major air base at Dhahran, which it continued using until 1962 and used again for a decade starting with the 1991 Gulf War.

The United States and Britain had by this stage launched invasions of Sicily, Italy, and southern France from bases in the Middle East, and were supplying massive quantities of lend-lease equipment to the Soviet Union across Iran, which was occupied by British, Soviet, and American troops. Saudi Arabia was only one link in this vast wartime chain, which stretched right around the globe, but the kingdom had one crucial characteristic, besides its strategic position and its possession of vast reservoirs of petrochemicals beneath its soil: It was one of only two independent states in this crucial Middle Eastern region that had never been occupied by the troops of European colonial powers and had no foreign bases on its soil. Moreover, Ibn Sa'ud had twelve years earlier signed an exclusive agreement for the exploration and exploitation of its oil reserves with an American consortium of companies that became the Arabian-American Oil Company, ARAMCO. This consortium had thereby secured the first major exclusive American oil concession in the Middle East, heretofore an exclusive British preserve.

President Roosevelt was thus meeting with the absolute ruler of a nation with something unique to offer the United States: an alliance with a Middle Eastern power that was not already part of another great power's sphere of influence. This gave American access to oil and bases in the kingdom even more meaning. Moreover, importantly for the coming postwar era, Saudi Arabia's ruler was staunchly anticommunist, and he did not have to worry about a large body of nationalist public opinion, as did governments in other major Middle Eastern countries like Egypt, Iraq, Syria, and Iran, where large urban populations, organized into political parties, enjoying slowly growing literacy and attached to a culture of newspapers and books, were deeply anticolonial and suspicious of foreign bases and foreign concessions.

Nevertheless, because of his concern about his standing both in the Arab world and with public opinion in his kingdom, however rudimentary it may have been, the Saudi king felt unable to go along with the request of his American interlocutor that all the Jewish survivors of the Nazi holocaust be settled in Palestine. He stressed that happy though he was to cooperate with the United States, he insisted on the importance of one issue—Palestine—about which he said: "What injury have Arabs done to the Jews of Europe?"[10] In response, in April 1945, just before Roosevelt died, the president sent a letter to Ibn Sa'ud confirming what he told him in response to the concerns over Palestine he had expressed during their meeting: that the United States would consult with both Arabs and Jews before acting in Palestine, where it would never act against Arab interests.[11]

Roosevelt's successor, Harry Truman, was to deny initially that the United States had ever made such commitments.[12] Although he was later provided with Roosevelt's April 1945 letter by the State Department, in the Palestine policy Truman crafted over the next few years he proceeded to violate both of his predecessor's commitments—to consult with both Arabs and Jews before taking action over Palestine and to do nothing there that would harm the Arabs. Four American diplomats based in the Middle East who had been brought back to Washington in October 1946 to brief Truman were left cooling their heels for over a month because the president finally told them, his advisers "felt that it would be impolitic to see his Ministers to Arab countries, no matter how briefly, prior to the November Congressional elections." It was to this group that Truman uttered the infamous words: "I'm sorry, gentlemen, but I have to answer to hundreds of thousands who are anxious for the success of Zionism; I do not have hundreds of thousands of Arabs among my constituents."[13] Not surprisingly in light of these views, starting with Truman's presidency, the issue of Palestine became a continuing irritant to the Saudi monarchy in its dealings with Washington. It remains so to the present day. It has, however, been an irritant that most Saudi and other Arab leaders came to accept as the price of doing business with the indispensable power of the United States.

By giving an oil concession to an American consortium in 1933, the Saudi monarch had already managed to assert his independence of Great Britain's heretofore exclusive influence over his kingdom, which the king had long resented bitterly.[14] Whether farsighted, fortunate, or both, between 1933 and his meeting with Roosevelt, Ibn Sa'ud managed to link his dynasty firmly to the growing power of the United States, well before many other world statesmen realized the future superpower's full potential. In the end, this crucial connection was to prove more important to him and to his five sons who have succeeded him as kings since 1953 than were their concerns about Palestine.

Washington early on perceived Saudi Arabia's economic and strategic value to postwar planning. Beyond this, it soon turned out to have the world's largest proven oil reserves. Oil produced by ARAMCO was crucial to Europe's postwar recovery, to keeping oil prices extremely low for several decades after World War II, and to increasing the profits of the big American oil companies that dominated the world oil market. Furthermore, Saudi Arabia was one of the first countries in the Middle East where the United States was free to establish bases without having to take permission from, or incur the jealousy of, the traditional powers that dominated the region—Britain and France.[15] The Dhahran air base was particularly useful to American global airlift capabilities and for rescue, reconnaissance, and combat aircraft, as a link in the chain of bases strategically located along the Soviet southern frontiers. This was particularly the case in the early years of the cold war, when American strategic bombers such as the B-29 had a limited range.[16] Feeling pressure from Arab nationalist sentiment and the anticolonial propaganda of the Egyptian regime, which intensified in the late 1950s, the Saudi government requested termination of the basing arrangement in 1961, and the US Air Force ceased to base units there the subsequent year, although American contract personnel continued to run the airfield for the Saudi government. The US Air Force ceased to need the base in the early 1960s when the development of longer-range weapons systems made it possible to give up several American bases, including Dhahran and later Wheelus Field in Libya.

It was not until after the advent of a completely different post–cold war American strategy, one involving a large-scale, long-term, multicountry American military presence in the Middle East, that starting in 1991 US forces were once again based at Dhahran, as well as in Kuwait, Bahrain, Oman, Qatar, and elsewhere in the region. This new strategy came after the demise of the USSR removed any existential nuclear danger to the United States itself. However, these newly arrived American forces in the Middle East were not directed against "international communism" and its proxies, as was the case from the mid-1940s through the early 1970s, but rather against local Middle Eastern actors. These were clearly entirely different purposes than those for which US bases in this region were first envisioned.

III

As the cold war penetrated the Middle East and as the United States gradually replaced Britain and France as the dominant Western power in the region, the US-Saudi connection continued to be important. It was cemented in 1957 by the adherence to the Eisenhower Doctrine of the new Saudi monarch, King Sa'ud.[17] This follow-up to the Truman Doctrine—which ten years earlier had marked the first formal American recognition that the cold war had extended to the Middle East—was enunciated by President Dwight D. Eisenhower before a joint session of Congress in January 1957. In it Eisenhower proclaimed American support for any Middle Eastern government targeted by "overt armed aggression from any nation controlled by International Communism."[18] King Sa'ud's public adhesion to the American camp in the Middle East through his acceptance of this doctrine was a major coup for the United States. American policy thereby separated Saudi Arabia from Egypt, its erstwhile ally in inter-Arab politics, and a vocal advocate of nonalignment, even as the Egyptian regime of Gamal 'Abd al-Nasser gradually moved closer to the Soviet Union.

For the next decade, Saudi Arabia and Egypt came to constitute the main poles of two opposed camps within the Arab world, which engaged in what Malcolm Kerr described as the "Arab cold war."[19] These camps in turn came to be closely aligned with the United States and the Soviet Union. By this process, a regional cleavage with its own logic and specificity was subsumed into the great cold war divide. This grafting of the cold war between the United States and the Soviet Union onto preexisting Middle Eastern rivalries and conflicts significantly exacerbated those conflicts in many cases. At the same time, the involvement of the Americans and the Soviets in internecine local quarrels provided opportunities for Middle Eastern clients to extract support from their superpower patrons, which the latter sometimes were obliged to extend against the better judgment of key policymakers.[20]

Saudi Arabia's value to the United States was soon to emerge in yet another sphere: the ideological arena. One of the key convergences of the cold war era in the Middle East was that between the Soviet Union and leftist and Arab nationalist movements in their various forms, including Nasserism, the Ba'th Party, multiple varieties of Arab socialism, the different Arab communist parties, and other radical parties and groups. Although this Soviet-Arab coalition seemed united by anticolonialism, a commitment to state-led development, contempt for "bourgeois democracy," and some other shared values, it was in fact a profoundly uneasy agglomeration of forces. There were deep divergences and suspicions. There were also sometimes open conflicts between its disparate component parts and between many of these parties and the various Arab regimes on the one hand and the Soviet Union on the other. Thus, almost immediately after the Iraqi revolution of 1958, the communist party in Iraq found itself at odds with the Nasserists, Ba'thists, and other Arab nationalists. This rapidly developed into a lasting conflict that only became more bitter and sanguinary as time went on. The Egyptian regime and the Soviets eventually were obliged to take sides with their respective squabbling Iraqi protégés, while keeping their bilateral relations as normal as possible.[21] Notwithstanding these problems, which eventually emerged between would-be allies, for a time, in the mid-1950s through the early 1970s, this grouping of Arab leftists and nationalists appeared to be a formidable coalition, particularly when aligned with a growing number of nationalist Arab regimes and with the USSR. Indeed, in the context of the "Arab cold war," this coalition seemed to be a winning one, as it claimed to represent the future in the battle against the backwardness of the traditional monarchies and conservative regimes associated with the United States.

This radical wave seemed to place the United States and its allies in a highly unfavorable position. To this apparently unbalanced situation, Saudi Arabia brought the powerful ideological weapon of Islam. This was something the Saudis were uniquely positioned to do, given the centuries-old alliance between the royal family and the rigidly orthodox Wahhabi religious establishment and given the kingdom's special place as the location of two of the three most holy places in Islam—Mecca and Medina. Particularly after the competent, pious, and ascetic King Faisal took over from his older brother Sa'ud in 1962, Saudi Arabia focused more intensively on Islam as the backbone of its resistance to the self-proclaimed "progressive" Arab regimes. It sponsored various pan-Islamic entities as a counterweight to the pan-Arab bodies and parties dominated by Egypt. It spent its oil wealth liberally on spreading the kingdom's puritanical and dogmatic Wahhabi form of Islam and on other forms of religious propaganda all over the world. Finally, Saudi Arabia gave refuge to Islamist political activists persecuted by secular Arab nationalist regimes in Egypt, Syria, Iraq, and elsewhere. These included members of the outlawed Muslim Brotherhood, some of whom had already been spotted by Western intelligence agencies as potentially useful proxies in the cold war struggle with the radical Arab protégés of the Soviet Union.

Saudi Arabia's use of Islam as an ideological tool was thus a major addition to the arsenal of the United States and it allies among the conservative forces in the Arab and Islamic worlds, which in the mid-1960s seemed largely on the defensive in the face of the Soviet-backed "progressive" Arab regimes. This tool proved so useful that it eventually became an important part of the American ideological arsenal in the cold war, used by the US intelligence services not only in the Arab countries but also in Pakistan and South Asia, Southeast Asia, Soviet Central Asia, and other parts of the Islamic world. Surprising though it may seem today, given the demonization of radical, militant political Islam in American public discourse, for decades the United States was in some respects *the* major patron of earlier incarnations of just these extreme trends, for reasons linked to the perceived need to use any and all means to wage the cold war.[22]

There was of course a price attached to this cold war–driven approach, not least in terms of the ideals and principles which Americans like to believe their foreign policy is based on. While the Soviet Union aligned itself with authoritarian nationalist regimes, American policy backed absolute monarchies in Saudi Arabia, Iran, and the Arab Gulf states (with the exception of Kuwait) and other nondemocratic, authoritarian regimes in Jordan, Tunisia, Morocco, Pakistan, and elsewhere from the late 1940s until the 1970s as part of this same cold war strategy. In so doing, the United States laid little or no stress on promoting democracy, constitutionalism, or human rights in the Middle East. Indeed, the United States had previously helped to subvert Middle Eastern democracies by actions such as supporting the Husni Zaim coup against the constitutionally elected President Shukri al-Quwwatly in Syria in 1949, organizing with Britain the overthrow of Iran's democratically chosen prime minister Muhammad Mussadiq in 1953 and imposing an autocratic regime under Mohamed Reza Shah, and providing Lebanese President Camille Chamoun with the funds to bribe his way to achieving a parliamentary majority in the 1957 elections.[23] In some cases when the United States subverted democracy in the Middle East, Islam served as a screen or an ideological adjunct, in Iran, for example, where some elements of the religious establishment became part of the American-supported anti-Mussadiq coalition in 1953. This approach was welcome to the absolutist, antidemocratic elites of the conservative states with which the United States was aligned.

The long-standing inattention of American policymakers to the promotion of democracy and human rights in the Middle East, as well as their cold war sponsorship of radical Islamic groups and trends, acquire significance in light of more recent conflict with militant, radical Islamic political movements. Some of these groups, like the Taliban and al-Qa'ida, are lineal descendants of ones the United States was allied with for decades. The cold war alliance between the United States and these Islamic movements produced bitter fruit long after the cold war was over. However, this alliance with a politicized, militant, and often extreme form of Islam was a direct function of American policy in the Middle East and beyond during much of the cold war.

This ideological tool was crucial in rallying conservative forces in the Middle East and beyond at the height of the civil war in Yemen from 1962 to 1967. Egyptian troops and air power backed the pro-Nasserist Yemeni Republicans, and Saudi Arabia and its conservative regional allies supported the royalists financially and militarily in a desperate seesaw struggle on the southwestern borders of the Saudi kingdom. Behind both sides in this conflict stood their superpower patrons, the United States and the Soviet Union. The banner of Islam and American backing became the cement that brought together a disparate coalition throughout the Arabian Peninsula and the Gulf. This coalition included Yemeni royalist and tribal forces, the governments of Jordan and Oman, which faced their own radical domestic oppositions, and farther afield the governments of Pakistan and Iran under the shah. Included as well in this American-led coalition were elements of the underground Muslim Brotherhood in Egypt, Syria, and Iraq. As part of this sub rosa regional conflict, while Saudi Arabia supported its allies in the Yemeni civil war with weapons and money, Jordan and Iran sent military advisers and some military units to the neighboring Dhofar region of Oman to fight against a radical Marxist guerrilla movement that opposed the sultan's regime and the British advisers who propped it up, while British troops fought to hang on to Aden and South Yemen against a tenacious insurgency.[24] On the other side, radical groups and Arab nationalist regimes, such as those of Egypt, Algeria, and Iraq, as well as the Soviet Union, gave extensive military support to the Yemeni Republicans, the Popular Front for the Liberation of Oman and the Arabian Gulf fighting in Dhofar, and the South Yemeni insurgents.

Since forces aligned with the United States claimed to defend the Middle East against atheistic communism and its secular Arab nationalist allies, a particular form of militant political Islam thus provided an ideological banner and a critical rallying point. The instrumental employment of radical Islamism as a tool of policy continued to provide a lasting focus for American, Saudi, and Pakistani regional policies, reaching its apogee during the Afghan war against the Soviet occupation from 1979 to 1988, and eventually spawning the Taliban and al-Qa'ida. This was long after the high tide of radical Arab nationalism had ebbed in the wake of the crushing defeat inflicted by Israel in June 1967 on Egypt and Syria, and after Egypt and other Arab countries had ended their alignment with the Soviet Union. However, the monster spawned in the waning days of the cold war continued to thrive long after it had ended.

IV

The events of the "Arab cold war" just described were only one example of the many ways in which the larger American-Soviet cold war had a major impact on the Middle East. The alignment of each of the superpowers with one or another side of the Arab-Israeli conflict was another. Starting in the 1960s and until the end of the cold war in 1991, the United States backed Israel, while the Soviet Union supported most of the Arab states engaged in the conflict. This fixed alignment did not, however, go back to the earliest phase of the Arab-Israeli conflict, the Palestine war of 1947–1949. During that crucial formative period, both the United States and the USSR were ranged on the same side: They both voted in the UN General Assembly in 1947 to partition Palestine in a way that gave the Jewish minority 55 percent of the country. Both raced to recognize the independence of the new Jewish state that resulted from that decision on May 15, 1948, and both surreptitiously helped to arm Israel during the war that ensued. Soviet arms, delivered through Czechoslovakia in the summer of 1948, were crucial to Israel's ultimate military victory.

The main reason for the United States taking the position it did, against the professional advice of the State Department and the Pentagon, was simple, and was summed up in President Truman's words quoted earlier regarding the composition of his constituents.[25] The Soviet position, which shifted from anti-Zionism to support of the creation of Israel in a few short months, owed a great deal to Stalin's obsessive concern about Britain's power in the Middle East, which he did not seem to realize was waning rapidly; his suspicions of what he saw as British Arab clients like Transjordan, Iraq, and Egypt; and his mistaken belief that a Jewish state might align itself with the USSR.[26]

Israel and the Soviet Union soon drifted apart, with Israel moving closer to the United States and the Soviet Union eventually developing closer relations with Arab countries that sought to free themselves from direct and indirect control by the old European colonial powers. Thereafter, Britain and France became the main arms suppliers to Israel, which used their weapons to win its next two wars against

Arab states, the Suez war against Egypt, which Israel fought in alliance with the British and French in 1956, and the war of June 1967 against Egypt, Syria, and Jordan. Crucially, France also provided Israel with the wherewithal to produce nuclear weapons, which it did surreptitiously starting in the mid-1950s.[27]

The tripartite Anglo-French-Israeli invasion of Egypt in 1956 marked another moment when the United States and the USSR found themselves on the same side, in opposing the aggression of the two old colonial powers and their Israeli ally against Egypt. This came at one of the high points of the cold war, when Soviet forces were engaged in bloodily suppressing the Hungarian uprising, and the United States and the Western powers were loudly decrying Soviet brutality. Over Suez, however, the two superpowers both opposed the tripartite attack on Egypt, albeit—as in 1948—for different reasons. The Soviets were happy to point to Western imperialist aggression while they put down an uprising in their own imperial backyard. Meanwhile, President Eisenhower was furious at Britain and France for acting without consultation, for doing so with overtly neocolonial motives, and for distracting world public opinion from Soviet behavior in Eastern Europe. The subtext of American displeasure was that Britain and France did not know their place in the new world of the cold war, where there were only two superpowers, and Washington made all important decisions on the Western side.[28]

The Suez war was the last time until the end of the cold war that the superpowers found themselves on the same side of the Arab-Israeli conflict. Soon the Arab cold war began, the Eisenhower administration's limited sympathy for the Egyptian regime of Gamal 'Abd al-Nasser was exhausted, and the American-Soviet rivalry ratcheted up in the Middle East. The Eisenhower Doctrine resulted from this escalation. It was directed not just at the Soviet Union but at Arab states with which the USSR was aligned, such as Egypt, which in the Manichean vision of Secretary of State John Foster Dulles were "controlled by International Communism."[29] The Soviet Union had been supplying Egypt with arms since 1955 (the original arms deal here too was made via Czechoslovakia) and soon was supplying other Arab countries as well. Thereafter the USSR provided aid for the construction of Egypt's Aswan Dam, after the United States reneged on its commitment to do so. The United States was arming Saudi Arabia, Iran, and other allies, and by the 1960s had begun to supply Israel with weapons, initially surreptitiously via West Germany. This arms supply relationship became more overt in the subsequent administrations of John F. Kennedy and Lyndon B. Johnson, as the former sent Hawk antiaircraft missiles and the latter A-4 Skyhawk attack bombers to Israel.

The 1967 war, however, marked the full alignment of the United States with Israel and the beginning of Israel's heavy reliance on American weapons systems, starting with the top-of-the-line F-4 Phantom fighter-bombers supplied by the Johnson and Nixon administrations. The massive dependence of Israel on billions of dollars annually in US military and economic aid came a few years later, following the 1973 war. By this time, the United States had come to see Israel as its most valuable ally in the Middle East region in the global struggle with the USSR and its proxies. It fitted perfectly into the Nixon administration's strategy of Vietnamization—finding local proxies to serve US interests—and it was seen as more valuable even than Iran under the shah, as was shown by American willingness to deliver to Israel weapons that neither Iran nor NATO allies received.

Policymakers in the Johnson and Nixon administrations faced a scenario in which they saw the USSR and China as pinning the United States down in Southeast Asia at little cost to themselves through what they myopically perceived as their Vietnamese proxies. They looked to Israel to even the score against the Soviet Union's proxies, Egypt and Syria, at little direct cost to the United States. The Soviets in turn could not allow themselves to be left behind. They upped the ante further after the 1967 war by writing off Egypt and Syria's debts for military equipment destroyed or captured by Israel during the war, and by delivering massive amounts of new arms, notably surface-to-air missiles, including the SAM-2, SAM-3, and the new SAM-6. The two superpowers raised the stakes during the 1968–1970 war of attrition along the Suez Canal, when the Egyptians pushed their air defenses to the edge of the Suez Canal, making possible a crossing of this great antitank barrier a few years later. During this fierce phase of the Arab-Israeli wars, Soviets advising Egyptian air defense crews directly engaged in combat, and the most advanced antiaircraft missiles and radar were sent to Egypt. Naturally, the United States countered with deliveries of top-of-the-line military equipment to Israel.[30]

Finally, in the 1973 war, Nixon and Secretary of State Henry Kissinger ordered the airlift of massive quantities of military equipment to Israel when its stocks were in danger of running out. This escalatory sequence from 1967 until 1973 was driven, incidentally, as much by the clients on both sides as by the competition between their superpower patrons, as Israel refused to negotiate seriously with Egypt in spite of American remonstrance, and the Egyptians insisted on a military option in spite of the deep reluctance of the Soviet military.[31] Throughout this six-year period, both superpowers sent their respective allies advanced weaponry and became more directly committed themselves. In the final stages of the 1973 war, the United States placed its armed forces worldwide on a general nuclear alert, Def-Con 3, in response to reports that several Soviet paratroop divisions had been placed on alert and that the USSR was shipping nuclear warheads to its forces in the Mediterranean.[32] The Soviets were reacting to Israel's refusal to obey a UN-mandated cease-fire, as its troops continued to roll toward Cairo after crossing the Suez Canal. In a message to Nixon, Soviet Communist Party general secretary Leonid Brezhnev demanded a joint superpower intervention to end the war, failing which the Soviets threatened to intervene unilaterally. They were apparently on the point of doing so when Kissinger raised the ante by ordering a nuclear alert and belatedly calling a halt to the Israeli advance. Though this event has received less attention than the Cuban missile crisis a decade earlier, here again the superpowers had seemingly been brought to the brink of a nuclear confrontation, this time by their proxy competition in the Arab-Israeli arena.

By this point, the cold war rivalry as played out through the Arab-Israeli conflict had taken on a dynamic of its own. This can be seen in the behavior of Richard

Nixon and Henry Kissinger and in the actions of their Soviet opposite numbers. Nixon and Kissinger's objective was to expel the Soviets from Egypt and to win that country over to the side of the United States. This objective incidentally fitted in perfectly with the aims of Egyptian President Anwar al-Sadat, who was eager, together with his military high command, to get out from under the Soviet thumb and receive the American support he eventually did win. The Soviets' aim was to retain their foothold in the region at all costs. Much of their large military presence in Egypt by this point—over 20,000 "advisers"—was in fact involved in maintaining a naval base under exclusive Soviet control that was used to keep track of the movements of US submarines carrying submarine-launched ballistic missiles (SLBM) in the Mediterranean.

For both superpowers, these and other cold war aims were far more important than the ups and downs of the Arab-Israeli conflict itself or peace between Arabs and Israelis.[33] Partly in consequence of the single-minded concentration of both of the superpowers on besting each other, that conflict came no closer to final resolution for the duration of the cold war. There were a number of efforts toward such a resolution, most of them desultory: a brief single session of a peace conference at Geneva in 1973; three disengagement agreements negotiated by Henry Kissinger, two between Egypt and Israel and one between Syria and Israel; the American-Soviet joint communiqué of 1977 calling for a comprehensive Middle East peace settlement to be negotiated at a multilateral peace conference; and the 1979 Egyptian-Israeli peace treaty that emerged after President Jimmy Carter's 1978 mediation at Camp David. Yet in spite of these initiatives, no resolution of the conflict was consummated. Achieving advantages in their rivalry with one another ultimately was far more important to the superpowers than was peace in the Middle East, which consequently got relatively low priority in their efforts in the region.

V

There are many other instances of how the overarching cold war rivalry distorted outcomes in the Middle East. Decisions on economic development, domestic policies, the balance of forces between political parties, and majority-minority relations within states in the region were affected by the machinations of the Soviets and the Americans in their unceasing rivalry with one another. To take one case, consider the tragic example of how the Kurds in Iran, Iraq, and Turkey became pawns in regional rivalries that came to be subsumed in the confrontation between the superpowers. The episodes of this ill-starred story began with the proclamation of the Kurdish Mahabad Republic in January 1946, when Soviet troops were still occupying northern Iran, including Iranian Kurdistan. This initiative marked the establishment of the first autonomous Kurdish entity, one that Stalin initially supported but soon abandoned.[34] One of the key leaders of the Mahabad Republic, its defense minister, the Iraqi Kurdish leader Mullah Mustafa Barzani, escaped and ended up in the Soviet Union. He returned in 1958 to his native Iraq, where his

Kurdish Democratic Party launched a series of revolts against different governments in Baghdad, including a major uprising with Iranian, American, and Israeli support against the Ba'th regime in 1974–1975. This ended with the betrayal of the Kurds in the 1975 Algiers agreement between Iran and Iraq with the collusion of Henry Kissinger. The United States had blessed the Iran-Iraq accord, which entailed the United States and Iran abandoning their support for the ongoing Kurdish revolt against the Iraqi regime that these two powers had helped instigate. Thereafter Kissinger told an appalled aide: "Covert action should not be confused with missionary work."[35]

The Iraqi regime slaughtered, with gas and other means, thousands of Kurdish villagers in the course of the Iran-Iraq war of 1979–1988, during which the superpowers played both sides of the street in their tireless efforts to gain advantage over each other. Thus the United States and its allies encouraged the Iraqi Ba'thist regime to go to war with the Islamic revolutionary government in Iran, supplying Iraq with the means to engage in gas warfare against Iran (and also its own Kurdish population), while the Reagan administration later surreptitiously contacted Iran as part of the illegal Iran-Contra conspiracy, delivering to it much-needed parts for Hawk SAM missiles. The Soviets, meanwhile, were no less callous and self-serving, supplying arms to the Iraqi forces while also selling armored vehicles and missiles to the Iranians. In all of this, the Kurds were left to their fate by the two superpowers, which cynically exploited them against what they perceived as each other's regional proxies, and then just as cynically dropped them when they were no longer of any use. This recurring trope in Kurdish history, of adoption and then abandonment by great power protectors, which had its precedent in similar behavior by the British at the end of World War I,[36] risks being repeated once again in northern Iraq, whenever the overextended United States is finally obliged to retreat from that distant, landlocked region.

Even as the Iran-Iraq war, which devastated the Kurds as well as both warring countries, was starting, the Soviet Union made an ultimately fatal decision to invade Afghanistan to prop up a crumbling pro-Soviet regime. In so doing, it sent the Red Army across a cold war line that had not been crossed since the end of World War II, and set off alarm bells all over the Western world. The Carter administration responded vigorously by supplying support to anti-Soviet Afghan guerrillas, the mujahidin, in a bid to bleed Soviet forces. Carter was succeeded in the White House by the much more assertive Reagan administration, which saw in Afghanistan an opportunity to do much greater harm to the Soviet Union. Indeed, Afghanistan opened for the Reagan team the long-sought prospect of bringing down the entire "Evil Empire." Reagan's administration included a number of the most vigorous proponents of the aggressive prosecution of the cold war since the mid-1950s. In some senses they were more aggressive than even Dulles had been: For all his messianic anticommunist bluster, Eisenhower's secretary of state had been committed to the cold war doctrine of containment propounded by the pragmatic George Kennan.[37] By contrast, many of the neoconservatives in the Reagan administration favored a radical strategy of "rolling back" communism, a belligerent approach that had never become established doctrine in Washington, even at the height of the cold war. With the most viscerally anticommunist administration since that of Herbert Hoover in office, rollback of regimes perceived to be under Soviet influence the world over became its policy.

Activating the old radical Islamist allies with which it had worked during the cold war and the Arab cold war, the CIA under William Casey, with the support of the Saudi, Pakistani, and other intelligence services, helped to field a force of Afghans, together with Arab volunteers and others that it brought in from all over the Islamic world. This eventually proved to be more than a match for the Soviet occupation forces and their Afghan allies, who went down to a staggering defeat. But after the bloodied Red Army crossed back into the Soviet Union in 1988, the lethal, divided, and ill-disciplined mujahidin movement created by these cold warriors eventually metastasized into forces that continued to engage in an endless war that engulfed Afghanistan. That war still rages there, today largely directed against the United States. Militant networks that grew out of the thousands of Arab and other Muslim volunteers brought to Afghanistan by the American and allied intelligence services developed into al-Qa'ida. All of these brutal, nihilistic, and violent organizations and forces are ghosts of the cold war, bastard children born of the blowback of a now conveniently forgotten era.

Soon after the Soviet Union was defeated in Afghanistan and after the Iran-Iraq war ended in mutual exhaustion, the Soviet empire in Eastern Europe and the rest of Eurasia began to crumble, and the Soviet Union itself finally disappeared in 1991. The cold war was over, but its tragic sequels, its toxic debris, and its unexploded mines continue to cause great harm until the present day. The tragic outcome of 9/11 represents one of these sequels, the evil work of the distant but very real ghosts originally conjured up by the United States to wage the last phases of the cold war. The cold war is over and the Soviet Union is no more, but those ghosts are still with us, in the Middle East and elsewhere.

VI

Did the cold war in the Middle East prevent the United States from exercising unfettered hegemony over that region until the Soviet Union was out of the way? Or was the American perception of Soviet power exaggerated, and was it in fact less of an obstacle to American domination of the Middle East than it may have seemed? My inclination is toward the latter view. The Middle East, like most of the other major arenas of cold war rivalry, was immediately adjacent to the USSR. There were no such cold war battlefields in the immediate vicinity of the United States, with the exception of Cuba, and for a brief period in the 1980s in parts of Central America. Thus, from soon after 1945, it was the United States that was containing the Soviet Union and stationing forces and strategic weapons all around the USSR's frontiers and those of its satellites and not vice versa.

Even after the USSR detonated an atomic bomb in 1949, shifting the strategic balance somewhat in its favor, it had no assured delivery system for nuclear weapons until the deployment of intercontinental ballistic missiles (ICBM) in the mid-1960s. Thereafter, both powers soon became capable of destroying one another many times over. These are all indications, nevertheless, of the great superiority of the United States over the USSR. This superiority was most importantly based on the far greater economic power of the United States and its postwar dominance of the European and Japanese economies; the two alone produced more than the Soviet economy little more than a decade after World War II.

To be sure the USSR also had certain advantages. By its very location it dominated the Eurasian landmass, and it had vast land armies. It also had an initial ideological advantage in Europe because of the presence of strong communist parties there, and a similar advantage in much of the developing world in the face of the persistence of European colonialism. This ideological edge operated in the Middle East for a time. Although the USSR was a great power, in many respects it was not truly a superpower, lacking the economic might of the United States or the global reach that the latter enjoyed with its fleets, air forces, and its far-flung military bases. All of these American strategic advantages can be seen operating in the Middle East, where a quiet struggle was waged, first in the Mediterranean, when in the 1960s the US Navy first based Polaris SLBM-carrying submarines targeting the USSR and the Soviets sought naval and air bases in the region to counter them. These advantages could be seen operating again in the 1970s when the US deployment of longer-range Poseidon SLBM-carrying submarines turned the Persian Gulf, the Arabian Sea, the Red Sea, and the Indian Ocean into a similar theater of naval competition. In the Middle East and elsewhere, the United States was taking the initiative by stationing strategic weapons in the backyard of the USSR, not vice versa. Thereafter, the United States was able to use its formidable economic power to help wean Egypt and other Arab states away from their former Soviet patrons with generous promises of aid.

Thus, while the struggle for influence in the Middle East seesawed back and forth, and at times looked desperate to some in Washington, it was the United States that always had the upper hand strategically. This became apparent when formerly radical Arab nationalist regimes like that of Egypt under Sadat in the 1970s and later that of Iraq under Saddam during the Iran-Iraq war defected to the American side. For all the rhetoric in Washington about countries in the Middle East "controlled by international communism" in the 1950s, these Arab regimes and their elites were never drawn ideologically to the USSR. Quite the contrary, all of them were deeply, fundamentally anticommunist, and none were staunchly anticapitalist (the sole exception in the entire Middle East was South Yemen). Even where communist parties had a role in the domestic politics of Middle Eastern countries, communists were never even close to being in control of them. The attraction of Middle Eastern rulers to both sides in the cold war was purely based on naked power. As it became apparent to most Middle Eastern elites that the United States was richer and more powerful than the Soviet Union, they eventually tended to gravitate toward Washington. Even the revulsion caused by Washington's bias in favor of Israel was not enough to alienate many Arab governments.

We have seen this in the case of Saudi Arabia. It was equally true of other reliably pro-American regimes. After Sadat's "apostasy" in leaving the pro-Soviet camp in 1972, it became increasingly clear that the United States could have its Israeli cake and eat it too, something that still appears true today.

Notes

1. This chapter is adopted from Rashid Khalidi, *Sowing Crisis: The Cold War and American Dominance in the Middle East* (Boston: Beacon, 2009).

2. For the text, see Winston Churchill, "The Sinews of Peace," in Mark A. Kishlansky, ed., *Sources of World History* (New York: HarperCollins, 1995), pp. 298–302.

3. A. C. Grayling, *Among the Dead Cities: The History and the Moral Legacy of the WWII Bombing of Civilians in Germany and Japan* (New York: Walker, 2006), p. 159, notes Churchill's thinking as early as 1944 about rearming Germany to help in an expected confrontation with the Soviet Union.

4. Roberts notes in "Stalin and Soviet Foreign Policy," in M. Leffler and D. Painter, eds., *The Origins of the Cold War,* 2nd ed. (London: Routledge, 2005), pp. 42–57, that Soviet policymakers' private expressions of their views track closely with their public statements.

5. An exception is Odd Arne Westad, *The Global Cold War: Third World Interventions and the Making of Our Times* (Cambridge: Cambridge University Press, 2005).

6. Recent works include Yezid Sayigh and Avi Shlaim, eds., *The Cold War and the Middle East* (Oxford: Oxford University Press, 1997); Salim Yaqub, *Containing Arab Nationalism: The Eisenhower Doctrine and the Middle East* (Chapel Hill: University of North Carolina Press, 2004); Nigel Ashton, ed., *The Cold War in the Middle East: Regional Conflict and the Superpowers, 1967–1973* (London: Routledge, 2007).

7. See Mahmood Mamdani, *Good Muslim, Bad Muslim: America, the Cold War, and the Roots of Terror* (New York: Pantheon, 2004); and Chalmers Johnson, *Blowback: The Costs and Consequences of American Empire,* 2nd ed. (New York: Holt, 2004).

8. William Eddy, *FDR Meets Ibd Saud* (1954; reprint, Vista, CA: Selwa, 2005).

9. Daniel Yergin, *The Prize, The Epic Quest for Oil, Money, and Power* (New York: Free Press, 1991), pp. 403–405.

10. Eddy, "FDR Meets Ibd Saud," p. 33.

11. US Department of State, *Foreign Relations of the United States, 1945* (Washington: Government Printing Office, 1969), 8:698.

12. Ibid., p. 755.

13. Eddy, "FDR Meets Ibd Saud," pp. 34–35.

14. See H. St. John Philby, *Arabia of the Wahhabis* (London: Constable, 1928); and *Saudi Arabia* (New York: Praeger, 1958); as well as Elizabeth Monroe, *Philby of Arabia* (London: Faber, 1973).

15. Libya, a former Italian colony, was another such country, and a US airfield that accommodated over 4,000 airmen and a wing of nuclear-armed strategic bombers was set up there, and was vacated only in 1969.

16. Until the first intercontinental bomber, the B-52, came into service in the late 1950s, and before intercontinental ballistic missiles and submarine-launched ballistic missiles were deployed in the 1960s, the American nuclear arsenal was carried by bombers of the Strategic Air Command (SAC), whose maximum ranges were less than

4,000 miles. They needed bases around the periphery of the Soviet Union in order to reach targets deep in the Soviet hinterland. Middle Eastern bases were particularly important to provide SAC bombers with the ability to reach targets to the east of the Urals and in Central Asia and Transcaucasia, where much of Soviet oil production and industry, especially military industry, were located.

17. Sa'ud ibn 'Abd al-'Aziz succeeded his father, 'Abd al-'Aziz ibn Sa'ud, on the old king's death in 1953.

18. The text can be found at: http://coursesa.matrix.msu.edu/~hst203/ documents/ eisen.html.

19. In Malcolm Kerr's book, *The Arab Cold War: 'Abd al-Nasir and His Rivals, 1958–1970*, 3rd ed. (London: Oxford University Press, 1971).

20. Alvin Z. Rubinstein, *Red Star on the Nile: The Soviet-Egyptian Influence Relationship Since the June War* (Princeton: Princeton University Press, 1977); and Waldemar Gallman, *Iraq Under General Nuri: My Recollections of Nuri Al-Said, 1954–1958* (Baltimore: Johns Hopkins Press, 1964), chaps. 4–5.

21. Hanna Batatu, *The Old Social Classes and the Revolutionary Movements of Iraq: A Study of Iraq's Old Landed and Commercial Classes and of Its Communists, Ba'thists, and Free Officers* (Princeton: Princeton University Press, 1978), pp. 764–973.

22. One of the best accounts of this American strategy can be found in M. Mamdani, *Good Muslim, Bad Muslim.*

23. For Iran, see Kermit Roosevelt, *Countercoup: The Struggle for Control of Iran* (New York: McGraw-Hill, 1979); and James Bill, *The Eagle and the Lion: The Tragedy of American-Iranian Relations* (New Haven: Yale University Press, 1988). For the Syrian and Lebanon cases, see Wilbur Crane Eveland, *Ropes of Sand: America's Failure in the Middle East* (New York: Norton, 1980). Eveland was a key figure in US intelligence activity in Syria and Lebanon.

24. For this period see Fred Halliday, *Arabia Without Sultans: A Political Survey of Instability in the Arab World* (London: Penguin, 1974), as well as the indispensable Kerr, *Arab Cold War.*

25. Eddy, "FDR Meets Ibd Saud," pp. 34–35. See also John Snetsinger, *Truman, the Jewish Vote, and Israel* (Stanford: Hoover Institution Press, 1974).

26. Arnold Kramner, *The Forgotten Friendship: Israel and the Soviet Bloc, 1947–53* (Urbana: University of Illinois Press, 1974).

27. Avner Cohen, *Israel and the Bomb* (New York: Columbia University Press, 1998), pp. 49ff.

28. Herman Finer, *Dulles over Suez: The Theory and Practice of his Diplomacy* (Chicago: University of Chicago Press, 1964); Diane Kunz, *The Economic Diplomacy of the Suez Crisis* (Chapel Hill: University of North Carolina Press, 1991); and Wm. Roger Louis and Roger Owen, eds., *1956: The Crisis and Its Consequences* (Oxford: Oxford University Press, 1989).

29. Selim Yaqub, *Containing Arab Nationalism: The Eisenhower Doctrine and the Middle East* (Chapel Hill: University of North Carolina Press, 2004); Irene Gendzier, *Notes from the Minefield: United States Intervention in Lebanon and the Middle East, 1945–1958* (New York: Columbia University Press, 1997); and David W. Lesch, *Syria and the United States: Eisenhower's Cold War in the Middle East* (Boulder: Westview, 1992).

30. Yaakov Bar-Siman-Tov, *The Israeli-Egyptian War of Attrition, 1969–1970: A Case-Study of Limited Local War* (New York: Columbia University Press, 1980); Edgar

O'Ballance, *The Electronic War in the Middle East, 1968–70* (London: Faber, 1974); and Lawrence Whetten, *The Canal War: Four-Power Conflict in the Middle East* (Cambridge: MIT Press, 1974).

31. Mohamed Heikal, *The Road to Ramadan* (London: Collins, 1975).

32. Kissinger did not even consult Nixon on this move. Robert Dallek, *Nixon and Kissinger: Partners in Power* (New York: HarperCollins, 2007). On the 1973 war, see ibid.; Saad el-Shazly, *The Crossing of Suez: The October War 1973* (London: Third World Center, 1980); Chaim Herzog, *The War of Atonement* (London: Weidenfeld & Nicolson, 1975); Zeev Schiff, *October Earthquake: Yom Kippur 1973* (Tel Aviv: University Publishing, 1974).

33. Khalidi, *Sowing Crisis,* pp. 125–137.

34. See Khalidi, *Sowing Crisis,* chap. 2, for details.

35. Jonathan C. Randal, *After Such Knowledge, What Forgiveness: My Encounters with Kurdistan* (New York: Farrar, Straus & Giroux, 1997).

36. Susan Meisalas with Martin van Bruinessen, *Kurdistan: In the Shadow of History* (New York: Random House, 1997).

37. Published under the pseudonym X as "The Sources of Soviet Conduct," *Foreign Affairs,* July 1947.

PART TWO

Arab-Israeli War and Peace

CHAPTER 11

THE 1967 ARAB-ISRAELI WAR

US Actions and Arab Perceptions

Fawaz A. Gerges

On more than one level the June 1967 Arab-Israeli war (also known as the Six Day War) was a watershed in the recent history of the Middle East. In particular, the confrontation radically transformed the nature of regional politics and the relationship between local states and the superpowers. On the one hand, the Arab-Israeli dispute became the most dominant single foreign policy issue in the external relations of the Arab states. The main focus of regional instability shifted from inter-Arab politics to Arab-Israeli interactions. The war also set the stage for the contemporary Arab-Israeli peace process. For the previous ten years, the dispute between Israel and the Arabs had been kept in the "icebox," moving neither toward resolution nor toward war.[1] In this sense, the Six Day War was a catalyst that forced Israel and the Arabs as well as their superpower patrons to participate in the quest for peace. On the other hand, the bloody escalation of the Arab-Israeli conflict made local players much more dependent on their superpower allies. As a result, the Arab-Israeli conflict became increasingly entangled in the US-Soviet cold war rivalry. Thus, bipolarity on the international stage was reflected on the regional level. The increased reliance of the local states on the superpowers restricted their freedom of action and compromised their independence.

This chapter examines the impact of the 1967 Arab-Israeli war on Arab nationalist perceptions regarding the input that the United States had in the crisis, in order to examine how these perceptions influenced Arab attitudes toward the US and Soviet roles in the peace process. I will argue that the Six Day War had a dev-astating, negative impact on Arab views regarding the US role, as well as on Arab beliefs in the efficacy of the Soviet Union and its reliability as a superpower ally. Although Arab nationalists, particularly in Egypt, were highly critical and suspicious of President Lyndon B. Johnson, they recognized the indispensable and pre-ponderant role of Washington in the post–1967 peace process. They believed the United States wielded much influence over its client—Israel—and held most of the cards in the peace process.

In contrast, Arab rulers, and not just Egyptian President Gamal 'Abd al-Nasser, became conscious of the limited nature of Soviet power and prestige in world pol-itics. Their experiences with the Soviet Union during the 1967 crisis convinced them that Moscow did not have the means or the will to defend the Arabs. This belated realization played a decisive role in the mellowing of Egyptian radicalism during the post-1967 period and, one might venture to claim, in the revolutionary reorientation of Egyptian foreign policy throughout the 1970s.

Thus, this chapter must address several critical questions: How did the Arab confrontational states, particularly Egypt, respond to their crushing defeat at the hands of Israel in June 1967? How did they perceive the role of the superpowers in the war, and did their perceptions of the two contrasting superpower positions influence their behavior toward the peace process? What was the impact of the US-Soviet rivalry on the dynamics of peacemaking? Why did President Johnson aban-don previous US support for the 1949 armistice regime, and how did this radical change in US policy complicate the quest for peace? To what extent did the dra-matic alteration in the regional balance of power inhibit both Israel and Arab rulers' willingness and ability to compromise? In this sense, did the 1967 war sow the seeds of a bloodier conflagration in the Middle East?

ARAB PERCEPTIONS OF THE US ROLE
IN THE 1967 ARAB-ISRAELI WAR

The polarization of the Arab-Israeli conflict along East-West lines was directly re-lated to the crushing defeat of the Arab states in 1967 and their perceptions that the United States had colluded with Israel to destroy the "revolutionary Arab regimes which had refused to be a part of the Western sphere of influence."[2] Nasser, the leading Arab nationalist, believed that his regime was the main target of the US-sponsored Israeli attack. He told Mohamed Heikal, a confidant of his, that Johnson succeeded in "trapping us." As for Nasser, this collusion entailed a complex set of political and diplomatic tricks and maneuvers. Moreover, the Egyptian lead-ership—not just Nasser—believed that the Johnson administration indirectly col-luded with Israel by covering its flanks and neutralizing the Soviet Union and by deliberately deceiving Egypt and lulling it into a state of complacency.[3]

The Egyptians pointed to the fact that although the United States had secured from Egypt a commitment not to fire first, it failed to extract a similar pledge from Israel. They said that Egypt was under overwhelming pressure by the United States and the Soviet Union not to fire first. They argued that the Johnson administration impressed on Soviet leaders the urgent need to call upon its Egyptian ally to desist from any military adventure. To show his goodwill, Nasser declared publicly that he would not be the one to initiate hostilities. He said he was given the impression that Israel had also committed itself not to shoot first.[4]

Little wonder, then, that the Arab nationalists were very bitter after Israel's pre-emptive strike on June 5. They felt overwhelming resentment and anger for the Johnson administration, fueled initially by official Egyptian and Jordanian accusations that the United States had participated alongside Israel in the first air attacks against the Arab forces.[5] Although unfounded, these accusations served to confirm a widely held Arab stereotype of US hostility. In particular, the Egyptians felt deceived by the United States; they also believed that the United States had involved the Soviets subconsciously in its strategy to mislead Egypt.

Nasser asserted that the US government helped Israel in several ways by providing it with intelligence and weapons. For example, Israel's attack on the USS *Liberty*—a US intelligence ship stationed off the Sinai coast on June 8—convinced the Egyptian leader of Johnson's complicity: The *Liberty* supplied Israel with critical intelligence about Egyptian military installations. In this context, Nasser claimed that Johnson had known and had approved of Israeli war plans in advance. As Nasser put it, the US role in the war was a continuation of its shutting off of aid to Egypt: Having failed to subdue Egypt through economic warfare, Johnson instigated Israel to use physical force instead.[6] Nasser said the United States "must be made to feel the brunt of its collusion with Israel. We must bring the weight of mobilized Arab anger to bear on her. The severing of relations is imperative."[7] This perception, or rather mis-perception, was shared by all the confrontation Arab states (most importantly, Egypt, Syria, and Iraq), which promptly broke diplomatic relations with Washington.

To understand the rationale behind Arab perceptions, one has to focus on the nature of the relationship between the Johnson administration and the Arab na-tionalist forces, particularly on the steady deterioration of US-Egyptian relations since the end of 1964. The gradual suspension of US food aid to Egypt beginning in 1965, coupled with the direct supply of arms to Israel and other conservative states in the area, embittered Egyptian leaders and convinced them that Johnson was not only determined to humiliate and starve their country to death, but also was working closely with their regional enemies to overthrow the revolutionary Arab governments.[8] In September 1965 the Egyptian ambassador to Washington informed a senior US diplomat that the Egyptian leadership believed that the US Central Intelligence Agency (CIA) was seeking to topple the Nasser regime.[9]

By the end of 1966 Nasser seemed to have lost hope for US policy, viewed as irredeemably pro-Israeli and anti-Egyptian.[10] The mood in Washington was equally hostile: "We're not angry [with Nasser]; we're fed up," wrote Harold Saunders, a key National Security Council (NSC) official dealing with the Middle East.[11] The US ambassador to Egypt, Lucius Battle, also said that a good deal of uncertainty and tension and a general sense of discouragement existed in US-Egyptian rela-tions. The two countries, asserted the ambassador, were on a "slippery slope headed toward confrontation of the 1957–58 type." He warned his superiors in Washington to bear in mind that they were approaching a watershed in their relationship with Egypt.[12]

THE ARAB VIEW OF THE US ROLE IN THE PEACE PROCESS

The general Arab view of the US role in the 1967 war and in the subsequent peace process should be studied squarely within this polarized context of suspicion and distrust. The Arab nationalists had no faith in the Johnson administration to act as a neutral mediator in the quest for peace. To them, an identity of interests existed between the White House and Israel, manifesting itself in Johnson's unequivocal support of Israel in the United Nations (UN) General Assembly and Security Council and subsequent actions, which were designed to ensure Israel's military superiority over all its Arab neighbors.[13] Arab rulers had a fixation with the United States that, in their opinion, determined questions of war and peace in the Middle East. They failed to appreciate the complexity of US-Israeli relations and the wide degree of autonomy that Israeli leaders exercised in their ceaseless quest for absolute security.

In both 1956 and 1967, Nasser and his Arab counterparts did not consider seriously the possibility that Israel, by manipulating the polarized international system, was capable of acting on its own in the pursuit of its national interests, with or without superpower collusion. Israel was simply seen as an instrument and agent of the Western powers and imperialism, performing at the behest of its masters; Israel was not working for itself alone but was serving as a US tool to dominate the Arab world. In the words of Algerian President Houari Boumedienne, "Israel played a secondary role in the 1967 war. The battle was American, and only the performance was Israeli." Likewise, Nasser said that the United States—not Israel—was the main party with which to discuss the occupation of Arab territories.[14] Although some of this was merely hyperbole, Arab politicians really believed that the United States held the key to war and peace in the region. Reading the recollections, speeches, and some minutes of the meetings of Arab officials, one gets the impression that Johnson had the power and the means to force Israel to withdraw to the prewar borders but did not want to employ them.[15]

Despite the vehemence of his attack on US policy, Nasser was in no position to confront the United States in the region. When the dust settled over the desert, Nasser found the bulk of his army destroyed, the Sinai occupied, his coffers empty, and his political career in jeopardy. Unlike the war of 1956, Nasser could not turn a military defeat into a political victory. In fact, the Six Day War was markedly different from the Suez crisis. In 1956 Nasser could rightly claim that Egyptian capabilities were no match for the combined forces of Britain, France, and Israel. In spite of his efforts, Nasser could not repeat the same political performance in 1967. The "most powerful state in the Middle East" had been decisively beaten and humiliated by a young, vigorous, and small nation.

As a result, Nasser's status and position in the Arab world were weakened as well. With the totality of defeat, Nasser's long-term goal of constructing a new Arab order disappeared. Undermined were the symbols and ideas of secular Arab nationalism that had served as the building blocks for this order. The revolutionary ideal was discredited in Arab politics. In inter-Arab relations, the overall balance of forces shifted dramatically in favor of the Arab conservatives, who held the power of the purse and who shaped the politics of the inter-Arab state system during the post-1967 period.

Furthermore, the Arab nationalists could no longer rely on the sympathy of world public opinion or on the active intervention of the superpowers. They did not understand the changed international situation in the late 1960s. The United States was bogged down in Vietnam and was not terribly focused on the Middle East. Likewise preoccupied at home and abroad, the Kremlin leadership was building bridges to the West in the hope of gaining economic and political concessions. The Soviets were against a war in the Middle East that might involve them in a direct clash with the United States (and thus endanger their new approach to the West).[16] The Arab radicals were mistaken in their assumption that the Soviets would intervene in a Middle East war. Such thinking was symptomatic of the prevailing, pervasive tendency of the regional actors to inflate their own importance. After the 1967 war, Nasser told his colleagues that he had not weighed carefully the changes in Soviet foreign policy after the death of Soviet leader Nikita Khrushchev.[17]

More significant to the Kremlin leadership were the nuclear stalemate with the United States and the perennial question of international security. In the Six Day War, US and Soviet policymakers communicated at the highest levels to contain the conflict and to prevent its spread and expansion. They exerted considerable pressures on their local allies to accept a cease-fire. Although the war was short, the superpowers used the hotline more than once to clarify any misunderstanding that might force them into an unwanted confrontation. In the aftermath of the war, top US and Soviet officials held talks to try to find a political solution.[18]

Although the Soviets were critical of Israel's actions in June 1967 and were supportive of the Arabs, they did not take concrete measures—except to promise to resupply arms—to help their friends. The Soviets could not even offer their Arab allies much support in the UN Security Council because of US objections to any resolution stipulating that Israel withdraw behind the 1949 armistice lines.[19] It was not until June 10 that the Soviet Union took drastic steps to halt the Israeli advance on the Syrian front. According to Johnson, Soviet Premier Alexei Kosygin used the hotline to inform him that as the result of Israel's ignoring all UN Security Council resolutions for a cease-fire, a very crucial moment had arrived. Kosygin foresaw the risk of a "grave catastrophe" unless Israel unconditionally terminated its military operations within the next few hours. Otherwise, the Soviet premier warned that his government would take all "necessary actions, including military." In addition, the Soviet Union severed diplomatic relations with Israel and threatened to take stronger measures unless the latter ceased hostilities immediately.[20]

Although he recognized that the Soviet Union was sensitive about its special relationship with Syria, Johnson said that he was determined to resist Soviet intrusion
in the Middle East. His immediate response was to issue orders to the US Navy
Sixth Fleet to move closer to the Syrian coast so as to send a warning signal to the
Kremlin: "There are times when the wisdom and rightness of a President's judgment are critically important. We were at such a moment. The Soviets had made
a decision. I had to respond."[21]

But neither the United States nor the Soviet Union had the stomach for a clash.
The Soviets knew that pressure from the US government was the only way to stop
an Israeli advance deep into Syria. Their warning to Johnson was designed to impress upon him the need to halt Tel Aviv's march toward Damascus. Soviet calculations proved correct. According to senior Israeli officials, on June 10 the Johnson
administration informed its ally that the situation had reached a dangerous point
and that Soviet intervention was no longer inconceivable. Israel agreed to a cease-
fire on the same day, following the occupation of the Syrian Golan Heights.[22]

A crisis between the superpowers was thus averted. Their high-level contacts
had effectively prevented an open clash between them. As the CIA put it, the Soviet
Union had no intention of intervening militarily in the war and so did what it
could to avoid confrontation. Another major concern of the Kremlin leadership,
argued a CIA intelligence assessment, was to forestall a disastrous Arab defeat that
would make the Kremlin the target of Arab criticisms.[23] As a superpower, the Soviet
Union was more concerned about its relationship with the United States than with
any abstract obligations to its regional partners. The logic of superpower politics
took priority over other interests.

Given the ambivalent position of the Soviet Union, one would have expected
Nasser to swallow his pride and mend fences with the Johnson administration. In
the case of the Suez conflict, Nasser knew that it was the United States rather than
the Soviet Union that ultimately forced the tripartite coalition to cease fire and
withdraw. In 1967, however, Nasser believed that Johnson unleashed Israel's military action against Egypt to topple his progressive regime. Unlike Eisenhower, who
played the leading and most effective role in thwarting the tripartite aggression,
Nasser asserted that Johnson played a decisive role in Israel's swift victory over the
Arabs.[24]

By using the last weapon in his arsenal—severing diplomatic relations with the
US government—and by his accusations against the United States, Nasser embit-
tered Johnson and made him more determined to prevent Nasser from regaining
a position of pan-Arab leadership. The US president made it clear that the United
States "could not afford to repeat the temporary and hasty arrangements" between
Egypt and Israel after Suez. Johnson now had the opportunity to try a different
approach, by supporting Israel's hold on the newly occupied territories pending
Arab consent to make peace with Israel.[25]

Indeed, as soon as the fighting started, Johnson, as former ambassador Richard
Parker puts it, "showed a clear and lasting bias in favor of Israel and a disregard for
the public commitments he and his administration had made to oppose aggression

from any quarter."[26] The United States became more closely allied with Israel in opposition to vital Arab interests. The extremely pro-Israeli stand of US public opinion, coupled with Arab hostility and Johnson's dislike of Nasser, enabled Johnson to adopt a policy of "unquestioning support for Israel."[27] The extent of the Arab defeat took US officials by surprise. They had expected Israel to win but were unsure about the duration or immediate results of an Arab-Israeli contest. On the first day of the war, the uncertainty and uneasiness of the administration were reflected in its call for all combatants to work for a cease-fire and return to old positions before the start of hostilities.[28]

The US stand changed dramatically, however, as soon as the completeness of Israel's victory became known. In a memorandum to the president on June 7, his special assistant, Walt Rostow, wrote that the Israeli victory created new conditions that the US government quickly should move to exploit. The following day Rostow warned that the greatest risk would be to fail to appreciate the political consequences of Israel's military triumph. He summarized the US official position as being opposed to any UN resolution that would require Israel to concede war gains except in return for an Arab-Israeli final settlement.[29] No doubt Rostow was fully aware that the new bargaining situation created by the war was asymmetrical.

The Johnson administration hoped to use the new asymmetrical situation to extract peace treaties and recognition of Israel's existence from the Arabs. Some US officials argued that the humiliating defeat of Egypt and Syria provided the United States with a golden opportunity to take "big" political measures in the region, since "Soviet policy was in ruins."[30] Even before the war was over the administration had concluded that Nasser's fate was sealed. US diplomats in the field were certain that a general anti-Nasser convulsion would shake Egypt and the Arab world; indeed that the domestic survival of his regime was in doubt, as was the allegiance of other Arab states.[31]

US intelligence agencies also believed that the Egyptian leader's days were numbered, and they began to think seriously about the post-Nasser era. Likewise, the US Department of State thought that the fall of Nasser's regime would lead not only to the reestablishment of US relations with Egypt, but also to the resurrection of US interests in the whole Arab arena.[32] The dominant view in Washington was that no quick palliative solutions or temporizing compromises should be accepted. In the words of the undersecretary of state for political affairs, Averell Harriman, the United States would never have another opportunity as propitious to deal with the underlying problems besetting this turbulent region—"so vital to our own and Western Europe's security."[33] Ironically, Nasser interpreted the US position as motivated by a desire to freeze the present situation, hoping that his regime, along with all revolutionary Arab regimes, "would fall, to be replaced by another more receptive to U.S. interests, or alternatively to instill utter despair in us, driving us to make peace with Israel on its conditions."[34]

The basic outlines of US long-term strategy were defined as follows: (1) cessation of hostilities between Israel and its Arab neighbors; (2) Arab recognition of Israel; (3) support of moderate Arab forces—the leader of which was Saudi Arabia—at the expense of the Arab radicals: Egypt, Syria, and Iraq; (4) a bigger role for Turkey and Iran in the Middle East; (5) regional arms control arrangements; and (6) a new mechanism for social and economic development.[35] In US eyes, the denouement of the war provided a great opportunity to solve the festering Arab-Israeli conflict and to redraw the political map of the region. A central element in this strategy was to cut Nasser's prestige and influence in the Arab world and revise regional political alignments.

Achievement of this objective would require the active involvement of Turkey, Iran, and Israel. For a decade these states had campaigned hard to become integral players in the inter-Arab state subsystem. According to an intelligence assessment by the CIA, before the war Israel had hoped to construct a loose coalition of Iran, Turkey, Iraqi and Syrian Kurds, and moderate Arabs. It follows that the primary Israeli war aim was the destruction of Nasser as the leader of the pan-Arab nationalist movement. If that goal could be achieved, Israeli officials assumed that Israel, Turkey, and Iran would become the dominant regional actors by representing an overwhelming balance of military power.[36]

In the aftermath of the war, both Israel and Iran lobbied the US government to support more substantial roles for them in the area. Israeli officials informed their US counterparts that their victory over the Arabs created new opportunities to build a more viable order in the Middle East. They argued further that the United States and its regional allies would be the main beneficiaries of this order.[37] The shah of Iran also informed the Johnson administration that "Nasser must be eliminated as otherwise he [could] again inflame Arab sentiments." Iran would be more than pleased, he added, to play a more active part and to be a solid pillar in the region, as Japan did in the Far East.[38] (Indeed, some time later, the Nixon Doctrine of 1969 envisaged hegemonic roles for Iran in the Gulf and Israel in the Fertile Crescent. President Richard M. Nixon and his assistant for national security, Henry Kissinger, saw Iran and Israel as the policemen and the protectors of US interests in the region.)[39]

These arguments impressed the Johnson administration, which accepted Tel Aviv's view that no withdrawal should take place except in return for a peace agreement. Johnson placed the major responsibility for the war on Egypt and refused to pressure Israel to concede any territories, as Eisenhower did in 1957. He said Israel must be accepted as a reality in the area and must be recognized by the Arabs.[40] Johnson spelled out five principles that were essential to peace: (1) the recognized right to national life (for all parties to the dispute); (2) justice for the (Palestinian) refugees; (3) innocent maritime passage (through the Suez Canal and the Strait of Tiran); (4) limiting the arms race (in the region between Arabs and Israelis); and (5) political independence and territorial integrity (for all). Both the Israelis and the Arabs saw Johnson's Five Great Principles of Peace as wholly supporting Israel. The convergence of interests between the United States and Israel was almost complete, marking the beginning of a special relationship between the two countries.[41] Thus, the Six Day War brought about a major shift in US policy toward the Middle East.[42] The president and his aides decided not to return to the old, failed policy supporting the 1949 armistice regime. This attitude explained the administration's posture of distant reserve toward the question of Arab-Israeli peace.[43]

THE ARAB VIEW OF THE SOVIET ROLE

Given their perceptions of an unholy US-Israeli alliance, the Arab confrontation states—Egypt, Syria, and Iraq, with the exception of Jordan—felt compelled to turn to the Soviet Union for political and military support. They recognized, however, the limited nature of Soviet power and influence.[44] The Soviet failure to provide direct military assistance to the Arabs had important repercussions on Soviet-Arab relations. Egyptian, Iraqi, and Algerian leaders were disappointed with the lack of tangible Soviet assistance. They suspected the Soviets of either being "scared of the Americans" or of having sacrificed their Arab allies on the altar of détente with Washington. Egyptian officials criticized the Soviet Union for actually playing the role demanded of it by Johnson during the crisis in May and June; some senior Egyptian officials were skeptical about the value of Moscow as a friend, whereas others even suspected a collusion between the United States and the Soviet Union. Arab rulers realized that the security requirements of their superpower ally vis-à-vis the United States took priority over Middle East regional concerns.[45]

This realization convinced the Arabs that their alliance with the Soviet Union was tactical rather than strategic. In this context, the Six Day War marked a watershed in Arab-Soviet relations. The Arabs questioned the nature of their alliance with the Kremlin; though Israel enjoyed full protection by the United States, the Arabs did not receive an equal Soviet commitment.[46] It could be argued that one of the main reasons for the decline of Soviet influence in the Arab world in the early 1970s lay in Arab perceptions of Moscow's stand during the war.

Yet despite the feeling of abandonment and indignation, Nasser and the other Arab nationalists could not afford a final divorce from the Communist giant—especially after they cut their political links with the United States and Great Britain. The Soviet Union became their last refuge. Nasser believed that the regional and global configuration of forces were in US and Israeli favor, thus he needed Soviet military and political support to rebuild his military and to counterbalance US and Israeli hegemony. Immediately after the war Nasser moved swiftly to end the ill feeling that was souring Arab-Soviet relations. Nasser publicly praised Kremlin leaders for their political, economic, and military assistance. He informed Soviet officials that he wanted to strengthen and deepen Egyptian-Soviet relations and that he was ready to sign any pact to organize and structure the relationship between their two countries on a more permanent basis.[47] Moscow's deepening involvement with Egypt and Syria took the Arab-Israeli conflict still deeper into the cold war rivalry between the superpowers. The Arab-Israeli dispute became a global-military-strategic problem, not a regional-political problem.[48] The peace process thus became entangled in the web of great power politics.

To the Soviets, the immediate results of the war must have been gratifying. Nasser's crushing defeat humbled him, and he became more receptive to Soviet requests. No longer could he afford to challenge Moscow's influence in the region, as he had in 1959; this reassured the Soviets. By regulating the flow of arms to Egypt and Syria, the Kremlin would have a greater impact on their policies. Nasser was left in no doubt as to Moscow's preference for a peaceful solution to the Arab-Israeli conflict.[49] Time and again, the Soviets would procrastinate and decline to supply their Arab friends with offensive weapons. The war had taught the Soviets the need to exercise more control over their regional allies, and the war's aftermath enabled them to do so. In the next three years the question of arms deliveries became one of the most effective clubs the Soviets wielded over the Arabs.[50]

The Egyptians were frustrated with their treatment by the Kremlin. In fact, Anwar Sadat described the period after the war as a clash between Egypt and the Soviet Union.[51] In the long run, Soviet behavior bred suspicion and bitterness in Arab ranks, especially in Egypt. Sadat claimed that one of the reasons motivating Nasser to accept the 1970 Rogers Initiative—a peace initiative by US Secretary of State William Rogers—was Nasser's belief that the Soviet Union was a "hopeless case."[52] Hence, it was a only matter of time before the Egyptians would rebel against what they perceived to be Soviet heavy-handedness.

In the short term, Soviet political and material influence increased considerably in the Arab world. Soviet leaders kept their promise to restore lost Arab inventories, with the exception of offensive weapons. Soviet military personnel also were sent in increasing numbers to Cairo and Damascus to assist in defense of deep strategic and industrial targets. However, the flourishing Soviet presence in the region was tactical and temporary, the product of a devastating upheaval that left Egypt, the nerve center of the Arab order, with few international options to pursue. The Arabs could not help comparing US support of Israel with the Kremlin's lukewarm commitment to the Arabs. Thus, the seeds of mistrust and suspicion had been sown in Arab-Soviet relations. Although Nasser could not distance himself from his Soviet ally, he eventually reopened his relationship with the United States, and by the time of his death from natural causes in 1970 he had come to recognize the indispensable role of Washington in the peace process. Sadat claimed that Nasser had told him that "whether we like it or not, all the cards of this game [i.e., the Arab-Israeli conflict] are in America's hands. It's high time we talked and allowed the U.S.A. to take part in this."[53]

Although Sadat's account is exaggerated and self-serving, it is also important, as it foreshadows the future direction of US-Egyptian relations. More than once Nasser tested the degree of US commitment to a balanced approach to the Middle East crisis. For example, following Richard Nixon's election to the presidency in 1968, Nasser decided to make a fresh start with the United States by initiating a dialogue with the new US leader. In fact, Nasser and Jordan's King Hussein informed Nixon that they were prepared to accept a diplomatic solution with Israel and that they were constrained neither by Syria's opposition nor by opposition from other Arab radicals. Egyptian Prime Minister Mahmoud Fawzi also told

Nixon privately that as part of a regional settlement Israel would have freedom of navigation in the Suez Canal. The Egyptians hoped that the Nixon administration would reciprocate by adopting evenhanded policies toward the Arabs and the Israelis. They were disappointed, however, with the lack of a positive US response. According to scholar William Quandt, Kissinger was not persuaded. Thus, the Nixon administration did not change its attitude and maintained close ties with Israel by preserving Israel's military superiority over Arab neighbors without pressing its leaders to withdraw from recently occupied Arab territories.[54]

Nasser still thought that Nixon—unlike Johnson—could play a positive role in the Arab-Israeli conflict. In May 1970, the Egyptian leader personally appealed to Nixon to adopt an evenhanded policy and become actively engaged in the quest for peace. He said Egypt had not given up on the United States, despite US military and political support to Israel: The United States must either order Israel to withdraw from the recently occupied territories or, if it was unable to go that far, refrain from extending any further assistance to Israel as long as the latter occupied Arab lands. Although Egypt and the United States did not have diplomatic relations, Nasser said this did not prevent the two countries from cooperating to achieve peace.[55] According to Sadat, this appeal to Nixon implied a desire on Nasser's part to pursue a political course of action.[56] Although Nixon responded to the appeal, and Rogers in fact outlined a peace initiative, Nasser and the United States could not overcome differences. It would take Nasser's successor (ironically, that turned out to be Sadat) and other new leaders to revive the old connection with the United States—at the sole expense of the Kremlin.

THE KHARTOUM SUMMIT

Nasser accepted the convening of a summit of Arab heads of state in Khartoum, Sudan, at the end of August 1967. As to the Arab militants—Syria, Iraq, Algeria, and the Palestine Liberation Organization (PLO)—it was their feeling that a counteroffensive was urgently needed to stem the tide of US advance in the region. In their view, the termination of diplomatic relations with the United States was not adequate to force it to change its policy. Thus, the Syrians, Algerians, Iraqis, and Palestinians called for a complete boycott of the United States and for a strategic alliance with the Soviet Union. They argued that the peace process would lead to Arab surrender and a US-Israeli dictate. On the regional level, they advanced the idea of a popular war against Israel and of a revolutionary crusade against the conservative Arab regimes. The Syrian rulers, in particular, took an anti-Western posture and poured abuse on reactionary Arab regimes that had remained on the sidelines during the latest round of Arab-Israeli hostilities. Syria boycotted the Khartoum Summit because it refused to accept Arab reaction as a partner.[57]

However, the clarification of the Soviet position played a decisive role in Nasser's decision to accept the convening of the summit. Its purpose was to define a collective Arab strategy toward Israel and the West. In Khartoum, Nasser joined the Arab moderates in supporting a political rather than military solution to the Arab-Israeli conflict. They also agreed to keep the dialogue with the West, and they opposed the militants' proposal to suspend Arab oil production.[58] An oil embargo, Nasser argued, would harm Arab economies more than those of the West and would almost certainly antagonize the West. Nasser's new realism manifested itself in his unwillingness to ask the conservative Arab regimes to sever diplomatic relations with the US government. He also informed Jordan's King Hussein that he was free to pursue a separate negotiated settlement—including signing a defense treaty with the United States—to recover the West Bank and Jerusalem.[59]

Nasser's behavior was designed not only to mend his fences with the Arab conservatives, but also to keep open lines of communication with the United States. He said he wanted to give the United States an opportunity to prove to its few remaining Arab friends that it was serious about reducing its total alignment with Israel. Nasser was not convinced by the arguments of the militants to cut all links with Washington. The war and its aftermath made the Egyptian leader acutely aware of the influential weight of the United States in the region. As Nasser himself put it, "Political positions cannot be built on myths but facts. We do not want and cannot fight America." Thus, the Egyptian leader asked Saudi King Faisal to serve as his channel of communication with the Johnson administration.[60]

Nasser parted company with the Arab radicals on the Arab-Israeli conflict itself: He was not impressed by their call for a total war against the Jewish state. He knew full well that the regional balance of power favored Israel, which had won the sympathy and respect of world public opinion and a decisive edge in international diplomacy. Nasser also took into account the superpower agreement to resolve the problem by political means. Moreover, as mentioned previously, both the Soviet Union and the nonaligned movement informed the Arabs that they would prefer to see a peaceful way out of the Arab-Israeli labyrinth.[61]

For all these reasons, the Egyptian president joined the moderates in Khartoum in support of a political rather than military solution to the conflict. This fact should not be confused by the summit's three declarations on Israel—"no peace, no negotiations, no recognition." The Sudanese premier noted that the three no's were adopted as an instrumental response, a political gesture, to the uncompromising stand of the PLO. Afterward, Nasser, Hussein, and other Arab officials made it clear both publicly and privately that they were prepared to live in peace with Israel in return for Israel's complete withdrawal from Arab territories occupied in 1967 and for a just solution to the Palestine problem. The summit, noted Hussein, empowered Egypt and Jordan to seek a political solution. In particular, Hussein was convinced that a political solution was the only feasible option open to the Arabs. This belief led him to coordinate his efforts with the United States as well as to serve as a link between the United States and Egypt.[62]

It was within this spirit that Egypt and Jordan accepted UN Security Council Resolution 242, which was adopted unanimously by the major powers in November 1967. This resolution called for the withdrawal of Israeli armed forces from territories—not "the" territories—occupied in the recent conflict and the termination of the state belligerency between Israel and its Arab neighbors.[63]

Nasser subsequently accused Johnson of supporting Israel in resisting the implementation of the terms of Resolution 242; instead the Johnson administration applied considerable political pressure in an attempt to force Egypt (and Jordan) into a separate peace settlement with Israel: The basis of any agreement with Egypt centered on total Israeli withdrawal from all occupied Egyptian territories in return for Egypt terminating the state of war with Israel. Nasser refused to conclude a separate deal with Israel and called for a comprehensive solution: "The issue is not only about withdrawal from Sinai. It is much bigger than that. The issue is to be or not to be." To Nasser, accepting a separate agreement with Israel meant coming to terms with the reality of defeat and abandoning the core of the Arab policy upon which he had built his political career.[64]

The Egyptians were angered when Johnson started to develop intimate ties with Tel Aviv. They believed that Johnson's actions were not only confined to safeguarding Israel, but also assisting it in its occupation of Arab lands. To Nasser and his colleagues, the US president was pushing Egypt to depend further upon the Soviet Union for military, economic, and political support. Egyptian Foreign Minister Mahmoud Riad said that Nasser felt puzzled by the element of self-destruction in US policy that was driving the Arabs into Soviet arms: "The United States leaves us no choice."[65] Egyptian leaders could not understand the radical change in the US position toward the peace process after the 1967 war, especially Johnson's abandonment of previous US support for the 1949 armistice regime. They believed that the US-Israeli drive aimed at "forcing Egypt to accept the fait accompli in the hope that the Arab area would surrender to U.S. and Israeli demands."[66]

This was another attempt by Johnson, asserted Nasser, to humiliate the Arabs, thus adversely affecting US-Arab relations. By the end of 1967, given Nasser's perception of Johnson's hostility, he had concluded that the peace process was dead as long as the balance of power favored Israel; it was only by restoring this imbalance that the United States would be induced to reassess its position. Nasser said that redressing the imbalance, and escalating military pressure, would have a radical impact on the whole Middle East situation, particularly on the positions of the superpowers, and would convince the superpowers of the need to stop maneuvering and to act decisively. Thus, Nasser's subsequent choice of a "war of attrition" can be seen as a result of the lack of progress toward a political settlement in the two years after the 1967 war and of his desire to break the political and military stalemate, something Anwar Sadat would do as well in 1973.[67]

CONCLUSION

Although the Six Day War set the stage for the Middle East peace process, it did not motivate or force Israel and the Arabs to reach a compromise. Israel's overwhelming victory over the Arabs brought about a radical shift in the regional balance of power in its favor. This shift in the configuration of forces, coupled with the strong pro-Israeli position of the US government, hardened the position of the two antagonists. Although most Arab rulers declared their readiness to live in peace with their Jewish neighbor, none of the Arab confrontational states—except for Jordan—was willing to conclude formal peace treaties with Israel. They were very weak militarily for any risky initiative on the diplomatic front. For Nasser and his Arab counterparts, to give the sort of commitments the United States and Israel were demanding would have meant accepting the reality of defeat, thus endangering the very survival of their regimes. Furthermore, despite their rude awakening in June 1967, Arab leaders were not yet ready to come to terms with Israel; they were still prisoners of their historical fears and prejudices.

Israel, on the other hand, was a satisfied power. As a result of their swift victory over the Arabs, Israeli officials demanded a high price for their withdrawal from some, but not all, of the recently occupied Arab territories. Given the disarray, fragmentation, and impotence of the Arab world and unwavering US support, some Israeli elements believed that they could indefinitely hold on to the occupied Arab territories. By the time UN Resolution 242 was passed, Israel was no longer interested in exchanging land for commitments of any kind from the Arabs. As the then deputy assistant secretary of state for Near Eastern affairs, Rodger Davies, put it: "Israel's appetite had grown with the eating."[68]

The diplomatic stalemate in the Middle East was directly related to the deepening polarization of the Arab-Israeli conflict along East-West lines. As mentioned previously, Arab nationalist perceptions of US involvement in the 1967 war influenced their attitudes toward the US role in the peace process. They believed that the Johnson administration had colluded with Israel against the forces of Arab nationalism. Subsequent US abandonment of its previous support for the 1949 armistice regime reinforced the widely held Arab view of US hostility.

As a result, Arab nationalists did not trust the United States to act as a neutral mediator in the quest for peace; they turned instead to the Soviet Union for political and military succor—despite their recognition of the limited nature of Soviet power—hoping to redress the regional imbalance. Moscow's further involvement with Egypt and Syria took the Middle East crisis still deeper into the cold war rivalry between the superpowers. The entanglement of the Arab-Israeli conflict in the web of great power politics complicated the peace process and made Israel and the Arabs less willing to compromise. Thus, far from being a catalyst for peace, the 1967 war sowed the seeds of yet another bloody conflagration in the region.

Notes

I want to thank former ambassador Richard Parker, Professor William Quandt, Dr. Avi Shlaim, and Professor Chris Taylor for reading and commenting on an earlier version of this chapter.

1. William B. Quandt, *Peace Process: American Diplomacy and the Arab-Israeli Conflict Since 1967* (Washington, DC: Brookings Institution and University of California Press, 1993), p. 1.

2. *Wataiq 'Abdel-Nasser: Khutab, ahadit, tasrihat: Yanayir 1967–Disember 1968 [Abdel-Nasser's Documents: Speeches, Discussions, and Declarations, January 1967–December 1968]* (Cairo: Markaz al-dirasat al-siyasiya wa al-istratijiya bi Al-Ahram, 1973), p. 246 (here-

inafter this series will be referred to as *Wataiq Nasser, 1967–1968*). Shortly after the war, Nasser told his colleague, Vice-President Zakaria Muhieddin, that Johnson was determined to get rid of Nasser. See Tharwat Akasha, *Mudhakkirati fi al-siyasa wa al-thaqafa [My Memoirs in Politics and in Culture]*, vol. 2 (Cairo: Maktaba al-madbuli, 1988), pp. 490, 501–502.

3. *Wataiq Nasser, 1967–1968*, p. 226; Mahmoud Riad, *The Struggle for Peace in the Middle East* (London: Quartet Books, 1981), pp. 36–37; Mohamed Heikal, *1967: Sanawat al-galayan, Harb al-talateen sana [1967: The Years of Upheaval, the Thirty Years War]*, vol. 1 (Cairo: Markaz Al-Ahram litarjama wa al-nashr, 1988), p. 846.

4. *Wataiq Nasser, 1967–1968*, p. 226; Riad, *The Struggle for Peace in the Middle East*, pp. 36–37; Heikal, *1967: Sanawat al-galayan*, p. 846; Mohamed Heikal, *Nasser: The Cairo Documents* (London: New English Library, 1972), p. 219.

5. H. M. King Hussein, *Harbuna ma'a Israil [Our War with Israel]* (Beirut: Dar al-nahar lilnashr, 1968), pp. 67–69.

6. Beginning in 1965, Johnson applied economic pressure against Nasser by reducing the flow of foreign aid to Egypt. *Wataiq Nasser, 1967–1968*, pp. 226, 243–248; Lieutenant General Salah al-Din al-Hadidi, *Shahid ila harb sab'a wa sitteen [Witness to the 1967 War]* (Cairo: Maktaba al-madbuli, 1974), p. 180. Diya al-Din Baybars, *Al-asrar al-sakhsiya li 'Abd al-Nasser [The Personal Secrets of Nasser as Told by Mahmoud al-Jayar]* (Cairo: Maktaba al-madbuli, 1976), p. 165; Ahmed Hamroush, *Qissa taura 23 Yulio: Karif 'Abd al-Nasser [The Story of the 23 July Revolution: The Autumn of 'Abd al-Nasser]*, vol. 5 (Cairo: Maktaba al-madbuli, 1984), pp. 138–139, 141; Mahmoud Riad, *Mudhakkirat: America wa al-'arab [Memoirs: America and the Arabs]*, vol. 3 (Beirut: Dar al-Mustaqbal al-'Arabi, 1986), pp. 40–42; Mohamed Heikal, *1967: Al-infijar, Harb al-talateen sana' [1967: The Explosion, the Thirty Years War]*, vol. 3 (Cairo: Markaz Al-Ahram liltarjama wa al-nashr, 1990), pp. 756, 846, 876.

7. Riad, *The Struggle for Peace in the Middle East*, p. 25.

8. *Wataiq Nasser, 1967–1968*, p. 336; Abdel Meguid Farid, *Min muhadarat ijtima'at 'Abd al-Nasser al-'arabiya was duwaliya [From the Minutes of 'Abd al-Nasser's Arab and International Meetings, 1967–1970]* (Beirut: Mu'assasa al-abhat al-'arabiya, 1979), pp. 120–121; Hamroush, *Qissa taura 23 Yulio*, vol. 5, pp. 82–83; Ahmed Youssef Ahmed, *Al-dawr al-Misri fi al-Yaman, 1962–1967 [The Egyptian Role in Yemen, 1962–1967]* (Cairo: Al-Hai'a al-Misriya al-amma ilkitab, 1981), p. 319.

9. US Department of State, Memorandum of Conversation, Subject: US-U.A.R. Relations, 17 September 1965, in *The Lyndon B. Johnson National Security Files, the Middle East: National Security Files, 1963–1969* (Frederick, Md.: University Publications of America, 1989), reel 8 of 8 (hereinafter, this series will be referred to as *LBJ Files*).

10. Riad, *The Struggle for Peace in the Middle East*, p. 16; Tom Little, *Modern Egypt* (London: Ernest Benn, 1967), p. 231; Hamroush, *Qissa taura 23 Yulio*, vol. 5, pp. 83–84, 94; Mohamed Heikal, *Sphinx and Commissar: The Rise and Fall of Soviet Influence in the Arab World* (London: Collins, 1978), pp. 161–162, 165–167.

11. Hal Saunders, Recommend Clearing Cable from Hare to Battle with Added Final Sentence, 4 June 1966, in *LBJ Files*, reel 8 of 8.

12. Cairo to Secretary of State, No. 3062, 25 May 1966 [sections one and two of two], in ibid.

13. Mohammed Fawzi, *Harb october am 1973: Dirasa was durus [The October War of 1973: A Study and Lessons]* (Beirut: Dar al-Mustaqbal al-'arabi, 1988), p. 5; Riad, *The Struggle for Peace in the Middle East*, p. 27; Mohamed Hafez Ismael, *Amin Misr al-quami*

fi asr al-tahadiyat [Egyptian National Security in the Challenging Age] (Cairo: Markaz Al-Ahram lilnashr, 1987), p. 125.

14. *Wataiq Nasser, 1967–1968,* p. 495; Heikal, *1967: Al-infijar,* pp. 914, 933; Mohamed Heikal, *The Road to Ramadan: The Inside Story of How the Arabs Prepared For and Almost Won the October War of 1973* (India: Natraj Publishers, 1981), p. 47; Riad, *The Struggle for Peace in the Middle East,* pp. 76–77.

15. Riad, *The Struggle for Peace in the Middle East,* pp. 25, 37, 39. Riad, *Mudhakkirat,* vol. 3, p. 45.

16. Robert Stephens, *Nasser: A Political Biography* (Middlesex, England: Penguin, 1971), p. 521; Richard Parker, "The June War: Whose Conspiracy?" *Journal of Palestine Studies* 21(4) (Summer 1992), pp. 15–17; Abdel-Latif A. Baghdadi, *Mudhakirat [Memoirs],* vol. 2 (Cairo: Al-maktab al-Misri al-hadit, 1977), p. 277.

17. Heikal, *1967: Al-infijar,* pp. 725, 733, 895; Baghdadi, *Mudhakirat [Memoirs],* vol. 2, pp. 275–276.

18. Draft Message to Chairman Kosygin, 8 June 1967, in *LBJ Files,* reel 1 of 8; Lyndon B. Johnson, *The Vantage Point: Perspectives of the Presidency, 1963–1969* (New York: Holt, Rinehart, and Winston, 1971), p. 298.

19. Memorandum for Mr. Rostow: The Security Council Meeting of 6 and 7 June 1967, in *LBJ Files,* reel 1 of 8.

20. The states of Eastern Europe, with the exception of Romania, also broke off diplomatic relations with Tel Aviv. Pravda, 10 June 1967; Johnson, *The Vantage Point,* p. 302; Moshe Dayan, *Story of My Life* (London: Weidenfeld and Nicolson, 1976), p. 304; Abba Eban, *An Autobiography* (London: Weidenfeld and Nicolson, 1977), p. 423.

21. Johnson, *The Vantage Point,* p. 302.

22. The weight of evidence indicates that Washington turned a blind eye toward Israel's offensive campaign against Syria. Israel's foreign minister at the time, Abba Eban, noted that some US officials informed him that Syria should not be allowed to escape injury. On June 8 these officials were worried lest the UN Security Council adopt a cease-fire resolution, thus leaving Syria off the hook. During the debate on whether to storm the Golan Heights, Eban told the Israeli cabinet that Washington would be delighted if Syria were beaten. Declassified US documents also show that US officials hoped that Israel would "go fast enough" to create a "de facto" situation on the Syrian front before the UN Security Council passed a cease-fire resolution. The USS *Liberty* incident, however, indicates that the Johnson administration did not sanction Israel's attack on Syria. We still do not know the whole story behind Israel's attack on this US-flagged intelligence-gathering ship in the eastern Mediterranean, killing thirty-four men, although some believe it was a deliberate attempt by Israel to keep Washington in the dark as to its intentions vis-à-vis the Golan Heights rather than an accident, as the Israelis claim. The recently declassified US documents do not provide any critical insights as to Israel's motives. For evidence on the US stand toward the Golan issue, see Walt Rostow to President, 6 June 1967, in *LBJ Files,* reel 1 of 8. See also Eban, *An Autobiography,* pp. 421–422; William B. Quandt, *Decade of Decisions: American Policy Toward the Arab-Israeli Conflict, 1967–1976* (Berkeley: University of California Press, 1977), p. 63; Steven L. Spiegel, *The Other Arab-Israeli Conflict: Making America's Middle East Policy, from Truman to Reagan* (Chicago: University of Chicago Press, 1985), p. 151; Dayan, *Story of My Life,* p. 304.

23. US Central Intelligence Agency (CIA), Memorandum for Walt W. Rostow, Subject: Objectives of the Middle East Combatants and the USSR, 6 June 1967, in *LBJ Files,* reel 1 of 8.

24. *Majmu'at Khutab wa tasrihat wa bayanat al-ra'is Gamal Abdel-Nasser, 23 Yulio 1952–1958 [The Collected Speeches, Declarations, and Statements of President Gamal 'Abd al-Nasser, 23 July 1952–1958]*, vol. 1 (Cairo: Hai'a al ist'lamat, n.d.), p. 617; *Wataiq Nasser, 1967–1968*, pp. 226, 243–248; Riad, *The Struggle for Peace in the Middle East*, p. 37; Sa'id Mar'iy, *Awraq siyasiya: Min'azma Mars ila al-naksa [Political Papers: From the March Crisis to the Disaster]* (Cairo: Al-maktab al-Misri al-hadit, 1978), p. 362; Salah Nasr, *Abdel-Nasser wa tajriba al-wahda [Nasser and the Unity Experience]* (Cairo: Al-watan al-'arabi, 1976), vol. 1, p. 281; Heikal, *1967: Al-infijar*, p. 846; Heikal, *Sphinx and Commissar*, p. 72.

25. During his first meeting with King Hussein after the war, President Johnson informed his guest that he was "angry" with Egypt. H. M. King Hussein, *Mahammati kamalik [My Profession as King]* (Jordan: Al-sirka al-'arabiya iltiba'a wa nashr, 1978), p. 221. See also Hussein, *Harbuna ma'a Israil*, p. 95; Johnson, *The Vantage Point*, p. 303; Quandt, *Peace Process*, pp. 51, 54, 62; and Stephens, *Nasser: A Political Biography*, p. 522.

26. Richard B. Parker, *The Politics of Miscalculation in the Middle East* (Bloomington: Indiana University Press, 1993), p. 121.

27. Quandt, *Peace Process*, p. 61; Parker, *The Politics of Miscalculation*, p. 129; Robert Stookey, *America and the Arab States: An Uneasy Encounter* (London: John Wiley, 1975), p. 217.

28. Harriman to the President and Secretary of State, No. 19914, 6 June 1967, in *LBJ Files*, reel 1 of 8.

29. Walt Rostow to the President, No. 299, 7 June 1967; and Department of State to Embassy Paris, No. 209550, 8 June 1967, in ibid.

30. Department of State to Embassy Tehran, Subject: Middle East Crisis, No. 209086, 7 June 1967, in ibid.

31. Cairo to Secretary of State, No. 3292, 7 June 1967, in ibid.

32. Ibid. CIA, Memorandum for Walt W. Rostow, 6 June 1967; and Department of State, Subject: Middle East Crisis, Embassy Tehran, No. 209086, 7 June 1967, in ibid.

33. Harriman to the President, No. 6577, 8 June 1967; and Department of State to Embassy London, No. 208887, 7 June 1967, in ibid.

34. Riad, *The Struggle for Peace in the Middle East*, p. 83; Riad, *Mudhakkirat*, vol. 3, p. 73; *Wataiq Nasser, 1967–1968*, p. 306; Amin Huweidi, *Hurub Abdel-Nasser ['Abd al-Nasser's Wars]* (Cairo: Dar al-mauqif al-'arabi, 1982), p. 149.

35. Walt Rostow to the President, No. 299, 7 June 1967; Department of State to Embassy London, No. 208887, 7 June 1967; and NSC Memorandum for Walt Rostow, Subject: Reactions to Your Paper of 7 June 1967, 8 June 1967, *LBJ Files*, reel 1 of 8.

36. Richard Helms, CIA, to Walt Rostow, Subject: Israeli Objectives in the Current Crisis—Soviet Policy Miscalculation, 6 June 1967, in ibid.

37. Embassy Tel Aviv to Secretary of State, No. 3998, 7 June 1967, in ibid.

38. Department of State to Embassy Tehran, Subject: Middle East Crisis, No. 209086, 7 June 1967; and Harriman to the President, No. 6577, 8 June 1967, in ibid.

39. Henry Kissinger, *White House Years* (Boston: Little, Brown, 1979), p. 1262; George Lenczowski, *American Presidents and the Middle East* (Durham, N.C.: Duke University Press, 1990), pp. 116–140; Quandt, *Decade of Decisions*, p. 9.

40. Johnson, *The Vantage Point*, pp. 303–304; and Quandt, *Peace Process*, p. 55.

41. David Kimche and Dan Bawly, *The Sandstorm, the Arab-Israeli War of June 1967: Prelude and Aftermath* (New York: Stein and Day, 1968), pp. 279, 281; Riad, *The Struggle for Peace in the Middle East*, pp. 39, 55; Quandt, *Decade of Decisions*, p. 64.

42. Strong US support of Israel in the post–Nixon Doctrine and post–Jordanian civil war period was not as big a shift in US foreign policy as popularly thought. All that Nixon did was to carry further the change in US policy toward Israel that was inaugurated by Johnson after the 1967 war.

43. NSC, Memorandum for Walt Rostow, 8 June 1967, *LBJ Files*, reel 1 of 8; Quandt, *Peace Process*, pp. 54, 57.

44. *Wataiq Nasser, 1967–1968*, pp. 221, 226, 242–243; Baghdadi, *Mudhakirat [Memoirs]*, pp. 274–275, 298–299.

45. *Wataiq Nasser, 1967–1968*, pp. 221, 226, 242–243; Heikal, *1967: Al-infijar*, p. 754; Cairo to Secretary of State, No. 3292, 7 June 1967; Soviet Objectives in the Middle East, No. 41, 2 January 1968, *LBJ Files*, reels 1 and 7 of 8, respectively; Riad, *The Struggle for Peace in the Middle East*, pp. 29–30, 36–37; Riad, *Mudhakkirat*, vol. 2, p. 46; Hamroush, *Qissa taura 23 Yulio*, vol. 5, pp. 126–163, 188–189; Heikal, *Sphinx and Commissar*, p. 181; Stephens, *Nasser: A Political Biography*, p. 511.

46. Anwar Sadat, *In Search of Identity: An Autobiography* (London: Collins, 1978), pp. 172–173; Munir Hafez, "Al-tarik al-sirri lihukm Gamal Abdel-Nasser," *Rose al-Yusif*, No. 2498, 26 April 1976, pp. 22–23; Baghdadi, *Mudhakirat [Memoirs]*, vol. 2, p. 298; Anouar Abdel-Malek, *Egypt: Military Society, the Army Regime, the Left, and Social Change Under Nasser*, trans. Charles Markmann (New York: Random House, 1968), p. viii; Heikal, *Sphinx and Commissar*, p. 191; Heikal, *1967: Al-infijar*, pp. 773, 916–918; Hamroush, *Qissa taura 23 Yulio*, vol. 5, p. 186.

47. *Wataiq Nasser, 1967–1968*, pp. 261, 268; Riad, *The Struggle for Peace in the Middle East*, pp. 42–45; Farid, *Min muhadarat*, pp. 29–30, 34, 41; Fawzi, *Harb october am 1973*, pp. 189, 194–195; Heikal, *Sphinx and Commissar*, p. 193; Hamroush, *Qissa taura 23 Yulio*, vol. 5, p. 186.

48. Stookey, *America and the Arab States*, p. 215.

49. Riad, *The Struggle for Peace in the Middle East*, pp. 49–50, 84; Farid, *Min muhadarat*, pp. 40, 52, 54–61; Fawzi, *Harb october am 1973*, p. 346; Heikal, *1967: Al-infijar*, pp. 788, 914; Heikal, *Sphinx and Commissar*, pp. 185–188; Huweidi, *Hurub Abdel-Nasser*, p. 150; Hamroush, *Qissa taura 23 Yulio*, p. 288.

50. Heikal, *1967: Al-infijar*, pp. 896, 912–913, 936; Heikal, *Sphinx and Commissar*, p. 195; Riad, *The Struggle for Peace in the Middle East*, p. 48; Sadat, *In Search of Identity*, pp. 181, 196.

51. Cited in Sadat, *In Search of Identity*, pp. 187, 197; Heikal, *Sphinx and Commissar*, pp. 193–194.

52. Sadat, *In Search of Identity*, p. 199. The Rogers Initiative was a limited diplomatic initiative designed to convince the Israelis and Egyptians to "stop shooting" and "start talking." The US-proposed cease-fire went into effect in August 1970.

53. Ibid., p. 198.

54. *Wataiq Nasser: Khutab, ahadit, tasrihat: Yanayir 1969–Siptember 1970 [Nasser's Documents: Speeches, Discussions, and Declarations, January 1969–September 1970]* (Cairo: Markaz al-dirasat al-siyasiya wa al-istratijiya bi Al-Ahram, 1973), p. 303 (hereinafter, this series will be referred to as *Wataiq Nasser, 1969–1970*); Riad, *The Struggle for Peace in the Middle East*, pp. 94, 96; Heikal, *Sphinx and Commissar*, p. 198; Quandt, *Peace Process*, p. 77.

55. *Wataiq Nasser, 1969–1970*, pp. 371–372.

56. Sadat, *In Search of Identity*, p. 198.

57. T. Petran, *Syria* (London: Ernest Benn, 1972), p. 201. Syrian rulers were silent, however, about their own procrastination and passivity during the first two days of

fighting and about their slow response to Egyptian and Jordanian urgent appeals for help. On June 6, in its report on the military situation on the Israeli-Jordanian front, the US embassy in Jordan made note of Syria's poor response—the "bare minimum to help out since [the] beginning of the conflict." See Amman to Department of State, No. 4098, 6 June 1967, *LBJ Files,* reel 1 of 8. This stand should be measured against the fact that since the early 1960s, Damascus had been pushing the Arab world toward an armed confrontation with Israel. The behavior of the Syrian leaders, writes Patrick Seale, could be explained by the scale and speed of the war that caught them off-balance and mentally unprepared for Israel's all-out, highly mobile blitzkrieg. Patrick Seale, *Asad of Syria* (London: I. B. Tauris, 1988), pp. 138–139, 144; Majid Khadduri, *Republican Iraq: A Study of Iraqi Politics Since the Revolution of 1958* (London: Oxford University Press, 1969), p. 291; Marion Farouk-Sluglett and Peter Sluglett, *Iraq Since 1958: From Revolution to Dictatorship* (London: KPI, 1987), p. 100; Hamroush, *Qissa taura 23 Yulio,* p. 202; Riad, *The Struggle for Peace in the Middle East,* p. 55; Stephens, *Nasser: A Political Biography,* p. 521.

58. Farid, *Min muhadarat,* p. 81; Hussein, *Harbuna,* p. 97; Heikal, *1967: Al-infijar,* pp. 932, 935; Stookey, *America and the Arab States,* p. 213.

59. Hussein insisted, however, on a collective Arab strategy toward the question of peace with Israel. Riad, *Mudhakkirat,* vol. 3, pp. 47–48; Hussein, *Mahammati kamalik,* p. 228.

60. A few months earlier Nasser had asked his prime minister to discuss with US officials the possibility of a peaceful solution to the Arab-Israeli conflict. The head of the Egyptian intelligence was also told to maintain contacts with the CIA. In November 1967, Nasser publicly declared that Egypt was talking to the United States because "we could not let anger determine our policy." *Wataiq Nasser, 1967–1968,* pp. 248, 288; Farid, *Min muhadarat,* p. 98; Riad, *Mudhakkirat,* p. 50; Hamroush, *Qissa taura 23 Yulio,* pp. 288–289, 342–343.

61. Mohamed Ahmed Mahgoub, *Democracy on Trial: Reflections on Arab and African Affairs* (London: Andre Deutsch, 1974), p. 145; Riad, *The Struggle for Peace in the Middle East,* p. 54.

62. Mahgoub, *Democracy on Trial,* p. 146; United Arab Republic, No. 41, 2 January 1968, *LBJ Files,* reel 7 of 8; *Wataiq Nasser, 1967–1968,* pp. 289–290; Hussein, *Harbuna,* p. 97; *Majmu'at khutab al-malik Hussein: 25 'ammn min al-tarikh, 1952–1977 [The Collected Speeches of King Hussein: 25 Years of History, 1952–1977],* vol. 1 (London: Samir Mutawi's Company for Publication, 1978), p. 662; Wasfi Tal, *Kitabat fi al-qadaya al-'arabiya [Writings on Arab Issues]* (Jordan: Dar al-liwa lisihafa wa nashr, 1980), p. 486; Saad Abu Wardiya, *'Amaliya itiakad al-qarar fi siyasa al-Urdunn al-kharijiya [The Making of Jordan's Foreign Policy]* (Jordan: Daira al-taqafa wa al-funun, 1983), p. 251; Peter Snow, *Hussein: A Biography* (London: Barrie and Jenkins, 1972), pp. 198, 251; Riad, *The Struggle for Peace in the Middle East,* pp. 38, 53–56; Farid, *Min muhadarat,* p. 92; Hamroush, *Qissa taura 23 Yulio,* pp. 235, 244; Stephens, *Nasser: A Political Biography,* p. 523.

63. Although the French text included the definite article, its absence from the English text was partly to preserve ambiguity and partly a product of US pressure in the United Nations. The removal of the definite article affected later interpretations of UN Resolution 242, especially by the Israelis.

64. *Wataiq Nasser, 1967–1968,* pp. 429, 481, 590; *Wataiq Nasser, 1969–1970,* p. 301; Riad, *The Struggle for Peace in the Middle East,* pp. 91–92; Riad, *Mudhakkirat,* pp. 76, 80, 94, 103; Mohammed Fawzi, *Mudhakkirat al-Fariq awwal Mohammed Fawzi: Harb*

al-talat sanawat, 1967–1970 (Damascus: Tlasdar, 1986), p. 202; Huweidi, *Hurub Abdel-Nasser,* p. 152.

65. Riad, *The Struggle for Peace in the Middle East,* pp. 25, 38, 77; Fawzi, *Harb al-talat sanawat,* p. 192; Heikal, *1967: Al-infijar,* p. 887.

66. *Wataiq Nasser, 1967–1968,* p. 498; Riad, *The Struggle for Peace in the Middle East,* p. 39.

67. As a result of the stalemate in the diplomatic arena, the situation deteriorated significantly in the Middle East in spring 1969. Fighting erupted along the Suez Canal, and in April Nasser announced the abrogation of the cease-fire, signaling the onset of the War of Attrition, which lasted until the Rogers Initiative cease-fire in August 1970. *Wataiq Nasser, 1967–1968,* pp. 289–290; Riad, *The Struggle for Peace in the Middle East,* pp. 75, 77–78, 88, 101; Huweidi, *Hurub Abdel-Nasser,* p. 147; Heikal, *1967: Al-infijar,* p. 937; Heikal, *Sphinx and Commissar,* pp. 191–192; Heikal, *The Road to Ramadan,* p. 56; Stephens, *Nasser: A Political Biography,* p. 518.

68. Cited in Parker, *The Politics of Miscalculation in the Middle East,* p. 128.

CHAPTER 12

FLAWED STRATEGIES
AND MISSED SIGNALS

Crisis Bargaining Between
the Superpowers, October 1973

Janice Gross Stein

On the night of October 24, 1973, the Soviet Union proposed joint military intervention with the United States to end the fighting that had begun when Egypt and Syria attacked Israel eighteen days earlier. After intense fighting, as well as massive Soviet and US airlifts of military supplies to the belligerents (the Soviet Union to Egypt and Syria, the United States to Israel), the Egyptian army was in a perilous position. Israel's forces had crossed the Suez Canal and, despite a cease-fire ordered by the United Nations (UN) Security Council, had advanced to cut off Egypt's Third Army. Moscow warned that if joint US-Soviet action were impossible, it would consider taking unilateral action to halt Israel's military offensive. In response, the United States alerted its nuclear and conventional forces worldwide in an attempt to deter Soviet military intervention. The superpowers found themselves in a dangerous confrontation.

The crisis had developed when least expected, after Soviet General Secretary Leonid Brezhnev and US Secretary of State Henry Kissinger had jointly negotiated the terms of a cease-fire on October 23. Both leaders wanted to stop the fighting and to avoid a crisis between their countries. Moreover, they shared the same tactical objectives: In the wake of Israel's stunning battlefield successes, the United

States now fully shared the Soviet Union's interest in ending the war before the Egyptian Third Army was destroyed. Brezhnev and Kissinger were also in constant communication with each other. Under these conditions, no crisis should have occurred. Yet, despite shared objectives and an agreement negotiated between Moscow and Washington, a serious crisis erupted, one that ended in confrontation.

Good bargaining might have averted the crisis and avoided the confrontation, since the zone of agreement between the United States and the Soviet Union was really very wide. At the least, bargaining strategies that read intentions more or less accurately and were signaled clearly could have minimized the damage from a confrontation. Bargaining should certainly not exacerbate the crisis and create the confrontation. Yet both Soviet and US strategies made the crisis more, not less, difficult to manage, contributed heavily to the confrontation, and did long-term damage to the relationship. Bargaining by both superpowers in 1973 was deeply flawed and potentially dangerous. This chapter explores Soviet and US strategies at the end of the 1973 Arab-Israeli war as a textbook case of inappropriate bargaining.

THE CONTEXT OF THE CONFLICT

Egypt and Syria launched a surprise attack against Israel on October 6, 1973. President Anwar Sadat of Egypt decided to go to war because he had lost hope that negotiation could successfully address the issue of Israel's occupation of the Sinai Peninsula. He felt his diplomatic overtures regarding an agreement over the Sinai in the few years preceding the war had been ignored by both Israel and the United States, and therefore he believed that war was his only recourse to reactivate diplomacy and improve his bargaining position. Israel's control of the Sinai, the Golan, the West Bank, and the Gaza Strip emerged from the 1967 Arab-Israeli war, which was precipitated by Egypt's expulsion of a UN peacekeeping force (in place since the end of the 1956 Suez crisis) and a blockade of the Strait of Tiran.

The fighting on both fronts was intense. Israel's army, caught by surprise, took several days to launch a counteroffensive, and it succeeded only after very heavy fighting pushed Syria's army back across the cease-fire lines. The Soviet leadership, anticipating serious Syrian and Egyptian military losses, began a massive airlift and sea lift to its allies, and US President Richard M. Nixon and Secretary of State Kissinger, after an agonizing debate, decided to match the Soviet airlift with a US airlift to Israel. The choice was so difficult because Kissinger was determined to seize the opportunity provided by the war to fracture the Soviet-Egyptian alliance and position the United States as the linchpin of postwar negotiations between Egypt and Israel (and simultaneously not endanger the primary administration foreign policy focus, i.e., détente; however, both superpowers became, through the airlifts, implicated in the war through their respective client-states in the region).

Once assured of resupply, Israel's armies went on the offensive against Egypt and penetrated Egyptian lines on the western bank of the Suez Canal. As the threat to Egypt grew, Brezhnev invited Kissinger to Moscow to negotiate a cease-fire resolution to be put before the UN Security Council. When the cease-fire went into effect, there were no UN observers in the field to determine the positions of both belligerents. A few hours after Egypt and Israel accepted the cease-fire Brezhnev and Kissinger had negotiated, fighting renewed on October 23. Egypt and Israel each accused the other of violating the cease-fire first, but the Israel Defense Forces (IDF) clearly took advantage of the violations to complete the encirclement of the Egyptian Third Army.

In Moscow the crisis developed in two phases. As fighting continued on October 23 and 24, Brezhnev anticipated a catastrophic military defeat of Egypt and a concomitant blow to the reputation of the Soviet Union as ally and arms supplier to the Third World. The road to Cairo was undefended and Egypt was on the verge of military disaster. Brezhnev also felt pressed for time. By October 24, the Soviet Union had only hours to prevent an Egyptian defeat. Here too, his sense of urgency was grounded in reality.

The second phase of the crisis began for Soviet leaders after the United States alerted its forces worldwide. Brezhnev and the Politburo were surprised and angered by the US alert; they met on October 25 for eight hours, in an angry and tense session. In this final phase of the confrontation, Politburo members did not worry about an intentional attack by the United States. Nevertheless, they were intensely angered and greatly disappointed by the US action and seriously concerned about the possibility of inadvertent escalation.

In Washington, the crisis also developed in two distinct but related phases, each following the other in rapid succession. In both phases, US officials perceived a threat, but the nature of the threat changed rapidly under the pressure of events during the course of thirty-six hours. Within hours after his return from Tel Aviv on the morning of October 23, Kissinger learned of the cease-fire violations and received an urgent message from Brezhnev. He worried about the consequences of the destruction of the Egyptian Third Army for US relations with Egypt—and with the Soviet Union. "The Egyptian Third Army on the east bank of the Canal was totally cut off," Kissinger explained. "A crisis was upon us."[1]

Nixon and Kissinger knew that the destruction of the Egyptian Third Army was unacceptable to Moscow. They also shared the Soviet objective of preventing an Egyptian defeat because it would seriously compromise their central objective of creating a postwar political monopoly. Kissinger not only understood Soviet constraints, he shared the estimate regarding the limited time available before the Egyptian Third Army would collapse. From early on October 23 until the evening of October 24, Kissinger identified a threat to US objectives, empathized with Soviet concerns, and considered it urgent to halt Israel's offensive.

Once Brezhnev proposed joint intervention and then warned that he would consider acting if necessary to stop the fighting, the nature of the crisis changed dramatically. Kissinger framed the problem as a threat not only to US interests in the Middle East but to US interests worldwide. If the United States backed down, he believed, its bargaining reputation in future encounters with the Soviet Union would be fundamentally compromised.[2] From Washington's perspective, the crisis was now primarily in the US-Soviet relationship. Kissinger, unlike his Soviet counterparts, did not worry about the risk of inadvertent escalation but focused on the threat to the US reputation for resolve.

Although they considered the risk of war to be low, Kissinger and his colleagues in the White House Situation Room nevertheless felt an acute sense of urgency. If the Soviet Union intended to send troops, they would do so in a matter of hours. They had very limited time to find an appropriate way to signal their determination to resist any deployment of Soviet forces in the Middle East. Although leaders in Moscow and Washington felt pressed for different reasons, the sense of urgency was real and shared, though not equally, in both capitals.

US COMPELLENCE

I begin with an analysis of US bargaining with Israel. Thirty-six hours elapsed between reports of the first violations of the cease-fire and Kissinger's receipt of Brezhnev's letter on the night of October 24. Initially, Kissinger made a less than vigorous effort to compel Israel to hold its hand. By October 24, however, *before* Brezhnev issued his threat, Washington tried vigorously to compel Israel to stop the fighting. US compellence succeeded, but it was too late. The threat to the Egyptian Third Army had provoked Brezhnev to raise the specter of unilateral intervention. There was also a fundamental ambiguity in US strategy: As the United States repeatedly warned Israel against the "destruction" of the Third Army and urged an immediate end to the fighting, it tacitly acquiesced in its encirclement. And an encircled Third Army was a ticking time bomb.

On October 23, Kissinger learned from Israel that all roads to the Egyptian Third Army had been cut. He immediately tried to arrange a second cease-fire through the United Nations in collaboration with Moscow. Israeli Prime Minister Golda Meir, in a "blistering communication," informed Kissinger that Israel would not comply with or even discuss the proposed resolution.[3] Kissinger did not threaten Israel but persisted, over its objections, in negotiating a second cease-fire. He noted that it called for a return to a line that "we had carefully not specified."[4] In so doing, he signaled Jerusalem that the United States was willing to tolerate, at least for the moment, an IDF encirclement of the Egyptian Third Army.[5]

When Kissinger learned of renewed fighting early on the morning of October 24, he made a vigorous effort to compel Israel to observe the cease-fire. He threatened to leave Israel alone if its actions provoked Soviet intervention.[6] In an effort to underline the seriousness of US intent, Kissinger asked Alexander Haig, the president's chief of staff, to call Israel's ambassador in the United States, Simcha Dinitz, to demand, on behalf of the president, an immediate end to offensive military action by Israel.[7] Israel's response was positive but laced with ambiguity: The IDF was trying to absorb Egyptian fire without responding, it would not try to advance, and Israel would keep the US ambassador in Israel, Kenneth Keating, fully informed "in a further effort to calm the Secretary and demonstrate Israeli good intentions."[8]

Even though US efforts to stop the fighting succeeded, the trapped Egyptian Third Army was still at risk because it had nearly exhausted its food, water, and medical supplies. By the time Ambassador Dinitz assured Kissinger that the fighting had stopped, desperate Egyptian President Anwar Sadat had already made his request for joint action by the United States and the Soviet Union.

Thus, US compellence worked, but it was too little and too late to do any good. Although Israel had promised not to advance any further, Kissinger observed that "this [the Israeli reply] left open the possibility of a war of attrition designed to use up Egyptian supplies and force the surrender of the Third Army."[9] The United States had not yet tried seriously to compel Jerusalem to permit food and medical supplies for the Third Army through their lines. Joseph Sisco, assistant secretary of state for Near Eastern and South Asian affairs, explained why the United States concentrated so heavily on an end to the fighting:

> We put enormous pressure on Israel on October 23 and 24. We pressed first on the ceasefire, then on the siege of Suez City, and finally on the encirclement of the Third Army. We pressed hardest on the ceasefire, because that was the first priority: We wanted to stop the fighting. The distinction among the three issues was not that sharp in our minds. We concentrated on what we had to accomplish urgently. We succeeded in stopping the fighting by the afternoon of October 24.[10]

Shortage of time and fast-moving events on the battlefield led Kissinger to concentrate on the urgent and difficult task at hand.

It is not surprising, then, that it took the extraordinary threat from the United States to abandon Israel to face Soviet intervention alone to compel Jerusalem to halt its military operations. Even then, the United States achieved only the first of several objectives. Kissinger understood that he was asking Israel to exchange a tangible gain on the battlefield for a vague US promise about a peace process in the future and acknowledged how difficult it was for Israel's cabinet to see the logic of this kind of concession.[11] Given his understanding of the forces propelling Israel's behavior, it is surprising that he expected to succeed in compelling Israel to observe the cease-fire before it had consolidated its military victory. Despite its dependence on the United States for military and diplomatic support, Tel Aviv framed the conflict very differently than did Washington. The Israeli leaders used every resource at their disposal to secure the military victory they and their population desperately wanted. Under these conditions, only an extraordinary effort would permit US compellence to succeed.

THE SOVIET RESORT TO COMPELLENCE

On October 24 at 9:35 p.m. Washington time, Ambassador Anatoliy Dobrynin, the Soviet envoy to Washington, called Kissinger with an urgent letter from Brezhnev. Dobrynin read Kissinger the most important passages:

> Let us together, the USSR and the United States, urgently dispatch to Egypt
> the Soviet and American military contingents, to insure the implementation

of the decision of the Security Council of October 22 and 23 concerning the cessation of fire and of all military activities and also of our understanding with you on the guarantee of the implementation of the decisions of the Security Council. . . . It is necessary to adhere without delay. I will say it straight that if you find it impossible to act jointly with us in this matter, we should be faced with the necessity urgently to consider the question of taking appropriate steps unilaterally. We cannot allow arbitrariness on the part of Israel.[12]

When Brezhnev sent his letter to Nixon, there was significant activity by Soviet paratroops and naval forces. On October 23, Moscow ordered two of its amphibious ships, which had been anchored off the coast of Syria, to steam for Egypt.[13] Early the next morning, a Soviet helicopter carrier and two destroyers were moved from their positions off Crete to relieve the Soviet anticarrier group covering the USS *Independence*. Four Soviet airborne divisions were on ready-to-move status and an in-flight command post was also established in the southern Soviet Union.[14] Preparations were made for the imminent departure of several airborne units, and transport aircraft were loaded. Communications nets surged with activity, and flight plans for the next day were changed.[15] The Soviet Union also halted its airlift to Egypt, thereby freeing significant numbers of transport aircraft.[16]

Soviet officials all agree that Brezhnev's proposal of joint US-Soviet military action was a serious signal, for the appeal to the United States was genuine. However, it was based on a misunderstanding that grew directly out of the drafting of the cease-fire agreement, with an attached memorandum of understanding, by Foreign Minister Andrei Gromyko and Kissinger in Moscow. The third clause of the draft cease-fire resolution provided for negotiations "under appropriate auspices." To clarify the meaning of the phrase, Gromyko and Kissinger also prepared an additional document that was not made public. The document read:

> It is understood that the phrase "under appropriate auspices" in Point 3 of the resolution shall mean that the negotiations between the parties concerned will take place with the active participation of the United States and the Soviet Union at the beginning, and thereafter, in the course of negotiations when key issues of a settlement are dealt with. Throughout the entire process of negotiation, the United States and the Soviet Union will in any case maintain the closest contact with each other and the negotiating parties.[17]

Brezhnev did not see either the private document, which was initialed by Gromyko and Kissinger, or the final text of the cease-fire resolution, which was drafted hurriedly by Kissinger, Sisco, and Gromyko and quickly cabled from Moscow to the United Nations and to Cairo and Damascus. President Sadat interpreted "appropriate auspices" as a US-Soviet guarantee to enforce the cease-fire if necessary.[18] The Soviet ambassador to Egypt, Vladimir Vinogradov, reported Sadat's understanding that the United States and the Soviet Union had "guaranteed" the cease-fire to Moscow.

The confusion arose when the Politburo met on October 23 to discuss the appropriate response to the continued violations of the cease-fire. At the meeting, members of the Politburo argued that the agreement reached in Moscow "obligated" the United States and the Soviet Union to take the steps necessary to implement the resolution that had been adopted by the UN Security Council. Victor Israelian, then the head of the Department of International Organization in the Soviet Foreign Ministry, was present at almost all the Politburo meetings and took detailed notes. He explained:

> The formula "under appropriate auspices" was interpreted as joint action by the USA and the USSR to guarantee the ceasefire in the Near East. For instance, [Prime Minister Alexei] Kosygin suggested at the Politburo meeting that a joint Soviet-American team of military officials should be sent to observe the ceasefire. His idea was that this group should include 200 or 250 observers from each of the two states. Kosygin was supported by Ustinov. They thought that this step should be agreed upon with the Americans and that the Americans should be reminded that, when Kissinger visited Moscow, an agreement was reached to "act as guarantors."[19]

The interpretation given the critical clause by Brezhnev and Kosygin did not go unchallenged at the Politburo meeting. Gromyko explained how the term "under appropriate auspices" had been interpreted in the document that he and Kissinger had initialed. He insisted that the dispatch of Soviet and US personnel would require approval by the UN Security Council; most likely, China would veto such a resolution. Besides, Gromyko added, there were already UN personnel in Cairo.[20]

Kosygin irritably dismissed Gromyko's objections: "That's all formalities. They [the UN Truce Supervisory Organization personnel] are dead souls," he insisted. "The fact is that both we and the Americans committed ourselves to carrying out the Security Council decision and we should proceed from that assumption. Action is needed."[21] Brezhnev was adamant that the United States and the Soviet Union should cooperate in sending military personnel as "guarantors" of the cease-fire. At his urging, the Politburo agreed to make this suggestion to the United States.[22]

Thus, Brezhnev was signaling a serious intent to cooperate in enforcing an end to the fighting. He hoped that the United States and the Soviet Union would act together to enforce the cease-fire as the capstone of détente. The first part of his letter to Nixon was not a threat but an offer of collaboration based on what he thought was a joint understanding of their responsibilities. As bizarre as the proposal would sound in Washington, collective enforcement action was considered realistic in Moscow.[23]

The last sentence of Brezhnev's letter to Nixon is more controversial. Brezhnev warned that "if you find it impossible to act jointly with us in this matter, we

should be faced with the necessity urgently to consider the question of taking appropriate steps unilaterally."[24] Brezhnev did not explicitly threaten the use of military force, but his tone was menacing. This sentence was not in the original draft
of the letter prepared for Brezhnev by Gromyko. Brezhnev added the warning at
the last moment before the letter was sent.[25]

There is debate about the course that Brezhnev would have followed if the
United States rejected the proposal for joint action. There is good evidence that
Brezhnev was bluffing, that he was not prepared to act unilaterally and send Soviet
forces to Egypt. Some Soviet officials considered that the Soviet Union would actually have sent forces if the fighting had not stopped. Vadim Zagladin, who was
deputy director of the International Relations Department of the Central Committee, reported that Soviet leaders considered military intervention in the Cairo
region.[26] Anatoliy Gromyko, who was in the Soviet Embassy in Washington on
October 24, was more cautious: "The Soviet Union seriously considered intervention. The plan was to send troops to the Cairo region. We would have put a cordon
around Cairo. On the other hand, we were anxious not to get involved in the fighting. Some of my colleagues might say that this [Brezhnev's letter] was only a form
of political pressure."[27] General Yuri Yakovlevich Kirshin of the Red Army confirmed that military leaders were asked to prepare contingency plans for the optimum use of Soviet paratroopers.[28]

Soviet officials with more detailed knowledge of the Politburo meeting deny
that the Soviet Union would have sent troops to Cairo. They insist that Brezhnev's
threat was a bluff. Ambassador Dobrynin, who was in Washington on October 24
but in close contact with Soviet leaders, doubted that the Soviet Union would have
sent troops.[29] Georgi Kornienko, head of the US desk in the Soviet Foreign Ministry and one of the four members of the special working group drafted to work
with the Politburo, was adamant: "I am absolutely certain that there were no plans
to send Soviet forces to the Middle East. They were put on alert to put pressure on
the Americans."[30] Israelian insists that the warning was a bluff, that the Soviet
Union had no intention whatsoever of sending troops to Egypt: "Kulikov [the chief
of staff of the military] opposed sending any officers there. He opposed sending
even observers without a disengagement of Israeli and Egyptian forces. Members
of the Politburo had not the slightest desire, on any level, to send forces. There
might have been some contingency planning by the military, but there was no intention to send forces."[31]

At the Politburo meeting on October 23, there was no discussion whatsoever
of sending regular forces, only military observers. The Politburo did not meet on
October 24, before Brezhnev's letter was sent, nor did it discuss his message after
the fact. Gromyko drafted the message for Brezhnev and the two walked and talked
with a few colleagues in the corridor.[32] "It was not a considered decision," Israelian
explained. "No formal decision was ever made by the Politburo to threaten military
intervention. Brezhnev added the threat to put pressure on Nixon to get the fighting stopped. He wanted to put pressure on the United States. He thought it was a
clever thing to do."[33]

The threat to consider unilateral action to stabilize the cease-fire was the last in a series of steps taken by the Soviet Union, all with a common political purpose. In the first instance, Brezhnev hoped that joint action with the United States would end the fighting. The threat that the Soviet Union might act alone was added at the last moment to signal to the United States the seriousness of Soviet interests at stake. Brezhnev hoped that if joint action were impossible, the threat that the Soviet Union would consider sending forces would be enough to compel the United States to stop Israel, that the visible preparation of Soviet troops and his warning would succeed in stabilizing the cease-fire and remove the danger to Cairo.

Brezhnev acted in response to four reinforcing considerations: the failure of intensive negotiations with the United States to stop the fighting; the need to safeguard the political position of proponents of détente at home; the reputation of the Soviet Union as a reliable ally; and the multiplicative effect of anger fueled by a sharp sense of betrayal. Counteracting these pressures was a keen appreciation of the risks of any deployment of forces and the desire to avoid a confrontation with the United States.

The first three motives are obvious and easily understood. Brezhnev's decision was also motivated by fury at what he considered to be Kissinger's duplicity. Brezhnev, prone to intensely emotional reactions, suspected—wrongly—that Kissinger had deliberately deceived him and encouraged Israel to violate the cease-fire. Soviet officials, in interviews, referred again and again to Brezhnev's acute sense of betrayal and anger on October 24. Dobrynin described Brezhnev's reaction in vivid detail: "He was very emotional. He felt deceived by Nixon and Kissinger. I was worried about our relations with the United States and worried that Brezhnev's anger with Nixon and Kissinger would lead him to do something rash."[34] Kosygin was also infuriated. At the Politburo meeting on October 25, he charged that "Kissinger visited Moscow, lied to us, went to Tel Aviv, and fraternized with the Israeli people."[35] Israelian recalled that "the fact that the United States refused to cooperate in regulating the Near-Eastern crisis irritated us and made us suspect that Kissinger was acting behind the back of the Soviet Union."[36] Soviet officials felt especially betrayed because they thought that Kissinger had violated the rules of the game that had been mutually agreed upon during the meeting in Moscow.

The pressures acting on Brezhnev could well have led him to decide to send forces to Egypt if Israel did not halt its military offensive and Cairo became directly threatened. The Soviet Union certainly had the capability to move forces quickly to Cairo West Airfield. Soviet General Alexander Ivanovich Vladimirov insists that had the Soviet Union wanted to send paratroops to Egypt, it would have taken very little time; four paratroop divisions were at full readiness and needed only twenty-four-hour notice before they could board transport aircraft for deployment.[37] The Soviet Union did not have the airlift capability for four divisions, but some movement of troops could have begun quickly.[38]

Soviet leaders, however, were sensitive to the risks of escalation and confrontation that could grow out of a deployment of Soviet conventional forces in Egypt. "Of course, it was a situation of the utmost danger," explained Anatoliy Gromyko.

"The possibility that the Soviet Union would be involved in military action was real. . . . There was a real possibility of escalation, the consequences of which I cannot envisage."[39] Brezhnev worried about the escalation that could result from any deployment of Soviet troops. His fear of escalation led him to reject any Soviet military involvement in the fighting. As soon as the war began, he repeatedly made his opposition to the dispatch of Soviet troops clear to his colleagues in the Politburo and to President Sadat. It is very likely that when Brezhnev added that last threatening sentence to an otherwise temperate draft message, he was driven by anger and intense emotion. Anxious about the fate of Egypt, despairing of diplomacy, and angry at Kissinger's alleged deceit—yet fearful of the escalatory consequences of unilateral intervention—Brezhnev decided first to propose joint intervention, and then to bargain through bluff. He saw no alternative.[40]

Brezhnev miscalculated badly. His attempt at compellence did not accomplish his immediate or long-term political purposes. The United States misread the message intended and responded with a worldwide alert to signal its own resolve. The Soviet threat failed utterly to elicit the desired response.

THE US RESORT TO DETERRENCE

The United States responded to the Soviet threat with a worldwide alert of its forces.[41] At 11:41 p.m., about an hour after the meeting began in the White House Situation Room, Admiral Thomas Moorer, the chairman of the Joint Chiefs of Staff, issued orders to all military commands to increase readiness to Defense Condition III (DEFCON III).[42] At 12:20 a.m. on October 25, US intelligence reported that eight Soviet Antonov-22 transport planes were scheduled to fly from Budapest to Egypt within the next few hours and that elements of the East German armed forces had been alerted. In response, the 82nd Airborne Division was ordered to be ready to deploy within four hours. At 12:25 a.m., the aircraft carrier *Franklin Delano Roosevelt* was sent to the eastern Mediterranean and the carrier *John F. Kennedy*, with its task force, was ordered to move at full speed from the Atlantic to the Mediterranean.[43]

Those who participated in the meeting in the White House Situation Room on the night of October 24 were divided in their estimate of Soviet intentions. Some thought the Soviet Union was bluffing; others thought that Moscow would send a limited number of forces to Egypt. Brezhnev's letter and the intelligence data on Soviet military preparations were consistent with both a bluff and a serious intent to deploy forces in the Middle East.

These differences were not important as to the appropriate response chosen by US officials. Those who thought that the Soviet Union might deploy a limited number of forces were determined to deny the Soviet Union political and military opportunity in the Middle East. Those who thought that the Soviet Union was bluffing also accepted the necessity of an alert. Secretary of Defense James Schlesinger, Moorer, and Haig agreed with Kissinger that an alert was the appropriate response to Brezhnev's challenge. Schlesinger argued that even if the probability of Soviet military action were low, the United States must demonstrate that it could act firmly.[44]

The alert served two purposes. If the Soviet Union was indeed intent upon unilateral military action, the alert's immediate objective would be to deter the Soviet deployment. The Nixon administration determined to deny Moscow this opportunity to introduce military forces into the Middle East. Secondarily, the alert was designed to bank resolve and build reputation for future bargaining. If Brezhnev was bluffing, the alert would "educate" the Soviet leadership. It was imperative to demonstrate resolve to convince Brezhnev that the United States could not be coerced by Moscow. Washington wanted to demonstrate resolve firmly, visibly, and quickly. Everyone present at the White House meeting agreed quickly on the necessity of an immediate, highly visible signal that would be noticed rapidly by Soviet leaders and would either "shock" them into abandoning any intention to intervene with military force or would call their bluff.[45]

The worldwide alert was a singularly inappropriate signal on the part of the United States. It was ineffective, potentially dangerous, and ill-considered. It was inherently ineffective because in the context of the Middle East any kind of nuclear threat was disproportionate and not credible. It was potentially dangerous because it moved up the ladder of escalation and increased the risk of confrontation with the Soviet Union. Even more alarming, US leaders made their decision with little attention to the technical and operational requirements of the alert, its risks, or its likely consequences. The alert was chosen in haste, with little consideration either of its capacity to deter Soviet military intervention or of the alternative measures that might have constituted an effective signal with a reduced risk of escalation.

The alert of the 82nd Airborne was also not a carefully crafted signal. William Quandt, then on the staff of the US National Security Council, provides a detailed—and vivid—description of the decision in the White House:

> Later that night, we got a fragment of a message, the tail end of a message, suggesting the imminent arrival of Soviet forces at Cairo West airfield. Kissinger was frantic. He ordered Atherton [the deputy assistant secretary of state for Near Eastern and South Asian affairs] and me to draft a plan to send U.S. troops to the Middle East, immediately, but not to Israel. Atherton and I were bewildered. Where would the forces go? Kissinger replied that he did not know, but that the forces could not go to Israel, but that a plan was to be prepared immediately to deploy forces in the Middle East. This was the only time that Atherton and I were totally confused. We could not conceive of how to meet the request.[46]

After he briefed the president early the next morning, Kissinger recalls, "Nixon was determined to match any Soviet troop buildup in the area."[47] When asked what kind of conventional military action he wanted, Kissinger replied: "We would have put down the 82nd Airborne if the Soviets had sent forces. We never got to that point. We never discussed it. It would have been very dangerous. That's why you get paid, for doing the dangerous jobs."[48]

The possibility of failure of this deterrence received no serious attention, and no contingency plans were in place. There was no discussion of where US troops were to be deployed, nor of the likelihood of combat with Soviet forces. "We had no plan for blocking [Soviet] intervention," confirms Peter Rodman, then special assistant to Kissinger. "We didn't think about it."[49] Thus, instead of considering the consequences and their options should deterrence fail, US leaders merely hoped that deterrence would succeed.

If the Soviet Union had sent forces to Egypt, and the United States had responded with a conventional deployment of its own, even limited encounters between the two forces in the context of a worldwide alert could easily have escalated to a broadening of the conflict. The Soviet Union might have mobilized additional forces in response. Under this not-so-unlikely scenario, the worldwide alert could have worked against the localization and termination of the fighting in the Middle East—the principal objective of both Moscow and Washington.

THE IRRELEVANCE AND RELEVANCE OF DETERRENCE

"The Soviets subsided," Kissinger claims, "as soon as we showed our teeth."[50] His argument suggests that despite strategic and conventional parity, and despite an acute domestic crisis in Washington (that being the Watergate scandal), the US strategy had persuaded Soviet leaders that Nixon was willing to risk war to block unilateral intervention by Moscow.[51] Soviet leaders purportedly reevaluated the likely costs of intervention, changed their minds, and decided not to send troops to Egypt.

If deterrence is to work, the leaders who are considering military action must change course because they reconsider the likely costs and consequences in the face of the threatened deterrent. Even *before* the United States alerted its forces, however, Brezhnev had no intention of sending Soviet forces to Egypt. As early as October 8, he instructed Ambassador Vinogradov to emphasize Soviet determination not to become involved in the fighting.[52] Again, this time on October 15, during the Politburo meeting, Brezhnev warned Kosygin against misleading Sadat. Although the Soviet government was willing to continue military support to Egypt on a large scale, it would "under no circumstances participate directly in the war."[53] Brezhnev's threat to consider unilateral action was a bluff, issued in frustration at the failure of diplomacy to stop the fighting and in anger at what Brezhnev considered Kissinger's duplicity. Since Brezhnev had no intention of sending forces, deterrence could not have changed his mind. At best, it was irrelevant.

The consequences of the US strategy were not irrelevant. Soviet leaders were genuinely bewildered by the alert; they could not decipher the US "signal." They were also provoked and deeply angered by an action that they could not understand. Shortly after Soviet intelligence picked up signs of the alert, Brezhnev convened the Politburo early on the morning of October 25. The meeting was attended by almost all members, and discussion continued for more than eight hours. General Kulikov began with a briefing on the US alert, including the alert of strategic nuclear forces.

Members of the Politburo had great difficulty interpreting the political intent of the alert. "They could not understand it," Israelian explained. "They asked: 'Are they [the Americans] crazy? The Americans say we threaten them, but how did they get this idea?'"[54] Gromyko was advised by Kornienko, Mikhail Sytenko, who then headed the Department of the Near East, and Israelian that the US reaction was provoked by the last sentence of Brezhnev's letter to Nixon.[55] Brezhnev was incredulous when this explanation was suggested at the Politburo meeting. "Could this be the reason?" he asked. "Could Nixon choose an alert based on this one sentence? But this man Nixon knows that I stopped the airlift as a demonstration of my willingness to cooperate."[56]

Soviet officials were divided in their assessments of the causes and purposes of the alert. Brezhnev thought that Nixon had ordered the alert to demonstrate that he was as courageous as John F. Kennedy—the strong man in a crisis.[57] This interpretation was widely shared by Politburo members. "It seemed to the Politburo," Israelian recalled, "that Nixon's decision was determined mainly by domestic politics. In a situation of growing emotions surrounding Watergate, Nixon had to demonstrate that he was a 'strong president' and that the United States needed him."[58] Many Soviet officials saw the alert as so inconsistent with the ongoing negotiations and the frequent communications between the two capitals that they could find no explanation other than Watergate. The preeminent Soviet expert on US politics, Georgi Arbatov, put it bluntly: "The American alert was designed for home consumption."[59]

However, not all senior officials agreed that the alert was largely a response to Watergate. Kornienko, who was present as an aide to Gromyko at the Politburo meeting, thought that the alert was designed to intimidate the Soviet leadership: "The DEFCON III alert was taken seriously in Moscow. Some of us saw it as an attempt to intimidate us from sending forces to the Middle East. The alert was not dismissed as a response to Watergate. We took it seriously."[60] Dobrynin thought that the alert was intended to intimidate the Soviet Union and to demonstrate resolve for US public opinion.[61]

Irrespective of their conclusions as to the purposes of the alert, Brezhnev and other members of the Politburo were "very emotional, very angry," according to Israelian. "There was no feeling of fear, but of great disappointment and anger."[62] According to Dobrynin, Brezhnev was so emotional because he "felt deceived by Nixon and Kissinger." Dobrynin was concerned "that Brezhnev's anger with Nixon and Kissinger would lead him to do something rash. I was furious, too."[63]

Thus, Politburo members debated the appropriate response to the alert within a highly charged emotional atmosphere. A significant minority supported a military response to the US "provocation." Marshal Andrei Grechko acknowledged that a large-scale mobilization of forces would be very expensive, yet he still recommended the mobilization of 50,000 to 75,000 troops in Ukraine and the northern

Caucasus.[64] Dmitri Ustinov, then secretary of the Central Committee in charge of defense production; Andrei Kirilenko, a loyal Brezhnev supporter; K. F. Katushev, responsible for liaison with ruling Communist parties; Yuri Andropov, then head of KGB, the Soviet intelligence agency; and Kosygin all supported the mobilization of some Soviet forces in response to the alert. "We should respond to mobilization," Andropov argued, "by mobilization."[65] Ustinov thought that Soviet forces should be mobilized without public announcement.

Marshal Grechko also urged the Politburo to order the 1,500 Soviet soldiers in Syria to occupy the Golan Heights. "In the past," he exclaimed, "we have never asked anybody if we could send our troops and we can do the same now."[66] His proposal clearly was not a response to the desperate plight of the Egyptian Third Army but a reaction to what he considered a US attempt at intimidation.

Gromyko, Kirilenko, and Kosygin spoke vigorously against the proposal to involve Soviet troops in the fighting. "We shall send two divisions to the Near East," Kosygin argued, "and in response the Americans will send two divisions as well. If we send five divisions, the Americans will send their five. . . . Today nobody can be frightened by anybody. The United States will not start a war and we have no reason to start a war."[67] Kosygin dismissed the US threat as not credible. He did not oppose Soviet involvement in the Middle East because he was intimidated by the United States but rather because of the futility of Soviet intervention.

The discussion grew more heated until the usually silent Brezhnev finally put the question: "Comrades, if we do not react at all, if we do not respond to the American mobilization, what will happen?"[68] Nikolai Podgorny, who formally held the office of president of the Soviet Union, Gromyko, and Boris Ponomarev, who headed the International Department of the Central Committee, agreed that Soviet interests would not suffer if Moscow decided not to respond to the US alert with its own military measures. These officials agreed with the general secretary that the crisis in US-Soviet relations should be resolved by political rather than military measures.

The Politburo then discussed the possibility of sending Gromyko immediately to Washington to confer personally with Nixon. Kosygin recommended that Gromyko express Moscow's bewilderment at the US alert and discuss the possibility of sending Soviet and US observers to monitor observance of the cease-fire. Kosygin's proposal to signal Soviet interest in a cooperative solution in this highly visible manner received no support in the Politburo. In fact, Brezhnev argued that to send a representative to Washington after the United States had alerted its forces would be interpreted as "weakness."[69] He rejected any Soviet attempt at reassurance in the face of the US attempt at deterrence.

In an emotional speech, Brezhnev summarized the Soviet Union's eventual response to the US alert: "The Americans say we threaten them," he said, "but they are lying to us."[70] Thus, he insisted again that the Soviet Union had given the United States no grounds to alert its forces and that a Soviet mobilization in response would accomplish nothing. In strong language, Brezhnev reemphasized his opposition to any preparatory military measures.

The US attempt at deterrence provoked anger, disappointment, and bitterness among Soviet leaders. What US officials regarded as a signal of resolve, Soviet officials interpreted as an attempt to intimidate or a response based on domestic political weakness. Bewildered and angered, a significant group within the Politburo proposed the mobilization of Soviet forces *in response* to the alert. Although Brezhnev opposed a military response, he too could not understand the intent of the alert. Angered by the alert, he rejected a proposal that Gromyko attempt to reassure Nixon personally of Soviet intentions, even though Soviet intentions were benign. Thus, the US strategy had made the confrontation more difficult to resolve. Following the Politburo meeting, Brezhnev wrote to President Nixon that although the Soviet Union had chosen not to respond with military measures, the US action was unprovoked and not conducive to the relaxation of international tensions.[71] Under a different leader, the Politburo might well have chosen differently.

THE FAILURE OF SOVIET COMPELLENCE

The Soviet strategy of threatening unilateral intervention if the fighting did not stop in the Middle East might well have resolved the crisis. In a nutshell, Brezhnev was trying to compel the United States to press Israel to stop the fighting. Once the cease-fire was stabilized and the safety of the Egyptian Third Army was assured, the crisis would most likely have ended. We have already shown how Soviet bargaining provoked escalation by leading the United States to issue a worldwide military alert. The evidence also suggests that the Soviet threat did not resolve the crisis. Like its US counterpart, it was both irrelevant and provocative.

By the time Brezhnev's letter arrived in Washington the fighting had stopped. Ironically, Brezhnev's threat only interrupted the US efforts to compel Israel to allow food and medical supplies to reach the trapped Egyptian Third Army. Kissinger, who had been actively trying to prevent the destruction of the Third Army, stopped pressing Israel immediately after he received Brezhnev's letter on the evening of October 24; he did not resume these efforts until the following morning—after it was apparent that the crisis between the United States and the Soviet Union would be resolved. Kissinger then pressed Israel to permit nonmilitary supplies to reach the Third Army despite the fact that Brezhnev had made no such demand in his letter. By the time the United States finally extracted a commitment from Israel on October 26 to permit a onetime convoy to reach the Third Army, the crisis was over.

The critical period was the thirteen hours from 7:00 p.m. on October 24, when Dobrynin first informed Kissinger of Brezhnev's letter, until 8:00 a.m. the next morning, when President Sadat withdrew his request for intervention by Soviet and US forces. It seemed unlikely to Kissinger that Moscow would send forces without Egyptian consent. During that period, Kissinger met several times with Israel's ambassador to Washington but made no request that Israel break its encirclement of the Third Army. Instead, Israel's leaders received a request from Kissinger for a contingency plan to destroy the Third Army. In the face of the

Soviet threat, Kissinger subtly encouraged Israel to consider escalating military action. When asked directly long after the crisis was over, Kissinger confirmed his refusal to be coerced: "The Soviet threat backfired. Only after the Russians caved in, did I turn on the Israelis. After the Soviets threatened, I asked the Israelis to develop an option to defeat the Third Army. Only after I knew that the Russians were caving in, did I press the Israelis really hard on Friday [October 25]."[72]

The United States responded to Soviet strategy by redefining the problem as a test of US resolve and ceased its attempts to compel its ally, Israel.[73] It might be argued that Soviet compellence nevertheless increased US incentives to coerce Israel once the crisis between Moscow and Washington passed. The evidence does not sustain this argument. The United States had tried to compel Israel to observe the cease-fire before the Soviet Union issued its threat. Nixon and Kissinger had also decided—again, before the Soviet ultimatum—that they would not permit the destruction of the Egyptian Third Army.[74] Kissinger had also begun his attempt to coerce Israel to permit the resupply of the Third Army before the Soviet Union raised the issue with the United States. And Nixon and Kissinger also worried about a confrontation with Moscow before Brezhnev sent his letter. Thus, the evidence suggests strongly that the United States would have compelled Israel to accept a cease-fire and allow resupply of the Third Army even in the absence of a Soviet threat because of its overriding interest in establishing a relationship with Egypt that would endure after the war was over.

The Soviet attempt at compellence was not only unnecessary but also irrelevant, poorly constructed, and counterproductive: Soviet leaders did not have real-time battlefield intelligence and were unaware that the fighting had stopped by the time Brezhnev's letter arrived in Washington; Brezhnev's threat was poorly constructed in that it did not raise the critical issue of the supply of the trapped Third Army; it was counterproductive because it interrupted the US attempt to coerce Israel. Soviet bargaining provoked precisely the responses it had wanted to prevent: an interruption of US efforts to save the Egyptian Third Army and a worldwide alert of US forces that threatened the confrontation that Brezhnev wanted above all to avoid.

THE CRISIS IS RESOLVED

When the Soviet Union decided not to respond to the US alert with military measures, the process of escalation stopped. A halt in escalation was necessary but insufficient to resolve the crisis. To settle the crisis, the Soviet Union had to withdraw its threat to consider unilateral military intervention. Brezhnev did so implicitly on October 25 when he accepted Nixon's offer to send US and Soviet observers to monitor the cease-fire. Later that day, the Soviet ambassador to the United Nations supported a resolution in the UN Security Council (Resolution 340) to dispatch a peacekeeping force that, by convention, excluded Soviet and US forces.

"It was not the military threat," according to Anatoliy Gromyko, "but diplomacy that finally found a solution."[75] As Brezhnev was concluding his emotional speech at the Politburo meeting, Konstantin Chernenko, acting informally as secretary to the Politburo, passed to him the text of Nixon's letter (actually drafted by Henry Kissinger). Brezhnev read the long letter aloud to the Politburo, emphasizing what he considered two particularly conciliatory phrases: "I agree with you that our understanding to act jointly for peace is one of the highest value and that we should implement that understanding in this complex situation"; and, "In the spirit of our agreements this is the time not for acting unilaterally, but in harmony and with cool heads."[76] Nixon's proposal provided the Politburo with a face-saving opportunity to end the crisis without confrontation. It was accepted "with relief," and the Politburo ended its meeting.[77]

Several important considerations help to explain Soviet acceptance of a political solution to the crisis. Foremost, Soviet leaders did not consider the stakes in the Middle East to be worth the risk of confrontation and war. When Politburo members began their first meeting after the US alert, the first issue they discussed was whether the Soviet Union was prepared to confront the United States and fight a large-scale war. Despite the differences within the Politburo, the unanimous answer was "no." Kosygin put it bluntly: "It is not reasonable to become involved in a war with the United States because of Egypt and Syria."[78] Andropov, Kirilenko, Ponomarev, Gromyko, Kosygin, and Grechko all made essentially the same point.[79]

The belief that the Soviet relationship with Egypt and Syria was not worth a war with the United States was widespread. "Nobody shared Arab war aims," Israelian said. "Sadat was not Castro. Our relationship with him was not the same."[80] Although the reputation and the interests of the Soviet Union were heavily engaged in Egypt, the Soviet-Egyptian relationship had long been troubled.[81] The Politburo was angered by Egyptian military incompetence, by Sadat's expulsion of Soviet military advisers, and by his failure to heed its advice. Soviet stakes in the region were high but tempered by ideological, military, and personal differences between Arab and Soviet leaders. The Politburo was therefore not prepared to risk a US-Soviet confrontation to save Sadat. Even after he listened to a pessimistic evaluation of Egypt's military situation, Brezhnev said to his colleagues: "We must tell Sadat, 'We were right. We sympathize with you but we can't reverse the results of your military operations.'"[82]

A second consideration was the importance Brezhnev personally attached to good relations with the United States. Brezhnev considered détente the outstanding accomplishment of his foreign policy. Even before the alert, Brezhnev recognized that a deployment of Soviet forces in Egypt would seriously complicate the Soviet relationship with the United States. He therefore strongly preferred a diplomatic solution within the framework that he had negotiated with Kissinger when Kissinger had come to Moscow.

In large part because Brezhnev prided himself on his personal relationship with the US president, he was deeply angered by "Nixon's action." Anger can lead to ill-considered and risky actions because people who are emotionally aroused are less likely to think through the consequences of their choices. In this case, the Soviet Union did not do so because of the impact of crosscutting emotions. Although

Brezhnev was angered and disappointed by the US alert, he was also angry with Sadat for consistently ignoring Soviet advice. Anger pulled in opposite directions. These crosscutting emotions moderated Brezhnev's reaction and reduced the impact of his anger at the United States. He was therefore able to temper his response.

One other factor contributed significantly to the resolution of the crisis. There was an important asymmetry in the perceptions of Moscow and Washington as to the actual risks of war. Leaders in Moscow worried about a confrontation between Soviet military forces and those of Israel if Soviet troops were sent to Egypt. They feared that a Soviet-Israeli conflict could easily escalate into a wider engagement that could draw in the United States. Politburo members worried that actions they might take might lead inadvertently to war. "The steps we take," Kirilenko urged, "should not lead to war."[83]

Analysts who argue today that the crisis was resolved because the United States manipulated the risk of war miss the fundamental point.[84] Soviet leaders worried about the risk of war as a consequence of *their* military deployment, *before* the US alert. Their evaluation of the risks of war worked in favor of crisis resolution. It served as a powerful incentive to search actively for a political solution and as a brake on a military response to the US alert. However, US leaders did not consider the risk of war and confrontation with Soviet forces to be significant even after their alert. Fortunately, the asymmetrical pattern of the fear of war worked in favor of crisis resolution. Soviet leaders, who worried seriously about escalation, had to make the critical decision about a response to the US alert.

CONCLUSION

Bargaining is usually ineffective when the two sides maintain radically different understandings of the context. As to the US-Soviet bargaining in 1973, messages were framed in one context and interpreted in another. It is not surprising that the interpretation of critical signals bore no relationship to the intentions of the signal senders. Attempts both to demonstrate resolve and to cooperate failed. Signals had a nearly random, hit-and-miss effect. The crisis, as we have seen, was resolved in spite of the bargaining strategies of both superpowers.

To the extent that bargaining had any impact, it was largely negative because of the way it reinforced Soviet images of the United States as unreliable, unpredictable, and duplicitous—and US images of the Soviet Union as aggressive and treacherous. Ironically, the bargaining process between the two superpowers not only failed to resolve the crisis but damaged the long-term relationship between them. Inappropriate strategies triggered a self-reinforcing cycle of conflict that led to the progressive deterioration of the relationship between the superpowers for the remainder of the decade.

After the 1973 Arab-Israeli war, Brezhnev and the proponents of détente faced a growing barrage of criticism from colleagues who alleged that the United States had tricked the Soviet leadership and used the war as a cover to exclude the Soviet Union from Egypt. Although Kissinger had not engaged in any deliberate deception of the Soviet leadership during the war, he seized the opportunity after the war to initiate a process of negotiation between Egypt and Israel that led to two successive disengagement agreements and culminated ultimately in the Camp David accords in 1978 and the subsequent Egyptian-Israeli peace treaty in 1979. The Soviet Union was almost entirely excluded from this process. Although the United States achieved its strategic objectives in the heartland of the Middle East and successfully moved the two most powerful parties in the region to a peace agreement, flawed bargaining during the crisis of October 1973 marked the beginning of the end of détente between the superpowers. Suspicion and distrust weakened the advocates of détente in both Moscow and Washington and contributed to a "second cold war" between the United States and the Soviet Union that would last for more than a decade.

Notes

1. Henry Kissinger, *Years of Upheaval* (Boston: Little, Brown, 1972), p. 571.
2. Henry Kissinger, interview by author, New York, 19 June 1991.
3. Kissinger, *Years of Upheaval*, p. 573.
4. Ibid.
5. Former member of Prime Minister Meir's staff, interview by author, April 1988.
6. In his book, Kissinger wrote: "It was clear that if we let this go on, a confrontation with the Soviets was inevitable. . . . I told Dinitz [Israel's ambassador to Washington] that the art of foreign policy was to know when to clinch one's victories. There were limits beyond which we could not go, with all our friendship for Israel, and one of them was to make the leader of another superpower look like an idiot. I said to Dinitz that if Sadat asked the Soviets, as he had us, to enforce the cease-fire with their own troops, Israel would have out-smarted itself." Kissinger, *Years of Upheaval*, p. 576.
7. Hanoch Bartov, in his *Dado—Arbaim Ve'Shmoneh Shanim V'Esraim Yom (Dado— 48 Years and Twenty Days)*, 2 vols. (Tel Aviv: Ma'ariv Book Guild, 1978), vol. 1, p. 592, reports that every five minutes that morning, calls were coming in from the White House warning Israel to stop its offensive. Israel was informed that Kissinger was boiling with rage. This biography of General David Elazar, the chief of staff of the Israeli Defense Forces (IDF) during the war, is based on the private papers of the chief of staff, which are not yet publicly available.
8. Cited by Kissinger, *Years of Upheaval*, p. 579.
9. Ibid.
10. Joseph Sisco, interview by author, Washington, 17 April 1991.
11. Kissinger, *Years of Upheaval*, p. 573.
12. Cited by Kissinger, ibid., p. 583.
13. Galia Golan, "Soviet Decisionmaking in the Yom Kippur War," in Jiri Valenta and William Potter, eds., *Soviet Decisionmaking for National Security* (London: George Allen and Unwin, 1984), pp. 185–217; and Bradford Dismukes and James McConnell, *Soviet Naval Diplomacy* (New York: Pergamon Press, 1979), p. 203.
14. There is some controversy as to how many airborne divisions were moved to the status of ready-for-combat that day. All seven divisions had been on alert since October 11, but some analysts claim that only one airborne division moved to ready-to-move status on 24 October. See Raymond Garthoff, *Détente and Confrontation:*

216JANICE GROSS STEIN

American-Soviet Relations from Nixon to Reagan (Washington, DC: Brookings Institution, 1985), pp. 377–378, n. 68. Hart maintains that three of the seven divisions were placed on ready-to-move status on 10 October and the remaining four early on 24 October. See Douglas M. Hart, "Soviet Approaches to Crisis Management: The Military Dimension," *Survival* 26(5) (September-October 1984), pp. 214–222.

15. Hart, "Soviet Approaches to Crisis Management."

16. The Politburo was not told of these military measures. When he was asked at the Politburo meeting on 25 October about Soviet military movements, Marshal Andrei Grechko, responsible for defense, responded that they were routine military maneuvers. Victor Israelian, interview by author, State College, Pa., 8 January 1992. Evgeny Pyrlin, the deputy director of the Middle East division in the Soviet Foreign Ministry in 1973, confirms that during the October War, "Grechko frequently replied to questions from his Politburo colleagues, 'I just informed Comrade Brezhnev about this,' and all questions became useless. As a rule the Minister of Defense was authorized to order military actions short of the mobilization of reserves and the reinforcement of armored and air divisions. To be frank, Mr. Grechko as the Minister of Defense had wide liberty of action and sometimes didn't inform the political leadership of the details." Evgeny Pyrlin, "Some Observations (Memoirs) About the Arab-Israeli War (1973)," unpublished memorandum commissioned for this project, Moscow, August 1992, p. 5. Andrei Alexandrov-Agentov, a senior aide to Brezhnev in 1973, explained that "Brezhnev liked and trusted Grechko. Very often, Grechko, confident of Brezhnev's trust, authorized measures of military preparedness without Brezhnev's knowledge or approval. He had a free hand." Andrei M. Alexandrov-Agentov, interview by author, Moscow, 19 August 1992. Alexandrov was a career diplomat whom Brezhnev had borrowed from the Ministry of Foreign Affairs when he became chairman of the Presidium of the Supreme Soviet.

17. Victor Israelian, personal communication, 9 March 1992.

18. Victor Israelian, interview by author, State College, Pa., 8 January 1992. In his message to Kissinger on 23 October, Sadat asked the United States to "intervene effectively, even if that necessitates the use of forces, in order to guarantee the full implementation of the cease-fire resolution in accordance with the joint US-USSR agreement." Cited by Kissinger, *Years of Upheaval,* p. 574.

19. Victor Israelian, "The Kremlin: October 1973," unpublished monograph, p. 22.

20. Ibid., p. 23.

21. Ibid., p. 21, and personal communication, 9 March 1992.

22. Israelian, "The Kremlin: October 1973," p. 23.

23. Vadim Zagladin (then deputy director of the International Relations Department of the Central Committee), interview by author, Moscow, 18 May 1989.

24. Cited by Kissinger, *Years of Upheaval,* p. 583.

25. Victor Israelian, interview by author, State College, Pa., 8 January 1992.

26. Vadim Zagladin, interview by author, Moscow, 18 May 1989.

27. Anatoliy Gromyko, interview by author, Moscow, 18 May 1989.

28. General Yuri Yakovlevich Kirshin, interview by author, Moscow, 17 December 1992.

29. Dobrynin, interview by author, Moscow, 17 December 1992.

30. Georgi Kornienko, interview by author, Moscow, 17 December 1991.

31. Victor Israelian, interview by author, State College, Pa., 8 January 1992.

32. Israelian is not certain how this last sentence was inserted. "It is difficult for me to say to whom this idea belonged originally. It is possible that it was born during one of Brezhnev's lobby interviews with his closest colleagues from the Politburo and was immediately put into the message." Israelian, "The Kremlin: October 1973," p. 24.

33. Victor Israelian, interview by author, State College, Pa., 8 January 1992.

34. Anatoliy Dobrynin, interview by author, Moscow, 17 December 1991.

35. Israelian, "The Kremlin: October 1973," p. 27.

36. Ibid., p. 23.

37. General Alexander Ivanovich Vladimirov, interview by author, Moscow, 18 December 1991. William Colby, director of the CIA in 1973, insists that Soviet forces did not need much coordination with Egypt to deploy. "They had a mission there. All they needed was landing times at Cairo West and they could have gotten those at the last moment." William Colby, telephone interview by author, 11 January 1992. On the other hand, Admiral Nikolai Amelko, deputy chief of the Soviet navy in 1973, argued that the deployment of paratroopers would have required air, logistical, and marine support, which would have required some coordination and time. No such request was made to the Soviet navy in October 1973. Admiral Nikolai N. Amelko, interview by author, Moscow, 18 December 1991.

38. Raymond Garthoff, personal communication, 9 July 1992. Garthoff estimates that it would have taken a considerable length of time to move the full four divisions.

39. Anatoliy Gromyko, interview by author, Moscow, 18 May 1989.

40. Alexander Kislov, Deputy Director of IMEMO, interview by author, Moscow, 18 May 1989. Garthoff, *Détente and Confrontation,* p. 383, concurs with this interpretation of Brezhnev's intentions.

41. Secretary of Defense James Schlesinger and Secretary of State Kissinger made the decision to alert US forces, in consultation with the director of the CIA, William Colby, the chairman of the Joint Chiefs of Staff, Admiral Thomas Moorer, and the president's chief of staff, Alexander Haig, who was with the president in his personal quarters. Present as well in the Situation Room of the White House were the deputy assistant to the president for National Security Affairs, General Brent Scowcroft, and Commander Jonathan T. Howe, the military assistant to the secretary of state at the National Security Council.

42. President Nixon did not participate in the discussions, was not informed of the alert when it was ordered, and only approved the alert retroactively at about 3 a.m. on the morning of 25 October. Overwhelmed by the growing scandal of Watergate, the president was reportedly drunk and exhausted upstairs in his personal quarters in the White House. *Inquiring into the Military Alert Invoked on October 24, 1973,* 93rd Congress, House of Representatives, Report 93–970 (Washington, DC: US Government Printing Office, 14 April 1974, 74–09780), p. 3.

43. Barry M. Blechman and Douglas M. Hart, "The Political Utility of Nuclear Weapons: The 1973 Middle East Crisis," *International Security* 7(1) (Summer 1982), pp. 132–156; Garthoff, *Détente and Confrontation,* p. 379; and Kissinger, *Years of Upheaval,* pp. 587–589. At 3:30 a.m., sixty US B-52 bombers were ordered back to the United States from Guam. This had been a long-standing objective of the Pentagon, but the State Department had objected to a visible reduction of the US commitment in Southeast Asia. Under the rubric of the DEFCON III alert, the Pentagon ordered their return.

44. Steven L. Spiegel, *The Other Arab-Israeli Conflict: Making America's Middle East Policy, from Truman to Reagan* (Chicago: University of Chicago Press, 1985), citing interview of Schlesinger, p. 264. William Colby confirmed that "nobody had any problems. Schlesinger and Moorer went along. They had no problems with it." William Colby, telephone interview by author, 11 January 1992.

45. Kissinger, *Years of Upheaval,* p. 584.

46. Interviews conducted by author: William Quandt, Washington, DC, 7 December 1988; and Alfred (Roy) Atherton, Washington, DC, 15 March 1990.

47. Kissinger, *Years of Upheaval,* p. 593.

48. Henry Kissinger, interview by author, New York, 19 June 1991.

49. Peter Rodman, interview by author, Washington, DC, 24 April 1991.

50. Kissinger, *Years of Upheaval,* p. 980.

51. For an explicit version of this argument, see Blechman and Hart, "The Political Utility of Nuclear Weapons," pp. 151–152.

52. Israelian, "The Kremlin: October 1973," pp. 5–6.

53. Ibid., pp. 13–14.

54. Ibid., p. 29.

55. Victor Israelian, interview by author, State College, Pa., 9 January 1992.

56. Ibid.

57. Ibid.

58. Israelian, "The Kremlin: October 1973," p. 26.

59. Georgi Arbatov, interview by author, Moscow, May 19, 1989. Kissinger also had worried about the impact of Watergate but for quite different reasons. At the meeting in the Situation Room of the White House on the night of 24 October, he and his advisers speculated about whether the Soviet Union would have challenged a "functioning" president. His concern about the weakness of the president made Kissinger all the more intent on signaling resolve through a worldwide alert. "We are at a point of maximum weakness," Kissinger said, "but if we knuckle under now we are in real trouble. . . . We will have to contend with the charge in the domestic media that we provoked this. The real charge is that we provoked this by being soft." Kissinger, *Years of Upheaval,* p. 589. It was not only the US media but most of the Soviet leadership that accused Nixon and Kissinger of manipulating domestic politics. The Politburo, however, did not see the domestic crisis in Washington as a weakness to exploit but as a source of American irresponsibility.

60. Georgi Kornienko, interview by author, Moscow, 17 December 1991.

61. Anatoliy Dobrynin, interview by author, Moscow, 17 December 1991.

62. Victor Israelian, interview by author, State College, Pa., 9 January 1992.

63. Anatoliy Dobrynin, interview by author, Moscow, 17 December 1991.

64. The Soviet alert system is designed to allow conventional alert readiness to be raised to high level without alerting any strategic nuclear forces. Joseph J. Kruzel, "Military Alerts and Diplomatic Signals," in Ellen P. Stern, ed., *The Limits of Military Intervention* (Beverly Hills, Calif.: Sage, 1977), pp. 83–89, 98.

65. Israelian, "The Kremlin: October 1973," p. 27.

66. Ibid.

67. Ibid.

68. Ibid., p. 28; and Victor Israelian, interview by author, State College, Pa., 9 January 1992.

69. Israelian, "The Kremlin: October 1973," p. 28. Gromyko also did not want to go to Washington.

70. Ibid., p. 29.

71. Israelian, "The Kremlin: October 1973," p. 28; also cited by Kissinger, *Years of Upheaval,* p. 608.

72. Henry Kissinger, interview by author, New York, 19 June 1991.

73. Garthoff concurs that the alert and the Brezhnev letter that prompted it did not end the crisis or resolve the situation. He argues that the Brezhnev letter did not serve to reinforce US readiness to curb Israel, which was in any case the product of US policy, but slowed it down. See Garthoff, *Détente and Confrontation,* pp. 380 and 383.

74. On 23 October, Nixon and Kissinger had decided to prevent the destruction of the Third Army and Kissinger had so informed Israel. Kissinger, *Years of Upheaval,* pp. 571, 573; and William Quandt, *Decade of Decisions: American Policy Toward the Arab-Israel Conflict* (Berkeley: University of California Press, 1977), p. 194.

75. Anatoliy Gromyko, interview by author, Moscow, 18 May 1989.

76. Israelian, "The Kremlin: October 1973," pp. 29–30.

77. Ibid., p. 30.

78. Ibid., p. 26.

79. Ibid.

80. Victor Israelian, interview by author, State College, Pa., 8 January 1992.

81. Leonid Zamyatin, an official of the Ministry of Foreign Affairs who subsequently headed the TASS news agency, put the relationship in context: "Egyptian-Soviet relations began to deteriorate under Nasser, who was pro-Soviet in his foreign policy but repressive toward Communists at home. We had even lower expectations of Sadat because of our dealings with him when he was in charge of the Aswan Dam project. He was a pain in the neck, always trying to renegotiate contracts. We became more cautious." Leonid Zamyatin, interview by author, Moscow, 16 December 1991.

82. Israelian, "The Kremlin: October 1973," p. 29.

83. Ibid., p. 26.

84. Blechman and Hart, "The Political Utility of Nuclear Weapons," pp. 132–156.

CHAPTER 13

THE UNITED STATES AND ISRAEL

The Nature of a Special Relationship

Bernard Reich and Shannon Powers

The relationship between the United States and Israel has been characterized as special by scholars, observers, policymakers, and diplomats alike. Irreducible to any one factor, the relations are strengthened by the multiple bonds on which they are founded even while not being codified in a formal alliance. The origins of this complex, multifaceted relationship antedate the establishment of the Jewish state in 1948 and find expression in continuing US support for the survival, security, and well-being of Israel. American presidents since Harry Truman have acknowledged the shared values between the two countries, and affirmations of a special relationship have become a common refrain in presidential statements and speeches. For instance, President Barack Obama has declared that "the deep bonds of friendship between the United States and Israel remain as strong and unbreakable as ever."

This perspective tends to confirm the Arab view, in the wake of the 1967 Arab-Israeli war (also known as the Six Day War), that there existed a preferential and exclusive US-Israeli relationship. However, in spite of the broad-scale commitment on the part of the United States to Israel at a very significant level, there are, as in any relationship of this sort, also areas of discord.

One major factor bolstering the US-Israeli relationship has always been the US Congress. Congress plays a significant role in the relationship, as it is both empowered and limited by constitutional and practical factors. Formally, Congress is vested with the spending authority, and therefore retains substantial decision-making power when it comes to foreign aid, answering such questions as what (economic and military assistance, loans or grants, and so on), how much, and to whom. Not only is Congress a crucial element in determining what aid Israel gets, it also helps to determine which Arab parties (such as Hamas after its election victory in 2005) do not receive aid. Congressional influence, however, extends beyond its formal authority over the allocation of aid, as Congress frequently issues its opinions, in the form of bipartisan declarations and resolutions, on both central issues and seemingly unrelated matters that are connected to the Israel factor.[1]

Congressional concerns about a Jewish state can be traced back to at least 1922, when Congress unanimously supported the Balfour Declaration (which President Woodrow Wilson had endorsed earlier) in the Lodge-Fish Resolution.[2] Since then, it has repeatedly passed resolutions in support of Israel during Middle East crises, particularly in recognizing Israel's right to defend its security and condemning attacks within its borders. The rhetorical power of these statements helps draw attention to Israel's position and secure the continued cooperation of the executive branch during periods of disagreement. Recently, amid tensions between the Obama and Netanyahu administrations, 333 members of Congress signed on to a letter sent to Secretary of State Hillary Clinton reaffirming their commitment "to the unbreakable bond that exists between the [US] and the State of Israel."[3]

When it comes to American support for Israel, however, Congress is not simply acting on its own volition. A major source of congressional power on the issue stems from its representation of American public opinion. Public opinion polls over the years continue to reflect the concern of American voters for Israeli security and their strong preference for candidates who are supportive of Israel.

Despite the staunch support America provides Israel, the US-Israeli relationship is not the exclusive one that is often portrayed by Arab spokesmen and others advocating a different orientation to Israel in US policy. This has become increasingly clear in recent administrations—Clinton's attempts to implement the Oslo Accords, George W. Bush's two-state vision and his Road Map for a final settlement of the Israeli-Palestinian conflict, and Obama's efforts at resuscitating peace negotiations through proximity talks. Although there was a period of exclusivity favoring Israel following the events of the Six Day War, this lack of a dual relationship began to change after the Yom Kippur War of 1973.[4] It was also during the Yom Kippur War that a massive US airlift of ammunition and military equipment proved essential to Israel in its response to the Egyptian and Syrian military attacks. By 1977 and Jimmy Carter's inauguration into office, a period had begun in which Arab (especially Egyptian) views were factored into the process and affected US policy. Some of the Arab states (but not yet the Palestinians and the Palestine Liberation Organization, PLO) became increasingly important from a foreign policy perspective because they were seen as moving in a general direction toward peace. Thus there was a change from exclusivity to dual-factor diplomacy.

The generalized image of a "positive only" US-Israeli relationship therefore ignores the fact that within that linkage there is, has been, and probably will continue to be dissonance on a wide range of issues, both procedural and substantive. As in any relationship, there is a certain frustration when one actor does not perform in the way that the other would prefer. One actor might be obstinate and problematic, and the decision makers involved may have difficult personalities. For example, in the spring and summer of 1990 in Israel (the national unity government fell, Labor Party leader Shimon Peres attempted to form a government, and Yitzhak Shamir of the Likud Party eventually formed one), clear US preferences were reflected in the public and private comments of the senior policymakers and decision makers in the George H. W. Bush administration; the United States was not a disinterested, dispassionate, and uninvolved observer. Although a direct effort to affect the situation cannot be identified from the record, there was a clear view of US preferences. Moreover, the US position probably played a role in the ultimate selection of Labor's Yitzhak Rabin as the new prime minister and the formation of a new government under his leadership in 1992. In a similar way, Israeli ambassadors have also made clear, although disowning any efforts to do so, their views concerning preferred policymakers and policies in the United States.

The positive elements in the US-Israeli relationship, as well as the overall cordial and congruent nature of the partners' concerns and policies in the region, have not prevented negative factors from manifesting themselves. When President Jimmy Carter, President Anwar Sadat of Egypt, and Prime Minister Menachem Begin of Israel met at Camp David in September 1978, there was discord on many elements of the March 1979 Egyptian-Israeli peace treaty despite the ultimate agreements; some issues were left for later clarification and resolution. During the subsequent autonomy negotiations, which began in May 1979, agreement was reached on some issues but not on the major questions.

During the administrations of Prime Ministers Menachem Begin and Yitzhak Shamir, there were disagreements between the United States and Israel on a wide range of issues, including Israel's bombing of the Osirak nuclear reactor in Iraq (1981), Israeli annexation of the Golan Heights (1981), Israeli bombing of PLO facilities in Beirut (1982), the war in Lebanon (1982), the Sabra and Shatila camp massacres (1982), the Jonathan Pollard espionage affair, and Israeli involvement in the Iran-Contra arms-for-hostages deal. There were questions about the intifada and Israel's response to it (which also led to image problems for Israel in the United States and the questioning of its methods) as well as Israel's reaction to the plan offered by US secretary of state George P. Shultz and various efforts in 1988 to deal with these and related matters.

There have been disagreements on the deportation of Palestinians (whether in large numbers or small) from the occupied territories and on the building of Israeli settlements in disputed territory. These were particularly acerbic during the tenures of George H. W. Bush and Yitzhak Shamir. There was, and is, policy dissonance as to the status of Jerusalem; the United States retains its embassy in Tel Aviv and does not accept Israel's unilateral declaration of Jerusalem as its capital. This remains the case despite the fact that the Jerusalem Embassy Relocation Act of 1995 requires the move of the US embassy from Tel Aviv to Jerusalem. Other legislation also reflects some ambiguity on this matter in US law and policy. And there have been broader policy questions on such matters as the sale of AWACS (airborne warning and control system) aircraft to Saudi Arabia during the administration of Ronald Reagan, the establishment of a dialogue between the United States and the PLO in 1988, and Arab terrorism and the appropriate Israeli response to it over an extended period. During George H. W. Bush's tenure, tensions emerged over Israel's role (or, more properly, nonrole) in the 1991 Gulf War as well as discord over the subsequent Madrid peace conference (1991). In 2010 the administration of Barack Obama clashed with Benjamin Netanyahu over housing construction in East Jerusalem.

Such disagreements are to be expected. The framework in which the United States and Israel have interacted has changed over time, and policies have changed to reflect the altered environment. The US-Israeli relationship had its origins when the United States and Soviet Union were competing for supremacy following World War II. Both superpowers courted Israel in their efforts to incorporate new states into their spheres of influence. Israel was seen as a valuable prize in the newly important, oil-rich Middle East. Nevertheless, within the US government there was substantial disagreement concerning the appropriate policy, and US support for the Jewish state was a presidential decision, often opposed by the senior bureaucrats in the Departments of State and Defense. Today the US-Israeli relationship operates within the confines of a new world order in which there is neither an alternative superpower nor US-Soviet competition to curry the favor of states or regional groupings.

A second difference is to be found in the perspectives of a small country confronting a large country, each seeing the world through a different lens. The United States is a superpower with global interests; Israeli interests are more regional and narrow, and there are more life-and-death concerns.

Finally, while the bond between the United States and Israel has remained constant, the meaning and content of that bond has varied over time. During the first decades after Israel's independence the relationship was grounded primarily in humanitarian concerns, in religious and historical links, and in a moral-emotional-political arena. The United States remained aloof from Israel in the strategic-military sector. The United States and Israel eventually developed a diplomatic-political relationship that focused on the need to resolve the Arab-Israeli conflict. Though they agreed on the general concept, they often differed on the precise means for achieving that end. Despite a growing positive connection between the two states, especially after the 1967 Six Day War, appreciation of the linkage, especially in the strategic sphere, remained limited.

RELATIONS BETWEEN THE CARTER ADMINISTRATION AND ISRAEL

The accession of both Jimmy Carter and Menachem Begin to office in 1977 inaugurated a new period in the relationship, characterized often by increased public tension and recrimination. Egyptian president Anwar Sadat's peace initiative also reduced the exclusivity of the US-Israeli relationship that had been established after 1967 as a consequence of Soviet policy and the ruptures of relations between some Arab states and the United States.

The Carter and Begin administrations became divided over numerous issues that directly affected the US-Israeli relationship. They were in accord in some aspects, however, as on the need to achieve peace and foster the security of Israel. Yet they would often disagree on the methods and mechanisms best suited to achieving those goals, the preferred end results, and the modalities that best served national interests. There were questions regarding the poor personal chemistry between policymakers on both sides as well. Senior US and Israeli officials were not always compatible, and this affected the countries' ever evolving relationship. Mutual dislike and mistrust extended beyond Carter and Begin into the Reagan administration; the United States was unhappy with Begin and his successor, Yitzhak Shamir, and Israel had strong anxieties about Defense Secretary Caspar Weinberger and his policies. There were disagreements concerning the nature of the situation in the region, often focusing on alternative intelligence estimates of the threat to Israel's national security.

Carter's tenure was filled with episodes of discord between the United States and Israel that generated numerous efforts by each power to influence the policies of the other. Israel's major success was in connection with the October 1, 1977, US-Soviet joint communiqué. Although proclaimed with great fanfare by the Carter administration, Israel was able to secure abandonment of the communiqué within a matter of days by mobilizing Israel's traditional supporters in the US Jewish community and non-Jewish supporters in Congress and elsewhere. It took advantage of strong public sympathy for Israel as well as strong public views against reinvolving the Soviet Union in the peace process.

The Carter administration had its most noteworthy success in effecting change in the Israeli position at Camp David and in the Egyptian-Israeli peace treaty. The main techniques included high-risk/high-visibility presidential involvement and Carter's suggestion that Israel could not allow the failure of this president, who might then transfer the blame to Israel in Congress and public opinion. Israel was also influenced by the administration's continuing economic and military assistance.

THE REAGAN TENURE

Ronald Reagan came to office with a very different perception of Israel and its importance. His campaign rhetoric concerning Israel went beyond the customary pledges of friendship, suggesting strong and consistent support for Israel and its perspective regarding the Arab-Israeli conflict. He saw Israel as an important ally and an asset in the struggle against the Soviet Union. He was opposed to dealing with the PLO until that organization dramatically changed its policies by renouncing terrorism, accepting United Nations Security Council Resolution 242, and acknowledging Israel's right to exist (which it eventually did in 1988). This pro-Israel perspective was retained and reiterated after he took office.

The US-Israeli relationship during the eight years Reagan held office was generally characterized by close positive ties, but there were also specific, divergent interpretations regarding the regional situation, the peace process, and Israel's security needs. Israel bombed an Iraqi nuclear reactor near Baghdad and PLO positions in Beirut during the summer of 1981, and it took action on other issues when it believed its national interest was at stake—even when it understood this would lead to clashes with the United States. The United States strongly opposed the raid on the Iraqi reactor, questioned the Beirut bombings, and postponed the delivery of previously contracted F-16 aircraft to Israel. Other issues emerged, including disputes about settlements in the territories occupied by Israel in the 1967 war and Israel's concern about a perceived pro-Saudi tendency in US policy manifested, in part, by arms supplied to Saudi Arabia, including F-15 enhancements and AWACS. Israeli anxiety was heightened when the Reagan administration suggested that a proposal to resolve the Arab-Israeli conflict put forward by then Crown Prince Fahd of Saudi Arabia (the so-called Fahd Plan) in August 1981, which Israel had rejected, had some merit.

Reagan sought to reassure Israel that the United States remained committed in helping it to retain its military and technological advantages over the Arab states. In fact, Israel was drawn to a Reagan administration proposal of cooperation, and on November 30, 1981, the United States and Israel signed a Memorandum of Understanding on Strategic Cooperation (MOU) in which the parties recognized the need to enhance strategic cooperation to deter threats to the region from the Soviet Union. For the Begin government, it represented an important achievement, suggesting an improved relationship with the United States, and it mitigated some of the negative effects of US sales of AWACS and other advanced weapons systems to Saudi Arabia. But this positive aura dissipated in December 1981 when Israel decided to alter the status of the Golan Heights by extending Israeli law, jurisdiction, and administration to that area. The action generated swift negative reactions in Washington, including US support for a UN resolution of condemnation and the suspension of the MOU. Israel was stunned by the extent of the US reaction; Israel's strongly negative response included Begin's castigation of the US ambassador to Israel.

Although Israel's Golan decision exacerbated tensions, the turning point was Israel's 1982 invasion of Lebanon, which called into question the links between the United States and Israel and led to clashes over the nature and extent of Israel's military actions and the US effort to ensure the PLO's evacuation from Beirut. US forces, which had been withdrawn from Beirut following the PLO's evacuation, returned there after the massacres of Palestinians by Lebanese Phalangists at the Shatila and Sabra camps in September 1982, leading to the burdensome involvement of US marines in the turmoil of Lebanon.

The war also precipitated the Reagan "fresh start" initiative of September 1, 1982, which sought to reinvigorate the Arab-Israeli peace process by taking advantage of the opportunities presented by the new situation in Lebanon. Israel, which was not consulted in advance, saw the proposals as detrimental because they departed from the conceptual framework of Camp David and seemed to determine prematurely the outcome of negotiations on several points, including the status of Jerusalem and the future of the West Bank and Gaza. There were other concerns as well, and these led Israel to reject the initiative. That action, coupled with the refugee camp massacres, resulted in a sharp deterioration in Israel's standing in US public opinion and in further disagreements with the Reagan administration, causing months of rancor. However, by the summer of 1983 the US-Israeli relationship reverted to its earlier positive levels as a consequence of Israel's Kahan Commission's report (which found Israel bore indirect responsibility for the Shatila and Sabra massacres), the failure of Jordan's King Hussein to join the peace process, the increase in Soviet involvement in Syria, the signing of the US-promoted Lebanon-Israel agreement of May 17, 1983, and the Syrian-Soviet opposition to it. The United States and Israel appeared linked by a congruence of policy that included recognition of Israel's strategic anti-Soviet value, their mutual desire for peaceful resolution of the Arab-Israeli conflict, as well as a parallelism concerning Lebanon and the future of that country. This comported well with Reagan's initial perceptions of Israel and presaged a period of positive relations, given tangible expression at the end of November 1983, when President Reagan and Prime Minister Yitzhak Shamir reached agreement on closer strategic cooperation.

Israel and the United States worked together to bring about the May 17, 1983, agreement between Israel and Lebanon that dealt with shaping the Lebanese government in conjunction with Israeli withdrawal and an eventual Israeli-Lebanese peace treaty. (The agreement was never implemented due to opposition from Syria and Syrian-supported groups in Lebanon; indeed, Syria, and through it the USSR, was excluded from the May 17, 1983, negotiations and resented it.) At the same time, the major issues of discord in the relationship, which centered on the West Bank and Gaza and the Reagan "fresh start" initiative, were not addressed in any meaningful way. There was an air of good feeling that pervaded both the executive and legislative branches of the US government.

Reagan faced other difficult times. The Pollard affair became a prominent issue.[5] Although this intelligence disaster captured headlines in both countries, had some short-term repercussions, and remains on the US-Israeli agenda, it has had little tangible or lasting effect on overall relations. A much more serious issue was the US effort to secure the release of its hostages in Lebanon through arms sales to Iran, which erupted, in November 1986, into a public scandal that became known as the Iran-Contra affair. This infamous chapter in US history involved active Israeli participation in the planning and execution of some operations of the US National Security Council and demonstrated the high level of strategic cooperation between the two governments during the Reagan administration.

Although interaction ranged over a variety of issues, both countries placed an overarching focus on the peace process throughout Reagan's second term. The concept of an international peace conference became more central during 1987, although little progress was made toward convening such a conference. Israel and the United States agreed on two prerequisites for Soviet participation: the regularization of Soviet Jewish emigration, and the restoration of Soviet ties with Israel, broken at the time of the 1967 Six Day War.

The onset of the Palestinian intifada in December 1987 led to public disagreement over the methods Israel employed to contain the violence and restore law and order. Israel's use of live ammunition provoked protests by the State Department as early as January 1988. Israel's deportation of Palestinian civilians charged with inciting the demonstrations led the United States to vote in favor of a UN resolution calling on Israel to refrain from "such harsh measures [which] are unnecessary to maintain order." Although the State Department minimized the significance of the US vote, describing it as a disagreement among friends that did not affect the broader relationship, this was the first time since 1981 that the United States had voted for a resolution critical of Israel. Secretary of State Shultz referred to US support for Israel as "unshakable." As the violence continued and the United States launched the Shultz initiative to seek an accord, however, tensions continued to grow.

Despite this setback, the Reagan administration marked a time of unprecedented growth in relations. Ronald Reagan saw Israel as a strategic asset, but there were other positive factors—a free-trade arrangement, intelligence exchanges, and high-level joint groups on political-military and related issues—as well as the more prosaic intercourse of a relationship between two friendly states. US economic and military assistance reached $3 billion per annum in essentially all-grant aid, and special grants helped Israel to deal with particular economic problems. Strategic cooperation between the United States and Israel reached new levels during this period, and on April 21, 1988 (in the Jewish calendar, the fortieth anniversary of Israel's independence), the two states signed a memorandum of agreement that institutionalized the emerging strategic relationship. Growing links in the military sphere involved joint military exercises, sales and purchases of equipment, training, and related activities. Israel also gained status as a major non-NATO ally.

In Algiers in November 1988 the Palestine National Council (PNC) decided to declare the establishment of a Palestinian state, and the policy environment changed dramatically, with repercussions for the George H. W. Bush administration. This declaration was accompanied by ambiguous statements concerning the peace process, Israel, and terrorism. However, on December 14, 1988, in a press conference in Geneva, PLO leader Yasser Arafat read the script articulating a change in PLO views toward Israel and the Arab-Israeli conflict, renouncing terrorism, recognizing Israel's right to exist, and accepting UNSC Resolutions 242 and 338. Arafat thereby met the conditions for beginning a dialogue between the United States and the PLO that had first been enunciated by then secretary of state Henry Kissinger. The same day as the Algiers statement, Secretary of State George Shultz formally announced, "The United States is prepared for a substantive dialogue with PLO representatives." The US ambassador to Tunisia, Robert Pelletreau, was designated as the only authorized channel for that dialogue. This official opening helped the incoming Bush administration to avoid what might have been a difficult issue; at the same time, it moved the process to another level. Skepticism remained, and the administration sought to reassure Israel that "those who believe that American policy is about to undergo a basic shift merely because we have begun to talk with the PLO are completely mistaken."

THE GEORGE H. W. BUSH TENURE

President George H. W. Bush took office in January 1989 with no long-range strategic plan or specific policies for the Arab-Israeli issue or the Gulf region of the Middle East. The end of the cold war, the implosion of the Soviet Union, the collapse of the Warsaw Pact, and the emerging new democracies in Eastern Europe preoccupied the administration and Congress and entranced the media and public. The Iran-Iraq war had given way to a cease-fire, the departure of Soviet troops altered the hostilities in Afghanistan, and a dialogue with the PLO, established in the last days of the Reagan administration, continued. Within the context of a changing international system the Middle East was not a high national priority.

Much of Bush's first year in office was marked by a coolness on various issues, especially those relating to the peace process. Broad-scale concord, on such matters as the need for peace through direct negotiations, and specific-issue discord, for instance, on questions relating to a land-for-peace exchange and related themes, increasingly seemed to be the measure of the US-Israeli dialogue. Nevertheless, substantial US economic and military aid to Israel continued.

During the first year and a half of the Bush administration, Israel and the United States were preoccupied with the effort to begin a negotiating process between Israel and the Palestinians. Bush administration frustration with the Yitzhak Shamir government was obvious in its preference for a Shimon Peres–led government after a successful vote of no-confidence terminated the tenure of the Israeli government in the spring of 1990 and in its voiced concerns about the prospects for peace after Shamir succeeded in constructing a new government in June 1990. The peace process was moribund when the Iraqis invaded Kuwait in August 1990, attributable (at least in the eyes of the Bush administration) in large measure to the policies of the Shamir government in Israel.

During the Gulf crisis and the war against Iraq, Israel was relegated to a marginal role. Its position as a strategic asset seemed diminished, and there was a widespread view in the Bush administration that Israel was not tactically relevant to potential actions in the Arabian Peninsula and the Persian Gulf. During the crisis, Israel did not serve as a staging area for forces nor as a storage depot for military materiel, nor was it utilized for medical emergencies. There was a conscious US effort to build a broad-based international force with an Arab component to oppose Saddam Hussein. Israel was not to be used as a tool to break the coalition. From the outset Israel was concerned that it was not part of the coalition. There was no publicly identified role for Israel, given US objectives in the crisis, although the Israelis did endorse the firm and rapid US reaction to Iraq.

When Iraq bombarded Israel with scud missiles, however, the United States was prompted to take a more determined stance with Israel. Responding to the entreaties of President Bush, Israel refrained from taking military action against Iraq. Other factors swayed Israel against taking reprisals, including the arrival of US Patriot missile batteries and US cajoling in a crucial telephone conversation between President Bush and Prime Minister Shamir. Deputy Secretary of State Lawrence Eagleburger made an important visit to Israel.

The resumption of the Arab-Israeli peace process in the aftermath of the Gulf War revived traditional Israeli concerns about the United States as something less than a wholly supportive and reliable ally. This was further complicated by the chemistry (or the lack thereof) between US and Israeli leaders and by concerns about specific Bush administration policies. Differences before the Gulf War were exacerbated when the United States pressed for movement on an Arab-Israeli peace process even as Israel remained unconvinced that the Arab world was ready to move in that direction. Within several months of the Gulf War cease-fire, the US-Israeli relationship was again characterized by discord and tension, and much of the newly created goodwill was dissipated by disagreements over the modalities and substance of the peace process and other matters. Tensions developed as the Bush administration appeared to link proposed housing loan guarantees, essential to the settling of Soviet Jews in Israel, to Israel's actions on settlements in the West Bank and Gaza Strip and its responsiveness to the peace process. In testimony before the US House Subcommittee on Foreign Operations of the Appropriations Committee on May 22, 1991, Secretary of State James Baker observed, "I don't think that there is any bigger obstacle to peace than the settlement activity that continues not only unabated but at an enhanced pace." In the autumn of 1991 tensions became public when Bush asked Congress to postpone consideration of Israel's request for US guarantees of $10 billion in loans. Ultimately the administration placed conditions on the loan guarantees that were impossible for the government of Israel to accept, and the matter was dropped in the spring of 1992 with recriminations by both sides.

The Bush administration clearly favored the Labor Party over Likud (and Yitzhak Rabin or Shimon Peres over Yitzhak Shamir), both in 1990 (during the period of the vote of no-confidence and the formation of a new Israeli government in June) and in the 1992 Knesset elections. Despite numerous denials and claims to the contrary, the Bush administration and the Shamir government were not harmonious on many of the issues central to peace in the Middle East. The outcome of the June 1992 elections in Israel, with Yitzhak Rabin replacing Shamir as prime minister, was welcomed by the Bush administration as a significant and positive factor that would alter the regional situation, the prospects for progress in the Arab-Israeli peace process, and the nature of the US-Israeli relationship. In late June 1992 Secretary of State Baker called for a quick resumption of Middle East peace talks, reflecting the administration's view that the elections had resulted in the demise of a hard-line Likud government and thereby facilitated the prospects for success in the peace negotiations. They saw the onus now falling on the Palestinians and other Arabs to make serious compromises and proposals for peace.

At the same time, the overall tenor of US-Israeli relations improved, and tensions were relieved. When Rabin visited the United States in August 1992, he and Bush focused on resuming the positive aspects of the US-Israeli relationship. Bush noted that "the meetings were also significant for the tone of the discussions. Our time together can best be described as a consultation between close friends and strategic partners." The two leaders announced that they had reached an accord, with the Bush administration supporting loan guarantees for Israel. President Bush noted that "we understand the position [of the Rabin government concerning settlement construction] and all I will say is that I salute this change. We salute what the Prime Minister is trying to do. We understand his position. He understands our position. And obviously, we would not be going forward with this loan guarantee if we did not salute the change."

Bushed stressed US determination to see the Arab-Israeli peace process through in a speech to a joint session of Congress on March 6, 1991: "A comprehensive peace must be grounded in United Nations Security Council Resolutions 242 and 338 and the principle of territory for peace. This must provide for Israel's security and recognition, and at the same time for legitimate Palestinian political rights. Anything else would fail the twin tests of fairness and security."[6] Baker's visits to the Middle East in the spring and early summer of 1991 made it clear that there was no agreement among the concerned parties to convene a conference between the Arab states and Israel that would lead to bilateral negotiations between Israel and the bordering states still at war with Israel. The issues in contention included the venue of a conference (whether in the region or elsewhere), what powers and authority it would have (whether primarily ceremonial or substantive in nature), under whose auspices it should be conducted (whether the United Nations would be a factor), which Palestinians and other Arabs could and would attend, and what prior commitments must be made by the participants.

Eventually Baker convened the Madrid peace conference at the end of October 1991. The conference was attended reluctantly by the parties, who retained substantial concerns about its nature and expected little of value to come from it. The conference did not achieve a substantive breakthrough, although it eliminated the procedural barriers to direct bilateral negotiations between Israel and its immediate neighbors when the Israeli and the Syrian, Egyptian, Lebanese, and Jordanian-Palestinian delegations met at an opening public session and an official plenary session and delivered speeches and responses. Bilateral negotiations between Israel and each of the Arab delegations followed.

The Madrid conference was followed by bilateral talks in Washington later in 1991, talks that directly or indirectly contributed to the September 1993 Israel-PLO Declaration of Principles, the October 1994 Israeli-Jordanian peace, and Israeli-Syrian talks focusing on the Golan Heights. The first rounds achieved accord on nonsubstantive matters, primarily the time and venue of future meetings. Progress was measured primarily by the continuation of the process rather than by significant achievements on the substantive issues in dispute. The wide gap between the Israeli and Arab positions was not narrowed in these initial encounters, and it could not be bridged by outside actors (such as the United States and the former Soviet Union). The United States adhered to its role as facilitator and refrained from intervening on substantive matters. It was not a party to the bilateral talks, and its representatives were not in the room or at the negotiating table, although it did meet separately with the parties and heard their views.

In the bilateral negotiations the Israeli-Palestinian and Israeli-Syrian negotiations were the most central and most difficult. In the case of both Jordan and Lebanon the general perception at the time was that agreements would be relatively easy to achieve, although they would have to await the resolution of the Syrian and Palestinian talks. In the case of Syria the central issue was peace and security and the future of the Golan Heights, with little likelihood of compromise in the short term. In the Israeli-Palestinian discussions the disagreement centered on the Palestinian desire for self-government and the Israeli opposition to that goal. Compromise was elusive, as the positions were mutually exclusive. However, Israeli proposals for Palestinian elections in the territories and the reality of the situation in the region suggested areas for continued negotiation, ultimately leading to the Oslo bilateral negotiations that resulted in the signing of the Israel-PLO Declaration of Principles on the White House lawn in September 1993.

A related and parallel process included multilateral discussions on several regional issues and an initial organizing conference convened in Moscow in January 1992. The goal was to achieve progress on important regional issues, even without a political solution, which would reinforce the earlier bilateral negotiations. The five permanent members of the UN Security Council and a number of other important powers (including the European Community and Japan) were represented in Moscow. Despite some initial difficulties over the question of Palestinian participation and representation, the talks continued to fortify the bilateral process.

Despite the achievements symbolized by the Madrid conference and the subsequent bilateral and multilateral discussions, by the time of the Israeli and US elections in 1992 no substantive breakthrough had occurred and no specific achievement (beyond continuation of the process) had been accomplished. Nevertheless, the Baker team seemed optimistic in the spring of 1992; although the differences between the parties were still wide, they would eventually narrow, and then it would be possible to bridge the gaps. Policy under the Clinton administration continued to emphasize the US role of facilitator.

THE CLINTON TENURE

The accession of the Clinton administration to office in 1993 and the Rabin government in 1992 provided the basis for a continuation of the relationship, but in a more positive mode, with strong and improving personal and country-to-country relations focusing on the Arab-Israeli peace process inaugurated in Madrid. The United States reassured Israel that its commitment to Israeli security would be sustained. And a strong positive personal relationship seemed to develop between the American president and his Israeli prime minister counterpart.

The relationship between Clinton and Rabin continued to become more intimate as the peace process, begun at Madrid and amplified by Oslo, continued to make progress. Each achievement seemed to be marked by an added positive glow to both the personal chemistry and the political accord between the two partners. The unusual nature of this relationship was revealed when Rabin was assassinated in November 1995. Clinton appeared to be personally moved by the death of his peace partner and issued the famous statement "Shalom, *chaver*" (good-bye, friend), which struck close to the heart of their dealings. The substantial size and level of the US delegation to the funeral was unprecedented, and it reaffirmed the connection between the two states and reflected the close personal ties forged between the two leaders.

The success of Benjamin Netanyahu in his race against Shimon Peres (Rabin's foreign minister and alter ego in the peace process) in the first-ever popular election of a prime minister in Israel in the spring of 1996 illustrated again the unusual nature of the connection. The Clinton administration, seeking continuity in the peace process, clearly preferred that Shimon Peres succeed. Some noted that the Clinton team all but campaigned for Peres (and some of Peres's opponents argued that the US government had gotten involved in Israeli domestic affairs). Despite the outcome, the relationship endured, and the United States continued to support Israel's security and quest for peace. There was a lack of personal chemistry between Clinton and Netanyahu, but many in the Republican-dominated US Congress endorsed Netanyahu's approach.

The period of Netanyahu's tenure in some ways resembled that of Menachem Begin in the relationship between the United States and Israel on the issues of the peace process. The Clinton administration continued to press for progress on the peace process begun at Madrid and expanded in Oslo and by subsequent Israeli accords with the Palestinians and with Jordan. The prime minister of Israel reflected skepticism of the Palestinian position and showed a deep-seated concern for an arrangement that would ensure Israel's security as well as a personal goal of ensuring the stability of his governing coalition. Consequently he acted with considerable deliberation and pursued a pace seen by the Clinton administration as far too slow. Clashing positions were reflected in numerous public (and private) conflicts between the two parties. By the middle of 1998 the Clinton administration presented an ultimatum to Israel that was ignored and then faded from public view. The two states pursued the peace process and clashed with each other. But the administration often was not backed by Congress, which seemed more sympathetic to the Netanyahu approach and position and provided public and private positive reinforcement to the Israeli government.

These episodes and others in the Clinton tenure reflected the themes that marked the Carter-Begin relationship and characterized the broader relationship between the United States and Israel, which centered on endurance and continuity in the quest for peace and Israeli security and on discord concerning the means and procedures (as well as some of the content) of the process to best achieve those ends.

Ehud Barak's election as prime minister of Israel in May 1999 brought to power a native-born Israeli with professional experience as an officer in the Israel Defense Forces (IDF). The Clinton administration viewed it as an opportunity to resume peacemaking; expectations were high that he would be a prime minister in the mold of Rabin, his mentor and friend. Barak set out on an ambitious diplomatic program and, with Yasser Arafat, set February 12, 2000, as the target date for preparing a framework agreement for an Israeli-Palestinian permanent peace settlement, to be completed by September 12, 2000. Israelis and Palestinians had a large number of meetings, and there was extensive involvement by the United States.

The Clinton administration, by choice and through developments, maintained the Middle East peace process at the center of its policy world. From the outset, the Clinton administration was engaged at its most senior levels in the bilateral and multilateral negotiation process. Negotiations between Israel and the Palestinians resumed soon after Barak's election, but little progress was made.

As the Clinton administration entered its final year in office, accelerated efforts suggested a possible tripartite summit involving Clinton, Barak, and Arafat. But the parties were far apart. The objective of the negotiations in July 2000 at Camp David (generally referred to as Camp David II) was to put together a package that Barak believed would generate acceptance and recognition from the Palestinians, which had eluded Israelis to that point, on the basis of a two-people, two-state solution in the region. But this was not to be. Arafat rejected the Barak proposals, left the negotiating table, and thereby provided the basis for the al-Aqsa intifada, which soon brought violence to the area. The Clinton tenure ended without an Israeli-Palestinian peace accord and with the area engulfed in violence.

THE GEORGE W. BUSH TENURE

A month after George W. Bush was elected president in November 2000, Ehud Barak announced his resignation as prime minister to seek a renewed mandate to pursue peace with the Palestinians. In the special prime ministerial election held on February 6, 2001, Ariel Sharon defeated Barak in a landslide victory with 62.7 percent of the vote. Bush congratulated Sharon, saying, "Our bilateral relationship is rock solid, as is the US commitment to Israel's security."

In his inaugural speech to the Knesset on March 7, 2001, Prime Minister Sharon, like his predecessors, remarked on the importance of the special relationship between the United States and Israel. "We shall work toward deepening our special relations with our great friend and ally, the United States."

The ascension of George W. Bush to the presidency and the election of Ariel Sharon as prime minister of Israel brought an end to the Oslo peace process, in which President Clinton had participated actively. Initially Bush took a hands-off policy toward the Arab-Israeli problem, wary of investing the kind of political capital Clinton had spent for such a meager return. Eventually Sharon and Bush would establish their own special connection. Significantly, while the Bush administration called for an end to Arab-Israeli violence and initially put the onus on Arafat to publicly call for the termination of violence, it signaled its determination to be less active, suggesting it would not emulate the Clinton administration's deep involvement in the details of the conflict.

By early spring 2001 the position of the new Bush administration had begun to emerge, and it seemed to dovetail with the program of the Sharon government. Assistant Secretary of State Edward A. Walker Jr., in testimony before the Subcommittee on Middle East and South Asia of the Committee on International Relations of the House of Representatives on March 29, 2001, noted: "Our country has vital strategic and economic interests in the region, and we believe that these interests will best be served by a peace that can be embraced by Israelis, Palestinians, and the region as a whole. We also have a vital and strategic interest in the survival and well-being of Israel."

At the annual policy conference of the American-Israel Public Affairs Committee (AIPAC), Secretary of State Colin Powell, while articulating the administration's laissez-faire stance on the peace process, disparaged Arafat: "Leaders have the responsibility to denounce violence, strip it of legitimacy, stop it. . . . the United States stands ready to assist, not insist." Exactly one decade earlier, on March 19, 1991, then chairman of the Joint Chiefs of Staff, Colin Powell, had declared before the same group: "We have stood with Israel since the day of its founding. We have stood with Israel throughout its history. We have demonstrated again and again that our roots are intertwined, as they are with all nations who share our beliefs in openness and democracy. So let there be no question that America will stand by Israel in the future." On March 19, 2001, Powell repeated those words: "I am proud to say that these words remain true." He further declared:

> There is a special friendship linking America with Israel, just as George Bush said before your conference one year ago when he was a governor of the state of Texas. I stand here today to emphasize this friendship another time. It includes all sides of life. This strong relationship ranges from areas of politics and economics to areas of security and culture. This relationship between two democratic systems will continue strong like a rock. It represents an unconditional relationship, deep-rooted and broad, a link built upon history, interests, values and ideologies. We are resolved in maintaining this special relationship with Israel and the Israeli people. We realize that Israel exists in a region of extreme danger. Therefore we will work and examine means to consolidate our valuable strategic cooperation with Israel in order to protect its military superiority.

Bush enlisted Sharon's support in developing a national missile defense shield, and Sharon was happy to oblige, given that Israel was the target of several rogue states. Furthermore, 87 senators and 209 representatives in Congress joined Sharon in pushing Bush to not invite Arafat to the White House, to close the PLO's Washington office, and to cut US aid to the Palestinian Authority until Arafat publicly called for an end to violence against Israel. As violence continued to flare between Israelis and Palestinians after Sharon's election, efforts to halt it, to restore confidence between the parties, and to resume negotiations became the core of US efforts to facilitate a peace process between Israel and the Palestinians.

The situation was dramatically altered by the September 11, 2001, attacks on the United States. The Bush administration worked to create an international coalition to respond to terrorism, focusing on Osama bin Laden and the al-Qa'ida movement. Al-Qa'ida's terrorist attack on the United States had the effect of postponing any new US efforts on the Arab-Israeli conflict and redirecting the Bush administration's priorities into leading the country in a war on global terror, particularly against Islamic extremism in the Middle East. The United States could now identify with Israel in profound new ways, having experienced terrorist attacks on its homeland for the first time, and it could empathize with Israel's decision to strike unilaterally against terrorists. At the same time, Osama bin Laden continued to link the attacks to the plight of the Palestinians and attributed that to unequivocal US support for Israel—a view widely accepted in the Arab and Muslim worlds.

In a press conference on October 11, 2001, President Bush noted that his administration would continue to focus on resolution of the Arab-Israeli conflict within the context of continued US-Israeli friendship. At the same time, he noted: "I also stated the other day that if we ever get into the . . . process, where we can start discussing a political solution in the Middle East, that I believe there ought to be a Palestinian state, the boundaries of which will be negotiated by the parties so long as the Palestinian state recognizes the right of Israel to exist, and will treat Israel with respect, and will be peaceful on her borders." But negotiations to end violence and resolve the Arab-Israeli conflict were held hostage to the continued violence that erupted in the wake of the failure of the Camp David talks.

A year after the termination of the Middle East peace process launched at Madrid, the new efforts seemed to be moving in the opposite direction. Arafat was unwilling or unable to halt Palestinian terrorism and violence against Israelis, thereby incurring Israeli responses and US concern, frustration, and disappointment. In late January 2002, Bush publicly expressed his disappointment in Arafat for his involvement in an arms shipment that could escalate Palestinian violence against Israel and for his failure to prevent terrorism. Despite US sympathy and empathy for Israel, and a strong bond on many matters, the United States proved unable to stop the cycle of violence, restore confidence, and get the Israelis and Palestinians back to the negotiating table.

Infuriated by Arafat's rhetoric and inaction, the United States generally viewed Israel's acts against Palestinian terrorists as defensive and placed the burden on Arafat to stop the violence. It could hardly do otherwise, given that by the end of 2001 the United States had ousted the Taliban from power in Afghanistan for harboring al-Qa'ida terrorists. "Obviously Israel has the right to defend itself, and the president understands that clearly," White House spokesman Ari Fleischer said on December 3, 2001.

On December 12, 2001, the Israeli Security Cabinet determined that Arafat was responsible for deadly attacks against Israel and stated, "Arafat is no longer relevant." The Bush administration soon adopted a similar position, and in June 2002 Bush called on the Palestinian people to "elect new leaders, leaders not compromised by terror."

The ensuing period was marked by Arafat's continued failure to lead the Palestinians to substantive peace negotiations and by the inability of Mahmoud Abbas, his successor, to make progress. The United States was increasingly preoccupied by the global war on terrorism and the war in Iraq—both issues that reaffirmed many of the positive factors in the US-Israeli relationship. In this environment, Prime Minister Ariel Sharon launched a plan for the unilateral withdrawal of all Israelis from the Gaza Strip, which Sharon outlined in a visit to Washington. On April 14, 2004, in a joint news conference at the White House, Bush recognized Israel's right to retain some territory and settlements in the West Bank. Bush called Sharon's plan both "historic" and "courageous." The implementation of the Sharon unilateral withdrawal was hailed by the Bush administration as a positive step forward.

When Sharon formed the new Kadima political party in late 2005 and called for parliamentary elections in early 2006, questions arose about the progress of the peace effort and the nature of the US-Israeli relationship in the second Bush term.

In the aftermath of Sharon's stroke and incapacity, Ehud Olmert became prime minister of Israel in March 2006. In a telephone call in early January 2006, Bush reiterated his intention to continue implementing Sharon's vision for advancing the peace process in the region. The Hamas victory in the Palestinian elections later that month raised additional concerns. These were summarized by Bush in remarks on May 4, 2006:

> As you know, I'm a strong believer in democracy and free elections, but that does not mean we have to support elected officials who are not committed to peace. Hamas has made it clear that they do not acknowledge the right of Israel to exist, and I've made it clear that so long as that's their policy, we will have no contact with the leaders of Hamas. Hamas must accept the demands of the international community to recognize Israel, disarm and reject terrorism, and stop blocking the path to peace.

As in earlier periods, the US-Israeli relationship did not change significantly.

On February 1, 2006, President George W. Bush said that the United States would rise to Israel's defense against Iran if needed and denounced the president of Iran for "menacing talk" against Israel. In an interview aboard *Air Force One*, Bush said, "I am concerned about a person that, one, tries to rewrite the history of the Holocaust, and two, has made it clear that his intentions are to destroy Israel. . . . Israel is a solid ally of the United States; we will rise to Israel's defense if need be." When asked if he meant that the United States would rise to Israel's defense militarily, Bush replied, "You bet, we'll defend Israel."

The 2006 Lebanon war between Israel and Hezbollah further dimmed prospects for a peace agreement. The Bush administration made one last major attempt at obtaining a peace accord between Israel and the PLO at the November 2007 Annapolis conference, but those efforts proved futile.

Bush and Sharon had established a firm relationship based on a strong opposition to terrorism of the type the United States faced, especially after 9/11, and with which Israel could empathize, having been the target of terrorist attacks for much of its existence. The congruence of their approach to dealing with this threat moved the two leaders closer together over the years, but there were elements of discord on the peace process. Sharon was not enthralled by the Road Map, and Bush expected more concessions from Israel toward the Palestinians.

BARACK OBAMA AND BENJAMIN NETANYAHU

In the fall of 2008, Olmert resigned as prime minister amid allegations of corruption, and Tzipi Livni was designated acting prime minister. Although she managed to piece together a coalition government, Benjamin Netanyahu was given the mandate to form a government coalition following the February 2009 Knesset elections. His right-of-center government included Labor and Shas with Avigdor Lieberman of Yisrael Beiteinu as foreign minister.

Earlier in January, Barack Obama had come to power amid Israeli concern about his commitment to the historic but unofficial alliance between their countries. Despite recognition of his senatorial voting record as generally supportive of Israel and his pledge that "Jerusalem will remain the capital of Israel and it must remain undivided," several senior advisers to the Obama campaign were perceived by Israelis as insensitive to their security situation. Moreover, Obama's new approach to the exercise of US global power, including his overture to the Muslim world and proposals for negotiating with adversaries such as Iran and Syria, left many Israelis concerned that an Obama administration would adopt policies that were incompatible with Israel's interests or inimical to its security.

There were concerns about Obama's sympathies on a more personal level as well. His statement that "nobody is suffering more than the Palestinian people," and his expression of concern for the dire situation in Gaza, led Israelis to question whether Obama was sympathetic to their situation as well, and whether the McCain-Palin team was in fact the more reliable friend of Israel. Obama's close association with Reverend Jeremiah Wright of the Trinity United Church of Christ further fueled the fire of suspicion because of Wright's praise for Louis Farrakhan, his 1984 visit to Libyan leader Muammar el-Qaddafi, and his strong criticism of Israel. Although Obama ultimately distanced himself from Wright, for much of the Israeli public, it was done too late, and too begrudgingly, to quell their concerns.

The first year of Obama's presidency did not bring any significant breaks in the US-Israeli relationship, but it was tense. Some of the tension stemmed from personal differences between Obama and Netanyahu as they tested the boundaries of their new working relationship, while others derived from the different interests of a regional versus a global power, and especially Obama's determination to do things differently than his predecessors, primarily his stated desire to improve the US image in the Islamic world.

This affected US-Israeli relations in two ways. First, Obama seemed to adjust the exclusivity of the US-Israeli relationship by engaging the Muslim world more directly than any prior president. His first formal television interview as president was granted to *Al-Arabiya*, an Arabic-language channel. He also delivered within his first one hundred days in office a major address at Cairo University, where he invoked the Quran and highlighted that America and Islam "need not be in competition." While this outreach did not detract directly from the US-Israeli friendship, some were concerned because Obama did not conduct a parallel outreach to Israeli audiences. Second, the Obama administration seemed determined to get tougher on Israel. Some former American envoys to the region have argued that the United States was not doing Israel any favors by acceding to its demands, and the Obama administration appeared to take that perspective seriously. On the Palestinian-Israeli peace process and on Iran's nuclear program, the Obama administration's perspective has not been wholly congruent with that of Israel. Obama has sought to engage Iran's Islamic regime diplomatically on the nuclear issue, refusing to set a timetable even while Netanyahu repeatedly gives warning that "the clock is ticking" as Iran's program approaches the point of irreversibility.

The United States and Israel further disagreed over how best to achieve an Israeli-Palestinian peace accord, as Netanyahu at first refrained from explicitly endorsing a two-state solution, and Obama made a complete freeze of all settlement construction in the West Bank a central point of contention. Israeli officials were quick to reject such a demand, insisting on the right to "natural growth," a formula that had been at least tacitly accepted by the Clinton and Bush administrations. However, modifications in each position were soon forthcoming. In a speech at Bar Ilan University Netanyahu formally accepted the two-state solution, and later he unilaterally imposed a temporary freeze on settlement activity in the West Bank with an exemption for synagogues and some units already under construction. The United States appeared to ease its pressure on Israel and even praise its actions, but minor flare-ups, primarily over construction activity, continued. In an interview with Fox News, Obama said, "I think that additional settlement building does not contribute to Israel's security. I think it makes it harder for them to make peace with their neighbors. I think it embitters the Palestinians in a way that could end up being very dangerous." However, there is general agreement regarding negotiations on an Israeli-Palestinian peace accord immediately and without preconditions.

Although the Obama-Netanyahu relationship has been somewhat unsteady and both leaders have looked to the broader constituencies they represent for political leverage, they have continued to recognize the mutual benefits of the historic friendship between their two countries and have continued to find ways to accommodate each other. An illustrative example can be found in the tensions that flared up between the two governments over Israeli housing construction in the Ramat Shlomo neighborhood in East Jerusalem.

While Vice President Joe Biden was paying a visit to Israel, the Israeli Interior minister announced the approval of new housing construction in the Ramat Shlomo neighborhood. Questions immediately arose about the continuity of the special relationship as members of the Obama administration condemned the Israeli decision. Within days, however, American and Israeli leaders were working to minimize the dispute and reaffirm the linkages between the two states. It is to be expected that the United States and Israel will continue to have periodic disagreements as their respective policy stances diverge in predictable ways due to their different global interests and commitments, their size and geographic position. Differences over specific policies, however, should not be mistaken for a rift in the strong ties that bind the countries together in their special relationship based on shared values and interests. Even during this episode, neither American public opinion nor Congress wavered in its solidarity with, and support for, Israel. In her address before the annual meeting of the American-Israel Public Affairs Committee (AIPAC), the largest pro-Israel lobby group in the United States, Secretary of State Hillary Clinton reiterated the American disapproval of Israeli construction in East Jerusalem and the West Bank, stating that it undermines the "mutual trust and endangers the proximity talks that are the first step toward the full negotiations that both sides say they want and need. And it exposes daylight between Israel and the United States that others in the region hope to exploit." At the same time she strongly conveyed that such policy differences do not threaten the enduring relationship between the United States and Israel: "And let me assure you, as I have assured you on previous occasions with large groups like this and small intimate settings, for President Obama and for me, and for this entire Administration, our commitment to Israel's security and Israel's future is rock solid, unwavering, enduring, and forever."[7]

It appears that the United States and Israel will manage their differences as other presidents and prime ministers have before them, and their special relationship will endure. As President Obama stated after a White House meeting with Netanyahu in the July 2010, "the bond between the United States and Israel is unbreakable. It encompasses our national security interests, our strategic interests, but most importantly the bond of two democracies who share a common set of values and whose people have grown closer and closer as time goes on."[8]

ENDURANCE AND CONTINUITY

Israel's special relationship with the United States revolves around a shared ideology and positive perception and sentiment evident in public opinion and official statements. It is also manifest in political and diplomatic support and tangible military and economic assistance, even though this has not been enshrined in a legally binding commitment joining the two in a formal alliance. Despite the extensive links that have developed, the widespread belief in the existence of the commitment, and the assurances contained in various specific agreements, the exact nature and extent of the US commitment to Israel remains imprecise. Israel has no mutual security treaty with the United States, nor is it a member of any alliance system requiring the United States to take up arms automatically on its behalf.

The US commitment to Israel has taken the generalized form of presidential statements (rather than formal documents) reaffirming the US interest in the political independence and territorial integrity of all Middle East states, including Israel.

It has largely been assumed that the United States would come to Israel's assistance should it be gravely threatened; this perception has become particularly apparent during times of crisis. Despite this perception and the general feeling in Washington (and elsewhere) that the United States would take action if required, there is no assurance that this would be the case. Israeli leaders continue to be interested in military and economic assistance as the primary tangible expression of the US commitment.

From Israel's perspective, the United States is an indispensable if not fully dependable ally. It provides Israel, through one form or another, with economic (governmental and private), technical, military, political, diplomatic, and moral support. Indeed, Israel is the largest recipient of US aid. It is seen as the ultimate resource against potential enemies, it is the source of Israel's sophisticated military hardware, and its interest in lasting peace is central to the Arab-Israeli peace process. Although there is this substantive relationship, there is also an Israeli reluctance, bred of history, to abdicate control over decision making on security matters.

The two states maintain a remarkable degree of congruence on broad policy goals. The policy consensus includes the need to prevent war, at both the regional and international levels, the need to resolve the Arab-Israeli conflict, and the need to maintain Israel's existence and security and to help provide for its economic well-being. At the same time, however, there will continue to be a divergence of interests that derives from a difference of perspective and overall policy environment. The United States has broader concerns resulting from its global obligations, whereas Israel's perspective is conditioned by its more restricted environment. Israel's horizon is more narrowly defined and essentially limited to the survival of the state and a concern for Jewish communities and individuals that goes beyond the frontiers of the Jewish state.

Despite the generally positive nature of the relationship since 1948, Israelis tend to recall a series of negative episodes as well. They highlight the 1947 arms embargo and the subsequent refusal to provide military equipment or other assistance during the War of Independence and the period that followed; Dulles's aid suspensions and general unfriendliness; US actions in connection with the Suez war of 1956 and Israel's subsequent withdrawal from the Sinai Peninsula and the Gaza Strip; and the disappointing lack of action by the United States just prior to the 1967 Six Day War in support of its 1957 pledge concerning freedom of passage for Israeli shipping in the Strait of Tiran.

There has also been a divergence on methods and techniques employed, as well as discord on specific issues. During the Six Day War there was a clash over Israel's mistaken attack on the US intelligence ship USS *Liberty*. In May 1968 there was disagreement over Israel's control of the islands of Tiran and Sanafir. The United States and Israel disagreed on the matter of reprisals by Israel in response to Arab *fedayeen* (literally, "self-sacrificers") actions and on the limits placed on the refugees from the West Bank in the wake of the Six Day War. There was major disagreement concerning the value of a great power to resolve the Arab-Israeli conflict, Israel's need for military supplies, and the status of the occupied territories. They have differed over the construction of settlements in the occupied territories and whether they are legal and whether they are in fact obstacles to peace. They have argued over Israel's desire for significant changes in the pre–Six Day War armistice lines as contrasted with the US perspective that there be "insubstantial alterations" or "minor modifications." The two states will continue to hold divergent views on the several elements of the Palestinian issue, particularly the West Bank's future, the rights of the Palestinians, and the delineation of a Palestinian homeland, entity, or state. These differences became increasingly obvious in the Carter and Reagan administrations.

In many respects, the issue of Jerusalem has highlighted the areas of discord. The United States has supported the Partition Plan designation of Jerusalem as a separate entity and has stressed the international character of the city while refusing to recognize unilateral actions by any state affecting its future. The United States refuses to move its embassy to Jerusalem and maintains it in Tel Aviv.[9] This stance has placed the two states in conflicting positions continuously from 1947 to the present, since Israel has declared Jerusalem to be the capital of the state and has insisted on the reunification of the city since the Six Day War. Israel's increasing dependence on the United States and the areas of policy discord suggest possible reemployment of various forms of pressure utilized previously, including the withholding of economic aid as in the mid-1950s, military aid decisions and delivery slowdowns since 1967 (such as the slow response to Israeli requests during the 1973 war), joining in United Nations censures, moral persuasion, private and open presidential letters, and similar devices.

The general consensus on major issues does not ensure agreement on all aspects or specifics of each problem. As the dialogue has increasingly focused on details, rather than broad areas of agreement, there have been disturbances in the relationship. Israel and the United States understand that this is inevitable but seek to minimize the areas of discord. Strains in the relationship are probably inevitable, given the extensive nature of the issues considered in the dialogue. Foreign Minister Yitzhak Shamir described the situation to the Knesset in these terms in September 1982:

> Our relations with the United States are of a special character. Between our two nations there is a deep friendship based on common values and identical interests. At the same time differences between our two countries crop up occasionally, chiefly on the subject of our borders and how to defend our security. These differences of opinion are natural; they stem from changing conditions, and they express our independence and our separate needs. . . . Israel is a difficult ally, but a faithful and reliable one. We are certain that what we have in common with the United States is permanent and deep while our disagreements are ephemeral. The permanent will overcome the ephemeral.

In presenting his government to the Knesset in July 1992, Prime Minister Yitzhak Rabin defined the relationship in these terms: "Sharing with us in the making of peace will also be the United States, whose friendship and special closeness we prize. We shall spare no effort to strengthen and improve the special relationship we have with the one power in the world. Of course we shall avail ourselves of its advice, but the decisions will be ours alone, of Israel as a sovereign and independent state."

Changing administrations in Washington and governments in Jerusalem have all affected the nature and content of the links between the United States and Israel within the broad parameters of the enduring special relationship. The broad patterns of concord on the more strategic and existential issues are accompanied by disagreement on the specifics of many of the elements of the Arab-Israeli conflict and on the means to achieve congruent objectives.

At Israel's birth the United States seemed to be a dispassionate, almost uninterested midwife—its role was essential and unconventional but also unpredictable and hotly debated in US policy circles. Today, decades later, some of the policy debate continues, and there are periods of tension in the relationship. Some of this reflects personality clashes and related differences between US and Israeli leaders. But there is little doubt about the overall nature of US support for its small and still embattled ally.[10]

Notes

1. An example of the latter is found in Strobe Talbott's confirmation hearings for deputy secretary of state, when congressional queries and votes tended to focus on what Talbott had written more than a decade earlier on the Arab-Israeli conflict, when he was seen as critical of Israel.

2. Public Resolution no. 73, 67th Congress, 2nd sess., September 21, 1922.

3. Letter by Representative Steny Hoyer (D-MD) and Representative Eric Cantor (R-VA) to Secretary of State Hillary Clinton Reaffirming the US-Israel Alliance (with Dear Colleague), March 26, 2010. The full text of the letter is available at http://tinyurl.com/4s393hg.

4. To a great extent this was a consequence of major Arab states rupturing diplomatic relations with the United States. Then Washington largely viewed the region through an Israeli prism, and it was difficult for the Arab states to gain the sympathy and understanding of the American people.

5. Jonathan Jay Pollard, a US Navy intelligence analyst, was arrested in November 1985 and charged with spying. Pollard pleaded guilty in June 1986. Israel denied that its senior officials had knowledge of or had approved any espionage activities against the United States. Shimon Peres apologized and promised a full investigation.

6. The full text is in the *New York Times,* March 7, 1991.

7. Hillary Rodham Clinton, Remarks at the 2010 AIPAC Policy Conference, Washington Convention Center, Washington, DC, March 22, 2010. The full text of Secretary Clinton's remarks is available at http://tinyurl.com/yfl8cxz.

8. Transcript of Remarks by Prime Minister Benjamin Netanyahu and US President Barack Obama, The White House, July 6, 2010. The full text of President Obama's remarks is available at http://tinyurl.com/4m6jefx.

9. Despite the Jerusalem Embassy Relocation Act of 1995, President Clinton and his successors did not move the embassy to Jerusalem to avoid disrupting the peace negotiations.

10. For example, in remarks before the 2010 General Assembly of the Jewish Federations of North America in November 2010, Vice President Joe Biden said, "This administration represents an unbroken chain of American leaders who have understood this critical strategic relationship, one in which we will not yield one single inch . . . The ties between our countries are literally, literally unbreakable. Our common values are interwoven in our cultures, in our mutual interests, none more urgent than the shared struggle against the scourge of violent extremism and terrorists." Remarks by Vice President Joe Biden before the 2010 General Assembly of the Jewish Federations of North America in New Orleans, November 7, 2010.

CHAPTER 14

FROM MADRID AND OSLO TO CAMP DAVID

The United States and the Arab-Israeli Conflict, 1991–2001

Jeremy Pressman

From 1991 to 2001, Arab-Israeli relations were characterized by diplomatic triumphs as well as familiar problems. The multilateral peace conference at Madrid, the secret Oslo negotiations and agreement, the return of Palestine Liberation Organization (PLO) leaders to historic Palestine, and Israel's disengagement from Gaza all seemed to herald an era in which the contentious aftermath of the 1967 war might finally be addressed and resolved. Yet bus bombings, checkpoints, and most importantly, the second Palestinian uprising *(intifada)* reminded all the participants that neither side had abandoned the use of force in its relations with the other.

Throughout the 1990s, first under President George H. W. Bush (1989–1993), a Republican, and then under President Bill Clinton (1993–2001), a Democrat, the United States remained deeply involved in Arab-Israeli relations. In 1991, the Bush administration capitalized on major changes in regional and world politics to jump-start the peace process at Madrid. US officials sought to negotiate agreements and then shepherd their implementation through intensive involvement in negotiating details and logistics. Secretaries of State James Baker III, Warren Christopher, and Madeleine Albright expended great effort on the issue and frequently met with Arab and Israeli officials; they often traveled to the region to further negotiations. President Clinton regularly hosted the Israeli prime minister and the PLO chairman, Yasser Arafat, at the White House. He traveled to Geneva to meet with Syrian President Hafiz al-Asad in January 1994, and the presidents met again in March 2000 when Clinton thought an Israeli-Syrian deal was likely. When the second *intifada* erupted in late 2000, US diplomats unsuccessfully worked to bring it to an end.

US diplomatic efforts from 1991–2001 came the closest yet to achieving the long-sought-after American goal of a comprehensive Arab-Israeli peace, but in the end the conflict was not resolved. Israel and Jordan inked a peace deal, and the fact that Israel now has signed peace treaties with two of its neighbors was in part due to Washington's diplomatic diligence. But Israeli-Palestinian agreements collapsed in violence despite enormous US investments in the peace process. Moreover, Israel and Syria came close to signing an agreement in 1999–2000, but they could not bridge the last differences over the exact border delineation of an Israeli withdrawal from the Golan Heights. A wide range of political and procedural errors blocked the achievement of both agreements. Near the end of Clinton's presidency, the Arab-Israeli negotiating failures at Shepherdstown, Geneva, and Camp David were part of a disappointing conclusion to ten years of talks. The US inability to contain the second *intifada* only reinforced the distance between the American interest in a comprehensive peace and the reality on the ground.

Throughout this period, Israeli prime ministers were either cognizant of the importance of US-Israeli ties or paid the price for challenging Washington. The three Israeli leaders from the left-wing Labor Party—Yitzhak Rabin, Shimon Peres, and Ehud Barak—had fewer problems because their efforts to advance the peace process dovetailed with US interests. The challenge was for right-wing Likud Party leaders—Yitzhak Shamir and Benjamin Netanyahu. In 1992, Shamir's reelection bid suffered from the US-Israeli fight over loan guarantees and Israeli settlements. In 1999, Netanyahu's record of undermining the peace process led to strains in the US-Israeli relationship.

In the next section, I describe changes in the international and regional distribution of power that opened the door to Arab-Israeli diplomacy. I then address the Oslo agreements (1993, 1995) and some of the specific reasons why the Israeli-Palestinian process failed. I consider the tenures of Benjamin Netanyahu and Ehud Barak, the failed Camp David summit (2000), and the Clinton Plan and final talks at Taba, Egypt, in January 2001. In the closing section, I consider four broader explanations for why Israeli-Palestinian and Israeli-Syrian talks never led to peace agreements. I conclude that political and procedural factors, not conflicting objectives or violent opposition, best explain the failures.

SHIFTING POWER: THE PATHWAY TO MADRID

After shifts in the global and regional distribution of power set the stage for the Arab-Israeli peace talks of the 1990s, the United States played an important role in bringing the parties together for diplomatic talks. The end of the cold war and the 1991 Persian Gulf war eliminated the Arab military option against Israel. Whether the military option meant attacking Israel or trying to acquire parity in the arms race, the Arab side's only hope was based on Soviet military and financial support. Only Soviet support could give the Arab armies access to weapons that could meet US/Israeli weapons on the battlefield. Only Soviet subsidies and aid could facilitate the Iraqi and Syrian purchase of such weapons.[1]

The Soviet decision in 1987 to stop subsidizing Syrian arms sales strongly reinforced the trend that had started when Egypt made peace with Israel in 1978–1979 and thereby greatly reduced the possibility of a coordinated Arab attack against Israel. After the reformist Soviet leader Mikhail Gorbachev told Syrian President Hafiz al-Asad of the change in Soviet policy, Syria dropped its pursuit of strategic parity with Israel; Damascus had no choice. The Arab side could still resort to violence through guerrilla war and terrorism through proxies, but it could not seriously challenge Israel in the conventional military arena. Since that time, the only Arab strikes against Israel have been by substate actors such as Hamas, Lebanon's Hizbollah, Palestinian Islamic Jihad, and various factions of the Palestine Liberation Organization (PLO).

The Soviet decision was followed in 1991 by the expulsion of Iraq from Kuwait by a US-led coalition. Not only did the United States reverse Iraq's occupation of Kuwait, but it also destroyed a significant amount of Iraqi arms. The UN Security Council (UNSC) sanctioned the creation and enforcement of "no-fly zones" in southern and northern Iraq where Iraqi aircraft were barred. UN inspectors traveled around Iraq and sought evidence of nonconventional weapons; they destroyed Iraqi weapons stocks and equipment. US forces remained stationed in Saudi Arabia, the Persian Gulf waters, and in smaller Gulf states. Iraq was contained, and the possibility of Iraqi soldiers joining other Arab forces for an attempt from the east to cut Israel in half was gone (though the Israeli fear of an attack on its eastern front lingered).

Taken together, the end of the cold war and the Persian Gulf war meant the Arab side lacked the numbers and the external support to match Israel in the strategic realm. This did not guarantee a turn toward diplomacy, but it did make such a possibility much more likely.

The end of the cold war and, ultimately, the collapse of the Soviet Union did not dampen US interests in achieving a comprehensive settlement of the Arab-Israeli conflict. One might have expected that the demise of the only other superpower and longtime US rival for power and influence in the Middle East might have eased US concerns about Arab-Israeli disagreements. Yet the Bush and Clinton administrations, which governed in the period between the cold war and the al-Qa'ida threat, nonetheless invested heavily in regional diplomacy. The United States remained dependent on Middle East oil, and the continuance of the Arab-Israeli conflict complicated US relations with Arab oil exporters; at a minimum, the possibility of another Arab oil embargo emerging after a future Arab-Israeli clash could not be wholly dismissed. Furthermore, Israel's security remained a central US commitment. Arab-Israeli peace agreements made Israel more secure and reduced the likelihood of a demand for US political or military intervention in a crisis situation similar to the wars in 1967 and 1973.

The United States, then, exploited the opening created by changes in the global and regional balance of power to bring about the first multilateral Arab-Israeli peace conference since the 1970s. The US effort, led by Secretary of State James Baker III, sought to bring together Israel and its neighboring Arab rivals—Jordan, Lebanon, and Syria.[2] In part, the United States was indebted to Syria for its membership in the anti-Iraq coalition. The PLO was not invited; instead, the Jordanian delegation, which included Palestinians from the occupied territories, was seen as representing both Jordan and the Palestinian people. During the summer of 1991, after intense US diplomatic lobbying, all the key parties agreed to attend a conference. The opening meeting was held in Madrid, Spain, from October 30 to November 1, 1991. It produced no breakthroughs and largely served as a forum for the public repetition of uncompromising positions.

The Madrid talks were followed by two types of negotiations, bilateral and multilateral, but the negotiations soon stalled.[3] The bilateral talks consisted of Israeli-Syrian, Israeli-Lebanese, and Israeli-Jordanian meetings and were usually held in Washington. With the collapse of the Soviet Union in December 1991, the United States was the sole superpower, and officials hoped to use US primacy to advance the cause of Middle East peace, leveraging its predominant position in the region and the goodwill it had generated by liberating Kuwait in the Gulf War earlier in the year. The talks, however, devolved into dueling press conferences at which the respective diplomats commented on the lack of progress after each day's sessions.

THE OSLO AGREEMENTS

In 1993, as the bilateral talks dragged on, Israeli Prime Minister Yitzhak Rabin and PLO Chairman Yasser Arafat both signed off on secret unofficial talks in Oslo, Norway. Rabin did not expect much to come of the talks and probably saw them as a pet project of Shimon Peres, his foreign minister, and Yossi Beilin, deputy foreign minister.[4] Yet in August 1993, the two sides initialed a breakthrough agreement, what soon became known as the Declaration of Principles. Unlike most of the other diplomatic milestones during this period, the United States was not involved in the Oslo talks because Norway initiated and hosted the meetings. Both parties wanted to shun the inevitable attention commensurate with US involvement, and for Israel, it has always been an objective to deal one-on-one with Arab parties in negotiations, where it can maximize its leverage and avoid American pressure to make unwanted concessions.

In the June 1992 elections, Rabin had promised a breakthrough with the Palestinians. At a meeting of the Labor Party's central committee in March 1992, for instance, Rabin suggested a time frame of six to nine months for reaching an autonomy agreement.[5] Rabin believed that resolving the Israeli-Palestinian conflict in the short term would help Israel both avoid antagonism from potential strategic threats such as Iran in the long term and lock in US support for Israel.

Arafat was struggling to come to terms with the impact of the first *intifada* and the Gulf War. The PLO backed Iraq, the losing side in the Gulf War; Arab Gulf financial support dried up as a result. By 1992–1993, the *intifada* had slowed and lost some of its popular character and appeal. Arafat was still on the outside of the occupied territories, while younger Palestinian leaders on the inside had established a vibrant institutional infrastructure. In order to sustain Palestinian daily life and resistance to the occupation during the first *intifada,* Palestinians developed a range of political and social welfare organizations. To Tunis-based PLO leaders, these new organizations were potential rival centers of political power.

The Declaration of Principles (DOP), signed on the White House lawn on September 13, 1993, launched the public phase of the Oslo process. That the DOP was signed on the White House lawn was a testament to how quickly the United States recognized the potential value of the agreement. Washington had not been involved in negotiating the deal, but Clinton officials used the White House ceremony to signal US backing for the agreement as well as to indicate that henceforth US diplomatic muscle would support the implementation of the agreement. The parties themselves also probably recognized the value of the United States as a future guarantor, broker, and funder.

The DOP did not resolve the core Israeli-Palestinian issues such as the future status of Jerusalem, Israeli settlements, or Palestinian refugees. Nor did it explicitly call for a Palestinian state alongside Israel or a freeze on Israeli settlement building in the occupied territories. Israeli Foreign Minister Shimon Peres, on flying to California and presenting the Oslo agreement to Secretary Christopher and Dennis Ross in August 1993, explained why: "The logic, Peres stressed, was to build a network of cooperation so that the harder issues would become resolvable in a very different climate."[6]

Instead of dealing with these "harder issues," the DOP set up a five-year transitional period in which Israel would gradually redeploy from the Gaza Strip and West Bank, starting with Gaza and the West Bank city of Jericho. Further withdrawals were contingent on security matters, as explained in the DOP: "Further redeployments to specified locations will be gradually implemented commensurate with the assumption of responsibility for public order and internal security by the Palestinian police. . . ." The Palestinians would develop a quasi-government, the Palestinian Interim Self-Government Authority (later known more simply as the Palestinian Authority), hold elections, and develop a "strong police force." Talks on the most difficult issues, "permanent status negotiations," would start by the beginning of the third year of the transitional period. Permanent or final status issues included core disputes over "Jerusalem, refugees, settlements, security arrangements, [and] borders." Article XV created nonviolent mechanisms for resolving disputes.

The Israelis withdrew from Jericho and much of Gaza in mid-1994, and Arafat and many other Tunis-based PLO leaders entered Gaza. This brought Arafat and the leaders of the PLO back into the center of Palestinian politics and gained the PLO legitimacy with the United States. After concern about marginalization and financial troubles, the PLO saw the DOP, however imperfect, as an opportunity for gaining political power and fiscal support. PLO acceptance was a sign of the movement's weakness, not strength.

Meanwhile, Israel and Jordan signed a peace treaty on October 26, 1994, after years of clandestine elite ties. Israeli leaders and Jordan's Hashemite monarchy had long met in secret. Yet because the majority of Jordan's population was Palestinian, Jordan had been unwilling to reach a public agreement with Israel prior to an Israeli-Palestinian breakthrough. The Oslo agreement changed the environment and gave Jordan the political cover it needed to solidify cooperative relations with Israel as well as regain the good graces of Washington after tacitly backing Iraq in the 1991 Gulf War. The United States helped facilitate the treaty, but Israel and Jordan had no fundamental disagreements and needed only limited outside assistance.

Rabin's election also ushered in an intensive period of Israeli-Syrian contacts from 1993 to 1995. It was a period in which the United States played an active role, and Israelis and Syrians made progress on a number of practical issues. The two sides traded diplomatic phrases: Rabin said "the depth of the withdrawal will reflect the depth of peace." In May 1993, Asad offered "full peace for full withdrawal." In 1993–1994, Rabin secretly agreed to a full Israeli withdrawal from the Golan Heights to the June 4, 1967, line, though exactly how to delineate that line remained a point of debate. US officials carried messages between Rabin and Asad just before Rabin opted for the Oslo (Israeli-Palestinian) track in August 1993. At a meeting with Clinton in Geneva on January 16, 1994, Asad spoke of a strategic decision for peace and "a new era of security and stability in which normal, peaceful relations among all shall dawn anew." Clinton traveled to Damascus in October of the same year, and Christopher frequently met with Asad and Rabin as well. In June 1995, the United States hosted the Israeli and Syrian chiefs of staff in Washington for talks on security matters at which a good deal of progress was made.[7]

Meanwhile, on September 28, 1995, the Israelis and Palestinians signed a second major agreement that detailed additional territorial changes in the West Bank. The agreement, Oslo II, created three types of West Bank land: Area A under Palestinian security and civil control, Area B under Palestinian civil control and Israeli security control, and Area C under Israeli security and civil rule. The territorial withdrawals of Oslo II proceeded slowly and were never fully implemented. The sides repeatedly disagreed on the exact size, timing, and location of agreed-upon withdrawals, but Israel was the ruling power so it had the final say. By the outbreak of the second *intifada* in September 2000, the majority of the West Bank, including all Israeli settlements, remained as Area C. About 17 percent of the West Bank was Area A and another 23 percent was Area B.[8]

Unlike the first Oslo agreement, Oslo II was partially the result of intensive US diplomacy, though not of the level of the late 1990s and 2000. Secretary of State Christopher and, in later years, Secretary of State Albright were willing to spend time and political capital nailing down Israeli-Palestinian agreements. US diplomats, including Martin Indyk, Aaron David Miller, and Dennis Ross, moderated, cajoled, proposed, and persuaded until the Arabs and Israelis found common ground on issues both large and small. At times, US diplomats called on other American officials, such as CIA Director George Tenet, to play a role with one or both sides.

From 1993 to 2001, the Oslo process proceeded more slowly than planned and ultimately failed to lead to a final resolution of the conflict. At the popular level, neither Palestinian expectations of freedom of movement, economic improvement, and statehood nor Israeli hopes for peace, security, and a normal life were met. Expectations had been high. At the DOP signing ceremony in 1993, Arafat expressed Palestinian hopes: "My people are hoping that this agreement which we are signing today marks the beginning of the end of a chapter of pain and suffering which has lasted throughout this century . . . [and that it] will usher in an age of peace, co-existence, and equal rights."[9] Rabin sought a break with the past: "We wish to open a new chapter in the sad book of our lives together, a chapter of mutual recognition, of good neighborliness, of mutual respect, of understanding. We hope to embark on a new era in the history of the Middle East."[10] These unmet expectations, especially on the Palestinian side, fueled growing disenchantment with the Oslo talks and greater sympathy for confrontational and violent policies that eventually crystallized into the second *intifada*.

In particular, the Oslo process suffered from four developments. First, some Palestinian groups, including Hamas and the Palestinian Islamic Jihad, attacked and killed Israeli civilians. To Israelis, terrorist bus bombings inside pre-1967 Israel suggested that they were not safe personally and that the process was not leading to normalization and peaceful relations. The wave of bus bombings in February–March 1996, for instance, killed and wounded hundreds of Israelis and contributed to the defeat of Prime Minister Shimon Peres in the May 1996 elections.

Second, some Israeli Jewish settlers used terrorist violence against Palestinians, mostly in the West Bank. The first Hamas suicide bombings came after an Israeli settler killed twenty-nine Palestinians at the Ibrahimi Mosque in Hebron on February 25, 1994. Most of the settler attacks, however, were less dramatic and often resulted in injury and property destruction rather than death. Yet when coupled with the civilian casualties from Israel Defense Forces (IDF) counterterror operations, they had a corrosive effect on Palestinian views of Israeli intentions.

Third, Israel continued to massively develop the West Bank settlements, including building a network of Jewish-only bypass roads that crisscrossed the West Bank. From 1993 to 2000, the number of Israeli settlers increased by at least 117 percent in Gaza and at least 46 percent in the West Bank (not including East Jerusalem where settler growth was also large).[11] In the 1990s, Israel stopped authorizing new settlements but still allowed the building of new "neighborhoods" for existing settlements. Israeli settlers also proceeded to set up tens of unauthorized outposts, a practice that mushroomed after Ariel Sharon became prime minister in 2001.[12]

Fourth, Israel used collective punishment, such as checkpoints, home demolitions, closure and curfews, bureaucratic procedures, and targeted assassinations, to advance its security objectives. For example, approximately 670 Palestinian homes in the West Bank (including Jerusalem) were destroyed from September 1993 to

June 1998.[13] Israel also implemented a policy of revoking permission to live in Jerusalem from Palestinians who could not prove the center of their life was in Jerusalem; Palestinians had to prove that their work, family, education, and housing centered on Jerusalem rather than elsewhere in the West Bank or abroad. Over 1,600 Palestinians and their families were removed in this way from 1996 to 1998, according to Israeli officials.[14] Palestinians often rejected Israel's security justifications for these policies and instead highlighted Israel's desire for continued control of the West Bank. A process Palestinians thought would lead to the end of the occupation instead seemed to be leading to its intensification.

While Washington was deeply involved in the negotiations, the United States refrained from coercing either party. With one exception in the 1990s, the United States did not provide aid directly to the Palestinian Authority, so it could not threaten to withhold aid if the PLO or PA failed to fulfill their commitments.[15] Although Israeli settlement expansion was changing the reality on the ground in the West Bank and undermining Palestinian support for the Oslo process, the United States did not exert significant pressure. The United States deducted the costs of settlement expansion from multibillion-dollar loan guarantees Israel had secured from the United States, but this was a marginal punishment that had a limited practical effect. With only a few exceptions, the United States has long been reluctant to threaten Israel.[16]

On November 4, 1995, Israeli Prime Minister Yitzhak Rabin was assassinated by an Israeli Jew. The killing deeply affected the personal chemistry of US-Israeli relations. Clinton and Rabin had developed a warm relationship in the first years of Clinton's presidency; the young president enjoyed interactions with Rabin, an older, seasoned politician. Reflecting on Rabin's death, Clinton later wrote, "We had become friends in that unique way people do when they are in a struggle that they believe is great and good . . . . I had come to love him as I had rarely loved another man."[17] At Rabin's funeral, Clinton's comment "shalom chaver" (goodbye friend) captured their friendship and came to embody the profound sense of shock and loss felt by many Israelis. Although Arafat was also a frequent visitor to the White House, the relationship between Clinton and Arafat, though cordial, lacked the personal chemistry of the Clinton-Rabin ties.

NETANYAHU AND BARAK

The Rabin assassination exacerbated Israeli-Palestinian problems. Not only was Rabin gone, but he was replaced six months later by Benjamin "Bibi" Netanyahu, who campaigned against the Oslo process. A wave of Palestinian bus bombings in February–March 1996—a response to Israel's assassination of Palestinian bomb maker Yahya Ayash in January—had the effect of reinforcing Netanyahu's criticism of Rabin's replacement, Shimon Peres.

With Netanyahu's electoral victory, the United States was then challenged with the task of getting a harsh opponent of the Oslo process to implement it and continue negotiations. Some agreements were signed, such as the Hebron Protocol (January 15, 1997) and the Wye agreement (October 23, 1998), but Bibi's overall stance further undermined Israeli-Palestinian relations. US officials worked hard to keep Netanyahu's government committed to the Oslo agreements, but in doing so they usually gave some ground as the contents of past agreements were renegotiated. The Hebron agreement (1997), for instance, relaxed the expectations contained in the Oslo II agreement (1995) for further Israeli withdrawals from parts of the West Bank. As Israel slowed the negotiations and the pace of the withdrawals, Netanyahu's relations with both Arafat and Clinton became strained.

The Wye agreement was classic US-led Middle East diplomacy and typified US efforts in 1996–1999 to keep the peace process afloat, but the agreement's actual impact was limited. The United States invited Arafat and Netanyahu to the Wye River Plantation in Maryland for intensive discussions. Clinton, along with the terminally ill King Hussein of Jordan, worked at an agreement until the two parties signed a deal on West Bank land, Palestinian prisoner releases, the Palestinian charter, and other issues. The agreement led to some modest progress, but relations quickly soured. Clinton traveled to Israel and Gaza in December 1998 to try to aid the faltering process.

The Israeli government changed again when the left-leaning Labor Party and Ehud Barak defeated Netanyahu and his Likud Party in elections on May 17, 1999. Although Barak signed an Israeli-Palestinian protocol at Sharm el-Sheikh, Egypt, in September 1999, he chose to first move aggressively on the Israeli-Syrian front. Despite Palestinian concern, the United States backed Barak's focus on Syria. The United States finally hoped to capitalize on the commitment of Yitzhak Rabin and his successors to withdraw from the Golan Heights to the June 4, 1967, line, the line that Syria demanded in order to sign an agreement.

After high-level talks in December 1999, Israeli and Syrian negotiators met in Shepherdstown, West Virginia, in January 2000. Barak was concerned about opposition in Israel to a full withdrawal, and the talks failed. In March 2000, Syria thought it had a US commitment that Israel would agree to the June 4, 1967, line, as opposed to the 1923 international boundary or other possible borders. Asad and Clinton met in Geneva expecting a momentous breakthrough, but the meeting immediately broke down when it became clear that Israel was proposing a modified version of the June 4, 1967, line. Barak, with US knowledge, decided not to offer Syria a complete return to the June 4, 1967, line, and so the two sides failed to come to an agreement.[18] Having failed to secure an agreement with Syria, in which Barak also hoped to come to an agreement regarding Lebanon, Israel unilaterally withdrew its soldiers from southern Lebanon in May 2000. On June 10, 2000, Asad died.

During the first part of Barak's term, Palestinian attacks on Israelis nearly ceased. Israeli-Palestinian security cooperation and Palestinian hopes that Barak's new government would lead to a two-state breakthrough combined to usher in greater quiet in Israel. In 1999 and the first ten months of 2000, only seven Israelis were killed in terror attacks—including just one inside pre-1967 Israel.[19] According to Ami Ayalon, the head of Israel's Shin Bet at the time, Palestinian political hope led to a drop in Palestinian mass support for violence and an increased willingness on the part of Palestinian security personnel to combat it.[20] Some have argued that Israel squandered this period of Israeli-Palestinian calm by focusing on Syria instead of pursuing high-level Israeli-Palestinian talks.

CAMP DAVID SUMMIT

In the spring of 2000, during Clinton's last year in office, Barak turned his attention to the Palestinian track after the failure with Syria. Perhaps hoping to recapture the Scandinavian magic of Oslo, the two sides held secret talks in Stockholm, Sweden, to deal with the core issues, but these negotiations broke up inconclusively after word of the talks leaked to the media. Israel soon decided to pursue a high-level, high-stakes summit to resolve the conflict. Barak, long a skeptic of Oslo's incrementalism, felt this was the only way to test whether Arafat would commit to a final agreement instead of offering only more interim steps and indecision. Palestinian leaders resisted in part because they feared the intensity of joint American-Israeli pressure in a closed summit, but US cajoling caused Palestinian leaders to set aside their concerns. President Clinton announced on July 5, 2000, that Israeli and Palestinian delegations had agreed to join him at his presidential retreat, Camp David.

Many explanations have been offered for the failure of the American-Israeli-Palestinian summit of July 11–25, 2000, but all parties contributed to its demise. The conventional wisdom that Israel made a generous offer and the Palestinian negotiators rejected it out of hand is not backed up by the evidentiary record.[21]

The United States made a number of procedural errors. Washington pressured a reluctant Palestinian leadership to attend, promised not to blame the Palestinians if the summit failed, and then reneged on that promise. US diplomats had not lobbied other Arab leaders to support Palestinian concessions on Jerusalem and did not have a workable fall-back plan for the summit should an overall agreement prove impossible. After meeting Israeli-Palestinian resistance, US officials quickly backed away from tabling written drafts of compromise language on sticky issues. At least in hindsight, the gap between Israel and the Palestinians on all the core issues entering the summit was wider than one would want coming into a meeting at the highest levels.

Israel attended the talks with unrealistic expectations about the Palestinian bottom line. During the summit, Israel rejected Palestinian sovereignty in the Arab parts of East Jerusalem and limited the Palestinian territory in the West Bank to two or three noncontiguous chunks of, at most, 91–92 percent (and by other measures as little as 77 percent) of the entire West Bank.[22] Why Israel thought the Palestinians would accept this package is a lingering historical puzzle. In general, Barak often seemed to assume he knew best and could compel others to follow his lead, but this approach failed at Camp David, much as it did on other issues during his short tenure as Israeli prime minister. At the summit itself, he did not engage Arafat, even though Arafat would have to sign off on any of the central Palestinian concessions on Jerusalem and refugees that were needed to strike a deal. Some Israeli and US diplomats also mistakenly thought that the unofficial final status agreement negotiated in 1995 between Palestinian Mahmoud Abbas and Israeli Yossi Beilin, known as the Beilin–Abu Mazen agreement, could serve as a rough blueprint for the summit.

Palestinian negotiators operated from a defensive position, fearful that Israel and the United States would try to compel them to accept the unacceptable. The Palestinians were largely reactive and never tabled a detailed proposal that went much beyond international law and UN resolutions. Contrary to many claims, however, the Palestinians did present a map of the West Bank proposing the Israeli annexation of 2–3 percent of the West Bank. The delegation was beset by power struggles, as was common under Arafat's long rule of the Palestinian national movement. Arafat's rejection of a key aspect of Jewish history—the site of the ancient Jewish temple in Jerusalem's Old City—undermined his credibility.

Some promising ideas solidified at the summit, however. The Palestinians agreed to the idea of swapping land for a few major settlement blocs in the West Bank that Israel wanted to annex, though how narrow or expansive such blocs should be remained a contested issue. Israel's idea of dividing Jerusalem was a breakthrough, even if Israel did not offer Palestinian sovereignty in all Arab areas in East Jerusalem. As they had indicated in prior negotiations, the Palestinians were willing to allow Israeli sovereignty in Jewish neighborhoods of East Jerusalem.

After the summit, quiet talks continued into August and September 2000, but just as the United States was about to present its own plan, the second *intifada* erupted.[23] Ariel Sharon, then the leader of the Israeli parliamentary opposition, visited the Temple Mount in Jerusalem on September 28, and Palestinian protests broke out and escalated. The Tanzim, an offshoot of the nationalist Fatah movement, welcomed the confrontation as a way to compel by force what Israel refused to give up at the negotiating table: control of the West Bank. The IDF, as planned, responded to the Palestinian protests with massive force, hoping that this would quickly quell the rioting. It had the opposite effect, and by the end of October 2000, Israeli forces had killed 116 Palestinians compared with 11 Israeli dead.[24] Once the fighting was under way, Arafat felt the Palestinians could gain further regional and international support and thereby put pressure on Israel if the fighting continued; top Palestinian leaders did little to restrain Palestinian fighters. A Clinton-led summit of leaders at Sharm el-Sheikh in mid-October 2000 and other diplomatic efforts to end the violence failed.

THE CLINTON PLAN AND TABA

On December 23, 2000, President Bill Clinton brought together negotiators from both sides and finally presented a US plan for a two-state solution. His proposal, the Clinton Plan, called for Palestinian sovereignty in Gaza and about 97 percent of the West Bank.[25] Palestinian refugees could stay in their host countries, return to the Palestinian state, or settle in small areas of land handed over by Israel as compensation for Israeli territorial annexations in the West Bank. Though Israel would annex settlement blocs in the West Bank, more isolated settlements would presumably be dismantled. Israel and third-party states could also choose to absorb some Palestinian refugees, but they were not required to do so.

Clinton called for a division of Jerusalem with Palestinian sovereignty in the Arab areas of East Jerusalem, and Israeli sovereignty in West Jerusalem and the Jewish areas of the east side. He offered two possible compromises for Jerusalem's Temple Mount (Muslims call it the Haram al-Sharif, or Noble Sanctuary), a location holy to both Jews and Muslims. The Clinton Plan also dealt with security matters. In order to pressure the parties, the United States insisted that the plan would be considered a valid proposal only until Clinton left office on January 20, 2001. The plan's continuing relevance today testifies to the bankruptcy of this idea.

The Israeli government accepted the plan but offered reservations. Privately, Barak sent Clinton a long and still-classified letter detailing his concerns, including misgivings about the refugee formulation.[26] In public, Barak rejected Clinton's call for Palestinian sovereignty over the Temple Mount/Haram al-Sharif. In practice, this meant a rejection of Clinton's compromise for sovereignty in the holy sites.

The Palestinian response has been the subject of much controversy, but it too was a technical acceptance with significant reservations. Arafat accepted the plan on January 2, 2001, in a face-to-face meeting with Clinton but offered reservations. Arafat accepted Israel's sovereignty over the central Jewish holy site known as the Wailing Wall but not over the entire ancient temple wall of which it is a part; he objected to Israeli use of West Bank airspace; and he requested a different framework for dealing with Palestinian refugees.[27]

The Clinton Plan was closely followed by Israeli-Palestinian negotiations at Taba, Egypt, during January 21–27, 2001. According to most participants and observers, the talks were substantive, and the parties made progress,[28] although the United States was not involved at a time when strong US mediation could have been very helpful. The negotiators issued an optimistic concluding statement: "The sides declare that they have never been closer to reaching an agreement, and it is thus our shared belief that the remaining gaps could be bridged with the resumption of negotiations following the Israeli elections."

On February 6, Ariel Sharon defeated Ehud Barak in Israeli elections. Upon taking office, Prime Minister Sharon chose not to engage in high-level talks, and the George W. Bush administration, itself having just come to power on January 20, accepted that approach.

Because both the Israeli-Syrian and Israeli-Palestinian negotiations ended in failure, the discussions that took place concerning a deeper US strategic role in the Arab-Israeli arena have been overlooked. Had the Israeli-Syrian negotiations gone differently, for instance, US monitors and peacekeepers might have been sent to the Golan Heights to supervise an Israeli-Syrian deal. The United States also agreed to a request from Arafat for US peacekeepers in the Jordan Valley. In July 2002, two years after the Camp David summit, Bruce Riedel, a former member of the US National Security Council staff, revealed that at the summit Israel proposed "a formal mutual defense agreement including a commitment by the United States to come to the assistance of Israel in the event of attack in the future, enshrined in a treaty to be ratified by the Congress and the Knesset." Israel also wanted the United States to include Israel under the US nuclear umbrella. Israel's draft treaty was an expansion of discussions that had focused on the Israeli-Syrian talks. At Camp David, Israel also sought billions of dollars for new arms and access to advanced US military technology such as Tomahawk cruise missiles and F-22 aircraft.[29]

THE FAILURE OF THE PEACE PROCESS

Why did the Israeli-Palestinian and Israeli-Syrian negotiations fail to lead to final peace agreements? In a broad sense, why did the Arab-Israeli peace process of 1993–2001 fail? In this concluding section, I consider four possible explanations and find that political and procedural mistakes, including missteps by Washington, doomed the talks.[30] The claim that one or more parties did not want a peace agreement is the least persuasive explanation despite its widespread popularity.

The actors did not want peace. One or more of the parties to the conflict did not actually want peace, so the failure of the talks helped them achieve their true objectives. Participation in the process was a ruse, perhaps to appease the United States and the international community. Negotiators could talk forever without actually reaching a final agreement that would require real sacrifice in exchange for concrete gains. The Palestinians did not want peace; they wanted a single Palestinian state in place of Israel. Israel did not want peace but rather the occupation and annexation of the West Bank, Gaza, and the Golan Heights. Syria would never accept normal, peaceful relations with Israel.

The evidence does not support this claim. Israel, Syria, and the Palestinians invested massive diplomatic energy and political resources in the process. Each expended great amounts of political capital domestically in order to pursue the negotiations; they took risks in the domestic arena that might undermine their hold on power. All agreed to policies that would not be popular at home. For example, Israel agreed to the division of Jerusalem and withdrawal from the Golan Heights; the Palestinians agreed to allow Israeli annexation of some settlements in Jerusalem and elsewhere in the West Bank; and Syria accepted normalization with Israel. When Israel recognized that the offer at Camp David had been insufficient, they continued to negotiate (as did the Palestinians). Barak's government paid the ultimate political price: It fell apart over a deal with the Palestinians. When Asad came to Geneva to meet with Clinton in March 2000, the Syrian delegation was massive, because Asad expected to need many officials to iron out all the details of the peace agreement. Israel's offer at the Camp David summit was imperfect for Palestinians only because they truly believed they would be bound by the agreement. If instead they had hoped to use the new state of Palestine as a springboard for a military attack on Israel, the difference between receiving 92 percent or 97 percent of the West Bank and many other stipulations would not have mattered.[31]

One caveat to the idea that Israelis and Palestinians are ready to compromise on all the core issues is that the negotiators do not have a clear solution to the problem of who would control the Temple Mount/Haram al-Sharif in Jerusalem. While the contours of an agreement on all the other issues are clear, the division of this sacred area is still unsettled.

Procedural errors undermined the negotiations. On the Israeli-Palestinian track, the way in which the process was constructed and carried out led to its failure. The initial terms of the 1993 Declaration of Principles were too favorable toward Israel. With no explicit mention of a Palestinian state or a settlement freeze, the agreement was bound to run into trouble. The process was too gradual, and this left opponents much time and many opportunities to thwart the drive toward peace. It was driven by elites, and this left out the Israeli and Palestinian publics. They were never conditioned to accept the compromises that would be needed. Along the way, as I noted above with the US performance at the Camp David summit, the handling of the actual negotiations was frequently botched. Everyone wanted an agreement, but the pathway was too rocky and ill conceived.

While much of this critique is accurate in terms of identifying the shortcomings of the Oslo process, it implicitly suggests that a balanced, rapid process with both leader and popular participation was a realistic possibility in 1993. It was not. Israel's general power advantage translated into a negotiating advantage, one that Israel, like any state in that position, would not willingly give up. Conditioning one's people is difficult without telegraphing to the other negotiating party in advance the concessions one will accept. Negotiators hold concessions close to their chests; they try not to broadcast them in public.

Furthermore, the gradualism of the Oslo process was the only approach likely to gain sufficient Israeli and Palestinian support so that it could be sustained. A more rapid move to a two-state solution on the June 4, 1967 lines would never have gotten off the ground. In part, the gradualism itself makes possible the posthoc view that Oslo was too gradual. Everyone has come to expect much more than what, in 1993, seemed like a monumental leap. In other words, the Oslo breakthrough conditioned people on both sides to be able to expect much more— a more lasting rapprochement—and therefore makes the initial approach seem misguided.

This explanation has mostly focused on the Israeli-Palestinian track, but the Israeli-Syrian process may also have suffered. First, the competition for Israeli and US attention between the two negotiating tracks slowed the talks. The best example was probably in August 1993 when Rabin weighed talks with Syria against the Oslo track and chose the latter at the (temporary) expense of the former. Second, Israel and Syria did not engage in consistent high-level negotiations. Months often went by without much interaction. The United States could have done more to speed up the Israeli-Syrian process, a claim that carries over to the next explanation.

Despite some limitations, then, the wide array of procedural mistakes and political decisions is the best explanation of the failure to reach agreements. Israelis, Palestinians, and Syrians were close, but they tripped themselves up, and the United States, the central mediator, failed to steer them in the right diplomatic direction on too many occasions. The problems were not just at Camp David or Geneva in

2000 but ran throughout the entire period. In the next section, I address the US failings more specifically. But while I treat the second and third explanations separately, they fit together quite well.

The United States was too passive. The United States failed to do its job as mediator, facilitator, and enforcer. The United States failed to monitor the parties and sanction actors who failed to uphold their agreed-upon commitments. During Clinton's first term, William Quandt argues that Washington could have forced the pace of all the negotiations rather than letting the talks drag and risk squandering a window of opportunity. He further claims that the United States did not always press Netanyahu when the Israeli government was ambivalent about the Oslo process.[32] The United States convened meetings at the highest level only to see them fail at Shepherdstown, Geneva, and Camp David. By the time the top leaders reached such meetings, US officials should have ensured that the odds of failure were low.

Another version of the idea that US failings stalled the drive for peace is that the United States should have coerced Israel in order to advance the process. Israel was the more powerful party, and only US efforts could counterbalance Israel's advantage and lead to an equitably structured negotiating framework. If the Oslo process failed in part because Israel could dictate the terms of the DOP and continue settlement expansion, the only leverage resided in Washington. The second alternative, then, to the gradual process as it unfolded was a process with a much stronger US role. But this is not just about the opening of the talks; it also would have required a strenuous US policy along the way to ensure success.

Still, for this to have been a viable US approach, one would have to completely ignore a core tenet of US policy: strong Israeli-US relations. As noted earlier, the United States has generally been unwilling to coerce Israel with sanctions or other material threats. Israel has many domestic supporters, including many elected and appointed officials, who balk at pressuring Israel and criticize presidential administrations who contemplate a coercive approach.

The opponents of the process bested supporters. On the Israeli-Palestinian track, the peace process failed because opponents used violence to dash euphoric expectations and prevent the timely implementation of agreements. Most terrorist attacks led to a temporal delay in the negotiations and caused supporters to question where this process was really headed. Israeli settlers who rejected territorial compromise continued to build and expand, often with the support of sectors within the Israeli government. In short, opponents used political and military means to thwart the diplomatic process. Israel and certainly Palestinians are not unitary actors; those opposed to compromise have plenty of avenues for undermining the process.

On the Israeli-Syrian front, little evidence has emerged from Syria that opponents of a deal with Israel undermined Hafiz al-Asad's strategic decision for a peace. On the Israeli side, segments of the Israeli public that opposed withdrawal from the Golan Heights spoke out and used the domestic political process to build momentum against the Rabin government. In a crucial domestic political challenge, a handful of members of parliament broke with Rabin over the Golan issue.

On the Israeli-Palestinian front, violent opponents were a major impediment, but they were an impediment all parties could have expected. Actors seeking to end a conflict regularly face opponents, and they must be able to manage such challenges. To place primary blame for the negotiating failure on the heads of opponents is to let off too easily the organizers and governments. The violence was greatly damaging, but leaders need to anticipate it and minimize the damage to the political process. In a sense, the procedural explanation is more persuasive because it subsumes the issue of addressing opposition attacks on diplomacy. Perhaps only a robust, resilient, well-managed process could have succeeded, and this is where US officials came up short. The United States is left with a good amount of material upon which to build the next time around, but Washington had hoped for much more than a recipe book for future Arab-Israeli talks.

Notes

I would like to thank Robert Blecher, Arie Kacowicz, and Henry Krisch for thoughtful comments on an earlier draft. I presented a version of this chapter at the annual conference of the International Studies Association in March 2006.

1. In theory, an alternative to Soviet funding for arms would have been financial support from the Arab Gulf states. But with the end of the cold war, those states did not step in to replace Soviet support.

2. Egypt and Israel had signed a peace treaty in 1979.

3. The multilateral negotiations included five working groups with participants from both inside and outside the Middle East: arms control and regional security, environmental issues, refugees, regional economic development, and water.

4. On Rabin's dismissive attitude, see David Makovsky, *Making Peace with the PLO: The Rabin Government's Road to the Oslo Accord* (Boulder: Westview, 1996), pp. 27 and 51. On the Oslo process more generally, see Graham Usher, *Palestine in Crisis: The Struggle for Peace and Political Independence After Oslo* (London and Chicago: Pluto Press in association with Transnational Institute and Middle East Research & Information Project, 1997); Geoffrey Kemp and Jeremy Pressman, *Point of No Return: The Deadly Struggle for Middle East Peace* (Washington, DC: Brookings Press, 1997); Uri Savir, *The Process: 1,100 Days That Changed the Middle East* (New York: Random House, 1998); Mahmud Abbas (Abu Mazen), *Through Secret Channels* (Reading, UK: Garnet, 1995); and Yossi Beilin, *Touching Peace: From the Oslo Accord to a Final Agreement* (London: Weidenfeld & Nicolson, 1999).

5. Efraim Inbar, "Labor's Return to Power," in *Israel at the Polls, 1992,* ed. Daniel J. Elazar and Shmuel Sandler (Lanham, MD: Rowman & Littlefield, 1995), pp. 27–43, at p. 35.

6. Dennis Ross, *The Missing Peace: The Inside Story of the Fight for Middle East Peace* (New York: Farrar, Straus & Giroux, 2004), p. 116.

7. On Israeli-Syrian relations during these years, see Ross, *The Missing Peace;* Sadik al-Azm, "The View from Damascus," *New York Review of Books* 47, no. 10, June 15, 2000; and Itamar Rabinovich, *The Brink of Peace: The Israeli-Syrian Negotiations* (Princeton: Princeton University Press, 1998).

8. A separate territorial regime was developed in the West Bank city of Hebron.

9. "Declaration of Principles on Interim Self-Government Arrangements, Texts and Speeches, the White House, Washington, 13 September 1993," *Israel's Foreign Relations: Selected Documents,* Volume 13–14: 1992–1994, http://www.israel-mfa.gov.il/mfa/go.asp?MFAH0jhko.

10. http://www.mfa.gov.il/MFA/Archive/Peace+Process/1993/Remarks+by+PM+Yitzhak+Rabin+at+Signing+of+DOP+-+13.htm, accessed February 22, 2006.

11. The Foundation for Middle East Peace (fmep.org), citing the statistical abstract of Israel, puts the 1993 figures at 3,000 (Gaza) and 117,000 (West Bank). The foundation's November-December 2000 report, citing Israeli Ministry of Interior officials on July 28, 2000, puts the Gaza figure for 2000 at 6,700. The foundation's September-October 2000 report puts the West Bank at 200,000. For 2000, the CIA World Factbook puts the figures at 6,500 and 171,000, respectively.

12. By unauthorized, I mean that the Israeli government did not formally authorize them, though arms of the government provided support. To most of the world, outposts and settlements in the West Bank (including East Jerusalem) are both illegal under international law.

13. The Palestinian Society for the Protection of Human Rights & the Environment (LAW), "House Demolitions since the Oslo Agreement," http://www.lawsociety.org/Reports/reports/1998/hdlist.html.

14. Human Rights Watch, *World Report 1999,* http://www.hrw.org/hrw/world-report99/mideast/israel.html. See also "Israel 'quietly deporting' Palestinians," *BBC News* (online), September 15, 1998.

15. Jeremy M. Sharp, "US Aid to the Palestinians," *CRS Report for Congress,* February 2, 2006, p. 4.

16. The exceptions include policies in the Dwight D. Eisenhower administration following the Suez War in 1957; the initial intent, perhaps, of the Ford administration's "reassessment" in 1975; and the Bush-Baker-Shamir loan guarantee debate in 1991–1992.

17. Bill Clinton, *My Life* (New York: Alfred A. Knopf, 2004), p. 679.

18. For more on Barak and the Israeli-Syrian process, see Jeremy Pressman, "Lost Opportunities," *Boston Review* 29, no. 6, December 2004-January 2005, pp. 44–46, http://bostonreview.net/BR29.6/pressman.html (book review of Dennis Ross's *The Missing Peace*). See also Charles Enderlin, *Shattered Dreams: The Failure of the Peace Process in the Middle East, 1995–2002* (New York: Other Press, 2003); Frederic C. Hof, "The Line of June 4, 1967," *Middle East Insight,* September-October 1999, pp. 17–23; and Akiva Eldar, "Who never misses an opportunity to miss an opportunity?" *Ha'aretz,* August 12, 2003.

19. "Fatalities in the First Intifada," http://www.btselem.org/English/Statistics/First_Intifada_Tables.asp, accessed January 9, 2006.

20. "New Tries for Mideast Peace," *New York Times,* October 31, 2003.

21. Jeremy Pressman, "Visions in Collision: What Happened at Camp David and Taba?" *International Security* 28, no. 2 (Fall 2003), pp. 5–43. See also Enderlin, *Shattered Dreams;* Ross, *The Missing Peace;* and Clayton E. Swisher, *The Truth About Camp David: The Untold Story About the Collapse of the Middle East Peace Process* (New York: Nation Books, 2004).

22. Pressman, "Visions in Collision," p. 17. For more on differences among the Israeli negotiators during the Oslo years, see Arie Kacowicz, "Rashomon in Jerusalem:

Mapping the Israeli Negotiators' Positions on the Israeli-Palestinian Peace Process, 1993–2001," *International Studies Perspectives* 6 (2005), pp. 252–273.

23. Jeremy Pressman, "The Second Intifada: An Early Look at the Background and Causes of Israeli-Palestinian Conflict," *Journal of Conflict Studies* 22, no. 2 (Fall 2003), pp. 114–141.

24. "Fatalities," http://www.btselem.org/english/Statistics/Casualties.asp, accessed December 1, 2005. The best article on the Israeli belief that force would end, not escalate, the confrontation is Ben Kaspit, "Israel is not a state that has an army but rather an army that has a state attached to it," *Ma'ariv*, September 6, 2002, pp. 8–11, 32 of Rosh Hashanah supplement; and Ben Kaspit, "The Army Will Decide and Approve," *Ma'ariv*, September 13, 2002, pp. 6–10 of sabbath supplement (in Hebrew but English translations available on the Web).

25. I have used 97 percent as shorthand for more complex details. The plan called for 94–96 percent of the West Bank plus an additional land swap of 1–3 percent. By land swap, the negotiators meant that a small amount of pre-1967 Israel, equal to 1–3 percent of the area of the West Bank, would be annexed by the new Palestinian state in exchange for the areas of the West Bank annexed to Israel.

26. For some of the contents of Barak's letter, see Gilead Sher, *The Israeli-Palestinian Peace Negotiations, 1999–2001: Within Reach* (New York: Routledge, 2006), pp. 206–207.

27. Ross, *The Missing Peace*, p. 11. For Arafat's reservations letter to Clinton, see Clayton E. Swisher, *The Truth About Camp David*, pp. 399–401. The Palestinian Negotiations Support Unit (NSU) also wrote a letter. See http://www.nad-plo.org/inner.php?view=nego_nego_clinton_nclinton2p, accessed March 21, 2006.

28. Pressman, "Visions in Collision," pp. 21–22.

29. Bruce Riedel, "Camp David—The US-Israeli Bargain," bitterlemons.org, July 15, 2002, edition 26, http://www.bitterlemons.org/previous/bl150702ed26extra.html, accessed March 9, 2006.

30. One additional explanation is that Rabin's assassination blocked peace. In relation to the Israeli-Syrian talks, see Yoav Stern, "Report: Bishara acted as Syria-Israel mediator in 1990s talks," *Ha'aretz*, March 17, 2006. Stern quotes from an interview that former Syrian Vice President Abed al-Halim Haddam gave to the Israeli newspaper *A-Sinara:* "Syria was ready for peace. As for Israel, it seemed like Israel was ready for it but he [Rabin] was killed."

31. For instance, minutes from a PLO central council meeting in October 2000 revealed, according to a press report, "readiness to give up 3 percent of the West Bank in a territorial exchange, as well as readiness to recognize Israeli sovereignty in the Jewish Quarter [of Jerusalem's Old City]." The minutes asserted the right of return for refugees, but, quoting the document, "there's nothing against providing compensation" instead. Israel captured and released the document. See Akiva Eldar, "Trite of return or the refugees problem," *Ha'aretz*, June 26, 2003.

32. William Quandt, *Peace Process* (Berkeley: University of California Press; and Washington, DC: Brookings Institution Press, 2001), pp. 339 and 352.

CHAPTER 15

GEORGE W. BUSH, BARACK OBAMA, AND THE ARAB-ISRAELI CONFLICT

Robert O. Freedman

During the first two years of Barack Obama's presidency numerous media comparisons were drawn between the policies of the Obama administration and the George W. Bush administration, particularly in regard to the Arab-Israeli conflict, where the policies of the two administrations have diverged the most sharply. This chapter will compare the two administrations and then draw a number of conclusions about similarities and differences in the policies of the two administrations.

GEORGE W. BUSH AND ISRAEL

The policy of the Bush administration toward Israel and the Arab-Israeli conflict moved through six distinct stages. First, from the inauguration until 9/11, Bush was generally supportive of Israel while distancing his administration from the Arab-Israeli conflict. Second, from 9/11 to June 2002, the Bush administration actively sought to solve the Israeli-Palestinian conflict in order to build Muslim support for his war against the Taliban in Afghanistan and the coming war against Iraq. The third stage, from June 2002 to Arafat's death in November 2004, witnessed periodic attempts by the United States to facilitate an Israeli-Palestinian settlement; the Road Map of April 2003 was the best example. A policy was also developed that called for democratization of the Arab world as a means of preventing terrorism. The fourth period, from the death of Arafat in November 2004 to the Hamas election victory of January 2006, witnessed an attempt to boost Arafat's successor, Mahmoud Abbas, while coordinating with the Palestinians Israel's plan for a unilateral withdrawal from Gaza. The fifth stage, from January 2006 to June 2007, was marked by increasing difficulties for the United States in Iraq, which drew the administration's attention away from the Arab-Israeli conflict. At the same time the United States encountered problems with its democratization program in the Arab world, which had foundered. To make matters worse, the United States found itself confronted with increasing conflict between Israel and the Palestinians and, in the summer of 2006, a war between Israel and Hizbollah. The final stage, from July 2007 to January 2009, witnessed a final, unsuccessful effort by the Bush administration to achieve a Palestinian-Israeli peace agreement, highlighted by the November 2007 Annapolis conference.

FROM THE INAUGURATION TO 9/11

When the George W. Bush administration took office in 2001, it had a number of reasons not to continue Clinton's activist policy toward the Arab-Israeli conflict. First, Bush had witnessed the major effort Clinton had made and the relatively meager results he had achieved. Bush, seeking to distinguish himself from Clinton, chose not to follow Clinton's path. Second, even if he had wanted to, Bush was unwilling to risk his limited political capital (he had won a very narrow victory in a hotly disputed election) and wanted to save it for more promising policy initiatives, such as his tax cuts and ABM (antiballistic missile) programs. As a result, the administration distanced itself from the Arab-Israeli conflict, as shown when Dennis Ross, who had been the special US mediator for the Arab-Israeli conflict, resigned in January 2001 and was not replaced.

Distancing itself from the Arab-Israeli conflict—and the ongoing al-Aqsa intifada—however, did not mean that the administration had distanced itself from Israel. On the contrary—and much to the discomfiture of Arafat and other Arab leaders—Bush quickly developed a close and warm relationship with Israeli Prime Minister Ariel Sharon, who was invited to visit the White House in mid-March 2001.

On the eve of the visit, the new American secretary of state, Colin Powell, gave a major speech supportive of Israel to the pro-Israel AIPAC lobbying organization. In the speech he echoed Israel's position that the starting point for peace talks had to be the end of violence. In a clear slap at Arafat, Powell publicly stated that "leaders have the responsibility to denounce violence, strip it of legitimacy [and] stop it." Powell also asserted the Bush administration's position that the United States would assist in but not impose a peace agreement: "The US stands ready to assist, not insist. Peace arrived at voluntarily by the partners themselves is likely to prove more robust . . . than a peace widely viewed as developed by others, or worse yet, imposed."[1]

In a meeting several days later, Bush again reassured Sharon that the United States would facilitate, not force, the peace process. Bush also sought to enlist

Sharon in his campaign to develop a national missile defense system, something to which the Israeli leader, whose country was a prime target of such rogue states as Iran and Iraq, was only too happy to agree. Sharon, for his part, pressed Bush not to invite Arafat to the White House unless Arafat publicly called for an end to the violence, a request endorsed by nearly 300 members of Congress (87 senators and 209 House members), who also called on Bush to close the Washington office of the PLO and to cut US aid to the PA if the violence did not cease.[2]

The one bit of American activism on the peace process during this period came following the publication of the Mitchell Report in mid-May. The report contained a series of recommendations for ending the rapidly escalating Israeli-Palestinian conflict, first and foremost "a 100 percent effort to stop the violence."[3] While Israel accepted the recommendation, with Sharon ordering a cease-fire, a series of Palestinian terrorist attacks that Arafat either could not or would not stop undermined the cease-fire. Visits by the new assistant secretary of state for Near Eastern affairs Nicholas Burns, CIA chief George Tenet, and Powell himself failed to resuscitate the cease-fire.[4] Indeed, the escalating violence was now punctuated by Palestinian suicide bombings against Israeli civilian targets such as pizza parlors and discotheques, attacks that were strongly denounced by the United States. It is quite possible that the Bush administration, having witnessed the failure of its one major activist effort to resuscitate the Israeli-Palestinian peace process, concluded that its original hands-off policy toward the conflict was the correct one, and until 9/11, it distanced itself from the conflict. All of this, of course, would change after 9/11.

FROM 9/11 TO JUNE 2002

Immediately after the terrorist attacks on the World Trade Center and the Pentagon, the United States changed its hands-off policy toward the Israeli-Palestinian conflict and sought to build a coalition, including Muslim states, against Osama bin Laden and his al-Qa'ida terrorist organization. In an effort to gain Arab support, the United States announced its support of a Palestinian state and exercised a considerable amount of pressure on Sharon to agree to a meeting between Israeli foreign minister Shimon Peres and Arafat to establish yet another cease-fire, even though Palestinian violence had not stopped as Sharon had demanded as the price for talks. Frustrated by this US policy, Sharon called it the equivalent of British and French policy at the 1938 Munich conference, where Czechoslovakia had been sold out to the Nazis. His comments drew a retort from the White House press secretary, Ari Fleischer, who called them "unacceptable."[5]

This was to be the low point in the US-Israeli relationship under Bush. Following its rapid military victory in Afghanistan, the United States embarked on a twofold strategy. The first part, trying to reinvigorate the Israeli-Palestinian peace process, was warmly greeted by US European allies and by pro-US governments in the Arab world. The second part of the strategy, threatening to carry the war from Afghanistan to other supporters of terror, especially Iraq, met with far less support.

The US effort to invigorate the Israeli-Palestine peace process began with a speech by President Bush at the United Nations in November 2001, where he said, "We are working for the day when two states—Israel and Palestine—live peacefully together within secure and recognized boundaries." However, in a clear warning to Arafat to crack down on terrorists, he also added, "Peace will come when all have sworn off forever incitement, violence, and terror. There is no such thing as a good terrorist."[6] Bush also pointedly did not meet Arafat at the United Nations as his national security adviser, Condoleezza Rice, noted: "You cannot help us with al-Qa'ida, and hug Hizbollah or Hamas. And so the President makes that clear to Mr. Arafat."[7] The United States backed up Rice's words by adding Hamas, Islamic Jihad, and Hizbollah to its post–September 11 terrorist list.

The next step in the US peace effort came on November 19 with a major speech by Secretary of State Colin Powell on the US view of a solution to the Israeli-Palestinian conflict.[8] In his speech Powell strongly condemned Palestinian terrorism, noting that the al-Aqsa intifada was now mired in "self-defeating violence." He also stated that although the United States believed that there should be a two-state solution to the conflict—with two states, Palestine and Israel, living side by side within secure and recognized borders—"the Palestinians must make a 100 percent effort to stop terrorism, and that this effort required actions, not words: Terrorists must be arrested." Powell emphasized that "no wrong can ever justify the murder of the innocent," that terror and violence must stop now, and that the Palestinians must realize their goals through negotiations, not violence. He further asserted—possibly in response to Arafat's call for the return to Israel of more than 3 million Palestinian refugees, which would upset Israel's demographic balance—that the Palestinians must accept the legitimacy of Israel as a Jewish state.

While emphasizing that the United States and Israel were closely "bound together by democratic tradition" and that the United States had an "enduring and iron-clad commitment to Israeli security," Powell indicated that Israel too had to make concessions for peace to be possible. These included a stop to settlement expansion and an end to the occupation of the West Bank and Gaza, which "causes humiliation and the killing of innocents." In conclusion, Powell stated that the United States would do everything it could to facilitate the peace process, "but at the end of the day the peoples have to make peace," a position very similar to the one Powell had held when he joined the cabinet nearly a year earlier.

In order to implement the US vision of peace outlined by Powell, in addition to promises of economic aid, Assistant Secretary of State William Burns and former Marine general Anthony Zinni were dispatched to meet with Israeli and Palestinian delegations to reach a cease-fire that would lay the basis for the resumption of peace negotiations. In an effort to facilitate the Zinni mission, President Bush put his personal prestige on the line by writing to five important Arab leaders—King Abdullah II of Jordan, President Hosni Mubarak of Egypt, King Mohammed VI of Morocco, Saudi Crown Prince Abdullah (who had publicly praised Powell's speech), and President Ben-Ali of Tunisia—asking for their help in persuading "the

Palestinian leadership to take action to end violence and get the peace process back on track."[9]

On November 27, soon after Zinni's arrival in the Middle East, two Palestinian terrorists, one of whom was a member of Arafat's Fatah organization (the other was from Islamic Jihad), killed three Israelis and wounded thirty others in Afulah, a town in northern Israel. Zinni responded to the violence in a balanced way: "This is why we need a cease-fire. Both sides have suffered too much."[10] Zinni then met with Arafat, asking him to end the violence, but even as they were meeting, Palestinian gunmen fired at the Israeli Jerusalem neighborhood of Gilo from the neighboring Palestinian suburb of Beit Jala—despite an explicit October promise by Palestinian leaders not to do so.[11] The next day three more Israelis were killed as a suicide bomber attacked a public bus near the Israeli city of Hadera.[12] This time Zinni's response was much stronger: "The groups that do this are clearly trying to make my mission fail. There's no justification, no rationale, no sets of conditions that will ever make terrorist acts a right way to respond."[13] Zinni's words, however, did not stem the tide of terrorism. Two days later suicide bombers killed ten Israeli teenagers who had gathered at the Ben Yehudah pedestrian mall in Jerusalem. This time Arafat condemned the attacks, stressing not the loss of life by Israel but the negative political effect the suicide bombers were having on the Palestinian world image.[14]

By now, Zinni was furious, as he saw his mission literally going up in flames: "Those responsible for planning and carrying out these attacks must be found and bought to justice. This is an urgent task and there can be no delay or excuses for not acting decisively. The deepest evil one can imagine is to attack young people and children."[15] President Bush, whose prestige had been put on the line by the Zinni mission, also responded strongly: "Now more than ever Chairman Arafat and the Palestinian Authority must demonstrate through their actions, and not merely their words, their commitment to fight terror."[16]

Arafat seemed to get the message, if rather belatedly, from US political pressure and from Israeli military retaliation. On December 16, he called for an immediate cease-fire, condemning both suicide attacks and the launching of mortar attacks.[17] Nonetheless, the Palestinian leader did not root out the Hamas and Islamic Jihad organizations from Gaza and the West Bank; rather, he negotiated a tenuous truce with them (a tactic later repeated by Mahmoud Abbas in March 2005), something that was clearly unsatisfactory to the Israeli government. Arafat was kept penned up in Ramallah by Israeli tanks, and in a further blow to his prestige, he was prohibited from leaving his compound to attend Christmas services in Bethlehem.

Three weeks after Arafat's call for a cease-fire, Israeli forces captured a ship in the Red Sea, the *Karine A*, which held fifty tons of concealed weapons, including C-4 explosives and Katyusha rockets—clearly weapons of terrorism. Arafat's initial denial that the Palestinian Authority had anything to do with the vessel further undermined his credibility, both in Israel and in the United States.[18] In response to heavy pressure by the United States, Arafat eventually arrested several of the

Palestinian officials involved, including a major general in his own security forces and an officer in the Palestinian Authority's naval police.[19]

Meanwhile, Hamas broke the truce by attacking an Israeli military outpost in Gaza, killing four soldiers and claiming the attack was in retaliation for Israel's seizure of the *Karine A*.[20] Israel retaliated, destroying, among other things, the runway of the Palestinian airport in Gaza, and after a terrorist attack against an Israeli bar mitzvah party in Hadera, in which six Israelis were killed and thirty wounded, Israel blew up the main Palestinian radio transmitter.[21]

Thus ended the first year of the Bush administration's efforts to resolve the Israeli-Palestinian conflict. Despite two major US efforts, one in June and one in November-December 2001, Palestinian terrorism, which Arafat was unable, or more likely unwilling, to control (he had long used terrorism as a political weapon) had sabotaged US efforts to resolve the Palestinian-Israeli conflict. Nonetheless, both Arab states and the European Union (EU) continued to urge the United States to get more engaged in the search for an Arab-Israeli peace. In response, in a remarkably frank interview with the *New York Times* on February 28, 2002, Colin Powell stated, "We have not put it [the search for an Arab-Israeli peace agreement] on the back burner. What that [US engagement] usually means is 'Go and force the Israelis to do something.' That's what many people think when they say 'Get more engaged' or 'You're standing on the sidelines. You haven't made Israel blink in the face of violence.'"[22]

Meanwhile, President Bush had sent his vice president, Dick Cheney, who often took a much harder line than Powell, to the Arab world in an effort to build Arab support for a planned US attack on Iraq. Cheney was met with strong Arab calls for the United States to work out a solution to the Israeli-Palestinian conflict before engaging in a war with Iraq. This position apparently convinced President Bush to send Zinni back for another try at achieving a cease-fire. To facilitate the Zinni visit, Sharon made a major concession by lifting his demand for the passage of seven days without violence before talks could resume. The atmosphere of the Zinni visit was further improved by the announcement of an Arab-Israeli peace plan suggested by Saudi Arabia. This plan would be introduced at the Arab summit scheduled for the end of March in Beirut and involved Arab recognition of Israel in return for Israel's return to its 1967 boundaries and a fair solution to the Palestinian refugee problem. To help reinforce the momentum for peace, the United States pushed for a new UN Security Council resolution, Resolution 1397, on March 13, 2002, which called for a two-state solution to the Israeli-Palestinian conflict; the end of violence, incitement, and terrorism; and the resumption of negotiations based on the Tenet and Mitchell plans.[23]

Unfortunately, the diplomatic momentum for peace was shattered by another series of Palestinian terrorist attacks just as Zinni was seeking to consolidate a cease-fire and the Arab summit was taking place in Beirut. On March 27, the first night of the Passover holiday, twenty-nine Jews were murdered and more than one hundred wounded at a Passover Seder in the coastal resort town of Netanya. This attack was followed by suicide bombings in Jerusalem, Tel Aviv, and Haifa over the next three days, bombings that killed seventeen people and wounded eighty-four. These events precipitated an Israeli attack on Arafat's compound in Ramallah, followed by a sweep into the major Palestinian cities of the West Bank, in what Sharon called Operation Defensive Shield.

As these events were unfolding, the United State at first strongly backed Israel, with Powell noting, "Sharon made concessions, while Arafat backed terrorism."[24] Then, when mass demonstrations broke out in the Arab world, which may have worried Bush as he stepped up his preparations for an attack on Iraq, the president decided to once again involve the United States. In a major speech on April 4, 2002, after first denouncing terrorism and noting that "the chairman of the Palestinian Authority has not consistently opposed or confronted terrorists nor has he renounced terror as he agreed to do at Oslo," Bush called for the Israelis to withdraw from the West Bank cities they were occupying.[25] Bush also announced that he was sending Powell to the Middle East to work out a cease-fire. Several days later, the president urged the Israelis to withdraw "without delay," but then he ran into a firestorm of domestic criticism for pressuring Israel.[26] First, the neoconservatives, who were the intellectual lifeblood of the administration, attacked Bush for urging Sharon to withdraw, claiming the Israeli leader was fighting terrorism just as the United States was fighting terrorism after 9/11. Second, evangelical Christians, a large and energetic base of Bush's core constituency, also attacked Bush for pressuring Israel.[27] Third, on April 15, 250,000 people rallied for Israel on the Mall in Washington, a demonstration organized by the US Jewish community; the demonstration also included evangelical Christians among its speakers. The message of the rally was that the United States should support Israel's fight against Palestinian terrorism, which was similar to the antiterrorist policy of the United States after 9/11. Finally, the administration was severely criticized by influential members of Congress, including Republican House majority leader Tom DeLay, a strong friend of Israel.[28]

Another factor prompting Bush to change his position was Arafat's continued sponsorship of terrorism. When Arafat's wife came out in support of suicide bombings as a legitimate form of resistance against Israeli occupation, and the Israelis gave the United States documents showing that Arafat had not only tolerated terrorism but had helped finance it, Bush further turned against the Palestinian leader. On May 26, while on a state visit to Russia, Bush noted that Arafat "hasn't delivered. He had a chance to secure the peace as a result of the hard work of President Clinton and he didn't. He had a chance to fight terrorism and he hadn't."[29]

As Palestinian terrorist attacks continued to proliferate, Sharon, who had pulled Israeli forces out of the cities of the West Bank in May 2002, sent them back in June, this time with minimal criticism from the United States. Indeed, in a major speech on June 24, Bush called for a "new and different Palestinian leadership" so that a Palestinian state could be born. In the most anti-Arafat speech in his presidency, Bush stated:

I call on the Palestinian people to elect new leaders, leaders not compromised by terror. I call upon them to build a practicing democracy, based on tolerance and liberty. If the Palestinian people actively pursue these goals, America and the world will actively support their efforts. If the Palestinian people meet these goals, they will be able to reach agreement with Israel and Egypt and Jordan on security and other arrangements for independence. And when the Palestinian people have new leaders, new institutions, and new security arrangements with their neighbors, the United States of America will support the creating of a Palestinian state whose borders and certain aspects of its sovereignty will be provisional until resolved as part of a final settlement in the Middle East.

Today, Palestinian authorities are encouraging, not opposing, terrorism. This is unacceptable and the United States will not support the establishment of a Palestinian state until its leaders engage in a sustained fight against the terrorists and dismantle their infrastructure. This will require an externally supervised effort to rebuild and reform the Palestinian security services. The security system must have clear lines of authority and accountability and a unified chain of command.[30]

While Bush chided the Israelis somewhat on settlement activity, the brunt of the president's ire was clearly on Arafat, and with this speech Bush formally joined Sharon in ruling out Arafat as a partner in the peace process.

US POLICY FROM JUNE 2002 TO ARAFAT'S DEATH IN NOVEMBER 2004

Following the June 24 speech, US foreign policy in the Middle East had two main objectives. The first was to work with the European Union, Russia, and the United Nations as part of a "diplomatic quartet" to fashion a Road Map leading to a Palestinian-Israeli peace settlement. The second was to build a large coalition to prepare for war with Iraq.

In designing the Road Map with the European Union, Russia, and the United Nations, the Bush administration faced a major problem. Although the United States had written off Arafat as a suitable partner for peace, as had Israel, the other three members of the Quartet had not, and this discrepancy caused problems in subsequent diplomacy. In addition, the presentation of the Road Map, which the Quartet began planning in July 2002, was delayed on numerous occasions and was not made public until the completion of the major combat phase of the Anglo-American invasion of Iraq at the end of March 2003. As a result, many Middle East observers felt that the Road Map was aimed at merely assuaging the Arabs while the Bush administration was preparing to attack Iraq.[31] Indeed, in the run-up to the war in September 2002, when the Israelis laid siege to Arafat's compound in Ramallah following another series of brutal suicide bombings, the United States chose to abstain on, rather than veto, a UN Security Council resolution condemning the Israeli action, with Condoleezza Rice reportedly telling the Israeli government that the United States expected a speedy resolution of the siege because it "doesn't help" US efforts to galvanize support for the campaign against Iraq.[32]

In any case, following delays on account of the Israeli elections of January 2003 (in which Sharon's Likud Party scored an impressive victory) and the invasion of Iraq, which began in late March, the Road Map was finally published on April 30, 2003. At the time, it appeared that Bush, spurred on by his ally, British Prime Minister Tony Blair, wanted to prove his critics wrong by demonstrating that he was genuinely interested in an Israeli-Palestinian peace agreement. According to the Road Map, which the Bush administration announced with great fanfare, the Palestinians, in phase one of the three-phase plan leading to a Palestinian state, had to "declare an unequivocal end to violence and terrorism and end incitement against Israel and undertake visible efforts on the ground to arrest, disrupt, and restrain individuals and groups conducting and planning attacks on Israelis anywhere."[33] Second, the Palestinians had to appoint an "empowered" prime minister and establish a government based on a strong parliamentary democracy and cabinet and have only three security services, which would report to the empowered prime minister. By these measures, the United States hoped to weaken, if not eliminate, Arafat's power base and in his place create an "empowered" prime minister who would be a proper partner for peace. For its part, Israel, under phase one of the Road Map, had to refrain from deporting Palestinians, attacking Palestinian civilians, and confiscating or demolishing Palestinian homes and property. And as the "comprehensive security performance" of the Palestinians moved forward, the Israeli military had to "withdraw progressively" from areas occupied since September 28, 2000, dismantle settlement outposts erected since March 2001, and "freeze all settlement activity [including natural growth of settlements]."

With Bush at the peak of his international influence as a result of the apparent military victory in Iraq, Arafat was compelled to accede to the Road Map's demands to create the post of prime minister to which senior Palestinian leader Mahmoud Abbas, also known as Abu Mazen, was appointed. Yet this appointment appeared to be a ploy; it soon became evident that Mahmoud Abbas was not the "empowered" prime minister the United States had in mind, since Arafat retained control over most of the Palestinian security forces. Apparently the United States had overlooked this fact in the hope that Abbas, who, unlike Arafat, had never been demonized by either Sharon or the Israeli public, had sufficient power to be a credible negotiating partner for Israel. Although the Palestinian Authority accepted the Road Map, Hamas, Islamic Jihad, the al-Aqsa Martyrs Brigade, and the Tanzim (young militants tied to Arafat's Fatah organization) did not. Israel, albeit with a number of reservations, also accepted it. When the Road Map was published, it was attacked by eighty-eight US senators, who asserted that the Road Map's position against Palestinian terrorism was not as strong as that in Bush's statement of June 24, 2002.[34]

Initially the Road Map was greeted with optimism, and on June 29, 2003, Abbas succeeded in eliciting a ninety-day *hudna*, or truce, from the leaders of Hamas, the Tanzim, and Islamic Jihad, though not from the al-Aqsa Martyrs Brigade.

Although Israeli military leaders worried that the terrorist groups would use the ninety-day period to rebuild their forces and armaments (especially the Qassem rockets that had been fired into Israel from Gaza), Sharon proved willing to take a chance on the *hudna*. He called for withdrawing Israeli forces from northern Gaza and Bethlehem; closing some checkpoints hindering traffic between Palestinian villages and cities; shutting down some illegal outposts on the West Bank (although other outposts were set up); releasing some Palestinian prisoners (though far fewer than the Palestinians wanted), including an elderly terrorist who had killed fourteen Israelis in 1975; and loosening work restrictions on Palestinians.

President Bush sought to move the peace process forward by meeting with both Abbas and Sharon in Washington in July 2003, although differences over Israel's construction of its security wall proved to be problematic during Bush's talks with the two leaders.[35] Meanwhile, during the *hudna*, attacks on Israel continued, including the murder of Israeli civilians, although the number of attacks decreased significantly from the period preceding the *hudna*. In addition, Abbas worked to lessen anti-Israeli incitement, painting over some of the anti-Israel slogans displayed on walls in Gaza. However, the key demand of both Bush and the Israelis—that Mahmoud Abbas crack down on the terrorists—was not met, primarily because Arafat refused to allow it. Nonetheless, Abbas tried to convince the United States that he could negotiate a permanent truce with the terrorist groups. While some in the US State Department seemed to be willing to go along with Abbas, Sharon was not, and as attacks on Israelis continued during the *hudna*, Sharon decided to retaliate by attacking the Hamas and Islamic Jihad terrorists who were seen as responsible. Then, on August 19, less than two months into the *hudna*, a terrorist attack in Jerusalem killed twenty-one Israelis, including a number of children. In response, Sharon stepped up his attacks on the terrorists, which led Hamas to declare an end to the *hudna*. Soon afterward, blaming both Arafat and Israel for a lack of support, Abbas resigned and the peace process again came to a halt.

In the aftermath of Abbas's resignation, with the peace process stalled, the United States again distanced itself from the Israeli-Palestinian peace process, as the Bush administration increasingly concentrated on the deteriorating situation in Iraq. Bush did, however, begin to push a policy of democratization for the Middle East. Influenced by Israeli politician Natan Sharansky's book *The Case for Democracy*,[36] Bush came to argue that there were two major reasons why the United States should push to democratize the Middle East. First, if young men had a chance to participate politically in their societies by joining political parties, demonstrating in the streets for their political positions, enjoying freedom of the press, and playing a role in choosing their nation's leaders through fair elections, they would be less likely to become terrorists. Second, democracies were less likely to fight each other than autocratic or totalitarian states. Thus, the administration's reasoning went, if the Middle East became more democratic it would be less likely to spawn terrorists and would be a more peaceful region of the world. Bush's democratization policy also benefited Israel. As the only genuine democracy in the region (with the partial exception of Turkey), Israel was not only an antiterrorist ally of the United States but a democratic one as well.

While Bush was formulating his democratization policy, Sharon was developing a new strategy of his own—the unilateral withdrawal from Gaza. This was conceived in part as an initiative to prevent other diplomatic efforts from being imposed on Israel (such as Yossi Beilin's Geneva initiative),[37] and in part to preserve Israel as both a Jewish and a democratic state by ending Israeli control over the approximately 1.4 million Palestinian Arabs living in the Gaza Strip.[38] At the same time Sharon decided to make a major effort to speed up construction of the Israeli security fence between Israel and the West Bank to prevent Palestinian terrorist attacks on Israel. The fence, however, did not run along the old 1967 border but took in a swath of land on the West Bank.

By early 2004 the United States and Israel began detailed bargaining on the unilateral withdrawal and the security fence, and under US pressure (and that of the Israeli Supreme Court), Sharon agreed to move the security fence closer to the 1949 armistice line. According to then Israeli ambassador to the United States Daniel Ayalon, Sharon also agreed to add four settlements in the northern part of the West Bank to his disengagement plan.[39]

The result of the bargaining was a meeting between Sharon and Bush in Washington in mid-April 2004 that was structured not only to reinforce the Sharon disengagement initiative but also to help each leader politically. Thus Bush went a very long way toward supporting Sharon's policies. Not only did he welcome Sharon's disengagement plan as "real progress" and assert that the United States was "strongly committed" to Israel's well-being as a Jewish state within "secure and defensible borders," but he also went on to reject any Palestinian right of return to Israel: "It seems clear that an agreed just, fair, and realistic framework for a solution to the Palestinian refugee issue as part of any final status agreement will need to be found through the establishment of a Palestinian state, and the settling of Palestinian refugees there, rather than in Israel."[40]

Bush also reinforced Israel's position that it would not fully return to the 1949 armistice lines and that any final agreement would have to reflect the settlements Israel had built since 1967: "In light of new realities on the ground, including already existing population centers, it is unrealistic to expect that the outcome of final status negotiations will be a full and complete return to the armistice lines of 1949."

Finally, Bush reaffirmed Israel's right to self-defense against terrorism, noting that "Israel will retain its right to defend itself against terrorism including taking action against terrorist organizations." This statement not only endorsed Israel's right to go back into Gaza to fight terrorism but also implicitly endorsed Israel's strategy of assassinating the leaders of Hamas, a process that continued during the spring and summer of 2004.

In his meeting with Sharon, Bush also made a number of gestures to the Palestinians. Not only did he reaffirm his commitment to a two-state solution to the Israeli-Palestinian conflict and call for Israel to freeze settlement activity and remove unauthorized outposts, but he also put limits on Israel's security wall, asserting, "As the government of Israel has stated, the barrier being erected by Israel should be a security rather than a political barrier, should be temporary, and therefore not prejudice any final status issues including final borders, and its route should take into account, consistent with security needs, its impact on Palestinians not engaged in terrorist activities." Nonetheless, returning to the theme he had emphasized since 9/11, Bush demanded that the Palestinians "act decisively against terror, including sustained, targeted, and effective operations to stop terrorism and dismantle terrorist capabilities and infrastructure."

Clearly Sharon had scored a great diplomatic success with his visit, and he heaped lavish praise on President Bush. After noting that the disengagement plan "can be an important contribution" to the president's Road Map for peace, he went on to state, "You have proven, Mr. President, your ongoing, deep, and sincere friendship to the State of Israel and to the Jewish people. . . . In all these years, I have never met a leader as committed as you are, Mr. President, to the struggle for freedom and the need to confront terrorism wherever it exists."

Needless to say, for a president now deeply engaged in an election campaign against John Kerry, a liberal senator from Massachusetts, who normally could expect to get the vast majority of Jewish votes, Sharon's words were extremely helpful to Bush, especially in pivotal states like Florida with its large Jewish population. Indeed, not only did Bush strongly support Sharon on the disengagement plan, but the Bush administration also sent a twenty-six-page booklet, *President George W. Bush: A Friend of the American Jewish Community*, to American Jewish organizations, stressing Bush's commitment to the state of Israel and to the world Jewish community. Prominent themes in the booklet were Bush's opposition to terrorism aimed at Israel and his opposition to PLO leader Yasser Arafat. The booklet stated, "For Yasser Arafat the message has been clear. While he was a frequent White House guest during the last administration, he has never been granted a meeting with President Bush."[41] In another effort to court Jewish support, Bush reportedly overrode State Department opposition to create an office at the State Department to monitor the rising tide of anti-Semitism around the world. Perhaps reflecting on the political nature of the proposed office, an unnamed State Department official told the *Washington Times*: "It's more of a bureaucratic nuisance than a real problem. We are not going to fight a bill that has gained such political momentum."[42] Finally, on the eve of the US presidential election, Bush sent National Security Adviser Condoleezza Rice to address the AIPAC meeting in Florida. The very fact of her presence, despite an ongoing FBI probe of a Pentagon analyst who had allegedly passed secrets to AIPAC, underlined the great importance the Bush administration placed on getting Jewish support in the election.[43]

Bush won the 2004 election by 3.5 million votes, and soon Arafat, seen by both the United States and Israel as the main obstacle to an Israeli-Palestinian settlement, died. Arafat's death set the stage for another US attempt to revive the Arab-Israeli peace process.

US POLICY FROM ARAFAT'S DEATH TO THE HAMAS VICTORY IN THE PALESTINIAN ELECTIONS

In the aftermath of Arafat's death and the reelection of George W. Bush, the situation initially appeared to improve, as far as US policy in the Middle East was concerned. First, the promotion of Condoleezza Rice to US secretary of state added coherence to US policy, as the old rifts between the State Department, on the one hand, and the White House and the Defense Department, on the other, were minimized. In addition, as Defense Secretary Donald Rumsfeld's influence declined because of the increased problems the United States was encountering in Iraq, Rice became the unquestioned administration spokesperson on foreign policy, especially on the Middle East. Second, the US democratization plan for the Middle East appeared to score some major triumphs with democratic elections being held in Iraq, Lebanon, and the Palestinian Authority. The PA held an election to choose Yasser Arafat's successor, and in what international observers considered a fair and democratic election, Mahmoud Abbas, a Fatah leader who had served a brief term as Palestinian prime minister under the Road Map, was elected with 60 percent of the votes. What made Abbas such an appealing candidate for the United States was his regular denunciation of terrorism as inimical to Palestinian interests. Thus, with the Abbas election, the two main strands of US post-9/11 Middle East policy—the fight against terrorism and support for democratization—came together, and it was not long before Abbas was welcomed to the White House with full pomp and ceremony, a privilege that had been denied to Arafat, whom the Bush administration saw as closely linked to terrorism. Sharon, for his part, made a series of gestures to Abbas in February 2005, including the release of seven hundred Palestinian detainees and agreement to a cease-fire. In order to help Abbas strengthen his position in the PA, the United States dispatched Lieutenant General William Ward to reorganize the Palestinian armed forces and James Wolfensohn, the former head of the World Bank, to help develop the Palestinian economy. Unfortunately, neither proved to be very effective. Ward was unable to transform the disparate Palestinian military groups into an effective fighting force, and he was replaced by Major General Keith Dayton. As far as Wolfensohn was concerned, despite his heroic efforts—including the use of his personal funds to facilitate the purchase by the Palestinians of Israeli greenhouses in Gaza—the Palestinian economy remained problematic.

While US-Palestinian relations got off to a good start after the election of Abbas, the new Palestinian leader took a risky gamble in March 2005. In an effort to achieve harmony among the contending Palestinian forces, he signed an agreement with Hamas and several other Palestinian organizations (but not Islamic Jihad) providing that, in return for a cease-fire with Israel, the only mode of interaction among the Palestinians would be "dialogue."[44] This agreement ran counter to Israeli and American calls for Abbas to crack down on Hamas and the other Palestinian terrorist organizations. This issue became particularly pressing as Israel prepared to disengage from Palestinian territories during the summer of 2005, pulling out Israeli settlements and military forces from Gaza as well as Israeli settlements from the northern West Bank. While Hamas had signed the cease-fire agreement, Islamic Jihad had not, and there were concerns that the Iranian-supported organization might disrupt the Israeli disengagement. While this disruption never materialized, Islamic Jihad did undertake a number of terrorist attacks against Israel in 2005, and the Israeli government responded with "targeted killings" (assassinations) of Islamic Jihad operatives.

The main problem for Israel, however, was Hamas, and unless Abbas moved against the Islamic organization, Israel would not take him seriously as a peace partner. Abbas, however, appeared more interested in creating Palestinian solidarity than in satisfying Israel. Indeed, in responding to my question in late June 2005 in Ramallah about why he had chosen not to crack down on Hamas after his strong victory in the Palestinian presidential elections, Abbas replied, "What, and have a Palestinian civil war!"[45] Unfortunately for Abbas, two years later the Palestinian civil war between Fatah and Hamas did occur, at a time when Abbas was much weaker and Hamas much stronger than in June 2005.

Despite Abbas's failure to crack down on Hamas, Secretary of State Condoleezza Rice sought to facilitate cooperation between Israel and the Abbas-led Palestinian Authority as the disengagement took place. Thus she helped to negotiate a number of agreements between Israel and the PA, including one to haul away debris from the destroyed Jewish settlements (the PA had demanded their destruction), another on the modus operandi of the crossing points between Gaza and Egypt and between Gaza and Israel, and a third agreement on travel between Gaza and the West Bank. While the disengagement went relatively smoothly, despite the protests of Jewish settlers in Gaza, the next issue to arise was the election for the Palestinian Legislative Council (PLC). Abbas had postponed the elections from their original July 2004 date to January 2006, in part so he could get political credit for the Israeli withdrawal, and in part because he could not settle the rifts between the old and young guards of his Fatah organization. A key issue in the elections was whether Hamas would run and, if so, under what conditions. Israeli Prime Minister Ariel Sharon initially opposed Hamas participation in the elections, citing the Oslo Accord requirement that no "racist" party could run in the elections; since Hamas continued to call for the destruction of Israel, it was clearly racist. Only if Hamas renounced terrorism and recognized Israel's right to exist should it be allowed to run, Sharon asserted. The United States, however, took a contrary position. In part because forbidding Hamas to participate would hurt the US democratization plan for the Middle East, and in part because Abbas had promised to finally crack down on Hamas after the PLC elections, Rice pressured Sharon to allow Hamas participation. The Israeli leader, perhaps preoccupied with domestic politics (he had broken away from his Likud Party and formed the new Kadima Party in November 2005, four months before the Israeli parliamentary elections), gave in to the US pressure. It was a decision that both the United States and Israel would come to regret.[46]

US POLICY FROM THE HAMAS ELECTORAL
VICTORY TO ITS SEIZURE OF GAZA

Capitalizing on Fatah's corruption, the PA's inability to provide law and order in the West Bank, and the continued divisions between Fatah's old and young guards, Hamas swept to a massive victory in the January 25, 2006, PLC elections. Hamas representatives were quick to claim that their victory was due to their policy of resistance against Israel.[47] The Hamas victory created a major dilemma for the United States, as its two main policies in the Middle East—the war against terror and support for democratization—had now come into direct conflict with each other. A terrorist organization, Hamas, utilizing democratic means, had taken control of the Palestinian legislature, and a Hamas leader, Ismail Haniyeh, had become the new Palestinian prime minister. Meanwhile Israel faced another challenge: Sharon, who had suffered a massive stroke in early January 2006, was no longer Israel's prime minister. His replacement, as acting prime minister, was his Kadima colleague Ehud Olmert, who not only had to prepare his new party for the March 28 Israeli elections but also had to deal with the Hamas election victory. Olmert quickly decided Israel would have nothing to do with Hamas unless it changed its policies toward Israel, a position embraced by most of the Israeli political spectrum. Rice quickly convened the Quartet (the United States, the EU, the UN, and Russia), which agreed not to have any dealings with the Hamas-led Palestinian government until Hamas renounced terrorism, agreed to recognize Israel, and acceded to the agreements signed between Israel and the PLO, including Oslo I, Oslo II, and the Road Map. Russia, however, soon broke with the Quartet consensus by inviting a Hamas delegation for an official visit to Moscow. In April 2006, after the United States and the EU, seeing no change in Hamas policy, had decided to cut all aid to the PA (except "humanitarian" assistance), Russia again broke ranks with its Quartet colleagues by offering the PA economic assistance.

The newly elected Israeli government led by Olmert refused to have anything to do either with Abbas (who was considered ineffectual) or with the Hamas-led Palestinian government. For its part, the new Hamas government repeated its refusal to recognize Israel or make peace with it, and supported, as "legitimate resistance," continued attacks on Israel whether in the form of Qassem rockets fired from Gaza into Israel or in the form of suicide bombings such as the one on April 17, 2005, which claimed ten Israeli lives.[48] Meanwhile, as Israel was confronting a Hamas-led government in the Palestinian territories, it also had to face a rising threat from Iran. After two years of on-and-off negotiations with the European Union over its secret nuclear program, Iran broke off negotiations in August 2005 and announced it was moving ahead with nuclear enrichment. Making matters worse for Israel, which along with the United States feared that Iran was on the path to developing nuclear weapons, the newly elected Iranian president, Mahmoud Ahmadinejad, called for Israel to be "wiped off the map" and declared that the Holocaust was a myth.⁴⁹ While the United States was highly supportive of Israel in the face of the Iranian leader's provocative statements (Bush, on February 1, 2006, had stated, "Israel is a solid ally of the United States; we will rise to Israel's defense if need be."),⁵⁰ the Israeli leadership had to question whether the United States, increasingly bogged down in both Iraq and Afghanistan (where the Taliban had revived), would act to eliminate the nuclear threat from Iran, or whether Israel would have to do the job itself.

Meanwhile, Israel's relations with the Hamas-led Palestinian government continued to deteriorate, with stepped-up shelling of Israeli territory from Gaza and Israeli retaliation. Then, in the summer of 2006, full-scale war broke out, first with Hamas and then with Hizbollah following the kidnapping of Israeli soldiers. In looking at US-Israeli relations during both conflicts, we find a number of similarities. The Bush administration has seen both Hamas and Hizbollah as terrorist organizations linked to Syria and Iran and, as such, enemies of the United States. Consequently, when Israel was fighting both terrorist organizations, it was on the same side of the barricades as the United States, and the United States adopted a strongly pro-Israeli position in both conflicts. Thus it vetoed a UN Security Council resolution condemning Israel for its bombardment of the Gaza town of Beit Hanoun, from which rockets were being launched into Israel, and condemned both Iran and Syria for their aid to Hizbollah in its war against Israel.

In the second Lebanon war, however, there was one additional factor that influenced US policy. The anti-Syrian Fuad Siniora government, which had come into office in Lebanon following the departure of Syrian forces in 2005, was seen as an ally of the United States, and one of the few remaining successes of its democratization program. Consequently the United States sought to ensure that if the Israeli-Hizbollah fighting did not enhance Siniora's position, by weakening Hizbollah, at least it would not hurt it. Thus, for the first two weeks of the war, the United States gave full diplomatic backing to Israel, hoping it would destroy Hizbollah, the Siniora government's main opposition. However, in late July, after an Israeli attack in Qana aimed at a Hizbollah bunker accidentally killed sixty Lebanese civilians,⁵¹ it had become clear that Israeli dependence on its air force to deal with Hizbollah was not working,⁵² and that Siniora's position was being threatened by the growing popularity of Hizbollah, which was successfully "standing up to Israel." This situation also negatively affected the governments of US allies Jordan, Egypt, and Saudi Arabia. Consequently the United States began to work for a cease-fire, and the result was UN Security Council Resolution 1701, which called for moving the Lebanese army to the Israeli border and expanding the UN troops in southern Lebanon to fifteen thousand. Israel was less than happy with the cease-fire because it did not lead to the disarming of Hizbollah or to a cessation of Syria's transfer of weapons to Hizbollah.

In the aftermath of the Israeli-Hizbollah war, US secretary of state Rice, who had originally spoken of a "new Middle East" emerging from the conflict, sought to build on the fears of rising Iranian influence in the region following the political victory of Iran's ally, Hizbollah. She tried to construct an anti-Iranian Sunni Arab bloc of Jordan, Egypt, Saudi Arabia, and the United Arab Emirates and to align it with Israel against Iran and its allies, Hizbollah and Hamas. Helping Rice in this project was Saudi Arabia's decision to revive the 2002 Arab peace plan, which offered Arab state recognition of Israel if it withdrew to its pre–1967 war boundaries and agreed to a "fair" settlement of the Palestinian refugee problem. Unfortunately for Rice, the Democratic victory in the November 2006 US congressional elections weakened the Bush administration, which had already been damaged by the failures in its Iraq policy and in the Hurricane Katrina recovery effort. This Democratic victory gave rise to a feeling, especially in the Middle East, that Bush had become a "lame duck" president, and that any serious discussion of peace should wait until his successor took office in January 2009. Nonetheless, Rice urged Olmert to negotiate with Abbas; the United States continued to try to strengthen him militarily while Hamas and Abbas's Fatah clashed increasingly. The fighting stopped temporarily as a result of a Saudi-sponsored agreement in Mecca in February 2007. The agreement established a Palestinian national unity government, but neither the United States nor Israel was pleased with the platform of the new government, which was dominated by Hamas and positioned itself closer to Hamas than to Fatah.[53]

FROM THE HAMAS SEIZURE OF POWER IN GAZA TO OPERATION CAST LEAD AND THE END OF THE BUSH ADMINISTRATION

Rice's efforts to expedite the Israeli-Palestinian talks got an unexpected boost in June 2007, when Hamas seized Gaza and Fatah cracked down on Hamas in the West Bank. While the Hamas seizure of Gaza was a blow to Palestinian unity, it did provide the Bush administration with the opportunity to try to make the West Bank a showcase while Gaza, under a tightening Israeli blockade because of Hamas rocket fire and the continued imprisonment of Israeli soldier Gilad Shalit, who had been captured in 2006, would stagnate. Thus the United States began a major program of economic aid to the West Bank and stepped up its efforts to train Fatah's West Bank security forces, a policy continued by Bush's successor, Barack Obama. At the same time the Bush administration promised Israel $30 billion in military assistance over the next decade and pledged to maintain Israel's qualitative military edge over its Middle Eastern enemies.[54] However, the Bush administration not only refused to attack Iran's nuclear installations but also opposed an Israeli attack on Iran, despite the fact that Iran's leaders were rejecting International Atomic Energy Agency (IAEA) requests for information about the possible weaponization of Iran's nuclear fuel, which Iran was continuing to enrich despite opposition from the United States, the European Union, and the IAEA.[55]

As the Bush administration was seeking to strengthen Abbas's Fatah-led West Bank economically and militarily, it was also seeking to build an anti-Iranian coalition of forces, primarily made up of Sunni Arabs, to support a renewed effort to achieve an Israeli-Palestinian peace settlement. In November 2007 the Bush administration convened a major international conference at Annapolis, Maryland, bringing together the leading Arab states (including Syria), the Quartet, representatives of the World Bank and the Islamic Conference, along with Israeli leader Ehud Olmert and Palestinian leader Mahmoud Abbas. The purpose of the conference was to give an Arab and international imprimatur for the renewed peace talks, thereby giving Abbas additional political cover against Hamas. The fact that the Arab League, in March 2007, had again come out with its peace plan (first introduced in 2002 at the height of the al-Aqsa intifada) was seen as also being helpful to Abbas. Nonetheless, the difficulties the two sides had in even agreeing to an opening joint statement foreshadowed the negotiating problems that lay ahead, although with the help of Condoleezza Rice a joint statement was worked out—literally at the last minute—which stated the goal of the meeting: "We agree to immediately launch good faith bilateral negotiations in order to conclude a peace treaty, resolving outstanding issues, including all core issues, without exception . . . and shall make every effort to conclude an agreement before the end of 2008."[56]

To facilitate the negotiations, a number of committees were set up to deal with the major issues dividing Palestinians and Israelis, although the principle that "nothing is agreed until everything is agreed" made it difficult to monitor the day-by-day success of the negotiations. In order to expedite the negotiations, Rice made numerous trips to the Middle East, and according to Bush in his memoirs, *Decision Points*, Olmert made a very significant offer to Abbas covering the central issues in the conflict under which (1) Israel would return the "vast majority" of the West Bank to the Palestinians, (2) a tunnel would be built linking the West Bank and Gaza, (3) a limited number of refugees would return to Israel, with the rest of the returning refugees going to the new Palestinian state, (4) Jerusalem would be the joint capital of both Israel and the Palestinians, and (5) the holy places would be administered by a panel of "nonpolitical elders." According to Bush, Olmert was to travel to Washington and deposit the offer with the US president. Abbas would then announce that the plan was in line with Palestinian interests, and Bush would convene the two leaders to finalize the deal.[57]

Unfortunately for all concerned, the deal was not consummated. Bush blames the fact that Olmert was under investigation on a series of corruption charges, and Abbas did not want an agreement with an outgoing Israeli prime minister.[58] While there is truth to the Bush assertion (Olmert was forced to step down as prime minister; Israeli foreign minister, Tzipi Livni, became acting prime minister; and new Israeli elections were set for February 2009, when Livni proved unable to put together a ruling coalition), there was more to the story than Olmert's weakness. After the defeat of his forces in Gaza, Abbas was also seen as a weak leader, while Bush by the time of the Annapolis conference, with Congress now controlled by the Democrats and facing continued difficulties in Iraq and a renewed insurgency in Afghanistan, was very much a lame duck president.

While Olmert and Abbas negotiated, the border between Israel and Gaza heated up. A Hamas-Israel cease-fire had become increasingly shaky, and by the end of

November 2008 Hamas forces had begun to fire volleys of rockets into Israel, making life in Israeli regions north and east of Gaza increasingly difficult for Israeli civilians. By the end of December 2008, Israel had decided on a policy of massive retaliation for the Hamas rocket attacks, and it mounted a major invasion of Gaza under the code name Operation Cast Lead. Unlike the Israeli-Hizbollah conflict of 2006 where the United States, after the first two weeks of that conflict, had pressured Israel to stop fighting in order to preserve the pro-Western Siniora government, this time Israel was fighting Hamas, an organization on the US terrorist list. Consequently the United States gave full backing to Israel. However, this was to be the last Middle East policy decision taken by the Bush administration, which was replaced on January 20, 2009, by the administration of Barack Obama.

THE OBAMA ADMINISTRATION AND THE ARAB-ISRAELI CONFLICT: A PRELIMINARY APPRAISAL

One of the Obama administration's first acts after taking office was to appoint former US senator George Mitchell as special envoy to the Arab-Israeli peace process. Mitchell had previously served as the mediator of the Northern Ireland peace agreement and had also played a role in the Israeli-Palestinian conflict. This demonstrated Obama's serious interest in achieving an Arab-Israeli peace settlement. A major challenge to Obama's peace process efforts, however, came less than a month after he took office. The Israeli elections of February 10, 2010, brought into office a right-of-center Israeli government under the leadership of Benjamin Netanyahu—the same Netanyahu who had clashed with Obama's Democratic predecessor, President Bill Clinton, in the 1996–1999 period. It wasn't long before Netanyahu and Obama clashed, due in part to their different worldviews and in part to their different Middle East priorities.

OBAMA'S APPROACH TO WORLD AFFAIRS

In all US presidential transitions, especially when the outgoing president has been in office for two terms, the new incumbent seeks to demonstrate that his policies are different from his predecessor's. This was the case when George W. Bush replaced Bill Clinton, and it was also the case when Barack Obama replaced Bush. Thus when Obama took office, he made a major effort to show that in foreign policy he would replace the unilateralism of the Bush era with a policy of outreach to countries that had come into sharp conflict with the United States during the Bush administration. These included Iran, Syria, Cuba, Venezuela, Russia, China, North Korea, and Myanmar. The Obama administration apparently assumed that if you meet your opponents halfway, they will reciprocate. While such an assumption appeared to be dangerously naive to many critics, including those in Israel, the administration held fast to this policy during its first year. A second aspect of the administration's approach involved outreach to the Muslim world. In speeches in both Turkey and Egypt, Obama sought to portray the United States as a friend of the Muslim world, despite the US wars in Iraq and Afghanistan. To emphasize this point, Obama played down the Islamic nature of the terrorism, much to the displeasure of conservatives in the United States, who condemned him for giving a free ride to Islamic terrorism.[59] A third aspect of the new policy was a cooling of ties with Israel, after the warm, if not cozy, relationship of the Bush years. Obama appeared to feel that such a cooling would help the United States appear more evenhanded and consequently facilitate US efforts to solve the conflict. Thus early in his administration, Obama called for a halt in settlement construction, including in Jerusalem, despite the understanding reached by Bush and Sharon in April 2004. In addition, despite trips to Egypt, Turkey, and Saudi Arabia, Obama did not visit Israel, despite being urged to do so by a number of American Jewish organizations, including those affiliated with the liberal J Street movement. Reinforcing the chill in relations was the fact that while Obama was a left-of-center liberal, Netanyahu was a right-of-center conservative. Gone were the days when the conservatives Bush and Sharon could easily relate because they saw the world through the same lens. Indeed, in the very first public meeting between Obama and Netanyahu in May 2009, the tension between the two leaders was clearly visible.

In addition to their different political perspectives, Obama and Netanyahu differed on Middle East priorities. To Netanyahu, Iran was the primary issue. With Iranian President Mahmoud Ahmadinejad calling for Israel to be wiped off the face of the earth and rapidly developing Iran's nuclear capability, Netanyahu pressed Obama to take action against Iran. For Obama, however, the priority was to try to get the Iranians to change their policies by dialogue, not force, and during his first year in office, Obama made numerous appeals to the Iranian regime for improved relations, only to be continually rebuffed. For his part, Obama saw a solution to the Arab-Israeli conflict as the priority in the Middle East, seeing such a solution both as a means of weakening Iran's proxies, Hizbollah and Hamas, pulling Syria away from Iran, and rallying the Sunni Arab world against Iran, if it failed to respond to his outreach policy.[60] Here again, the settlement issue was key as Obama felt that by getting Israel to stop settlement building in Jerusalem and the West Bank, the resumption of Palestinian-Israeli negotiations would be facilitated and an overall settlement of the conflict brought closer.[61] Unfortunately for Obama, as he would later ruefully admit, he did not understand the changes in Israeli politics that had been caused by the Israeli-Hizbollah war of 2006 and the Israeli-Hamas war of December 2008–January 2009.

ISRAEL'S MOVE TO THE RIGHT

The Israeli elections of 2009 reflected a clear move to the right by the Israeli body politic. Netanyahu's right-wing Likud Party jumped from twelve to twenty-seven seats, and the right-of-center Yisrael Beiteinu Party of Avigdor Lieberman rose from eleven to fifteen seats. At the same time, the left-wing Meretz Party dropped from five to three seats and the left-of-center Labor Party fell from nineteen to thirteen seats. In explaining the shift to the right, analysts noted that the policy of unilateral withdrawals had not achieved peace. After Ehud Barak unilaterally withdrew from southern Lebanon in 2000, Israel had to endure repeated rocket attacks leading up to a major war with Hizbollah in 2006, which the centrist Kadima Party did not wage effectively. Similarly, after Israel withdrew both settlements and military bases from Gaza in 2005, Israelis experienced increased rocket fire from Gaza, which Hamas had seized in 2007, leading to the major Israeli invasion of Gaza in December 2008. Given these events, the majority of Israelis were wary of further withdrawals, which, as Netanyahu pointed out in the campaign, would bring Tel-Aviv and Ben Gurion airport into rocket range. Also, they were highly suspicious of the Palestinians; the split between Hamas and Fatah made any final Israeli-Palestinian peace agreement a distant possibility, at best. Making matters worse was a general feeling that Palestinian Authority leader, Mahmoud Abbas, was well-meaning but weak, and that his prime minister, Salam Fayyad, was honest but had no political base. In addition, the stance of Israel's Arab community (20 percent of the Israeli population) had become problematic to Israel's Jewish majority, as the leaders of the Arab community increasingly sided with Israel's Arab enemies while demanding that Israel as a Jewish state be replaced with Israel "as a state of its peoples."[62] Given this turn to the right, Obama's pressure on Israel was received coldly, and Obama's popularity, as measured in Israeli polls, fell to single digits.[63]

Consequently Netanyahu took a hard line on the Middle East peace process, refusing to agree to a two-state solution to the Israeli-Palestinian conflict and promoting an active Jewish settlement program in the West Bank. Under heavy US pressure, however, he modified his position. Thus in June 2009, in a speech at Bar-Ilan University in Israel, Netanyahu agreed to a two-state solution, with the important qualification that Jerusalem would remain united under Israeli control. Then in November 2009 Netanyahu also agreed to a ten-month partial settlement construction ban, excluding Jerusalem.

By the beginning of 2010, the split between Obama and Israel seemed to be narrowing. Obama had begun to take a tougher stand on Iran, after the Iranian government, now beset by increasing domestic dissent, continued to rebuff Obama's call for improved ties and rejected international efforts to deal with Iran's nuclear enrichment efforts. In addition, a tougher tone had begun to enter the Obama administration's diplomatic vocabulary, after the apparent failure of outreach efforts toward Venezuela, Cuba, Myanmar, and North Korea. As far as Israel was concerned, Obama had publicly stated in a *Time* magazine interview on February 1, 2010, that he had "overestimated" the US ability to get the Israelis and Palestinians to engage in a "meaningful conversation" because of the domestic political problems both sides faced.[64] Consequently the United States backed off from its calls for a full settlement freeze and accepted the partial freeze proposed by Netanyahu. Nonetheless, given this apparently improving situation in US-Israeli relations, a crisis erupted in mid-March 2010, when US Vice President Joe Biden was in Israel.

There were several aspects of the crisis. First, after a great deal of effort, the United States had coaxed Palestinian Authority leader Mahmoud Abbas to agree to resume peace talks with Israel, albeit at the low level of indirect or proximity talks under which the US Middle East special envoy, George Mitchell, would shuttle between the two sides. Biden's trip to Israel was aimed, in part, to add the US imprimatur to the start of the talks that had been endorsed by the Arab League, thus giving Abbas a modicum of legitimization. However, as the date of Biden's visit to Israel approached, the situation in East Jerusalem became more explosive. The Israeli government, either with Netanyahu's active support or with his toleration, had begun to accelerate the construction of Jewish housing in Arab-populated neighborhoods of East Jerusalem such as Silwan and Sheikh Jarrah, while at the same time destroying Arab-owned housing in these neighborhoods and elsewhere in East Jerusalem because they had been built without the municipal permit, which, under an Israeli catch-22 policy, is almost impossible for East Jerusalem Arabs to obtain.

This had inflamed Arab opinion. The Palestinians saw these actions as further attempts by Israel to unilaterally extend its control over areas they wanted for their future Palestinian state. The Palestinians see control over Arab East Jerusalem as vital because, for both political and religious reasons, they want it as the capital of their long-hoped-for Palestinian state. With the Jewish construction in Arab East Jerusalem, this hope was rapidly slipping away. Thus the announcement, in the midst of Biden's visit, that Israel was going to construct an additional 1,600 homes in East Jerusalem, even though the construction was to take place in the all-Jewish neighborhood of Ramat Shlomo, was the straw that broke the camel's back as far as the Palestinians were concerned, and they refused to enter into the indirect negotiations to which they had committed. This, in turn, undermined not only the Biden mission but also the months-long diplomacy the Obama administration had been actively pursuing to get the Israeli-Palestinian talks under way. Netanyahu's response that he had been unaware of the announcement before it had been made was seen as specious by the Obama administration, which appeared to lose trust in the Israeli leader. Following the fiasco of the Biden visit, where heated words were exchanged between Netanyahu and high-ranking members of the Obama administration, a debate appeared to break out in the administration as to what to do.[65] One group argued that it was time for the United States to come up with its own plan for an Israeli-Palestinian peace settlement and in well-placed leaks in the *New York Times* and *Washington Post* in early April, the Obama administration was portrayed as actively considering coming up with its own peace plan.[66] Advocates of this position cited then CENTCOM commander David Petraeus's argument in a mid-March 2010 policy paper that the Arab-Israeli conflict was damaging the US position in the Middle East, although in the thirty-five-page paper the conflict was mentioned only twice,[67] and Petraeus later claimed that his position had been misunderstood.[68] However, others in the Obama administration argued that the United States could not want a solution more than the parties themselves did. In a news conference at the end of April President Obama appeared to come down midway between the two positions, thereby enabling the United States to keep both options open. Thus on the one hand Obama stated:

> Even if we are applying all of our political capital to that issue [solving the Israeli-Palestinian Conflict], the Israeli people through their government, and the Palestinian people through the Palestinian Authority, as well as other Arab States, may say to themselves—we are not prepared to resolve this—these issues—no matter how much pressure the United States brings to bear—and the truth is, in some of these conflicts the United States can't impose solutions unless the participants in these conflicts are willing to break out of old patterns of antagonism. I think it was former Secretary of State James Baker who said, in the context of Middle East peace, we can't want it more than they do.

On the other hand, Obama also noted that an Israeli-Palestinian peace was a "vital national security interest of the United States," and that "what we can make sure of is that we are constantly present, constantly engaged," and he also said "I'm going to keep at it."[69]

Meanwhile, as discord between the Obama administration and Netanyahu continued, nearly three hundred members of the United States Congress, who were sympathetic to Israel, had made their position clear in a letter to Secretary of State Hillary Clinton in late March, in which they expressed "deep concern" over the US-Israeli crisis:

> The US and Israel are close allies whose people share a deep and abiding friendship based on a shared commitment to core values including democracy, human rights, and freedom of the press and religion. Our two countries are partners in the fight against terrorism and share an important strategic relationship. A strong Israel is an asset to the national security of the United States and brings stability to the Middle East. We are concerned that the highly publicized tensions in the relationship will not advance the interests the US and Israel share. Above all, we must remain focused on the threat posed by the Iranian nuclear weapons program to Middle East peace and stability.[70]

Perhaps heeding the call of Congress, or perhaps realizing that the United States could not move the peace process forward without a good working relationship with Israel, the Obama administration moved in early May to resume its efforts to convene the indirect talks between Israel and the Palestinians and also to improve relations with Israel. The indirect talks were resumed, and the United States made a major gesture to Israel by granting it an additional $205 million in military aid over and above the $3 billion Israel was already getting, to help it expand its Iron Dome antimissile system that would help protect Israel against rocket attacks from Gaza and Lebanon.[71] Netanyahu appears to have reciprocated by putting a de facto freeze on construction in East Jerusalem. At the same time, however, Obama's effort to eliminate nuclear weapons from the world, an effort that appeared partially aimed at putting additional pressure on Iran to scrap its nuclear enrichment program, came into conflict with Israel's need for nuclear weapons as a deterrent against a possible attack by its enemies. Consequently Israel was unhappy with the US decision in late May 2010 at a review session for the Nuclear Nonproliferation Treaty to support a call for Israel to join the treaty, a development that would force it to disclose and then give up its nuclear weapons. Israel was further concerned that the conference's final document did not mention Iran's failure to comply with IAEA demands to stop the enrichment of uranium. US support for the document contrasted sharply with that of the Bush administration during the 2005 treaty review conference when the United States refused to sign a similar declaration calling for Israel to join the treaty.[72]

Despite this disagreement, US-Israeli relations appeared to be on the upswing by July. The United States had refused to join the Arab and Turkish condemnation of Israel over the incident of May 31 in which Israel intercepted a Gaza-bound flotilla and killed nine Turkish Islamists who were resisting the Israeli capture of one of the ships in the flotilla (the others surrendered peacefully). In July, Netanyahu again visited Washington, and this time his reception was much more cordial than during his previous visit in March. Obama, after meeting Netanyahu, stated, "The US will never ask Israel to do anything that undermines its security" and also emphasized that the bond between Israel and the United States was "unbreakable."[73]

By early September US diplomacy had scored a minor breakthrough when Abbas, with the backing of the Arab League, had finally agreed to enter into direct negotiations with Israel. The timing was, however, problematic. The end of Israel's partial settlement freeze was set for September 26, just three weeks after the formal start of the direct negotiations. Despite a great deal of pomp in Washington, little was actually accomplished in the three weeks of direct talks, and when the partial settlement construction freeze ended, Israel resumed construction in the settlements and East Jerusalem, actions that Obama called "unhelpful." Abbas broke off negotiations.[74]

At this point the United States floated an offer to Netanyahu to get him to extend the settlement building moratorium for an additional ninety days. The hope was that a general border delineation could be worked out by that time so that future Israeli settlement construction would take place only in areas that Abbas and Netanyahu agreed would remain part of Israel under a land swap arrangement. Reportedly, the offer included providing Israel with an additional twenty F-35 Stealth fighter planes (Israeli had already planned to buy twenty), a US-Israeli security treaty, and US pledges to protect Israel against efforts by the Palestinian Authority to get the UN Security Council to vote for the establishment of a Palestinian state, even without an agreement with Israel.[75] Despite this generous offer, Netanyahu refused to accept the US initiative, which was subsequently taken off the bargaining table. Meanwhile the United States and Israel continued to differ over policy toward Iran. In the face of strong urging by Israel, the United States continued to resist calls for an attack on Iran, arguing that the sanctions that the United States, the EU, and the UN Security Council had enacted against Iran were the proper path. As Secretary of Defense Robert Gates noted, "We even have some evidence that [Supreme

Religious Leader, the Ayatollah] Khameini now [is] beginning to wonder if [Iranian President] Ahmadinejad is lying to him about the impact of the sanctions on the economy. And whether he is getting the straight scoop in terms of how much trouble the economy really is in. . . . A military solution as far as I am concerned . . . it will bring together a divided nation. It will make them absolutely committed to obtaining nuclear weapons . . . and they will just go deeper and more covert."[76]

CONCLUSION

In comparing the Bush and Obama policies toward Israel and the Arab-Israeli conflict, we find similarities and differences. Both administrations committed themselves to Israel's security. Of the $5 billion in US foreign aid, Israel is the recipient of $3 billion, 60 percent of the total. In a 2007 memorandum of understanding with Israel, the Bush administration committed the United States to supply Israel with $30 billion in security assistance over the next decade. The Obama administration not only agreed to continue funding security assistance to Israel at that level but also added $205 million to it to support Israel's Iron Dome antirocket system. Neither the Bush administration nor the Obama administration supported Israel's calls for an American attack on Iran's nuclear installations, and both were hesitant to support an Israeli attack on Iran as well.

Despite these similarities, there have been a number of differences, and in the mind of the Israeli public at least, they tend to outweigh the similarities. First and foremost have been the differences over Israeli settlement building. While no US administration has formally supported the building of Israeli settlements in the West Bank and East Jerusalem, George W. Bush in April 2004 tacitly supported Israel's continued building in the major settlement blocs when he stated, "in light of new realities on the ground, including already existing population centers, it is unrealistic to expect that the outcome of the final status negotiations will be a full and complete return to the armistice lines of 1949." By contrast, early on in his administration Obama came out strongly against settlements not only in the West Bank outside the settlement blocs, but also in the settlement blocs and in Jerusalem as well. While Netanyahu agreed to a partial settlement freeze, one not including East Jerusalem, the settlement issue has been a major cause of conflict between Israel and the Obama administration, reaching a peak during the visit of Vice President Joe Biden to Israel in March 2010.

A second difference can be seen in the differing worldviews of the two administrations. George W. Bush was a conservative with a black-and-white understanding of terrorism, one that was reinforced by 9/11. In this, both Prime Minister Ariel Sharon, a conservative, and Prime Minister Ehud Olmert, a moderate conservative, were on the same wavelength as Bush, and this reinforced their relationship. By contrast, Obama is a liberal, and his view of the world has clashed with that of Netanyahu, a conservative. A third difference can be seen in the different approaches to Iran. In his first term Bush sought to isolate Iran. In his second term he proved willing to cooperate with key European Union states in their efforts to get Iran to stop enriching uranium, but relations between the United States and Iran remained hostile during Bush's entire term of office. By contrast, Obama's outreach policy toward Iran—which so far has not persuaded Iran to stop enriching uranium—was seen as the height of naïveté by Netanyahu, who saw the time spent by Obama in trying to win over the Iranian leadership as more time for Iran to develop its nuclear weapons.

A related outreach program by the Obama administration involved Syria—which the Bush administration sought to isolate, especially after the assassination of Lebanese Sunni leader Rafiq Hariri in 2005. Obama apparently hoped that by warming up relations with Syria, he could influence the Syrians to stop the infiltration of anti-US fighters into Iraq, as well as break Syria's ties with Iran and stop aiding Hamas and Hizbollah. So far that policy has stalled as well, due to a legacy of mistrust between the two countries. United States sanctions and United Nations resolutions directed against Syria have dampened initial enthusiasm on both sides that significant progress could be made in the bilateral relationship. Yet another difference between Netanyahu and Obama lies in Obama's pursuit of a nuclear-free world. Obama appeared to the Israelis to be sacrificing their interests by failing to insist that Israel should not be pressured to give up its nuclear weapons until after a comprehensive Middle East peace agreement had been achieved.

Another major difference between the two administrations has been their approaches to the Arab-Israeli peace process. Bush, after 9/11, sought to end the al-Aqsa intifada and create a Palestinian state living in peace alongside Israel. While the Obama administration has had the same goal, Bush's post-9/11 efforts, unlike Obama's, tended to be episodic, and all but ceased after both the Zinni mission to the Middle East and the 2003 Road Map were sabotaged by Palestinian terrorism. After Arafat died and Mahmoud Abbas was elected president of the Palestinian Authority, the United States moved ahead with its peace plan, since Abbas, unlike Arafat, was a strong opponent of terrorism. Unfortunately for Bush, however, Abbas proved to be a weak leader, and the US democratization program, which had become a centerpiece of the administration's policy in the Middle East, foundered when Hamas won the Palestinian Legislative Council elections in January 2006. Bush's strategy suffered another blow when Prime Minister Sharon suffered a massive stroke in January 2006, soon after his unilateral withdrawal from Gaza. The Palestinian government collapsed when Hamas seized power in Gaza in June 2007, signaling a major split in the Palestinian movement. By that time, with the war in Iraq going badly and with the Democrats having won control of both houses of the US Congress in the midterm election of 2006, Bush was very much a lame duck president. His subsequent efforts at peacemaking at the Annapolis conference in November 2007 did not prove successful, although if one is to believe Bush's memoirs the two sides did come close. However, the fact that the Bush administration came to an end as war was raging between Israel and Hamas illustrates the failure of the Bush administration's peacemaking strategy.

Obama, by contrast, has had a very different approach. Unlike Bush's episodic approach to Middle East peacemaking, Obama's was continuous, although he has had to revise his strategy on several occasions. In part this was due to a desire to show he was different from Bush. Thus while Bush was inactive in pursuing the Arab-Israeli peace process at the start of his presidency, Obama on his second day in office appointed George Mitchell as his special Middle East mediator. Obama also undertook a major outreach effort to the Muslim and Arab worlds with speeches in Turkey and Egypt in an effort to show that despite the fact that the United States was involved in wars in two Muslim countries, Iraq and Afghanistan, it was not at war with Islam. To emphasize this point Obama downplayed the Islamic nature of terrorism—much to the displeasure of US conservatives. At the same time, he appeared to deliberately cool ties with Israel.

Essentially, Obama's peacemaking strategy has had four phases through the end of 2010. Through most of 2009, he sought to get Israel to agree to a two-state solution to the Israeli-Palestinian conflict and stop building settlements; the PA under Abbas to return to direct negotiations with Israel; Syria to cut its ties to Hamas, Hizbollah, and Iran; and Saudi Arabia and the Gulf Emirates to make confidence-building gestures to Israel such as allowing Israeli civilian overflights of their countries and visits by Israeli businessmen. This ambitious plan, however, did not prove successful. Netanyahu did accept a two-state solution, albeit with conditions, and adopted a ten-month partial settlement freeze (not including East Jerusalem). But Abbas did not agree to direct negotiations; Syria did not cut ties with Hamas, Hizbollah, or Iran; and Saudi Arabia and the Gulf Emirates refused to make confidence-building measures with Israel. This led the Obama administration to undertake a reappraisal of its policy at the end of 2009, and by February 2010 the administration had decided on a more modest policy. Obama himself acknowledged in a *Time* magazine interview in February 2010 that the United States had overestimated its ability to bring about a settlement and now sought to get indirect or proximity talks under way between Israel and the Palestinians. Joe Biden's visit to Israel in mid-March 2010 was supposed to kick off the talks, but instead precipitated a crisis in US-Israeli relations as the Israeli government embarked on plans to add 1,600 housing units in East Jerusalem. The crisis led to another reappraisal of US policy.

Obama, however, did not endorse the suggestion to issue his own peace plan, and he went back to indirect talks. The indirect talks did not bear fruit, however, other than to finally get Abbas's agreement to enter into direct talks with Israel, something that took place in early September 2010 with Obama and Secretary of State Clinton looking on. Yet this appeared to be too little and too late as Netanyahu's partial settlement freeze ended on September 26, and the Netanyahu government then reverted to its old policy of settlement building, leading Abbas to break off negotiations. The United States then made a major offer of security assistance to Israel, including the provision of twenty F-35 fighter aircraft to Israel in return for a ninety-day extension of the settlement freeze. Israel declined the offer.

In sum, while there have been important similarities between the George W. Bush and Obama administrations in their policies toward Israel, particularly in providing military aid to help ensure Israeli security, there have also been major differences, particularly over Israel's settlement-building policy and over the Arab-Israeli peace process. Given the differences that have become noticeable over the first two years of the Obama administration, we may well expect more differences to emerge over the remaining years of the Obama presidency.

Notes

1. Cited in Roula Khalaf, "Powell Sets Out Bush Line on Middle East," *Financial Times*, March 20, 2001.

2. Alan Sipress, "Lawmakers Criticize Palestinians," *Washington Post*, April 6, 2001.

3. For the text of the Mitchell Report, see *Ha'aretz*, May 6, 2001.

4. For Tenet's effort to help work out an Israeli-Palestinian peace agreement, see George Tenet, *At the Heart of the Storm: My Years at the CIA* (New York: HarperCollins 2007), chaps. 4–6.

5. Cited in Aluf Benn, "Sharon Calls Powell After White House Blasts PM Comments," *Ha'aretz*, October 5, 2001.

6. For the text of Bush's speech, see *New York Times*, November 12, 2001. See also Serge Schmemann, "Arafat Thankful for Bush Remark about 'Palestine,'" *New York Times*, November 12, 2001.

7. Cited in Bill Sammon, "Bush Will Not Meet with Arafat," *Washington Times*, November 9, 2001.

8. For the text of Powell's speech, see "United States Position on Terrorists and Peace in the Middle East," November 19, 2001, www.state.gov/secretary/rm/2001/6219.htm.

9. Janine Zacharia, "Bush Asking Arab Nations to Pitch in for a Secure Peace," *Jerusalem Post*, November 25, 2001.

10. Cited in Eric Schmitt, "Envoy Forges Bonds and Reaps Benefits," *New York Times*, November 28, 2001.

11. See James Bennet, "US Envoy Meets Arafat and Asks for End of Violence," *New York Times*, November 29, 2001.

12. Avi Machlis, "Israeli Bus Blast Casts Shadow on Peace Process," *Financial Times*, November 30, 2001.

13. Joel Greenberg, "Envoy to Middle East Assails Palestinian Militants," *New York Times*, December 1, 2001.

14. Cited in Lee Hockstadter, "Bomber in Bus Kills 15 in Israel," *Washington Post*, December 3, 2001.

15. Ibid.

16. Cited in Peter Herman, "Terrorists Kill at Least 15 in Israel," *Baltimore Sun*, December 2, 2001.

17. Clyde Haberman, "Arafat Demands Halt in Attacks against Israelis," *New York Times*, December 7, 2001.

18. For a discussion of this point, see David Frum, *The Right Man: The Surprise Presidency of George W. Bush* (New York: Random House, 2003), p. 256. Frum was a speechwriter for Bush from January 2001 to February 2002. See also Bob Woodward, *Bush at War* (New York: Simon & Schuster, 2002), p. 297.

19. Lee Hockstadter, "Arafat Arrests Three in Arms Incident," *Washington Post*, January 12, 2002.

20. Mary Curtius, "Hamas Takes Responsibility for Attack," *Los Angeles Times*, January 10, 2002.

21. Amos Harel, "IDF Plans to Hit More PA Targets, Voice of Palestine Radio Torched in Ramallah, Police Bombed in Tulkarm," *Ha'aretz*, January 20, 2002.

22. Todd S. Purdum, "Powell Says US Will Grab Chances at Middle East Peace," *New York Times*, February 28, 2002.

23. The text of UN Security Council Resolution 1397 is on the United Nations website.

24. For Powell's comments, see "Excerpts from Powell's News Conference of March 29, 2002," *New York Times*, March 30, 2002. See also Tracy Wilkinson, "Israel Corners a Defiant Arafat," *Los Angeles Times*, March 30, 2002.

25. Woodward, *Bush at War*, p. 34.

26. Ibid.

27. Israel has been carefully cultivating the support of evangelical Christians. The Israeli ambassador to the United States, Daniel Ayalon, regularly visited evangelical churches to thank them for their support, which he has called "so important in this day and age"; cited in James Morrison, "Israel Gives Thanks," *Washington Times*, Embassy Row sec., November 27, 2003. See also James Morrison, "Praying for Israel," *Washington Times*, Embassy Row sec., October 28, 2003, citing Ayalon speaking in an evangelical church in Tampa, Florida, where he stated, "The American Christian community is a bedrock of support for the State of Israel and its people."

28. Howard Kohr, executive director of AIPAC, called DeLay, the former House majority leader, "one of the more important, resolute, and outspoken supporters of Israel"; cited in Juliet Eilperin, "Mideast Rises on DeLay's Agenda," *Washington Post*, October 16, 2003.

29. Cited in "Bush Slams Arafat but Sees 'New Attitude' in Some PA Leaders," *Ha'aretz*, May 26, 2002.

30. For the text of the Bush speech, see *Washington Post*, June 25, 2002.

31. The skepticism was reinforced in December 2002, when neoconservative Elliot Abrams was made Condoleezza Rice's deputy for Arab-Israeli affairs on the National Security Council. For a view of Abram's evolving thinking and his relationship with other neoconservatives, see Connie Bruck, "Back Roads: How Serious Is the Bush Administration About Creating a Palestinian State?" *New Yorker*, December 15, 2003.

32. Cited in Aluf Benn, "US Telling PM That the Muqata Siege Undermining Plans for Iraq," *Ha'aretz*, September 29, 2002.

33. The text of the Road Map is found on the US Department of State website, April 30, 2002.

34. For the text of the letter of the eighty-eight senators, see *Journal of Palestine Studies*, Summer 2003, p. 185.

35. Elaine Monaghan, "Bush Praises Palestinian Leader's Courage," *Times of London*, July 26, 2003; Guy Dunmore, "Bush Attacks Israelis for Building of West Bank Wall," *Financial Times*, July 26, 2003; and Brian Knowlton, "Sharon Meets with Bush but Says Security Fence Will Still Go Up," *International Herald Tribune*, July 30, 2003.

36. Natan Sharansky, *The Case for Democracy: The Power of Freedom to Overcome Tyranny and Terror* (New York: Public Affairs, 2004). See also Joel Rosenberg, "Two Great Dissidents: Natan Sharansky's Vision and President Bush's," *National Review*, November 19, 2004. For an early critique of the democratization program, see Thomas

Carothers and Marina Ottoway, eds., *Uncharted Journey: Promoting Democracy in the Middle East* (Washington, DC: Carnegie Endowment, 2005).

37. See Yossi Beilin, *The Path to Geneva: The Quest for a Permanent Agreement, 1996–2004* (New York: RDV Books, 2004).

38. For an analysis of Sharon's disengagement strategy, see David Makovsky, *Engagement Through Disengagement: Gaza and the Potential for Renewed Israeli-Palestinian Peacemaking* (Washington, DC: Washington Institute for Near East Policy, 2005). See also Robert O. Freedman, "Sharon: The Evolution of a Security Hawk," *Midstream*, May-June 2004.

39. Cited in Nicholas Kralev, "White House Urged West Bank Action," *Washington Times*, August 13, 2004.

40. All quotations from Bush's and Sharon's speeches are taken from *Ha'aretz*, April 15, 2004.

41. Cited in Nathan Guttman, "President Bush Woos the Jewish Vote," *Ha'aretz*, August 12, 2004.

42. Cited in Nicholas Kralev, "Anti-Semitism Office Planned at State Department," *Washington Times*, October 14, 2004. See also "State Department Opposes Anti-Semitism Bill," *Washington Post*, October 14, 2004.

43. Cited in Nathan Guttman, "Kerry and Bush Send in Top Guns to Woo AIPAC," *Ha'aretz*, October 26, 2004.

44. The agreement was published on the Associated Press website, March 17, 2005.

45. Mahmoud Abbas, interview by author, Ramallah, June 26, 2005.

46. In a *Financial Times* interview on April 20, 2007, Rice clung to the democratization policy, stating, "I'll choose elections and democracy, even if it brings to power people that we don't like . . . Without reform and democratization you're going to have a false stability in the Middle East which will continue to give rise to extremism"; interview, "What the Secretary Has Been Saying," on the US State Department website.

47. Hamas leader Mahmoud Zahar said Hamas would not renounce the right to armed resistance against Israel to keep the money flowing from Europe and the United States: "I'm sure Israel will disappear as the Crusaders and other empires disappeared. All of Palestine will become part of the Arab and Islamic land—as the Koran promised"; cited in Paul Martin, "Leader Likely to Cut Ties with Israel," *Washington Times*, January 27, 2006.

48. Cited in Greg Meyer, "Suicide Bombing in Israel Kills 9; Hamas Approves," *New York Times*, April 18, 2006.

49. Iran's policy toward Israel is discussed in Robert O. Freedman, *Russia, Iran, and the Nuclear Question: The Putin Record* (Carlisle, PA: Strategic Studies Institute of the US Army War College, 2006), pp. 32–36.

50. Cited in Bernard Reich, "The United States and Israel: A Special Relationship," in David W. Lesch, ed., *The Middle East and the United States*, 4th ed. (Boulder: Westview, 2007), p. 221.

51. Cited in Marina Grishina and Yelena Suponina, "Qana Tragedy: Russia and UN Urge Immediate Cease-Fire in Lebanon," *Vremya Novosti*, July 31, 2006. For Bush's view of the war, see George W. Bush, *Decision Points* (New York: Random House, 2010), pp. 413–415.

52. Elli Lieberman, "Israel's 2006 War with Hizbollah: The Failure of Deterrence," in Robert O. Freedman, ed., *Contemporary Israel* (Boulder: Westview, 2009), pp. 317–358.

53. Hassan M. Fattah, "Accord Is Signed by Palestinians to Stop Feuding," *New York Times*, February 9, 2007.

54. For an analysis of the US efforts to bolster Israeli security, see the report by Andrew J. Shapiro, assistant secretary of state for political-military affairs, delivered to the Brookings Institution, July 16, 2010.

55. The leading US opponent to an American attack on Iran was Secretary of Defense Robert Gates, who was appointed to his post by George W. Bush in 2006 and retained by Barack Obama. For Bush's view of a possible US attack on Iran, see George W. Bush, *Decision Points,* pp. 417–420.

56. For the text of the joint statement, which Bush read at the opening of the Annapolis Conference, see Walter Laqueur and Barry Rubin, eds., *The Israel-Arab Reader* (New York: Penguin, 2008), pp. 625–626.

57. Bush, *Decision Points,* pp. 408–409.

58. Ibid, p. 410.

59. A leading critic of the Obama administration's policy on Islam has been the conservative *Washington Times*, whose editorials and op-eds regularly condemn Obama for being weak on Islam.

60. According to the Wikileaks revelations, by 2006 most of the Sunni Arab leaders were already vehemently anti-Iranian and some, like Saudi Arabia, were urging a US attack on Iran's nuclear installations, a development that by 2009 Obama was undoubtedly aware of. Nonetheless, Obama seems to have thought that an Israeli-Palestinian peace agreement would made it easier for these Arab leaders to rally their people against Iran. See David E. Sanger, "Around the World, Distress over Iran," *New York Times*, November 28, 2010.

61. In his June 2009 Cairo speech, Obama said, "The US does not accept the legitimacy of continued Israeli settlements." Cited in Ethan Bronner, "New Focus on Settlements: Obama Pressures Israelis over West Bank, but Effort to Stop Growth Faces Hurdles," *New York Times*, June 6, 2009.

62. As'ad Ghanem and Mohamad Mustafa, "Coping With the Nakba: The Palestinians in Israel and the 'Future Vision' as a Collective Agenda," *Israel Studies Forum* 24, no. 2 (2009): 52–66.

63. Cited in Gil Hoffman, "Only 6 % of Israelis see US Government as pro-Israeli," *Jerusalem Post Online*, June 19, 2009.

64. Barack Obama, interview by Joe Klein, *Time*, February 1, 2010.

65. Yossi Alpher, "Too Many Constraints on the Administration," in *The US-Israel Crisis and the Peace Process*, Bitterlemons online, March 22, 2010.

66. See, for example, Helene Cooper, "Weighing an Obama Plan to End a Middle East Logjam," *New York Times*, April 8, 2010.

67. See the statement of General David H. Petreus before the Senate Foreign Relations Committee on the future of the US Central Command, March 16, 2010.

68. Natash Mozgavaya, "Petreus to Ashkenazi: I Never Said Israeli Policy Endangers US," *Ha'aretz*, March 27, 2010.

69. Cited in Hilary Leila Krieger, "Forcing the Peace," *Jerusalem Post*, April 30, 2010.

70. Cited in Natasha Mozgavaya, "Nearly 300 Congress Members Declare Commitment to US-Israeli Bond," *Ha'aretz*, March 27, 2010.

71. AFP Report, "Obama Seeks Funds to Boost Israeli Rocket Defenses" *Turkish Daily News*, May 16, 2010.

72. Janine Zacharia and Mary Beth Sheridan, "Israel Angry at Being Singled Out in Action Plan on Nuclear Weapons," *Washington Post*, May 30, 2010.

73. Cited in Sheryl Stolberg, "Easing Tension with Obama, Israeli Leader Will Push Talks," *New York Times*, July 6, 2010.

74. Cited in Barak Ravid, "Obama: East Jerusalem Building Plans Unhelpful to Peace Efforts," *Ha'aretz*, November 9, 2010.

75. For descriptions of the proposed US-Israeli deal, see Charles Levinson, "Netanyahu Supports US Plan for Freeze," *Wall Street Journal*, November 15, 2010; and Joel Greenberg, "Netanyahu Moves on US Incentives for Construction Freeze in West Bank," *Washington Post*, November 15, 2010.

76. "US Defense Chief Says Iran Sanctions Working, Argues Against Military Strike," *Ha'aretz*, November 16, 2010.

PART THREE

Allies and Enemies in the Gulf and Beyond

CHAPTER 16

AMERICANS AND THE MUSLIM WORLD—FIRST ENCOUNTERS

Robert J. Allison

Before the geographic area we now call the Middle East was called the Middle East, before the British colonies on the North American mainland became the United States, and before petroleum powered the world's economy, Americans and Muslims had a strange and profound encounter. This encounter was part of the long afterglow of the Crusades, as when English mercenary John Smith, fighting for the Austrians against the Ottoman Turks, was captured in Transylvania. Smith killed his Muslim captor and escaped, returning by way of Russia to England, which he left again, this time to sail west and found the colony of Jamestown. In 1645, as novelist and naval historian James Fenimore Cooper tells us, a ship built in Cambridge, Massachusetts, fought an Algerian ship in the Atlantic, in what Cooper called the first American naval battle. In the 1680s, New Yorkers raised money to redeem sailors captured in North Africa, and in 1700, an American sailor returned to Boston from captivity in Algiers. The Puritan clergy used his story of captivity and resistance to Islam to bolster the faith of their flocks.

Eighteenth-century American and European literature made the Muslim world a counterpoint to the idea of individual autonomy, the central feature of the emerging American ideology. Political writers, such as John Trenchard and Thomas Gordon in England, the authors of *Cato's Letters,* and Charles Secondat Montesquieu in France, author of the *Persian Letters* and *Spirit of the Laws,* used Muslim states such as Morocco, Turkey, and Algiers as examples of how not to construct political societies. The American colonists who rebelled against England in 1776 and then set to forming their own political society had not only read these books, but they had incorporated them into their way of thinking. In the Barbary states of North Africa, and in the Ottoman Empire, at least as it was presented to them by European writers, Americans saw an example of the kind of political society they did not want to create.

Travelers and other observers saw signs of decay in Muslim societies, and Americans were determined to avoid the causes and thus prevent the symptoms. The most influential book on the subject was the Abbé Volney's *The Ruins, or a Survey of the Revolution of Empires* (1792), a meditative reflection drawn from his travels in Egypt and Syria. *The Ruins* speculated on how the great Mesopotamian civilization came to collapse, and Volney found the answer in political intolerance fed by religious fanaticism. President Thomas Jefferson found Volney's *Ruins* so important that he undertook to translate it, enlisting the help of American diplomat and poet Joel Barlow.

This ideological picture of the Muslim world was colored by the experiences of American sailors held captive in Algiers, Tripoli, and Morocco. Between 1785 and 1815, a dozen American ships were captured by the North African states, who held the sailors hostage. This captivity forced American leaders to grapple with a variety of problems: What was the responsibility of the US government to its citizens? Should the United States pay ransom for citizens held captive? Should the United States pay tribute to foreign powers in order to protect its citizens? Different American leaders had different responses to these questions. John Adams calculated that paying tribute to Algiers would be less expensive than fighting a war, that Americans were the most reluctant people on earth to pay the kind of taxes that would be required to build a navy, and since Britain and France paid tribute to Algiers, there was no harm in the Americans emulating their example. Thomas Jefferson, on the other hand, believed it would be essential to American liberty to fight Algiers and Tripoli, not only to protect American citizens but to demonstrate to England and France that the Americans were a different sort of people, who would not engage in the kind of corrupt diplomacy of Europe. Jefferson's assertion of America's "difference" won the day, and one of his administration's first acts in 1801 was to send an American fleet to the Mediterranean to blockade Tripoli. The pope praised the American navy for subduing Tripoli, accomplishing what the Christian nations of Europe had been unable, or unwilling, to do.

The captivity of American sailors in Algiers raised another issue, directly related to the idea that Americans were less corrupt and more noble than Europeans and that the Americans had created a political society whose virtue would endure forever. The Americans who wrote about their captivity in Algiers called the experience slavery. The irony of Americans being held as "slaves" in Africa was lost on very few. Benjamin Franklin's last published work was a parody of a Georgia congressman's defense of African slavery in America, putting the Georgian's words in the mouth of a Muslim official justifying the enslavement of Christians in Algiers. Royall Tyler, author of the first American play, wrote a novel entitled *The Algerine Cap-*

tive, connecting American captivity in Algiers to American complicity in the African slave trade.[1]

American misunderstanding of the Muslim world rested on a profound ignorance of the Islamic religion, Muslim society, and the wild misinterpretations of the prophet Muhammad, who was known to eighteenth-century European and American writers as "Mahomet." Puritan minister Cotton Mather contrasted the liberty with which Europeans and Americans could reason with the tyranny of Muslim society. Heaven shone on *"our Parts of the Earth"* in allowing "Improvements of our *modern Philosophy,"* while no follower of the "thick-skull'd Prophet" was permitted to question the scientific truths revealed to Muhammad.[2]

We do not know where Mather learned about Muhammad, but the only English-language biography of Muhammad had been written in 1697 by Anglican clergyman Humphrey Prideaux. Prideaux's interest in Muhammad was only coincidental to his real purpose, which was to expose the folly of religious indifference. Prideaux had planned to write a major work on Constantinople's fall to the Muslims in 1453. But his growing alarm at the state of English society, the "giddy humour" with which too many young people embraced "fashion and vogue" rather than religion, and the ease with which men and women criticized the church, alarmed Prideaux, and he wrote his book on Muhammad as a sober warning. Mecca had been a prosperous trading town, the people had been more attentive to their commercial interests than to their spiritual needs, they had allowed the faith of their fathers to degenerate, and Muhammad had exploited their religious laxity to impose his own religious and political agenda. The Muhammad emerging from Prideaux's work, and from the other English-language tracts on Islam, was an ambitious man. His ambition found a religious outlet, and the Meccan merchants' religious indifference allowed him to secure his religious tyranny.[3]

Prideaux's "Mahomet" was a warning sign in the young American republic of the 1790s. Many Americans welcomed the French revolution that enshrined liberty and reason in the place of monarchy and tradition. But others worried about the consequences, and in France's revolution they saw an anarchy that would ultimately be replaced by a tyrant. Vice President John Adams reached back into French history, writing a series of essays warning about the consequences of anarchy and disorder. In England, Edmund Burke warned in *Reflections on the Revolution in France* that liberty would be the victim of equality. Thomas Paine responded to Burke with his *Vindication of the Rights of Man,* which seemed, on its arrival in America, to be as much an answer to Adams as to Burke. Secretary of State Thomas Jefferson had an advance copy of Paine's pamphlet and sent it to the printer with a note praising Paine's attack on "the political heresies" that had lately sprung up, confident that "our citizens would rally again round the standard of common sense." Paine's book was printed in America with Jefferson's endorsement on the cover. American readers took Jefferson's jab at "political heresies" as a reference to Vice President Adams. In response to this perceived attack on Adams, his son, John Quincy, writing under the name Publicola, compared Jefferson to "the Arabian prophet" who called on "all true believers in the Islam of democracy to draw their swords," and paraphrasing the Muslim creed "There is no God but Allah, and Muhammad is his Prophet," the younger Adams had Jefferson and his zealous supporters shouting, "There is but one Goddess of Liberty, and Common Sense is her prophet."[4]

The situation seemed similar to that of seventh-century Mecca. Jefferson was a well-born, respectable man like Prideaux's Muhammad, but by countenancing the free thought of Thomas Paine and others, he would ultimately destroy the liberty he pretended to defend. In 1795, a Philadelphia publisher specializing in religious works published the first American edition of Prideaux's *Life of Mahomet*, and Prideaux's preface, warning of the dangers of infidelity and religious indifference, seemed especially pertinent in the new nation.

But this was not the only possible reading of Prideaux's *Mahomet*. The Adams administration, which took office in 1797, tried to quell the political storm by imposing a sedition act, making it a crime to criticize or bring ridicule upon the president. One of the fifteen victims of the act was Vermont Congressman Mathew Lyon, who was sent to federal prison for suggesting that President Adams appointed men to office for their political loyalty rather than their accomplishments and that the president was fond of pomp and parade. (Lyon was reelected to Congress while in prison.) Having seen how far criticizing the president directly would take him, Lyon's son James, a printer, launched an indirect criticism. While his father was in jail, James Lyon published the second American edition of Prideaux's *Life of Mahomet*, this one without the preface warning of infidelity. Without this preface, the book takes on a different cast, and the Mahomet is a religious zealot who will tolerate no opposition and forbids "all manner of disputing about his religion," just as Adams and the Federalists had forbidden political disputes. Prideaux's conclusion could not have been more eloquently phrased for Lyon's purpose: "And certainly there could not be a wiser way devised for upholding of so absurd an imposture than by thus silencing, under so severe a penalty, all manner of opposition and disputes concerning it."[5] If Lyon had said this, his prison term would have been extended.

A second biography of Muhammad appeared in America in 1802, with the descriptive title *The Life of Mahomet; or, the History of that Imposture which was begun, carried on, and finally established by him in Arabia: and which has Subjugated a Larger Portion of the Globe, than the Religion of Jesus has yet set at Liberty.* The anonymous author found Islam to be "deeply affecting to a Philanthropic heart," as it degraded men and women "to the rank of brutes by the consummate artifice and wickedness" that had been created by one man, the prophet Muhammad. Islam had so depraved its adherents that this author thought they could be saved only by Christian conquest to free them from "that system of blasphemy and iniquity by which they are at present enslaved." Missionaries and teachers would be helpless against the rulers who used "carnal weapons" on their subjects and respected no argument but force.[6]

Muslim societies were more than distant symbols. In 1785 and 1793, Algiers captured a dozen American ships and held over one hundred American sailors captive. In this crisis, Susanna Rowson, an English actress living in America, wrote a play, *Slaves in Algiers, or, a Struggle for Freedom.* Loosely basing it on Cervantes's *Il Cautivo,* Mrs. Rowson added a tangled family dynamic to make her story current with an American audience. Although the Western characters Constant, Augustus, Olivia, and Rebecca are essential to the plot, the story centers on Fetnah, who has been sold into the dey's harem by her father, the merchant Ben Hassan, who began his career as a London rag merchant and had betrayed everything in his quest for wealth—he had left England for Algiers, had converted from Judaism to Islam, and finally had sold his daughter to the dey because he and Fetnah's mother "loved gold better than they did their child."[7]

Ben Hassan will do anything for money; Fetnah, though the Dey's "chosen favorite," laments her imprisonment in the splendid palace. "I like them very well," she says of the luxury surrounding her, "but I don't like to be confined." She asks, is "the poor bird that is confined in a cage [because it is a favorite with its enslaver] consoled for the loss of freedom? No! tho' its prison is of golden wire, its food delicious, and it is overwhelmed with caresses, its little heart still pants for liberty: gladly would it seek the fields of air, and even perched upon a naked bough, exulting, carrol forth its song, nor once regret the splendid house of bondage."

Fortunately for Fetnah, at this moment Rebecca arrives in Algiers "from that land where virtue in either sex is the only mark of superiority. . . . She was an American." Rebecca, also consigned to the dey's seraglio, assures Fetnah that "woman was never formed to be the abject slave of man" and stirs Fetnah's natural love of liberty. Fetnah declares, "I feel that I was born free, and while I have life, I will struggle to remain so." Fetnah accepts the struggle, and the virtuous Americans even convince the dey to accept it, telling him to "sink the name of subject in the endearing epithet of fellow-citizen," and he agrees to "reject all power but such as my united friends shall think me incapable of abusing." The Americans tell the dey to prove by his conduct "how much you value the welfare of your fellow creatures," as they return to the land "where liberty has established her court," hoping for the day when "Freedom" will "spread her benign influence" through every nation.[8]

The Americans in Susanna Rowson's play are great teachers, teaching the dey how to be a better ruler and teaching the people of Algiers to be good citizens. The American war against Tripoli (1801–1805) gave the Americans more opportunities to teach the lesson of American prowess and virtue. From the first naval engagement in August 1801 until the peace treaty was signed in June 1805, Americans regarded the war as a constant lesson in their own distinctive national character. President Jefferson was determined to cut the American military budget, to chastise Tripoli, and to do both as a lesson to European nations on proper modes of international conduct. Jefferson's decision to blockade Tripoli rather than launch a direct attack and to blockade using the smallest possible force led to disaster, as the *Philadelphia,* the second-largest ship in the American fleet, ran aground off Tripoli in October 1803. But the navy turned this disaster into a triumph, as Lieutenant Stephen Decatur and a small crew disguised themselves and a captured Tripolitan vessel and sailed into Tripoli harbor in February 1804, destroying the *Philadelphia* without losing a man. Americans saw Decatur's deed as evidence of their own prowess and courage. The naval bombardment of Tripoli in August 1804 gave further proof of American courage, and when Tripoli and the United States signed the treaty onboard the USS *Constitution* (the first time a Barbary state signed a treaty on an enemy warship), it confirmed for Americans their new place in the world.[9]

Barely a year after the war began, a play conveying this message was performed on the New York stage. No copies survive of *The Tripolitan Prize, or, American Tars on an English Shore.* We know it only from a caustic review by Washington Irving. The American tars reach the English shore after being chased by a Tripolitan ship—it seems a violent storm in the Mediterranean sent both ships to the English Channel, where they fight it out. Improbable as this may have been, it allowed the Americans to win their battle against Tripoli within sight of England, and on the stage, crowds of Englishmen and women watched the American victory. Irving noted with sarcastic disgust that the American audience, particularly those in the galleries, spent the entire play "hallooing and huzzaing" the American captain and his crew onstage. The captain bellowed at one point, "What! an American Tar desert his duty!" and the American audience responded, "Impossible! American Tars forever! True blue will never stain!!" The battle, Irving wrote, was "conducted with proper decency and decorum," after which "the Tripolitan very politely gave in—as it would be indecent to conquer in the face of an American audience."[10]

We do not have such rich records of the audience response to other literature written in response to the Tripolitan war. But these cultural effusions—plays, poetry, novels, and paintings—all convey the same themes the audience celebrated in *The Tripolitan Prize* and *Slaves in Algiers.* Joseph Hanson's 1806 poem, *The Musselmen Humbled, or a Heroic Poem in Celebration of the Bravery Displayed by the American Tars, in the Contest with Tripoli,* said that the Americans had won the war against Tripoli as they were armed with "the formidable powers of justice and freedom," which gave them "that invincible courage, which terrified and overcame the plundering vassals of the tyrannical bashaw." Hanson asked, "[W]hat can be effected by the slaves of tyrants? who fight for plunder and despotic masters: who defend no laws, but such as are oppressive; and protect no pow'r, but that which disrespects 'em."[11]

An 1812 play by Bostonian James Ellison, *The American Captive, or Siege of Tripoli,* saw this same reason for the American victory. In the play, Abdel Mahadi had seized power in Tripoli from his older brother, Ali ben Mahadi, whom he said was too weak to rule. Ali was "too mild to reign," he had "courted peace, and peace attain'd created heavy taxes!" Instead of peace, Ali should have "courted the crimson hand of war." Abdel, on the other hand, will use *"plunder"* to preserve his power and save his subjects from "that damn'd abyss, to which my brother's mild and milky reign had doom'd them." Plunder alone "can prop our sinking realm" and save it from the "misery and want" brought by peace. Ali's daughter, Immorina, and her fiancé lament this triumph of *"ambition"* over *"virtue,"* taking solace that while "*crime* may for a season triumph," only "*virtue*" can secure "a monarch's bliss, his count[r]y's welfare, and his subjects' love."[12]

As in Rowson's *Slaves in Algiers,* this debate on internal affairs is enriched by the arrival of American captives. In this play, one of Abdel's cruisers has captured an American ship. The arrival of Americans causes great excitement in Tripoli, as one Tripolitan woman asks Immorina, "Do you know what *Americans* are?" Immorina answers, "*Men,* are they not, like other men?" "Pshaw," the old woman says, the Americans are "*Indians!* Yes indeed, *Indians!*" They would scalp any man or woman they caught, "and I'm sure this proves them not to be *men.*" Immorina corrects her. The Indians, she says, are the natives of America but only "inhabit the western regions of that vast country, and are savage, and barbarous, like our wild Arabs." On the other hand, "those whom we denominate Americans" are like the Europeans in "customs and manners," are civilized, polished, enterprizing, brave, and hospitable.[13]

The civilized, polished, enterprising, brave, and hospitable Americans are represented in this play by Captain Anderson, the captured master of the ship. Anderson and Abdel form a striking contrast of American and Tripolitan power. In their first meeting, Abdel is decked out in a "sumptuous Turkish habit," his turban decorated with a large diamond crescent, his jeweled sash barely hiding the dagger on his hip. Abdel asks Anderson if his father is a noble. Anderson replies, "If to be the son of him who served his country, in the time of peril, be that which you call noble, I am of the most noble extraction, but if, from pamper'd lords and vicious princes, alone descend the gift, then I am not." Anderson's father bore "the proudest title man can have"—he was "An honest man."[14]

Anderson contrasts not only with the corrupt and gaudy Abdel but also with other American characters in the play. Jack Binnacle, one of Anderson's crew, wonders why the United States does not simply "blow Algiers, Tunis, and Tripoli up, and put an end to these nests of pirates?" Anderson applauds Binnacle's spirit and pledges to "fight till my heart-strings snap" rather than "be tributary to any nation," but he wants a permanent solution. Simply destroying the coastal cities would allow marauders like Abdel to move into the interior. Anderson wants to reform Tripoli so tyrants like Abdel cannot flourish. Anderson's plan, carried out with the help of Princess Immorina and the Jew Ishmael, is to escape from Tripoli, secure support from the navy for the deposed Ali, who will return to power and end the depraved power of Abdel once and for all.[15]

To the tune of "Washington's March," Anderson and Ali return to Tripoli, and Anderson prays "to be granted that heroic courage, that energy of soul, which so distinguish'd the father of my country, the matchless hero of the western world." Anderson kills the despotic Abdel, declaring that "*A slave* has power to strike a *tyrant* dead." Although Immorina tells Anderson that he now ranks "among the Prophets," the American is more interested in being placed alongside Washington.[16]

As in Susanna Rowson's *Slaves in Algiers,* and *The Tripolitan Prize,* Anderson in *The American Captive* teaches the Muslim tyrant a lesson. A contemporary American songwriter promised that if any despot dared insult the American flag, "We'll send them Decatur to teach them 'Good Manners.'"[17]

And yet some American writers questioned the ability of their country to teach moral lessons to others. In the spring of 1787, while her father, the American minister to France, toured the southern part of that country, sixteen-year-old Martha Jefferson wrote to keep him informed of events in the world. Germany, Russia, and Venice, she reported, were at war against Turkey, and the plague had struck in Spain. She only briefly mentioned these world events, but then she found a story that captured her interest. "A virginia ship comming to spain," she wrote, "met with a [Algerian] corser of the same strength. They fought and the battle lasted an hour and a quarter. The Americans gained and boarded the corser where they found chains that had been prepared for them. They took them and made use of them for the algerians themselves." Martha saw the irony in this turn of events. But instead of relishing the American victory, she saw only compounded tragedy. "They returned to virginia from whence they are to go back to algers to change the prisoners to which if the algerians will not consent the poor creatures will be sold as slaves." The Algerians had wanted to enslave the Americans, a fact that might have justified their own enslavement. But not to Martha Jefferson, who asked her father, "Good god have we not enough? I wish with all my soul that the poor negroes were all freed. It greives my heart when I think that these our fellow creatures should be treated so terribly as they are by many of our countrymen."[18]

The capture of American sailors, who were put to work in Algiers or Tripoli, touched Americans' consciences. The plight of these "slaves" in Algiers and Tripoli stirred Americans to raise money for their redemption. The Americans could boast that they had created a society different from the tyrannies of the Old World, but the captivity of Americans in North Africa reminded them that this was not the case. In Ellison's *The American Captive,* Jack Binnacle, a captive sailor, tells Hassan the overseer about America. "It's a charming place, Mr. Overseer; no *slavery* there! All freeborn sons!" Hassan answers, "No Slavery, hey? Go where the Senegal winds its course, and ask the wretched mothers for their husbands and their sons! What will be their answer? *Doom'd to slavery, and in thy boasted country, too!*"[19]

A New England newspaper ran an item in 1794 headed "Profession versus Practice," a satire on fugitive slave ads, and an attack on "ranting southern demagogues," like Thomas Jefferson, who preached "*universal equality*" while practicing "*piratical barbarity.*" The ad promised a reward for the return of an "American slave" to his master, "Ibrahim Ali Bey" of Algiers. It described the slave as an "ungrateful Villain" and "incorrigible infidel," who refused to renounce "his Christian errors" and had escaped with a "borrowed" manumission certificate. Freed slaves, the ad warned, were lending their freedom papers to other slaves, who used this "new invented species of *robbery*" to escape. How odd, the ad concluded, that these Christians would think this sharing was "*meritorious.* What strange, absurd ideas the Christians must have of *merit.*"[20]

The true story of a free black man helping an enslaved African escape appeared in several New England papers in 1795 and was paired with the story of an American captive redeemed from Algiers. Cato Mungo, reportedly an African prince, was returned by benevolent friends to Ouidah, in West Africa, and George Burnham, an American captain from New York, was ransomed by friends in 1794. Cato Mungo and George Burnham's stories were paired under the heading "Curses of Slavery," and the pairing made Burnham's suffering seem slight. Cato Mungo gave a "long and melancholy account of the treatment of the poor Africans in that land of cruelty" and suggested that Africans take "some measures" to redeem "such of our brethren as it would be in our power to restore to their families and connections." He repeated in horror that "several of the Royal family of this kingdom" were now "doing drudgery in the kitchens of the *United States!!!*"[21]

Cato Mungo had been helped to escape by Mawyaw, a free black man living in Connecticut, where slavery was still legal. Although slaves in Connecticut were treated more decently than were slaves in other states, they were still slaves. Mawyaw had helped Cato Mungo escape to Massachusetts, where slavery had been abolished in 1783. Connecticut's legislature had recently rejected an emancipation plan, Mawyaw reported, allowing "self-interest" to check its benevolence. Although the state was giving away millions of dollars' worth of public lands, "their souls were not large enough" to free African slaves. The legislators "did not think themselves justifiable in taking away the property of individuals," Mawyaw reported. He was not surprised: He noted that Americans "could not find in themselves generosity enough" to redeem their countrymen "now in slavery in the kingdom of Algiers." Americans were in no position to assert their moral superiority to the Algerians.

Benjamin Franklin's last published essay carried this same theme. Franklin, as president of Pennsylvania's antislavery society, had signed a petition to Congress in 1790 calling for an end to the slave trade. Franklin may have expected this to be his last public act. But a Georgia congressman, James Jackson, took to the floor of the House to denounce Franklin for suggesting that slavery was morally wrong. Jackson blasted Franklin and the Quakers, who had also submitted an antislavery petition, for being overzealous moral meddlers whose ignorant and misguided efforts at reform would undermine both the American economy and the well-being of the slaves. Slavery, Jackson said, was justified by religion, economics, politics, and history. The Georgians who enslaved Africans lifted their slaves out of barbarism and taught them the Christian virtues. If the slaves were freed, Jackson said, it would ruin Georgia's economy, since no one would work in the rice fields and these blacks would not work unless they were forced to do so. And what would happen to the freed people? They would not stay and work, and if they moved to the frontier, the Indians would kill them. Georgia's keeping of slaves was the benevolent option, as it taught slaves Christianity and allowed them to cultivate Georgia's rice.

Franklin read Jackson's speech in the *Federal Gazette* in March 1790. Franklin knew he had to reply. No American political leader had ever publicly said that slavery was a good thing: All had been committed to its extinction. Jackson's speech marked a change. Franklin knew he had to respond. Franklin had written his first newspaper essay more than seventy years earlier, had later tangled with Cotton

Mather and the British ministry in print, and knew how to devastate an adversary. He wrote his response to Jackson under the name "Historicus" and said he liked Jackson's speech very much. It reminded him of something he had read many years before, a speech given by the dey of Algiers.

Sidi Mehemet Ibrahim, the dey of Algiers, had given a speech similar to Jackson's in 1687. Franklin said he had read it in a book called *Martin's Account of his Consulship*.[22] The dey was provoked by a group of religious zealots, the Erika, or "Purists," who had petitioned Sidi Mehemet to abolish Christian slavery and piracy, which the Erika said were unjust and against the teachings of the Qur'an. Franklin then quoted Sidi Mehemet's speech, which turned out to be James Jackson's speech, with Erika substituted for Quakers and Christian slaves substituted for Africans. James Jackson's argument justifying the slavery of Africans in America also justified the enslavement of Americans in Africa.

Algiers should not give up enslaving Christians, Sidi Mehemet warned, as it would ruin the nation's economy merely to gratify "the whims of a whimsical sect." He asked, "If we forbear to make slaves" of Christians, "who in this hot climate are to cultivate our lands? Must we not then be our own slaves?" As for the freed slaves, Sidi Mehemet and Jackson both feared they would not easily make the transformation to freedom. If the Christians stayed, they could not be considered the equals of Muslims. They would not "embrace our holy religion; they will not adopt our manners; our people will not pollute themselves by intermarrying with them."

They would become "beggars in our streets" and would pillage Algerian property. They would not work unless they were forced to do so, and if sent to the frontiers, they were too ignorant to establish a "good government" and would be massacred by wild Arabs. They were not to blame for their ignorance or weakness—these were traits they brought with them from their backward homelands, where most peasants, Spanish, Portuguese, French, and Italian, were treated as slaves. The Algerians had improved their lives by allowing them to work "where the sun of Islamism gives forth its light." Sending the freed people home would be denying them this benefit; it would send them "out of light into darkness."

After listening to Sidi Mehemet's arguments, the leaders of Algiers decided, according to Historicus, that to go on record as saying that slavery violated moral law was "at best *problematical*." Algiers would hold on to slavery, and so, in 1790, would the United States. Franklin had made up the Erika, Sidi Mehemet, and *Martin's Account of his Consulship*. But unfortunately, he had not made up James Jackson. The similarities between Jackson's real speech and Sidi Mehemet's fictional one showed that "men's interests and intellects operate and are operated on with surprising similarity in all countries and climates, whenever they are under similar circumstances."

Franklin knew this better than most of his countrymen. They thought they had seen in the Muslim world all that they hoped to avoid in the new world: political and religious tyranny, subjugation of women, and craven self-interest. They also believed that they had created a political system that would prevent these evils, or at least hold them in check. Americans had developed an image of themselves and their society by looking at the Muslim world, holding an image of people and places that helped them, they thought, construct their own nation and identity. But Franklin told them their image of themselves was wrong, only partly because they carried in their heads a hopelessly distorted picture of Muslim history and society.

Notes

1. For more on these themes, see Robert J. Allison, *The Crescent Obscured: The United States and the Muslim World, 1776–1820* (New York: Oxford University Press, 1995); Ray Watkins Irwin, *The Diplomatic Relations of the United States with the Barbary Powers, 1776–1816* (Chapel Hill: University of North Carolina Press, 1931); and James Field, *America and the Mediterranean World, 1776–1882* (Princeton: Princeton University Press, 1969). On the general perceptions of Islam in the West, see Norman Daniel, *Islam and the West: The Making of an Image* (Oxford: Oneworld, 1993).

2. Cotton Mather, "The Christian Philosopher" [1721] reprinted in *Cotton Mather* (n.p.).

3. Humphrey Prideaux, *The History of the Life of the Great Imposter Mahomet* (Philadelphia: Stewart and Cochran, 1796), 2–3.

4. Merrill D. Peterson, *Thomas Jefferson and the New Nation: A Biography* (New York: Oxford University Press, 1970), 438, 440.

5. Humphrey Prideaux, *The True Nature of Imposture, Fully Displayed in the Life of Mahomet* (Fairhaven, Vt.: James Lyon, 1798), 76–77.

6. *The Life of Mahomet; or, the History of that Imposture which was Begun Carried on, and Finally Established by Him in Arabia; and Which has Subjugated a Larger Potion of the Globe, than the Religion of Jesus has Yet Set at Liberty. To Which is Added, an Account of Egypt* (Worcester, Mass.: n.p., 1802), 83–84, 85.

7. Susanna Haswell Rowson, *Slaves in Algiers, or a Struggle for Freedom* (Philadelphia: n.p., 1794), 5.

8. Ibid., 9–10, 65–68, 71, 72.

9. For a striking example of this, see the song written by Francis Scott Key honoring the heroes of Tripoli, which in verse and cadence became the foundation of the "Star-Spangled Banner," which he wrote a few years later during the War of 1812 against England. Allison, 204–206.

10. Irving's review from the *New York Morning Chronicle,* quoted in William Dunlap, *History of the American Theatre* (New York: J. and J. Harper, 1832), 301–302.

11. Joseph Hanson, *The Musselmen Humbled; or a Heroic Poem in Celebration of the Bravery Displayed by the American Tars, in the Contest with Tripoli* (New York: n.p., 1806), 3, 7–9.

12. James Ellison, *The American Captive, or Siege of Tripoli* (Boston: n.p., 1812), 9, 12, 35.

13. Ibid., 24–25.

14. Ibid., 20–21.

15. Ibid., 18–19, 37–38.

16. Ibid., 34, 51.

17. *New York Evening Post,* 15 March 1806.

18. Martha Jefferson to Thomas Jefferson, Paris, 3 May 1787. *Papers of Thomas Jefferson,* Julian Boyd et al., eds. (Princeton University Press, 1950–), 11:334.

19. Ellison, *American Captive,* 37–38.

20. "Profession vs. Practice," Boston *Federal Orrery,* 24 November 1794; Boston *Mercury,* 25 November 1794; Newburyport *Morning Star,* 26 November 1794.

21. "Curses of Slavery," *Rural Magazine, or Vermont Repository* (March 1795), 118–124. Cato Mungo's story was reprinted in Salem *Gazette,* 13 January 1795; Boston *Federal Orrery,* 29 January 1795; Portsmouth *Oracle of the Day,* 31 January 1795. For African Muslims enslaved in America, see Allan D. Austin, *African Muslims in Ante-Bellum America* (New York: Routledge, 1996).

22. Benjamin Franklin, "On the Slave Trade," *The Works of Benjamin Franklin,* Jared Sparks, ed. (London: Benjamin Franklin Stevens, 1882), 2:517–521.

CHAPTER 17

THE UNITED STATES IN THE PERSIAN GULF

From Twin Pillars to Dual Containment

Gary Sick

The United States arrived reluctantly as an active player in the Persian Gulf, but after a quarter-century of resistance, turmoil, and false starts, it emerged as the unquestioned military and political power in the region. In some respects this was merely the story of how the United States slowly reconciled itself to assume the role originated by the British in the nineteenth century. British interests, however, were never identical to US interests, and the underpinnings of US policy by the turn of the century bore little resemblance to the classic British defense of its eastern lines of communication.

The interests of the United States in the Persian Gulf region have been very simple and consistent: first, to ensure access by the industrialized world to the vast oil resources of the region; and second, to prevent any hostile power from acquiring political or military control over those resources. Throughout the cold war, the most immediate threat was the Soviet Union; after the Soviet collapse, Iran and Iraq became the primary targets of US containment efforts.

Other objectives, such as preserving the stability and independence of the Gulf states or containing the threat of Islamic fundamentalism, were derivative concerns and were implicit in the two grand themes of oil and containment. Preoccupation with the security of Israel was a driving factor in US Middle East policy for half a century, and developments in the Arab-Israeli arena sporadically influenced US policies in the Persian Gulf (and vice versa). Especially after the end of the cold war, the Israeli factor began to assume much greater importance in the formulation of US policy in the Gulf.

The slow unfolding of US policy contributed to (and occasionally was the victim of) the development of the modern Persian Gulf. This chapter focuses on a few key turning points, where seemingly unrelated US policy choices eventually resolved themselves into a surprisingly coherent strategic posture.

THE TWIN PILLAR POLICY

Prior to World War II, US involvement in the Persian Gulf was minimal. The first sustained encounter with the region was in the nineteenth century, in the days of the great clipper ships.[1] The Persian Gulf and Indian Ocean were regarded as a British preserve, and US political, commercial, and military contact with the region was extremely rare.[2]

The US Middle East Command was established during World War II to oversee the supply route of war materiel to the Soviet Union. Its 40,000 US troops constituted the largest US deployment to the region from that time until Operation Desert Storm in 1991. The small US naval contingent (Middle East Force) that was established in 1947 relied on British hospitality at Jufair on Bahrain Island.

The British announcement in 1968 that it intended to withdraw from its historic position east of Suez came as an unwelcome shock in Washington, which had long relied on the British presence as an essential component of its Soviet containment strategy along the immense arc from the Suez Canal to the Malacca Straits. It also came at the worst possible moment, since US forces were increasingly strained by commitments in Vietnam and Southeast Asia.

The Nixon administration undertook a major review of US Persian Gulf policy when it took office in 1969. This was part of a global effort to redefine US security interests at a time of competing demands on US military forces and a growing reluctance by the American public to support what were seen as potentially costly foreign commitments. The result of this effort was the Nixon Doctrine, which placed primary reliance on security cooperation with regional states as a means of protecting US interests around the world. In the Gulf, it was decided to rely heavily on the two key states of Iran and Saudi Arabia, a strategy that quickly became known as the "Twin Pillar policy."[3]

From the beginning, it was recognized that Iran would be the more substantial of the two "pillars" because of its size, its military capabilities, its physical juxtaposition between the Soviet Union and the Persian Gulf, and the willingness of the shah (unlike the Arab states of the region) to cooperate openly with the United States on security matters. This very special relationship between Washington and Tehran was sealed in May 1972 during the visit to Tehran of President Nixon and his national security adviser, Henry Kissinger.

In two and one-half hours of conversations over two days, a deal was struck in which the United States agreed to increase the numbers of uniformed advisers in

Iran and guaranteed the shah access to some of the most sophisticated nonnuclear technology in the US military arsenal. The shah, in return, agreed to accept a key role in protecting Western interests in the Persian Gulf region. All of this was summed up with startling candor at the end of the meetings, when President Nixon looked across the table to the shah and said simply, "Protect me."[4]

This moment was the culmination of several decades of tumultuous political relations between the United States and Iran. In 1953, the Eisenhower administration had carried out a "countercoup" that restored the shah to the throne and ended the political career of nationalist leader Muhammad Mussadiq.[5] By this act, the United States at once lost its political innocence with regard to Iran and guaranteed that it would be held permanently responsible—at least by Iranian popular opinion—for the Iranian ruler's excesses and cruelties. In 1963, a fiery religious leader, Ruhollah Khomeini, led the opposition to a bill that, among other things, extended diplomatic protection to American military advisers. This rebellion, which in retrospect was a rehearsal for the revolution of 1978–1979, led to Khomeini's fourteen-year exile. Although most Americans were scarcely aware of this incident, the Iranian opposition was convinced that the shah was acting on behalf of the United States.

The agreement between President Nixon and the shah in 1972 transformed the previous client relationship. Iran was on the brink of becoming a major power in the oil market and now had free access to the US arsenal of modern weaponry. This was formally acknowledged when Iran agreed to become the protector of US interests in the region, and the shah increasingly felt emboldened to lecture his great power ally on politics, economics, and strategy. The United States in turn reduced its intelligence coverage of Iran's internal politics and relied on the shah for assistance in putting down the Marxist rebellion in Dhofar, for an assured energy supply at the time of the oil embargo of 1973, and for support in political and military operations in the Middle East and Africa as well as Vietnam.

This role reversal went almost unnoticed in the Persian Gulf and elsewhere, however. In Iran, the image of a compliant shah responding to orders dictated in Washington remained vividly implanted in the national psyche. As a consequence, when the revolution exploded in the late 1970s, the United States had the worst of both worlds. It had relinquished much of its independent capacity to assess and influence Iran's internal politics, but it was popularly suspected of orchestrating every move by the shah's regime.

The Twin Pillar policy also involved a tripartite covert action with Israel to destabilize Iraq by supporting a Kurdish rebellion against Baghdad. This plan was adopted in May 1972 during the Nixon-Kissinger visit; it collapsed in 1975 when the shah unilaterally came to an agreement with Saddam Hussein and abandoned the Kurds. It established a precedent for viewing the Persian Gulf as an extension of the Arab-Israeli conflict and for US-Israeli cooperation in the region.[6]

The collapse of the shah's regime in February 1979 was the death knell for the US Twin Pillar policy. From the beginning, the policy had been predicated on a close personal relationship with the shah. With his departure and the arrival of a hostile Islamist regime in Tehran, the United States was left strategically naked in the Persian Gulf, with no safety net.

THE CARTER DOCTRINE

This blow was compounded in February 1979 by reports of an incipient invasion of North Yemen by its avowedly Marxist neighbor to the south. This event, coming in the wake of the Marxist coup in Afghanistan in April 1978, the conclusion of the Ethiopian-Soviet treaty in November 1978, the fall of the shah, and the assassination of US Ambassador Adolph Dubs in Kabul in February 1979, created the impression that the United States had lost all capacity to influence regional events. That impression was strengthened when Turkey and Pakistan followed Iran in withdrawing from the Central Treaty Organization in March.

Washington responded by dispatching a carrier task force to the Arabian Sea and by rushing emergency military aid to Yemen and the airborne warning and control system, or AWACS, to Saudi Arabia. The United States also undertook a systematic effort to develop a new "strategic framework" for the Persian Gulf. By the end of 1979, the outlines of a strategy had been sketched in, including initial identification of US forces for a rapid deployment force and preliminary discussions with Oman, Kenya, and Somalia about possible use of facilities. Nevertheless, when the US embassy in Tehran was attacked in November, a high-level review of US military capabilities drew the sobering conclusion that US ability to influence events in the region was extremely limited. In late November, when there were serious fears that the US hostages were in danger of being killed, a second aircraft carrier was sent to the area and two additional destroyers were assigned to the Middle East Force.

The Soviet invasion of Afghanistan just before Christmas in 1979 reawakened fears of a Soviet drive to the Persian Gulf and Indian Ocean. The practical effect of the Soviet invasion was to terminate the efforts of the Carter administration to seek mutual accommodation with the Soviet Union, including support for the SALT II treaty. This policy shift was articulated by Carter in his State of the Union address of January 23, 1980: "Any attempt by any outside force to gain control of the Persian Gulf region will be regarded as an assault on the vital interests of the United States of America, and such an assault will be repelled by any means necessary, including military force."

This declaration, which quickly came to be known as the Carter Doctrine, bore a remarkable resemblance to the classic statement of British policy by Lord Lansdowne in 1903, when he said the United Kingdom would "regard the establishment of a naval base, or of a fortified port, in the Persian Gulf by any other power as a very grave menace to British interests," an act that would be resisted "with all the means at our disposal."[7] The statement clearly established the United States as the protecting power of the region and effectively completed the transfer of policy responsibility in the Persian Gulf from the British to the Americans.

When Carter made this statement, it reflected US intentions rather than capabilities. By the time the Reagan administration arrived in Washington in January 1981, it would have been accurate to say that the US security structure in the Persian Gulf region was more symbol than reality—at least as measured in purely military capacity.[8] Nevertheless, it was equally apparent that the developments of 1980 marked a major threshold in the evolution of US strategy and a new conviction that this region represented a major strategic zone of US vital interests, demanding both sustained attention at the highest levels of US policymaking and direct US engagement in support of specifically US interests. That was without precedent.

The Reagan administration adopted the Carter Doctrine and over the following seven years succeeded in putting more substantial military power and organization behind its words. The Rapid Deployment Joint Task Force (RDJTF) was reorganized in 1983 as a unified command known as the Central Command, based at MacDill Air Force Base in Tampa, Florida, with earmarked forces totaling some 230,000 military personnel from the four services. Its basic mission reflected the two themes that had wound through US regional policy from the very beginning: "to assure continued access to Persian Gulf oil and to prevent the Soviets from acquiring political-military control directly or through proxies."

THE IRAN-IRAQ WAR (1980–1988)

Despite the shadow of Soviet military power, all threats to oil supplies and to regional stability came not from Russia and its allies but from political developments within the region. The first of these was the Arab oil boycott at the time of the Arab-Israeli war of 1973, which nearly tripled the price of oil and sent Western economies spinning into a serious recession. The second was the Iranian revolution, and the third was the Iran-Iraq war, which Iraq launched with a massive invasion in September 1980.

The United States asserted its neutrality at the beginning of the war, then later tilted unofficially in favor of Iraq as Iran drove back the Iraqi forces and counterattacked across the border. In 1985–1986, as part of a "strategic opening" to Iran coupled with an abortive effort to free US hostages in Lebanon, the United States and Israel undertook a series of secret contacts and substantial arms transfers to Iran that effectively shifted US policy—at least at the covert level—toward Iran. When the revelation of these arrangements created consternation and threatened US relations with the friendly oil-producing states of the Gulf, the United States reversed field sharply and adopted an openly pro-Iraqi position.[9]

During much of the war, the United States and many other powers adopted a hands-off posture, content to see these two abominable regimes exhaust each other on the battlefield, particularly since the war was having relatively little impact on oil supplies or prices.[10] That nonchalance began to fade in 1985–1986 when Iran began to retaliate for Iraqi air attacks against its shipping in the Gulf by using mines and small armed boats against neutral shipping en route to Kuwait and Saudi Arabia.

In late 1986, Kuwait asked both the United States and the Soviet Union to place Kuwaiti tankers under their flag and provide protection. The Soviet Union agreed to reflag three Kuwaiti tankers, and the United States quickly followed suit by re-flagging eleven. The United States moved a substantial number of naval ships into or near the Gulf and began escorting tanker convoys to and from Kuwait.[11] Iran's indiscriminate use of mines led other NATO navies to send minesweepers and other escort ships to the Gulf to protect international shipping.

Although the reflagging decision was seen at the time as a temporary US re-sponse to a specific problem, in retrospect it was a fundamental turning point. For the first time since World War II, the United States assumed an operational role in the defense of the Persian Gulf, with all that implied in terms of development of infrastructure, doctrine, coordination with NATO allies, and direct collaboration with the Arab states on the southern littoral. President Reagan's military interven-tion thus confirmed President Carter's assertion that the Gulf was of vital interest to the United States and that the United States was prepared to use military force in pursuit of that interest. Although the Carter Doctrine addressed the prospective threat from the Soviet Union, its first major implementation involved a regional state, anticipating the massive international coalition that repelled Iraq's occupation of Kuwait in January 1991.

FROM WAR TO WAR

United Nations (UN) Security Council Resolution 598 was passed unanimously by the Security Council on July 20, 1987, calling for an immediate cease-fire be-tween Iran and Iraq. This set off a full year of acrimonious debate, punctuated by sporadic missile bombardments of cities and further attacks on oil tankers.[12] A new element in this escalation of the war was the expanded use of chemical weapons by Iraq against civilian targets. Iraq had used poison gas extensively in earlier cam-paigns, but the targets had been Iranian military forces. On the evening of March 16, 1988, Iraq conducted two bombing raids against the village of Halabjah, which Iranian forces were about to enter. The bombs caught the local Iraqi Kurdish vil-lagers in their homes and in the street, killing at least 2,000 civilians. The UN dis-patched an investigating team that confirmed the atrocity. But Iraq was unrepentant. Foreign Minister Tariq 'Aziz wrote to the UN secretary-general that "in their legitimate, moral, and internationally approved self-defense, our people are determined to use all available abilities and means against the criminal in-vaders."[13] In fact, in the succeeding months, Iraq used poison gas more frequently and against a wider range of targets, including civilians, than at any previous time in the war. The UN Security Council passed Resolution 612 on May 9, 1988, man-dating an immediate end to the use of chemical weapons in the war and holding out the prospect of sanctions against violators, but it had no effect.

During this same period, the Soviet Union announced its intention to withdraw its military forces from Afghanistan by the end of 1988. This resulted in the signing of an accord between Afghanistan and Pakistan on April 14 in Geneva, with the United States and the Soviet Union as co-guarantors.

Throughout this period, political cohesion in Iran was breaking down, and the continued use of mines in the Gulf set off a new round of clashes with US forces.[14] Iraq went on the offensive against Iran's disorganized and disheartened military forces, recapturing the Fao Peninsula in a lightning attack on April 18, then proceeding to push back Iranian forces all along the front. In mid-May, apparently with assistance from Saudi Arabia, Iraq carried out a devastating attack on the Iranian oil transfer site at Larak Island in the southern Gulf, destroying five ships, including the world's largest supertanker.[15] Antiwar sentiment began to appear openly in demonstrations in major Iranian cities. And most disturbing of all for the divided leadership, persuasive evidence began to accumulate that Khomeini was severely ill and virtually incapacitated.

On July 3, a commercial Iranian aircraft was shot down by the USS *Vincennes*, killing all 290 passengers and crew. This terrible accident, coming at the end of a seemingly endless series of defeats, underscored the despair of Iran's position. On July 18, the Iranian foreign minister sent a letter to the UN secretary-general formally accepting Resolution 598. Two days later, Khomeini sent a "message to the nation," read by an announcer, associating himself with the decision, which, he said, was "more deadly than taking poison."[16]

Iraq was taken by surprise and initially resisted accepting a cease-fire, while continuing its mopping-up operations. Iraq also continued to demonstrate a contemptuous disregard for the Security Council and for world opinion on the use of chemical weapons. A UN investigative team presented its report to the Security Council on August 1, finding that "chemical weapons continue to be used on an intensive scale" by Iraq. Only hours later, Iraq launched a massive chemical bombing attack on the Iranian town of Oshnoviyeh. However, as international pressure mounted, Saddam Hussein finally agreed to accept a cease-fire on August 6. A UN observer force was rushed to the region, and a cease-fire went into effect on August 20, 1988.

The end of the war provided an opportunity for the George H. W. Bush administration to reconsider its support for Saddam Hussein in the wake of revelations about Iraq's use of chemical weapons against its own population, the genocidal Anfal campaign against the Kurds, and Iraq's efforts to develop nuclear weapons and other weapons of mass destruction. The policy of limited cooperation with Iraq, however, remained intact. This policy became an embarrassment after the defeat of Iraq in the 1991 Gulf War, when claims were leveled that the US government had chosen to ignore warnings that agricultural credits might have been diverted to the purchase of military equipment. The most sensational charges of criminal responsibility were never substantiated, and the so-called Iraqgate scandal faded after the 1992 US presidential elections. However, documents made available to the Congress and the media did demonstrate persuasively that the Bush administration had pursued a largely uncritical policy toward Iraq during the period between the end of the Iran-Iraq war and the Iraqi invasion of Kuwait.[17]

At a minimum, this policy of tolerance and inattentiveness may have contributed to a false sense of security on the part of Saddam Hussein as he prepared to invade his neighbor to the south. The US ambassador to Baghdad, April Glaspie, was widely criticized for failing to warn Saddam Hussein about the possible consequences of an attack, but any fair-minded review of the record would reveal that she was accurately reflecting the policy of the president and secretary of state during this interwar period.[18]

THE SECOND GULF WAR

When Iraqi forces crossed the border into Kuwait at 1 a.m. on the morning of August 2, 1990, they set in motion a series of events that would transform US policy in the Persian Gulf. It marked a turning point in US relations with the Arab states of the Gulf, as pointed out by F. Gregory Gause III elsewhere in this volume. The cooperation between the United States and the Soviet Union on a matter of high strategy and military policy, which would have been unthinkable only a few years earlier, marked the undeniable end of the cold war.[19] The successful creation of a very large international coalition under the auspices of the UN and under the direct leadership of the United States aroused expectations for both the UN and peacekeeping, some of which was expressed in President George H. W. Bush's use of the phrase "a new world order" in relation to the Gulf intervention.[20]

The eventual use of missiles by Iraq against Israel underscored the relationship between the Arab-Israeli conflict and Gulf policy more clearly than at any time since the oil embargo of 1973. The immediate imposition of a draconian sanctions regime against Iraq, and its continuation over a period of many years, demonstrated both the extent and limitations of collective nonviolent coercion by the international community. The combined use of air power, lightning-fast ground mobility, and high-tech weapons—many for the first time in combat—in a computerized battlefield environment wrote a new chapter in the conduct of modern warfare and raised some troubling new questions.[21] The media, and especially television, brought these events into the world's living rooms with an intimacy and immediacy that may have been unprecedented in its universality.

Saddam Hussein's forces were ejected from Kuwait with minimal combat casualties.[22] On March 3, US General Norman Schwartzkopf met with an Iraqi military delegation at Safwan airfield in southern Iraq, and the Iraqis quickly agreed to allied terms. Almost immediately, revolts against Saddam Hussein's regime broke out among the Kurds in northern Iraq and among the Shi'a in southern Iraq. Initially President Bush declared that Iraq was violating the terms of the cease-fire by using military helicopters to put down the revolts. He reversed himself almost immediately, however, stating that "using helicopters like this to put down one's own people does not add to the stability of the area. . . . We are not in there trying to impose a solution inside Iraq."[23]

The distinction was critical. Over the following weeks, Iraqi forces brutally suppressed the uprisings and arguably preserved Saddam Hussein's position of power. The rationale for the change was spelled out two weeks later by White House spokesman Marlin Fitzwater, who noted, "There is no interest in the coalition in further military operations." Arab officials, he said, were advising Washington: "Let

Hussein deal with this, then the dust will settle and he's going to have to pay the piper for the war over Kuwait. Or at least that is what we are counting on."[24]

In an interview with David Frost, General Schwarzkopf said he was "suckered" by the Iraqis into agreeing to permit helicopters to fly, ostensibly to move top officials between cities, when they really intended to use helicopter gunships against the rebels.[25] Five years later, also in an interview with David Frost, George H. W. Bush commented on Saddam Hussein and the postwar situation: "I miscalculated. . . . I thought he'd be gone." With regard to the Safwan meeting, Bush noted, "I think he took us by surprise. . . . We might have handled the flying of helicopters differently. . . . So I think there's room for some ex post facto criticism here."[26]

Whatever the rationale, the US decision to permit Saddam Hussein to use advanced weaponry to suppress the internal revolts after the war made the United States an accessory after the fact to a massacre and ensured, whether inadvertently or not, that Saddam Hussein would retain power in Iraq. When the extent of the repression became known, and as Kurdish refugees began flooding across the border into Turkey, the United States, together with France and Great Britain, established so-called no-fly zones in the north and south. This gesture undoubtedly saved some lives and effectively prevented Saddam Hussein from reestablishing total control over the Kurdish territories. It was, however, much too late to save the many thousands of Iraqis who had spontaneously attacked the symbols of Ba'thist rule in the weeks after the allied victory.

THE CLINTON ADMINISTRATION AND DUAL CONTAINMENT[27]

On May 18, 1993, two months after President Clinton took office, Martin Indyk of the National Security Council staff spelled out the broad outlines of what he called America's "dual containment" policy in the Persian Gulf.[28] Traditionally, the United States had pursued a policy of balancing Iran and Iraq against each other as a means of maintaining a degree of regional stability and to protect the smaller oil-rich Arab states on the southern side of the Gulf. That was the purpose of the Twin Pillar policy, and it was implicit in subsequent tilts toward Iraq and (briefly) Iran during the Iran-Iraq war. Indyk, however, proclaimed the policy bankrupt and rejected it "because we don't need to rely on one to balance the other." Iraq was boxed in by UN sanctions, Iran was nearly prostrate after the eight-year war with Iraq, and the United States was the predominant power in the Persian Gulf with the "means to counter both the Iraqi and Iranian regimes."[29]

Iraq

The objective of the policy with regard to Iraq was to sustain the coalition that had defeated the armies of Saddam Hussein in Operation Desert Storm and to ensure that Iraq complied with all United Nations resolutions. The United States characterized the existing regime in Iraq as criminal and irredeemable and favored maintaining the sanctions until Saddam Hussein was gone.[30] This position created difficulties with other members of the UN Security Council, since Article 22 of the enabling Resolution 687 specified that the sanctions would be lifted once Iraq had eliminated and accounted for all of its weapons of mass destruction.

In the years after the adoption of the policy, the United States reportedly budgeted approximately $15 million per year for covert actions to destabilize the Saddam Hussein regime and for support of various Iraqi opposition groups.[31] The US Central Intelligence Agency attempted to organize several operations to depose Saddam Hussein, including a major covert action just before the Clinton administration took office and at least two others in 1995 and 1996.[32] These operations were unsuccessful.

There was very little debate in the United States about the desirability—even the necessity—of maintaining strict sanctions against the government of Saddam Hussein. The substantial American consensus in favor of severe sanctions could be attributed in large measure to the Iraqi leader himself. The nature of his attack on Kuwait, the looting and killing and burning that followed, his ruthless suppression of dissent, his near-genocidal tactics against his own people, the discovery that he was much closer to having nuclear and chemical weapons than had been supposed, his systematic obstruction of UN investigations including physical interference and mass falsification of documents, and his continued military forays and threats whenever he believed he could get away with it—all of these firmly implanted an image of utter evil and constant threat. That image underscored and reinforced US insistence on what was the most elaborate network of sanctions ever imposed on a member state of the UN.

There was, however, considerable sympathy in the United States for the plight of the people of Iraq, who bore the worst of the brunt of two wars and stringent economic sanctions. This popular concern was no doubt a factor in the US decision to acquiesce in the limited sale of Iraqi oil under terms negotiated by the UN in 1996.[33] The United States insisted, however, that the misery of the Iraqi people was directly attributable to Saddam Hussein, who callously used the deprivation of his own people as a bargaining chip.[34]

In June 1993 and in September 1996, the United States launched cruise missiles against targets in Iraq. The first case was retaliation for evidence of an Iraqi plot to assassinate former President George H. W. Bush in Kuwait. The second was in retaliation for Iraqi ground force incursions in northern Iraq in cooperation with the Kurdish Democratic Party.[35] On several occasions, the United States surged military forces into the region in response to Iraqi threats or failure to comply with UN Special Commission (UNSCOM) inspections. In February 1998, the United States appeared to be poised for a massive strike against Iraq, when it refused to permit inspection of presidential sites. That crisis was resolved only when the UN secretary-general, Kofi Annan, went to Baghdad and negotiated a memorandum of understanding with the Iraqi president.[36]

The bottom line, however, was that the United States, with significant help from a number of friends, allies, and the UN Security Council, was generally successful in keeping Saddam Hussein in what Secretary of State Madeleine Albright called a "strategic box." By mid-1998, this policy was losing support from the Arab states, which felt that the Iraqi people were being unfairly punished for the misbehavior of their rulers, and from states such as Russia, France, and China that had major political and financial interests in Iraq. The international consensus was preserved, however, primarily because of the unrelenting intransigence and belligerence of the Iraqi leader.

Iran

The other target of dual containment, Iran, posed a very different set of problems. The dual containment policy called for Iran to (1) cease its support of international terrorism and subversion, (2) end its violent opposition to the Arab-Israeli peace talks, and (3) halt efforts to acquire weapons of mass destruction. President Bush had made a hopeful reference to Iran in his Inaugural Address in January 1989, saying, "Goodwill begets goodwill. Good faith can be a spiral that endlessly moves on."[37] However, there was no talk of goodwill by the Clinton administration. Instead, US officials developed a special vocabulary in which Iran was routinely branded as a "rogue," "terrorist," "outlaw," or "backlash" state. This relentless drumfire of attacks—the mirror image of Iranian depictions of the United States as the "Great Satan"—had its effects in the media, in the Congress, in the public, and in the attitudes of lower-level bureaucrats. With a Democrat in the White House and the Republicans in control of the Congress, a domestic political contest developed over which party could be most vigorous in promoting US policies to deal with Iran.

The debate was galvanized in 1995 when the US oil company Conoco announced that it had signed a $1 billion contract with Iran to develop the Sirri gas field in the Persian Gulf. Although perfectly legal, the prospect that this deal would breach the wall of containment around Iran generated such a wave of outrage that the company was forced to renounce it. The Congress and the American-Israel Public Affairs Committee (AIPAC) began preparing legislation that would end all trade with Iran and punish any corporations that engaged in investments there. President Clinton, who was preparing for his reelection campaign, quickly preempted this by issuing two executive orders that made it illegal for American oil companies to operate in Iran and established penalties for any US citizen or corporation doing business with Iran.[38] Both decisions were announced by senior administration officials before major Jewish organizations. The US business community, apparently intimidated by the public outcry, remained silent on the matter.[39]

This process was replayed in presidential election year 1996. The Congress prepared a bill that would impose sanctions on any foreign corporation that invested $20 million or more in the Iranian oil and gas sector. Libya was later added on the floor of the Senate, and the bill became known as the Iran-Libya Sanctions Act (ILSA). Although the bill was certain to create serious problems with America's allies, the Congress saw ILSA as an opportunity to take a public stand against terrorism. The bill passed 415-0 and was signed into law by President Clinton.

In May 1997, Seyyed Mohammed Khatami was elected to a four-year term as president of Iran in a stunning electoral surprise. He conducted a grassroots campaign on the issues of rule of law, civil society, and dialogue among competing ideologies. His campaign struck a resonant chord with the Iranian population, particularly among women and the burgeoning population of young people, many of whom had no memory of the ancient regime. Paired against the well-known speaker of the Majlis (parliament), who represented revolutionary orthodoxy, Khatami attracted the largest number of voters in Iranian history and won a decisive victory with 69 percent of the vote. He carried all of the urban centers in Iran and virtually every province. In August, his reformist cabinet was accepted without exception by the Majlis.

Although Khatami was widely regarded as a candidate of domestic issues, it was his foreign policy moves that attracted the most attention during the first year of his term. In December 1997, Iran played host to the Organization of the Islamic Conference, where it won plaudits for its conciliatory positions and moderation. Iran called for closer cooperation with the UN, an institution it had shunned as a Western tool after the revolution. Iran began a concerted effort to improve its relations with Saudi Arabia and its other Arab neighbors in the Persian Gulf region, with some substantial initial success.

In January 1998, Khatami made an unprecedented "Address to the American People" in the form of an interview on CNN.[40] He praised the achievements of American civilization, went as far as an Iranian politician could go in expressing regret for the hostage crisis, and spelled out very clearly Iran's positions on all of the major issues of concern to the United States.

> On terrorism: "Any form of killing of innocent men and women who are not involved in confrontations is terrorism. It must be condemned, and we, in our turn, condemn every form of it in the world."
>
> On the peace process: "We have declared our opposition to the Middle East peace process, because we believe it will not succeed. At the same time, we have clearly said that we don't intend to impose our views on others or to stand in their way."
>
> On weapons of mass destruction: "We are not a nuclear power and do not intend to become one."

Washington responded to the Khatami initiative cautiously but generally positively.[41] The United States toned down its rhetoric and took some small steps to improve relations. But problems remained. Less than sixty days after Khatami took office, the French oil company Total, together with state-owned partners Gazprom of Russia and Petronas of Malaysia, concluded a $2 billion deal to develop an Iranian gas field. These negotiations, which had been under way since Conoco withdrew in 1995, placed Total and its partners in apparent violation of ILSA, which mandated US sanctions against any company investing more than $20 million in the Iranian oil and gas sector.[42]

In May 1998, the United States announced that it would waive the provisions of ILSA on grounds of national security. That decision was due almost entirely to pressure from America's European allies, but it was nevertheless received positively in Tehran.[43] The United States also announced a major redeployment of its Persian Gulf forces, sharply reducing the number of ships and aircraft permanently stationed in the region. This was due primarily to cost factors and personnel pressures, but again it was received positively by Tehran. There was growing awareness among Washington strategists that the initial assumption that the United States alone could confront both Iran and Iraq may have been exaggerated. At a minimum, as the threat from Iran appeared to be declining, the United States could ill afford to deliberately cultivate enemies.

On June 17, 1998, Secretary of State Albright delivered a major speech that responded almost point by point to the issues that Khatami had addressed in his interview six months earlier.[44] The speech was notable for its conciliatory tone and for the absence of the rhetoric that had characterized US statements about Iran over the previous five years. The speech offered no specific new policies or initiatives, but it held out the prospect for a new beginning:

> We are ready to explore further ways to build mutual confidence and avoid misunderstandings. The Islamic Republic should consider parallel steps. If such a process can be initiated and sustained in a way that addresses the concerns of both sides, then we in the United States can see the prospect of a very different relationship. As the wall of mistrust comes down, we can develop with the Islamic Republic, when it is ready, a road map leading to normal relations. Obviously, two decades of mistrust cannot be erased overnight. The gap between us remains wide. But it is time to test the possibilities for bridging this gap.[45]

CONCLUSION

By the end of the twentieth century, the United States had become a Persian Gulf power in its own right. Its political, military, and economic footprint in the region was greater even than the governments of the region themselves. Its role as security guarantor was not in doubt, and its prestige and influence were at their zenith.

Less clear was what the future might hold, and how the United States might choose to exercise its power in its new role as the sole superpower. History provided no reliable guidance. For more than a half century, the United States experimented, often clumsily, with stratagems of all sorts in a variety of circumstances. In the end, as in the cold war, its interests were preserved, and it emerged as the dominant power. The challenge for the future would be to blend military power with diplomacy in a region that could no longer be sequestered from the broader issues of the Middle East, international politics, and the global economy.

Notes

1. These early contacts led to a treaty with the sultanate of Muscat and Oman in 1833, which is still recalled on occasions of state with Oman.

2. The following comments draw on the author's article "The Evolution of US Strategy Toward the Indian Ocean and Persian Gulf Regions," in *The Great Game: Rivalry in the Persian Gulf and South Asia,* ed. Alvin Z. Rubinstein (New York: Praeger, 1983), pp. 49–80.

3. For a more detailed account of this period, see Michael A. Palmer, *Guardians of the Gulf: The Growth of American Involvement in the Persian Gulf, 1833–1991* (New York: Free Press, 1992).

4. A detailed account of this episode and its implications can be found in Gary Sick, *All Fall Down: America's Tragic Encounter with Iran* (New York: Random House, 1985), pp. 14ff.

5. See Chapter 3 by Mark Gasiorowski in this volume.

6. For a more detailed account, see James A. Bill, *The Eagle and the Lion: The Tragedy of American-Iranian Relations* (New Haven, Conn.: Yale University Press), 1988, pp. 204–208. Israel had a well-developed strategy, known as the Doctrine of the Periphery, to outflank its hostile Arab neighbors by promoting relations with non-Arab states on the fringes of the conflict. In the case of Iran, this took the form of a very close strategic relationship for more than twenty years.

7. Cited in J. C. Hurewitz, *The Persian Gulf After Iran's Revolution,* Foreign Policy Association Headline Series 244, April 1979, p. 22.

8. Former secretary of defense James Schlesinger drew attention to this fact in an article questioning whether the RDJTF was rapid, deployable, or even a force. See "Rapid(?) Deployment(?) Force(?)," *Washington Post,* September 24, 1980.

9. For a detailed examination of this episode, see Theodore Draper, *A Very Thin Line: The Iran-Contra Affair* (New York: Hill and Wang, 1991).

10. The casualty figures for the Iran-Iraq war are often exaggerated. Mohsen Rafiqdust, the former head of the Iranian Revolutionary Guard Force, told Robert Fisk of the *Independent* (June 25, 1995) that 220,000 Iranians were killed and 400,000 wounded during the Iran-Iraq war. That is roughly consistent with Iranian official statements and with independent Western estimates. Iraq has never published any figures on its losses, but Amatzia Baram, a specialist on Iraq at Haifa University, has estimated that 150,000 Iraqis were killed (*Jerusalem Quarterly* 49 [Winter 1989], pp. 85–86). If the standard ratio of two wounded for every man killed is applied, Iraq may have had 300,000 wounded. Thus, an informed estimate of total losses on both sides would equal approximately 370,000 killed and some 700,000 wounded, which is imprecise but plausible. In the case of Iraq, this casualty level is roughly comparable to US losses in the Civil War.

11. The substantial deployment of US forces to the Gulf was hastened—as was congressional approval—by the Iraqi missile attack on the USS *Stark* on May 17, 1987. Although the buildup was intended to counter Iran, the Iraqi attack galvanized public attention and underlined the threat to shipping in the Gulf.

12. Iraq was much better equipped than Iran, and it fired three to four missiles to every Iranian missile. The only confirmed use of poison gas was by Iraq—against Iranian troop formations and some civilian sites in Kurdish territory. For a more detailed examination of this armed negotiation, see Gary Sick, "Slouching Toward Settlement: The Internationalization of the Iran-Iraq War, 1987–88," in *Neither East Nor West: Iran, the Soviet Union, and the United States,* ed. Nikki Keddie and Mark Gasiorowski (New Haven, Conn.: Yale University Press, 1990), pp. 219–246.

13. Letter to the secretary-general of March 28 (*FBIS,* March 30, 1988).

14. One mine struck the USS *Samuel B. Roberts,* and on April 18, 1988, US forces hit two Iranian oil platforms, Nasr (near Sirri Island) and Salman (in the joint Iran-Oman Lavan field), cutting Iran's oil production by some 50,000 barrels per day. In the same action, two Iranian frigates were sunk, another was severely damaged, and four gunboats were damaged or sunk. In 1996, Iran brought a suit against the United States in the International Court of Justice seeking compensation for the loss of the oil platforms on the grounds that the attacks were a violation of international law and contrary to the terms of existing US-Iranian agreements.

15. The bitter dispute between Iran and Saudi Arabia over Iran's participation in the annual *hajj* deepened the distrust between these two states. Saudi Arabia stepped up its direct support for Iraq, apparently permitting Iraqi aircraft to utilize Saudi air-fields during raids on Iranian oil facilities in the southern Gulf. On April 26, 1988, Saudi Arabia broke diplomatic relations with Iran.

16. *FBIS,* July 21, 1988. On July 25, Khomeini made a six-minute appearance on television from the balcony of his residence. He appeared extremely frail and did not speak.

17. For example, see Murray Waas and Douglas Frantz, "US Gave Data to Iraq Three Months Before Invasion; Persian Gulf: Documents Show Intelligence Sharing with Baghdad Lasted Longer Than Previously Indicated," *Los Angeles Times,* March 10, 1992, p. 1 (one of a series of investigative reports). See also "News Conference, Rep. Jack Brooks (D–TX), Rep. Charles Schumer (D–NY): Special Prosecutor Criminal Dealings with Iraq Prior to Iraqi Invasion of Kuwait," *Federal News Service,* July 9, 1992.

18. A verbatim text of Glaspie's meeting with Saddam Hussein on July 25, 1990, was later released by the Iraqi government and was published by the *New York Times* on September 23, 1990, p. 19. Glaspie, in testimony before the Senate Foreign Rela-tions Committee on March 20, 1991, characterized the transcript as about 80 percent accurate, but with some key passages edited out.

19. See Chapter 15 by Robert O. Freedman and Chapter 9 by Georgiy Mirsky in this volume.

20. Speech by President Bush from the Oval Office, January 16, 1991, two hours after the bombing campaign against Iraqi positions had begun.

21. See, for example, "Needless Deaths in the Gulf War: Civilian Casualties During the Air Campaign and Violations of the Laws of War," *Middle East Watch Report,* Human Rights Watch, New York, November 1991.

22. According to official counts, allied deaths were 146 Americans (35 by friendly fire), 24 British (9 by American fire), 2 Frenchmen, 1 Italian, and 39 among various Arab allies. Baghdad has never given an official count of its casualties, but postwar analyses concluded that Iraq's uniformed losses were far smaller than previously esti-mated, perhaps as low as 1,500 deaths. Estimates of civilian casualties were uncertain and varied greatly from one observer to another. See John G. Heidenrich, "The Gulf War: How Many Iraqis Died?" *Foreign Policy* 90 (Spring 1993), pp. 108–125. The As-sociated Press on March 9, 1993, provided an overview of the various estimates.

23. *New York Times,* March 15, 1991, p. 13.

24. *New York Times,* March 27, 1991, pp. 1, 9.

25. *New York Times,* March 28, 1991, pp. 1, 18.

26. *Dow Jones News,* January 15, 1996.

27. The following analysis draws extensively on the author's article "Rethinking Dual Containment," *Survival: The IISS Quarterly* 40, no. 1 (Spring 1998), pp. 5–32.

28. Martin Indyk, "The Clinton Administration's Approach to the Middle East," Keynote Address to the Soref Symposium on "Challenges to US Interests in the Middle East: Obstacles and Opportunities," *Proceedings of the Washington Institute for Near East Policy,* May 18–19, 1993, pp. 1–8. Martin Indyk at the time of this speech had just joined the National Security Council staff. He later became the US ambassador to Israel and then assistant secretary of state for Near East affairs.

29. Indyk, "The Clinton Administration's Approach to the Middle East," p. 4.

30. See, for example, the remarks by Secretary of State Madeleine K. Albright at Georgetown University, Washington, DC, March 26, 1997, as released by the Office of the Spokesman, US Department of State.

31. Elaine Sciolino, "CIA Asks Congress for Money to Rein in Iraq and Iran," *New York Times,* April 12, 1995, p. 1.

32. All of these operations were publicly confirmed after the event by former senior officials of the US government. See Don Oberdorfer, "US Had Covert Plan to Oust Iraq's Saddam, Bush Adviser Asserts; Effort to Remove Leader Came 'Pretty Close,'" *Washington Post,* January 20, 1993, p. 1; and ABC News, "Unfinished Business—the CIA and Saddam Hussein," transcript no. 97062601-j13, June 26, 1997. There have also been detailed reports in the *Los Angeles Times, New York Times,* and other media.

33. Initially, Iraq was permitted to sell up to $2 billion of oil in two 90-day periods after each authorization. The first sales began on December 10, 1995. In 1998, the terms were extended to permit total sales of $4.5 billion—more than the Iraqis were physically capable of producing, given the low price of oil at the time. The sales contracts were monitored closely by the UN, and the proceeds were allotted to humanitarian relief and repayment of claims from the war and to cover UN expenses in Iraq.

34. United Nations Special Commissioner Rolf Ekeus estimated that Iraq deliberately deprived itself of more than $100 billion in revenues by refusing to cooperate with UN weapons inspections. See "For the Record," *Washington Post,* January 31, 1997.

35. This attack was particularly controversial since the targets were in the south and unrelated to the ground attack in the north.

36. See "Memorandum of Understanding Between the United Nations and the Republic of Iraq," Associated Press, February 24, 1998.

37. See the text of the Inaugural Address in the *New York Times,* January 21, 1989, p. 10. Iran welcomed this remark and responded by helping to free the US hostages in Lebanon. It is a sore point with Iran that this gesture, in their view, was never reciprocated by the United States.

38. See Executive Order 12957 of March 15, 1995, and Executive Order 12959 of May 6, 1995.

39. For a detailed analysis of the politics associated with the developments of Iranian sanctions, see Laurie Lande, "Second Thoughts," *International Economy,* May-June 1997, pp. 44–49.

40. The transcript of this interview with Iranian President Mohammed Khatami was posted on the CNN website immediately after it was aired on January 7, 1998. Large portions of the text were published in a number of newspapers the following day.

41. Even before the Khatami election, many senior policy observers and former US officials were calling for changes in the dual containment strategy. These voices included two former national security advisers, a former secretary of defense, three former assistant secretaries of state for Near East affairs, and the former commander of US forces in the Persian Gulf, among others.

42. The trigger level had been reduced automatically from $40 million to $20 million on the first anniversary of the legislation in August 1997.

43. The European Union threatened to take the case to the World Trade Organization if the United States imposed sanctions on the French company, on grounds that the US policy was in violation of international trade agreements.

44. Secretary of State Madeleine K. Albright, Remarks at 1998 Asia Society Dinner, Waldorf-Astoria Hotel, New York, New York, June 17, 1998, as released by the Office of the Spokesman, June 18, 1998, US Department of State.

45. Ibid.

CHAPTER 18

FROM "OVER THE HORIZON" TO "INTO THE BACKYARD"

The US-Saudi Relationship in the Gulf

F. Gregory Gause III

The 1990–1991 Gulf crisis and war, prompted when Saddam Hussein invaded Kuwait on August 2, 1990, represented a turning point in the close but complicated relationship between the Kingdom of Saudi Arabia and the United States. Although the Saudis had relied on US security guarantees as an essential element of their defense policy since the 1940s, they had, at least since the 1960s, preferred to play down the military aspect of US-Saudi relations to their own public and to regional audiences in the larger Arab and Muslim worlds. And though the rulers of the kingdom did call on US military assistance in times of crisis previous to the Iraqi invasion of Kuwait, it was largely limited to air and naval forces. Never before had US ground troops in such numbers been stationed in the kingdom. Never before had the Saudi regime confronted such a stark choice in terms of declaring its ultimate reliance on the United States for its security.

This chapter sets out the essential security dilemma faced by the Saudis, explaining why the regime must rely on outside power protectors when faced with a direct threat from larger regional neighbors, despite the problems such a choice poses. It then briefly reviews the history of the US-Saudi security relationship, highlighting the tensions Riyadh has experienced in trying to maintain its defense links to Washington while asserting, for domestic and regional audiences, its independence from the United States. The background of the Saudi decision to invite

US and other forces into the kingdom after Saddam Hussein's invasion of Kuwait is examined, along with developments in the US-Saudi relationship since the Gulf War, including the fallout for bilateral relations, the 9/11 attacks, and the Iraq war.[1]

THE SAUDI DEFENSE DILEMMA

The Saudi defense policy dilemma is the direct product of the country's oil wealth and the political strategy the regime has chosen for using that wealth. Oil makes the kingdom important to the rest of the world, but oil wealth also increases its vulnerability in a number of important ways. Most obviously, it makes Saudi Arabia a potential target for larger ambitious neighbors, as the Iraqi invasion of Kuwait clearly demonstrated. On a deeper and less obvious level, the characteristics that oil wealth has brought to domestic politics exacerbate Saudi security problems. The Saudi regime's ability to mobilize its population for defense is limited by the ethos of the particular type of rentier state the kingdom has become. State demands on citizens, such as military service, are avoided to circumvent demands from citizens to have a say in state policy. The size of the Saudi population, small relative to potentially threatening neighbors, complicates defense planning, as well as the inability to fully utilize existing human resources.

A strategy of self-reliance in defense and security is both inadequate and politically troublesome for Saudi Arabia. The inadequacy of self-reliance is to some extent a simple matter of numbers. According to the 1992 census, the Saudi population was 16.9 million, of which 12.3 million were citizens.[2] Since then, the citizen population (not including foreign workers) has increased to almost 19 million. Iran's population is more than 70 million. But numbers are not the whole story. The Saudi citizen population is not that much smaller than Iraq's. The combined population of the members of the Gulf Cooperation Council (GCC) is very close to that of Iraq. Despite the demographics, no one in 1990 suggested that the Saudis by themselves or with their GCC allies could confront the Iraqi invasion of Kuwait.

Furthermore, the political context of the states renders a policy of self-reliance even less feasible than the numbers suggest. Mobilizing citizen manpower into the armed forces would require obligatory military service, a state demand on its citizens that the United States, for example, has chosen to avoid. A ruthless and efficient authoritarian state like Saddam's Iraq or Asad's Syria can extract a large proportion of its manpower from society for military purposes. States animated by revolutionary fervor, like Iran in the 1980s, or by democratic ties of loyalty between citizen and state, like Israel (for its Jewish citizens), can call on the population for military service and receive an enthusiastic response. Saudi Arabia (and the other Gulf monarchies) lacks these kinds of mobilization abilities.

This is attributable to the type of rentier state the Saudis have chosen to build with their oil money. The Saudi social contract as it has developed since the early 1970s, if not before, rests on the state providing benefits *to* citizens, not extracting resources (taxes and service) *from* them. Instituting a national service requirement would upset that implicit deal between state and society. In the West, the need to mobilize citizen armies contributed to pressures for popular participation in government. The ruling families in the Gulf want to avoid exacerbating the already growing demands in their societies for greater participation. Moreover, from the perspective of rulers who remember the Arab military coups in the 1950s and 1960s, recruiting into the armed forces people whose loyalties to the regime are questionable would decrease rather than increase security.

Military recruitment strategies in the kingdom reflect these social realities. There is no military draft in Saudi Arabia; military service is voluntary. Discussions in official Saudi circles immediately after the Gulf War about doubling the size of the armed forces, which would probably have entailed some kind of draft or obligatory service, were shelved.[3] Military service is not among the top professions in the country in terms of social status. With economic opportunities relatively plentiful for young, better-educated male citizens who are competent and ambitious, the incentives to join the military are limited.

Moreover, there are official and unofficial barriers to military recruitment of some groups within the kingdom. Saudi Shi'a (who make up approximately 10 percent of the Saudi citizen population) rarely join the military and even more rarely advance in the officer corps, a result of government discouragement and social custom within the community.[4] There are persistent reports, unconfirmed and unconfirmable officially, that those who do not hail from Najd (Central Arabia) cannot advance in the military hierarchy and are barred from certain sensitive positions (e.g., fighter pilot). Needless to say, fully half of Saudi Arabia's human resources—female citizens—are not available for military service. Taken together, these factors mean that the kingdom cannot and will not mobilize human resources for military purposes with the same efficiency as larger (or even some smaller) neighbors. Demographic, social, and political constraints combine to rule out a policy of self-reliance in security matters.

A simple comparison of Saudi Arabia to other regional powers as to the size of armed forces relative to population points out the barriers to military mobilization. In 1990, the last time Saudi Arabia was involved in an international war, the Saudi armed forces, including active-duty National Guard forces, totaled 111,500. Iraq, with less than double the Saudi citizen population, had a military establishment at least five times as large in 1990. Syria, with roughly the same population (only 2 million greater), had a standing armed force of over 400,000 in 1991. Jordan, with less than half of the Saudi citizen population, had an active force of 101,000 in 1991, nearly the same size as the Saudi forces. Israel, also with less than half of the Saudi citizen population, had a standing force of 141,000 and a reserve force of over 500,000 in 1991.[5]

The political and demographic barriers to full utilization of the military manpower resources in the kingdom, combined with the number of potential military threats in the region, dictate that the Saudis seek outside allies. It is logical, in such a situation, that a small state should seek the most powerful ally it can find in order to deter potential enemies—and win a fight, if necessary. Thus the US-Saudi security relationship makes much sense for Riyadh. But because the nature of the security threats facing the Saudi regime are not limited to military invasion by a larger neighbor, its relationship with the United States becomes more complicated.

The lack of firm, institutionalized political links between the Saudi regime and its society opens up a new set of threats in the foreign policy sphere. It is not just military attack that the Saudi regime worries about; it also fears *political* intervention originating from abroad, based on the powerful transnational ideological platforms of pan-Arabism and Islam, aimed at stirring up its own domestic populations against it. A succession of ambitious regional figures have used propaganda and subversion, as well as military pressure, against the kingdom: Gamal 'Abd al-Nasser of Egypt in the 1950s and 1960s, Ayatollah Khomeini in the 1980s, and Saddam Hussein in 1990–1991. In the 2000s a Saudi citizen, Osama bin Laden, tried to rally support against the regime from abroad and encouraged al-Qa'ida sympathizers in the country to attack it. None of these challengers succeeded in bringing down the Saudi regime, but they all left their mark on the minds of rulers. The irony is that, having built substantial bureaucratic and coercive infrastructures, the Saudi regime is less susceptible today to this kind of foreign ideological pressure and domestic subversion than it may have been in the past. Citizens' interests are much more focused on domestic agendas rather than on glorious but impractical transnational agendas. But it is difficult for the rulers to appreciate this change when little, if any, citizen input into the foreign policy decision-making process is tolerated.

Close ties with the United States open up the Saudi regime to attacks by regional enemies. Charges that the rulers have forfeited the country's independence in exchange for US protection have been staples of Arab propaganda since the 1950s and Iranian propaganda since the revolution in 1979. Such charges are aimed at encouraging the Saudi population to oppose the regime and shake its stability domestically. As will be considered below, the US connection in the military sphere is disquieting to at least some part of the Saudi public, so these kinds of charges are seen by the Saudi rulers as having some potential to create domestic problems for them. This is the Saudi dilemma when it comes to relations with the United States: Military security rationales require the US link, while domestic security imperatives require that the link be as unobtrusive as possible. Walking this tightrope has not been an easy task for the Saudis.

THE BACKGROUND TO THE US–SAUDI SECURITY RELATIONSHIP

US interests in Saudi Arabia began in 1933, when King 'Abd al-'Aziz granted an oil concession to Standard Oil of California (SOCAL). Although SOCAL gave the king better terms than he could expect from British Petroleum, then awash with oil from Iran and Iraq, there was also a strategic element in the Saudi decision to grant the concession to a US company. Britain was the patron of the Hashemite regimes in Jordan and Iraq, rivals of the Al Sa'ud whom 'Abd al-'Aziz had ejected from Hijaz less than a decade previously. Britain was also the protecting power of the smaller Gulf and South Arabian states and directly ruled Aden. With the exception of Yemen, Saudi Arabia was surrounded in the 1930s by British power. And though 'Abd al-'Aziz was careful to maintain friendly relations with London (risking civil war in the late 1920s to stop raids by his fanatical Wahhabi followers, the Ikhwan, into Iraq and Transjordan), he also sought support from other outside powers to balance British influence. Thus his desire for some political connection to the United States is understandable.

Washington initially hesitated to respond to Saudi political overtures. It was not until World War II that US policymakers began to perceive strategic interests in the Gulf area. Even then, the region was viewed largely as a British preserve in the global division of influence between Washington and London. In 1942 and 1943, the United States supplied lend-lease financial aid to the kingdom, whose two main sources of revenue—oil production and pilgrimage traffic—had been severely curtailed by the war; it did so not directly but through Great Britain. It was only in 1944 that US aid began to go directly to Riyadh, in exchange for the rights to use the large air base at Dhahran. The historic meeting of King 'Abd al-'Aziz and President Franklin Roosevelt on the latter's yacht in the Great Bitter Lake of the Suez Canal in 1945 was the first direct contact between leaders of the two countries.

Despite this new channel, the United States continued in the late 1940s to resist Saudi requests for a direct military alliance, which the Saudis wanted to counter the British-backed Hashemites. Although the United States sent numerous messages to Riyadh supporting the independence and the territorial integrity of the kingdom, a formal alliance was ruled out. The most the United States was willing to offer in terms of a military relationship was to supply some equipment and dispatch a training mission in 1951, in exchange for a five-year extension of the Dhahran base rights.[6]

Even though the United States was reluctant to make a formal alliance commitment to Saudi security at this time, Washington was hardly indifferent to the kingdom. The importance of oil as a strategic commodity was underlined by the World War II experience, and US economic and military planners began to see the Gulf as a centrally important area in overall US strategy. Although the ambitious plans of Harold Ickes, which would have essentially nationalized US oil interests in the kingdom during the war, fell afoul of congressional and oil company opposition, Washington sought to cement its economic relationship with Riyadh after the war by encouraging the US oil consortium that formed the Arabian-American Oil Company (ARAMCO) to provide more financial support to the Saudi regime. By granting the oil companies the right to deduct from their US taxes the increased share of oil revenues they paid to the Saudis, Washington in effect subsidized the Saudi regime, allowing the oil companies to pay 50 percent of their oil revenues from the kingdom to Riyadh without affecting their bottom line. The fifty-fifty deal, originally implemented in Venezuela, was applied to Saudi Arabia in 1950.[7]

In the 1950s, the pattern of Saudi desire for a close US security relationship and US reticence to give formal defense commitments was reversed. US military supplies to the kingdom during the 1950s were substantial (though not in comparison to what would come later)—well over one hundred tanks of various types and thirty-seven aircraft.[8] King Sa'ud was the first Arab leader to be received in the White House after the announcement of the 1957 Eisenhower Doctrine, which was aimed at containing communism in the Middle East.[9] However, the costs to Saudi Arabia in terms of regional and domestic politics of the close relationship with the United States became more apparent as the 1960s approached. The fall of monarchical regimes in Egypt and Iraq, in part because of domestic reactions to their close associations with Britain and British bases in those countries, brought home to the Saudis that an outside power link was not an unmitigated blessing. The pressures that built up around the rise of Gamal 'Abd al-Nasser and his brand of Arab nationalism in regional politics made association with Western powers a domestic and regional liability.

Thus the Saudi dilemma became acute. Just as the US link became important for military security, its political ramifications became very negative. The Saudi regime walked the tightrope. Military purchases from the United States were essentially halted from 1958 to the mid-1960s, as identification with the United States became more dangerous and the regular army came to be seen as a threat to the domestic security of the regime. The lease on the US air base at Dhahran was allowed to expire in 1962 (its military usefulness to the United States for cold war purposes was much diminished with the advent of intercontinental and sea-launched ballistic missiles). However, when Egyptian air units in Yemen began to attack areas across the Saudi-Yemeni border in 1962, the Saudis requested that US fighter planes stationed at Dhahran fly demonstrative sorties over Saudi cities as a warning to Cairo.[10] In 1965 the US military supply relationship with Saudi Arabia was renewed with the supply of Hawk antiaircraft systems.

Events in the late 1960s combined to increase US military interest in Saudi Arabia and to lessen Saudi fears of the domestic and regional consequences of their US tie. The announced British intent to withdraw from relationships with the smaller Gulf monarchies increased the US strategic interest in the Gulf. Still mired in Vietnam, the United States had no intention of taking on new defense commitments in any formal way in the Gulf, but US strategy was aimed at encouraging Iran, and to a lesser extent Saudi Arabia, to build up military forces (with US weaponry) and act as regional proxies for US interests. With increasing oil revenues in the early 1970s (before the price shock of 1973), Saudi Arabia's weapons purchases from the United States increased from $15.8 million in 1970 to $312.4 million in 1972.[11] With Egypt's defeat in the 1967 Arab-Israeli war and the concomitant decline in importance of Nasserist pan-Arabism in the region, the political risks of association with the United States went down. Yet this is exactly the time Saudi Arabia chose to assert its independence from the United States, in a very risky manner—the oil embargo and oil price increases of 1973–1974. In the minds of many Saudis, risking confrontation with the United States over Arab-Israeli issues at that time was their country's finest hour.

This brief period of confrontation with the United States quickly ended. The fourfold increase in oil prices made Saudi Arabia that much more central to US policymakers and made the United States that much more important to Saudi Arabia economically, both as a consumer of oil and as a location for Saudi investments. The new oil wealth deepened the Saudi linkages to the United States. In the military sphere Riyadh directed the vast majority of its arms spending toward the United States. US training missions instructed Saudi forces in the new weaponry. The US Army Corps of Engineers undertook enormous building projects in the kingdom. As Saudi Arabia was now a more valuable prize, its need for an outside protector increased. In January 1979, as the Iranian revolution was unfolding, the Saudis requested a display of military support from the United States, which complied by sending a squadron of F-15s to the kingdom (though it was publicly announced that the planes would not be armed in order not to irritate the new Iranian government).[12] In October 1980, at the outbreak of the Iran-Iraq war, US AWACS (airborne warning and control system) aircraft were dispatched to the kingdom to strengthen its air defenses. Finally, with Iranian attacks on Saudi and Kuwaiti shipping growing in the 1980s, US naval forces were sent to the Gulf in 1987 to protect that shipping. Though the original request came from Kuwait, the US forces also escorted shipping bound for Saudi Arabia.

In the financial sphere, Saudi petrodollars were recycled through US (and British) banks, the Saudi government became a major purchaser of US Treasury bonds, and Saudi private wealth found investment opportunities in the United States. At an April 1993 meeting in Washington on US-Gulf business links, sponsored by the US Department of Commerce, the GCC, and the American-Gulf Chamber of Commerce, it was reported that direct Gulf investment in the United States totaled $407 billion as of the beginning of 1992.[13] As oil prices were (and still are) denominated in US dollars, the real return to Saudi Arabia of its oil sales depended on the strength of the US currency. The sinews binding the United States and the Saudi regime became stronger and more ramified as a result of the oil price increases of the 1970s.

Yet the dilemma for Saudi policymakers of the domestic and regional consequences of a close relationship, at least publicly, with the United States remained. Whereas Arab nationalist pressures might have declined in the region, the Islamic political resurgence, represented in part by the Iranian revolution, was equally hostile to a US military presence in the kingdom and equally able to address Saudi citizens over the head of their government. The Saudis refused to support the Camp David Accords, despite heavy US pressure to do so. When Reagan administration officials came calling in Riyadh at the beginning of 1981 to encourage Saudi Arabia to sign up for Secretary of State Alexander Haig's strategic consensus policy for the Middle East, with its emphasis on US military access to regional bases, the Saudis politely refused. The GCC, of which Saudi Arabia is the largest and most important member, in its first summit meeting in May 1981 declared member states' desire "for keeping the entire region free of international conflicts, particularly the presence of military fleets and foreign bases."[14] Even as the US Navy was escorting Saudi shipping in the Gulf in 1987–1988, the Saudis were very concerned to emphasize that US forces had no basing rights in the kingdom. For the Saudis, a US presence "over the horizon," close enough to come to the kingdom's aid but far away enough to avoid the political problems associated with the US connection, was the ideal situation.

This dilemma of needing the United States in the security sphere but fearing the domestic and regional consequences of public identification with the United States forms the backdrop to the Saudi decision to invite US and other foreign forces into the kingdom in early August 1990.

THE US-SAUDI RELATIONSHIP AND THE GULF WAR

The Saudi decision to invite hundreds of thousands of US troops, as well as other foreign units, to the kingdom was a major change in the nature of the US-Saudi relationship. It can only be understood in light of the existing relationship between Saudi Arabia and Iraq. Riyadh had supported the Iraqi war effort against Iran politically and financially. Since the end of that war in 1988, the Saudis had been unable to resume their preferred geopolitical position of rough equidistance between the two larger Gulf powers. Ideological differences with Iran remained a serious stumbling block. Although there was certainly no love in Riyadh for Saddam Hussein, there was a continuing belief that a strong Iraq was necessary to balance Iranian ambitions.

Thus Saudi Arabia's initial response when Iraq began to raise demands against Kuwait in the summer of 1990 was to seek a negotiated settlement that would give the Iraqis some tangible gains. The Saudis were noticeably silent when Baghdad threatened Kuwait on the issue of Kuwaiti oil production, in some measure because they themselves wanted to see Kuwait abide by its OPEC (Organization of Petroleum Exporting Countries) production quota. At the OPEC meeting of July 25–27, 1990, Kuwait agreed to cut its production to the quota level. When Iraq continued to pressure Kuwait, the Saudis and President Hosni Mubarak of Egypt joined in a mediation effort in late July that resulted in the Kuwaiti-Iraqi meeting of August 1 in the Saudi city of Jeddah, just one day before the invasion.

Circumstantial evidence indicates that although no detailed Saudi-Egyptian plan was put forward to the parties at Jeddah, the thrust behind their mediation effort was to extract some concessions from Kuwait to mollify Saddam. Mubarak revealed after the invasion that he had told the Kuwaitis that they should make an offer including border modifications and financial aid to Iraq.[15] Saudi decision makers have not been as revealing about their stance in those days, but there are indications that Riyadh had about the same idea. The Saudis had pressured Kuwait before the invasion to reduce their oil production to their OPEC quota, as Saddam had demanded.[16] Crown Prince Hassan of Jordan told an interviewer that on August 2, King Fahd had asked King Hussein of Jordan to get the Iraqis "to withdraw to the disputed area" on the border, not completely out of Kuwait.[17] Yemeni President 'Ali 'Abdallah Salih said that on August 5 King Fahd had told him that Kuwait had been mistaken in its hard-line policy toward Iraq.[18]

Comments by Saudi defense minister Prince Sultan ibn 'Abd al-'Aziz in late October 1990 also give some hint as to the Saudi stand. Prince Sultan, after assuring that Saudi Arabia would not accept any solution short of unconditional Iraqi withdrawal from Kuwait and the return of the Kuwaiti government, referred to the general Saudi position on how to settle inter-Arab problems. He said that "any Arab who has a right vis-à-vis his brother Arab must assert it, but not by means of using force. This is an undesirable thing." He indicated that Saudi Arabia "is among those who call for Arab national security, including brotherly concessions from Arab to Arab, whether such a right is established or more doubtful." He went on to say that "it is not a bad thing for any Arab country to give a brother Arab country land, or money, or access to the sea."[19] The Western press saw Sultan's remarks as a signal of Saudi willingness to compromise with Iraq.[20] However, given that the quote came directly after Sultan's direct refusal to accept anything but an unconditional Iraqi withdrawal from Kuwait, it might be more accurate to interpret his remarks as an indication of what Saudi policy was *before* the invasion, defending Saudi efforts at avoiding this crisis and indirectly criticizing the Kuwaitis for refusing to compromise.

The Saudis' sense of shock and betrayal at the Iraqi invasion reflected not only the unprecedented nature of the action but also the feeling that Saddam had reneged on a tentative agreement that the Saudis had constructed for his benefit.[21] Their perception of Saddam's ultimate intentions must have been colored by this very specific sense that the Iraqi leader could not be trusted to keep his commitments. Little else can explain the relatively quick decision by the Saudis to abandon their historical position regarding US ground forces. Although much has been made of the two-day delay in making this decision and of the hints of differences of opinion within the Saudi royal family over it, more striking is the ease with which the Saudis reversed their past aversion to an open US military presence in the kingdom and the lack of substantial opposition within the ruling elite to that policy. Even if some members of the royal family were unhappy with the decision, they did not make a public or even a quasi-public issue out of their objections. The religious establishment, which might also have been expected to oppose the deployment of US troops, officially approved the policy in a fatwa (religious judgment) by Shaykh 'Abdallah bin 'Abd al-'Aziz bin Baz, the senior cleric in the kingdom.[22]

Once they accepted the US military presence, the Saudis were in effect committed to the US strategy of confrontation with Saddam. Between mid-August 1990 and late February 1991 Saudi Arabia took a backseat to US political and military leaders in the crisis. During this period the regime used its propaganda organs, diplomatic weight, and financial clout to garner support within the Arab and Muslim worlds for its policy. Although attracting considerable political and some military support from other governments in the region, the regime's efforts to persuade

Arab and Muslim public opinions of the legitimacy of the decision met with much less success.

As the crisis proceeded, and particularly in the postcrisis period, some of the old reservations about a high-profile US military presence in the kingdom began to resurface. In late November 1990, King Fahd, in a speech to the country, denied that Saudi Arabia had made any agreements for the permanent stationing of foreign forces in the kingdom.[23] In a statement to the press immediately after the Gulf War, Saudi defense minister Prince Sultan referred to a US commitment to withdraw its forces from the kingdom once their mission was completed.[24] In September 1991, during one of the US confrontations with Iraq over application of the United Nations (UN) resolutions, Prince Sultan expressed misgivings about the very public way in which the United States was using Saudi Arabia as a military staging area against Iraq and urged Washington to spread its deployments out to Kuwait and even to capture an airfield in Iraq itself to use as a base.[25] During subsequent US-Iraqi confrontations in October 1994 and September 1996, Sultan reiterated his reluctance to allow the United States to use Saudi facilities to stage attacks on Iraq.[26] Saudi Arabia, unlike the smaller Gulf monarchies, did not negotiate a formal defense agreement with the United States in the wake of the war.[27]

The continuing worry in the Saudi regime about limiting to the greatest extent possible the public profile of its US military connection stems from fears about the domestic consequences of that connection. It is within Islamic political currents in the kingdom that disquiet about the role of the United States is greatest. During the crisis there were some limited indications of discontent within religious circles about the US military presence.[28] After the Gulf War, indications of unease from Islamic political circles over the new relationship between the kingdom and the United States emerged more clearly. In the spring of 1991, over four hundred religious officials and political activists addressed a petition to King Fahd regarding changes they wanted to see in the kingdom's policies. Although the bulk of the petition dealt with domestic issues, the signers also called on the government to avoid alliances that run counter to Islamic legitimacy and to acquire arms from a variety of sources, including the building of a domestic arms industry.[29] Both of these statements could be read as a warning about overreliance on the United States.

The clearest indication of opposition to the direction of US-Saudi relations came in a detailed, forty-six-page Memorandum of Advice directed to the king in the summer of 1992 and signed by more than one hundred Islamic political activists. The bulk of the memorandum, like the shorter petition mentioned above, dealt with domestic affairs. It did, however, clearly challenge the foreign policy lines set down by the kingdom in the wake of the Gulf War. It called for an end to the practice of giving loans and gifts to what it termed "un-Islamic" regimes like "Ba'thist Syria and secular Egypt," pointing to the folly of funding Saddam's Iraq during its war with Iran. It said that the Gulf crisis pointed out the "lack of correspondence between the enormous military budgets and the number and capabilities of the forces" and called for expanding the army to 500,000 men (an increase of at least 400 percent), obligatory military training, the diversification of foreign arms sources, and the building of a domestic arms industry. The signers criticized the government for not supporting Islamic movements but rather providing aid to states that "wage war" against such movements, like Algeria, and called for strengthening relations with all Islamic tendencies, be they states, political movements, or individuals.

The signers of the memorandum were very leery of the close relations the government had with Western regimes, "which led the assault against Islam," and particularly in "following the United States of America in most policies, relations and decisions, like the rushing into the peace process with the Jews." It urged the government to "avoid any kind of alliance or cooperation which serves imperialist goals" and to "cancel all military treaties and conventions which impinge on the sovereignty of the state and its independence in administering and arming its military." The memorandum was particularly scathing regarding the kingdom's reliance on arms supplies from the United States, a country that "gives us what it wants, denies us what it does not want us to have, exploits us in times of trouble, and bargains with us during times of calamity."[30]

In November 1995, a bomb destroyed the Riyadh office of the American training mission working with the Saudi National Guard. Five Americans and two Indian employees of the mission were killed. Four Saudis were arrested for the bombing and confessed on television to being members of the Islamic opposition. They were executed in May 1996.[31] Less than one month later, in June 1996, a car bomb exploded in front of an apartment building housing US Air Force personnel in Dhahran (in Saudi Arabia's Eastern Province). Nineteen Americans died and nearly four hundred Americans, Saudis, and others were wounded. The American personnel, most of whom helped maintain air reconnaissance of the no-fly zone in southern Iraq, were subsequently moved from Dhahran to an isolated desert air base south of Riyadh.[32]

These indications of domestic opposition to a high-profile US role in Saudi security plans should not obscure the fact that the US-Saudi security relationship after the Gulf War was extremely close. Between August 1990 and the end of 1992 Saudi Arabia placed weapons orders worth more than $25 billion with US arms manufacturers.[33] The centrality of Saudi arms purchases for US suppliers was made clear in the January 1994 agreement between Riyadh and five of the largest US military contractors, allowing the Saudis to stretch out payments for many of those weapons.[34] Falling oil prices and the depletion of financial reserves during Desert Storm placed fiscal constraints on the Saudi government in the 1990s, but it remained the most important foreign customer for US weapons manufacturers during that decade. Military consultations between the two countries continued at the highest levels.[35] The economic importance of the kingdom for the United States was underlined by the Saudi decision in February 1994 to buy $6 billion in commercial aircraft from US rather than European companies. President Bill Clinton personally lobbied Saudi leaders, including King Fahd, on the issue.[36]

CONCLUSION: THE POST–SEPTEMBER 11 RELATIONSHIP

Even after the experience of the Gulf War, the dilemma that characterizes Saudi relations with the United States remains. The need for a US security link is clear. Much of the reluctance to acknowledge that need before the Saudi public and the region has disappeared. Yet the Saudi leadership continues to feel at least somewhat constrained by important elements of domestic public opinion in codifying that relationship in an open military alliance or in formally and publicly permitting US military bases in the kingdom. This tension in US-Saudi relations predates the Gulf War and continues despite that extraordinary phase in the history of security ties between Washington and Riyadh. It is a permanent part of the relationship.

The permanence of this tension was underlined by the fallout for US-Saudi relations from the terrorist attacks on New York and Washington on September 11, 2001. The involvement of so many Saudis in that operation—Osama bin Laden, although stripped of his citizenship in 1994, comes from a prominent Saudi family, and fifteen of the nineteen hijackers were from the kingdom—led many in the United States to question Saudi political stability and reliability as an ally. The fact that bin Laden made his opposition to the US military presence in Saudi Arabia a centerpiece of his propaganda unnerved the Saudi rulers. They knew this issue resonated with their public. Thus, at a time when the United States expected full and open cooperation from all its allies, Saudi Arabia sought to put some public distance between itself and Washington, denying the United States use of Saudi bases for military strikes on Afghanistan.[37] Tensions rose as the media in both countries traded hostile barbs. The Iraq war of 2003 changed the strategic picture in the Gulf region, removing Washington's need to maintain substantial air force units in Saudi Arabia. In April 2003, the United States announced that it would withdraw the air force unit that had been stationed in the kingdom since the end of the Gulf War. By the end of 2010, only small American military training missions remained in Saudi Arabia.

Despite those tensions, substantial Saudi-US cooperation occurred in the aftermath of September 11, including Saudi permission for the United States to coordinate the air wars over both Afghanistan in 2001 and Iraq in 2003 from a command and control center in Saudi Arabia. American special forces were also permitted to use Saudi territory as a base for operations in Iraq, though the Saudi government kept this fact from its public. Both governments insisted that the bilateral relationship remained strong, and by 2010 there were numerous indications that the crisis in the relationship produced by the 9/11 attacks had passed. When al-Qa'ida began a campaign of attacks within Saudi Arabia itself in 2003, the two countries cooperated on intelligence and counterterrorism issues. By the mid-2000s, the tension that had developed in the immediate post-9/11 period had given way to intense interaction against a perceived common enemy.[38]

The changed regional security situation in the wake of the Iraq War also brought Saudi Arabia and the United States together. Both Washington and Riyadh became increasingly focused on the security threat posed by the growth of Iranian power in the region and by Iran's nuclear program. Their common perception of the Iranian threat provided a new incentive for military cooperation, ending what remained of the post-9/11 estrangement. In October 2010 the Obama administration formally notified Congress of plans for Saudi Arabia to buy as much as $60 billion worth of arms from American companies, including fighter jets, attack helicopters, missiles, and missile defense technologies. The package will tie the Saudi military to American arms supply and training for the next two decades.[39] Riyadh has been generally supportive of American diplomatic efforts to solve the Arab-Israeli conflict in recent years, as much to limit Iran's ability to exploit the issue in Arab public opinion as to support the Palestinian nationalist movement. It also has cooperated with the United States to contain Iranian influence in Lebanon. While the Saudi regime recognizes that its close ties to the United States continue to present public opinion problems domestically, particularly on Arab-Israeli issues, its national security and domestic regime security interests have become so inextricably linked to its American alliance that the circumstances under which it would end its close ties with the United States are difficult to imagine.

Notes

1. Much of the material in this chapter has been culled from previous work the author has done on security and political issues in the Gulf area. See F. Gregory Gause III, *Oil Monarchies: Domestic and Security Challenges in the Arab Gulf States* (New York: Council on Foreign Relations Press, 1994); "Saudi Arabia: Desert Storm and After," in *The Middle East After Iraq's Invasion of Kuwait,* ed. Robert O. Freedman (Gainesville: University Press of Florida, 1993); "Gulf Regional Politics: Revolution, War, and Rivalry," in *Dynamics of Regional Politics: Four Systems on the Indian Ocean Rim,* ed. W. Howard Wriggins (New York: Columbia University Press, 1992); and *The International Relations of the Persian Gulf* (Cambridge: Cambridge University Press, 2010).

2. Results of the Saudi census were reported in the *New York Times,* December 18, 1992, p. A8. The demographic analysis firm Birks Sinclair and Associates, publisher of the *Gulf Market Report* with long experience in the region, estimated the 1992 Saudi population to be 12.3 million, of whom 8.1 million were citizens. The Birks Sinclair estimate was cited by Roger Hardy, *Arabia After the Storm: Internal Stability of the Gulf Arab States* (London: Middle East Programme Report, Royal Institute for International Affairs, 1992). For a 2010 population estimate, see *al-Hayat,* KSA ed., August 5, 2010, http://ksa.daralhayat.com/ksaarticle/169301.

3. See *New York Times,* October 13, 1991, pp. 1, 18; October 25, 1991, p. A9, for references to the Saudi proposals. Since that time there have been no moves to expand the size of the Saudi military.

4. Leaders of the Saudi Shi'a community addressed a petition to King Fahd in 1991. In it they complained of a "quarantine" keeping Saudi Shi'a out of the armed forces. Practically identical versions of this petition can be found in *Makka News,* April 6, 1991, and in *Arabia Monitor* 1, no. 6 (July 1992). The former was published by the Organization of the Islamic Revolution in the Arabian Peninsula, an Iranian-supported exile group with a US post office box in Bowling Green, Kentucky. The latter was a monthly newsletter published in Washington by the International Committee for

Human Rights in the Gulf and Arabian Peninsula. Both ceased publication as a result of an agreement between the Saudi government and Saudi Shi'a activists in late 1993. *Washington Post,* October 16, 1993, p. A15; *New York Times,* October 29, 1993, p. A11.

5. Figures taken from International Institute for Strategic Studies, *The Military Balance, 1990–91* and *The Military Balance, 1991–92* (London: Brassey's for the International Institute for Strategic Studies, 1990, 1991).

6. Nadav Safran, *Saudi Arabia: The Ceaseless Quest for Security* (Cambridge: Harvard University Press, 1985), pp. 58–69.

7. For an account both of Ickes's plans and the 50-50 deal, see Daniel Yergin, *The Prize* (New York: Simon & Schuster, 1991), chaps. 20–22.

8. Safran, *Saudi Arabia,* pp. 103–104.

9. King Sa'ud had his own agenda, aimed at strengthening the Saudi position in the region, in backing the Eisenhower Doctrine. Those ambitions led to some strains in the US-Saudi relationship. See David W. Lesch, *Syria and the United States: Eisenhower's Cold War in the Middle East* (Boulder: Westview, 1992), pp. 127–189; and Lesch, "The Saudi Role in the 1957 American-Syrian Crisis," *Middle East Policy* 1, no. 3 (1992).

10. Safran, *Saudi Arabia,* pp. 92–96.

11. US Congress, House of Representatives, Committee on Foreign Affairs, Subcommittee on Near East, *New Perspectives on the Persian Gulf,* 93rd Congress, 1st sess. (Washington, DC: Government Printing Office, 1973), p. 47.

12. Safran, *Saudi Arabia,* p. 301.

13. *al-Hayat,* April 23, 1993, p. 12.

14. R. K. Ramazani, ed., *The Gulf Cooperation Council: Record and Analysis* (Charlottesville: University Press of Virginia, 1988), doc. 9, p. 28.

15. *New York Times,* November 8, 1990, p. 14.

16. *New York Times,* July 18, 1990, pp. D1, D5; July 25, 1990, p. 8; July 27, 1990, p. 2.

17. *New York Times,* September 21, 1990, p. 1.

18. *New York Times,* October 26, 1990, p. 11.

19. *al-Hayat,* October 22, 1991, pp. 1, 7.

20. *New York Times,* October 23, 1990, p. 1; October 27, 1990, p. 4.

21. In a speech to Saudis in early January 1991, King Fahd emphasized the sense of personal betrayal he felt when he heard that Saddam had invaded Kuwait. *New York Times,* January 7, 1991, p. 10.

22. The full text of the *fatwa* can be found in *al-Sharq al-'Awsat,* August 21, 1990, p. 4.

23. *al-Sharq al-'Awsat,* November 28, 1990, p. 3.

24. *al-Hayat,* March 14, 1991, p. 1.

25. *New York Times,* September 30, 1991, p. A5.

26. Charles Aldinger, "Saudis Declined to Base US Arms," Reuters online, November 4, 1994; "Saudi Against Hosting US Raids on Iraq," Reuters online, September 11, 1996.

27. Ranking Saudi official, interview by author, Jeddah, October 1992. *New York Times,* October 13, 1991, pp. 1, 18; October 25, 1991, p. A9.

28. See remarks by Dr. Safar al-Hawali, dean of Islamic Studies at 'Umm al-Qura University in Mecca, published by the *New York Times,* November 24, 1990, p. 21. See also *New York Times,* December 25, 1990, p. 6.

29. The author obtained a copy of the Islamist petition from sources in Saudi Arabia. English-language versions of this petition can be found in Foreign Broadcast Information Service—Near East and South Asia (FBIS/NESA), May 23, 1991, p. 21 (translation of a version published in the Cairo newspaper *al-Sha'b*); *Makka News*, no. 8, June 16, 1991; and Middle East Watch's *Empty Reforms: Saudi Arabia's New Basic Laws*, pp. 61–62.

30. The author obtained copies of the Memorandum of Advice in Saudi Arabia. All translations are mine. One of the copies was dated Muharram 1413, which corresponds to July 1992, indicating that it was in circulation before the fall of 1992, when Western news organizations reported on it (*New York Times*, October 8, 1992, p. A6).

31. For an interesting discussion on the background of one of those executed, see Ethan Bronner, "In Bomber's Life, Glimpse of Saudi Dissent," *Boston Globe*, July 7, 1996.

32. John C. Roper, "US Saudi Arabia Agree on Troop Move," United Press International online, July 31, 1996.

33. Arms Control Association, *US Arms Transfers to the Middle East Since the Invasion of Kuwait—Fact Sheet, October 8, 1992* (Washington, DC: Arms Control Association).

34. *New York Times*, February 1, 1994, p. A6.

35. International Institute for Strategic Studies, *The Military Balance 1997/98* (Oxford: Oxford University Press, 1997), pp. 26, 140.

36. *New York Times*, February 17, 1994, p. 1.

37. *Washington Post*, January 18, 2002, p. A1.

38. On the course of post-9/11 American-Saudi relations, see Gause, *International Relations of the Persian Gulf*, pp. 144–148.

39. *Los Angeles Times*, October 21, 2010, http://tinyurl.com/272kuxg.

CHAPTER 19

THE IRAQ WAR OF 2003

Why Did the United States Decide to Invade?

Steve A. Yetiv

History offers no bigger question: Why do nations choose to go to war instead of pursuing other strategies for achieving their ends? This question has been salient for ages, and it is no less germane today for anyone trying to understand why the United States decided to invade Iraq in March 2003. The United States decreased its presence in Iraq in 2009 and 2010, consistent with President Barack Obama's 2008 campaign pledge to do so. This action may well bring a fascinating chapter in American foreign policy to a close. What was once a force of over 140,000 troops was trimmed to approximately 50,000 troops by September 2010. The remaining force is intended to continue to train, advise, and support Iraqi forces and fight al-Qa'ida. All forces are slated to be removed by the end of 2011, but some may stay behind to play critical roles. Changes can be made in the overall force structure in the coming years depending on security realities on the ground in Iraq and political realities in Washington.

It will take years to discover if Iraq can stabilize after American forces leave or to what extent it will fall prey to al-Qa'ida and affiliated terrorists, sectarian strife, and the vagaries of being a developing country next to major regional powers, chiefly Turkey and Iran, that view achieving influence in Iraq as an important security goal. Whatever happens, the question of why the United States invaded will remain salient in understanding Iraq and the Middle East, as well as the broader question of why countries go to war. In this sense, the Iraq war is both a fascinating case study and also a classic issue in world affairs that ties to the massive literature on war and peace across multiple disciplines.

The question of why the United States decided to invade Iraq is all the more intriguing now that we know that the invasion and occupation, while felling a brutal dictator and bringing important elements of democracy to Iraq, was so difficult and costly. Indeed, over 4,400 US service personnel were killed in Operation Iraqi Freedom since the invasion started on March 19, 2003, and well over 30,000 were wounded in action. Hundreds of soldiers from other countries were killed as well, and many thousands of Iraqis lost their lives. The nonpartisan Congressional Research Service estimates that the United States *will have spent almost $802 billion on funding the war by the end of fiscal year 2011.*[1] Others argue that this figure will be far higher when we account for the impact of the war on the US budget and economy, on the health of the soldiers returning home, and in terms of the broader opportunity costs of having spent much money on war that could have been used elsewhere.

Many of the central documents regarding why the United States invaded Iraq will not be declassified for some time, and key policymakers have not yet allowed substantial on-the-record interviews that might be used, along with these documents, to piece together a more comprehensive explanation of American behavior. Nonetheless, it is possible to offer at least a sensible sketch of the key reasons for going to war. This chapter first describes the events leading up to the war and then considers the primary and possible secondary motivations for going to war.

THE EVENTS PRECEDING THE 2003 WAR

Saddam Hussein cooperated with President Bush and his administration in painting himself as an incorrigible, dangerous dictator despite the fact that he was deprived of weapons of mass destruction and struggling at home. Iraq's record of defiance was not in doubt, although the decision to choose war against Iraq was controversial. Iraq had defied sixteen United Nations resolutions passed between 1991 and 2002, starting with United Nations Security Council (UNSC) Resolution 687, which was the most important. It mandated full disclosure of all of Iraq's ballistic missile stocks (above a range of 150 kilometers) and production facilities, all nuclear materials, chemical and biological weapons and facilities, and cooperation in their destruction. Paragraphs 10–12 required Iraq to "unconditionally undertake not to use, develop, construct, or acquire" weapons of mass destruction (WMD). UNSC Resolution 687 also forced Iraq to accept the UN-demarcated border with Kuwait, the sovereignty of Kuwaiti territory, and UN peacekeepers on the Iraq-Kuwait border.[2]

In his speech to the United Nations on September 12, 2002, President Bush demanded that Iraq comply immediately with the previous sixteen UN resolutions. He claimed that because Iraq was continuing to pursue the acquisition of weapons of mass destruction and missile delivery systems, it represented a "grave and gathering danger" to American and global security. He pointed out that the United Nations had struggled with Iraq for a dozen years to ensure its compliance with the demands of UNSC Resolution 687 and that Iraq defied its provisions, thus creating a credibility crisis regarding UN resolve. He held out the prospect that UN inspectors could find Saddam's WMD, but he also asserted that the United States was willing to act unilaterally, observing that it is not possible to "stand by and do nothing while dangers gather."

Washington pushed hard to pass the seventeenth resolution against Iraq on November 8, 2002. UNSC Resolution 1441 required Baghdad to admit inspectors from the UN Monitoring, Verification, and Inspection Commission and the International Atomic Energy Agency and to comply fully with all foregoing resolutions.[3] The resolution, which was passed unanimously by the UN Security Council, suggested the use of force against Iraq if it committed a "material breach" or serious infraction in cooperating with efforts to identify and destroy its WMD capability. However, the notion of "material breach" was interpreted differently among the Security Council members.

France, Russia, and China preferred to avoid war and certainly opposed war on Washington's and London's terms and timetable, yet none of the three threatened to veto Resolution 1441. However, France and, to some extent, Russia did attempt to change some of the resolution's language in order to put the brakes on a move toward war, limiting such authorization to the case of serious violations by Baghdad.[4]

For its part, Iraq moved to comply with Resolution 1441 by allowing UN inspectors back into the country and by submitting 12,000 pages and several compact discs of information to the United Nations, which supposedly described its weapons capabilities. Baghdad asserted that it lacked WMD programs and had no WMD in storage. Unfortunately, these disclosures were viewed as incomplete.

Chief UN weapons inspector Hans Blix issued a report in January 2003 that was critical of Iraq's "efforts to disarm and cooperate with UN inspectors."[5] He observed that serious questions remained about Iraq's chemical and biological weapons capability, which he believed was not accurately or fully disclosed in Iraq's report to the United Nations. Not surprisingly, the Bush administration found Iraq's lack of cooperation highly problematic. Secretary of State Colin Powell asserted that American experts had found the Iraqi declaration to the United Nations to "be anything but currently accurate, full, or complete" and that the declaration "totally fails to meet the resolution's requirements."[6] As Powell explained to the UN in his now famous appearance on February 5, 2003, "We haven't accounted for the anthrax, we haven't accounted for the botulinum, VX, both biological agents, growth media, 30,000 chemical and biological munitions."[7] Feeling the rising tide of international condemnation, Saddam responded by granting greater access to UN inspectors in Iraq. He may have thought that he could foil US efforts to gather international support for an invasion of Iraq, without revealing the fact that there were actually very few or no WMD in the country. On February 10, 2003, Blix offered a more optimistic account of Iraq's cooperation, seeing a new "positive attitude on the part of the Iraqi regime," and asked for more time for inspections.[8]

While Russia, Germany, and France seized on Blix's report to thwart the American and British drive toward war, Washington and London proved recalcitrant.

They may well have concluded that Saddam was simply engaging in more games with UN inspectors, that his track record suggested no real interest in completely ridding the country of WMD, and that inspections were therefore doomed to fail. From their perspective, if Saddam did have these weapons, he would not help UN inspectors find them, and without his help, they could remain hidden. Meanwhile, even if they did find WMD, they could not be confident that they had uncovered all of them or that, after they left, Saddam would not rebuild some of the weapons programs.

Partly as a result of this skepticism and partly because Iraq, in the view of the United States and Britain, did not meet the conditions of UN Resolution 1441 or previous UN resolutions, the United States and Britain drafted an eighteenth resolution against Iraq, which, in essence, called for war. To pass this resolution, the United States needed the support of nine of the fifteen Security Council members, while avoiding a veto by any of the four other permanent members of the Security Council. Although the Security Council had unanimously supported Resolution 1441, the underlying differences among them on going to war complicated US efforts to pass the new resolution. Russia threatened to veto it, although Moscow avoided an open breach with Washington. Russian President Vladimir Putin had supported earlier US efforts to contain and defang Iraq and had lent tentative support for war, but on a much slower timetable; he could not endorse a war that was viewed in Russia and the rest of the world as rushed or ill-advised.[9]

France interpreted Resolution 1441 as a warning to Iraq to comply more fully with UN inspectors, not as a casus belli. After France threatened to veto the eighteenth resolution, possibly with backing from China and Russia, the United States and Britain shifted their strategy, especially when they learned that some of the smaller countries on the UN Security Council would not support their action.

The United States and Britain offered somewhat different justifications for war, but they were convinced that Iraq's violation of the previous seventeen UN resolutions gave them sufficient basis for using force. Citing this rationale, they presented Saddam, his sons, and key Iraqi elites with an ultimatum: Leave the country within forty-eight hours or face war. Saddam rejected the ultimatum, possibly fearing that the United States would eventually track him down wherever he went or perhaps believing that he could survive the American-led onslaught and eventually resurrect his regime. In retrospect, it seems likely that he and his generals had plans to stand down and disperse into a guerrilla movement, with greater chances of evicting American forces from Iraq through a war of attrition. The minutes of a meeting of his top commanders, chaired by Saddam, support this interpretation.[10]

Operation Iraqi Freedom was launched against Iraq on March 19, 2003, with a massive air attack, an assault referred to with overcharged bravado as Operation Shock and Awe. Bombs struck their targets precisely, carrying a message that the United States was serious about change in the Middle East. Saddam's regime fell to this massive onslaught, but the security and political debris that was left in its wake would continue to bedevil the United States and its allies, who were bent on rebuilding Iraq in the Western image.

THE KEY MOTIVATIONS FOR GOING TO WAR

States offer different reasons for war, some of which are biased and would be hotly contested by their adversaries and probably by some of their allies as well. The United States offered three reasons for invading Iraq.[11] Although we should not accept them uncritically, and they probably do not capture the full story of American motivations, they appear to be central to the Bush administration's decision.

First, the United States was concerned about Iraqi WMD programs. On August 14, 2002, national security adviser Condoleezza Rice chaired a meeting that laid out US goals in Iraq in a draft of a national security presidential directive entitled "Iraq: Goals, Objectives, and Strategy." President Bush signed the directive, making it official policy, on August 29. The document emphasized the desire of the US government to overthrow Saddam Hussein's regime in order to eliminate its WMD, to end its threat to the region, to create democracy in Iraq, and to contain the threat of a WMD attack on the United States or its allies.[12]

In June 2001, the CIA reported that although the evidence was not fully clear, it appeared that Iraq had used the period between 1998 and 2001 to rebuild prohibited WMD programs.[13] In October 2002, a special national intelligence estimate more clearly articulated those accusations: "Iraq has continued its weapons of mass destruction programs in defiance of UN resolutions and restrictions. Baghdad has chemical and biological weapons as well as missiles with ranges in excess of UN restrictions; if left unchecked, it probably will have a nuclear weapon during this decade."[14]

In one key document, President Bush warned that if the Iraqi regime were "able to produce, buy, or steal an amount of highly enriched uranium a little larger than a single softball, it could have a nuclear weapon in less than a year."[15] In September 2002, he cited a British intelligence report indicating that Iraq could launch a chemical or biological attack forty-five minutes after the order was given to do so.[16] The administration also described Iraq as capable of using WMD against the United States, a position that was not shared by the intelligence analysts who wrote the October 2002 national intelligence estimate.[17]

Senior administration officials repeatedly asserted that Iraq sought to rebuild its nuclear program and obfuscate the existence of nuclear facilities by placing them underground or camouflaging them. In this view, inspections would not be able to detect or halt these activities, and even if they could, Iraq would resume them once the inspectors left the country.[18] In the case that Iraq did not yet possess nuclear capabilities—a scenario characterized as unlikely—the administration believed that Iraq had the intellectual infrastructure and intent to produce them. In the eyes of administration officials, that alone was enough of a threat after 9/11 to justify US action against Iraq. The administration did not trumpet this argument, however, because it was less marketable than other arguments for war.[19]

The attacks of September 11 raised the stakes high enough that the administration had a low level of tolerance for WMD in the hands of a dictator, especially one with Saddam's record of aggression. Vice President Dick Cheney asserted in

August 2002: "If the United States could have preempted 9/11, we would have, no question. Should we be able to prevent another, much more devastating attack, we will, no question."[20] From this perspective, irrefutable facts about Iraq's capabilities and intentions were unnecessary; Saddam had given the administration enough reason to have serious doubts about his intentions in a post-9/11 environment. As Bush asserted in his January 28, 2003, State of the Union speech, a "brutal dictator, with a history of reckless aggression, with ties to terrorism, with great potential wealth, will not be permitted to dominate a vital region and threaten the United States."[21]

President Bush described Iraq, Iran, and North Korea in his now famous January 29, 2002, State of the Union message as part of an "axis of evil" against which preemptive force might have to be used. Later, on September 28, 2002, Bush elaborated on the Iraq problem: "The danger to our country is grave and growing. The Iraqi regime possesses biological and chemical weapons, is rebuilding facilities to make more and . . . is seeking a nuclear bomb, and with fissile material could build one within a year."[22]

A second rationale for going to war was Iraq's purported ties to terrorism. The administration's assertion that Iraq had supported al-Qa'ida was buoyed by the fact that a majority of Americans (53 to 64 percent in an August 2002 Gallup poll) believed that Saddam was directly involved in the 9/11 attacks.[23]

Prior to the attacks of September 11, 2001, the Bush administration was not especially concerned about al-Qa'ida. Policy tended to side with the Clinton administration, which had worked through domestic law enforcement agencies in an attempt to eliminate the al-Qa'ida threat. One exception was the unsuccessful effort in President Clinton's embattled second term to assassinate bin Laden with a missile strike at an al-Qa'ida training camp in Afghanistan. The Bush administration was more fixed on the al-Qa'ida threat than the Clinton administration, yet it failed to take timely action to address it. Reflecting the broader tenor among high-level Bush administration officials, national security adviser Condoleezza Rice was slow to respond to suggestions made in a key memo by counterterrorism coordinator Richard Clarke to take action against al-Qa'ida, and she was subsequently accused of ignoring the threat prior to 9/11.[24] Ironically, on September 10 she was in the process of preparing a national security directive on how to eliminate the terrorist threat posed by al-Qa'ida.[25]

After September 11, the Bush administration appeared to be concerned about, even obsessed with, the connection between WMD and terrorist organizations, as reflected in many speeches by top American officials, including Vice President Cheney.[26] To what extent the Bush administration manipulated intelligence to support the war may not be fully known for some time. Clearly administration officials were concerned that Iraq could be supporting transnational terrorists. Evidence for this interpretation can be found in the now famous Downing Street memo, which summarizes discussion in a July 23, 2002, meeting when British Prime Minister Tony Blair conferred with his top security advisers. In the memo (actually the minutes of the meeting), the head of Britain's MI6 intelligence service reports on his high-level visit to Washington: "Bush wanted to remove Saddam through military action, justified by the conjunction of terrorism and WMD. But the intelligence and facts were being fixed around the policy."[27]

Even though the link between al-Qa'ida and Iraq was tenuous at best,[28] it was Saddam's misfortune that Iraq represented precisely what the Bush administration feared after 9/11: a dictator developing WMD with connections to terrorist groups. Bush described his post-9/11 perception of Saddam in an interview with Bob Woodward: "All his terrible features became much more threatening. Keeping Saddam in a box looked less and less feasible to me."[29] In Rumsfeld's words, "We acted because we saw the existing evidence in a new light, through the prism of our experience on September 11," a perspective that was obsessed with America's vulnerability to states with WMD and connections to terrorists.[30]

Even Secretary Powell appeared to be persuaded to some extent that Iraq posed a threat, although he may have been playing the role of obedient soldier to the president and vice president. In his crucial speech to the UN on September 12, 2002, he warned that Saddam had used terrorism for decades: "Saddam was a supporter of terrorism long before these terrorist networks had a name, and this support continues. The nexus of poisons and terror is new. The nexus of Iraq and terror is old. The combination is lethal."[31]

Some scholars have argued that the administration used the WMD threat to justify a war that it had decided to launch even before 9/11.[32] That is not likely. Not only did the 9/11 attacks give the administration a basis for garnering public support for war, which it had previously lacked, but the strategic priorities of the administration changed dramatically after the attacks.

Indeed, having been advised in the hours following the attacks that al-Qa'ida may well have planned the attacks on New York and Washington, Donald Rumsfeld reportedly asked for the existing military plans for an invasion of Iraq; his deputy, Paul Wolfowitz, also pushed for an immediate attack on Iraq, ahead of an invasion of Afghanistan.[33] Meanwhile, President Bush asked for contingency plans to attack Iraq if it were shown that Iraq was involved in the attacks or sought to exploit the crisis for its own gain.[34] Like Wolfowitz, Bush made it known early on that he thought Iraq was involved in the 9/11 attacks,[35] and he repeated the mantra that Iraq had had long-standing ties to terrorist groups that were capable of and willing to deliver weapons of mass death.[36] His information no doubt came, in part, from the CIA. On October 7, 2002, George Tenet, then director of the Central Intelligence Agency, sent Senator Bob Graham, the chairman of the Senate Select Committee on Intelligence, unclassified information that indicated the existence of a long-term relationship between al-Qa'ida and Iraq, including "solid reporting of senior level contacts between Iraq and al-Qa'ida going back a decade."[37]

In addition to the administration's concerns about Iraq possessing WMD and having established ties with al-Qa'ida, President Bush and his advisers had a third reason for going to war with Iraq. It was their intention to topple the autocratic regime of Saddam Hussein and democratize Iraq, so that it could then sow the seeds of democracy more broadly in the Middle East. Although the Bush administration did not initially focus on democratization as a rationale for war, it would be a mistake to assume that it was simply an afterthought.

Whereas President George H. W. Bush had been repeatedly criticized for lacking vision, his son exemplified vision, whatever one thinks of its merits, in the post-9/11 period. Although his vision may have come from the gut, it adhered to a unilinear view of history. In contrast to the cyclical view of history, which sees the afflictions of international relations repeating themselves over time, President George W. Bush held a firm belief in human progress—in this case, the democratization of a challenging region.[38]

On the evening of September 11, 2001, in the wake of the attacks in New York and Washington, well before the US decision to go to war in Iraq, Bush reassured the nation that the United States "would go forward to defend freedom and all that is good and just in our world."[39] He repeated that mantra ahead of the Iraq invasion, and he continued to repeat it throughout the long war that followed, emphasizing that the United States would support and spread democratic ideas.[40]

The objective of democratizing Iraq and the Middle East lost traction as time wore on, especially after WMD failed to turn up in Iraq and the al-Qa'ida connection to Saddam remained elusive. This approach was a sharp break with past US foreign policy in the region. Indeed, even the Clinton administration, which was proud of its support for human rights abroad, did not attempt to launch a democratization drive in the Middle East. Secretary of State Madeleine Albright explained US restraint in this region: "We have been afraid to push too hard for democracy, especially in Arab countries. We worry, perhaps with reason, that if radical Islamists obtain power through an election, there would be no more elections . . . and instability might be created."[41] By contrast, Condoleezza Rice, who became secretary of state in early 2005, held a different view: "For sixty years, my country, the United States, pursued stability at the expense of democracy in this region here in the Middle East, and we achieved neither. Now we are taking a different course. We are supporting the democratic aspirations of all people."[42]

In the administration's view, democratization could undermine the demons that drive transnational terrorism,[43] a theme that dominated the administration's list of priorities by 2004. In his State of the Union address on February 2, 2004, President Bush urged Saudi Arabia and Egypt to "show the way toward democracy in the region."[44]

THE CONCEPTUAL MOTIVATION FOR WAR: PREEMPTION VERSUS CONTAINMENT

The motivations for war discussed above are insufficient to explain the decision to go to war. After all, if WMD were so threatening, why didn't the Bush administration attack North Korea, which was a far greater threat than Iraq? If fighting terrorism was the key objective, administration officials could just as easily have decided to focus on strangulating al-Qa'ida globally rather than executing regime change in Iraq, even if they believed there was a Saddam/al-Qa'ida connection. If they were concerned about WMD and terrorism, administration officials might also have decided to ratchet up their containment of Iraq with increased military, political, and economic pressures instead of invasion and occupation. Why did they choose to go to war?

Simply put, after 9/11, the Bush administration did not believe that containment would work. The perception that Iraq had WMD and connections to terrorism further drove the change in American foreign policy away from containment and toward preemption, and preemption became the conceptual basis for invading Iraq.

To be sure, prior to 9/11, the administration viewed the policy of containment as problematic. As Bush pointed out, "I was not happy with our policy" since it was not toppling Saddam or changing his behavior. But prior to September 11, "a president could see a threat and contain it or deal with it in a variety of ways without fear of that threat materializing on our own soil."[45] That describes, roughly, the disposition of the Clinton administration, as well as that of the first Bush administration. Those earlier administrations were content with strengthening the containment effort against Saddam Hussein through "smart sanctions," which aimed at preventing Iraq from obtaining military goods while relaxing the embargo on trade items that Iraq's people needed. Prior to 9/11, Iraq was barely mentioned by top officials, except as a potential long-term threat, even though consensus had developed among them that Saddam's regime needed to be removed; regime change had become official American policy in 1998.[46]

After September 11, US policy toward Iraq changed dramatically from regime change through political means to regime change through the use of force.[47] The Bush Doctrine of preemption was articulated in the State of the Union address on January 29, 2002, and then formally outlined in the National Security Strategy of September 2002.[48] It was based partly on the notion that deterrence and containment may not succeed, and it emphasized the need to resort in appropriate cases to preemptive measures.[49] For Paul Wolfowitz, 9/11 was the "most significant thing" that generated a change in US foreign policy, and he cited it as one of the top ten events, if not the top event, of the "last one hundred years."[50]

The United States had always practiced preemption when necessary, but had never openly presented it as a strategy and then used it so brazenly to justify war on another country. September 11, however, altered the stakes. As President Bush put it, September 11 made it such that the "doctrine of containment just doesn't hold any water."[51] Bush asserted in a speech in Cincinnati in October 2002 that the United States had to take preemptive action because after September 11, the country could not "wait for the final proof—the smoking gun," which would come in "the form of a mushroom cloud."[52] America's threshold for terrorism had been lowered enough that Iraq became a key target for vigorous American action. Containment was a passive approach; now the United States would become much more proactive.

Regime change through the use of force was one key element of the broader policy of preemption, but the Bush administration also sought to stop terrorist attacks before they occurred through other means. Regime change was the most overt and the riskiest of these means.

FAULTY INTELLIGENCE

Wars historically have often been started because of miscalculations about the strength of other actors and the threats they pose. The Bush administration's conceptual shift toward preemption and war in Iraq was driven by faulty intelligence on Iraq's WMD and connections to al-Qa'ida. It may never be fully evident to what extent the administration, or particular members within it, manipulated this intelligence to justify war, but clearly the information was important in the decision to go to war. Indeed, poor intelligence created a specter of a much greater Iraqi threat than existed; it facilitated the administration's efforts to gain domestic and, to some extent, international support for war and predisposed key officials to believe that Iraq could be rebuilt and refashioned without the extraordinary challenges that would arise in the postwar period. Accurate intelligence would have made the option of going to war less palatable and more difficult to market.

In any case, the administration insisted that it had made a sound decision based on the evidence at hand, faulty as it was, and challenged criticism that it had cooked the books for war. Reflecting the administration's position, Powell asserted that he was "disappointed" that the intelligence was not on target but that the administration had not misled the world and the American people, because government officials had believed what they said about Iraq. "We thought Iraq had stockpiles of WMD."[53]

Two major official inquiries, one by the Senate Select Committee on Intelligence in 2004 and one by the Robb-Silberman Commission in March 2005, found no evidence that political pressure by the Bush administration had contributed to these intelligence failures.[54] The inquiries did find that Vice President Cheney and others had encouraged analysts to rethink their findings, but this did not lead to different conclusions. However, the inquiries did not have access to key White House documents. Moreover, while they found that political pressure by the administration did not contribute to intelligence failures, they left open the question of the extent to which the administration exaggerated the threat from Iraq and, in particular, Iraq's ties to al-Qa'ida to justify war.[55] In fact, one February 2002 declassified document from the Defense Intelligence Agency asserted that Ibn al-Shaykh al-Libi, a top member of al-Qa'ida in American custody, had intentionally misled American debriefers about Iraq's support for al-Qa'ida and shipments of illicit weapons to the terrorists. The administration repeatedly drew on his questionable testimony, as did Colin Powell in his February 2003 UN speech. Al-Libi withdrew his claims in 2004, but the administration's reliance on this shaky intelligence raised questions about the extent to which the administration dramatized, fabricated, or misunderstood Saddam's connection to al-Qa'ida.[56]

The link between Iraq and al-Qa'ida did not make much sense in the first place. As Saddam Hussein himself emphasized when interviewed by the FBI in 2004, he and Bin Laden were very different individuals, with sharply contrasting ideologies and goals, making it nonsensical for Iraq to cooperate with al-Qa'ida.[57] Bin Laden probably viewed Saddam as a corrupt, secular pan-Arabist, an infidel who was fit to be overthrown or killed. Meanwhile Saddam probably saw bin Laden as an irrational radical who tilted with windmills and had no program or workable ideology of his own. He was a threat to pan-Arabists and nationalists because he promoted a radical version of transnational Islam managed under Taliban-like states. He would target Saddam if he could as the prototype illegitimate and poor Arab leader.

OTHER POSSIBLE MOTIVATIONS FOR WAR

Many people around the world felt that the war against Iraq was unnecessary. If the war was not really intended to address some imminent threat from Iraq, they wondered, then what were its real aims?[58]

Oil Security and Alternatives to Saudi Energy

Millions of people in the Middle East and around the world believed that the war was about oil. According to a 2000 Pew Research Center opinion poll, 76 percent of those polled in Russia, 75 percent of those polled in France, 54 percent of those polled in Germany, and 44 percent of those polled in Great Britain believed that the war was driven by a "desire to control Iraq's oil."[59] Most Iraqis, it is fair to say, also held this view, which was prominent among both moderate and radical Islamists around the world. For his part, Osama bin Laden asserted in a 1998 interview that the Muslim world and Islam were under assault, noting that others "rob us of our wealth and of our resources and of our oil" and that "our religion is under attack."[60] This view of Americans stealing Middle Eastern oil was fairly constant in statements by al-Qa'ida and its affiliates.[61]

Although the United States obviously views access to Persian Gulf oil as "vital to US and global security," little evidence exists that it has sought to steal this oil.[62] For instance, it did not seize Iraqi oil fields or appropriate the proceeds from oil sales. However, access to oil reserves may very well have been one motivating factor for the invasion of Iraq.

First, the September 11 attacks created concerns about Saudi stability. Some of these concerns were rational and some were not, but they all influenced elite and general public opinion in the United States. The fact that fifteen of the nineteen hijackers came from Saudi Arabia raised questions about whether hatred for the United States was more endemic in the kingdom than previously believed. It also raised the question of whether they attacked the United States in order to create a schism in US-Saudi relations and thus undermine the legitimacy of the Saudi regime, which may have been their primary target.

Some were concerned that elements in the Saudi regime actually supported the terrorists, suggesting the existence of a radical element within the royal family itself. Others believed that the regime had turned a blind eye to the terrorists because the religious establishment in the country made it politically difficult to confront them. If any of these explanations were credible, the future of US-Saudi relations was potentially in jeopardy.

It made sense to secure Iraq's vast oil resources if Saudi Arabia was becoming unstable. The overthrow of Saddam Hussein could put Iraq's oil production in friendlier hands, and this would give the West greater ability to maintain the flow of oil in the event of political or security problems in Saudi Arabia. Even if the Saudi regime was stable, US-Saudi tensions could mount over time, thus making Iraq more important to diversifying oil supplies.

Second, regime change could allow for higher Iraqi oil production. Iraq is believed to have 112.5 billion barrels of known reserves, which places it second only to Saudi Arabia's 262 billion (approximately 25 percent of the world's proven oil reserves). Iraq's proven reserves are found in seventy-three fields, only one-quarter of which have been developed.[63] Other Middle East states such as Iran and Kuwait hold approximately 90 to 120 billion barrels, but those fields do not have the upward potential of Iraq's because they are already producing at a high rate. Iraq possesses 11 percent of the world's proven oil reserves, yet even at its peak production in 1979, it was producing only 5.5 percent of the world supply. Iraq's potential could have been viewed as enormous precisely because it has been hamstrung over the past twenty-five years. The Iran-Iraq war from 1980 to 1988, the 1991 Gulf War, subsequent UN sanctions, periodic American military attacks, and Saddam's own mismanagement and corruption further curtailed Iraq's potential and left its oil infrastructure in disarray.

Iraq's various conflicts with the UN resulted in a drop in oil production from an average of 2.0–2.6 million barrels per day (mb/d) from 1999 to 2001, due to sanctions delineated under UN Resolution 986. Production hit a high of 2.6 mb/d in 2000 (equal to 3.4 percent of world supply) and dropped to 1.7 mb/d by August-September 2002.[64] Some analysts believed that with a totally rebuilt oil infrastructure, Iraq could have increased oil production to an estimated 6 to 12 mb/d within a decade, partly because Iraq's oil is relatively underexplored and underdeveloped.[65] In early 1990, prior to the invasion of Kuwait, Baghdad had planned to raise production and export capacity to 6 mb/d by 1996.[66] After May 1997, Iraq's oil ministry worked assiduously to produce a postsanctions oil development plan, the latest version of which preceded the Iraq war of 2003 and had a goal of producing 6 mb/d within six years.[67]

Third, toppling Iraq's regime could have ended Iraq's threat to regional oil fields, at least in the near term. After all, Iraq's invasion of Kuwait had demonstrated that Saddam Hussein might be inclined once again to invade Kuwait or even Saudi Arabia. This was increasingly likely as international pressure and the UN sanctions began to wane, leaving Saddam greater room to maneuver in the region.[68]

These three factors may well have contributed to the Bush administration's decision to invade Iraq. Administration officials could not have underestimated potential problems with Saudi Arabia and the importance of oil to the American and global economy. Nor could they overlook the fact that Persian Gulf oil would only become more important as other sources of oil around the world began to peak and then dry up. Just how important the oil factor was as a national security concern in the administration's decision-making process, compared to other motivations, is unclear and hard to assess.

Oil, Halliburton, and American Oil Companies

Although national security may have motivated an interest in Iraqi oil, another potential explanation for invading Iraq is that Vice President Cheney, and his contacts in the oil world, could have benefited from large oil contracts after Iraq was liberated by American forces. With America dominating or influencing Iraq, the United States could more effectively compete for such contracts with countries such as France, Russia, and China, who already had a foothold in the region. Not only could the United States get a bigger piece of the pie, but the size of the pie itself would expand because Iraq could produce far more oil with Saddam gone, UN sanctions lifted, and foreign investment revitalizing Iraq's oil sector.

This view of American motivation for going to war smacked of deep cynicism and may have been promoted by the administration's detractors in order to embarrass top administration officials.[69] But Cheney's previous role as CEO of Halliburton, plus President Bush's own oil background, tend to reinforce this viewpoint.[70] The Bush administration's Energy Task Force, which was headed by Cheney, presented a draft report in April 2001 that stated, among other things, that the United States should reconsider sanctions against Iran, Iraq, and Libya, because they prohibited US oil companies from doing business in "some of the most important existing and prospective petroleum-producing countries in the world."[71] Moreover, immediately prior to the invasion of Iraq in early 2003, Halliburton's subsidiary, Kellogg, Brown & Root, received a multibillion-dollar contract from the Defense Department to repair oil fields and import consumer fuels in Iraq.[72]

Would Cheney have risked a national and global scandal to help a company for which he no longer worked, even though he had to know that the contract would be criticized? Although he still had Halliburton stock, would he risk a high-profile scandal for money?

Although mining Iraq's energy resources could benefit companies like Halliburton that support the infrastructure for oil production, it would not necessarily help oil producers. As more oil flowed from Iraq, the price of oil would likely decrease based on simple supply/demand dynamics. Big oil companies could benefit only if the profits from additional contracts in Iraq outweighed the losses they would face from decreased oil prices. Nonetheless, the factor of domestic oil and oil services companies benefiting from regime change in Iraq should be considered.

Father and Son: Personal Reasons

Was President Bush's decision to go to war in Iraq influenced by the fact that his father evicted Saddam Hussein from Kuwait in 1991 but left him in power? In this scenario, Bush Jr. invaded Iraq to finish the job that Bush Sr. started. He may have sought to shore up his father's legacy by finishing off a dictator who proved to be more resilient than his father and many others anticipated. Saddam's longevity embarrassed Bush Sr., not just because he survived the 1991 war when many thought he would fall, but because he continued to be perceived as a major threat, especially after September 11. Many people began to ask why the United States did not eliminate him in 1991, when it had the chance to do so. Thus if Bush Jr. invaded Iraq, he could benefit his father's legacy by removing the threat and proving that Saddam actually did have WMD and connections to terrorists. History would surely blame Bush Sr. if terrorists linked to Iraq bombed New York in 2015. Bush Jr. could make sure that never happened by taking matters into his own hands.

Then too, Bush Jr. may have sought to avenge Saddam's effort to assassinate his father during a 1993 visit to Kuwait. He did say that Saddam Hussein was "a guy that tried to kill my dad," suggesting an overt hostility toward the dictator.[73] Loyalty runs strong in the Bush family and Bush Jr. acted as an enforcer of loyalty in his father's administration, all of which suggests that a personal motive may have influenced President Bush's decision to overthrow Saddam Hussein in 2003.

Carving His Own Path

Perhaps Bush Jr. sought to mark out his own independent course as a determined leader despite his reputation as a follower, reacting to widespread criticism that it was actually Dick Cheney, one of Bush Sr.'s closest advisers, who ran the administration. This criticism could not have been lost on Bush Jr. and certainly not on his advisers, who may have thought a war would establish his credentials as a strong leader. Interestingly, when asked by Bob Woodward whether he had consulted with his father before making the decision to invade Iraq, Bush Jr. asserted, "There is a higher Father that I appeal to," dismissing his father's role in rather unambiguous terms.

Moreover, Brent Scowcroft, his father's influential national security adviser and close friend, argued in the *Wall Street Journal* against the Iraq invasion, asserting that containment was working well and warning that an invasion would impede the war on terrorism and destabilize the region.[74] Scowcroft's remarks may have reflected the views of Bush Sr., who seemed unhappy with his son's decision to go to war and had strongly opposed invading Baghdad in 1991. In any case, ignoring the advice of his father's key adviser, and possibly that of his father, suggests that he was determined to chart his own course.

Bush, God, and Religion

If Bush's father played a limited role in shaping his decisions, this was not the case for God Almighty. President Bush raised—significantly more than most presidents—the issue of religion and his relationship with God in his speeches. From his assertion on September 12, 2001, that he was in the "Lord's hands,"[75] to his constant rhetoric about the forces of good and evil, to his frequent references to the war on terrorism as a crusade,[76] Bush was prone to a religious interpretation of events.[77] His notion of "crusade" was quite different from that of most Muslims:[78]

He saw it as an effort to confront evil terrorists and those who supported them, whereas Muslims tended to interpret it in terms of their difficult historical experience with the brutal Christian Crusades.

In the spring of 2004 Bush referred several times to his belief that a higher source was guiding his actions. Historically, the United States had promoted the liberal tradition as a transnational set of ideas and largely kept religion out of politics. Indeed, it was an area in which the United States differed fundamentally from Islamist states. President Bush was not deviating significantly from that tradition, however, nor did the president speak for all Americans or administration officials. Nevertheless, his words were enough to raise questions in the Muslim world about a Judeo-Christian showdown with Islam. The fact that President Bush embraced Israel's leader, Ariel Sharon, added to this perception, because their close relationship fed speculation about a Zionist-Crusader conspiracy.

Seemingly Bush would be heavily criticized for his copious religious references, and to some extent he was. Yet even during the presidential election, the campaign of Senator John Kerry veered away from open criticism. Bush's religious imagery seemed to have struck a chord not only among Christian conservatives and evangelicals, who had a biblical interpretation of world events, but also among Americans who held negative views of Muslims even prior to 9/11.[79]

Possibly Bush saw Iraq through the prism of religion. The United States was a God-fearing Christian nation, and Iraq was fit for transformation. Of course, Iraq could not be Christianized, but the messianic impulse may have been part of what bolstered Bush's determination, an impulse that meshed well with his brand of American exceptionalism.

The Military-Industrial Complex

Factors particular to President Bush may have influenced the drive to war in Iraq. However, some observers, especially those inclined toward conspiracy theories, might say that the so-called military-industrial complex, whose notorious power and influence President Eisenhower warned Americans about, also had a role in the decision to go to war in Iraq. According to some thinkers, this complex of corporate and military organizations has a vested interest in going to war—high-profit military contracts, expanded military research budgets, and influence.

Invading Iraq could benefit the military-industrial complex. The armed forces could see President Bush as confirming their importance. The military-industrial complex could view the war as a ticket for producing and selling more and better weapons. The Defense Department could gain influence if the armed forces performed well, and the military might stave off budget cuts and base closings and gain support for new weapons programs. And the much-maligned CIA would have an important mission in the post–cold war era.

The Israel Lobby

Some speculate that the Israel lobby in Washington was connected to the American decision to invade Iraq.[80] This explanation seems unlikely. First, it is very hard to make a connection between the lobby and decision making in the Bush White House. That decision was made by a very few people—essentially Bush, Cheney, and Rumsfeld. The decision-making team, as far as we know, had little input from thinkers outside government or even from its own intelligence community. Second, the decision to invade can clearly be traced to the factors discussed in this chapter, which were immediate issues—the fear in the post-9/11 period of WMD in the hands of a dictator who had used WMD on his own people and had attacked Iran in 1980 and Kuwait in 1990.

CONCLUSION

The Iraq war was launched in March 2003, but US-Iraqi tensions had been building throughout the 1990s. Although the 1991 war had severely weakened Iraq, the wily dictator from Tikrit not only failed to cooperate with UN inspectors as mandated by UNSC Resolution 687 but acted as if he had WMD, which he evidently lacked. He may have thought that this pretense would send a signal to his real and imagined adversaries at both the domestic and international level that he was strong, that he could deter their attacks, even punish them with retaliation if need be. Yet by doing so, he constructed himself as the very threat that the administration of George W. Bush wanted to check and then eliminate after the 9/11 attacks. In this sense, Saddam was once again acting as his own worst enemy.

The United States appears to have invaded Iraq chiefly because it feared WMD in the hands of a dictator and assumed the worst about Saddam's connections to terrorists. These concerns were significantly heightened and reframed by 9/11. That tectonic event altered the prism through which Bush administration officials saw the world, particularly the potential threat posed by Iraq. This helps to explain why the United States saw Iraq so differently than did so many other countries around the world.

American fears were exacerbated by poor intelligence, which, viewed through the 9/11 prism, took on new meaning. Most likely, this intelligence was used selectively by some officials to justify a war that the administration thought was necessary. Although 9/11 created a potential strategic rationale for going to war against Iraq, it also allowed the administration to garner public support for war. That had been lacking even after the United States made regime change in Iraq its official policy in 1998.

By eliminating Saddam's regime and refashioning Iraq, the administration could also advance democratization in the Middle East. If terrorists were hatched partly because they lived in repressive societies, democratic "shock therapy" to the region, as romantic as it sounded, might ameliorate this problem. At the same time, the United States could help secure Iraq as a hedge against post-9/11 instability in oil-rich Saudi Arabia.

Domestic and personal motivations for war cannot be ruled out, but they do not appear to be as important as the primary factors. After all, they had not generated war earlier, in the absence of the critical factors outlined above.

Notes

1. http://tinyurl.com/2mf24r.

2. For the texts of major UN resolutions adopted in 1991, see *UN Security Resolutions on Iraq: Compliance and Implementation*, Report to the Committee on Foreign Affairs by the CRS (Washington, DC: Government Printing Office, March 1992).

3. For the text of the resolution, see http://tinyurl.com/5b12.

4. On this jockeying and for the draft of the resolution at this time, see *New York Times*, October 23, 2002.

5. Hans Blix, *An Update on Inspection*, Report of the Executive Chairman of UN-MOVIC to the United Nations Security Council, New York, January 27, 2003, http://tinyurl.com/65ewxz.

6. http://tinyurl.com/4sc68d9.

7. Powell's statement in front of the UN, excerpted in the *New York Times*, February 23, 2003.

8. Dafna Linzer, "Iraq Approves Inspectors' Use of U-2 Surveillance Planes, Iraqi Ambassador Says," Associated Press, February 6, 2003.

9. Thane Gustafson, *Changing Course? Iraq and the "New" US-Russian Relationship* (Cambridge, MA: Cambridge Energy research Associates, 2003), 2–3.

10. Yossef Bodansky, *The Secret History of the Iraq War* (New York: HarperCollins, 2004), 5.

11. On the war's motivations, see Lawrence Freedman, "War in Iraq: Selling the Threat," *Survival*, Summer 2004.

12. Bob Woodward, *Plan of Attack* (New York: Simon & Schuster, 2004), 155.

13. Cited in Freedman, "War in Iraq," 24.

14. Ibid., 5.

15. White House, "President Bush Outlines Iraqi Threat," October 7, 2002, http://www.whitehouse.gov.

16. Remarks by President Bush on Iraq in the Rose Garden, September 26, 2002, http://tinyurl.com/4owev9u.

17. http://tinyurl.com/2b9pfa.

18. Kenneth Katzman, *Iraq: US Efforts to Change the Regime* (Washington, DC: Congressional Research Service, October 3, 2002), 10–11.

19. On how the war was sold, see Chaim Kaufmann, "Threat Inflation and the Failure of the Marketplace of Ideas: The Selling of the Iraq War," *International Security* 29 (2004).

20. Dick Cheney, "The Risks of Inaction Are Far Greater Than the Risk of Action," Address to the 103rd National Convention of the Veterans of Foreign Wars, August 26, 2002.

21. The full text of the State of the Union address appears at http://www.gpoaccess.gov/sou/index.html.

22. Radio Address by the President to the Nation, Office of the Press Secretary, September 28, 2002.

23. See Philip H. Gordon, "Iraq: The Transatlantic Debate," Institute for Security Studies Occasional Paper 39 (November 2002): 15. For an argument that this connection did exist, see Laurie Mylroie, *Bush vs. the Beltway: How the CIA and the State Department Tried to Stop the War on Terror* (New York: Regan Books, 2003).

24. Memorandum from Richard A. Clarke to Condoleezza Rice, National Security Council, Washington, DC, January 25, 2001.

25. Bob Woodward, *Bush at War* (New York: Simon & Schuster, 2002), 34–35.

26. Dick Cheney, "Speech to the Council on Foreign Relations," Washington, DC, February 15, 2002, http://tinyurl.com/druxp.

27. Downing Street memo text, http://tinyurl.com/dubld.

28. See Kaufmann, "Threat Inflation and the Failure of the Marketplace of Ideas." For a view that the al-Qa'ida connection to Iraq was real, see Yossef Bodansky, *The Secret History of the Iraq War* (New York: HarperCollins, 2004), chap. 3.

29. Quoted in Woodward, *Plan of Attack*, 27.

30. Testimony by Secretary of Defense Donald H. Rumsfeld, Senate Armed Services Committee, Washington, DC, July 9, 2003, http://tinyurl.com/4dz2b6q.

31. Colin L. Powell, "Remarks to the United Nations Security Council," US Department of State, February 5, 2003, 19.

32. Some scholars argue that it did do so. See ibid.

33. See the account by former counterterrorism chief Richard Clarke, in Richard A. Clarke, *Against All Enemies: Inside America's War on Terror* (New York: Free Press, 2004), 30.

34. Testimony of National Security Adviser Condoleezza Rice, 9/11 Commission, April 8, 2004; Freedman, "War in Iraq," 18–19. On the impact of 9/11, see Woodward, *Bush at War*, 34–35; "US Decision on Iraq Has Puzzling Past: Opponents of War Wonder When, How Policy Was Set," *Washington Post*, January 12, 2003.

35. Woodward, *Bush at War*, 99.

36. Radio Address by the President to the Nation, Office of the Press Secretary, December 7, 2002.

37. Letter to Senator Bob Graham, October 7, 2002.

38. On this debate, see Robert W. Merry, *Sands of Empire: Missionary Zeal, American Foreign Policy, and the Hazards of Global Ambition* (New York: Simon & Schuster, 2005).

39. "Statement by the President in His Address to the Nation," September 11, 2001.

40. For instance, see the president's address to the American Enterprise Institute, February 26, 2003.

41. Madeleine Albright, *Madam Secretary: A Memoir* (New York: Hyperion, 2003), 416.

42. Steven R. Weisman, "Rice Urges Egyptians and Saudis to Democratize," *New York Times*, June 21, 2005, A1.

43. "Excerpts from President Bush's Remarks at the Air Force Academy Graduation Ceremony," *New York Post*, June 3, 2004, 33.

44. *New York Times*, February 3, 2005, A1.

45. Quoted in Woodward, *Plan of Attack*, 12.

46. Freedman, "War in Iraq," 15–16.

47. Katzman, *Iraq: US Efforts to Change the Regime*, 7–12.

48. On this doctrine, see Lawrence Freedman, *Deterrence* (London: Polity, 2004). The full text of the State of the Union address appears at http://tinyurl.com/4jf3set.

49. See George W. Bush, "National Strategy to Combat Weapons of Mass Destruction," White House, December 2002.

50. http://tinyurl.com/dea7.

51. Remarks by the president and British Prime Minister Tony Blair, White House, January 31, 2003, http://tinyurl.com/4rppavm.

52. Remarks by the president on Iraq, Cincinnati, Ohio, October 7, 2002, http://tinyurl.com/4bnsg3r.

53. Colin Powell on C-SPAN, December 8, 2004.

54. Select Committee on Intelligence, US Senate, *Report on the US Intelligence Community's Prewar Intelligence Assessments on Iraq,* July 7, 2004; Commission on the Intelligence Capabilities of the United States Regarding Weapons of Mass Destruction, *Report to the President of the United States,* March 31, 2005.

55. For instance, regarding Iraq's obtainment of nuclear materials from Niger, see Joseph Wilson, *The Politics of Truth: Inside the Lies That Put the White House on Trial and Betrayed My Wife's CIA Identity* (New York: Carroll & Graf, 2005), chap. 15.

56. Douglas Jehl, "Report Warned Bush Team About Intelligence Doubts," *New York Times,* November 6, 2005.

57. National Security Archive, Casual Conversation, June 28, 2004. http://tinyurl.com/mtz9gg.

58. See, for instance, David Hastings Dunn, "Myths, Motivations, and 'Misunderestimations': The Bush Administration and Iraq," *International Affairs* 79 (2003).

59. Cited in ibid., 280.

60. *Frontline* interview with Osama bin Laden, "Hunting the Enemy," May 1998.

61. See, for instance, Craig Whitlock, "Commandos Free Hostages Being Held in Saudi Arabia," *Washington Post,* May 30, 2004.

62. National Security Directive 54, White House, Washington, DC, January 15, 1991. Steve A. Yetiv, *Explaining Foreign Policy: US Decision-Making and the Persian Gulf War* (Baltimore: Johns Hopkins University Press, 2004).

63. On Iraq's potential, see Vincent Lauerman, "Gulf War II: Longer-Term Implications for the World Oil Market," *Geopolitics of Energy,* April 2003.

64. Dresdner, Kleinwort, Wasserstein Research, "Oil Prices Short-Term Strength Masking Longer-Term Weakness," *World Oil Report: 2002,* 2, July 24, 2002.

65. This figure represents the average of several different estimates. On Iraq's potential, see Fadhil J. Chalabi, "Iraq and the Future of World Oil," *Middle East Policy* 7 (October 2000). Iraq could eventually triple its current production capacity; see EIA, *Annual Energy Outlook 2002.*

66. Issam Al-Chalabi, *Iraqi Oil Policy: Present and Future Perspectives* (Cambridge, MA: Cambridge Energy Research Associates, 2003).

67. Lauerman, "Gulf War II."

68. John S. Duffield, "Oil and the Iraq War: How the United States Could Have Expected to Benefit, and Might Still," *Middle East Review of International Affairs* 9 (June 2005).

69. On these views, see, for instance, Michael Ratner, Jennie Green, and Barbara Olshansky, *Against War in Iraq: An Anti-War Primer* (New York: Seven Stories Press, 2003).

70. On the war's motivations, see Freedman, "War in Iraq," especially p. 9.

71. Quoted in Craig Unger, *House of Bush, House of Saud: The Secret Relationship Between the World's Two Most Powerful Dynasties* (New York: Scribner, 2004), 225.

72. See Erik Eckholm, "Now You See It: An Audit of KBR," *New York Times,* March 20, 2005, A4.

73. Remarks by President Bush on September 26, 2002.

74. Brent Scowcroft, "Don't Attack Saddam," *Wall Street Journal,* August 15, 2002.

75. Andrew J. Bacevich and Elizabeth H. Prodromou, "God Is Not Neutral: Religion and US Foreign Policy After 9/11," *Orbis* 48 (Winter 2004): 49.

76. *New York Times,* February 15, 2003.

77. Mark Juergensmeyer, "Religious Terror and Global War," in *Understanding September 11,* ed. Craig Calhoun et al. (New York: New Press, 2002).

78. Edward Peters, "The Firanj Are Coming—Again," *Orbis* 48 (Winter 2004): 3–19.

79. Fawaz A. Gerges, *America and Political Islam: Clash of Cultures or Clash of Interests* (Cambridge: Cambridge University Press, 1999), especially chap. 3.

80. See John J. Mearsheimer and Stephen M. Walt, *The Israel Lobby and US Foreign Policy* (New York: Farrar, Straus & Giroux, 2007).

CHAPTER 20

WHAT WENT
WRONG IN IRAQ?

Ali R. Abootalebi

The George W. Bush administration launched its invasion of Iraq in 2003 confident that American forces would liberate Iraq and would be met with welcoming crowds of Iraqis throwing flowers and blowing kisses. This euphoric entrance into Baghdad was to be followed, it was hoped, by a quick transition to a liberal secular democracy, if possible through the election of an American-friendly government composed principally of former exiles, in particular that of Ahmed Chalabi and his Iraqi National Congress (INC). With the impressive American military victory in Afghanistan and the creation of the friendly Karzai government in Kabul only a year earlier, it seemed the template had already been established. The situation in Iraq, however, remained uncertain as President Bush left office, and it remains untenable as of late 2010, almost two years into Barack Obama's presidency.

As of this writing the United States not only has failed to achieve its stated policy objectives in Iraq but has actually damaged its long-term policy goals in the Middle East region and reduced the likelihood of its victory in the "war on terror." Rather than establishing a stable democracy with a viable working economy, the invasion of Iraq instead brought the country to the brink of sectarian civil war, intensified sectarian divisions in the Iraqi political system, undermined regional and international public support for US foreign policy, and seriously weakened the US military.

For these reasons, the Iraq invasion of 2003 was a strategic mistake for the United States. It was the result of a combination of factors—principally the neoconservative imperial hubris that had infected the Bush administration since September 11, 2001, and inadequate knowledge of Iraqi society and culture among key decision makers. This latter factor also played a role in the many tactical errors made by US personnel in the planning stages of the invasion and in its immediate aftermath—all of which simply compounded the strategic mistake made in the decision to go to war. These include (but are not limited to) the decision to invade with a light force, the lack of postwar planning, the decision to quickly disband the Iraqi military, and the absence of comprehensive communication with the Shi'a community and its leadership.

This chapter provides a comprehensive explanation of why the US invasion of Iraq was a strategic mistake and accounts for the many tactical errors that were subsequently made in its implementation.[1] No such analysis would be complete, however, without some suggestions for how a transformed US policy might succeed in extricating its forces from the country while leaving behind a government somewhat amenable to its interests. These suggestions are discussed in the conclusion.

THE IRAQ WAR AS A STRATEGIC MISTAKE

The Shortsighted Neoconservative Vision

The strategic mistake of going to war with Iraq resulted from President Bush's miscalculation that the transition to stability and democracy in the aftermath of the invasion would be relatively easy. That the president was so misled was the direct result of a number of influential policy advisers, academics, and decision makers, many of whom adhere to the vision of American hegemony known as neoconservatism. Though the roots of this movement date back several decades, the neoconservative movement achieved unprecedented publicity and power through the so-called Project for a New American Century and the influence its members gained within the Bush administration.

Individuals in positions of influence who have been part of this neoconservative movement since 2000 include former vice president Dick Cheney; former secretary of defense Donald Rumsfeld; former deputy secretary of defense Paul Wolfowitz; former undersecretary of defense for policy Douglas Feith; Cheney's chief of staff, Lewis Libby; Zalmay Khalilzad (later US ambassador to Iraq); special assistant to the president and senior director for Near East and North African Affairs from 2002 to 2005, Elliot Abrams; and chairman, from 2001 to 2003, of the Defense Policy Advisory Board, Richard Perle.

The neoconservative push to invade Iraq was driven by a number of policy objectives. First, neocons desired to export secular democracy and free market capitalism to Iraq and the wider Middle East. Transforming Iraq into a democracy would lessen the threat it posed to its neighbors, thus allowing for the redeployment of US troops from Saudi Arabia, where their presence near Islam's holiest sites continued to incite Muslim anger. Second, replacing the Saddam regime with a US-friendly government would end its support for Islamic terrorists fighting Israel. Third, such a government would also aid the US goal of securing oil and gas pipelines from the Middle East, the Caucasus, and Central Asia. And finally, an invasion would end a twelve-year policy of economic sanctions and no-fly zones that were continuing to make the United States look ineffectual and weak. All of this could be achieved, they believed, through a rapid military campaign and the replacement of the Ba'thist regime with a mostly secular government composed principally of friendly exiled Iraqis.

Unable to justify the intervention on these policy objectives alone, the Bush administration appeared to fabricate a threat from Iraqi weapons of mass destruction (WMD) and to exaggerate the connections between the Saddam regime and international terrorism. The "Downing Street memo," as first reported on May 1, 2005, by the *Sunday Times* of London, revealed, for example, that British Prime Minister Tony Blair was told by the head of Britain's MI6 intelligence service, Sir Richard Dearlove, that in 2002 the Bush administration was selectively choosing evidence that supported its case for going to war and ignoring anything to the contrary.[2] James Risen of the *New York Times* provided vital additional background to the Downing Street memo in his book *State of War.*

Iraq's WMD program was in fact limited to mainly laboratory experimentation with chemical and biological substances, its stockpile of weapons having long been destroyed. Since the first Gulf War the UN inspection teams had successfully discovered and supervised the destruction of 90 percent of these weapons, and the regime itself disposed of its stockpiles for fear of potential reprisals. The evidence on Iraq's nuclear activities also pointed to a rudimentary program that never really recovered after the Israeli destruction of the Osirak nuclear plant in 1981. In October 2004, the head of the Iraq Survey Group (ISG), Charles Duelfer, announced that the group had found no evidence that Iraq had produced and stockpiled any WMD since 1991, when UN sanctions were imposed.[3]

Misreading Iraqi Society and Culture

The neoconservative vision failed to take account of Iraqi culture and society and underestimated the influence of Iran. The ethnic (Arabs, Kurds, Turkmen), religious (Shi'a, Sunni), and tribal divisions in Iraq were bound to become a source of instability once the repressive central government was toppled. Islam is the religion of 97 percent of the population, divided along Shi'a, 60–65 percent, and Sunni Islam, 32–37 percent, with Christians and other minorities constituting the rest. The Arab-Kurd divide in Iraq overlaps the Sunni-Shi'a divide, as the 15–20 percent Kurdish population overwhelmingly follows Sunni Islam.[4] The Shi'a clerical leadership continues to emphasize Iraq's Islamic character instead of ethnic and class divisions. While the future of ethnic relations remains uncertain, especially in the face of Kurdish historical aspirations for independence, it is the goal of the Shi'a and Sunni clerical leadership in Iraq and in neighboring Iran to promote Iraqi unity along with its Islamic identity. Indeed, given the current situation in Iraq, Islam is the only common denominator among the four main rival ethnic groups (including the small minority of Turkmen) capable of keeping Iraq unified. Secular democracy can be a very attractive solution for observers and policymakers from outside the region, as it evidently was to the Bush administration. But how can secular democracy take hold almost overnight in a society that has had entrenched religious institutions for fourteen hundred years? The experimentation with modernization elsewhere in the Middle East has usually resulted in weak societies and strong states, where power elites have continued to rule through political rhetoric and parochial sources of legitimization, including religion, personal charisma, and political repression and/or cooptation.[5] The rise of political Islam and its relative success in Iran in the mobilization and redirection of socioeconomic resources has raised hopes among sectors of the populace in Iraq and Muslims elsewhere. It is unlikely that a majority of Iraqis will abandon what is so familiar and dear— Islam—for an unknown imported ideology supported by the American and British occupiers and their cohorts among Iraq's secular elites.

The return, however, of Islam to the center stage of politics and society in the Middle East is not surprising. It need not be seen as a threatening force against political stability and democracy in the region. The interplay between Islam and politics in Iraq today is over the question of "effective governance," and not whether Islam is trying to totally dominate politics or to use the democratic process to destroy democracy for the sake of an Islamic theocracy. The question really should be whether political Islam can govern and whether Islam and democracy can coexist within particular Muslim (e.g., Iraqi) sociopolitical, economic, and cultural milieus. If this dilemma is not resolved, US fears about political Islam will seriously damage its interests in Iraq and in the Middle East in general.

Undermining the War on Terror

The resistance of the ex-Ba'thists, jihadists, and nationalists to the occupation, though motivated by different agendas, proved lethal. The jihadists, inspired by al-Qa'ida and Salafi and Wahhabi ideologies, have considered Iraq a potential base for continuing their jihad against the crusading West and their Iraqi allies. The Iraqi nationalists and ex-Ba'thists, on the other hand, saw their fight against occupation as a matter of Iraqi pride and lost socioeconomic resources and prestige. The insurgency used every means available in attacks on coalition forces and Iraqi government forces with the objective of either regaining lost power (the primary motivation of the ex-Ba'thists) or setting up a new Islamic base to counter the US presence in Iraq and its support of "corrupt" regimes in the Arab world (the goal of the jihadists).

The post-9/11 terrorist attack on American forces in Iraq revealed that al-Qa'ida is a multinational network of dedicated radical militants from all over the Muslim world, committed to an anti-Western, especially anti-American, campaign. The ultimate goal of al-Qa'ida is the eradication of Western influence and control over Muslim countries, especially the oil-rich Middle East. But equally important to al-Qa'ida operatives is the overthrow of "corrupt" governments in the Middle East and elsewhere in the Muslim world, who, with the support of the West, have abandoned the will of Allah—the establishment of just and viable Islamic governments. Osama bin Laden has cited US support for the "illegitimate" state of Israel in its conflict with the conquered Palestinians, the US military presence in Saudi Arabia and the Persian Gulf states and support for their corrupt regimes, and the long-standing US sanctions against innocent Iraqi people as the fundamental reasons behind his strong anti-American stance. One observer has succinctly summarized the challenge to American foreign policy in the Middle East:

> Two groups have come under examination in the "why do they hate us?" debate that has unfolded since September 11, 2001. One comprises the perpetrators of violence and terrorism—the Osama bin Ladens, the Mohammad Attas, and some suicide bombers. They are fanatics in every sense of the word. Their interpretations of politics and Islam are so extreme that they disparage the great majority of Muslim Middle Easterners as "unbelievers." They are not going to be deterred by debate, compromise, sanctions, or even the threat of death. The challenge they pose to the United States is a security issue, a matter to be dealt with through careful police work and military action. America's resources are adequate for dealing with this threat. The vastly larger group of Muslim Middle Easterners who express anger toward the United States and evince some sympathy for bin Laden pose a far more serious challenge. This group's members are afflicted by middle-class frustrations, governed by political systems that give them no voice, and burdened by economies that offer them few opportunities. They are witnessing a conflict over land and sacred places in which they perceive the United States as applying two standards of equity and two standards of measuring violence, each in favor of Israel. That resulting frustration and anger leads to expressions of sympathy for those who resort to violence against the United States.[6]

The Bush administration and its supporters claimed that Iraq had become a graveyard for militant jihadists and therefore the United States had become safer since the battleground had moved away from the homeland. However, it has become clear from various assessments by Israeli, British, and American sources that the invasion of Iraq created a new generation of Islamic jihadists who will continue to pose a serious threat to the United States for years to come. For example, the appearance of many self-starter terrorists, like the ones responsible for the attack on Madrid's public transportation system in 2004 and London's in 2005, and the Iraqi jihadist movement, including groups like Ansar al-Sunna and the Islamic Army of Iraq, negate the claim of a jihadist retreat in the aftermath of the Iraqi invasion.

Iraq in October 2010 appears more secure and has endured less jihadist activities, but it remains far from stable. The newly created al-Sahwa army helped eject many jihadists from Iraq, as Iraqi tribal youth were mobilized and paid to fight al-Qa'ida. The Status of Forces Agreement (SOFA) between the Iraqi government and the United States in October 2008 also signaled the withdrawal of US forces from Iraq by summer 2011, a central demand of Moqtada al-Sadr. Meanwhile, violence and killing continued. Iraq's Monitor of Constitutional Freedom and Bill of Rights revealed that in October 2010, 231 people were killed and 601 others wounded by exploding IEDs across Iraq in the first ten months of this year.[7] Political wrangling after the March 2010 parliamentary elections between Nuri al-Maliki and his State of Law party and Iyad Allawi's al-Iraqiyya party over the formation of an Iraqi government underlines the continuing sectarian nature of Iraqi politics.

The war in Iraq has also drawn resources away from the US war on terror. The nonpartisan Congressional Research Service estimates that the United States will have spent almost $802 billion on funding the war by the end of fiscal year 2011, with $747.6 billion already appropriated by mid-2010.[8] Nobel laureate Joseph E. Stiglitz and Harvard budget expert Linda Bilmes estimated the cost of the Iraq war in 2005 at $1–2 trillion, far higher than earlier estimates of $100–200 billion at the beginning of the war. The Stiglitz and Bilmes study included such costs as the long-term medical needs of war veterans and opportunity costs involving the war.[9] The authors upgraded their figures to the amount of $3 trillion and more in September 2010.[10] American and coalition troops dead in Iraq as of October 2010 stood at 4,427 Americans, 179 Britons, and a total 4,745 for the coalition.[11]

Further troubling for US interests is a widespread belief among Iraqis that the US presence in Iraq is not for the sake of their "liberation" but for their oil wealth and that the US military will remain in Iraq indefinitely. A 2006 survey of Iraqi attitudes toward Americans indicated that:

> Large majorities of Iraqis believe that the United States has no intention of ever withdrawing all its military forces from their country and that Washington's reconstruction efforts have been incompetent at best: Eighty percent of respondents said they believe the US intends to maintain permanent military bases in Iraq, including 79 percent of Shi'a Arabs, 92 percent of Sunnis, and two-thirds of Kurds, some of whose leaders have quietly suggested that Washington would be welcome to establish bases in Kurdistan in northern Iraq.[12]

Terrorism experts Peter Bergen and Alec Reynolds suggested in 2005 that the war in Iraq "will generate a ferocious blowback of its own, which—as a classified CIA assessment predicts—could be longer and more powerful than that from Afghanistan in the 1990s and beyond."[13] This is aside from the drastically declining popularity of the United States in the Arab and Muslim world, as indicated by various polls taken by the Pew Research Center for the People and the Press, Zogby, and CNN/Gallup.

COMPOUNDING THE STRATEGIC MISTAKE: TACTICAL ERRORS IN PLANNING AND IMPLEMENTATION

Too Few Ground Troops

Soon after the initial US and UK launch of "Shock and Awe" and the ground invasion on March 20, 2003, it became clear that an inadequate number of troops had been committed to the operation. When Baghdad fell in sixteen days, on April 5, it was attributed to American military strategy and technological superiority. Some elements of the Iraqi army put up stiff resistance in places like Nasariyah, but the scale of the resistance was far smaller than the expected house-to-house battle in Iraqi cities. The statue of Saddam Hussein in Firdos Square came down on April 9, but the potent and deadly American military lacked the numbers to both occupy and control vast Iraqi territories. As General Franks put it, the United States had sufficient combat forces in Iraq but did not initially have enough civil affairs, military police, and other units needed to establish order after major combat was over; the issue was not the level of forces, but their composition. Reporting on General Franks's assessment, Michael Gordon of the *New York Times* asserted: "This was partly a result of difficulties in getting all of the Central Command's force requests approved quickly at the Pentagon. He also admitted that delays in obtaining funds from Congress for reconstruction efforts and the decision of many foreign governments not to send troops had contributed to the continuing turmoil in Iraq."[14] General Franks stopped short of criticizing his boss, Donald Rumsfeld, but by then the gulf between the Pentagon and the commanders on the ground on military strategy was increasingly apparent.

Others have reached similar conclusions. The generals on the ground understood what a disaster they were creating in the race to reach Baghdad, which left in its wake an entire country full of places where Saddam Hussein's loyalists could regroup and prepare to carry on a permanent war. In *Cobra II*, Michael Gordon and General Bernard Trainor underscore that the generals in the field were overruled by directives from Washington. They argue that in addition to the actual war, there was an ongoing war between US field commanders, their own senior commander (General Tommy Franks, the head of Central Command), and civilian leaders in Washington. Gordon and Trainor contend that the US military's quick victory came despite the strategic miscalculations of senior civilian and military leaders and that the Bush team's misjudgments made the situation in Iraq far worse than it otherwise would have been.[15] Michael Gordon observed in late 2004:

> Looking back at that crucial time, officers, administration officials, and others provided an intimate and detailed account of how the postwar situation went awry. Civilian administrators of the Iraqi occupation raised concerns about plans to reduce American forces; intelligence agencies left American forces unprepared for the furious battles they encountered in Iraq's southern cities and did not emphasize the risks of a postwar insurgency. And senior American generals and civilians were at odds over plans to build a new Iraqi army, which was needed to impose order.[16]

Insufficient Planning

On April 14, 2003, the Pentagon declared an end to major combat operations after US forces took control of Tikrit in northern Iraq. The question no one was asking, however, was, What happened to the Iraqi army? The presumption seemed to be that the Iraqi army, facing certain destruction, had simply dissolved. But the Iraqi army had proven itself a loyal army with strong commitments to the Ba'thist ide-ology and the rule of the privileged Sunni Arabs. Speculations about Saddam's army making a grand stand in a battle of cities did not materialize, since the Iraqi army had learned the lessons of the first Persian Gulf war in 1991 on how deadly a direct confrontation with US forces can be. The Pentagon, however, had failed to anticipate and prepare for an unconventional guerrilla war. It should not have come as a surprise to the war planners that the core of the Iraqi army, the Repub-lican Guards, would fight the invasion, but on its own terms. In the 1991 war, the Iraqi army sacrificed thousands of its poorly trained and equipped peasant army to slow down the American liberation of Kuwait and the occupation of southern Iraq, while the elite Republican Guards suppressed the Shi'a and Kurdish rebellion and ensured the regime's survival. In October 2004 Condoleezza Rice put the blame for the insurgency primarily "on the fact that many Iraqi forces fled during the American push to Baghdad, only to fight another day."[17]

When Ambassador L. Paul Bremer III issued his decrees on May 16 and 23, 2003, disestablishing the Ba'th party and disbanding Iraqi armed forces, he was fu-eling the resistance with additional incentives for a prolonged guerrilla resistance to the occupation. The Ba'thists had ruled over Iraq since 1968, with strong ties to tribal leaders and an iron fist policy in suppressing Shi'a and Kurdish opposition. The Iraqi regime had survived eight years of a disastrous war with Iran and the hu-miliation of the first Persian Gulf War and then survived and even thrived under the United Nations sanctions regime throughout the 1990s. The declaration of these decrees could not undo a woven network of connections and privileges in Iraqi civil-military relations, and Paul Bremer should have known that. The hard core of the loyal Republican Guards had prepared to disband itself on the eve of the war but only to engage in a prolonged guerrilla fight later. The tactics and skills used by the insurgents in Iraq are testimony to the Guards' central involvement in the insurgency.

The chaos that fell on Baghdad after the fall of the regime exposed how ill-prepared the US forces were for dealing with the postconflict situation. The looting of Baghdad began almost immediately after coalition troops arrived in Baghdad. While the Baghdad National Museum was being looted, US troops were busy pro-tecting the oil ministry. The poorly protected munitions depots were looted, and nearly all government services came to a halt. The absence of police protection and the prolonged disruptions in electric, water, sewage, and other basic services con-tributed to the transformation of the initial low-intensity conflict into a much deadlier form of insurgency. On July 16, 2003, General John Abizaid called the increasing attacks on coalition troops a "guerrilla-type campaign," speculating that troops might need to be deployed for up to one year. The August 19, 2003, bomb-ing of the UN's Baghdad office, killing UN representative Sergio Vieira de Mello and twenty-one others, and the August 29 bombing in Najaf that killed eighty-three people, including the leader of the Supreme Council for the Islamic Revolu-tion in Iraq (SCIRI, later renamed Islamic Supreme Council of Iraq or Supreme Islamic Iraqi Council, ISCI or SIIC), Mohammad Baqir al-Hakim, were devastating blows to the United States and other coalition members as the new protectors of the Iraqi people. By then, the number of US combat deaths had reached 117, and more had died since the declared end of combat operations than had died during the initial combat.

In the first eight months after the invasion, the Bremer administration tried to recover international support for the coalition occupation of Iraq and legitimate the coalition troop presence. The creation of the twenty-five-member Iraqi Governing Council on July 13, 2003, and its August 14 UN Security Council approval were intended to mend earlier splits in the UN Security Council that positioned the United States and Great Britain on one side and France (and Germany) and, to a lesser degree, China and the Russian Federation on the other. Later, on November 15, Bremer's Coalition Provisional Authority (CPA) and the Iraqi Governing Council (IGC) signed an agreement to draft an interim constitution by February 28, 2004, and to transfer power by July 1, 2004. In the meantime, Bremer and the US military were caught by surprise as insurgents stepped up their deadly attacks and the Shi'a religious leadership began to flex its muscle. The number of US soldiers killed in Iraq reached five hundred on January 17, 2004, and soon the Grand Ayatollah Ali al-Sistani rejected the US proposal for indirect, caucus-style elections. Iraq's Shi'a leadership was not a part of the "grand coalition" of Iraqi exiles who were slated to govern postinvasion Iraq.

The insurgency was also fueled by ordinary Iraqis who joined the cause because of their loss of livelihood or because of humiliation suffered at the hands of the Americans. The injection of non-Iraqi foreign fighters and al-Qa'ida jihadists into the Iraqi theater served to strengthen the existing resistance, since the war with the coalition forces was already expected to be a long-term conflict.

Underestimating the Shi'a Factor in Both Iraq and Iran

Although Ahmad Chalabi and the mainly secular members of the Iraq National Congress (INC) had the attention and support of neoconservatives in Washington, a larger and more popular group of Iraqi oppositionists had spent years organizing in Iran, building the foundation of a future Islamic Iraq. The SCIRI and Hizb al-Da'wah had long established political and theological links between the seminaries in Qom (Iran) and al-Najaf (Iraq), with a clear vision that Iraq would one day become an Islamic republic. Given the traditional ties between the Shi'a leadership in Iran and the Shi'a leadership in Iraq, the Ayatollah Ali al-Sistani's stature in both the Shi'a and Sunni communities, and the suffering of Iraqi people under the secular Ba'thist regime, the clerics in Iraq were inevitably going to rise to the center stage of Iraqi politics. However, the United States made no serious contacts with the Shi'a leadership in Iraq prior to, or in the initial phase of, the invasion, and Jay Garner and Paul Bremer seemed oblivious to the gathering Shi'a power. Clearly the Shi'a leadership would have not agreed then, nor would it agree in the future, to submit to secular politics and an extended US military presence in Iraq. Nevertheless, the exclusion of prominent indigenous and exiled Shi'a clerics from plans for the future of Iraq certainly added to the mistrust of US intentions.

The clash between US forces and the militia loyal to the fiery and popular Shi'a leader Moqtada al-Sadr on April 4, 2004, was testimony not so much to the divisions within the Shi'a clerical leadership but to their preferred strategies. Despite the CPA issuing an arrest warrant for al-Sadr, his Mahdi Army fought US forces for seven weeks until the truce agreement on May 27. The truce was really the product of al-Sistani's call for al-Sadr to stop fighting in order to prevent a premature popular Shi'a rebellion, at a time when the mainly Sunni and Jihadi resistance to the coalition forces meant accepting, for the present, US meddling in Iraqi affairs. Ayatollah al-Sistani may adhere to the quietist school of Shi'a Islam—which calls for clerics to avoid direct involvement in politics—but his vision for the future of Iraq parallels his Shi'a counterparts in Iraq and Iran who oppose secular political governance and social relations. The Shi'a clerical leadership understands that in light of Sunni Arab and Kurdish opposition to a Shi'a-dominated state, it must enlist the cooperation of non-Shi'a sectors of the Iraqi population. Thus the key to its political success is the utilization of both cooperation (al-Sistani) and resistance (al-Sadr) to maintain its leverage. However, the Bush administration was oblivious to the networking power of the religious *hawzehs*—religious seminaries—in Iraq and Iran. There are millions of dedicated supporters among Shi'a and Sunni Islamic movements who, having rejected Ba'thism and despising foreign military occupation, continue to strive for an Islamic Iraq.

The United States, from the beginning, had decided to support secular forces in Iraq in both exile and indigenous communities. The Shi'a clerical power, including open clashes with the al-Mahdi army in Kufa, Karbala, Najaf, al-Kut, and Sadr City, was considered to be a direct challenge to US plans in Iraq. The creation of Iraq's interim administration under Ghazi al-Yawar as president and Ayad Allawi as prime minister was to promote a functional secular government to deal with Iraqis' daily problems. The success of the Allawi administration therefore depended on the position of secular forces in Iraq. However, the revelation of physical and sexual abuse of Iraqi prisoners in Abu Ghraib on April 23, the persistent insurgent attacks on Iraqis and coalition forces, including the beheading of Nick Berg, shown on a video on the Internet on May 11, and the deterioration of living conditions in Iraq continued to undermine the leadership of the US-supported interim administration. It should have come as no surprise when Ayad Allawi's Iraqi National List captured only a small percentage of the vote in the December 12, 2005, parliamentary election. The US administration's ignorance concerning the power of the Shi'a clerics and the unpopularity of the US-backed Iraqi politicians were reflected in a report. The codirectors of Conflicts Forum, a London-based group dedicated to providing an opening to political Islam, Alastair Crooke and Mark Perry, observed that "seventy-two hours before the Iraqi people voted on a new parliament, on December 12, 2005, we were told by a senior US administration official that 'detailed data received by the White House' pointed to a 'decisive win' for Ayad Allawi's Iraqi National List." Allawi's victory would turn the tables on the insurgents, this official said gleefully. "Sectarianism will be the big loser." Allawi's prospective triumph was trumpeted repeatedly over the next two days by US news networks quoting administration officials. Weeks later, after the results of the election became known, it was clear that the White House had overestimated Allawi's popularity. His party received just over 5 percent of the vote.[18]

What emerged by 2005 as a powerful alliance of Shi'a groups, the United Iraqi Alliance, was the natural outcome of the changed political environment in Iraq in the aftermath of the collapse of the Ba'thist regime. Despite their differences in leadership and organization, the leading Shi'a parties in the alliance, SCIRI and al-Da'wah, share aspirations for a religiously oriented Iraq, in close cooperation with their counterparts in Iran. It is no secret that leading Shi'a clerics and networks in Iraq and Iran (as well as in Lebanon) have overlapping and complementary personal and religious ties and experiences. There are prominent Shi'a clerics with their feet in both countries' main religious seminaries in al-Najaf and Qom. Ayatollah Ali al-Sistani, for example, was born in Iran but is the leading religious figure in Iraq. The late Grand Ayatollah Abul-Qassim Khoei was born in Iran in 1899 but moved to Iraq at age thirteen and took residence in the holy city of Najaf. The famous al-Sadr family has had a long history of prominent Shi'a clerical leadership in Iraq and Lebanon. The late Grand Ayatollah Sayyid Muhammad Baqir al-Sadr, who was born in al-Kadhimya, Iraq, and worked with Sayed Mohammed Baqir al-Hakim in forming the Islamic movement in Iraq, is the father-in-law of Moqtada al-Sadr and the cousin of both Mohammad Sadeq al-Sadr and Lebanon's Imam Musa al-Sadr. Ayatollah Sayed Mohammed Baqir al-Hakim, cofounder of SCIRI, fled to Iran in 1980 and, along with Iranian Ayatollah Modarresi, cofounded SCIRI. Moqtada Sadr is currently studying in Qom seminary to become an ayatollah. There are currently sixteen grand ayatollahs and twenty-two ayatollahs who are directly or indirectly active in the Qom religious seminaries, many with personal and religious ties with al-Najaf in Iraq.[19] The Bush administration's wishful thinking that Iraq would become a secular democracy was an act of self-deception.

Further endangering American goals in Iraq and Afghanistan are Iranian leaders' perceptions and policies. Tehran is nervous about the American (and NATO) military presence in Iraq and Afghanistan and the ensuing instability in both of these countries, including drastic increases in drug trafficking and ethnic tension, which have spilled over into Iran. Added to this concern is the well-established US infantry, naval, and aerial presence in the Persian Gulf and in the Caucasus and Central Asia. The socioeconomic and political challenges from within Iran, where two-thirds of the population is under thirty years old and national development has tangibly been hurt because of American economic, political, and diplomatic pressure, also have had security implications for this state. That is, the Iranian leadership strongly believes that the United States was intent on regime change in Iran, especially given the presence of powerful neoconservatives in the Bush administration. Iran's controversial nuclear program has further intensified American political pressure on the government of Iran.

Iraq has in the meantime become a playing card in the high-stakes poker game between Tehran and Washington, especially with the escalating financial and human cost of the war in Iraq and Afghanistan. The Obama administration's Iraq policy has not drastically differed from President Bush's. The reduction of American troops to 50,000 in summer 2010 was a positive step in stabilizing Iraq. The full implementation of SOFA that promises the full withdrawal of American troops from Iraq by summer 2011 must be viewed with skepticism, however. The likely scenario would see thousands of American troops remaining in American-built military bases across Iraq. In the end, the crisis in Iraq cannot be resolved without the cooperation of Iran, but the government in Tehran is trying to tie its leverage in Iraq to its ambitions for a civilian, and perhaps military, nuclear program.[20]

Iran is frequently cited as the biggest beneficiary of America's war on terrorism due to the removal of the Taliban in Afghanistan and Saddam in Iraq. But observers of the region hold differing opinions on how the situation in Iraq will impact Iranian policy. Some have argued that there is no unitary Iranian approach when it comes to Iraq. Michael Eisenstadt argues that "there are debates in Tehran that fall in along ideological as well as pragmatic fault lines." In this scenario, Iran would seek a US withdrawal from Iraq in the long run, but a "manageable" state of conflict would be in their short-term geostrategic interests, since this would keep the United States tied down in Iraq. The US military preoccupation in Iraq would work to Iran's advantage, given the controversy over Iran's nuclear program and the threat of UN sanctions or even military action by the United States, Israel, or both. F. Gregory Gause has a different perspective, contending that "a government [in Iraq] that is seen as a viable democratic model might be a source of embarrassment for Iran." Geoff Porter goes even further and argues that "if Iraq were to evolve into an Islamist democracy, this would be a bad example for Iran, which would be forced to entertain alternative forms of an Islamist state that differ from the current iteration."[21]

Although some Sunni Arabs have accused Iraqi leaders of allowing Shi'a Badr members to infiltrate Iraq's security forces and carry out sectarian violence, this does not indicate an Iranian conspiracy to destabilize Iraq for the sake of keeping American troops preoccupied and thus away from Iran.[22] It is true that SCIRI's military wing, the 12,000-strong Badr Brigades, has received financial and training support from Iran's Revolutionary Guard in the past, and Iran also supports Sadr's Mahdi Army, which on occasion has clashed with the Badr Brigades. (The Mahdi Army for now remains disbanded and inactive but could be quickly reactivated by orders from Moqtada al-Sadr.) But the Shi'a religious leaders in Iraq are the natural allies of Iran, no matter the differences in their tactics in dealing with the occupation. Furthermore, the Sunni religious leadership in Iraq does not necessarily see the Shi'a establishment as a primary enemy. The religious doctrinal differences between the two communities are somewhat significant, but both share the Quran, the *shari'a* (Islamic tradition), the Five Pillars of Islam, and the cultural foundations of the faith. Followers of the both sects of Islam have lived together for centuries without a history of communal clashes.[23] The Sunni-Shi'a divide in Iraq is mainly the result of political jockeying among major contenders of power in Iraq and has been exacerbated by American military and political presence, creating the perception that the Shi'a-dominated government is merely an American puppet government that is also being exploited by the Iranians. Shi'as in Iraq, Lebanon, the Persian Gulf states, and elsewhere see an opportunity to break away from their sociopolitical and economic deprivation through Islamic revivalism. Given the historic religious ties and the majority Shi'a population, Islam will certainly play a central, if not dominating, role in the future of any Iraqi government. The challenge to the United States is to prevent the establishment of an anti-American Shi'a-dominated or an anti-American Arab Sunni/Shi'a-dominated religious state. This is, however, exactly what is occurring. It is in the long-term American national interest to embrace a democratically, albeit religious, elected Iraqi (and Iranian) government, since the *ulama* (Islamic religious scholars) and Islamists are not inherently anti-American.

CONCLUSION

Contrary to political rhetoric by Bush administration statesmen, the United States is not seriously committed to establishing democracy in the Middle East. The United States has cast a blind eye to human rights abuses in Algeria, Egypt, Saudi Arabia, Jordan, Kuwait, Turkey, Afghanistan, Pakistan, Indonesia, and elsewhere in the Muslim world. President George W. Bush's initial reluctance to invest political capital and actively engage in the peace process has proven damaging to the Palestinian Authority and the Arab states in their dealings with Israel. Removing Saddam from power had little to do with the liberation of the Iraqi people. The connection between the two was mentioned, of course, usually with great enthusiasm, but as Lawrence Freedman stated: "Emancipation was not the reason why the Bush administration went to war or invoked international law to justify it. For Cheney and Rumsfeld, the war was about solving the Saddam problem rather than the Iraq problem, about bringing security rather than justice, about toppling the regime rather than building one. After all, the Bush administration had profoundly said that it was not in the business of nation building and would happily leave it to others."[24]

The US strategy to create a secular and democratic Iraq was unrealistic from the start, given Iraq's large Shi'a population, the Shi'a clerical power over their adherents, and their strong connections with religious and political establishments in neighboring Iran. Not only are the numerous strategic and tactical mistakes made in Iraq the result of bad judgment, but they also reflect a lack of fundamental understanding of the nature of Iraq's cultural, religious, and sociopolitical settings. The military and administrative mismanagement of Iraq has also played into the hands of Iraqi opposition to the American military presence. Ironically, these mistakes provide further justification for the decision makers to prolong indefinitely the US military presence in Iraq. The competition between the United States and Iraqi Islamists over the future of Iraq is likely to continue for years to come and will be extremely difficult to resolve.

The voting pattern of the March 2010 parliamentary election showed the persistence of sectarianism in Iraqi politics and thus the likelihood of external influence in Iraq's political development. The Sunni boycott of the 2005 parliamentary elections and sectarian politics in Iraq proved increasingly frustrating for Maliki and many Iraqis. Iraqi Shi'i voters withdrew their support for the highly sectarian ISCI that lost its dominance in local councils across the majority-Shi'i south in 2009 elections. Maliki then moved to reach out to Iraqiyya and Hiwar—the secular list with strong Sunni Arab backing—as his new nonsectarian allies. The Iranian reaction was to restore the old all-Shi'i alliance in preparation for 2010 elections. Ahmad Chalabi became Iran's new point man to help with an agreement between ISCI and Moqtada al-Sadr, while pressuring Maliki to distance himself from secular Ba'thist forces like Iyad Allawi and his al-Iraqiyya party.

A US-Iranian rapprochement is indispensible in stabilizing Iraq and securing the future of the Persian Gulf. Iran's desire to connect the future of Iraq (and Afghanistan) to negotiations over its controversial nuclear program and the future of Persian Gulf security is a logical means of advancing its national interests. Turkey, Syria, Jordan, Kuwait, and Saudi Arabia are other neighbors of Iraq with long-term competing and complementary interests in the composition of future Iraqi governments. Sunni-Shi'a power relations, the future of Kurdish autonomy and/or independence, and the future security of the Persian Gulf region are also central to the future of these countries. Iraq's Shi'a domination and Iran's rising power, however, gives Iran an edge in Iraq, and the United States must realize that.

The final resolution to the conflict in Iraq rests in a compromise over the division of political power and socioeconomic resources among the contending religious and ethnic rivals. The United States must understand that Islam and the *ulama* will continue to play a central role in Iraqi politics and society as both a divisive and a unifying force in the future. It is not unreasonable to assume that any long-term US military presence in Iraq will undercut the legitimacy of Iraqi governments and will be challenged by the Iranian and Syrian governments. The solution to this dilemma can be reached through political rapprochement with these governments to provide for a long-term Persian Gulf security and to improve chances for a final resolution to the Arab-Israeli conflict.

Notes

1. I would like to thank my colleague Stephen Hill for his very helpful comments and editorial suggestions on earlier drafts of this chapter. My thanks also go to the Office of Research and Sponsored Programs at the University of Wisconsin–Eau Claire for its continued support of my research.

2. Mark Memmott, "'Downing Street Memo' Gets Fresh Attention," *USA Today*, June 8, 2005. The memo refers to a meeting on Downing Street on July 23, 2002, attended by Blair, Attorney General Lord Goldsmith, Foreign Secretary Jack Straw, ex-defense secretary Geoff Hoon, Sir Richard, former head of the UK armed forces Admiral Lord Boyce, and head of the Joint Intelligence Committee John Scarlett.

3. BBC, "Report Concludes No WMD in Iraq," October 7, 2004.

4. Central Intelligence Agency, *World Factbook,* http://tinyurl.com/3o1o.

5. For a better understanding of Islam and state-society relations in the Middle East and Islamic world, see Ali R. Abootalebi, *Islam and Democracy: State-Society Relations*

in Developing Countries, 1980–1994 (New York: Garland, 2000); Oliver Roy, *Globalized Islam: The Search for a New Ummah* (New York: Columbia University Press, 2004); Gilles Kepel, *The War for Muslim Minds: Islam and the West* (Cambridge, MA: Belknap, 2004).

6. John Waterbury, "Hate Your Policies, Love Your Institutions," *Foreign Affairs*, January-February 2003, 58–68, at 58.

7. Press TV, October 29, 2010, http://tinyurl.com/4rowncm.

8. BBC, Iraq War in Figures, September 1, 2010, http://tinyurl.com/39yr7pt.

9. Pascal Riche, "The Cost of the War," *TPM Café*, January 5, 2006. The study included costs such as lifetime disability and health care for the over 16,000 injured, one-fifth of whom have serious brain or spinal injuries. It also analyzes the costs to the economy, including the economic value of lives lost and the impact of factors such as higher oil prices that can be partly attributed to the conflict in Iraq. The author's paper also calculated the impact on the economy if a proportion of the money spent on the Iraq war were spent in other ways, including investments in the United States.

10. Joseph E. Stiglitz and Linda J. Bilmes, "The True Cost of the Iraq War: $3 Trillion and Beyond," *Washington Post*, September 5, 2010.

11. Iraq Coalition Casualty Count, http://tinyurl.com/4upvlwy.

12. Jim Lobe, "Most Iraqis Doubt US Will Ever Leave," Inter Press Service, January 31, 2006. The survey was conducted by the Program on International Policy Attitudes (PIPA) at the University of Maryland for WorldPublicOpinion.org and conducted through face-to-face interviews of 1,150 randomly selected Iraqi adults in all eighteen Iraqi provinces in early January, three weeks after the December elections.

13. Peter Bergen and Alec Reynolds, "Blowback Revisited: Today's Insurgents in Iraq Are Tomorrow's Terrorists," *Foreign Affairs*, November-December 2005, 2–6, at 2.

14. Michael R. Gordon, "The Strategy to Secure Iraq Did Not Foresee a Second War," *New York Times*, October 19, 2004.

15. Michael R. Gordon and Bernard E. Trainor, *Cobra II: The Inside Story of the Invasion and Occupation of Iraq* (New York: Pantheon, 2006).

16. Gordon, "Strategy."

17. Ibid.

18. Mark Perry and Alastair Crooke, "How to Lose the War on Terror: Talking with the 'Terrorists,'" *Asia Times*, March 31, 2006. Crooke is the former Middle East adviser to European Union high representative Javier Solana and served as a staff member of the Mitchell Commission investigating the causes of the second intifada. Perry is a Washington, DC–based political consultant, author of six books on US history, and a former personal adviser to Yasser Arafat.

19. The extensive ties that bind the Shi'a *'ulama* in Iran, Iraq, Lebanon, and elsewhere are well known to observers of the Middle East. Basic information is available online at http://en.wikipedia.org/wiki/Qom.

20. For insight into Iran's nuclear program, see Ray Takeyh, "A Nuclear Iran: Challenges and Responses," *Council on Foreign Relations*, March 2, 2006.

21. On the role of Iran in Iraq, see Lionel Beehner, "Iran's Goals in Iraq," *Council on Foreign Relations*, February 23, 2006.

22. Ibid.

23. On the Sunni/Shi'a divide, see Vali R. Naser, "Sunni vs. Shi'a: Religious Rivalry in Iraq and Beyond," *Council on Foreign Relations,* November 3, 2005.

24. Lawrence D. Freedman, "Review Essay, Writing of Wrongs: Was the War in Iraq Doomed from the Start?" *Foreign Affairs*, January-February 2006, 129–134, at 130.

CHAPTER 21

THE PUSH AND PULL OF STRATEGIC COOPERATION

The US Relationship with Turkey in the Middle East

Henri J. Barkey

Not long before the 1974 Cyprus crisis, the US administration decided to move Turkey, along with Greece and Cyprus, from the Near East to Europe. This, of course, was just an organizational change within the State Department, but it would underlie much of Washington's approach to Turkey in the ensuing decades. The importance of Turkey, a major US ally during the cold war, was measured largely by its contribution to NATO's struggle against the Soviet Union. Its strategic location close to both the Soviet Union and the Middle East (one of the premier theaters for superpower rivalry) and control of the straits made Turkey vital to the United States. With the 1991 collapse of the Soviet Union, Washington continued to insist that Turkey was a European country and worked hard to firmly ensconce Ankara in Western institutions by championing its candidacy for European Union (EU) membership.

The new geopolitics of the post-Soviet space opened new arenas of economic and political opportunities for Turkey. It could demonstrate that it had a role to play in Central Asia and the Caucasus, hitherto ruled by Moscow, and, with the collapse of Yugoslavia and the subsequent conflicts in Bosnia and Kosovo, in the Balkans as well.

The 1990s witnessed an evolution in the Turkish-American relationship, which came to embrace many subjects and areas of common concern. In addition to traditional issues such as Greece and Cyprus, these included Iraq, Armenia, and Azer-

376

baijan, the post-9/11 war on terrorism, oil pipelines from the Caucasus and Central Asia, Turkish-Israeli rapprochement, and the future evolution of a European security infrastructure. Most importantly, US commitment to Turkey's EU candidacy has remained solid. Despite the confluence of issues, Ankara's view is somewhat jaundiced by the fact that it has not achieved a sense of parity in its relations with the United States. Criticism of its human rights practices in the 1990s by Washington was a constant irritant for Turkish authorities, who also harbored deep suspicions of US intentions in northern Iraq. Still, Turkey's devastating economic crisis in 2001 was a reminder of its deep dependence on Washington.

With the end of the cold war, Ankara's focus gradually shifted to the hitherto disregarded Middle East. Ironically, it is in the Middle East that the United States has found Ankara to be most relevant to its own policies and ambitions. During the 1990s, Saddam Hussein emerged as the single most important factor in US-Turkish relations as the Turks were critical to the US policy of containing Iraq. The 2003 Iraq war dealt Turkish-American relations a serious blow, primarily because Turkey refused to allow a second northern front against Baghdad and the concomitant transit of US troops through its territory. Ankara feared that the war would bring Iraqi Kurds much closer to independence, with serious implications for its own Kurdish population.

The 2002 advent of the AKP, a moderate Islam-oriented Justice and Development Party, brought new risks and opportunities to the relationship. On the one hand, the party's roots were in the anti-Western and anti-American Islamist movement of yesteryear and created the risk of a domestic political confrontation between it and the secular civilian and military establishment. On the other hand, the advent through the ballot box of a moderate Islamist party, committed to European integration, validated the US discourse on democracy.

By 2010, the US-Turkish relationship had soured; ironically, the change came about during the Obama presidency, an administration that was perceived far friendlier to Turkey, and despite the proliferation of arenas of cooperation such as the G20 and the UN Security Council. A new, self-confident Turkish foreign policy—which emphasized its centrality in global affairs, pushed for preeminence in adjoining regions, and disagreed sharply with Washington on critical issues—had emerged. While Ankara and Washington began to see eye-to-eye on Iraq, Iran, Armenia, and Israel, the acrimonious tone led some in Washington to question Turkey's direction.

This chapter focuses on the post–cold war Turkish-American relationship within the context of the Middle East, and for simplicity's sake I define the region to include the Caucasus and Central Asia as well. Despite a contextual focus on the Middle East, I consider other important US-Turkish issues as well.

RECENT ORIGINS

The Turkish-American relationship in the post–World War II era dates to Soviet leader Stalin's threats to both Greece and Turkey and the promulgation of the Truman Doctrine in March 1947. The Truman Doctrine marked the beginning of the cold war and containment policy and redefined Turkey's position in the world from a reluctant late participant in the war effort against the Axis powers to a frontline state in the fight against communism. Turkey, together with Greece, joined the NATO alliance in 1952. The change in external alliances was accompanied by an equally dramatic turn of events within Turkey: The one-party state established by Turkey's founder, Mustafa Kemal Ataturk, gave way—albeit slowly and reluctantly—to a multiparty political system, and the new leaders of Turkey remained closely attached to the United States.

The Democrat party that took over the reins of power in Turkey in 1950 was ostensibly more pro–United States and, more important perhaps, more market oriented. Once in power, the Democrat administration of Adnan Menderes took the lead in the creation of the 1955 Baghdad Pact, a bloc of countries that joined together to thwart Soviet advances into the Arab Middle East.[1] The Baghdad Pact, comprising Turkey, Iraq, Iran, and Pakistan, was short-lived because Iraq pulled out following the 1958 overthrow of the regime in Baghdad. The pact reinvented itself as the Central Treaty Organization (CENTO), although it proved to be of limited use.

The US-Turkish relations suffered from ups and downs because of the rivalry with Greece, another NATO ally. The island of Cyprus, home to Greeks and Turks, gained its independence from Great Britain in 1960. The intercommunal conflicts between majority Greeks and minority Turks on Cyprus often brought Turkey to the brink of invading the island in defense of the Turks. In 1964 a last-minute letter from President Lyndon Johnson threatening Ankara with serious repercussions should it invade the island is credited with stopping the Turkish government from pursuing this course. In 1974, however, following a coup in Cyprus inspired by the ruling military junta in Athens, Turkish troops intervened. Even though the initial July 1974 Turkish invasion—conducted under the auspices of the London agreement that had formally recognized Turkey, Greece, and Britain as guarantor powers for the island's communities—received mixed international reviews, the Turks followed it up by a second one in August. The latter resulted in the current status quo. The reaction to the second military action was quite drastic. The US Congress, in opposition to the administration's wishes, imposed an arms embargo on Turkey, which would last from 1975 to 1978, further embittering Turkish attitudes toward the United States. In reaction to the embargo, the Turkish prime minister, Suleyman Demirel, closed all US bases in Turkey except for those that had a specific NATO mission and announced the intention of his government to pursue a policy of rapprochement with Arab and Eastern Bloc countries.

Tensions with the United States coincided with a period of domestic turbulence in Turkey. Starting in the late 1960s, anti-Americanism, largely a mirror image of student movements in Europe and elsewhere around the globe, had permeated all levels of society.[2] In the 1970s, economic difficulties, coupled with the rise of militant left- and right-wing groups, seriously undermined Turkey's stability. The political system seemed to come under siege from every corner of the country and every political tendency; in addition to the left- and right-wing groups, Islamist and Kurdish organizations had also began to agitate. In turn, Turkey's instability began to worry Washington and its European allies.

Frayed Turkish-American relations began to mend with the lifting of the arms embargo in 1978 and more importantly with the rapid transformation of Turkey's immediate neighborhood. The Iranian revolution created a new revisionist anti-American power in a sensitive region and cost the United States an intelligence perch for eavesdropping on the Soviet Union. That same year, the Soviets invaded Afghanistan, and although Turkey would not figure prominently in the proxy war that Washington would initiate, the cold war was back on, emphasizing once again Turkey's strategic location. Washington, attuned to Turkey's geostrategic importance, was muted in its criticism when Turkish generals took power in September 1980 amid rising political violence and parliamentary deadlock.

The 1980s would usher in a new era in Turkish politics. The centerpiece of this decade was the economic reforms initiated by Turgut Özal. He first unleashed them in January 1980 for Demirel's government; he continued them as minister in charge of the economy during the military interregnum, and he accelerated them following his 1983 victory in the first elections since the coup. In effect, he single-handedly managed to transform Turkey's economy from an inward-looking one to an export-oriented one. Özal's success in the economic sphere brought a degree of self-confidence to Turkey, as the Turkish private sector started to export furiously, especially to Europe. In the years that followed, the economic reforms would be crucial in enhancing Turkey's attractiveness to the EU. Although Özal's approach found favor in Washington, nagging issues remained. Among them was the role of ethnic lobbies in Washington, primarily Greek and Armenian, in undermining the Turkish cause. The Greek lobby was seen as responsible for imposing the arms embargo in 1975, and Armenian groups succeeded in making the 1915 Ottoman genocide of Armenians a salient political issue. Attempts in Congress to pass resolutions recognizing the genocide brought about strong Turkish reactions, often overshadowing other diplomatic business. Ankara's troubles in Congress spurred it to seek its own allies in the United States.

US-TURKISH RELATIONS UNDER IRAQ'S SHADOW: PHASE I

Iraq's August 1990 invasion of Kuwait represented the first challenge of the post–cold war era. From then on, directly or indirectly, Iraq would cast its long shadow over US-Turkish relations. The Iraq issue is best analyzed in two phases: The first phase covers the period from the Gulf War to September 11, 2001; the second phase revolves around the 2003 US invasion of Iraq and the ensuing insurgency. Turkey's proximity to Iraq and the basing of US aircraft at the Incirlik air base to maintain a no-fly zone over northern Iraq after the conclusion of the Gulf War would make Turkey a linchpin in Washington's containment strategy of Baghdad. As long as Saddam Hussein ruled Iraq, US policy, as it evolved through the 1990s, could not be implemented without Ankara's help. The Gulf crisis also exacerbated the insurrection by Turkish Kurds in the country's southeastern regions. The often brutal methods employed by the Turkish state to combat this rebellion increasingly put it at odds with its US ally.

At the onset of the Kuwait crisis, President Özal—despite his limited powers as president and facing a great deal of opposition at home—managed to orient Turkish policy behind the United States and its allies in what he was sure would be the winning side. At his instigation, his government closed down Iraq's main export pipelines to the Mediterranean in anticipation of UN sanctions resolutions. Özal struck a cordial relationship with President George H. W. Bush during the crisis and proved quite willing to push his country even farther along the path of cooperation with the allies.[3] The opposition to his policies became so fierce that for the first time in Turkish history a chief of staff of the armed forces resigned in protest rather than cooperate with his president.[4]

When the defeated Iraqi regime turned on its own unruly population in 1991, the Kurds in the north, who had taken advantage of the Gulf War to rebel, began to flee in large numbers to the Iranian and Turkish borders, resulting in a massive refugee crisis. For Turkey, which was confronting a Kurdish insurgency of its own, the inflow of more Kurds into its territory was an unacceptable burden. As a result, the United States, with its allies, put together a force composed of aircraft and ground troops called Operation Provide Comfort (OPC) to force Iraqi troops out of northern Iraq and allow Kurdish refugees to return home. OPC, based in Turkey, required periodic approval by the Turkish parliament, and because of the acrimonious debates it generated, it became a source of tension between Washington and Ankara. These bitter debates were often marked by the quiet, last-minute intervention of the powerful Turkish military in favor of renewing the OPC's mandate. The process, however, did not serve either country well.

Turkish insecurities regarding OPC were directly related to the domestic Kurdish insurgency led by the Kurdistan Workers Party (PKK) and its leader, Abdullah Öcalan, which peaked around 1992. The government felt seriously threatened by the PKK taking advantage of Kurdish-controlled northern Iraq and the sympathetic populace in southeastern Turkey. As casualties mounted in the southeast, Turks feared the influence of the Iraqi Kurdish example. Iraqi Kurds, thanks to OPC, were no longer living as subjects of the Iraqi regime and had established their own government structures and had even organized their own elections. Ankara, moreover, was alarmed at the prospect of eventual Iraqi Kurdish independence and its demonstration effect on its own Kurds. As a result, Turkish policy in the 1990s was focused on discouraging Iraqi Kurds from breaking away and on encouraging Saddam's regime to peacefully reintegrate the north. As such, Turkish and American policy diverged significantly over Iraq. A principal proponent of this strategy in Turkey was none other than Bulent Ecevit, who in opposition became the most vociferous critic (together with the Islamist leader Necmettin Erbakan) of US policy and OPC in particular. Ecevit blamed the United States for planning to create a putative Kurdish state in northern Iraq.[5]

Over time, OPC was restructured, its land component removed, and its renewals routinized. It was renamed Operation Northern Watch (ONW). ONW and its southern counterpart represented a first line of defense for the United States against Saddam, and increased the psychological pressure on Baghdad by reminding it daily that it did not control its own territory. It would not be an exaggeration to argue that without ONW, Washington's Iraq policy could have collapsed. As the popularity of UN-imposed economic sanctions on Iraq waned in the late 1990s, ONW's importance grew.

However, this was not a one-way street, as ONW provided numerous benefits to Turkey. It was an important source of Turkish leverage in Washington, which always had to take account of Turkish sensitivities in Iraq and elsewhere for fear of jeopardizing ONW. ONW provided a cover for Turkish military incursions into northern Iraq in pursuit of PKK insurgents. More importantly, it crystallized US support for Turkey's position on the PKK as a terrorist organization and ensured Washington's collaboration in Öcalan's apprehension in February 1999 after his eviction from Syria.[6] Öcalan's capture was an important victory for Ankara as the PKK, in order to prevent the Turkish authorities from executing its leader, decided to halt its military operations and remove its fighters from Turkish soil to northern Iraq.

Despite the increasing collaboration between Washington and Ankara, Iraq remained a source of tension in Turkish-American relations throughout the Clinton administration. Turks were suspicious of US intentions in the region. They were convinced that their own Kurdish problem and the PKK insurgency could be attributed to the absence of "legitimate authority" in northern Iraq (which was controlled by two Kurdish factions at loggerheads with each other), the collapse of their trade relations with Baghdad following the Gulf War, and the imposition of economic sanctions on Iraq. They made it clear that their preference was the reunification of Iraqi territory under the control of the central government in Baghdad. This Turkish position ran counter to US preferences, but the internecine divisions within the Kurdish community between the Patriotic Union of Kurdistan (PUK) and the Kurdish Democratic Party (KDP)—led by Jalal Talabani and Masoud Barzani, respectively—would continue to undermine Washington's position.

The unresolved status of Iraq, particularly northern Iraq, and the prospect of Kurdish autonomy compelled Turkey to become an active player in northern Iraqi politics. In its determination to eradicate the PKK and prevent the deepening of Kurdish autonomy in the north, Ankara alternated its support among the different Kurdish factions. It sporadically engaged in large military incursions into the north, based troops there, and with time created the Iraqi Turkmen Front (ITF), composed of members of the Turkish-speaking minority in Iraq, as a counterweight to the Kurds and their aspirations. Trade between Iraq and Turkey flourished, especially after the oil-for-food UN resolution, which stipulated that Iraqi oil exports could be used to import food and medicine. Although this trade did not match prewar levels, it nonetheless provided Turkey with access to oil, including smuggled oil, and some leverage over the Iraqi Kurds (particularly the KDP). In order to support Ankara, which had complained bitterly about the losses it had incurred as a result of the Kuwait war, the United States insisted that a majority of the oil to be exported out of Iraq be transported through Turkish pipelines.

THE CONTEXT BEYOND IRAQ

Although Iraq was a dominating concern in the 1990s, other issues influenced and enriched the complex US-Turkish relations. Throughout the 1990s, the United States, concerned about Turkish domestic political stability, tried to fortify Ankara by endorsing its quest for European Union membership and by supporting it economically and pushing it to reform its archaic approach to human rights and ethnic relations. The latter effort often produced sharp differences between the two countries, yet Turkish-American relations were on the mend by the end of the decade. Ankara, not surprisingly, took a dim view of US interference in its domestic politics when the Clinton administration criticized Turkey's undemocratic practices and its repression of Kurdish rights and Islamic parties. Still, the US administration simultaneously pursued a number of initiatives designed to improve Turkey's regional standing, improve its EU membership chances, and strengthen its integration with the world economy.[7] These included the push for the construction of an oil pipeline from Baku to the Mediterranean port city of Ceyhan, which would make Turkey a major transit route for Caspian oil; the inclusion of Turkey on the list of the ten big emerging markets, requiring special US attention; and the push for the successful conclusion of negotiations for a customs union with the EU. Later on, when the EU snubbed Ankara at the 1997 Luxembourg summit, Washington undertook a relentless campaign to convince the Europeans that Turkey deserved consideration for membership.

Perhaps the most emblematic moment of this relationship occurred during President Clinton's visit to Turkey in autumn 1999. Spending a record five days in this country (including attendance at the OSCE [Organization for Security and Cooperation in Europe] summit), the president visited with the 1999 earthquake victims and gave a well-received speech at the Turkish Grand National Assembly.

One of the more fundamental changes in Turkish foreign policy after the demise of the Soviet Union and the Gulf War had been its burgeoning relationship with Israel. The dramatic proof of this transformation came about during the tenure of Prime Minister Necmettin Erbakan, perhaps the single most anti-Israeli and even anti-Semitic Turkish politician, who, under pressure from his armed forces, had to sign a military cooperation agreement with Israel. The nature of Turkish-Israeli relations was controversial. For some, it was a "strategic" relationship designed to radically change the balance of power in the Middle East, whereas others have seen it as a development that came about—albeit in an accelerated fashion—following years of deliberate neglect.[8] There were a number of reasons why Turkey decided to embark on cooperation with Israel. The Oslo agreements between Israel and the PLO in 1993 enabled Ankara to relax its approach to Israel. For the Turkish military fighting the PKK insurgency, an opening to Israel served to punish Syria, which had been harboring the PKK chief Öcalan. The close cooperation of Syria's northern and southern neighbors, the two most formidable regional military powers, was received with great alarm in the Arab world.

But among the most important reasons for the rapprochement was the perception in Turkey that improving relations with Israel would help Turkey in Washington. Absent an effective lobby of its own, Ankara had already begun to use its own Jewish citizens to lobby the United States. Still, this was not enough to counter what Ankara had come to believe was the influence of "evil lobbies" or "foreign elements," meaning the Greek-American and Armenian-American lobbies, with the US Congress.[9] In addition to these, human rights nongovernmental organizations had stepped up their criticisms of Turkey on Capitol Hill, especially with the intensification of the conflict in southeastern Turkey. Close cooperation with Israel would help Turkey's image in the generally Israel-friendly US Congress and mobilize Jewish American groups to lobby in Ankara's favor. From this perspective, the strategy worked; not only did the pro-Israel groups begin to help Turkey, but the courtship has survived the ups and downs of the Israeli-Palestinian conflict and volatile Turkish politics until 2008.

A second reason for the Turkish decision to seek a closer relationship with Israel also had to do with concerns about Washington's reliability as an arms supplier in an era of greater human rights sensitivities and raging counterinsurgency campaign against Kurds. Early during the Clinton administration, a helicopter sale got bogged down in the halls of Congress, forcing Ankara to withdraw the order rather than face the prospect of a humiliating rejection. Similarly, with other contracts subjected to these same criteria, Israel represented an alternative source of weapons. Given Israel's desire to develop markets for its relatively small arms industry and to improve relations with Turkey, it was unlikely that human rights or any other consideration would undermine such sales.

Israel derived important advantages such as the ability to train its air force pilots in Turkey, away from the very limited land space offered by Israel itself. The military dimension of the relationship was shrouded in secrecy and, therefore, attracted far more attention than it perhaps deserved. This is not to say that the military relationship was unimportant to either side—after all, Israeli aircraft began to routinely train in Turkey, and Israel successfully participated in contracts to sell Turkey a variety of weaponry—but rather that its strategic importance may have been overrated.

During the 1998 crisis with Syria over Öcalan, Damascus and the rest of the Arab world clearly perceived Turkey's greater self-confidence to be a direct result of its new relationship with Israel. Israeli leaders, by contrast, tried to signal Syria that they were not party to this escalation in tensions. The rest of the Middle East, especially Iran, viewed this relationship with alarm, as suggestions were made in the Turkish press that Israel would take advantage of its flight training to destroy Tehran's weapons of mass destruction capabilities. But there was another aspect to this Turkish-Israeli relationship that escaped scrutiny: the economic dimension.

Economic ties, unlike military ones, take much longer to bear fruit. While still lagging the close military ties, the Turkish-Israeli economic relationship blossomed with time, benefiting from the fact that Israel enjoyed a free trade agreement with the United States, which provided Turkish exporters with an additional means of reaching the lucrative American market.

As far as Washington was concerned, the Turkish-Israeli relationship was long overdue. The United States provided some incentives, but by and large it took the position that these two countries could decide on their own the limits to their relationship. Joint exercises, mostly search-and-rescue types, involving the US Navy with its respective counterparts from Turkey and Israel have been held at yearly intervals. When the first of these exercises was conducted, it gave rise to an outcry in the Arab world, whereas the second time it was barely noted. In 2002, however, the three countries extended these to include "comprehensive air maneuvers this year in an effort to improve combat readiness."[10]

Burgeoning ties between the two strong regional allies were welcomed by the United States and especially their extension—albeit before the collapse of the Oslo process—to another US ally, Jordan. This three-way relationship is an example of the "rise of new 'security geometries' or alliances in critical regions" in which the United States, by virtue of its dominant role in these countries' international relations, had the ability to influence the wider region in which they coexist.[11] This did not mean that the United States and Turkey saw eye to eye on all Middle Eastern issues. As much as Washington would have liked to enlist Ankara in its efforts to contain Iran, the fact of the matter was that Turkish-Iranian relations were complex and marked by both cooperation and competition befitting the remnants of two imperial powers. Whereas Turkey welcomed US support for the construction of the Baku-Ceyhan pipeline, Turks also went ahead with a gas pipeline originating in Iran, despite US efforts to isolate Iran. On the other hand, Turks, having complained of Iranian interference in their domestic affairs ranging from support for the PKK to Islamist terrorist groups or other Islamic organizations, were keenly aware of their neighbor's growing WMD threat and, hence, welcomed US attempts at limiting Tehran's capabilities.

US-TURKISH RELATIONS UNDER IRAQ'S SHADOW: PHASE 2

The George W. Bush administration taking the helm in January 2001 included many top officials who had advocated taking a much harder line against Saddam Hussein. The 9/11 attacks and the anthrax episode that shut down Capitol Hill simply provided the rationale for the administration's decision to topple the Iraqi leader. As a result, Iraq began to loom larger in US-Turkish relations.

The initial change in the Bush administration's priorities, its intention to pursue terrorists to the ends of the earth, suited Ankara well. First and foremost, for Turkey the al-Qa'ida threat was a vindication of its own discourse on terrorism. Ankara, therefore, was confident it would receive greater support against the PKK. Moreover, the obscurantist character of both the Taliban and al-Qa'ida enhanced the ruling secular Turkish civilian and military elites' view that making concessions to Islamists, whether in Turkey or in the Middle East, was the beginning of a slippery slope. Turkey was one of the first countries to offer Washington its support for the war on terrorism, and by announcing that Turkish troops would be the first to replace the British peacekeeping forces in Kabul, Ankara further enhanced its image. Turkey tendered not only materiel assistance but also its credentials as a Muslim ally of the United States at a time when many in the Islamic world began to perceive the war on terrorism as a war on Islam. The Ankara government offered its backing despite the fact that large majorities of the Turkish public, according to opinion polls, opposed not only the dispatch of troops to Afghanistan but also the conduct of the US war.[12]

The Afghan campaign was an opportunity to reverse the gains made by a fundamentalist Taliban regime that sought to undermine friendly Central Asian governments. Most importantly, by taking part in the military operations and helping to stabilize the region, Turkey won a chance to further enhance its reputation in the world.[13]

To Turkey's great consternation, the other shoe would soon drop. The Bush administration set its sights on Iraq, which would create a new set of complications in the relationship. Turkey's importance to Washington was tested early in the Bush administration when Ankara suffered from a disastrous economic crisis unleashed by a February 2001 fight between President Necdet Sezer and Ecevit. The rapid devaluation of the Turkish lira, the collapse of the banking sector under questionable loans, and the massive layoffs suffered by all sectors of the economy rendered Ecevit's coalition government weak and unpopular. The war on terrorism and Washington's reliance on Turkey for the conduct of its Iraq policy once again highlighted Turkey's strategic importance and convinced the Bush administration—despite internal critics such as Treasury secretary Paul O'Neill—that it deserved to be rescued through a massive bailout, whereas Argentina, undergoing an equally debilitating economic crisis, did not.

By the time Prime Minister Ecevit visited Washington in January 2002, Iraq had clearly moved to the top of the Bush agenda. Soon after his return from Washington, Ecevit started to publicly distance himself from Saddam Hussein and even warned Baghdad's ruler that unless he complied with UN resolutions, President Bush would act against him.[14] This turnabout in Ecevit's traditional stance regarding Iraq was noteworthy. He claimed to have made it clear to President Bush that should the United States decide to act against Iraq, Ankara expected to be consulted in advance. He also insisted on other conditions, including ensuring the safety of the Turkmen in Iraq, the inadmissibility of an independent Kurdish state in the north of Iraq, and the minimization of Turkish economic losses.

It would not be Ecevit's fate to lead Turkey during the 2003 Iraq war. The Justice and Development Party (AKP), led by former Istanbul mayor Recep Tayyip Erdogan, swept into power in November 2002 by winning one-third of the national vote but almost two-thirds of the parliamentary seats. War in Iraq would be an ironic conundrum to face for a leader who in the 1990s had been a devoted follower of the Islamist Erbakan but had now moderated his discourse. Erdogan, due to the political ban on him, had to temporarily relinquish the job of prime minister to his colleague Abdullah Gul, but he found himself immediately courted by President Bush. The US administration, in full war mode, was hoping to get Turkey's permission to have American troops transit Turkish soil to open a second front against Baghdad. After long and protracted negotiations, the moderate Islamist government decided to support the United States.

The Turkish government drove a hard bargain. It negotiated a large financial package to protect it from the potential negative economic side effects that the war would have entailed. More importantly, it received Washington's approval to enter northern Iraq in the wake of the US 4th Infantry Division to prevent another refugee crisis reminiscent of 1991. In reality, the Turks were anxious for their presence to be felt in northern Iraq as a deterrent to Iraqi Kurdish aspirations for independence.

Events did not turn out as expected. To everyone's surprise, when the government resolution endorsing the US request came for a vote in the Turkish parliament on March 1, 2003, it failed. Although more people voted in favor than against, there were enough members of parliament who abstained while remaining in the chamber that, under Turkish parliamentary procedures, were counted as no votes. The parliamentary resolution failed primarily due to AKP's mismanagement and inexperience. In a morning straw poll, party whips concluded that they had a fifty-vote margin to spare. There was also some confusion regarding the attitude of the military. Although the generals supported the deal, it was clear that both the AKP government and the Turkish General Staff, in view of public opposition to the deployment of US troops, were anxious to deflect responsibility to the other. In an interview with Fikret Bila, a *Milliyet* columnist, three days before the vote, a senior commander openly said that the armed forces opposed the deal with America.[15] The vote, but especially the perception that the military was unenthusiastic about it, elicited a sharp rebuke from deputy defense secretary Paul Wolfowitz. Still, as the United States continued to prepare for war, American Special Forces crossed Turkish territory into Iraq to liaise with Kurds and other oppositionists.

Turkish-American relations over Iraq deteriorated further after the March 1 vote. On July 4, 2003, US forces in control of northern Iraq arrested a number of Turkish Special Forces members in the Kurdish town of Sulaymaniyah on suspicion of colluding with ITF members to assassinate the governor of Kirkuk. The Turkish soldiers—who were in northern Iraq with American acquiescence—received the al-Qa'ida treatment: They were hooded and sent to Baghdad for further interrogation.[16] News of the incident shocked the Turkish public and officials, and the arrests became emblematic of the mistrust in Turkish-American relations. Turks began suspecting that the United States was not just intent on punishing Ankara for the March 1 vote. Given Washington's reliance on the Iraqi Kurdish factions, especially after the intensification of the insurgency, it appeared that the United States wanted to sideline Ankara in Iraq in favor of the Kurds. These suspicions were confirmed—

though incorrectly American officials would argue—when the American administrator for Iraq, Ambassador Paul Bremer, sided with the Iraqi Kurds to block a possible deployment of Turkish troops to central Iraq at Washington's request.

The continued war in Iraq further deepened Turkish anxieties about American aims, interests, and capabilities. Ankara expected that among US priorities as the occupying power would be the elimination of the PKK from its hideouts in northern Iraq, but the intensified insurgency prevented the US Central Command from engaging an organization that refrained from attacking American troops. After the PKK abandoned its unilateral cease-fire in 2005, the reluctance of the United States to take on the PKK became a continuous source of frustration in Turkey. The differences over the PKK represented only the tip of the iceberg. Turkey, which hitherto objected to the idea of a federal Iraqi state, had to acknowledge after the constitutional developments in Iraq that the new state was going to be federal in structure. Instead, Ankara articulated what it called "red lines" that it wanted respected—denying the Iraqi Kurds independence and the oil-rich city of Kirkuk. Ankara claimed that Kirkuk was a Turkmen city and any attempt at changing its ethnic composition would be unacceptable. By contrast, Iraqi Kurdish leaders insisted on the Kurdish character of the city and sought to return Kurdish refugees displaced by Saddam Hussein's ethnic cleansing in the 1980s and 1990s. Both the transitional administrative law and the new Iraqi constitution called for a referendum to determine whether Kirkuk would join the Kurdish provinces in a future federal Iraqi republic. If Kirkuk were to become part of the Kurdish federal entity, Turks feared that the city's oil riches would ultimately lay the foundation of a future independent Kurdistan.[17]

Turkish leaders continuously voiced concern over the conduct of US military operations. American actions in the northern Iraqi town of Tel Afer, where the majority of the population is of Shi'a Turkmen origin, and in Falluja were severely criticized by AKP leaders and parliamentarians. The AKP and its core constituencies viewed the war in Iraq (and in Afghanistan) as unjustly targeting Muslim populations. Correspondingly, anti-Americanism in Turkey reached unprecedented levels. The new AKP government had pushed the envelope successfully on critical issues such as the European Union and Cyprus—often in opposition to hard-line domestic interests. Hence it found itself vulnerable to accusations of inaction on the PKK bases in northern Iraq, unable to defend against PKK incursions and Iraqi Kurdish aspirations. Were the PKK to ramp up its activities, domestic pressure in Ankara would mount for cross-border military operations. In turn this would have a deleterious impact on relations with the United States.

THE NEW TURKISH FOREIGN POLICY IN THE MIDDLE EAST

The unpopularity of the Iraq war in the Middle East and the US inability to either control the insurgency or decisively end the conflict created a vacuum in the region. The AKP took advantage of this by first interjecting itself in the Syrian-Israeli negotiation process; Ankara managed to start a serious dialogue between those two enemies that would end with Israel's war on Hamas in 2008–2009. Turkey began to reassess its posture in the Middle East, emboldened by its dynamic economy, ranked sixteenth in the world, increasing visibility in international politics through such institutions as the G20 or the UN Security Council, its strategic location, and historical and cultural ties to the Middle East. Erdogan and his foreign minister, Ahmet Davutoglu, increasingly struck a different foreign policy in the region (and elsewhere around regions abutting Turkey). The Turkish government has set its sights on restoring relations with its neighbors, countries such as Iran, Iraq, and Syria with which it has had difficult and often tense exchanges. In part, this policy is driven by Turkey's insatiable need for new markets for its exports, which have become the mainstay of the economy as the Özal reforms of the 1980s have matured.

One of the most dramatic changes occurred in northern Iraq. Although Turkey had been an unabashed foe of the Kurdistan Regional Government (KRG), it implemented a 180-degree policy turn to emerge a close ally of the Kurdish quasi-state. It even opened a consulate in the KRG capital, Arbil, effectively recognizing that region's autonomous status within a federal Iraq.[18] In so doing, the Turks transformed themselves in the eyes of Washington from a nuisance if not problem to US objectives in Iraq into a reliable and helpful ally. In fact, Ankara helped the United States during the negotiations with Baghdad on the status of forces agreement. The change in policy was not done at the behest of Washington, but rather because the Turks changed their calculus on Iraq, in part driven by their own domestic Kurdish problem.

Another dramatic turnabout came in relations with Israel. Whereas it was no secret that the AKP leadership was not enamored with Israel, it decided to maintain relations, at times quite cordial, with Jerusalem because as the only regional country with good relations with everyone, it provided Turkey with an entrée few countries (save perhaps for Egypt) enjoyed. This did not prevent Ankara from criticizing Israel when it deemed necessary. The first shock to Israel occurred after the 2006 Hamas victory in the Palestinian elections; the AKP issued an invitation to Khaled Meshal, head of Hamas's armed wing based in Damascus and the one most responsible for the wave of suicide bombings that Israel suffered from over the years. The invitation to Meshal, who held no elective office, also shocked Washington, which had branded Hamas as a terrorist organization. Things would only get worse: When Israel attacked Hamas in Gaza at the end of 2008, soon after Israeli prime minister Ehud Olmert had visited Ankara to discuss the next phase of Syrian-Israeli talks, the AKP decided to unleash on Israel. For Erdogan this had become an almost personal issue, and he did not miss any opportunity to attack Israel publicly. Moreover, as tensions over Iran's suspected nuclear weapons program gathered steam, Erdogan decided to back Iran and focus on Israel's undeclared nuclear weapons, thus providing Tehran with critical diplomatic support and breathing room.

Gone were the days of an Israeli-Turkish alliance, as hyped as it may have been. Worse was to come, however. In May 2010, IHH, a militant Turkish Islamist NGO with connections to both the AKP and a history of activities in Afghanistan and elsewhere often in opposition to the United States, decided to run Israel's sea blockade of Gaza, but Israelis decided to prevent this action. Israeli requests that the flotilla be stopped from leaving Turkey were for the most part ignored. The resulting military operation in international waters was bungled by Israel, and nine of the IHH militants were killed. This proved to be the death knell for the Turkish-Israeli relationship. In Turkey, where Israel had never been popular, the IHH disaster and Israel's refusal to apologize meant that it had ceased to be an ally or a friend. Turkish officials openly said that if Israel refused to apologize and pay compensation, Jerusalem would find Ankara in opposition to its interests in every international forum. Erdogan's tough stand against Israel, his support for Hamas, and the flotilla crisis helped make him the most popular politician on the proverbial Arab street. The flotilla incident also forced the Israelis to relax their grip on Gaza. Turkey had gained a great deal of influence, some at the expense of traditional Arab countries such as Egypt.

The deteriorating relations with Israel and especially the vitriolic attacks by the AKP leadership even before the flotilla debacle had already alarmed Washington and opened the door for the questioning of Turkey's AKP among Israel supporters in Washington. However, US-Turkish relations were thrown into a tailspin because of Iran, not Israel. Erdogan's insistence that he had been assured of the peaceful intentions of Iran's nuclear program was followed by a Turkish-Brazilian-Iranian gambit designed to prevent the Security Council from passing additional sanctions on Iran. On May 17, 2010, Erdogan and Davutoglu joined their counterparts in Tehran to sign an accord that, according to them, represented the beginning of the end of the Iran nuclear crisis. Washington riposted by announcing that it had reached agreement with China and Russia, two countries hitherto reluctant to go along with sanctions on Tehran, that a new, tougher sanctions resolution would be presented to the Security Council.

When Brazil and Turkey voted against sanctions at the subsequent UNSC meeting, Washington was particularly upset at Ankara; that a member of the NATO alliance and an EU candidate country would side with Tehran against its Western allies unleashed a torrent of criticism against Turkey.[19] Turkey's indecisiveness, at the time of writing, on NATO's defense shield against possible Iranian missile deployment has further contributed to unease with Ankara in Western capitals. The perception that the AKP government always seemed to be siding with Muslim causes and countries, ranging from Omar al-Bashir in Sudan to Hamas in Palestine and Ahmedinejad in Iran, unnerved many in the Obama administration as many in Washington wondered aloud whether Turkey was abandoning the West. On Iran, while the Turks were anxious about rising tensions on their border, so soon after the Iraq quagmire, they misread US intentions and goals in Iran. For Washington, Iran is more than a regional security threat; it represents a challenge to the Obama administration's nonproliferation agenda and nuclear weapons reduction negotiations with the Russians. An Iran visibly progressing toward nuclear weapons would undermine the administration's nuclear reduction efforts in the US Congress. How Turkey positions itself on this issue will have important consequences down the road.[20]

The perception that Turkey was forsaking the West was a simplistic reaction to a country making the best of an improved strategic and political landscape. Whether Ankara sought to engage countries and movements that were anti-Western to bring them into the fold, as it claimed, or was trying to emerge as a regional power capable of determining (if not imposing) its own preferences on the Middle East and consequently assuming a greater role in international politics remains to be seen. The opening to Syria, despite the bravado emanating from Ankara, potentially can lead to long-term dividends.[21] In the case of Hamas, however, AKP's stand has undermined the Palestinian Authority but has not brought any gains. It is in Iraq where Turkey's policy approach has yielded the most by contributing to Iraq's stability.

In general, the AKP government has tried to distance itself from the United States but not break with it. Under the AKP, the new foreign policy is not so much an attempt to oppose Washington as it is to demonstrate that Turkey is an important power. In the minds of AKP leaders, Turkey's geographic location, its much improved economy, its military capabilities, and its historic connections to the Middle East and the Asian continent render Turkey a far more important power than it has aspired to be or been given credit for in the past. The repeated attempts at offering its good offices for mediation in a variety of conflicts, principally in the Middle East, are part and parcel of the AKP's efforts at making Turkey more visible and relevant. In the end, Turkey needs the United States and the European Union; there are no substitutes for them. Even if Ankara were to export more to the Middle East and elsewhere, the European market will continue to determine Turkey's competitiveness. By competing in the toughest market, the European one, Turkish exports obtain the qualitative edge needed to compete elsewhere. Similarly, the international respect and prestige that the AKP wants to earn for Turkey cannot come at the expense of its relations with the United States precisely because Ankara's close relationship with Washington, just as with the EU, remains one of its most compelling attributes.

CONCLUSION

Perhaps Turkey's greatest contribution to the United States, as Ian Lesser aptly argued, is a degree of freedom of action or power projection in adjacent areas.[22] Prior to 9/11, despite the vagaries of Turkish domestic politics as widely disparate political parties assumed power in Ankara, both countries had experienced a marked increase in common concerns and interests. This no longer holds true. The war in Iraq and the AKP ascendancy in Turkey have created some distance between them. This does not mean that the United States will no longer continue to support broad Turkish goals or come to its assistance, as in the crippling economic crisis of 2001. The changed Turkish policy on Iraq has provided both countries with a new avenue of cooperation where acrimony used to dominate.

The Turkish-American relationship will continue to be influenced by events outside the Middle East. Among the three most important are Turkey's progression along the European Union membership path, developments in Cyprus, which is also related to the EU, and relations with Armenia. In all three cases, the AKP government has taken risks and modified what previously were immutable preconditions, although it has fallen short of taking them to their logical conclusions. Turkey's rising international profile and self-confidence has distracted Ankara's leaders from further progress on these fronts. In part, it is because, at least on Cyprus, Europe has not been as forthcoming as it should have been. While some European leaders who have expressed reservations that Turkey's ultimate accession may hamper the EU process, Turkey remains a long way away from fulfilling the membership conditions. As a result, the EU relationship is likely to be a stormy one, with neither side completely satisfying the other's conditions.

Turkish-American relations have often surprised even the most seasoned observers. On the eve of the 2003 Iraq War, a leading Turkish columnist, Mehmet Ali Birand, observed that Turkish leaders who had long championed a strengthened strategic relationship with the United States were on the horns of a dilemma because of America's war preparations. In essence, he argued, the tables had been reversed: The United States would be asking Turkey to demonstrate its much-touted strategic commitment by supporting its actions in Iraq, and Ankara would have no choice but to comply.[23] Turkey, as the March 1 vote demonstrated, did not follow Birand's prescription. Nevertheless, the United States did not punish Ankara, as some had demanded, but instead sought to stabilize relations and offered a reduced economic package to help Turkey weather the crisis. Turkey and the United States have continued to maintain their relationship despite many ups and downs. And there is no reason to expect any radically new transformation in the future.

Notes

1. For an analysis of the period, see George S. Harris, *Troubled Alliance: Turkish-American Problems in Historical Perspective, 1945–1971* (Washington, DC; Stanford, CA: American Enterprise Institute; Hoover Institution, 1972); and Bruce R. Kuniholm, *The Origins of the Cold War in the Near East* (Princeton: Princeton University Press, 1980). Also see Elie Podeh's chapter in this volume on the Baghdad Pact.

2. Cengiz Çandar, "Some Turkish Perspectives on the United States and American Policy Toward Turkey," in *Turkey's Transformation and American Policy,* ed. Morton Abramowitz (New York: Century Foundation Press, 2001), pp. 128–131.

3. Morton Abramowitz, who was the US ambassador to Turkey at the time of the Gulf War, recounts his experience in obtaining Özal's permission to overfly Turkish territory and access to bases for the war in "The Complexities of American Policy Making on Turkey," in *Turkey's Transformation and American Policy,* pp. 153–156. Özal, in effect, was challenging the traditional cautious modus operandi of Turkish foreign policy; see

Malik Mufti, "Daring and Caution in Turkish Foreign Policy," *Middle East Journal* 52, 1 (Winter 1998): 48–49.

4. In his memoirs, the resigning chief of the general staff, Necip Torumtay, tells of Özal's preoccupation with northern Iraq and its possible benefits for Turkey; see Necip Torumtay, *Orgeneral Torumtay'in Anilari* (Istanbul: Milliyet Yayinlari, 1993), pp. 115–116. Whether Özal, if the opportunity arose, intended to occupy parts of Iraq such as Mosul or Kirkuk has never been clear. In a recent interview, the then commander of land forces, Dogan Güres, reflected on how Özal would complain about the injustice the British had done at the end of World War I by including those Turkish territories in Iraq. Although General Güres claims to have prepared plans for all possible eventualities, Özal never confirmed that this was his intention; *Yeni Safak* (Istanbul), December 31, 2001.

5. Baskin Oran, *Kalkik Horoz: Çekiç Güç ve Kürt Devleti* (Ankara: Bilgi Yayinevi, 1996).

6. Ecevit even publicly thanked the United States for its help in capturing Öcalan; Kemal Kirisci, "US-Turkish Relations: New Uncertainties in a Renewed Partnership," in *Turkey in World Politics: An Emerging Multiregional Power*, ed. Barry Rubin and Kemal Kirisci (Boulder: Lynne Rienner, 2001), p. 134.

7. For more on US-Turkish relations during the Clinton years, see Henri J. Barkey, "The Endless Pursuit: Improving US-Turkish Relations," in *Friends in Need: Turkey and the United States After September 11*, ed. Morton Abramowitz (New York: Century Foundation, 2003).

8. A representative sample of writings on this topic include Alan Makovsky, "Israeli-Turkish Relations: A Turkish Periphery Strategy?" in Barkey, *Reluctant Neighbor*, pp. 147–170; Ofra Bengio, *The Turkish-Israeli Relationship: Changing Ties of Middle Eastern Outsiders* (New York: Palgrave, 2004); Meliha Benli Altunisik, "Turkish Policy Toward Israel," in *Turkey's New World*, ed. Alan Makovsky and Sabri Sayari (Washington, DC: Washington Institute for Near East Policy, 2000), pp. 59–73; Amikam Nachmani, "The Remarkable Turkish-Israeli Tie," *Middle East Policy*, June 1998, 19–29; Anat Lewin, "Turkey and Israel: Reciprocal and Mutual Imagery in the Media, 1994–1999," *Journal of International Affairs* 54, 1 (Fall 2000): 239–261.

9. Yasemin Çongar, "The State of Turkish-American Dialogue, *Private View*, Spring 1999.

10. Metehan Demir, "Israel, Turkey, US to Hold Joint Air Maneuvers," *Jerusalem Post*, February 11, 2002.

11. Ian O. Lesser, "Western Interests in a Changing Turkey," in *The Future of Turkish-Western Relations*, ed. Zalmay Khalilzad, Ian O. Lesser, and F. Stephen Larrabee (Santa Monica, Calif.: RAND, 2000), pp. 56–57.

12. Some argued that the Turkish government did not really have a choice in the matter precisely because the United States had come to Turkey's rescue in a number of critical junctures, ranging from the 2001 economic crisis to Öcalan's capture and the push to convince the EU to make Turkey a candidate country. For a forceful exposition of this point of view, see Mehmet Ali Birand, "Türkiye'nin ABD'ye eli mahkum . . . " *Posta*, October 11, 2001.

13. Sedat Ergin, "Türkiye'nin Afganistan sinavi," *Hürriyet*, November 16, 2001.

14. See Cengiz Çandar, "Bagdat'tan Washington'a U dönus?" *Yeni Safak*, January 23, 2002; and *Hürriyet* (Istanbul), January 24, 2002.

15. Fikret Bila, "Ucaksavarlar kime?" *Milliyet,* February 26, 2003. The column got front-page billing with a headline that read, "Askerler Rahatsiz," or "The Soldiers Are Apprehensive." It was later revealed that Bila had talked to the Land Forces commander Aytac Yalman.

16. This appeared to be a rogue operation conducted by some in the special forces command without the knowledge of the higher-ups in the Turkish General Staff. See Henri J. Barkey, "Turkey and Iraq: The Perils (and Prospects) of Proximity," US Institute of Peace Special Report, July 2005, p. 10.

17. Ibid.

18. For more on Turkey's new Iraq policy, please see Henri J. Barkey, "Turkey's New Engagement in Iraq: Embracing Iraqi Kurdistan," US Institute Special Report #237, May 2010.

19. Steve Cook, "How Do You Say "Frenemy" in Turkish?" foreignpolicy.com.

20. Kadri Gürsel, "Türkiye 'Yeni Soğuk Savaş'ın Neresinde?" *Milliyet,* October 30–31, 2010. This is a two-part analysis that questions Turkey's position on the new cold war.

21. Kemal Kirisci, Nathalie Tocci, and Joshua Walker, "A Neighborhood Rediscovered: Turkey's Transatlantic Value in the Middle East," Brussels Forum Series papers, German Marshall Fund, March 2010.

22. Lesser, "Western Interests in a Changing Turkey," p. 71.

23. Mehmet Ali Birand, "Türkiye, ABD'ye 'hayir' diyemez," *Posta,* February 12, 2002.

CHAPTER 22

THE UNITED STATES
AND AFGHANISTAN

From Marginality to Strategic Concern

Marvin G. Weinbaum

Until September 11, 2001, when Afghanistan became the epicenter of concern over exportable global terrorism, American interest in the country had been mostly a by-product of the cold war with the Soviet Union. Yet Afghanistan was also for a time one of the least confrontational arenas of cold war politics. The United States, satisfied with a low-key, limited involvement, conceded Afghanistan as a zone of influence to its Soviet neighbor. A modest US development program, only credible enough to keep Kabul governments from falling entirely under the sway of the Soviet state, coexisted alongside Moscow's far larger aid effort. Desperately poor Afghanistan thus enjoyed a version of neutrality both profitable and non-threatening. However, US acquiescence to a dominant Soviet role in one pivotal sector, aid to the Afghan military, proved anything but benign.

The decade of the 1980s, preceded by the Soviet military's invasion of December 1979, changed everything for US involvement in Afghanistan. It was a period when US policy was dedicated, above all, toward forcing a Soviet withdrawal and featured a generous, covert program to assist an Islamic-inspired insurgency. Afghanistan, now at the very forefront of a geostrategic competition, suffered devastation to its state and society, even as the conflict contributed in large measure to ending the cold war.

With the departure of the last Soviet troops in early 1989, the United States felt no overriding national interest in Afghanistan, certainly none to match competing US global concerns. Nor did policymakers sense that the United States could contribute materially toward resolving a civil war that began with efforts to defeat a surviving Afghan communist regime and continued with fighting among the victorious mujahideen parties. It was the appearance and success after 1994 of the Taliban, initially a movement of nationalist-minded religious students, that revived Washington's attention to Afghanistan. Political intolerance, human rights abuses, and drug trafficking soon became synonymous with Taliban rule. But it was the presence of the regime's guest benefactor, Osama bin Laden, alleged mastermind of strikes against US embassies in East Africa, that provoked the United States to seek UN sanctions against the Taliban. The terrorist attacks on New York and Washington in September 2001 quickly transformed an American diplomatic offensive into a military action to root out international terrorism emanating from Afghanistan. The Taliban were routed but not defeated as their leaders, along with bin Laden's al-Qa'ida, found sanctuary in Pakistan. The lion's share of responsibility for helping to stabilize and reconstruct the Afghan state and society then devolved upon an initially reluctant United States. Over the next decade the United States would find itself even more deeply occupied in Afghanistan, leading a coalition of nations fighting to stave off a full-fledged insurgency. On the outcome of this counterinsurgency rests not only the direction of the Afghan state and the prospects for stability of a volatile region but also the future of America's strategic partnerships and their contribution to the global order.

THE KING'S AFGHANISTAN

Modern US-Afghan relations might have gone very differently had Washington not rejected requests as early as 1946 for modest military ties, mainly for purchasing arms, from the Afghan governments under Shah Mahmud and Sardar Daoud, both close relatives of King Muhammad Zahir Shah, whose long reign began in 1933. Kabul was rebuffed, however, by US administrations unwilling to forfeit opportunities to cultivate a relationship with the new, prospectively anticommunist state of Pakistan created in 1947. Given the antipathy over the common border between Afghanistan and Pakistan, the United States felt it more rewarding to choose against the smaller, landlocked country. This left Afghanistan scrambling for protection against Pakistan and for the means to fend off an actively imperialist postwar Soviet state. Even though a trade agreement had been signed with the Soviet Union in 1950, until Stalin's death in 1953, Moscow seemed dedicated mainly to increasing the number of communist satellite regimes. Afghanistan, like other nonaligned countries, was by 1955 eligible for military and economic aid, and Prime Minister Daoud welcomed Chairman Khrushchev's offer of $100 million in assistance for various development projects. The same year, Daoud won approval from a specially convened council of traditional leaders for a security treaty with Moscow. In 1956, the first in a series of agreements for arms with the Soviet Union and Eastern Bloc countries worth $32 million was signed. As with the development credits, this aid was to be repaid with bartered, although typically undervalued, Afghan commodities.[1] Pakistan had meanwhile signed on in 1954 to the Mutual Security Agreement, making it a military ally of the United States.

Although the Soviet Union was ceded the preeminent role in Afghanistan's economic development, the Afghan royal family and most government officials remained Western oriented, especially after the inauguration of a democratically elected government in 1965. Yet under Prime Minister Daoud, the Soviets were allowed to upgrade the army and air force, including officer training, thus opening the way for domestic communists to infiltrate and subvert the Afghan military and critical sectors of the bureaucracy. The Soviet state also made itself indispensable as it offered, as an alternative to Pakistan's port of Karachi, a northern trade route. Aside from becoming Afghanistan's major trading partner, Moscow also gave backing for a Daoud-initiated irredentist campaign to carve an ethnic state, to be called Pashtunistan, from most of northwest Pakistan.

Agreements between Kabul and Moscow had the effect of encouraging the United States to offer the Afghan government enough economic assistance to keep Afghanistan from falling effectively within Moscow's orbit. The decision did not come without an internal debate in Washington that went on for several years, beginning in 1954. It pitted those in the State Department who argued for liquidating US involvement in Afghanistan and others who, although not anxious for competition on a project-by-project basis, contended that aid was necessary to keep the Afghans from losing all chance to remain independent and neutral.[2] The Kabul government recognized the advantages accruing to Afghanistan from having the cold war adversaries bid against one another and welcomed aid as well from other donors, including China, West Germany, and Great Britain.

US assistance had actually begun in 1952 with loans for an ambitious water and agricultural development project in the country's southwest Helmand Valley region. By 1956, expanded US aid programs, supported by $15 million in grants, focused on teacher training and other educational programs and various other areas of technical assistance. Together with private American assistance groups, the agricultural, health, and communications sectors were assisted, and food aid was drawn from US surplus stocks. A Peace Corps program was initiated in 1962. Several major infrastructural projects received grants, including construction of a highway from Kabul to the Pakistan border and from Herat to the Iran frontier—in response to a far more ambitious Soviet national road program—and the construction of an international airport in the country's second-largest city, Kandahar. By 1974, the United States had given as much as $500 million in assistance in loans, grants, and commodities.

American diplomacy was also active. Afghanistan's long-standing quarrel with the shah of Iran's government over Afghan diversion of the waters of the Helmand River and a tributary had become more acute with US loans for new dams. Quiet US mediation finally brought the two sides together in a treaty signed in March

1973 that regulated and divided the waters.³ Washington also encouraged mediation by several friendly Islamic countries after Afghanistan's strong advocacy of Pashtunistan resulted in a Pakistan-imposed trade blockade that nearly brought the two countries to war in 1955. In both cases, US strategic interests dictated that it work to lessen tensions between Afghanistan and US-allied countries, lest Moscow be able to exploit further these territorial issues.

Still, the United States never received the political dividends that went to the Soviets. Moscow's projects gained more visibility and were seen as more directly impacting the lives of ordinary Afghans. Washington's development assistance also became less visible after 1956, when the largest projects were completed and funding dropped off considerably. Ironically, behind Washington's largely consistent thinking on Afghanistan from the 1950s through the 1970s lay a concern that were US involvement to deepen, especially through military assistance, it could provoke the Soviets to act more aggressively toward Afghanistan.⁴

Although foreign aid brought a measure of prosperity to some sectors of Afghan society, the country remained one of the world's poorest. The assistance also created a large financial debt to Moscow.⁵ More consequential still was that it released new social forces that politicized a country unprepared to absorb them institutionally. A new constitution, enacted in 1964 after King Zahir Shah ousted the autocratic Daoud in 1963, was supposed to usher in a more open, inclusive system of government. But the king blocked the formation of political parties after they were legislated by the elected parliament. Forcing political activity into more clandestine channels, especially in a country penetrated by foreign influences through aid dependency, would eventually pose a threat to Afghanistan's national integrity.

POSTMONARCHY IN THE 1970S

Taking advantage of cold war rivalries, Afghanistan had managed to escape forfeiting its nonalignment. The communist-led coup of July 1973 that removed Zahir Shah seemed finally to have ended Afghanistan's historic buffer state role. It brought back as president of a soon-to-be -ormed Afghan republic the former prime minister Daoud. Although Washington accorded recognition to the regime, it grew increasingly wary of Daoud's rule as he embarked on a domestic program with heavy socialist markings. Accompanying this was an expanded Soviet assistance program and the placement of the Afghan army under direct Soviet supervision.⁶ In contrast, US economic assistance programs to Afghanistan had already been feeling the pressure of Washington's heavy commitments in Southeast Asia.

Initially Daoud appeared as a front man for the dedicated Marxists who returned him to power. But the Afghan president's determination to marginalize his Afghan communist allies soon became evident. Although continuing to welcome Moscow's aid, Daoud was also uneasy about the heightened Soviet presence in the country and was aware of dissatisfaction among Afghans with his attempts at radical transformation of the society and economy. By 1977 Daoud was looking hard for economic and political alternatives that could lessen Moscow's influence. He found them in the region's Islamic states. Pro-Western Iran had, between 1973 and 1975, already given $50 million in assistance and, together with Saudi Arabia, was anxious to upgrade relations with the Kabul regime, promising aid at a level that could eventually dwarf assistance from the Soviet Union.[7]

The Carter administration's plans for Iran as a regional hegemon counted on more cordial relations being forged among Iran's neighbors. Iran, Saudi Arabia, Kuwait, and Japan were encouraged to provide economic assistance to Afghanistan.[8] While the US ambassador in Kabul, Theodore Eliot, encouraged the idea of greater "true" nonalignment by the Daoud government, no plan existed to break Kabul away from Moscow, much less for the United States to replace the Soviet Union. Daoud was nonetheless under criticism from the Afghan political left, for what were perceived to be gradually expanding ties to the United States. Daoud's change of direction was more apparent as he backed away from the Pashtunistan cause in reaching out for a better understanding with Pakistan's prime minister, Zulfiqar Ali Bhutto. When Bhutto was deposed in July 1977, his successor, General Zia ul-Haq, indicated that deliberations would continue, and Daoud accepted an invitation to visit Pakistan in March 1978.[9]

The Afghan leader's diplomatic maneuvering ended abruptly with a second coup in April 1978, soon to be called the Saur revolution. Although Moscow had misgivings about the growing independence of Daoud's foreign policy, the Soviets had apparently not engineered the overthrow, and Daoud had tried to respect the sensitive lines not to be crossed with his benefactors. Soviet advisers in the capital no doubt knew of the coup plans, and Moscow had worked hard leading up to the coup to bring together the two bitterly divided factions of the communist Peoples Democratic Party. But the coup was essentially homegrown, an act of revenge by local communists who had been shunted aside by the man they had brought back to power from political oblivion. As before, it required critical backing from units in the Afghan army. Daoud and members of his family, along with high-ranking officials in his regime, were summarily executed.

Further US aid cutbacks took place after the communist takeover. Against the background of a running debate between national security adviser Zbigniew Brzezinski and the State Department over how tough to get with the Soviet Union, it was decided to maintain a US presence in Afghanistan and, to the extent possible, to try to influence a communist leadership under President Nur Muhammad Taraki and Prime Minister Hafizullah Amin. US ambassador Adolph "Spike" Dubs, using his considerable diplomatic skills, appeared to have succeeded during 1978 in establishing working relations with the doctrinaire Marxist yet at times also nationalistic leadership.[10] But Soviet involvement in the country, including the arrival of many more military and civilian advisers, increased in the months following the coup, occasioning several private protests from Washington. When Dubs was kidnapped in February 1979, allegedly by religious fanatics, and then murdered during a suspiciously bungled rescue operation by Afghan government security forces and their Soviet advisers, Washington withdrew its aid program almost entirely and reduced its diplomatic presence in Afghanistan.

More than a year earlier a rural Islamic insurrection had begun against the communist government. Moscow blamed the opposition's success on Amin's insensitive and repressive policies, which it feared could lead eventually to a popular uprising. But when the Soviets in the summer of 1979 sought to eliminate Amin, leaving Taraki in full authority, the Moscow-hatched plot backfired, and Amin instead had Taraki killed. Desperate, and fully aware that the Soviets did not trust him and would seek revenge, Amin quietly sought to open channels to the United States and other countries, hoping to strike a deal to ward off Moscow. Washington, wanting no part of the unpopular, unsavory Amin, ignored his overtures. In late December, the Soviets invaded and killed Amin and his close associates and installed Babrak Karmal, leader of the more Moscow-pliant wing of the Communist Party. Moscow's decision to unleash the Red Army was probably motivated more by fear of rising discontent within the Afghan military than concern about a potent Islamic insurgency. The invasion also carried wider strategic importance, allowing Moscow to take full advantage of opportunities offered by the rapidly declining influence of the United States in the region, most notably in postrevolutionary Iran, which had been Washington's regional policeman only a short time earlier. From an intelligence standpoint, the invasion was an embarrassment. Despite mounting evidence of a troop buildup, the Carter White House was alerted too late for it to give the Brezhnev government a credible warning not to launch Soviet forces.[11]

JIHAD AGAINST THE SOVIETS

For the United States, the Afghan conflict was to become the last great battle of the US-Soviet ideological and military rivalry, and like their previous encounters, it was fought largely through surrogates. If US government policy could be faulted for failing to undertake the public and private diplomacy that might have deterred Moscow from invading Afghanistan, President Carter afterward, feeling personally deceived, reacted angrily. Through public statements as well as economic boycotts and international diplomacy, Moscow faced strong condemnation. More generally, the United States believed it was responding to Brezhnev's increasingly aggressive policies across the Third World. Washington undertook measures to beef up military facilities around the globe, along with efforts to improve relations with China and other countries considered well situated to thwart the Soviets. Taking on Pakistan as an ally in the fight was especially important because the United States had entered into newly combative relations with revolutionary Iran. Indeed, Pakistan could be conceived as strategic compensation for the loss of the shah's Iran. If nothing else, Pakistan was to be kept from falling into the Soviet sphere.

It was the view of many US analysts that the Soviets sought with their invasion of Afghanistan to realize a long-held dream of access to a warm water port. With Pakistan seen as the next target of an expansionist Soviet Union, the Carter administration offered Pakistan's General Zia ul-Haq direct US military assistance. Rejecting the program as inadequate, Zia claimed that Pakistan needed more than Carter's "peanuts" if it were to become the first line of defense against the Soviets, given the potential risks. Only when the incoming Reagan administration promised a far more generous long-term $3.2 billion package of economic assistance and military sales credits did Pakistan agree to become a frontline state, nurturing the insurgency against the Soviet army and Afghan communist forces.

In his partnership with the United States, Zia ul-Haq hoped that his regime would be able to shed the taint of illegitimacy and international ostracism that it had acquired with the military's 1977 coup against an elected, although faltering, Bhutto government. Direct military assistance from Washington would, most importantly, help Pakistan's military to upgrade defenses against India, a country with close ties to the Soviet Union. The possibility of handing Moscow a defeat in Afghanistan suited Zia's vision of creating friendly Muslim states in the region in order to give Pakistan "strategic depth" in the long struggle with India. At home, the Afghan war helped Zia to sustain his domestic control and delay restoration of meaningful democratic institutions.

Over the course of what became known as a jihad, or holy struggle, against the Soviets and their Afghan communist allies, the CIA carried the burden of US involvement. Eventually Washington found itself engaged in the most extensive and expensive covert warfare operation since Vietnam. The assistance to Afghanistan began modestly enough with $30 million going to the resistance forces in 1980, with Saudi Arabia generally matching US funding and the Chinese contributing weapons. Not until the end of 1984, when an allocation of $280 million was announced, was the decision reached by the Reagan administration to escalate the conflict sufficiently to aim for an outright Soviet military defeat. Support increased the following year to $470 million, and in 1987 to $630 million. In all, during the 1980s, the Afghan mujahideen received more than $2 billion from the United States, enough to train at least 80,000 fighters.[12]

Large sums of money were funneled to Pakistan's security organizations, notably to a newly empowered Inter-Services Intelligence directorate (ISI). Purchased weapons were distributed by the ISI among the several Peshawar-based mujahideen parties expected to carry the brunt of the fighting in Afghanistan. The ISI forced some coordination among these parties, although it showed favoritism toward the most radical and, ironically, most anti-American of the Islamic groups. More secular Afghan nationalists, many with close ties to the United States, were almost entirely excluded from the Pakistani-supervised insurgency.

CIA officials on the scene were not entirely bystanders. Detailed and extensive satellite intelligence was passed on to the resistance, as was training in more sophisticated weaponry and communications equipment.[13] But for the most part, Washington willingly delegated to the ISI orchestration of the war and rationalized the decision as giving discretion to those in a better position to assess the strategic picture and use the funds most effectively. In fact, allocations were made by Pakistan only secondarily on the basis of fighting prowess. Most handsomely awarded with arms were the parties that Pakistan felt it could trust and control.

The United States mostly looked the other way as Afghan resistance party leaders living in the border city of Peshawar, Pakistan, enriched themselves through stealing and selling hundreds of millions of dollars of arms.[14] CIA officials who were monitoring the insurgency also knew that the Pakistani army and refugee administrators were siphoning off arms and relief supplies. The partial appropriation of CIA shipments was condoned as a sort of commission to the Pakistan government for the burdens and risks it had assumed in backing the Afghan insurgency, even if a third of supplies never reached their intended recipients.

THE GENEVA ACCORDS

As early as June 1982, proximity talks had begun in Geneva that allowed Islamabad to avoid direct negotiations with the Marxist regime in Kabul, which it had refused to recognize. The stated objectives of the talks, held under UN auspices in successive rounds over six years, were to end foreign interference and intervention, to realize self-determination and a sovereign Afghanistan, and to repatriate refugees. Plainly, any agreements had to suit the superpowers' cold war strategies. The Soviet Union was deeply engaged in decisions at every stage. The United States, although seemingly more detached from the negotiations, monitored them closely and was present at the final session in Geneva in 1988. Throughout the talks, the United States carried on a dialogue with Moscow over Afghanistan, usually preceded by contacts with Islamabad. Pakistani negotiators, risking forfeiture of US military and economic aid, looked for cues from Washington. However, Pakistan's separate interests, motivated by concern over domestic instability and its own strategic logic, also weighed heavily.[15]

Differences prevailed in Washington over the Geneva negotiations, some linked to issues that touched only peripherally on the Afghan conflict. Cold war conservatives, doubting Moscow's sincerity at Geneva, saw no reason to let the Soviet military off the hook in Afghanistan, or at least only under the most humiliating terms. Pro-mujahideen lobbies, including many Afghan émigré groups that resented the exclusion of the Afghan parties from the deliberations, shared their suspicions of the Soviet's intentions at Geneva. Ideological hard-liners and jihad advocates were also anxious that an agreement leading to a Soviet withdrawal would not end arms shipments to the mujahideen. The Geneva talks were also influenced by US nonproliferation policies. Throughout the 1980s, lobbies on Capitol Hill pressed for Pakistan's compliance with US law and for the relinquishing of its clandestine nuclear weapons program. They demanded that Washington not continue to ignore Pakistani activity and insisted that the White House implement a legislatively imposed aid cutoff—with its obvious implications for the insurgency. These voices were countered by others who stressed Pakistan's contribution not only to the Afghan cause but also as part of a strategy backing Islamic alternatives to communism wherever they could be found.

Some critics of US policy on the left contended that the Soviets were prepared for a military pullout as early as 1983 and that the Reagan administration's desire to perpetuate a conflict bleeding the Soviet state delayed serious negotiations. Although Moscow may, in fact, have been ready to withdraw its armed forces earlier, it would have done so only with international recognition of its Afghan client and a reasonable certainty of the Kabul regime's survival. It was not until 1986, a year after Mikhail Gorbachev assumed power, that the Soviets decided against committing more troops and grew serious about recalling their forces, even if that meant leaving the Kabul government at some risk.

By this time, Moscow had begun to face up to the full economic and political costs of fighting the mujahideen. The Soviet leadership's decision was influenced by losses it sustained from the introduction of US shoulder-fired, ground-to-air Stinger missiles and the rising tide of domestic opposition to the war in the Soviet Union. Perhaps most of all, Afghanistan posed a prime obstacle to Gorbachev's plans for domestic economic and political reforms.

At the same time, the Reagan administration had begun to take the UN peace process more seriously and appeared ready to accept a nonaligned government in Kabul. Discussions between Washington and Moscow, suspended since 1982, resumed in mid-1985. With the Soviets signaling their readiness for a settlement, the hard-line opposition in Washington began to melt. Standing in the way of an accord in Geneva, however, was a lack of agreement on a timetable for the Red Army's withdrawal. Other issues, including verification of the pullout and a political formula for governing the country, also had to be resolved with Pakistan.[16]

Soviet willingness by early 1988 to accept a shorter time frame for withdrawal was not matched by agreements on foreign interference and a political settlement. But the United States, seeing no early possibility for an interim government, was anxious not to pass up the opportunity for a Soviet troop withdrawal. On the issue of intervention, both sides settled, in effect, for symmetry in allowing continued military assistance to their respective clients. However, President Zia wanted to hold out until an agreement was reached on a political arrangement that replaced the ruling Marxist regime. Moscow refused to accede to abandoning Afghanistan's communists by excluding them in a future government. Only direct personal intervention by President Reagan in a phone call to Zia induced the Pakistani president to sign the April 1988 Geneva Accords.

POST-SOVIET WITHDRAWAL

It was widely predicted that the Marxist government in Kabul would collapse in a matter of months after the last Soviet troops departed in February 1989. Plans were made in Washington to reopen an embassy in Kabul, and assistance was promised to help with postwar reconstruction. Meanwhile, US policy remained aimed at bringing down the Kabul regime through a military victory and replacing it with the Peshawar-based Afghan Interim Government, a collection of mujahideen parties. But Kabul's communist regime, well stocked with equipment needed to defend itself and continuing to draw economic support from Moscow, refused to surrender and was able to ward off military defeat for three more years. By 1990, Washington was anxious to halt the ongoing bloodshed and began to entertain the possibility that the Peshawar-based parties might have to accept a political reconciliation that involved a broad coalition, including perhaps communist elements.[17] An alternative strategy that might have tried to construct over several years a new political reality, bypassing both the communist and mujahideen leaders, found little support in either Washington or Islamabad. For its part, Pakistan, particularly its military establishment, was determined to install a government in Kabul over which it would be assured a strong influence. The Pakistani leaders felt that they could control the jihad parties in Kabul much as they had in Peshawar.

Without a Soviet presence in Afghanistan, Washington's military aid to the mujahideen declined; the authorization for arms in 1990 was cut to $50 million from $300 million the previous year. Moreover, supplies of weapons were more closely linked with proven fighting effectiveness, and deliveries slowed with increased evidence that some resistance groups were hoarding their war supplies. The Bush administration also began to question its continued assistance to strongly doctrinaire Islamic mujahideen groups, which now appeared to be obstacles to peace and resembled emerging radical forces across the Muslim world. Understandably, many in Pakistan viewed the US weakening commitment as premature, taken before Pakistan's interests in the region had been secured. Had the communist regime in Kabul not fallen in April 1992, a full US arms cutoff was probably inevitable.

The demise of the government of President Muhammad Najibullah, in power more than five years, followed closely on the heels of the breakup of the Soviet state. Then, despite a Pakistan-brokered accord among the victorious parties, they fought among themselves in a full-fledged civil war more devastating to Afghanistan's capital than was the previous phase of the conflict. Over most of the country, a warlord system instituted a criminalized economy based increasingly on smuggling, extortion, and increased opportunities for income from opium poppy cultivation. The circumstances also allowed for the continued presence of Islamic radicals from Arab and other Muslim countries receiving training and indoctrination much as they had during the anticommunist jihad. Large numbers of those in the camps were Pakistanis, some of whom would fight under the patronage of Pakistan's army in the Kashmir insurgency against Indian security forces.

With power ceded to the mujahideen parties, economic assistance replaced military aid. International assistance was slated for the resettlement of refugees, and the first steps were to be taken in rebuilding the battered economy. However, it quickly became apparent that serious programs of rehabilitation and reconstruction would have to wait until some force prevailed militarily and could begin to consolidate its authority over the country. Whatever sense of obligation was felt initially by the United States and others to join in rebuilding the country gradually dissipated. Between 1992 and the following year, US funding for Afghanistan dropped 60 percent, to $20 million.

US detachment carried the most immediate implications for Pakistan. With the Soviets gone from Afghanistan, the basis of a US partnership with Islamabad became outmoded, even dispensable. By 1990, Pakistan's nuclear program—which disqualified it for US assistance—was rediscovered. Presidential waivers that allowed for economic and military aid were no longer forthcoming, thus ending nearly a decade of assistance to Pakistan. As a result, the United States lost much of the leverage it had over Islamabad, including any chance that it could steer Pakistani policy on Afghanistan during the next decade.

The ubiquitous conspiracy theorists in Pakistan saw it differently, claiming that US disengagement in the region had been cooked up with the Russians. Allegedly the plot was designed to deny the mujahideen the full fruits of a victory that would threaten Moscow's control over its Central Asian republics and US influence in the Middle East. It would also thwart Pakistan's emerging contribution to a more powerful post–cold war Islamic world.[18] The reality was far simpler, however. Washington concluded that it had little to offer in finding a political solution and, unlike Pakistan, not a great deal at stake as factions eventually ruled Afghanistan. The consequences of what might emerge with a weak, factious state were not fully assessed. Although the rising drug trade from Afghanistan was a concern, there was little sense at the time that the trafficking, going mainly to Europe, could be stopped or that production, even if curtailed, would not shift to neighboring states. The threat posed under a system of warlords giving sanctuary to foreign extremists was not fully appreciated.

The period of mujahideen civil conflict was a low point for Pakistan. Having failed to install Gulbuddin Hekmatyar, its preferred Afghan commander in power in Kabul, Islamabad displayed its willingness to back any faction able to consolidate control and provide a reasonably stable government. Above all, Pakistan sought a regime capable of freeing the roads from banditry and other impediments to opening trade routes with Central Asia. Islamabad not only failed in its effort to find a leader or faction that could deliver but instead concluded that those occupying the formal seats of power in Kabul were moving toward closer ties with New Delhi.

TALIBAN RULE

The answer to Pakistan's search for surrogates in Afghanistan appeared to lie with the Taliban. Mostly students in Islamic schools, frustrated by the predatory militias controlling Kandahar and connecting roads, Taliban fighters easily overcame the local authority and set up a self-defined Islamic rule. Pakistan's Interior minister, Nasrullah Barbar, moved quickly to adopt this new force, as did the region's powerful trucking cartels. Above all, the Taliban's popular appeal was based on their ability to inject greater law and order, their seeming incorruptibility, and the hope of many ordinary Afghans that these idealistic young men would finally bring peace to the country. Over subsequent months, the Taliban encountered surprisingly little armed resistance as they carried their cause elsewhere in the country. By August 1995, the movement had routed the defenders of Herat, the largest city in the country's west. Only when, that autumn, the Taliban approached the capital, Kabul, and confronted for the first time a disciplined fighting force under veteran commander Ahmed Shah Massoud did they falter. It was also the first serious face-off for the mostly ethnic Pashtun Taliban against fighters from the second-largest ethnic minority, the Tajiks.

The Taliban capture of Kabul in September 1996 ushered in one of the more interesting interludes in US-Afghan relations. By this time, US interests in the country were beginning to revive. Increasingly, the country had become a source of heroin for the international market. Its chaotic political climate sheltered the military and ideological training of Islamic terrorists preparing to fan out globally with an anti-establishment Muslim and anti-American agenda. The Taliban offered another attraction. With the Taliban seemingly on the verge of victory across the country, the United States decided to establish contacts with the new regime. Some US officials believed that befriending the movement could yield early dividends. The Taliban seemed to lack a political agenda and thus stood in contrast to some mujahideen parties, notably that of Gulbuddin Hekmatyar, who was openly hostile toward the United States. Privately, the movement's leaders assured Washington that terrorism and drugs would have no place in their pious rule. The Taliban promised to end poppy growing and indicated a willingness to close down training camps for militants, expelling resident Arabs. The antipathy in Taliban beliefs for Shi'a Islam also recommended the Taliban for a role in the US hoped-for containment of Iran. By contrast, increasing contacts with Tehran by a Kabul regime headed by President Burhanuddin Rabbani, an ethnic Tajik, had sounded alarm bells in Washington. No doubt factoring into US policy through the mid-1990s were plans by an American-Saudi coalition of Union Oil of California (Unocal) and Delta oil companies to build gas and oil pipelines from Central Asia through Afghanistan to Pakistan and then to other Asian markets. But constructing these pipelines required that Afghanistan be largely pacified, and the Taliban emerged as the force most likely to secure the risky but potentially highly lucrative investment. The project appealed to Washington because if it succeeded, it would cut off investment for an Iranian route, thereby denying the Islamic republic the economic benefits of hosting the pipelines. Unocal expected to do business with the Taliban with its attractive promise of future revenue and jobs in an economic recovery. The company's intense lobbying in Washington succeeded in giving the strong impression that the commercial venture carried official US sanction.[19]

Although not yet considering formal recognition, Washington took tentative steps toward reestablishing an official American presence in Kabul. A series of trips by US officials in autumn 1994 explored reconstruction assistance as well as refugee repatriation, issues of drug trafficking, and the disposition of radical groups. But progress toward de jure recognition slowed abruptly in the weeks following the Taliban's occupation of Kabul. Evidence that the movement was not, in fact, about to sweep to a total military victory no doubt influenced policy. More importantly, narrow religious doctrines and repressive social policies that the Taliban had previously brought to bear elsewhere in the country were now applied with little modification to the capital city's more secular urban society. Human rights advocates in the United States, especially feminist groups, condemned the Taliban's governing, most notably their elimination of girls' schools and the near impossibility of women's employment. Banning of television and most forms of entertainment marked the Taliban as narrow-minded zealots. So too did their imposition of harsh punishments for criminal offenses, beginning with the murder and public display of the mutilated body of former Afghan President Najibullah after the capture of Kabul.

Public and private criticism of the Taliban increased during 1997, summed up by Secretary of State Madeleine Albright's description of the Taliban as "despicable" during a November visit to Pakistan. American policymakers became embittered when the 1998 bombings of US embassies in East Africa were traced to Afghanistan and the Saudi Arabian dissident Osama bin Laden, who had taken refuge in Afghanistan. For harboring the alleged perpetrator of these attacks and hosting training facilities for believed terrorists, the Taliban became the number one culprit and target for the United States. This was forcefully demonstrated by the cruise missile strike on these camps in August 1998. In hopes of forcing the Taliban to yield up bin Laden to justice and dismantle his al-Qa'ida organization, the United States imposed sanctions on the Taliban early in 1999. Washington also orchestrated the UN Security Council's approval of further sanctions in November 1999. To these were added yet another set of sanctions in January 2001. Several of the bans and boycotts were aimed at making it inconvenient for the Taliban leaders to travel and at cutting off their access to funds. Most effective would have been a halt in arms shipments to the Taliban, but it could not be accomplished without the cooperation of neighboring countries, most of all a reluctant Pakistan. The sanctions brought little change in the Taliban's capacity to fight or to pursue their domestic agenda.

Consumed with feelings of self-righteousness about Islam, the Taliban saw the international demands as a test of their leadership and faith. Increased isolation strengthened the hard-liners among the Taliban's senior officials. Worsening economic conditions made the leadership more reliant on the fund-raising activities of bin Laden and more amenable to his influence. With almost no contacts beyond his immediate entourage, Mullah Omar Akhund was encouraged in the belief that he had emerged as a transnational Islamic leader. Mullah Omar's March 2001 decision ordering the destruction of all the country's pre-Islamic statues—notably the colossal Bamian Buddhas—defied international opinion and ignored Islamic authorities he deemed less enlightened.

Slowly the United States and the international community came to appreciate that the Taliban operated with its own, frequently incomprehensible worldview. Many of the strategies that diplomats would ordinarily have expected to sway the Taliban's behavior had little or no effect. Once having decided that an Islamic dictum applied, the leadership cared little for whether Taliban policies damaged the regime politically and economically. Their unwillingness to relinquish bin Laden, although expressed in terms of principle, also reflected a reluctance to break faith with fighters and financial contributors loyal to the Saudi dissident.

The Taliban had picked up the pieces of a failed Afghan state and society, but were unable to construct much on their own. While improved law and order, as well as respect for the leaders' Islamic piety, brought popular appeal, there was growing frustration with the Taliban's style of rule. Local Pashtun commanders pragmatically allied with the Taliban were in many cases prepared to break with the regime but found the alternative ethnic Tajik-led opposition unacceptable. Close associates of Mullah Omar never challenged him, despite sharp differences. Perhaps the greatest fear among Taliban insiders was not being defeated by their northern adversaries but concern that in light of their inability to contribute to the country's rebuilding, they could not withstand a force promising to improve the lives of the people.

All signs pointed to the Taliban remaining ascendant for some time. The September 9, 2001, assassination of the Northern Alliance's skilled and charismatic commander Ahmed Shah Massoud left the Taliban well positioned to mount a campaign to bring the remaining 10 percent of the country under their control. Material assistance given to the opposition by Iran and Russia probably would have been insufficient to stave off a Taliban victory. But the balance of force changed entirely when the US-led coalition attacked the Taliban in October. The country was fated to move into a post-Taliban era where, unless a successor political structure was quickly erected and authority asserted countrywide, a return to the warlord system seemed inevitable. Uncertainty also prevailed over whether the international community would limit its involvement to rooting out supporters of terrorism or commit to bringing broad-based government and programs of rehabilitation and reconstruction.

THE KARZAI ERA

Afghanistan in the wake of the Taliban's departure became the first major application of the Bush Doctrine, which defined US policy as refraining from nation building. American interests might dictate the projection of military power globally, unilaterally if necessary, but the task of rebuilding states and societies would be left to a country's own people assisted by the international community. Consistent with this policy, Washington made only a minimal commitment of ground forces. Planned as the opening salvo in a broader war against international terrorism, the deployment of US troops would last long enough to hunt down the remnants of al-Qa'ida, especially bin Laden and the Taliban's top leadership. This "light footprint," as it was called, also meant that political authority would be handed off to the Afghans as quickly as possible. Above all, a mostly low profile sought to allay the impression that the outsiders, above all the Americans, might be there as occupiers, intending to impose their own order on Afghanistan.

Just weeks after the Taliban was ousted, the UN convened a conference in Bonn, Germany, that brought together leaders of the disparate groups that had opposed the Taliban. Hard negotiations, requiring behind-the-scenes interventions by the UN's special representative and observers from the United States and other countries, resulted in compromise agreements on a political framework and a timetable for forming a democratic constitutional system. Hamid Karzai, a Pashtun tribal moderate, was the preferred American choice to head the new government. His inoffensive credentials made him acceptable to most Afghans and unthreatening to the country's neighbors. A Loya Jirgah (Great Assembly), a traditional gathering of local and national figures, confirmed Karzai as an interim president in June 2002, and a national election in October 2004—held with international supervision and financing—gave him a clear popular mandate. A Loya Jirgah the previous year had approved an essentially liberal constitution that provided for strong presidential powers. In September 2005, Afghans voted in a parliamentary election whose results reflected much of the country's ethnic polarization and political fragmentation.

The limited American commitment had some unfortunate consequences. In the weeks following the Taliban's removal, the few troops deployed were unable to mount effective operations along the border with Pakistan. Contracting out much of the task of closing escape routes to the area's unreliable Pashtun tribal militias allowed bin Laden and his associates to flee. Nor was there much interest in providing forces to secure the rest of the country. On arrival, a 5,000-member multinational UN-sanctioned international security assistance force (ISAF) was, at the request of the US military, restricted in its peacekeeping activities to the Kabul area, presumably out of concern that needed American logistical support would be a distraction from US antiterrorist operations. The political and security vacuum countrywide was quickly filled by private armies headed by regional warlords and local commanders, many of them returning from exile. With a fledgling central government exercising no national writ, these militias acquired a large measure of autonomy and in the guise of defending local Afghans, proceeded to prey on them.

A light footprint policy that focused on American antiterrorism objectives had other adverse affects. Afghans expected that international largesse in the post-Taliban era would supply resources that would soon improve ordinary people's lives. Yet rebuilding the Afghan economy and rehabilitating its largely decimated infrastructure proceeded very slowly. A Tokyo conference attracting nearly sixty countries and international organizations in January 2002 elicited generous pledges of assistance to Afghanistan's social and economic sectors. Agriculture was slated to receive especially high priority. Over time, however, many donor countries failed to meet their obligations, citing Afghanistan's low capacity to absorb development assistance and the difficult security environment for executing aid projects.

Despite US reluctance to assume a nation-building role in Afghanistan, it immediately emerged as the leading aid donor. Total US aid appropriations, both military and nonmilitary, increased from $737 million in FY 2003 to $1.7 billion in FY 2004, to nearly $4 billion in FY 2005. An all-important highway from Kabul to Kandahar, Afghanistan's second-largest city, had been paved by December 2003 and there were palpable gains in the education and health sectors from US aid programs. But the larger picture was less promising. The benefits of US and international spending were unevenly distributed as Kabul and several other cities profited disproportionately from the proceeds of foreign assistance. Though critical to economic revival, agriculture development lagged badly. Projects designed to address Afghanistan's infrastructural deficits and generate income for large numbers of Afghans were also seriously delayed. After March 2003, the US preoccupation with the Iraq War precluded accelerated reconstruction and attention to poor governance and absence of security for Afghans.

Meanwhile an illicit Afghan economy, built mainly around opium poppy cultivation, was rapidly expanding. By 2005 Afghan opium poppy cultivation constituted at least half of the country's gross domestic product. It provided a far better income to around 2 million farmers than they would have earned by growing traditional crops. However, the corrosive effects of the drug economy on Afghan society and government were also apparent. So too was the fact that the Taliban insurgents were taking a cut from the lucrative drug trade. While the British remained the lead nation in a national poppy eradication program, in 2004 the United States began financing the training of special Afghan antinarcotics squads and sponsored programs providing alternative crops and livelihoods for farmers.[20] The Afghan president and others resisted pressures from Washington for an aggressive approach to drug eradication that included aerial chemical spraying. Karzai claimed that heavy-handed operations that would affect mostly small farmers could prove politically destabilizing. In reality, no enforcement stood much chance until the Kabul government was prepared to target government officials, including many at the highest levels, handsomely profiting from drug production.

The most explicit attempt to expand the presence of foreign forces and marry security with reconstruction began on a small scale in 2003 with the creation of provincial reconstruction teams (PRTs). Exclusively American at the outset, the PRTs consisted of mostly regular military personnel but also included civilians with various political and technical skills, and representatives of the Afghan Interior Ministry. Within three years there were twenty-five PRTs, with nearly half from other ISAF–contributing countries. The teams were expected to fund and supervise small rural development projects and improve local security for nongovernment organizations (NGOs) and international agencies engaged in relief and development work. Yet many NGOs objected on the grounds they were in fact endangered by the PRTs' development activities, which blurred the difference for Afghans between military and nonmilitary aims. More seriously, PRTs located mostly in the country's secure provincial capitals were a poor substitute for a fuller international presence at the district level where they could better connect with the Afghan people.

A narrative of missed opportunities best describes the US engagement with Afghanistan for the greater part of the first decade after 2001. An underresourced military effort, an uncoordinated, ineffective development strategy, and an indifference to the malfeasance of the Karzai government steadily eroded the favorable attitudes that most Afghans held toward the United States and the international community. By 2006 it had become clear that years of policy drift had allowed an initially low-level guerrilla campaign by the Taliban and two allied insurgent groups, the Haqqani Network and the Hesb-i-Islami of Gulbudeen Hekmatyar, to become a full-grown, lethal insurgency. Regrouped and well organized and equipped, the militants increasingly employed improvised explosive devices and suicide bombers. What had been mostly hit-and-run cross-border attacks from sanctuaries inside Pakistan had now morphed into an entrenched insurgency across much of Afghanistan's south and east. The Taliban found allies among dissident militias, criminal elements, drug traffickers, aggrieved individuals, and unemployed youth. The changing character of the conflict required a course correction, and in 2006 British and Canadian troops assumed combat roles in Taliban-dominated Helmand and Kandahar provinces, and the US military mission that had remained independent of ISAF was in large part folded into the multinational, NATO-led force.

A new start was undertaken to improve and accelerate training of the Afghan national army and police. From the outset, the Afghan security forces were identified as the cornerstone of a security policy that would eventually provide an exit from Afghanistan for the US military and its coalition partners. The Afghan security forces were expected to gradually assume responsibility for dealing with the country's rampant crime problem and take over the job of protecting the regime against its enemies. The United States took charge of rapidly expanding an army that in 2006 numbered 30,000.[21] Building a larger and more reliable police force presented even greater challenges. Most recruits are illiterate, and the police have long had a reputation for incompetence and corruption. To deal with high rates of attrition, salaries were increased for members of both the army and police. The United States picked up the training of both, and at the end of 2010 the army was expected to have over 240,000 and the police roughly 120,000 members. In total, the Afghan security force is projected to grow to more than 300,000, a level well beyond anything that the Afghan government can hope to afford without international funding.

A more concerted effort has been made to improve cohesion and cooperation among the international aid actors as well as devise a more coherent aid strategy. At a London Conference of aid donors in 2006, a repeated criticism was that there was no single organization to check and monitor where the foreign aid money was going and that only a small portion was under Afghan government control or was reaching the Afghan people. Differing aid philosophies and national interests resulted in weak coordination among donor countries. A five-year development strategy known as the Afghan Compact emerged from the London Conference that together with documents approved at conferences in Paris in 2008 and London and Kabul in 2010 constitutes a UN development assistance framework designed to provide greater coherence. In all of these conferences President Karzai has complained that his government controls only a minor fraction of the project aid that has been given by the international community since 2001. The rest is channeled through NGOs, international agencies, and private contractors that absorb the lion's share of the funds before they reach their intended recipients. The United States, which by 2010 had spent nearly $19 billion in nonmilitary expenditures in Afghanistan, bypassed Afghan ministries, citing their limited skills and lack of transparency in dispensing funds.[22] The 2010 London conference promised to increase the responsibility of the Kabul government for control over development aid to up to 50 percent through an existing international trust fund. The offer was conditioned, however, on government progress in strengthening its public financial management.

Plans for reform continue to be stymied by what many in the United States and international community see as President Karzai's toleration of corruption and incompetence at all levels of government. The Afghan president has been widely viewed as trying to satisfy the country's major power brokers rather than providing decisive leadership. His government's failures to deliver basic services, as well as the country's distrusted judicial system, are said to explain many of the insurgency's gains. Karzai, for his part, has expressed frustration with his American and ISAF allies for their conduct of the war. Positioning himself politically among Afghans for an eventual American and international departure, Karzai has strengthened his image as a nationalist by championing public expressions of anger over those military operations resulting in the death of innocent Afghan civilians. Karzai also accuses his allies of trying to deny him reelection by intervening in a disputed presidential election in August 2009. To demonstrate his independence, Karzai has pressed for reconciliation with the insurgency's top leaders. While American officials are skeptical of an early agreement with the Taliban or Haqqani Network, the United States has encouraged talks if only to avoid being tagged as the spoiler should negotiations go nowhere.

By 2009 the Taliban and its allied groups had erected shadow administrative structures throughout most of the country. They had infiltrated districts in the southwest and north with Pashtun populations once considered safe. These mounting threats, together with events outside Afghanistan, set the stage for a serious American reappraisal of the war effort. Military and political successes in Iraq meant that the United States could shift its attention to Afghanistan and consider what strategies had worked against the Iraqi insurgents. This refocus was assured by the election of a US president who had campaigned on the proposition that Afghanistan was where the real fight against international terrorism belonged. Soon after assuming office, President Obama called for a strategic review and announced in April 2009 a policy that prioritized the removal of a terrorist threat from al-Qa'ida through helping to stabilize Afghanistan. The Obama administration was presented with a comprehensive counterinsurgency plan that called for tens of thousands of additional US ground forces and a civilian surge to concentrate on helping to build state institutions. The US president in a December 2009 speech accepted the principles of the revised strategy, while providing fewer troops than requested by the military and with the caveat that US troops would begin leaving Afghanistan in July 2011.

The counterinsurgency approach was a variant of an approach General David Petraeus had devised for Iraq, which emphasized protecting population centers more than pursuing and destroying the enemy. It called for using the additional troops to clear the Taliban fighters from their strongholds and then holding those areas while internationally assisted Afghan government personnel win over local support through development projects and improved governance. The American military further banked on its successes against the insurgents in key provinces and districts having the effect of changing popular perceptions about which side would ultimately prevail. Once that happened, a political outcome was believed achievable by peeling away lower- and middle-level Taliban fighters from their ideological leaders.

Despite the disappointments of the Karzai era, few Afghans appear to welcome a return of the Taliban. Its rule demonstrated that it has no agenda for addressing the country's basic needs. Most Afghans continue to believe that international assistance, with the United States in a central role, is indispensable to the country's recovery. Afghan citizens realize that the country lacks the human and material resources to progress very far by itself. The insurgency has succeeded in creating enough disruption and intimidation for people countrywide to lose faith in the ability of international actors and the Kabul government to protect them and improve their lives. For the time being, most Afghans remain ambivalent in their loyalties. To recapture the kind of welcome that foreign forces and aid benefactors enjoyed for some years after 2001, Afghans must believe that costs of continued conflict are acceptable because the United States, above all, will not leave prematurely.

CONCLUSION

Afghanistan barely figured on the US foreign policy map until late in 1979. Even the Saur revolution in 1978, bringing Afghan communists to power, was tolerable. Washington's policy reflected a willingness to recognize, more or less, the Soviet's greater interest in Afghanistan and the American inability to do much about it. Only when the Soviet Union directly intervened militarily and was perceived to have wider strategic ambitions did that view change. But once the Soviet Union was gone, the United States quickly turned elsewhere, despite the unresolved conflict. Taliban rule prompted a refocusing, mainly around the issue of terrorism. Any possibility that the country would again fall off Washington's radar screen once sanctions against the Taliban yielded Osama bin Laden vanished with the events of September 11, 2001.

Inconsistencies in US policies and an inclination to downplay Afghanistan's significance call for further explanation. A good place to start is the steadfast perception of Afghanistan's remoteness, psychologically as well as geographically. The country's location helped to motivate Washington's conclusion during the cold war that with Afghanistan in the Soviet Union's backyard, the United States could not take responsibility for Afghanistan's security along with that of Pakistan's, and the country's chances of independence were actually best served by a slim US presence. Following the Soviet occupation, the problems likely to beset the Afghan state, however regrettable, initially appeared to be sufficiently parochial and distant enough not to impinge on vital American interests.

This failure to recognize fully the regional and global implications of an Afghan nation left turbulent and unreconstructed comes as a consequence of viewing Afghanistan as essentially unique and exotic. It is a picture that portrays the country as hopelessly primitive, rent by unresolved primordial conflicts. Tribal mores and religious fanaticism are thought to make the country largely ungovernable. The image held is of a country where, aside from delivering humanitarian aid, the normal prescriptions for building a viable modern economy and stable, democratic polity are probably not applicable. No doubt the Taliban's often erratic and unacceptable behavior contributed to this view. Even so, it is unfair to Afghan history and underestimates the potential for development and internal cooperation with the right kind of international assistance. Much of what currently seems congenitally an obstacle to Afghanistan's development economically and politically is in fact the consequence of more than a generation of war.

The United States probably underestimated its capacity to contribute to positive changes in Afghanistan. In spite of Washington's penchant for disengagement, throughout the country's civil war most Afghans continued to look to the United States, above all other countries, to help them secure a political settlement.[23] At the time, even some in the Taliban leadership saw little hope of forging a national recovery without the United States. Afghans have always found it difficult to imagine that after having been so supportive in the 1980s, American leaders could ignore their needs, especially since Afghan jihad helped bring down the Soviet state.

By allowing Afghanistan to descend into virtual anarchy and then succumb to an erratic, despotic theocracy, Washington had left the country vulnerable to exploitation by transnational extremists dedicated to working against American interests. Efforts to target these elements were fruitless until the United States embarked militarily on regime change. In dislodging the Taliban regime along with al-Qa'ida, Washington found itself, despite its predilections, saddled with responsibilities of helping to rebuild an Afghan state and economy.

A broad, sustained international commitment is required if Afghanistan is to have a promising future. The success in the post-Taliban era in evading a potential humanitarian crisis and in realizing the significant political and constitutional milestones has come only with UN-sanctioned, multinational involvement. The challenges confronting the country are many. Deep social and economic deficits leave Afghanistan among the world's most underdeveloped countries. Fledgling judicial and political institutions struggle to establish legitimacy and effective governance. The central government has yet to bring to heel influential regional power brokers. Banditry and corruption are uncontained, while drug production and trafficking distort the economy. Ethnic-linked contention for positions of power and resources threatens national unity. And still unresolved are constitutional issues that divide progressive reformers and religious conservatives.

The United States and the international community essentially have been buying time for Afghanistan. In providing resources and helping the country to fend off its enemies, they have hoped to offer the Afghan state an opportunity to acquire the capacity to address the basic needs of its citizens and provide them physical security. How and when to transfer to Afghan institutions greater responsibilities for development has been of critical concern, and both Afghans and their international benefactors will need to manage their expectations. It has been conceded that the country is not likely to witness strong central authority or shed its heavy reliance on outside benefactors in the foreseeable future. Nor is it likely to measure up to international legal and ethical standards without a more competent and legitimate legal system. At best, Afghanistan is seen as having to settle for becoming a normal less-developed country, albeit one that is sufficiently stable to resist becoming fertile soil for radical forces intent on mounting a regional or global threat. Instrumental to this outcome is the nonintervention of neighboring states and the confidence among Afghans that the international actors and especially the United States will not again desert them.

Yet the promise of continued American involvement in helping Afghanistan to achieve even a modest future is in some doubt. Continuing difficulty in reversing a resilient insurgency has led many to question whether a reinforced but belated counterinsurgency can succeed. Critics insist that a corrupt, unpopular Kabul government leaves the United States without a credible partner. The Afghan war is the longest in American history, and competing national priorities, not the least domestic economic concerns, bring criticism of its costs and doubts about its strategic benefits. An American public is increasingly skeptical that the United States should assume responsibility for assisting Afghans to realize democracy, human rights, and economic growth. Many accept the view that American interests in Afghanistan should be almost exclusively directed toward thwarting a return by al-Qa'ida, an objective believed achievable with a more targeted approach and a limited US presence in the country. This approach assumes that left to themselves, Afghans can sort out their own differences, and that sharing power and conceding parts of the country to the Taliban may be unavoidable. This benign view discounts the strong possibility of political retribution and ethnic cleansing in a renewed civil war, and the temptation of regional powers to intervene on behalf of their ethnic clients. Afghanistan might for a time recede to the margins of American foreign policy. But a disengagement from Afghanistan that leads to instability in a region where American stakes remain so high is almost bound to bring a repeat of US involvement, perhaps at an even higher cost.

Notes

1. Richard S. Newell, *The Politics of Afghanistan* (Ithaca: Cornell University Press, 1972), p. 128.

2. Leon B. Poullada and Leila D. Poullada, *The Kingdom of Afghanistan and the United States: 1828–1973* (Lincoln, NE: Dageforde, 1995), pp. 178–179.

3. Ibid., p. 183.

4. Thomas T. Hammond, *Red Flag over Afghanistan* (Boulder: Westview, 1984), pp. 26–27.

5. By 1979, the Afghans had received from the Soviet Union $2.5 billion in economic and military aid. Bhabani Sen Gupta, *Afghanistan: Politics, Economics, and Society* (Boulder: Lynne Rienner, 1986), p. 12.

6. Lawrence Ziring, *Iran, Turkey, and Afghanistan: A Political Chronology* (New York: Praeger, 1981), p. 97.

7. Ralph H. Magnus and Eden Naby, *Afghanistan: Mullah, Marx, and Mujahid* (Boulder: Westview, 1998), p. 62.

8. Hammond, *Red Flag over Afghanistan*, p. 38.

9. Ziring, *Iran, Turkey, and Afghanistan*, p. 97.

10. Ibid., p. 106.

11. Hammond, *Red Flag over Afghanistan*, pp. 105–106.

12. Barnett Rubin, *The Fragmentation of Afghanistan* (New Haven: Yale University Press, 1995), pp. 196–201. The full cost for the United States during the course of the anticommunist jihad is elsewhere put at $3.3 billion. Marvin G. Weinbaum, *Pakistan and Afghanistan: Resistance and Reconstruction* (Boulder: Westview, 1994), p. 172.

13. Mohammed Yousef and Mark Atkins, *The Bear Trap: Afghanistan's Untold Story* (London: Leo Cooper, 1992), pp. 93–94, 189–194.

14. Tim Weiner, *Blank Check: The Pentagon's Black Budget* (New York: Warner Books, 1991), p. 150. For a description of the CIA's covert assistance to the mujahideen during the 1980s, see Larry P. Goodson, *Afghanistan's Endless War* (Seattle: University of Washington Press, 2001), pp. 142–143.

15. Riaz M. Khan, *Untying the Afghan Knot: Negotiating Soviet Withdrawal* (Durham, NC: Duke University Press, 1991), p. 170.

16. Rasul Bakash Rais, *War Without Winners* (Oxford: Oxford University Press, 1994), pp. 123–124.

17. Ibid., p. 135.

18. Weinbaum, *Pakistan and Afghanistan*, pp. 92–93.

19. Ahmed Rashid, in *Taliban: Militant Islam, Oil, and Fundamentalism in Central Asia* (New Haven: Yale University Press, 2000), pp. 166–169, is among those who contend that US officials vigorously intervened on behalf of the Unocal bid. For a fuller discussion, also see Richard MacKenzie, "The United States and the Taliban," in *Fundamentalism Reborn? Afghanistan and the Taliban*, ed. William Maley (New York: New York University Press, 1998), pp. 96–100.

20. "Afghanistan: Post-War Governance, Security, and US Policy," Congressional Research Service, Report to Congress, March 17, 2006, pp. 44–45. In fiscal year 2004 the United States spent $220 million on drug eradication and raised it in 2005 to more than $500 million.

21. *New York Times*, October 13, 2010, p. A10.

22. Kenneth Katzman, "Afghanistan: Post-Taliban Governance, Security, and US Policy," Congressional Research Service report, June 25, 2010, p. 75.

23. Goodson, *Afghanistan's Endless War*, p. 181.

CHAPTER 23

IDEOLOGY AND IRAN'S
AMERICAN POLICIES, 1997–2008

Mark L. Haas

This chapter examines the root sources of Iranian enmity toward the United States during the Bill Clinton and George W. Bush presidencies. To what extent and in what ways was Iranian hostility toward America a product of the profound ideological differences dividing the two states? To answer this question I examine the perceptions and actions of different ideological factions within Iranian policymaking circles. If ideological variables were central to Iranian leaders' international relations, then different ideological factions should have pursued markedly different foreign policies toward the United States. If, however, different ideological groups advocated fairly similar policies toward America despite their domestic differences, then systemic variables—such as US power and policies—were more likely at the heart of Iran's actions toward America. The core issue examined in this chapter is of critical importance for effective decision making by American politicians. Only by understanding the root sources of Iranian leaders' views of the United States will American policymakers most effectively advance US interests in these relations.[1]

IRAN'S IDEOLOGICAL FACTIONS

There are a number of ways to define ideology. I define it as leaders' preferences for ordering domestic politics. Ideologies, in other words, are the specific principles by which different groups attempt to legitimate their claim to rule and the primary institutional, economic, and social goals that they try to realize in their states. Ideologies are identified by what politicians value most highly for their societies and the major differences that separate different political parties or groups from one another.

Elsewhere I have found that the degree of ideological differences (or the "ideological distance") dividing leaders of states frequently has a profound impact on their foreign policies.[2] The greater the ideological differences dividing decision makers in different states, the higher their threat perceptions and thus the greater the likelihood of hostile relations developing. Leaders dedicated to opposing ideological principles tend to assume the worst about one another's international intentions, and fear the subversive impact of the other on their society. The reverse patterns tend to hold the greater the ideological similarities uniting leaders. These relationships, as we shall see, held for Iran's interactions with the United States during the years examined in this study.

After 1996 Iranian leaders were divided into two main ideological groups, which I label ideological "reformers" and "conservatives" (the latter could also be labeled "ideological hard-liners").[3] Iranian conservatives' primary domestic objective was to preserve the political system established by Ayatollah Ruhollah Musavi Khomeini after the Iranian Revolution in 1979 (e.g., rule by clergy based on a narrow interpretation of Islamic law, governmental regulation of personal virtue, and a rejection of what conservatives perceived to be defining principles of Western culture: materialism, secularism, immorality, and the separation of religion from politics). Central to the conservative ideology was Khomeini's doctrine of *velayat-e faqih*, or rule by the jurisprudent (a reference to the office of the Supreme Leader of the Revolution, which is the most powerful political institution in Iran and one that is filled by a leading Shiite cleric). This doctrine asserts the necessity of clerics' political control, and it legitimates the Iranian theocracy.[4]

To Iranian conservatives, the religious dimension of the Islamic Republic of Iran (IRI) was much more important than the republican component. Indeed, some conservatives rejected democratic discourse and the related protection of political pluralism. According, for example, to Ayatollah Mesbah Yazdi, who was a close adviser to President Mahmoud Ahmadinejad, "the prophets of God did not believe in pluralism. They believed that only one idea was right."[5] Other conservatives claimed that the regime must be connected to and have some backing from the people. Democratic practices, though, were clearly subordinate to the preferences of the ruling clerics, especially the Supreme Leader.[6]

Conservatives believed that their ideological principles were antithetical to Western liberalism, and in order to preserve the former in Iran the latter had to be eliminated. According to the conservative candidate in the 1997 presidential elections, Ali Akbar Nateq-Nuri (who was widely expected to win): "Liberalism is a real threat for the country and it must be eradicated."[7] Or as two other conservatives asserted: "Western liberal culture is incompatible with Islamic culture," therefore only one or the other can survive.[8]

In contrast, Iranian reformers advocated important liberalizing changes for Iranian politics and society.[9] According to Mohammad Khatami, a leading reformer who was Iran's president from 1997 to 2005, the core political goal of reformers was to "introduce to the world the model of religious democracy."[10] Reformers, in other words, were trying to find a balance between liberal values and the Islamist system that had existed in Iran since 1979.[11] On the one hand, the goal of "religious democracy" represented a rejection of liberal tenets because it required that religious authorities have greater involvement in political affairs than was deemed acceptable in Western states, and meant that some individual freedoms must be compromised in order to maintain the religious identity of the regime. Leading reformers, including Khatami, argued that individuals did not have the right either to question Islamic tenets (i.e., many reformers denied the validity of freedom *from* religion) or to overthrow the Islamic Republic (people could reform the regime but not destroy it). As Khatami explained in a 1997 speech, "no person is at liberty to endanger the security of the society, the interests of the country . . . [or] scar the fundamentals of Islam."[12] According to reformers, only by maintaining the religious authority and identity of the regime could Iran maintain a level of morality and spirituality that Western democracies lacked.[13]

In other ways, however, reformers were in accord with core liberal principles, and thus in major ideological disagreement with Iranian conservatives. Although Iranian reformers wanted to preserve the religious identity of the state and thus some of the political power of clerics, reformers believed that this power as constituted was too great, which was leading to abuses. Thus Khatami asserted that the government's power in Iran should be criticized and balanced because "too much power leads to corruption, even if those who hold power are good people."[14] To reformers, the best way to balance and criticize government power was to better respect democratic values and rights, for example, establishing the rule of law, creating checks and balances among all the branches of government, exhibiting greater tolerance of different political opinions, and better protecting pluralism and minority rights.[15] Khatami's primary domestic objectives while president (in his own words) were to "institutionalize the rule of law" and protect the "freedom of individuals and the rights of the nation . . . [through] constitutionally guaranteed liberties, strengthening . . . the institutions of civil society . . . and preventing any violation of constitutional rights."[16] These goals, as one scholar summarizes, were "clearly inspired by the West."[17] According to Khatami, it was only by implementing these major liberalizing reforms that "our country and our society will be preserved."[18]

Iranian reformers' ideological objectives, in sum, were significantly closer to Western ideological principles than were those of Iranian conservatives. If ideological relationships play an important role in formulating foreign policies, then the differing domestic principles of Iranian reformers and conservatives should have led them to possess very different views and policies toward the United States. The next section demonstrates the accuracy of this prediction.

IDEOLOGY AND IRANIAN VIEWS
OF THE UNITED STATES

The four most important political bodies in Iran are the office of the Supreme Leader of the Revolution, the presidency, the parliament, and the Council of Guardians.[19] The Supreme Leader is by far the most powerful person in Iran. He is the commander of all military forces, and he appoints and dismisses the head of the judiciary, the president of state radio and television, and half of the members of the Council of Guardians (the head of the judiciary—another appointee of the Supreme Leader—proposes the remaining members of the Guardian Council, but these must be approved by parliament). The Supreme Leader also has a budget (the amount is undisclosed) that is independent of the president and parliament.

The president is Iran's second most powerful political figure. He appoints and dismisses ministers and controls the powerful Planning and Budget organization, which is important for establishing economic policy. The president is also the chairman of the National Security Council, which coordinates governmental activities involving defense, intelligence, and foreign policy.

Iran's parliament (Majlis) has considerable power, especially by Middle Eastern standards. It is responsible, among other things, for drafting legislation, ratifying treaties, and approving the state budget. The Council of Guardians, though, has the power to veto parliamentary legislation that the council's members judge to be incompatible with Islamic law. It can also reject candidates for any office who are deemed to be unsuitable based on a candidate's perceived Islamic convictions and loyalty to the regime.

Iranian conservatives have always controlled the Office of the Supreme Leader and the Guardian Council. Reformers controlled the presidency from 1997 to 2005 and parliament from 2000 to 2004, both of which were historical firsts. Although Iranian conservatives always possessed considerably more domestic power than reformers did, this does not mean that the latter's power from 1997 to 2005 was inconsequential. Reformers influenced policies in key ways, leading conservatives to lament the direction of Iranian decision making when reformers were at the zenith of their influence. Conservatives welcomed the reformers' parliamentary and presidential defeats in 2004 and 2005, precisely because they recognized that reformers were having an impact on policy that ran contrary to conservative preferences.[20] Indeed, so great was the perceived threat posed by reformers that key conservative leaders, including the Supreme Leader and Iranian Revolutionary Guard Corps (IRGC) commanders, were brought to the "conclusion that a counteroffensive was necessary for regime survival."[21] The result was a conservative consolidation in the 2000s as regime hard-liners further limited the power of the president in favor of the Supreme Leader and Revolutionary Guard.[22]

The ideological differences between Iranian reformers and conservatives resulted in very different views of the United States. To begin with, the huge ideological divide separating the United States from Iranian conservatives pushed the latter to see America as both an inevitable threat to Iran's security and a powerful force for domestic subversion. This does not mean that American power and various provocative policies (such as stationing troops throughout the Middle East and enacting economic sanctions against Iran) did not exacerbate conservatives' perceptions of threat. They clearly did. But conservatives understood the root cause of US-Iranian enmity as based in ideological differences. The ideological beliefs of US leaders caused Americans to adopt hostile policies toward Iran in the first place. As Nateq-Nuri explained, Iran's "struggle against America has its origin in our ideology." Consequently the United States by "its nature" was a permanent enemy of the IRI.[23] Supreme Leader Khamenei often made similar statements. In a 2003 speech, he claimed that "the primary reason for US hostility toward our country is the Islamic identity of our system." Earlier in the year, he asserted that "it is natural that our Islamic system should be viewed as an enemy and an intolerable rival by such an oppressive power as the United States, which is trying to establish a global dictatorship . . . It is also clear that the conflict and confrontation between the two is something natural and unavoidable."[24]

Conservatives also repeatedly referred to the danger of "cultural onslaught" from the West—spreading Western values such as materialism, secularism, and the separation of religion and politics. According to Khamenei, the West in general and the United States in particular "has targeted our Islamic faith and character."[25] At the same time that Khatami was saying that Western ideology had much to commend it (see below), Khamenei was blaming Western civilization for "directing everyone towards materialism while money, gluttony and carnal desires are made the greatest aspirations."[26] Nateq-Nuri similarly blamed the West for "spreading corruptions and obscenity; ridiculing sacred Islamic . . . traditions; propagating debauchery [and] raunchiness."[27] According to him, the West's "cultural onslaught" was attempting to destroy Iran's "ideology, religious thinking, national identity and religious values."[28] The secretary of the Guardian Council, Ayatollah Ahmad Jannati, was more succinct: "The enemy is trying to destroy Islamic culture."[29]

To be clear, conservative fears of subversion were based on much more than a worry that ideas from one society would diffuse to another. Conservatives believed that the US government was actively promoting its ideological principles in order to destroy the Islamic Republic. According to Khamenei speaking in 2003, "more than Iran's enemies need artillery, guns and so forth, [American leaders] need to spread cultural values that lead to moral corruption." Three years earlier, the Supreme Leader asserted that "I have now reached the conclusion that the United States has devised a comprehensive plan to subvert the Islamic system. This plan is an imitation of the plan that led to the collapse of the former Soviet Union."[30] This last statement came at a time when many analysts were comparing President Khatami and Iranian reformers to former Soviet premier Mikhail Gorbachev and Soviet New Thinkers.

To prevent ideological subversion to Western principles, Iran, to conservatives, had to preserve its hostility toward the United States. Economic, diplomatic, or strategic interactions ran the risk of legitimating American cultural values and corrupting pious Muslims to immoral ideological beliefs. For many in the Iranian right, the risks of ideological contagion were more important than material gain. Conservatives lambasted Iranians who advocated economic cooperation with America as dupes and US agents whose policies would create fifth columns for Iran's ideological enemies. Conservatives, in other words, viewed the United States as a major threat to their interests independently of America's "provocative" international policies (unless economic cooperation is perceived as aggressive). Khamenei was scathing in his opposition to globalization and, in his term, the "Westoxicated" elements in Iran that supported it: "Audio and visual waves, which are worse than warplanes, are being used to disseminate a rogue culture aimed at reasserting the domination of the enemies of Islam, paving the way for the imposition of unethical values and Westernized ideas to captivate and humiliate Muslims."[31] Mohsen Kadivar, a senior reformist cleric, summed up the conservative position: "When the West threatens isolation, [conservatives] welcome it. They cannot integrate. They feel if Iran integrated it would lose its Islamic identity."[32]

The more liberal ideological beliefs of Iranian reformers led them to a significantly lower threat perception of the United States. Indeed, given their emphasis on civil rights and institutional checks on governmental power, it is not surprising that members of this group looked on elements of Western culture with admiration. Once again, this does not mean that reformers wanted to replicate Western regimes. Rather, they asserted that they wanted to take what was best from Western ideology—chiefly the emphasis on the protection of individual liberty and minority rights and the institutions that helped achieve these goals, such as the separation of political powers, constitutionalism, and a thriving civil society—and unite it with the Iranian emphasis on personal virtue and piousness. Iranian reformers, in other words, hoped to get the freedom enjoyed in the West without its secularization and materialism. President Khatami, for example, claimed that the West has a "superb civilization." While Iran should neither imitate it "blindly" nor abandon Iran's "own identity," it should borrow the West's "good points" so as to "enrich our own culture." Unless Iran's leaders "correctly identify the positive and negative aspects of western civilization," Iran would not "develop" to the fullest extent possible.[33]

This admiration of Western ideology and the perceived need to borrow core institutional and normative aspects from it applied even to the United States. In fact, to some reformers the United States was especially deserving of respect and emulation. America is a free society with very high levels of technological and economic achievement, yet also very religious. In a January 1998 interview with CNN, President Khatami praised America because it was founded by Puritans who "desired a system, which combined the worship of God with human dignity and freedom." "What [Iranians] seek is what the founders of American civilization" pursued. "This is why we sense an intellectual affinity with the essence of American civilization."[34]

If Western ideology was to a significant extent to be admired and emulated, as reformers claimed, interaction with the United States was not nearly as threatening to Iranian interests as conservatives asserted. In fact, since reformers aimed to borrow from the West its best ideological elements so that Iran could reach the highest political, economic, and moral development possible, interaction with the United States was to be encouraged, not avoided—hence their interest in economic cooperation, political negotiations, and cultural exchanges with Western countries, including the United States. The scholar Anoushiravan Ehteshami succinctly expresses this point: "For many reformists . . . restoration of relations with the United States is vital for renewal at home."[35] International rapprochement, in short, could facilitate domestic liberalization.

Cooperation with the United States as a key means of spurring political and economic liberalization in Iran was among the outcomes that Iranian conservatives most feared, thereby contributing to their fierce attacks against reformers. As Daniel Brumberg explains, "Knowing that the reformers' support of normalization [with the United States] is organically linked to their quest for freedom and democracy, [conservatives were] determined to ensure their ultimate control over the debate on US-Iranian relations."[36] Whereas the more liberal ideology of Iranian reformers pushed them to see the United States as both a manageable external threat (thus making "normal" relations possible) and a potential support to their domestic interests, conservatives believed the opposite. Beginning in the next section, I demonstrate how the differing views of the United States held by Iranian reformers and conservatives affected their policies on two issues that were critical to American security: the development of nuclear weapons and responses to America's attacks on Afghanistan in 2001 and Iraq in 2003.

IRANIAN POLITICS AND
NUCLEAR WEAPONS, 1997–2008

The potential acquisition of nuclear weapons by Iran was a highly contentious international issue from 1997 to 2008, and it continues to be so at the time of this writing. The best chance of resolving this dispute is rooted in Iranian domestic politics. Iranian leaders do not possess a monolithic view of the benefits and costs of nuclear weapons. Instead, there is a continuing debate over this issue that largely corresponds with politicians' ideological beliefs.

Iranian conservatives for the most part are forceful advocates for Iran's nuclear weapons program, since they view other countries, especially the United States, as grave threats to Iran's security. To conservatives, the world is "a Hobbesian one of unremitting struggle, where predatory powers lurk to dictate and dominate and where the only currency is military power. Power, in this view, is the indispensable element for survival."[37] To Iranian conservatives, in other words, nuclear weapons would be a significant aid to Iran's safety in the face of mortal enemies. According to Ali Ardashir Larijani (who was appointed by Ahmadinejad to be secretary of the Supreme National Security Council and was Iran's top negotiator on issues of national security), in order to protect Iran from foreign threats "you have to find a way to be able to take the country's level and status to a point so as to automatically solve your national security problem, otherwise these pressure factors will always weigh on you." "If Iran becomes atomic Iran, no longer will anyone dare to challenge it."³⁸ In November 2004, the conservative newspaper and mouthpiece for the Supreme Leader, *Jumhuri-ye Islami*, similarly claimed that "it is obvious having access to advanced weapons shall cause deterrence and therefore security, and will neutralize the evil wishes of great powers to attack."³⁹

Most Iranian conservatives rejected various arguments against the acquisition of nuclear weapons, including claims that these armaments might diminish Iran's security by provoking other countries, especially the United States, into adopting aggressive policies to prevent this outcome. Ideological enmity led conservatives to believe that America would be hostile to Iran no matter what policies it adopted on the nuclear issue. Members of this ideological faction viewed US hostility to Iran's nuclear program as an excuse that the Americans were using to force ideological change. According to Khamenei, speaking in 2003, "what the United States, which has been spearheading the aggression against our Islamic revolution, expects from our nation and government is submission and surrender to its hegemony, and this is the real motive for US claims regarding weapons of mass destruction, human rights or democracy."⁴⁰

Conservatives believed that even if Iran abandoned its nuclear program, American pressure would continue because, according to army commander Mohammed Salimi, "the enemies of Iran are bent on changing the regime in Iran."⁴¹ In 2008 President Ahmadinejad stated that "the American government has been against our people for 30 years. They always find an excuse. When the nuclear issue was not on the agenda, they had imposed an embargo on false pretexts. The nuclear issue is only an excuse for the US administration to display its bad intentions against our people."⁴²

Iranian conservatives, in other words, tended not to view conflict with the United States as a product of the "security dilemma" (a realist concept that refers to the action-reaction cycle in which states attempting to make themselves feel safe frighten others into adopting more aggressive policies). If Iran and America were caught in a security dilemma, hostilities between the two states could be reduced if each adopted more reassuring policies. Iranian conservatives instead saw conflict with the United States as inevitable as long as the huge ideological gap dividing the two countries existed. Given these perceptions of implacable US enmity, conservatives saw little reason for Iran not to develop nuclear weapons. As one Iranian reformer explained, "If they [Iranian conservatives] think they are going to be damned [whether or not Iran develops WMDs], they might as well do as they please [and acquire these weapons]."⁴³

Iranian reformers possessed significantly different views of nuclear weapons. Most importantly, many advocated that Iran *not* develop these weapons, at least if this outcome meant sacrificing what they deemed to be more important objectives.

In the first place, many reformers believed both that economic development and industrialization should be among Iran's foremost political objectives, and that economic cooperation with the Western powers was indispensable for realizing these goals. Reformers understood that developing nuclear weapons would be doubly detrimental to these ends. The United States and its allies would likely respond to an Iranian nuclear weapons program by increasing the level of economic sanctions directed at Iran and rescinding any positive economic inducements—such as lifting existing sanctions and supporting Iran's candidacy to join the World Trade Organization (WTO)—that these countries had offered Iran to entice its leaders to not acquire these armaments.

Reformers, like conservatives, viewed the development of nuclear technology as potentially benefiting Iran's interests. Whereas conservatives saw nuclear weapons primarily as a means of protecting Iran from its foremost ideological enemy, however, reformers often viewed them as a means of leveraging more economic assistance from vital economic partners. Consequently, most reformers believed that Iran's nuclear weapons program should be sacrificed for the right economic price—a view that most conservatives rejected.[44]

The reformers' economic justifications for not developing nuclear weapons were reinforced by their understanding of the most effective means of protecting Iran's security. Iranian reformers agreed with conservatives that Iran should be free of foreign intimidation and interference in its internal affairs. In order to achieve these goals, however, reformers emphasized the need to develop cooperative, reassuring policies, especially regarding nuclear weapons.

For example, during Khatami's informal talks with US leaders after his election in 1997, his representatives relayed to the Americans that Khatami "understood [America's] concerns" about Iran's WMD programs, and that he and fellow reformers were willing to be "accommodating" on this issue.[45] Publicly, the president asserted that while Iran had the right to develop nuclear energy, the international community has "the right to be assured that [this technology] will be channeled in the right way."[46] Both reformers in parliament and reformist newspapers claimed that if Iran did not adopt reassuring policies, such as allowing international inspectors to examine Iran's nuclear facilities, foreigners would be justified in thinking that Iran's intentions were not peaceful.[47]

Reformers' calls for accommodating policies on the nuclear issue resulted from these individuals' ideological relationships with other states. As Shahram Chubin explains, "the reform faction [did] not have the same sense of [international] embattlement as their conservative counterparts." "Where [reformers differed] from the conservatives [was] in their view of foreign policy generally, specifically with reference to the value of détente, dialogue and cooperative security. Lacking a sense of [ideological] mission, and having a different conception of what Iran represents (a democratic republic as well as an Islamic one) the reformists [saw] interdependence and engagement [with the West] as desirable (and inevitable)."[48] Iranian reformers' affinity with core ideological attributes of Western states, in other words, pushed these individuals to possess reduced threat perceptions that allowed them to advocate reassuring policies and security cooperation to protect Iran's safety, rather than relying on the power of nuclear weapons and deterrent threats, as conservatives prescribed.

Skeptics might dismiss reformers' willingness to be accommodating on the nuclear issue as strategic rhetoric that was designed to fool foreign leaders about Iran's true intentions. They may have been buying time to develop nuclear weapons until they could present the world with a nuclear fait accompli, much as North Korea did in the 1990s and early 2000s.

There is important evidence that potentially supports this interpretation of Iranian policies. Most notably, Iran's nuclear weapons program appears to have been accelerated in 1999—two years after Khatami became president—and continued after reformers gained control of parliament in 2000.[49]

Whether the continued development of nuclear weapons in Iran even at the height of reformers' domestic power resulted from their interest in developing these armaments despite public statements to the contrary, or from conservatives' continued political dominance despite reformers' control of the presidency and parliament from 2000 to 2004, is unclear. We do not know enough about the internal workings of Iranian politics to answer this question. What is clear, though, is that once Iran's clandestine nuclear weapons program became public in 2002, leaders from Iran's various political factions responded quite differently. Whereas most conservatives advocated that Iran continue with its nuclear plans even in the face of international opposition, reformers adopted policies that were designed to address Western security fears.[50] In October 2003, for example, Khatami signed an agreement with France, Britain, and Germany (the EU-3) to suspend uranium enrichment. In December 2003, the president signed the Additional Protocol to the NPT, which allowed for short-notice international inspections of Iran's nuclear facilities. In November 2004, the Iranian government signed the Paris Agreement, which renewed its commitment to continue the suspension of uranium enrichment and related activities.[51]

After these developments, the International Atomic Energy Agency (IAEA) was able to declare in November 2003 that there was no evidence of an Iranian nuclear weapons program. Similarly, in a report issued in March 2005, Mohammad ElBaradei (the director general of the IAEA) stated that no new evidence of illicit nuclear activities had been discovered, and that Iran, as far as the IAEA could see, was in compliance with the Paris Agreement (ElBaradei did, however, express a suspicion at this time that Iran might not be fully cooperating with his agency's inspections).[52] In November 2007, the US government issued a national intelligence estimate that stated that "we judge with high confidence that in fall 2003, Tehran halted its nuclear weapons program."[53]

The claim that ideological reformers were genuinely committed to reassuring the West of Iran's nuclear intentions is supported by the fact that many of their policies were quickly reversed after the conservative Ahmadinejad was elected to the presidency in place of Khatami. Ahmadinejad was inaugurated on August 6, 2005. Within two days, Iran reneged on its commitments in the Paris Agreement and Additional Protocol. On August 8, the Esfahan nuclear facility resumed the conversion of uranium yellowcake into uranium hexafluoride, which is a gas that is necessary for making nuclear fuel.[54] In January 2006, Iran removed IAEA seals from enrichment sites. In February 2006, the IAEA board of governors referred Iran to the UN Security Council to begin discussions on imposing economic sanctions.[55]

Further corroborating the claim that reformers were genuinely interested in reaching a compromise with the United States and its allies on the development of nuclear technology is that, according to virtually all accounts, the domestic battles between Iranian ideological conservatives and reformers on this issue were extremely contentious. If these groups had actually agreed on the need to acquire nuclear weapons—and reformers' statements and actions indicating otherwise were meant to lull foreign powers into a sense of complacency until Iran could present the world with a nuclear fait accompli—domestic infighting on this issue would have been muted. Instead, politicians publicly and privately attacked one another for their positions on Iran's nuclear program (conservative rebukes of reformers' actions also show that the latter were having an important impact on policy, despite conservatives' greater domestic power).[56] For example, in April 1998 the commander of the IRGC, Yahya Rahim Safavi, gave a private speech to his officers that was subsequently leaked. In it, he criticized the direction of Iran's foreign policy, including its nuclear program, under President Khatami: "Can we withstand America's threats and domineering attitude with a policy of détente? Can we foil dangers coming from American through dialogue of civilizations? Will we be able to protect the Islamic Republic from international Zionism by signing conventions banning the proliferation of chemical and nuclear weapons?"[57] Similarly, in November 2004 former IRGC commander Mohsen Rezai condemned Khatami's cooperation with international inspectors and the "turning over our country's top intelligence documents" (as stipulated by the Paris Agreement and Additional Protocol).[58] To Rezai, Iran's security would have been better served by trying to intimidate the West by the power that Iran might have, rather than providing reassurances about the weapons it lacked. In April 2005, *Jumhuri-ye Islami* harshly criticized reformers' views of the United States and their resulting nuclear policies: "The core problem is the fact that our officials' outlook on the nuclear dossier of Iran is faulty and they are on the wrong track. It seems they have failed to appreciate that America is after our destruction and the nuclear issue is merely an excuse for them."[59]

The preceding statements reveal the different understandings held by Iranian conservatives and reformers concerning the nature of the US threat and how to address it. If reformers led by Khatami were not genuinely interested in nuclear arms control as part of overall negotiations with the United States, there would have been no need for conservatives to complain so bitterly about the direction of Iran's foreign policies, including its weapons programs. Instead, different ideological distances dividing various Iranian policymakers from their American counterparts resulted in significantly different international preferences for Iran's core security policies.[60]

IRANIAN POLITICS AND AMERICA'S WAR ON TERROR

Iran's ideological factions exhibited key differences on another set of critical international developments during the period under examination: America's reaction to the September 11 terrorist attacks, including the wars in Afghanistan and Iraq.

Once again, reformers were cooperative on these subjects, while ideological conservatives frequently tried to thwart US objectives.

Khatami's government was one of the first in the world to condemn the September 11 terrorist attacks. Within hours of the event, Khatami forcefully denounced them: "I condemn the terrorist operations of hijacking and attacking public places in American cities, which have resulted in the death of a large number of defenseless American people."[61] Conservatives, in contrast, reacted differently to 9/11. Many popular conservative papers denied that Muslims were behind the attacks, and instead claimed that either American or Israeli officials masterminded them. The purpose of this conspiracy was to provide the United States a pretext to initiate a crusade against Islam and assert American and Israeli imperialist ambitions throughout the Muslim world.[62]

Iranian reformers' support for the United States against terrorist groups after 9/11 was not just rhetoric. When the United States attacked Afghanistan in October 2001, the Iranian government provided important aid to US efforts. In the lead-up to the war, Iranian officials met with American representatives in Geneva and furnished intelligence about Afghanistan and the Taliban. During the war, Khatami's government allowed US transport aircraft to stage from airfields in eastern Iran, agreed to perform search-and-rescue missions for American airmen who were downed over Iran, allowed humanitarian supplies to offload in Iranian ports so as to reach parts of Afghanistan as fast as possible, and helped to facilitate cooperation between US forces and those of the Northern Alliance in Afghanistan. After the Taliban regime collapsed, the Iranians were instrumental in bringing various groups, especially ethnic Pashtuns, into the coalition government led by Hamid Karsai. Iran also developed close relations with this new pro-American government and provided aid for the reconstruction of the country, especially in the Herat region.[63]

Some Iranian assistance before and during the war in Afghanistan can be explained by factors that are unrelated to the ideological divisions among Iranian policymakers. Most importantly, Iran shared America's enmity for Taliban Afghanistan. Iran and Afghanistan had come close to war in 1998 after Taliban soldiers killed ten Iranian diplomats in Iran's consulate in Mazar-e-Sharif. The destruction of the Taliban regime thus coincided with Iran's interests.

Although common interests with America help explain some of Iran's policies after 9/11, factional politics also played a critical role. Iranian reformers and conservatives exhibited major policy differences during the war, despite their shared enmity toward Taliban Afghanistan. Some conservatives remained strongly opposed to helping America, and by January 2002 they so provoked the United States with various policies that they effectively sabotaged momentum toward rapprochement between the two countries. Reformers, in contrast, not only condemned these actions but hoped to use cooperation with the United States over Afghanistan as a springboard to improve substantially overall relations.[64] Thus, for example, in October 2001 a majority in the reformist-dominated Majlis called on the government not only to aid the United States in Afghanistan but to work for normalization of relations.[65]

The depth of Iranian reformers' interest in rapprochement with America is revealed by their collective response to increasingly provocative statements about Iran made by US leaders. Most notably, in the January 2002 State of the Union address President Bush labeled Iran as part of an "axis of evil" that threatened the United States and free peoples around the world. Although Iranian reformers were caught off guard and in many ways resented Bush's statement, a number of these individuals reacted to it in ways that were supportive of US interests. To begin with, reformers blamed conservative foreign policies for increasing tensions with America. In the aftermath of the axis of evil speech, many Iranian reformers "proved far more critical of their own foreign policy establishment than that of America . . . The dominant theme was 'who lost the United States?'"[66] Reformers in parliament and newspapers argued that provocative actions by conservatives in the international arena had left Iran isolated and feared, and thus vulnerable to an American attack.[67]

Even more significantly, reformist politicians and newspapers argued that domestic liberalization was ultimately the best, and perhaps only, way to defuse the US threat. In February 2002, 172 out of 290 members of the Majlis signed a petition that denounced illiberal policies, including "repressive measures against journalistic circles, political activists and students."[68] To reformers, Iran's illiberal domestic system was provoking and justifying American hard-line policies. As a direct result of this belief, "reformist newspapers warned the conservative establishment that the only way to preempt the imminent US threat was to democratize Iran's political system and allow other groups to participate in the process. In other words, internal legitimacy was the single best solution to preempt the external threat."[69] Consistent with this position, in September 2002 Khatami proposed a bill that would strengthen presidential powers at the expense of the Supreme Leader, and parliamentary reformers proposed another that would limit the power of the Council of Guardians to disqualify candidates running for office.[70]

This argument provides substantial support for a domestic-ideological understanding of international threats. To Iranian reformers, US hostility to Iran was not about relative power concerns or anti-Islamic sentiments consistent with "clash of civilizations" thinking. Instead, reformers asserted that American enmity was caused to a large degree by the repressive nature of the Iranian regime. Shrink the ideological distance dividing the United States and Iran by liberalizing Iranian politics, reformers asserted, and the United States would not attack Iran.[71]

At the same time that Iranian reformers were renewing their calls for domestic change, they were also pushing for normalization of relations with the United States—two interrelated objectives. Domestic liberalization in Iran would reduce US hostility, and improved relations would help provide the resources necessary for economic and political change. Hence reformers asserted that the United States "is an important country and is the key in solving some, if not most, of Iran's problems," including both political liberalization and economic modernization.[72]

Iranian conservatives opposed reformist policies on almost all the issues identified above. Some ideological conservatives, including Khamenei, exhibited streaks of pragmatism that inclined them to cooperate with the United States after 9/11. Hence, for example, Khamenei's decision to allow aid to the United States during the war in Afghanistan. A combination of external pressure from the United States, internal pressure from reformers, and the recognition of some common interests with America (e.g., shared enmity against the Taliban) were the key factors responsible for these more accommodating initiatives.

These factors working for more pragmatic relations by no means eliminated, however, conservatives' fierce ideological hostility to the United States. As Daniel Brumberg explains, even after 9/11 conservatives "held that the very survival of the country's Islamic revolution hinged on maintaining an ideological wall between Iran and the United States. Armed with this sacred conviction, they concluded that the reformist push for rapprochement was part of a conspiracy to destroy the Islamic Republic of Iran."[73] An editorial in *Jumhuri-ye Islami*, for example, stated that "the attempt to inculcate the proposition that negotiation with the US is the key to the solution of problems is an act of treason."[74]

Conservatives frequently acted on their staunchly anti-American sentiments by taking actions that had costly effects, most notably undermining progress toward rapprochement with the United States and heightening hostilities. Following US-Iranian cooperation during the war in Afghanistan in the fall of 2001, Iranian conservatives torpedoed the goodwill that these policies created. On January 3, 2002, Israel intercepted a ship, the *Karine A*, in the Red Sea. It was carrying an arsenal of weapons, including Katyusha rockets, antitank mines, rocket-propelled grenades, and 2.5 tons of explosives. The arms had been manufactured and loaded onto the ship in Iran. The cargo appears to have been destined for the Palestinian Authority.[75] This event demonstrated to many in the United States that Iran was not genuinely interested in rapprochement but remained dedicated to the destruction of the Middle East peace process. Parliamentary reformers in Iran indicated that conservative leaders and institutions (likely the Revolutionary Guards) were responsible for this development.[76]

US suspicions created by the *Karine A* affair were reinforced by growing evidence, after the war in Afghanistan began, that Iran was harboring al-Qa'ida leaders.[77] Iranian conservatives, apparently again led by members of the Revolutionary Guards, were most likely responsible for this development. Iran's intelligence minister, Ali Yunesi, acknowledged that "small and big-time elements of al-Qa'ida" were in Iran and that his agency (which was controlled by reformers) was apprehending them.[78] In February 2002 a majority of Iran's parliament, led by reformers, demanded an investigation into the *Karine A* affair and the harboring of al-Qa'ida members in Iran. Some reformers accused conservatives of adopting these policies in order to raise international tensions, which would facilitate increased domestic repression and the persecution of political opponents (i.e., reformers).[79]

While some conservatives like Khamenei approved, at least temporarily, pursuing accommodation with the United States, others (and perhaps even Khamenei) adopted actions that could only fuel America's enmity toward Iran. The *Karine A* affair and revelations about Iran's harboring al-Qa'ida members undermined progress toward improved relations that had been achieved in the fall of 2001 during the war in Afghanistan. Less than one month after the *Karine A* affair, Bush delivered his axis of evil speech, and two days after that national security adviser Condoleezza Rice commented that "Iran's direct support of regional and global terrorism [including continued support of Hamas and Hizbollah], and its aggressive efforts to acquire weapons of mass destruction, belie any good intentions it displayed in the days after the world's worst terrorist attacks in history."[80]

The conservatives' contradictory policies continued during the Iraq war. Iran and the United States possessed a number of important common interests in this conflict. Both states were enemies of Saddam Hussein. Neither state wanted to see Iraq ripped apart by civil war. A weak, divided Iraq could become a haven for hostile terrorists, most notably the Mujahedin-e-Khalq (the MEK is an Iranian group operating out of Iraq that is dedicated to the destruction of the IRI). Cooperation by the Iranians in Iraq would also help ensure that Iran was not America's next target.

These considerations led many of Iran's key decision makers from across the political spectrum to cooperate with the United States, at least during the first year of the war. Most importantly, according to one US analyst, "Tehran told its various proxy groups in Iraq not to resist the United States and instead participate in the US-led process of reconstruction . . . If the Iranians had wanted to cause chaos in Iraq, they could have easily done so in the darkest days after the war [began]."[81]

These cooperative policies did not last long, however. The United States became less likely to attack Iran as conditions in Iraq worsened, and the conservative Ahmadinejad was elected to the presidency in 2005. These two factors led to increasingly hostile policies toward America. By 2006 the US military claimed to have proof that Iran was providing significant aid, including training, money, and arms, to violent groups in Iraq that were targeting American troops. This aid apparently went to not only Shiite extremists but to Sunni groups as well, including al-Qa'ida affiliates. By 2007 Iranian aid to America's enemies was so extensive that US officials claimed that Iran was engaged in a "proxy war against American, British, and Iraqi forces."[82]

In sum, as in Afghanistan, Iranian conservatives had less interest in cooperating with the United States in Iraq, while reformers continued to argue for normalizing relations with America and increasing cooperation with it. Conservatives maintained relatively helpful policies in response to strong external and internal pressure. By 2005, these conditions were no longer met, and ideological hostility toward the United States once again dominated conservative decision making.

CONCLUSION

The analysis and findings in this chapter generate clear policy recommendations for American leaders. Most importantly, American decision makers should recognize the great significance that the domestic contest between Iranian conservatives and reformers has for US interests, and then do what they can to strengthen Iranian ideological reformers and weaken ideological conservatives.

Unfortunately, US leaders have frequently not followed these prescriptions. To key leaders in the Bush presidency, only a full-blown liberal regime change in Iran could significantly improve relations with America. In the absence of revolution, the ascension to power of different ideological factions within Iran's ruling circles would have little policy effect. Thus Bush officials claimed that the only meaningful political distinction in Iran from the American point of view was between the illiberal Iranian government (which was bound to be hostile to the United States regardless of factional shifts) and the Iranian people (who would cooperate with the United States once they possessed sufficient power). As one US official said in July 2002, "we have made a conscious decision to associate with the aspirations of the Iranian people. We will not play . . . the factional politics of reform versus hardline."[83]

The Barack Obama administration adopted a similar view, asserting that the international policy differences between Iranian conservatives and reformers were slight. In a June 2009 interview, Obama stated that from a national security perspective, there was little difference for America if the hard-liner Mahmoud Ahmadinejad or the reformer Mir Hussein Mousavi won the 2009 presidential elections. "Either way," asserted Obama, the United States is "going to be dealing with an Iranian regime that has historically been hostile to the United States, that has caused some problems in the neighborhood and is pursuing nuclear weapons."[84] Indeed, because Iranian reformers and conservatives were likely to pursue similar international policies toward America despite their domestic differences, in some ways it was better for the United States to have Iranian conservatives win the election. As a senior Obama official told the *Wall Street Journal*: "Had there been a transition to a new government [if Mousavi won], a new president wouldn't have emerged until August. In some respects, [Ahmadinejad's victory] might allow Iran to engage the international community quicker."[85]

Unlike the Bush administration—which adopted hard-line policies toward Iran with no regard for the relative power of Iranian reformers and conservatives—the Obama administration (at least for its first year in office) advocated accommodating actions regardless of domestic developments in Iran. Both sets of policies were mistaken. Because Iranian reformers and conservatives have prescribed very different policies in key areas, America has a fundamental security interest in affecting the domestic contest between these factions. This is difficult, but not impossible, to do. When Iranian conservatives dominate decision making, the United States should adopt hard-line policies, including economic sanctions and forceful deterrent actions. These policies are the most likely to thwart ideological conservatives' provocations, create incentives for more pragmatic conservatives to assert themselves, and provide evidence that reformers can use to demonstrate that their rivals' policies are ineffective and dangerous.

In order to isolate Iran when Iranian conservatives control policymaking without creating an anti-American, nationalistic reaction, simultaneous with hard-line policies, US leaders should make clear that a peaceful resolution of disputes is possible if Iran both makes progress on domestic reforms and adopts more accommodating foreign policies. Indicating that a "grand bargain" with America is possible even without a full-blown ideological revolution will further boost reformers' and pragmatists' justifications for increased power. Positive incentives, in sum, should accompany strong deterrent actions. Public diplomacy that demonstrates that Iran's international isolation is a result of hard-line policies and that America supports the advancement of human rights, the rule of law, and democracy in Iran are most likely to stimulate domestic debate in Iran in America's favor. When Iranian reformers possess significant political power, the United States should adopt cooperative policies that support these politicians (such as trade liberalization, the unfreezing of Iranian assets, and the normalization of relations), and American leaders should be willing to match reformers' offers of détente and rapprochement for as long as progress in these areas is being made.

Notes

1. For a more extensive development of the argument and findings presented in this chapter, see Mark L. Haas, *Ideologies and American Security in the Middle East* (New York: Oxford University Press, 2012), chap. 2.

2. Mark L. Haas, *The Ideological Origins of Great Power Politics, 1789–1989* (Ithaca: Cornell University Press, 2005).

3. For other scholars who adopt this taxonomy, see David Menashri, *Post-Revolutionary Politics in Iran: Religion, Society, and Power* (London: Frank Cass, 2001); Shahram Chubin, *Iran's Nuclear Ambitions* (Washington, DC: Carnegie Endowment for International Peace, 2006); Ali Gheissari and Vali Nasr, "The Conservative Consolidation," *Survival*, Summer 2005, pp. 175–190; Daniel Heradstveit and G. Matthew Bonham, "What the Axis of Evil Metaphor Did to Iran," *Middle East Journal*, Summer 2007.

4. Among the most powerful conservative leaders in the period under investigation were Ayatollah Ali Khamenei (Supreme Leader of the revolution), Mahmoud Ahmadinejad (president of Iran), Ayatollah Ahmad Jannati (head of the Council of Guardians), Ayatollah Mohammad Yazdi (head of the judicial system), Yahya Rahim-Safavi (commander in chief of the Iranian Revolutionary Guard Corps, IRGC), Mohsen Rezai (secretary of the Expediency Council and former commander in chief of the IRGC), and Ali-Akbar Velayati (adviser to the Supreme Leader on foreign affairs and former minister of foreign affairs).

5. Quoted in Ray Takeyh, *Hidden Iran: Paradox and Power in the Islamic Republic* (New York: Times Books, 2006), p. 36. See also Meir Litvak, "Iran: The Clerical Debate on Democracy and Islam," in Joshua Teitelbaum, ed., *Political Liberalization in the Persian Gulf* (New York: Columbia University Press, 2009), p. 275.

6. Litvak, "Iran," pp. 272–274.

7. Quoted in Mehdi Moslem, *Factional Politics in Post-Khomeini Iran* (Syracuse, NY: Syracuse University Press, 2002), p. 235.

8. Quoted in Moslem, *Factional Politics in Post-Khomeini Iran*, p. 108.

9. Leading reformers from 1997 to 2008 included Mohammad Khatami (president of Iran), Abdol Karim Soroush (a leading scholar and philosophical inspiration to many reformers), Ataollah Mohajerani (minister of Culture and Islamic Guidance), Abdollah

Nuri (vice president), and Mehdi Karrubi (speaker of parliament). Conspicuously absent from this list is 'Ali Akbar Hashemi Rafsanjani, who was one of Iran's most powerful politicians in the period under analysis. He was president of Iran from 1989 to 1997 and chairman of the Expediency Council since 1997 and chairman of the Assembly of Experts since 2007. I omit Rafsanjani from placement in an ideological grouping because his domestic-ideological preferences varied so much over the years that he may fairly be categorized as more of a political opportunist than someone with confirmed ideological principles. It is worth noting, though, that during each of Rafsanjani's ideological "phases," he advocated foreign policies that were largely consistent with an ideological explanation of international behavior. During his more liberal periods, he pushed for more pragmatic and cooperative policies toward the United States than did conservatives. When Rafsanjani allied with conservatives domestically, he also largely supported their international policies, including significant hostility toward both America and Israel. See Moslem, *Factional Politics in Post-Khomeini Iran*, pp. 128–148, 175–179; Wilfried Buchta, *Who Rules Iran? The Structure of Power in the Islamic Republic* (Washington, DC: Washington Institute for Near East Policy/Konrad Adenauer Stiftung, 2000), pp. 150, 202; Menashri, *Post-Revolutionary Politics in Iran*, pp. 149–150; Sanam Vakil, "Reformed Rafsanjani Could Be a Force for Change," *Financial Times*, June 16, 2005.

10. Quoted in Litvak, "Iran," p. 278.

11. Litvak, "Iran," p. 277. As one study of Iranian politics puts this point, reformers "synthesized Islamic moral concepts with modern Enlightenment political philosophy to argue that there was no inherent tension between democracy and Islamic society." Frederick Wehrey et al., *The Rise of the Pasdaran: Assessing the Domestic Roles of Iran's Islamic Revolutionary Guards Corps* (Santa Monica, CA: RAND, 2009), p. 15; see also Anoushiravan Ehteshami and Mahjoob Zweiri, *Iran and the Rise of the Neoconservatives: The Politics of Tehran's Silent Revolution* (London: I. B. Tauris, 2007), p. 10.

12. Quoted in Litvak, "Iran," pp. 290–291. On the preceding points, see ibid., pp. 290, 292, 298.

13. Litvak, "Iran," p. 297.

14. Quoted in Litvak, "Iran," p. 297.

15. Moslem, *Factional Politics in Post-Khomeini Iran*, p. 132; Daniel Brumberg, *Reinventing Khomeini: The Struggle for Reform in Iran* (Chicago: University of Chicago Press, 2001), pp. 175–176; Ehteshami and Zweiri, *Iran and the Rise of the Neoconservatives*, p. xiv.

16. Quoted in Brumberg, *Reinventing Khomeini*, p. 233.

17. Brumberg, *Reinventing Khomeini*, p. 233.

18. Quoted in Litvak, "Iran," p. 277.

19. For details see Buchta, *Who Rules Iran?* chaps. 1–8.

20. See Maximilian Terhalle, "Revolutionary Power and Socialization: Explaining the Persistence of Revolutionary Zeal in Iran's Foreign Policy," *Security Studies*, July 2009, pp. 576–577.

21. Wehrey et al., *Rise of the Pasdaran*, p. 83.

22. For details, see Gheissari and Nasr, "Conservative Consolidation."

23. Both quoted in Menashri, *Post-Revolutionary Politics in Iran*, p. 84.

24. Both quotations from Karim Sadjadpour, *Reading Khamenei: The World View of Iran's Most Powerful Leader* (Washington, DC: Carnegie Endowment for International Peace, 2008), p. 15.

25. Quoted in Menashri, *Post-Revolutionary Politics in Iran*, p. 214. See also Wehrey et al., *Rise of the Pasdaran*, pp. 32, 37–38.

26. Quoted in Menashri, *Post-Revolutionary Politics in Iran*, p. 214.

27. Quoted in Menashri, *Post-Revolutionary Politics in Iran*, p. 83.

28. Menashri, *Post-Revolutionary Politics in Iran*, p. 214.

29. Quoted in Moslem, *Factional Politics in Post-Khomeini Iran*, p. 109.

30. Both quotations from Sadjadpour, *Reading Khamenei*, pp. 17 and 18, respectively.

31. Quoted in Shahram Chubin, *Whither Iran? Reform, Domestic Politics, and National Security* (Oxford: International Institute for Strategic Studies, 2002), p. 24.

32. Quoted in Michael Slackman, "If America Wanted to Talk, Iran Would," *New York Times*, September 3, 2006, p. 4.4.

33. Quoted in Menashri, *Post-Revolutionary Politics in Iran*, p. 186.

34. Transcript of Interview with Iranian President Mohammad Khatami, January 7, 1998, http://tinyurl.com/6y8rumz.

35. Anoushiravan Ehteshami, "Iran's International Posture after the Fall of Baghdad," *Middle East Journal*, Spring 2004, p. 183.

36. Daniel Brumberg, "Dilemmas of Western Policies towards Iran," *International Spectator* 3 (2002): 74.

37. Chubin, *Iran's Nuclear Ambitions*, p. 33.

38. Quoted in Chubin, *Iran's Nuclear Ambitions*, p. 33.

39. Quoted in Colin Dueck and Ray Takeyh, "Iran's Nuclear Challenge," *Political Science Quarterly* 122, no. 2 (2007): 193.

40. Quoted in Sadjadpour, *Reading Khamenei*, p. 14.

41. Quoted in Chubin, *Iran's Nuclear Ambitions*, p. 76.

42. Quoted in "Turkish, Iranian Presidents Want diplomatic Solution of Iran's Nuclear Issue," BBC Monitoring Europe, August 15, 2008.

43. Quoted in International Crisis Group, Middle East Report no. 18, *Dealing with Iran's Nuclear Program*, October 27, 2003, p. 17.

44. Ray Takeyh, "Iran Builds the Bomb," *Survival*, Winter 2004–2005, p. 56; Chubin, *Iran's Nuclear Ambitions*, p. 32; Kenneth M. Pollack, *The Persian Puzzle: The Conflict Between Iran and America* (New York: Random House, 2004), pp. 378–379.

45. Quoted in Pollack, *Persian Puzzle*, p. 318.

46. Quoted in Shahram Chubin and Robert S. Litwak, "Debating Iran's Nuclear Aspirations," *Washington Quarterly*, Autumn 2003, p. 105.

47. Chubin and Litwak, "Debating Iran's Nuclear Aspirations," p. 105.

48. Chubin, *Whither Iran?* pp. 69, 84, respectively.

49. Chubin, *Iran's Nuclear Ambitions*, p. 8; Pollack, *Persian Puzzle*, p. 362.

50. These policies were strongly opposed by many Iranian conservatives. See Karl Vick, "Iranian Hard-liners Wary of Nuclear Deal," *Washington Post*, November 20, 2003; and Mehran Kamrava, "Iranian National-Security Debates: Factionalism and Lost Opportunities," *Middle East Policy*, Summer 2007, pp. 84–100. For details on Iran's covert nuclear weapons program that was made public in 2002, see International Crisis Group, *Dealing with Iran's Nuclear Program*.

51. Chubin, *Iran's Nuclear Ambitions*, pp. xiv–xx; International Crisis Group, *Dealing with Iran's Nuclear Program*.

52. Chubin, *Iran's Nuclear Ambitions*, pp. xiv–xx.

53. The document defined "nuclear weapons program" as "Iran's nuclear weapon design and weaponization work and covert uranium conversion-related and uranium enrichment-related work; we do not mean Iran's declared civil work related to uranium

conversion and enrichment." See National Intelligence Estimate, "Iran: Nuclear Intentions and Capabilities," November 2007, http://tinyurl.com/26hd2d. Other analysts, including some in the Bush and Obama administrations and the IAEA, questioned the accuracy of these assessments. See David E. Sanger and William J. Broad, "IAEA Suspects Iranian Nuclear Weapons Activity," *New York Times*, February 19, 2010.

54. Jenny Booth, "Iran Nuclear Plant Restarts Processing Uranium," *Times Online*, August 8, 2005.

55. Chubin, *Iran's Nuclear Ambitions*, pp. xviii–xx.

56. Chubin and Litwak, "Debating Iran's Nuclear Aspirations," p. 105; Chubin, *Iran's Nuclear Ambitions*, pp. 29–30.

57. Quoted in Farideh Farhi, "To Have or Not to Have? Iran's Domestic Debate on Nuclear Options," in Geoffrey Kemp, ed., *Iran's Nuclear Weapons Options: Issues and Analysis* (Washington, DC: Nixon Center, 2001), pp. 35–36.

58. Quoted in Chubin, *Iran's Nuclear Ambitions*, p. 56; see also Vick, "Iranian Hardliners Wary of Nuclear Deal."

59. Quoted in Dueck and Takeyh, "Iran's Nuclear Challenge," p. 195. See also Wehrey et al., *Rise of the Pasdaran*, p. 87.

60. Supporting these claims, as well as those made in the next section, is the fact that Khamenei frequently criticized the reformist-led sixth parliament (2000–2004) for being "pro-American" and "radical" in ways that were "contrary to many of the regime's interests." The Supreme Leader, in contrast, openly praised the conservative-dominated seventh parliament (2004–2008). According to Khamenei, the seventh parliament, unlike "the previous term, really stood firm on the nuclear issue." Similarly, Major General Hassan Firouzabadi, the chief of staff of the armed forces, warned before the 2008 parliamentary elections that reformers "must not be allowed to find their way into the Majlis again and to repeat their past performance" since reformers do "nothing but fulfill US interests . . . Has the Iranian nation not already tasted this bitter shame once?" Quoted in Akbar Ganji, "The Latter-Day Sultan: Power and Politics in Iran," *Foreign Affairs*, November-December 2008, pp. 52, 64, 58, respectively. Khamenei offered nearly identical praise of Ahmadinejad in comparison to Khatami. In 2009, the Supreme Leader lauded Ahmadinejad's domestic and international policies. Ahmadinejad, according to Khamenei, helped keep "alive the Khomeini legacy" by fighting against "encroaching secularism and westernization" that had recently threatened to poison Iran (i.e., during Khatami's presidency). Ahmadinejad also stood firm against the West, unlike his predecessor who wanted to submit to the West's "hegemonic designs." Quoted in Abbas Milani, "Obama's Existential Challenge to Ahmadinejad," *Washington Quarterly*, April 2009, pp. 70–71.

61. Quoted in Mohammad Ayatollahi Tabaar, "The Beloved Great Satan: The Portrayal of the US in the Iranian Media Since 9/11," *Journal of European Society for Iranian Studies*, Winter 2005, p. 66.

62. Tabaar, "Beloved Great Satan," pp. 64, 66–68.

63. Pollack, *Persian Puzzle*, pp. 346–347; Mohsen M. Milani, "Iran, the Status Quo Power," *Current History*, January 2005, p. 32.

64. According to Chubin, "reformists . . . clearly hoped to use [9/11] to strengthen links with the West and improve Iran's overall image" (Chubin, *Whither Iran?* p. 98). See also Hossein S. Seifzadeh, "The Landscape of Factional Politics and Its Future in Iran," *Middle East Journal*, Winter 2003, p. 73; Tabaar, "Beloved Great Satan," pp. 71, 74.

65. Pollack, *Persian Puzzle*, p. 348.

66. Ali M. Ansari, *Confronting Iran: The Failure of American Foreign Policy and the Next Great Crisis in the Middle East* (New York: Basic Books, 2007), p. 189.

67. Ray Takeyh, "Iran: Scared Straight?" *PolicyWatch*, May 3, 2002, http://tinyurl.com/4bcys4c; Brumberg, "Dilemmas of Western Policies Towards Iran," pp. 75–78.

68. Quoted in Takeyh, "Iran: Scared Straight?"

69. Tabaar, "Beloved Great Satan," p. 64; also p. 71.

70. Brumberg, "Dilemmas of Western Policies Towards Iran," p. 80.

71. As the scholar Farideh Farhi expresses this point, "reformists [claimed] that Iran would not be in such a precarious position [with the US] had there not been a conservative assault on elective institutions and the democratic aspirations of the Iranian people." Farideh Farhi, "Iran's Nuclear File: The Uncertain Endgame," *Middle East Report Online*, October 24, 2005, p. 9.

72. Tabaar, "Beloved Great Satan," p. 71. This statement is a summary account based on a survey of reformist newspapers. Its core idea—that the United States was key to solving Iran's problems—could not have been more different than conservatives' views. See also Chubin, *Whither Iran?* p. 84.

73. Daniel Brumberg, "End of a Brief Affair? The United States and Iran," *Policy Brief*, March 2002), p. 3, http://tinyurl.com/4nc6bqm.

74. Both quoted in Seifzadeh, "The Landscape of Factional Politics and Its Future in Iran," p. 73.

75. Pollack, *Persian Puzzle*, pp. 350–353.

76. A. William Samii, "Tehran, Washington, and Terror: No Agreement to Differ," *Middle East Review of International Affairs*, September 2002, p. 13 n. 65. http://tinyurl.com/4v7pwo9.

77. Douglas Jehl and Eric Schmitt, "Havens: US Suggests a Qaeda Cell in Iran Directed Saudi Bombings," *New York Times*, May 21, 2003.

78. Ray Takeyh, "Iranian Options: Pragmatic Mullahs and America's Interests," *The National Interest*, Fall 2003, p. 55; Pollack, *Persian Puzzle*, p. 358.

79. Samii, "Tehran, Washington, and Terror," p. 13 n. 65.

80. Quoted in Ariel Cohen, "Regional Powers in Central Asia Grapple with Expanding US Military Presence," *Eurasia Insight*, February 6, 2002. A senior US official told the *New York Times* that the *Karine A* incident "was a sign to the president that the Iranians weren't serious" about improving relations. Quoted in David E. Sanger, "Bush Aides Say Tough Tone Put Foes on Notice," *New York Times*, January 31, 2002.

81. Pollack, *Persian Puzzle*, p. 355. Not all prominent conservatives, however, wanted to refrain from the beginning of the war from trying to thwart US objectives in Iraq. IRGC commander Safavi, for example, appears to have argued for moving into southern Iraq in force to establish Shia protectorates. Khamenei appears to have made a compromise with these conservatives. The Supreme Leader allowed Iraqi intelligence operatives to deploy to Iraq and position themselves to fight a war but not to engage in conflict unless ordered to do so by Khamenei. This compromise shows once again the ambiguity of conservatives' policies despite some important common interests with the United States (see Pollack, *Persian Puzzle*, p. 357).

82. John F. Burns and Michael R. Gordon, "US Says Iran Helped Iraqis Kill Five G.I.'s," *New York Times*, July 3, 2007, p. A1. See also Mark Mazzetti, "Documents Say Iran Aids Militias from Iraq," *New York Times*, October 19, 2008.

83. Quoted in Brumberg, "Dilemmas of Western Policies towards Iran," p. 78. See also Takeyh, *Hidden Iran,* p. 129.

84. Quoted in Helene Cooper and Mark Landler, "For Obama, Pressure to Strike a Firmer Tone," *New York Times,* June 18, 2009.

85. Quoted in Jay Solomon and Chip Cummins, "Iran's Election Results Stoke Global Debate," *Wall Street Journal,* June 15, 2009.

CHAPTER 24

IS IT TIME FOR THE UNITED STATES TO GIVE UP ON ARAB LIBERALS?

Jon B. Alterman

In the months and years since September 11, 2001, the idea that the United States should promote democracy more actively in the Arab world has become commonplace. President George W. Bush spoke at length on the topic more than a dozen times, most explicitly during a November 6, 2003, speech at the National Endowment for Democracy. The president's embrace of the idea followed many months of pronouncements by senior US government officials addressing the need for political change in the Arab world—for American interests as well as those of the people in the region—and the need for the US government to play an active role in promoting such change.

Although democratization and reform in the Arab world are indisputably desirable, the US government is going about it in the wrong way. The US strategy, as it has been executed, is based on supporting traditional liberal elites who support liberal ideals as they are articulated in the West. In many ways, it is an obvious way to start. As a group, such reformers are intelligent, congenial, well educated, and fluent in English. Americans are comfortable with them, and they are comfortable with Americans.

But if we are honest with ourselves, we need to recognize that, as a group, such liberal elites are aging, becoming increasingly isolated, and diminishing in number.

These liberals are losing a battle for the hearts and minds of their countries, and populations are now driven toward younger and more disaffected personalities.

America's problems do not stop there, however. The United States faces three paradoxes. The first is that liberal elite reformers in much of the Arab world are already seen as clients of foreign powers and as collaborators in a Western effort to weaken and dominate the Arab world. Focusing attention and resources on these reformers runs the risk of isolating them still further, driving a deeper wedge between them and the societies we (and they) seek to affect. In such an event, US efforts are not only ineffectual; they are counterproductive. The second is that conservatives have intimidated liberals, many of whom have swung their support to existing authoritarian systems. Third, some of the most vocal proponents of democracy in the Middle East are Islamists—precisely the groups that most US policymakers are most interested in isolating.

US efforts to promote political openness and change in the Arab world would be far more effective if they stopped trying to coax the disparate sparks of comfortable liberal thought into a flame that sweeps through political systems. Instead, they should concentrate on affecting two targets: regional governments and mass publics. The United States also needs to be willing to work multilaterally to promote reform in a way it has been unwilling to do up to now. Greater openness and tolerance in the Middle East would indeed serve US interests. How US leaders try to achieve these outcomes, though, must change in major ways from past practices. If the stakes were lower, the United States could afford the luxury of taking an easier and less effective approach to political change in the Arab world. In today's environment, it isn't nearly sufficient.

In current talk about efforts to reform political life in the Middle East, the Eastern European example looms large. Not only did Eastern European communism crumble after decades of Western effort, but the end of the Soviet Union spelled the diminution, if not the end, of what had been the primary strategic threat facing the United States for a half century.

At its core, the Eastern European experience is thought of this way: Communist tyranny spread, while Western nations kept alive a flickering hope of freedom through overt radio broadcasting, covert support for oppositionists and "prisoners of conscience," and constant government-to-government pressure on human rights and political freedom. A robust policy of public diplomacy and cultural exchanges revealed the obvious: Communist lies about poverty in the West were just that, and the communist world was falling farther and farther behind a rapidly industrializing West.

On the governmental level, the Soviet quagmire in Afghanistan combined with the Ronald Reagan administration's stepped-up military spending to provoke an internal crisis. On the public level, a series of initiatives to support civil society groups hastened the collapse of corroded and crumbling governments in country after country.

Veteran "cold warriors" view their victory as the product of determination and vision. Unwilling to accommodate authoritarianism, they insisted on a policy of tireless confrontation with the Soviet Union and its clients. Unwilling to accept the inevitability of autocracy, they imagined a future for Eastern Europe that would be capitalist and free. The names of many of the most dedicated of these warriors are familiar today, and they were prominent figures in the administration of George W. Bush: Richard Perle, Paul Wolfowitz, and Elliott Abrams.

But what of the Middle East? After September 11, 2001, strategic thinkers proclaimed millennial Islamist terrorism to be the preeminent strategic threat facing the United States. But whereas the cold war represented a confrontation *between* governments, this new battle was one brought on by the *failure of* governments. As President Bush explained in London in November 2003, "In democratic and successful societies, men and women do not swear their allegiance to malcontents and murderers, they turn their hearts and labor to building better lives." He continued, "By advancing freedom in the greater Middle East, we help end a cycle of dictatorship and radicalism that brings millions of people to misery and brings danger to our own people."[1] The tools imagined are much the same as those used in the cold war: pressure on governments and fanning the flames of freedom, liberalism, and democracy throughout the Middle East.

While it is obvious to say that the Middle East is not Eastern Europe, it is unsettling to consider just how different the two environments are and how little these differences are acknowledged.

It is useful to start by thinking about the roles of elites vis-à-vis governments. Elites play many roles, but one of the most important for the purposes of the present discussion is the role of mediation. Elites often serve as a lubricant between foreign and domestic systems, using commonalities in travel, education, and language to bridge national divisions. The period of Western imperialism in the Middle East spanned most of the first half of the twentieth century, and in many countries it followed four centuries of Ottoman imperial rule. Throughout, elites played an important collaborative function. "Collaboration" here is not meant pejoratively, but rather in the way suggested by that great historian of British imperialism, Ronald Robinson, who writes of "two interconnecting sets of linkages . . . one consisting of arrangements between the agents of industrial society and the indigenous elites drawn into cooperation with them; and the other connecting these elites to the rigidities of local interests and institutions."[2]

Early-twentieth-century Levantine elites were a worldly bunch, often multilingual and tolerant, if a bit corrupt. Under their guidance, parliaments arose throughout the region, often unifying on the need to end European colonial rule. But as we know, many of the stories of the elites in the Middle East ended badly. Tales of self-indulgence and profligate spending only sharpened dismay at the Arab world's continued subjugation to European powers. Collaboration took on a negative coloration, as the elites were seen as too feckless to win true independence. The sin of the elites, in the eyes of many, was exemplified by the creation of the state of Israel, widely seen to be a solution to a European problem on the back of a weak and divided Arab nation.

When nationalist revolutions swept the Arab world in the 1950s, those revolutions were a repudiation of that weakness. Elites were tossed out as foreign fops, and new indigenous elites—Manfred Halpern's much-vaunted "new middle class"—set about defining a new and "truly authentic" form of Arabism.

In truth, traditional Arab elites have never recovered the high ground. Widely perceived to be agents of foreign interests—however one construes foreign in an Arab context—the old families have clawed their way back to influence but have largely done so on the terms of their tormentors. Liberalism remains suspect, part of a Western plot to weaken and subjugate rather than strengthen and liberate. Elite messengers and their messages remain besmirched.

Compare this to Eastern Europe, where it was the communists' utilitarian socialist universalism that was a foreign import. While one cannot quite point to a golden democratic past in Europe, there was not a sense, as there was in the Arab world, that the patrimony of liberal thinking was weakness and foreign domination—quite the opposite.

In addition, the role that elites play in any society is changing, driven by communications technology and a surge in popular culture. One need not accept the idea of a single global village to appreciate the familiarity—or at least, perceived familiarity—many people feel with societies half a world away. Whereas the old elites transcended the local through their travel and knowledge of foreign languages, newly emergent elites participate in a global, or at least regional, culture that may have little to do with dominant European-derived paradigms. The collaborative role that traditional elites have played is less mysterious, and the interests of foreign powers are more obvious to local audiences.

The rise of an increasingly independent popular culture has an important effect on our discussion. Elites have lost much of the agenda-setting role they enjoyed in years past. What matters most in attracting an audience now is having a message, not merely having an outlet. Stolid state-run broadcasters have seen their audiences desert them, and they have had to change their message. Audiences now control what they pay attention to, through Facebook, Twitter, and the Internet, not information bureaucrats. The broadcaster with his finger on the pulse of the public mood, not the one with the ear of the minister of information, plays the primary agenda-setting role in modern Arab societies. Such communication is increasingly unmediated, as television brings arguments and rebuttals straight into the living rooms of its viewers.

In an environment overflowing with clashing ideas that easily cross borders, it has long seemed that much of Arab discourse is centered around an idea of defining what is "authentically Arab." For years, part of such an identity involved support for the Palestinian cause. But in recent years, the explosion of communication from the grass roots has created competing notions of everything from music and style to religious practice, all of which affects people's daily lives. The Arab world is no more likely to arrive at a single conclusion of what it is to be an Arab than Americans are to arrive at a conclusion of what it is to be an American. However, this process is nonetheless defining what is "un-American" and, by extension, what is "un-Arab." Because of the legacy suggested above, old liberal elite views of a just Arab society are falling outside the bounds of Arabs' imagined common future.

Washington has many heirs to the liberal elite tradition in the Arab world. They often fill posts in the World Bank and other international institutions, work for the US government, or labor in academia. They talk of the misdirection of the Arab world and the need for change. We notice their accents when they speak English, and we hail them as authentic voices for change in the Middle East. But what Washington doesn't hear is that many of these people have accents when they speak Arabic as well. Their speech marks them as Arabs who have left, who have fundamentally compromised, or been compromised. One colleague used the evocative phrase "native aliens" to describe them; their most valuable commodity is that they have Western ideas but non-Western passports.[3]

In academic circles in the early 1990s, it was hard not to hear of Nawal al-Saadawi, the prominent Egyptian feminist, novelist, and physician who fled her own country under death threats. But I will never forget the words of one of my Egyptian professors, a prominent female professional in her own right, who practically spit in disgust saying (in Arabic), "She doesn't belong to us, she belongs to you."

For much of the 2000s, the Egyptian government appeared to be conducting a prosecutorial witch-hunt against Egyptian-American sociologist Saad Eddin Ibrahim. While the government officially accused him of misappropriating money from the European Union, the sponsor had no complaints about the use of funds. It was widely whispered that Ibrahim's misfortune had nothing to do with the funding and everything to do with his flamboyant criticism of so-called Arab republics that had hereditary rule—Syria in practice, and Egypt in theory, if presidential son Gamal Mubarak rose to the presidency. Ibrahim's case aroused little interest in Egypt, and his valedictory lap occurred in the United States rather than there. But when Senator Patrick Leahy speculated about earmarking $2 million for his NGO, the Ibn Khaldun Center, four prominent members of the board resigned in protest. All the while, not a single cent changed hands.

Three additional points are in order. The first is to make clear that all Arab liberals do not come from elite backgrounds. A good number—although probably a minority—come from modest backgrounds. But the fact remains that support for liberal ideals as they are promoted and articulated in the West remains almost entirely an elite province, whether that of those born into an elite rank or those who have come up into such ranks. What we often refer to as "like-minded individuals" form a distinctive group, and a decidedly elitist one.

The second point is that as old elites are pushed aside, new elites are emerging. Such elites come from religious backgrounds, the media, the military, or some combination. What is important to note here is that the new elites tend to come from sectors of their societies that are often illiberal, while old liberal elites are increasingly marginalized.

Conservative groups conduct an active, creative, and impressive array of activities and services that affect people's daily lives: providing care to the sick, food to the hungry, and spouses to the unmarried. They seek leadership positions in professional organizations and civic groups. All too often, Arab liberals' activities end when they deliver copy to their editor.

What has happened in the Arab world smacks a bit of what the sociologist William Julius Wilson described happening in black neighborhoods in Chicago in the 1960s and 1970s. Whereas segregation had created all-black communities that had both rich and poor, desegregation created black communities that were uniformly poor and had far higher incidents of violence and crime than had obtained during segregation. In the Arab world, liberal elites cluster ever more closely around Western embassies in capital cities and work in international institutions, while the bulk of the Arab world grows more angry, more desperate, and more estranged from those liberal elites with whom Western governments deal most often.

All putative liberals in the Middle East do not fall into this category. In religious and secular circles alike, new thinkers are emerging who seek to create new syntheses of "authentic" Arabness (or Islam) and modernity. As a group, they come to the idea of liberalization through different paths—some through socialism, and others through Islamism—and they have seen the failure of their previous ideologies. But such thinkers often go beyond the bounds of what Americans are comfortable with. Many reject the idea of secular government, and they embrace the idea of armed resistance, be it against Israel or the United States. They are committed to neither women's rights nor laissez-faire economics. To some in the West, their ideas seem like watered-down liberalism; to others, their ideas are an example of what Senator Daniel Patrick Moynihan used to refer to as "defining deviancy down." They are deeply wary of the United States government, and the United States government is deeply wary of them.

Instead, the US government during the Bush era sought to work with traditional partners, seeking to engage them through a program called the Middle East Partnership Initiative (MEPI), established by the Bush administration in 2002. MEPI identified economic cooperation as an initial step toward respect for rule of law, transparency, and an end to cronyism, but many of the partnership's first efforts consisted of conferences and training. Urgency in getting the partnership up and running meant grasping for low-hanging fruit, and an overwhelming push for women's empowerment helped limit participation mostly to capital city elites. One of the programs was, perhaps, typical. The Business Internship for Young Arab Women sought forty women between the ages of twenty-two and thirty with high proficiency in English to live in the United States for three to six months. However desirable this may have looked from a US standpoint, the number of women with such English skills was quite limited, yet not nearly as limited as the number whose families—both mothers and fathers—considered it appropriate for their daughters to live independently overseas at such a tender point in their lives. While the intent was noble, anyone with even a passing knowledge of the Middle East should have recognized what a small segment of Arab society would have benefited from such a program. And there is a chilling statistic: Of thirty-four civil society organizations listed as "partners" on the MEPI website, there was but one Arab organization among them.

MEPI is, of course, an overlay on existing aid programs in the Middle East, run either by the US Agency for International Development (USAID), US embassies, or both. In case after case, such programs are directed toward the activities of what can only seem to be a client class of Western-educated elites whose governments permit such activities so long as they remain politically inert. In Jordan, the embassy supports a panoply of semiroyal charities like the Noor Al Hussein Foundation, the Royal Society for the Preservation of Nature, and similar organizations. Indeed, Jordan's so-called nongovernmental organizations are so tightly tied into the government that they gave rise to the acronym GONGO, meaning "government-organized nongovernmental organization." In the words of one friend in the White House, the typical aid recipient in the Middle East is the son of an ambassador, with a German mother, who happens to run an NGO.

US efforts to promote democracy have also run aground on the hard shoals of reality. Throughout the region, concerted efforts at democratization have yielded results that are mixed at best. For example, many in the Bush administration expected Iraq to be the jewel of US efforts to promote political change in the Middle East, sweeping aside a brutal socialist dictatorship and installing a democratic, capitalist system that would be an inspiration throughout the Middle East. Hundreds of billions of American dollars later, Iraqi national politics are marked by sectarian strife, political dysfunction, and a growing Islamicization of public life. Ahmed Chalabi, the expatriate darling of many administration figures and the clear leader of the Iraqi opposition in exile before the fall of Saddam, polled only about 30,000 votes nationwide (out of approximately 12 million) in the December 2005 elections. Well-meaning efforts to train would-be Iraqi politicians and jump-start a political process have collapsed under assassinations, intimidation, and infighting. Iraq inspires far more fear than respect in the Middle East and stands as an example to many of how alternatives to an unsatisfactory status quo may be even worse.

The Palestinian Authority seemed poised for progress after the death of Yasser Arafat in November 2004, especially after then Prime Minister Mahmoud Abbas swept a multiparty election with more than 60 percent of the vote three months later. Early optimism gave way to pessimism, however, as Abbas was unable either to assert effective control over his own Fatah party and the Palestinian Authority or to make diplomatic progress with Israel and the United States. Worsening economic conditions, persistent corruption, and a complete breakdown in party discipline all contributed to the Hamas parliamentary victory in January 2006. Western denunciations of the party and its platform, combined with widespread hopes—even in the Arab world—for its failure, have left many wondering how the US government will square the circle between supporting democratic elections and sanctioning the victors of those elections.

The most interesting example may be Egypt, which was a critical test case of the Bush administration's democratization policy. Egypt is not only a key ally of the United States (on military cooperation, Arab-Israeli peace issues, and counterterrorism) but also a massive aid recipient, receiving more than $2 billion annually in military and financial assistance. President Hosni Mubarak appeared to be among the first Arab leaders to blink in the face of the US democratization strategy, announcing suddenly in February 2005 that he would open the presidential elections in September of that year to multiple candidates, instead of conducting it as a referendum on his presidency as in the past. Some observers saw this as a chink in the armor of authoritarian rule, and anticipation grew for both the presidential elections and the parliamentary elections that followed two months later. In the State Department, as in the White House, attention shifted toward Egypt.

The results were sobering. President Mubarak hardly broke a sweat in his campaign, handily defeating his rivals. The next closest finisher won less than 10 percent of the vote, and most challengers fared significantly worse. Egyptians hardly felt they had a viable choice. When parliamentary elections rolled around two months later, candidates from the Muslim Brotherhood (running as independents) did surprisingly well, and candidates from traditional opposition parties did surprisingly poorly. Egypt had broken up its elections into three rounds to ensure that a judge could monitor each polling station. Brotherhood gains in the relatively open first round were a shock to many in the ruling party; over the next two rounds, reports documented the return of old tactics such as voter intimidation and violence, ferrying government employees to boost votes for the ruling party, and shutting down polling stations. When the dust settled, the ruling party had maintained its grip on power, but the Muslim Brotherhood was by far the largest opposition group, winning 88 of the 454 seats. The rest of the opposition parties, including old leftist and socialist parties, won only a dozen seats in all. Perhaps most chillingly, President Mubarak's most prominent challenger, Ayman Nour, lost his seat in the parliament; a month later, the courts convicted him of fraud and sent him to prison, a symbol to many of what happens when one openly challenges the status quo. Nour had met several times with Secretary of State Condoleezza Rice, and as a secular opposition figure with a taste for populism, he was clearly operating in a political space that US government officials wanted to expand. It was also a space that the Egyptian government sought to regulate closely.

It is a risky venture for the US government to pursue a policy of democratization that concentrates on support for liberal voices in illiberal societies. Doing so can exacerbate US problems rather than solve them, driving deeper wedges between those with whom the United States seeks to work and those whose attitudes it seeks to influence. Liberal elites are not necessarily successful opinion leaders in their own communities, and closer ties to the West often serve to estrange them from, rather than embed them in, such communities. Think about it as a plant. If all of the sunshine and all of the nutrients come from one direction, it will not grow tall and strong—it will be weak and bent, and no amount of food or sunlight will make it right as long as it all comes from a single direction.

Greater tolerance, transparency, and openness in the Middle East would indeed serve US interests, and it would serve the interests of the people of the Middle East as well. But to be effective, efforts must be concentrated in three areas. The first is on the government-to-government level. As countless US government officials have recognized, the US government cannot go on doing what it has been doing, relegating these issues to the bottom of a long list of agenda items for bilateral discussions. However, in order to implement such a program effectively, we need to be alert to two dangers. The first is that it will fall into the trap of excusing repression as a necessary part of the war on terrorism. Foreign governments know how vulnerable the United States is on this issue, and they will attempt to use it to excuse a range of abuses. The US government should not take the bait.

The second is that the US government needs to consistently and aggressively push for greater freedom of association in the Middle East, even for those whose views it finds despicable. It is understandable that foreign governments are sensitive about US intervention in their domestic politics, but the veto that some exercise over any nongovernmental group taking money from overseas is unacceptable.

As part of these efforts, the United States must work much more with the broader publics in the Middle East. The US government needs to have far more modest goals with far broader segments of the population in the Arab world. The depth and breadth of animus against the United States poisons the environment for any values it espouses, and merely neutralizing some of this opposition would represent a significant advance.

In order to pursue such a strategy, the United States would need to work with an array of nontraditional partners. Some may say things the US government doesn't agree with on issues relating to women, Israel, or any of a number of issues. The US government needs to abandon the idea that cooperation with an individual or group means embracing their every belief. It need not and should not. In addition, the United States will have to move away from accounting rules that pose an intimidating, if not impenetrable, barrier to many groups. Fiduciary responsibility is necessary, but it must be a tool to promote accountability rather than a barrier to action.

Another area to think about in this regard is stepping up activities of American organizations that have nothing to do with the US embassy in a particular country. Corporations, foundations, NGOs, and a range of other groups could carry out activities successfully without the imprimatur—or encumbrances—of official US government endorsement. The US government should vigorously pursue such strategies on their own merits, as well as get around some of the problems mentioned above.

A third area of activity is greater coordination with other countries and groups of countries, particularly the European Union. Europeans share a quite similar analysis of trends in the Arab world, yet they are far more aware because they see large expatriate populations in their own countries threatening domestic security. Despite the deep commonality of goals between the Middle East Partnership Initiative and the Barcelona Process, neither side understands much about the other. There are at least two advantages to cooperation with the EU. The first is that the EU doesn't carry the stigma in the Middle East that the United States does, making it a less threatening actor on the domestic stages of the region. Equally important, however, coordinated pressure and incentives stand a far better chance of working than competing ones, diminishing the possibility that targeted countries would seek to play the United States against the EU and increasing the likely efficacy of outside efforts.

As mass protests movements rocked the governments of Tunisia and Egypt in early 2011, it is remarkable just how small a role traditional liberal elites played in those movements. Socially networked twenty- and thirty-year-olds, allied with the economically disenfranchised, found their movement focused and amplified by twenty-four-hour Arabic news channels. The traditional liberal elites, fully compromised by the ruling regimes, played no part in the fall of the governments they sought to open up. Instead, the masses in the streets made clear to their respective militaries that the status quo was no longer viable.

While Western states did not hasten the fall of these governments, there was something Western about movements that relied so much on the collective creativity of individuals. While it is hard to discern a clear set of priorities for the movements—indeed, it is easier to understand what they were against rather than what they were for—individual agency seems to have been a priority of many of the organizers. At the same time, many of the issues of the traditional left, such as secularism and a pro-Western orientation, seem to have been absent from the protestors' minds. In the early days, one might interpret these uprisings as an effort to create a sort of postmodern politics that eschew traditional parties and orientations but have liberal notions of tolerance at their core. Turning those postmodern politics into political results, however, is a task that none of these movements have yet done successfully.

How should one approach traditional Arab liberal elites in all of this? None of this is to argue that the US government should abandon them or cast them off. They continue to play valuable roles in our society and in their countries of origin. But Americans need to recognize that such liberals are unlikely to be effective catalysts for the change that all agree is necessary. Stepping up US support for these elites runs the risk of drawing them even further out from the societies we seek to influence, isolating them and pulling their societies even farther away from the direction in which we want them to go.

If the United States is to be successful in these efforts to promote political openness and change, it must keep in mind two things. The first is a healthy understanding of the limits of US abilities. The second is to remember that when others rely on us to create change, it diminishes the likelihood of that change actually occurring by delegitimizing its authenticity and by breeding complacency or passivity among those whose action is most needed.

There is another challenge facing the United States as well, and that is remembering that what is important is not how things sound and feel in Washington but how they sound and feel in the Middle East. In their classic book *Africa and the Victorians,* Robinson and Gallagher observed, "In the end it was the idea and the analysis of African situations in Whitehall, and not the realities in Africa as such which moved Victorian statesmen to act or not to act."[4] With so much high-level interest in the Middle East, the United States runs the risk of being guided by conventional wisdom rather than true knowledge. In that event, the outcomes would almost certainly be worse than those that many in Washington agree they need to be.

Notes

1. http://www.whitehouse.gov/news/releases/2003/11/20031119-1.html.

2. Ronald Robinson, "Non-European Foundations of European Imperialism," in *Studies in the Theory of Imperialism,* ed. Roger Owen and Bob Sutcliffe (London: Longman, 1972), p. 121.

3. I am grateful to Hakan Yavuz at the University of Utah for this phrase, although I absolve him of any responsibility for the other ideas expressed here.

4. Ronald Robinson, John Gallagher, and Alice Denny, *Africa and the Victorians: The Official Mind of Imperialism,* 2nd ed. (London: Macmillan, 1981), p. 21.

CHAPTER 25

ISLAMIST PERCEPTIONS
OF US POLICY IN THE
MIDDLE EAST

Yvonne Yazbeck Haddad

For more than five decades, the umbrella ideology of Islamism has cast a growing shadow as Islamist groups strive to create a unified ethos in order to enhance their own sense of empowerment in facing repressive regimes and what they view as Western and Zionist hegemonic policies in the Muslim world. Designed as an alternative to liberal humanism and socialism, as well as fundamentalist secularism and Marxism, Islamism has left itself vulnerable to attacks from various quarters, including the regimes of some Arab countries, secularists, Zionists, humanists, socialists, feminists, and most recently the government of the United States, which since 9/11 has dubbed Islamists as evil.[1] During the past twenty years, the US press and some people in the US academy and government have created a consummate stereotype, commonly identified as "Islamic fundamentalism" or "Islamic extremism."[2] In October 2006, President Bush identified the enemy but distinguished it from the religion of Islam: "Some call this evil Islamic radicalism, others militant jihadism, still others Islamo-fascism. Whatever it is called, this ideology is very different from Islam."[3] Individuals and groups who fall into this category tend more and more to be demonized by those who oppose or fear them, rendering them unworthy of being taken seriously in their criticism of US policies.[4] Thus Islamism as an ism increasingly provides a handy means of objectification for those who seek to undermine its legitimacy.

Currently a profound sense of victimization among Islamists has led to the development of a parallel stereotype: the alliance between Israel and the United States, which is generally depicted as "the Crusader-Zionist conspiracy," the Western demon bent on the eradication of Islam.[5] This perception has its roots in the worldview of the Muslim Brotherhood, "the mother of all Islamist movements" in Egypt. Hasan al-Banna, who founded the Muslim Brotherhood in 1928, identified a comprehensive venue of operations for his organization in order to realize his futuristic vision of a vibrant Muslim nation (*umma*). The focus was to be on the development of a new Muslim human being brought about through moral and spiritual rearmament, a new society actualized through economic development and social justice, and a new vibrant nation free of foreign domination. He perceived the Muslim nation to be in mortal danger as a consequence of the abolition of the office of the caliphate (the generally acknowledged leader of the Islamist community dating to the initial successor of the Prophet Muhammad) in 1924 by Mustafa Kemal Ataturk in Turkey. The caliph had provided a sense of Islamic unity maintained by commitment to Islamic values in societies governed by Islamic law. From his vantage point, foreign interests, at the time mainly British, appeared to work diligently to divide the Muslim world into nation-states to facilitate their subjugation and to insist on implementing the Balfour Declaration of 1917, which had promised a national homeland for European Jews in Palestine. For al-Banna, the Balfour Declaration not only perpetuated colonial interests in the area but continued European Crusader designs on the holy lands.

Many different views and perspectives are represented under the rubric of Islamism. It is currently popular in Western scholarship to distinguish between the mainline Muslim Brotherhood on one side and al-Jama'at al-Islamiyya, Islamic groups such as al-Takfir wa al-Hijra, al-Jihad, and al-Qutbiyyun in Egypt, Hamas of Palestine, and Hizbollah of Lebanon on the other. The Islamic groups are generally referred to as militants, extremists, or terrorists, whereas the Muslim Brotherhood and its affiliates in other Arab countries, such as the Islamic Action Front of Jordan and Jam'iyyat al-Islah of Kuwait, are perceived as more moderate and willing to participate in the democratic process.

Ahmad Kamal Abu al-Magd, a former cabinet member in the regime of Anwar Sadat in Egypt, distinguishes between five groups seeking Islamization. The first call themselves the Salafiyyun and are noted for their inflexible adherence to the classical teachings of Islam, leaving little room for modern reinterpretation.[6] The second group is the Sufis, who emphasize the spiritual dimension of Islam and focus their efforts exclusively on seeking a spiritual revival. The third group carries the banner of Islam but is in total rebellion against the prevailing Muslim condition. Attempting to move beyond Islam, they are nonetheless eager to hang on to Islamic slogans. The fourth group consists of several movements adamant in their demand for the reinstitution of Islamic law (*shari'a*) as the constitution of the state. For them, the control of political power is the most effective way to work for Islam. The fifth group that al-Magd identifies is composed of the moderate majority who believe in the use of reason in applying the teachings of Islam as a guide for life.[7]

Although all Islamists appear to agree on an agenda of bringing about the kinds of changes that provide empowerment and well-being for Muslim society, they differ on the means of actualizing change and on issues of political and religious pluralism in an Islamic state. Meanwhile, there is general agreement among Islamists and secularists that US foreign policy in the Middle East has been skewed in favor of Israel since the 1967 Arab-Israeli war (also known as the Six Day War, or June War). This perception has left an indelible mark on Islamist identity and its worldview. This chapter analyzes these perceptions and the Islamist response. It is based on Islamist literature, which is polemical on the Palestinian self-rule question and generally hostile toward Israel and US foreign policy. Illustrations used in this chapter are taken mainly from Islamist journals, newspapers, and other publications and are supplemented with interviews I conducted with Islamists in Jordan, Egypt, Kuwait, Tunisia, and the United States.

ISLAMISM: A REACTION TO DISEMPOWERMENT

Islamism is not a reactionary movement; it does not want to replicate the Islamic community of the Prophet Muhammad in the seventh century. Rather, it seeks control of the present and future of Muslim destiny.[8] From its inception it has been reactive, responding to direct and imagined challenges posed by internal conditions as well as its violent encounter, during the past two centuries, with a dominant West, which has insisted that the only universal values worth adhering to are those developed in the West during the Renaissance and the scientific revolution and embodied in rational, liberal, or Marxist thought. Its ideologues operate with a heightened awareness of the importance of monitoring events in the world, particularly those that affect their lives, and responding to them. They see themselves as manning a defensive operation, the responsibility of which is to safeguard society from total disintegration.[9]

Islamism was initially a reaction to a sense of internal decay in Muslim society. A central theme in most Islamist literature is a response to the deep awareness of Muslim backwardness, a critical assessment of what went wrong historically, and an effort to rectify the situation in order to bring about a vibrant future. Revival is seen by its advocates as a crucial means of infusing life into a community that is bogged down in centuries-old ideas and traditions that have led to the ossification of Islamic society, restricting its ability to adapt to the fast-changing reality of the modern world. The revivalists produced a literature that portrayed Islam as a forward-looking, creative, and open ideology receptive to movement and change. They sought to remove the shackles of Islamic society, freeing it from the constraints of past values and interpretations. Their goal was to initiate involvement in the unfolding history of the world, taking control of the lives of their constituency and participating in shaping the future. A unified community was seen as an essential component of this venture.

The challenge of modernity to the prevailing Islamic system arrived already formulated and fully developed, in an alien environment where a different set of issues was being addressed. Westernizers, both indigenous and foreign, perceived European models as prefabricated systems that were transferable and ready for borrowing and implementation because they had worked in the West; hence they advocated liberalism, secularism, and socialism. Since the 1967 Arab-Israeli war there has been a growing perception that imported, Western, ready-made models of development and modernization, touted as instant solutions for domestic and foreign problems, have failed to bring about the results hoped for by advocates. More importantly, they are perceived to have failed even in the West.

Islamism is a reaction to the denial of the right of self-determination. The lack of democratic institutions and the absence of governments that operate under the law and for the well-being of the people in the region are increasingly identified as major causes of backwardness. Islamist leader Tawfiq Muhammad al-Shawi of Egypt, for example, identifies such specifics as the following: the lack of freedom of determination (the right to choose the ruler) on the part of the polity and the lack of accountability on the part of the ruler; the fact that the *shari'a* has been replaced in most countries by laws legislated by governments; the separation of the law from government, that is, the replacing of an independent jurisprudence by a European model in which "law is the will of the state"; and the loss of a comprehensive unity, a by-product of Western efforts to divide and conquer.[10]

Islamism is a reaction against disempowerment and what is seen as the irrelevance of the nation-states created in the region as a result of the Sykes-Picot Agreement constructed during World War I, through which the British and the French artificially divided much of the Middle East into spheres of influence that were later sanctioned through postwar agreements into the Mandate system consisting of state units that had hitherto not existed. There is general consensus in Islamist literature that the dominant world order that has prevailed since the nation-states in the area were carved out has not allowed for the inclusion of Arabs as full citizens of the world. Arab nations and peoples have continued to be subservient to foreign domination, which Islamists describe as a continuing predatory relationship.[11] Their diagnosis is based on the belief that the core problem is the failure of these nation-states to adhere to the sources of strength in Islam itself that brought about the great and powerful Islamic civilization of the medieval world. In many cases, the analysis goes on to show that the ideology that is supposed to bring about the revival of Muslim society and its potency in the world, although cast in an Islamic idiom, continues to rely on Western standards and values as necessary for that revival.

Islamism is also a reaction to a profound feeling among Muslims that they have been victimized over the centuries at the hands of Western Christians. The litany of perceived outrages includes European treatment of Muslims during the Crusades. They cite the fact that Eastern Christians, Jews, and Muslims in Jerusalem were massacred by the Western invaders during the First Crusade whereas Salah al-Din (Saladin) treated the Crusaders magnanimously by giving them assurance of safe passage after he led the Muslim recapture of the city eighty-eight years later in 1187. It includes the *reconquista* in Spain during which a ruthless de-Islamization policy gave Muslims the options of conversion, expulsion, or execution. It includes the colonialist movements of the nineteenth and twentieth centuries, along with the activities of Christian missionaries. It also includes the reality that Muslims living in the Soviet Union were not allowed to practice their faith or study the tenets of their religion. And it includes the perception that for a century, Zionism has been one more element of the long and continuous effort supported by Christians to eradicate Islam and Muslims from the holy places. Bosnia and Kosovo are seen as further manifestations of European efforts to eradicate the indigenous European Muslim population.[12]

Along these lines, Islamists perceive Christian missionary activity as designed to separate Muslims from Islam. These efforts are believed to have been inspired by the long history of Christian fanaticism against Islam, culminating in the commissioning of missionaries to march under the banner of Christ into Muslim countries in order to convert them. The legacy of missionary sermons and speeches (now translated into Arabic) provides a rich illustration of the accuracy of this perception. For example, it has been noted that although there had been concern over the Jewish danger, the Bolshevik menace, and the yellow peril, Islam posed the greater danger since it alone is capable of expanding and forming a wall against imperialist interests.[13]

Islamism is a reaction to the demonization of Islam. Muslims are offended and angered at the way in which Islam has been defamed in inflammatory political statements, such as former US vice president Dan Quayle's comparison of Islamic fundamentalism to Nazism and communism,[14] and statements supporting Zionist interests in popular novels, such as Leon Uris's *The Hajj*.[15] Islamists are very aware that since the late 1970s there has been a dramatic increase in the number of articles in the US press dedicated to Muslim bashing. They tend to depict Muslims as irrational and vengeful and motivated by religious zeal and fanaticism that arise out of an innate hatred of the West, its Judeo-Christian heritage, and its secularist values. For Muslims, among the most infuriating statements was the 1990 Jefferson Lecture on "Islamic fundamentalism" by prominent Arab historian Bernard Lewis,[16] which generated a heated response from many sources. Islamists observe that Lewis identified historical and cultural differences as the causes of Muslim anger, completely ignoring the specific policies and actions of Western nations that foster the perception among Muslims that as long as the lives of Westerners are not at stake, fairness does not matter. One Muslim author wrote: "His twenty-six-page address was remarkable for the absence of the word 'Israel.' Nor was any mention made of the United States support of the Zionist state, which inflames Muslim passions worldwide. Any US diplomat who has served in a Muslim country or taken even a cursory glance at Muslim media can verify this feeling."[17] Since 9/11, American officials as well as evangelical Christian leaders have felt free to demonize Islam. William G. Boyken, deputy undersecretary of defense for intelligence and war fighting, recalled his service in Somalia and boasted: "I knew that my God was bigger than his. I knew that my God was a real God, and his was an idol." Former attorney general John Ashcroft stated, "Islam is a religion in which God requires you to send your son to die for him . . . while Christianity is a faith in which God sent his Son to die for you." Televangelist Benny Hinn preached: "This is not a war between Arabs and Jews. It is a war between God and the devil." Franklin Graham, in an interview on Beliefnet.com, said: "I believe the Qur'an teaches violence. It does not teach peace, it teaches violence." Other religious leaders focused their diatribe on the Prophet Muhammad, inflaming Muslim sentiments worldwide. Jerry Vines, former president of the Southern Baptist Convention, said, "Muhammad was a demon-possessed pedophile." In September 2002 Pat Robertson commented on *Hannity & Colmes*, "This man Muhammad was an absolute wild-eyed fanatic. He was a robber and brigand." Jerry Falwell, on *60 Minutes* on October 6, 2002, stated, "I think Muhammad was a terrorist."

Such distorted presentations of Islam are seen by Muslims as conscious efforts at revisionist history, inspired by contempt for Islam or motivated by political considerations in an attempt to maintain unwavering US support for Israel. They tend to validate for Islamists their perceptions that the West has a double standard by which it measures events in the area.

Islamism is increasingly a reaction to what is perceived as Western and Zionist fears of Islam. Although the theme of the "threat of Islam" may have been manufactured for Western political reasons, it provides a useful tool in recruiting young Muslims into the fold.[18] The "mighty" West and Israel, which have humiliated and subjugated Muslim nations, claim that they fear nothing but Islam. If the oppressors know the source of strength, they ask, when will the Muslims awake?[19]

Islamism is a reaction to Zionism. Israel's 1967 preemptive strike, which resulted in a devastating defeat of Jordan, Egypt, and Syria, is generally referred to as *'udwan*, or aggression. Its policies are perceived as Judaizing and aimed at disempowering, dispossessing, and displacing the Palestinians in an effort to destroy their identity. What is perceived as its persistent rejection of United Nations resolutions and violation of the Geneva Convention have fostered, nursed, and inflamed the Islamic response. It is enhanced by what is seen to be US intervention at the United Nations in support of these policies, which has made the international community ineffective in implementing resolutions that would uphold justice.[20] Israeli justifications for the confiscation of property as its divine right and Western silence regarding these activities elicited a response from Abdullah Kannun, a noted North African author and a member of the Higher Council of Islamic Research of al-Azhar, that is typical among Islamists. Advocating the Islamization of the conflict, he affirmed that although the Arabs are the protectors of Palestine, the land belongs to all Muslims. Consequently Muslims must be aware of the connection between Zionism and the kind of Christian religious zealotry that was experienced earlier by the Muslims during the Crusades: "The Palestinian issue is an Islamic, not only an Arab issue. Zionism is the stepdaughter of imperialism *(rabibat al-isti'mar)*. Imperialism is the hidden image of the Crusades undertaken by Western Christians against the Muslims of the East."[21]

On another level Islamism can be said to be a kind of mirror image of Zionism. It may be seen as an attempt to emulate what is perceived as a winning Israeli formula in which religious zeal, divine justification, scriptural proof-texting, and victimization are employed to mobilize Jewish as well as Euro-American Christian support for the state. For some Muslim observers, the essence of the issue is that the state of Israel is a Jewish state. "Zionism is therefore the means of the Jewish religion to realize itself, a means of the Jewish people to create their unity in confrontation with all others in the region," says Kamil al-Baqir, a leading Islamist.[22] The question thus remains: Why is it acceptable for Jews to have a Jewish state and not for Muslims to form an Islamic state? Islamist leader Abdullah Kannun notes that the "educated, civilized West is not ashamed to boast of its Christianity, to explain Zionism in its religious context, and to support it by quotations from the Bible, but the ignorant, underdeveloped East is ashamed to call for an Islamic revenge."[23]

ISLAMISM AND THE "DOUBLE STANDARD"

Islamism is a reaction to what is perceived as the double standard *(al-izdiwajiyya)* that is used by the West in its foreign policy in the Middle East. For example, in demonizing the Islamists, Westerners claim that there is no room for religion in the modern nation-state.[24] Islamists consider this hypocritical in light of Western support for Israel and enduring and prominent symbols of religiosity in the West, and they believe that it proves the double standard. Hence they believe that the West is not against religion per se but against Islam. "Pakistan and Israel," says one writer, "are two countries created solely on the basis of religion and faith. But you may read in the Western press that Pakistan is backward and reactionary because it has emerged in the name of religion. Nothing whatsoever of this nature is said about Israel."[25]

There is a growing perception among Islamists that Jews and Christians, driven by religious fanaticism, triumphalism, and imperialism, have been engaged in a "thousand-year war" with Muslims, which the latter are losing because they are not driven "by a parallel religious sentiment in order to repel this fanatic aggression."[26] Major events in the area have contributed to this perception, such as the civil war in Lebanon, which has cast an aura of suspicion on the allegiance of Arab Christians and the efficacy of Arab nationalism, the success of the Iranian revolution, which validated for the faithful the Qur'anic teaching that God will give victory to those who believe, and Operations Desert Shield and Desert Storm, which were widely perceived as a vindication of the projected Islamist worldview that blamed "the problem of Israel" on Western bigotry and religious fanaticism and were seen as a continuation of the Crusader-Zionist efforts to destroy Islam.[27]

Muslims have been intrigued by the fact that Israel and its supporters boast that it is the only democracy in the area. They note that it functions as a democracy "for Jews" while denying religious minorities—both Christian and Muslim—equal access to resources such as water,[28] housing,[29] health, education,[30] jobs, and the ability to purchase land. Some go so far as to argue that Israel's actions have been devoid of any compassion or human values.[31] The former executive secretary of Islamic Jihad in Palestine, Fathi Shikaki, said in an interview, "I would ask them how they could talk about justice, democracy, and human rights while a methodical process of genocide has been taking place for decades against the Palestinian people."[32]

Muslims are very aware of the double standard that comes into play when the US press, members of the academy, and some government officials label Muslims as extremists. They see that the charge of extremism is arbitrary depending on the interest of the accuser. According to Islamist leader 'Abd al-Baqi Khalifa, for example:

> Extremism is ascribed to violent events according to the interests of those who are making the judgement. For example, the war in Afghanistan prior to the Mujahideen was presented by the Soviet media as a war of evil people against the Russians who had come to Afghanistan to develop it and restore security to the area and prevent American domination over it. In the American and Western media it was depicted as a war of liberation undertaken by the Afghan people against an invading army.[33]

Khalifa further notes that the international press is under the influence of the decision makers and acts as their mouthpiece providing epithets for those they seek to criticize. Thus "the warriors of Abkhazia are separatists, the southerners in Sudan are [liberationists], the demonstrators in Moscow are criminals and in Peking are freedom lovers, the Kurds in Iraq are victims, in Turkey, they are professional criminals. These are the contradictory depictions that have made the word 'extremist' predominantly a kind of political curse word rather than a name for anyone in particular."[34]

Islamists perceive a pronounced discrepancy between professed US values and US actions; that justice, self-determination, and human rights appear to be victims of national interest; that in the last analysis "might makes right"; and that Muslims are rendered weak *(mustadh'afun)* by the empowerment of Israel. Aware of the enormity of the Holocaust and of European-Christian guilt for the sins of Nazism and anti-Semitism, they still question why Western society found a way to expiate those sins at the cost of Palestinian-Christian and Muslim lives. They note that the Ecumenical Council convened by the pope asked Christians to stop cursing Jews in the Catholic Church and that the World Council of Churches absolved the Jews from the historical events that led to the crucifixion of Jesus Christ. Yet, they ask, why is this the fault of the Muslims? Why, they ask, should the Arabs of Palestine pay the price for this error by the church with their homeland, their dignity, their present, and their future?[35] "When various churches compete to please Israel and flatter the Jews, does this point to anything but that the religious leaders have sold their conscience to Satan? . . . The Arabs [of Palestine] are threatened by general extinction, their homes are blown up, their villages eradicated from existence, and still [their efforts at] self defense are considered a crime and an insurrection. . . . This dreadful tribulation is bound to awaken sleeping Islam."[36]

ISLAMISTS AND THE ZIONIST LOBBY

Islamist literature depicts the West as dominated by the Zionist lobby. This image has had several mutations as Zionist influence is perceived to have gained control of the inner circles of policymakers who determine the destiny of the region. Interviews I conducted with Islamists in Egypt in 1985 made clear that they resented the double standard with which they were treated. One leader talked about the "evenhanded" policy, which was then the buzzword used by the administration to describe the habit of the West "to stroke Israel with the palm of their hand and whack us with the back." That same year, the joke in Jordan was, Why doesn't Israel want to become the fifty-first state of the United States? The answer: It would then have to be satisfied with being represented by two senators whereas now it has one hundred.

In interviews I conducted in 1989, the image of Zionist control of the US government became even more dominant. One Islamist depicted the United States as a colony of Israel (a view that is shared by Arab secularists). He compared the state of affairs in the United States with the former British rule over Egypt, noting that there were three specific areas in which British power manifested itself. First, Egyptians were not allowed to have an independent foreign policy but had to defer to Britain for direction. Second, there were foreign British residents in Cairo who made sure that Egyptian policy was in accord with the interests of Britain. Third, Egyptian tax revenues were sent to Britain to sustain its power. He drew the parallels by concluding, "What you have in the United States is a government that is unable to formulate an independent foreign policy without first asking how will Israel react. Secondly, the Congress is accountable to the Israeli lobby, which functions as a foreign agent placing the welfare of Israel above that of the United States. In the third place, the lobby assures the flow of billions of US tax dollars to Israel."

Unwavering support for the state of Israel in the US Congress is taken for granted by Islamists. Members of Congress were seen as fearful of losing their jobs if they questioned unqualified support for Israel. By being thus silenced, Congress was seen by Islamists as sanctioning acts of violence by Israel as well as supporting Israeli policies, through routine funding, of "dehumanizing" the Palestinian people. This did great damage to US credibility. One Egyptian Islamist referred to the "hostages on the Hill" in reference to the US Congress. The image has not improved. The influence of the Zionist lobby is perceived as being unprecedented in US history. With the ascendancy in the Bill Clinton administration of Martin Indyk, a former Zionist lobbyist who is perceived as supporting Likud policies, to the National Security Council in charge of US policy in the region, some Islamists referred to the "Israeli-occupied White House."[37] The election of George W. Bush did not bring about the hoped-for rectification in American foreign policy; rather, it ushered in the power of the neoconservatives, who are decidedly pro-Israeli.

US FOREIGN POLICY AND THE
GEORGE W. BUSH ADMINISTRATION

Muslims expected a more equitable policy from the George W. Bush administration. During the presidential debates, he had questioned the use of racial profiling legislated by the Clinton administration, which had targeted Arab Americans. Furthermore, in the estimation of Arab and Muslim Americans, a change in administration would remove the Israeli lobby from the center of policymaking. They had noted that the lobby was instrumental in defeating the reelection bid of George W. Bush's father (because it did not forgive his policy of demanding a halt to the construction and expansion of settlements on the West Bank). Consequently George W. received the endorsement of the major Muslim and Arab organizations, and a large number of Arabs and Muslims in the United States registered and voted for the first time, accounting for 2 percent of the votes received by the Bush-Cheney ticket. Muslims believe that their votes were the decisive margin in Florida. They had not paid attention to the promises he had made to the Zionist lobby. He was later to boast that he had borrowed twenty policy wonks from the American Enterprise Institute, noted as the home of neoconservatives and unconditional supporters of Israel.[38] In essence, while the Clinton administration relied on Zionists with connections to the Labor Party in Israel, the Bush administration utilized those who had a long-standing relationship with Benjamin Netanyahu of Likud.

From the beginning, President Bush wanted to keep his hands off the Arab-Israeli conflict. In the process, he allowed the Israeli authorities to continue to grind down the Palestinian resistance to the occupation. His public and highly publicized refusal to meet with Yasser Arafat, while repeatedly welcoming Prime Minister Sharon to the White House, sent an important message to Islamists that he was in total support of Israel and its policies. Whenever the Palestinians reacted to Israeli aggression, Bush blamed Arafat and the Palestinians. Such open support of Sharon infuriated Muslims and Arabs overseas; Sharon was particularly reviled because he was implicated in four massacres perpetrated against the Palestinians. They were particularly aggrieved when Bush met with Sharon after the Israeli shelling and demolition in Ramallah around the headquarters of Yasser Arafat. Bush had earlier expressed his frustration by saying, "Enough is enough," which led some to believe that he was finally disgusted enough to restrain what was perceived to be Israeli aggression. But upon meeting with Sharon, Bush declared him a "man of peace." This led the moderate Palestinian negotiator Saeb Erekat to say, "When I hear the president saying that Sharon is a man of peace after he has destroyed our way of life, and after the Jenin refugee camp, I don't know if this is not a reward for Israeli terrorism against the Palestinian people."

Another policy adopted early in the Bush administration that aggravated Islamists was its refusal to engage in a discussion of what was perceived to be Israeli racial policies. Their anger was demonstrated in Muslim publications all over the world when the United States and Israel walked out of the UN World Conference Against Racism, Racial Discrimination, Xenophobia, and Related Intolerance held in Durban, accusing participants that the conference had been "hijacked" by Israel's enemies. For Islamists that fact demonstrated once again America's lack of concern for Palestinians under what is perceived to be an oppressive Israeli occupation that openly discusses means of containing Palestinians within fences, transferring them to other countries, or getting rid of them because they do not fit into its definition of a Jewish state. One Islamist asked, "If this is not racism, what is?"

And then there was the 9/11 attack on the World Trade Center in New York and the Pentagon in Virginia, and Americans asked, "Why do they hate us?" Osama bin Laden's statement provided an answer that few US policymakers wanted to hear. He identified US foreign policy vis-à-vis the Arab-Israeli conflict, US containment of Iraq, which had degraded the lives of the Iraqi people and led to their suffering, and US troops stationed in the Gulf, who maintained American hegemony in the area and supported autocratic regimes. His message was blunted by a parade of former US policymakers, diplomats, and army brass who appeared on American television stations around the clock to assure the American public that they hate us because of our "democracy," our "culture," and our "values." And as Raghida Dergham of the Lebanese daily *al-Hayat* has said, not one dared to tell the American people that "it is the policy, stupid." The Arabs who perpetrated the horrible terrorist acts in the United States were suspected of being the same group that had hit American installations of command and control elsewhere: two embassies in Africa, the USS *Cole* in Yemen, and the Khobar Tower in Saudi Arabia where American troops lived. They had not attacked any of America's cultural monuments—not one Pizza Hut, McDonald's, or cathedral had been bombed. For those who continue to question whether there was any connection between the destruction of 9/11 and our foreign policy, Robert Fisk of the British *Independent* pointed to the fact that the last will of Muhammad Atta, who led the suicide bombers on 9/11, was written on April 18, 1996, the day of the Qana massacre. (On April 18, 1996, the Israeli army during Operation Grapes of Wrath in South Lebanon deliberately targeted the UN headquarters at Qana, which resulted in the massacre of more than one hundred women and children who had taken refuge there.)

After the attacks of 9/11, the Bush administration declared a "global war on terrorism." The attack on American soil was so momentous that it was deemed to have "changed America forever." To his credit, President Bush reached out to the Arab and Muslim American communities and assured them that the United States was waging war not against Islam but against terrorism. He called on the American people not to take out their anger and frustration on American Muslims. At the same time, his administration incarcerated more than 5,000 Arabs and Muslims using the hastily legislated Patriot Act. Racial profiling of Arabs and Muslims continues to be a common practice. Meanwhile, there was very little movement in adjusting US foreign policy to demonstrate more evenhandedness and justice. The Bush administration was caught in a double bind: If it altered its policies, it could be perceived as caving in to the terrorists; at the same time, the constant blaming of Palestinians for the bloodshed in Israel/Palestine and the daily saber-rattling for regime change in Iraq raised questions about US sincerity. The majority of Muslims overseas believed that the United States had declared war on Islam. The administration's policy, implemented by the American diplomatic corps, of trying to root out fundamentalist Islam from textbooks and *madrasas* in Muslim countries has infuriated Islamists. They have questioned what right "Mufti Bush" has to decide what true Islam is. The fact that the administration bombed the Taliban, which had not perpetrated 9/11, and the large number of Afghan civilian casualties raised suspicions that the motive was retribution. No one doubted US might and ability to destroy Islamists, but they reserved the right to think for themselves and to hold their own interpretations of the Qur'an. Many continue to question whether current policies are creating a new generation of Islamists who will seek to avenge what they perceive to be a war on Islam, despite the assurances by the Bush administration to the contrary, and they await justice for the Palestinians.

Western commentators point to the fact that various Arab governments appear to have wearied of the Palestinian leadership and the Palestinian cause. The Gulf War precipitated an exodus of Palestinians from yet another Arab country, Kuwait, while Operation Iraqi Freedom emptied them out of Iraq. That, however, does not translate into Muslim abandonment of the issue of Palestine and Jerusalem. For Islamists, the danger facing the Muslims is not "the Palestine problem" as much as the "problem of Israel." For Muslims, Palestine is a cause. It represents the demand for the right of a people to self-determination, democracy, and freedom. It is also the demand that the West recognize that an Arab person is equal to a European person or, as some Palestinians put it, that a European Jew is not better than a Palestinian Christian or Muslim and has no superior right to rob, destroy, expel, kidnap, or kill without consequences. Palestine is a demand for the end of the colonial era, an end to the era of "Christian arrogance"[39] and "Jewish insolence,"[40] a demand that the superior international Islamic law prevail, which would guarantee justice and freedom to Muslims and to religious minorities who dwell among them.

Islamists believe that American foreign policy has targeted them as worthy victims for annihilation. They hope that one day the West will wake up to the tragedy it has perpetrated. Those in the West may yet apologize for the destruction of Palestine; they may even offer restitution, but will they ever be able to correct the wrong that they have done? As Rashid Qabbani, the mufti of Lebanon, put it:

> The West has been brilliant in the crime of ridding itself of the Jewish problem and dumping it into the heart of the Arab world by supporting the Zionist entity and [establishing] Israel in Palestine in 1948. After WWII Western nations began seeking forgiveness from Israel for what Nazism had done to the Jews. Will the Western conscious[ness] awake one day to seek forgiveness for the crime which they committed by establishing Israel in Palestine and by evicting the Palestinian people from their homes and land? Will the West seek forgiveness for the suppression, terrorizing,

and humiliation that Israel has been meting out for fifty years to the oppressed Palestinian people and for the loss of their land at the hand of the
West? Should it occur, of what value will Western apology be? For it is the
West that daily provides Israel with the weapons of mass destruction, prepared for the annihilation of the Palestinians and the Arabs.[41]

OPERATION IRAQI FREEDOM AND ITS CONSEQUENCES

One of the transformations that took place post-9/11 was in President George W.
Bush himself, who referred to himself as the "war president."[42] After September
11, 2001, the president proceeded to plan for the invasion of Iraq, a plan promoted
by the neoconservative advisers in his administration.[43] In seeking the support of
the American people for the global war on terrorism, the Bush administration utilized a variety of themes, including creating a climate of fear about the alleged imminent danger from a nuclear attack by Saddam Hussein. When these assertions
were questioned, then national security adviser Condoleezza Rice, on September
8, 2003, retorted: "The problem here is that there will always be some uncertainty
about how quickly he can acquire nuclear weapons. But we don't want the smoking
gun to be a mushroom cloud." Furthermore, despite the fact that Saddam was a
secularist, he was initially depicted as an accomplice of al-Qa'ida. Later he was condemned as a monster who had gassed his own people (even though the biological
and chemical weapons are suspected to have been provided by the United States).
He could not be trusted with possessing weapons of mass destruction that he would
surely aim at the United States. At the same time, the propaganda for war provided
the public with a moral justification for attacking Afghanistan and Iraq, bathing
the war in the virtues of, among other things, liberating the oppressed women of
Islam from fanatical oppressive Islamists. The goal became the modernization and
democratization of Islamic society. Washington eventually promised the refashioning of Iraq as a beacon of democracy that would serve as a model for the entire
Middle East.[44]

Muslims took note of the fact that Operation Iraqi Freedom was a preemptive
war. From their perspective, there was no virtue in the attack. Although they de-
spised Saddam Hussein, they perceived the goal of the US-led invasion in more
sinister terms, as one that was driven by the motive of weakening the Arabs and
Muslims and empowering Israel. They accused the Bush administration of dealing
with the consequences of terrorism while turning a blind eye toward its causes.
Arabs and Muslims are aware that terrorism is a response to American policies that
empower autocratic regimes and implement Israeli and Zionist policies that are
harmful to Arabs and Muslims and therefore breed hatred. They noted that the
US government could not acknowledge this truth since it would indict itself, and
therefore it projects the blame on others. Hence the Bush administration declared
a global war on terrorism, in which it assumed a total monopoly in deciding the
nature of the war, its timing, its targets, the means to be utilized, and the manner
in which it would be conducted.[45]

Islamists saw the war in Iraq as a two-pronged attack that utilized military power and media deception. While various spokesmen of the Bush administration boasted about Shock and Awe to neutralize the Iraqi army and pacify the population, Islamists saw the attack as proof of American brutality and addiction to state terrorism in order to gain control of Iraqi oil fields. On Arab television American military tactics looked indistinguishable from those that Israel utilized in the occupied territories. The two occupations appeared to blend into a coordinated attack against Muslims, especially after US rhetoric conflated terrorism against the United States with resistance to Israeli occupation in Palestine and Lebanon. Shock and Awe did not cow Arabs and Muslims; rather, it inflamed their passions against the West and its supporters, a sentiment that spawned a large number of volunteers for the insurgency. The American media was perceived by Muslims as assuming the role of the self-censoring and embedded servant of hegemonic imperialist goals "which have no association with freedom or democracy."[46]

While a great deal of ink has been spilled discussing the war, its motives, goals, and conduct, two focuses of Islamist literature are worth noting: the growing rejection of violence as a tactic to achieve the goals of the Islamic movement and the continued rejection of perceived US schemes to bring the Muslim world under its cultural hegemony and to empower Israel over the Arabs and Muslims.

Several Islamist leaders have published *shari'a*-based interpretations that denounce terrorist bombings targeting civilians. They have also expressed their opinion that these bombings are based on a misinterpretation of Islamic teaching and have been counterproductive and therefore against the interests of Islam. The renunciation of violence by these Islamic groups was not a consequence of the demonstration of American resolve and power, whether in Afghanistan or in Iraq. For example, the Jama'ah Islamiyya, which was responsible for the first attack on the World Trade Center in 1993, renounced violence on July 5, 1997. They called for the cessation of armed operations and the shedding of blood as a means of achieving the goal of Islamizing society. This declaration was signed by its leadership and approved by Sheikh Omar 'Abd al-Rahman from his prison cell in the United States. The group split, and those who refused to subscribe to peaceful resistance perpetrated the terrorist activities in the late 1990s in Luxor, Upper Egypt, while others joined al-Qa'ida.[47]

This literature notes that violence has been counterproductive and has not achieved its goals. Hijacking airplanes has not put a stop to air travel in the world. Nor has targeting a bank eliminated the banking industry or kept people from dealing with banks. Likewise, bombings are not going to force the United States to alter its policies. Rather, violence has brought great injury to the cause and goals of the Islamic movement since it has led to the identification of jihad with terrorism, an interpretation promoted by many Israelis and the Americans as a way to delegitimate resistance movements in Palestine and Lebanon as well as in Chechnya and Iraq. Israeli and American rhetoric depicts all resistance as terrorism and asserts that "all Muslims are terrorists, the word Islam means terror, all are engaged in killing civilian women and children."[48] Thus some Islamist leaders have concluded that "*jihad* for the sake of *jihad*, fighting for the sake of fighting is the wrong model of *jihad*. It is an erroneous interpretation of this great Islamic duty."[49] This view contends that American aggression should not legitimate what is against the Islamic *shari'a*, the killing of innocent people. America's crimes against Arabs and Muslims are evident and cause a great deal of grieving; however, they should not be used as an excuse to weaken the *'umma* or provide the United States with an excuse to interfere in the internal affairs of Arabs and Muslims.[50]

The literature admits that the perpetrators are right that the US treatment of Muslims is laced with arrogance and contempt, evident in the legislation passed by Congress as the Sudan Peace Act,[51] the Iraq Liberation Act,[52] and the Syria Accountability Act,[53] while four hundred congressmen voted in support of a resolution to not put pressure on Israel to implement the Road Map, which would bring about the creation of a Palestinian state—despite the fact that the Road Map, from its inception to its final formulation, was an Israeli project.[54] It is also evident in the treatment of prisoners of war in Afghanistan, detainees at the prison at Guantanamo Bay in Cuba, and those held at the Abu Ghraib prison in Iraq. This treatment is seen in the Arab and Muslim worlds as an example of America's disdain for human rights as well as international conventions.[55] Islamists saw President Bush as a hypocrite and a liar not only because of the deception about the reasons for the invasion of Iraq but also because of the spin about the noble goals of the invasion. They noted, for example, that in a November 6, 2003, speech at the National Endowment for Democracy, he focused on the theme of democracy in the Muslim world. He commended the leaders of autocratic countries—Bahrain, Jordan, Kuwait, Morocco, Oman, Qatar, Saudi Arabia, and Yemen—but condemned the "Palestinian leaders who block and undermine democratic reform."[56] But when the Palestinians elected representatives he did not approve of, specifically the Hamas parliamentary victory in January 2006, Bush sanctioned the blockade of the freely elected Palestinian government, which was intended to starve it into submission.

Another peeve was the promotion by the Bush administration of the Greater Middle East Partnership project that was perceived to be an American political strategy to abrogate the Arab identity by adding far-flung Muslim nations under a new geographic umbrella.[57] The term Middle East was designed by colonial powers. Its geographic reach has always been elastic and flexible, determined by Western interests. In earlier times it had included Iran, Turkey, and Cyprus, but the greater Middle East had an even larger reach. To Islamists, its goal appeared to be the eradication of the Arab identity. They would become Middle Easterners instead of Arabs. Some perceived it as a reincarnation of an old project to refashion the Arab nations according to Western dictates and Israeli design. The idea had first been floated by Shimon Peres, former prime minister of Israel, by which he depicted the Middle East at peace, with Israel managing the area's resources and controlling its trade.[58]

Islamists remained suspicious of the Bush administration's goals in Iraq. They maintained that under the rubric of pluralism and democracy, the American government appeared to be in the process of dividing the country according to ethnic and sectarian identities. They noted that the record of the US occupation did not inspire hope. It was accused of insisting on giving US companies the right to develop the oil industry, robbing the Iraqis of their wealth. It was also accused of initially placing shady characters in charge of the Iraqi government, of allowing the theft of archeological treasures, and of subverting the intellectual and religious culture of Iraq by replacing the school curriculums with materials conceived and written in the United States.[59]

Suspicion of American motives is pervasive in the Muslim world. The fear is that the globalization promoted by the United States will result in the Americanization of Arab and Muslim culture. This Americanization can be imposed through "shock and awe" if necessary, with total disregard for any freedom of choice or democratic input by Muslims.[60] The hope in the Arab and Muslim worlds is that Americans will recognize that the international order that was unilaterally abrogated by the United States must be restored. The hope is that the American people will initiate that change.[61]

ISLAMISTS AND THE OBAMA ADMINISTRATION

The Arab and Muslim world welcomed the election of Barack Obama to the presidency of the United States with cautious optimism, anticipating a new era in American policy toward the Middle East. They had by the end of the Bush presidency been convinced that the United States had declared war on Islam and Muslims. They resented the wars in Iraq and Afghanistan that precipitated the deaths of thousands of civilians. They were outraged by the torture of prisoners in Guantanamo prison and by the support of Israeli confiscation and colonization of Palestinian lands and the building of walls that held the population on the West Bank in what appeared to be open-air prison. The Bush administration ended with what was perceived as a savage war on Gaza that targeted its population and their houses, hospitals, schools, and food. They were ready for change.

Ahmed Yousef, the chief political adviser to Hamas in Gaza, was quoted during the 2008 election campaign as saying, "We hope he (Obama) will (win)."[62] Noting Obama's public disavowal of former President Carter's plans to meet with Hamas without preconditions, Yousef said: "I understand American politics. This is the season for elections and everybody tries to be, sound like he is a friend of Israel."[63] Obama later made a speech before the American Israel Public Affairs Committee in Washington, DC, and argued that Israel's security was "sacrosanct" and that Israel should remain a "Jewish State."[64] The most controversial part was Obama's assertion that in "any agreement with the Palestinian people . . . Jerusalem will remain the capital of Israel, and it must remain undivided."[65] A four-minute video highlighting Obama's pro-Israel statements and featuring an Obama Loves Israel photo montage was compiled and distributed through the Internet.[66] The goodwill expressed by Yousef changed to disappointment: "[Obama's] remarks on Jerusalem cast doubt over the chances of peace . . . We reject the positions of Barack Obama because they are in contradiction with the traditional positions of the United States which considers that East Jerusalem is under occupation."[67]

The Arab-Israeli conflict continues to concern Muslims throughout the world, and the Obama administration appears unable to rein in the Israeli campaign to confiscate and colonize more Palestinian land by escalating the construction of more settlements in the West Bank and Jerusalem.

Upon taking office, President Obama announced a new initiative toward Muslim nations. Two days following his inauguration, he signed three executive orders regarding Guantanamo. The first established that prisoners of war would henceforth be "treated humanely and shall not be subjected to violence to life and person (including murder of all kinds, mutilation, cruel treatment, and torture), nor to outrages upon personal dignity (including humiliating and degrading treatment)"[68] while in detention under the authority of "the United States Government."[69] The second executive order provided that the detention facilities at Guantanamo Bay would be closed "as soon as practicable, and no later than 1 year from the date of this order."[70] Furthermore, it ordered that five hundred of the eight hundred prisoners detained at Guantanamo Bay were entitled to a review of their files and could be released or transferred to a third-party country.[71] The third executive order established the creation of a special task force whose mission was to "conduct a comprehensive review of the lawful options available . . . with respect to the apprehension, detention, trial, transfer, release, or other disposition of individuals captured or apprehended in connection with armed conflicts and counterterrorism operations."[72] Almost two years following the order to close Guantanamo Bay, the facility remains open and detains fifty prisoners who have yet to receive due process.

President Obama made other symbolic gestures toward the Middle East and Muslim world by delivering two major speeches, one in Istanbul (April 6, 2009) and the other in Cairo (June 4, 2009). The Cairo speech, in particular, was well-received by moderate Islamists[73] and viewed with cautious optimism by right-leaning Islamists.[74] Khalid Mishaal of Hamas in an interview with *Time* magazine moments after the speech said:

> Undoubtedly Obama speaks a new language. His speech was cleverly designed . . . The essence of the speech was to improve the US image and to placate the Muslims. We don't mind either objective, but we are looking for more than just mere words. If the United States wishes to open a new page, we definitely would welcome this. We are keen to contribute to this. But we [believe that cannot happen] merely with words. It must be with deeds, by changing the policy on the ground.[75]

This sentiment was shared by Fadel Soliman, director of the Bridges Foundation and Islamic *da'wa* activist, in a piece published in *Al-Ahram Weekly*: "visits and verbal messages do not bring change, but rather real work does."[76]

While the Obama administration changed several Bush policies, it failed to deliver any meaningful results on the Arab-Israeli conflict, the primary source of Muslim rage. For instance, while it publicly demanded that Israel cease the construction
of additional settlements in the occupied territories, it failed to pressure Israeli
Prime Minister Benjamin Netanyahu to alter his government's policy. This provoked criticism from some Islamists, including Hassan Nasrallah, the leader of
Hizbollah, who argued that Obama completely backed Israel. He noted, "We saw
how the US withdrew from [the demand to halt settlement construction) and
called on the Palestinians to return to the negotiation table with no preconditions.
Obama's deception has been exposed sooner than expected."[77]

Nevertheless, relations between the United States and Israel appeared for a while
to sour, most notably illustrated following a Netanyahu visit to Washington. It was
widely reported that Obama scolded the Israeli prime minister for his settlements
stance and for the findings illuminated in the Goldstone Report that determined
that Israel perpetrated war crimes during its war on Gaza.[78] Yet the United States
publicly supported Israel's rejection of the report. Then, on May 31, 2010, when
the Israelis boarded a flotilla of aid ships headed to Gaza and killed nine protesters
including an American citizen, it reinforced the perception that nothing had
changed and continued the process of the deteriorating relations between America
and the Muslim world.[79]

Other Middle East policy issues of interest to Islamist groups include the
Obama administration's position vis-à-vis Iran, which began with friendly gestures—
intended to launch diplomatic talks—but quickly changed into threats of additional economic sanctions through the United Nations. Both Ayman al-Zawahiri
and Osama bin Laden have argued that Obama is no different from Bush, citing
his support for Israel, his plan to continue the war in Afghanistan, and his decision
to keep Defense Secretary Robert Gates, a holdover from the Bush administration,
in his position.[80] Khalid Mishaal claimed that the Obama administration attempted
to intervene in internal Palestinian politics, contending that it tried "to foil Palestinian efforts to achieve the national reconciliation by pressuring Fatah leader Mahmoud Abbas not to go ahead with it."[81]

More recently, Isam al-Aryan, of the Muslim Brotherhood in Egypt, wrote an
article for *al-Akbar* (Beirut) under the title "A Letter to Barack Obama." He urged
Obama to refrain from backing authoritarian regimes, lamenting that these regimes
have surrendered their sovereignty and interest to outsiders. He also expressed bitterness toward American hypocrisy: "it is a matter of allegiance to your country
when you promote principles that are called upon by the American constitution,
and the values of freedom, respect of human rights, democracy and respect of the
will of people. By contrast, it is not a matter of allegiance to your country to keep
your armies . . . occupying all corners of the world. It is not a matter of faithfulness
to your principles to keep those detainees in jail without conviction and extract
false confessions from them by torture; and to use tyrants and autocrats who remain
in power because of your support."[82] Thus it is clear that to date most Muslims

have been disappointed that Obama's rhetoric has not been matched by hoped-for changes in American foreign policy.

Notes

1. For example, "The black intellectual trend has lately been able to make Islam a synonym to terrorism and darkness through the media which is controlled by the 'Muslim' states. He who prays five times a day is an iniquitous terrorist . . . she who wears a hijab is an iniquitous terrorist; he who reads the Qur'an is an iniquitous terrorist, and he who refuses usury, drinking, Eastern dancing, social dancing and mixing of men and women is an iniquitous terrorist; he who advocates the study of Islamic history and Islamic religion is an iniquitous terrorist; he who calls for an Islamic economic, cultural, political unity is an iniquitous terrorist. . . . Anyone who belongs to Islam is bloody and reactionary who must be destroyed. What would satisfy them is for the Muslims to abandon Islam and follow others in religion, thought, way of life and conduct . . . only then would it be proper to call them enlightened." Hilmi Muhammad al-Qa'ud, "Al-Fikr al-Aswad . . . wa al-Fitan al-Thaqafiyya," *al-Mujtama'*, December 28, 1993, p. 56.

2. In an interview, Fathi Shikaki, secretary-general of the Islamic Jihad movement in Palestine, protested the designation of terrorist. See Omar Maxwell, "No Peace Until Palestine Is Free," *Inquiry*, January 1993, p. 21: "I do not know how the Palestinian is described as a terrorist when his scream is a response to his pain and suffering while defending his land against Jewish Russian soldiers, who had never (and neither their fore-fathers) set foot in any inch of Palestine. The West's attempt to homogenize our countries is the source of all terrorism and chaos. We are calling for peace based on justice, rights and dignity. We must be dealt with as equals and as carriers of a great civilization. Only then will peace prevail in our region and the whole world."

3. "President Bush Delivers Remarks at the National Endowment for Democracy," October 6, 2006, http://tinyurl.com/4jcy7aj. "President Bush Delivers Remarks to the Joint Armed Forces Officers' Wives' Luncheon," Bolling Air Force Base, October 25, 2006, http://tinyurl.com/4q9unqz.

4. For example, "In recent days, the West has started to triumphantly declare that in today's world, Arabs do not matter. For them Muslims also do not matter and they would like to keep it that way. The media and Western political and propaganda machines are assiduously asserting that Islam is incompatible with civilization. Their main points are that Islam lacks democracy, is devoid of compassion and has no rights for women. In doing so they have splendid examples, or in fact props; Saudi Arabia is rendering the best service. It is allegedly run according to the Quran, so there is no democracy and no rights." Abdurrahman Abdullah, "The Final Battle for the Soul of Afghanistan," *Inquiry*, June 1992, p. 19.

5. See, for example, Muhammad 'Amara, *al-Ta'addudiyya: al-Ru'ya al-Islamiyya . . . wa al-Tahaddiyat al-Gharbiyya* [Proceedings of the Conference on Political, Sectarian and Ethnic Pluralism in the Arab World] (Herndon, VA: IIIT, 1993), pp. 1–34.

6. For a sampling of Salafi literature, see 'Abd al-Rahman 'Abd al-Khaliq, *al-'Usul al-'Ilmiyya li al-Da'wa al-Salafiyya* (Kuwait, 1982); 'Umar Sulayman al-Ashqar, *Ma'alim al-Shakhsiyya al-Islamiyya* (Kuwait, 1984). For a criticism of Salafi thought, see Muhammad Fathi 'Uthman, *al-Salafiyya fi al-Mujtama'at al-Mu'asira* (Cairo, 1982).

7. Ahmad Kamal Abu al-Magd, *Kitab al-Qawmiyya al-'Arabiyya wa al-Islam* (Beirut, 1980), pp. 32–33. For a different categorization, see Khurshid Ahmad, "Islam and the New World Order," *Middle East Affairs,* Spring-Summer 1993, pp. 10–11.

8. See Yvonne Yazbeck Haddad, "The Authority of the Past: Current Paradigms for an Islamic Future," in *The Authority of the Past,* ed. Toby Siebers (Ann Arbor: University of Michigan Institute for the Humanities, 1993). For Islamist discussions on the future, see Ahmad Kamal Abu al-Magd, "Al-Muslimun Da'wa li-Iqtiham al-Mustaqbal," *al-'Arabi,* March 1983; Fu'ad Muhammad Fakhr al-Din, *Mustaqbal al-Muslimin* (Cairo, 1976); 'Abd al-'Aziz Kamil, *al-Islam wa al-Mustaqbal* (Cairo, 1976); 'Abd al-Halim 'Uways, *al-Muslimun fi Ma'rakat al-Baqa'* (Cairo, 1979); Sayyid Qutb, *Islam: The Religion of the Future* (Chicago: Kazi Publications, 1977).

9. Muhammad al-Ghazali, *Ma'rakat al-Mushaf fi al-'Alam al-Islami* (Cairo, 1964); Muhammad al-Hasani, *al-Islam al-Mumtahan* (Cairo, n.d.); Muhammad Farag, *Al-Islam fi Mu'tarak al-Sira' al-Fikri al-Hadith* (Cairo, 1962); Muhammad al-Ghazali, *Kifah Din* (Cairo, n.d.); Muhammad Jalal Kishk, *al-Ghazu al-Fikri* (Cairo, 1975); 'Abd al-Sattar Fathallah Sa'id, *al-Ghazu al-Fikri wa al-Tayyarat al-Mu'adiya li al-Islam* (Cairo, 1977).

10. Tawfiq Mahmud al-Shawi, "Istratijiyya 'Ilmiyya li al-Tayyar al-Islami," *al-Mujtama',* December 28, 1993, p. 22.

11. Abdullah, "Final Battle," p. 19.

12. One author described the minarets of Yugoslavia in the following words: "This remains a living testimony to the glorious and often forgotten Islamic heritage of the last remnants of Europe's indigenous Muslim population, a people, a society, a civilization possibly on the verge of extinction. This is not a fate different from the fate experienced by the indigenous Muslims of Sicily, Italy, Spain, Portugal, Hungary, Malta, etc. many centuries earlier." Saffet Catovic, "Europe's Islamic Heritage in Jeopardy," *Inquiry,* January 1993, p. 28.

13. See Ziyad Muhammad 'Ali, *'Ida al-Yahud li al-Haraka al-Islamiyya* (Amman, 1982), p. 21.

14. Graduation speech at the US Naval Academy, Annapolis, Maryland, May 30, 1990.

15. "We Muslims are very distressed at the growing number of attacks of the Western Jewish American media against Islam. . . . We are prone to think that the Jewish and Zionist groups with all their great influence in the West and America have determined to turn the West against Islam and to push Christianity and Islam into a violent confrontation that will destroy both and keep the Zionists as winners." Ghannushi, interview, *al-Majalla,* December 28, 1993, p. 28.

16. See Bernard Lewis, "The Roots of Muslim Rage," *Atlantic Monthly,* September 20, 1990. An editorial by Charles Krauthammer appearing in the *National Review* reiterates the same ideas, as does "The New Crescent of Crisis: The Global Intifada," *Washington Post,* February 16, 1990. Cf. Daniel Pipes, "The Muslims Are Coming, the Muslims Are Coming," *National Review,* November 19, 1990, pp. 28–31.

17. Mowahid H. Shah, "A New Cold War Within Islam?" *Christian Science Monitor,* July 30, 1990, p. 19.

18. In an interview with the first secretary of the US embassy in Qatar, Yusuf al-Qaradawi is reported to have said: "It is not in America's interest to be an enemy of Islam, the Islamic forces and the Islamic movements that are balanced and moderate. However, there are individuals and powers who have an interest in maintaining that

Islam is something to fear and revile. They envision for American policy makers and to those in power that Islam is a frightening demon which represents what they call the green threat which they must be cautious of after the passing away of the red Communist threat. This in reality is a myth. For Islam, especially that represented by the moderate groups which we advocate, is not a danger to anyone." *al-Mujtama'*, December 28, 1993, p. 31.

19. David Ben-Gurion, the first prime minister of Israel, is reported to have said, "We fear nothing but Islam." Yitzhak Rabin reportedly declared, "The religion of Islam is our only enemy." And Shimon Peres warned, "We will not feel secure until Islam puts away its sword." 'Ali, *'Ida*, pp. 45–46.

20. 'Abd al-Hamid al-Sayeh, *Madha Ba'd Ihraq al-Masjid al-Aqsa?* (Cairo, 1970), pp. 23, 178ff.

21. Abdullah Kannun, "Al-Muslimun wa Mushkilat Filastin," in *Kitab al-Mu'tamar al-Rabi' li-Majma' al-Buhuth al-Islamiyya*, pp. 36, 38.

22. Kamel al-Baqir, "Jawhar al-Qadiyya al-Filastiniyya" [The Essence of the Palestinian Issue], in *Kitab al-Mu'tamar al-Rabi'* [Book of the Fourth Conference], p. 136.

23. Abdullah Kannun, "Makanat Bayt al-Maqdis fi al-Islam," in *Kitab al-Mu'tamar al-Rabi' li-Majma' al-Buhuth al-Islamiyya*, 2:39.

24. "And it was the West, champion of the separation of Church and State, cradle of secularism, that helped in the creation of this state founded on the idea of the return to the Promised Land. The intrusion of religion into politics didn't bother European socialists, nor American technocrats. Neither did it bother the atheists of Moscow who were the first to recognize the State of Israel." Habib Boulares, *Islam: The Fear and the Hope*, p. 25, as quoted in *Inquiry*, June 1992, p. 42.

25. Muhammad M. al-Fahham, "The Restoration of Jerusalem," in *The Fifth Conference of the Academy of Islamic Research* (Cairo: Government Printing Office, 1971), p. 53.

26. Muhammad al-Ghazali, *Qadhaif al-Haqq* (Kuwait, 1984), p. 109.

27. Yvonne Yazbeck Haddad, "Operation Desert Shield/Desert Storm: The Islamist Perspective," in *Beyond the Storm*, ed. Phyllis Bennis and Michel Moushabeck (New York: Olive Branch Press, 1991), pp. 248–260.

28. See Konstantin Obradovik, ed., *The Inalienable Rights of the Palestinian People* (London: Outline Books, 1985), pp. 292–301.

29. Ibid., pp. 245–291.

30. Munir Farah, "Impact on Education," in *Occupation: Israel Over Palestine*, ed. Naseer A. Aruri (Belmont, MA: AAUG, 1983), pp. 295–318; and Naseer Aruri, "Universities Under Occupation," in ibid., pp. 319–336.

31. See, for example, Hasan Khalid, "Kalimat al-Wufud" [Statement of the Delegates], *Kitab al-Mu'tamar al-Rabi': al-Muslimun wa al-'Udwan al-Israili* (Cairo, 1968), 2:29.

32. Maxwell, "No Peace Until Palestine Is Free," p. 22.

33. 'Abd al-Baqi Khalifa, "al-Tatarruf: Mafahimuh . . . Asbabuh . . . Nata'ijuh . . . 'Ilajuh," *al-Mujtama'*, November 23, 1993.

34. Ibid.

35. Al-Ghazali, *Qadhaif*, p. 223.

36. Ibid., p. 225.

37. "This is a surrender to the Jews who have assumed the power in the United States, so that the White House and those in it have become an instrument in the hand

of the Jews." "al-Wilayat al-Muttahida Taraf Munhaz Yad'am Isra'il wa-Atma'aha," *al-Majalla* 29, December 5, 1998, p. 9.

38. President Discusses the Future of Iraq, Office of the Press Secretary, White House, February 26, 2003.

39. See, for example, the repeated references to Crusader arrogance in Fathi Bakhkhush, "Daqqat Sa'at al-Jihad: al-Umma fi Khatar" [The Hour of Jihad Has Struck: The Nation Is in Danger], *Risalat al-Jihad*, November 1990. He condemns the US-led Desert Storm coalition: "The Crusaders have come this time with a military campaign under the leadership of oppressive America, arrogant with its devastating power" (p. 58). He also writes that the Islamic nationalist rejection of US policies in the region has enraged "oppressive American Crusaderism" because it perceives it as a "threat to its contending power and its [ability] to impose its arrogance on the world" (p. 59). He also calls the forces gathered for Desert Storm "the greatest terrorist Crusader force in history," which can only be resisted by a religious response. "If one of the characteristics of this age is that American arrogance has reached the highest peak, a parallel characteristic is the ability of armed believing nations to mire this arrogance in the dust" (p. 61).

40. Yitzhak Shamir is quoted as having boasted in a radio broadcast that "he is proud of the terrorist record of the Stern Gang including the assassination of Swedish Count Bernadotte on a United Nations Peace Mission in 1948, the assassination of Lord Moyen, the British Minister of State for Middle East Affairs, and the massacre of Deir Yasin." See "Kalla al-Sihyuniyya Haraka 'Unsuriyya" [No, Zionism Is a Racist Movement], *Risalat al-Jihad*, October 1991, p. 6. Cf.: "The Israeli enemy backed by the forces of imperialism, never ceases to disclose his real designs which are no less than wresting more Arab territories, and thereby impudently paying no heed to the legitimate rights of the Palestinian people." Abdul-Aziz Kamel, "The Opening Address," *Sixth Conference of the Academy of Islamic Research* (Cairo: al-Azhar, 1971), p. 17. Abba Eban, former Israeli ambassador to the United Nations, was reported to have said, "If the General Assembly were to vote by 121 votes to 1 in favor of Israel returning to the Armistice lines . . . Israel would refuse to comply with that decision." *New York Times,* June 19, 1967.

Several examples are cited by Fahmi al-Huwaidi, the popular Egyptian journalist, including the following: "The most recent example of 'good intent' comes from Morocco during the middle of January when the Moroccan government handed Israel the remains of Jews who drowned when their boat overturned while attempting to flee to Israel in the fifties. Israel's response to this gesture was insolent and in bad taste. It marked the event by placing a cornerstone for the erection of a monument to commemorate the victims in Maaleh Edumim, the large settlement established between Jerusalem and Jericho in the West Bank and which the Palestinians seek to have removed." Fahmi al-Huwaidi, "Bayn Bolard wa al-Shaykh Ahmad Yasin: Jawasisuhum Lahum Thaman wa-Munadiluna bila Thaman!" *al-Majalla,* January 30–February 5, 1994, p. 34.

41. Rashid Qabbani, "al-Gharb Yamuddu Isra'il bi-kul Aslihat al-Damar al Shamil," *al-Mujtama',* May 12–18, 1998, p. 25.

42. In his February 7 (broadcast on February 8), 2004, hour-long Oval Office interview with Tim Russert on NBC's *Meet the Press* (http://tinyurl.com/5rmscnj), President Bush declared himself to be a "war president." Bush: "I'm a war president. I make decisions here in the Oval Office in foreign-policy matters with war on my mind.

Again, I wish it wasn't true, but it is true. And the American people need to know they got a president who sees the world the way it is. And I see dangers that exist, and it's important for us to deal with them."

43. Grant F. Smith, *Deadly Dogma: How Neoconservatives Broke the Law to Deceive America* (Washington, DC: Middle East Policy, 2006).

44. Al-Rifa'i and Qubaisi, *Amerka*, p. 256. See also Muhammad Hasanain Haykal, *Al-Imbaratoriyya al-Amerikiyya wa Ighara ala al-Iraq* (Cairo: Dar al-Shuruq, 2003), pp. 239, 255.

45. Isam Na'man, *Al-Arab Ala Muftaraq Istishraf Tahadiyyat ma Ba'd September 11, 2001* (Cairo: Sharikat al-Matbu'at li al-Tawzi' wa al-Nashr, 2002), pp. 23–24.

46. Al-Rifa'i and Qubaisi, *Amerka*, pp. 238.

47. Osama Ibrahim Hafiz and Asim Abd al-Majid Muhammad, *Mubadarat Waqf al-Unf: Ru'ya Waqi'iyya wa Nazra Shar'iyya* (Cairo: Islamic Turath Bookshop, 2002). For publications against violence after 9/11 by the same press, see Hamdi Abd al-Rahman al-Azim, Najih Ibrahim Abdullah and Ali Muhammad Ali al-Sharif, *Taslit al-Adwa Ala ma Waqa' fi al-Jihad min Akhta*, 2002; Najih Ibrahim Abdullah and Ali Muhammad Ali al-Sharif, *Hurmat al-Ghulu fi al-Din wa-Takfir al-Muslimin*, 2002; Ali Muhammad Ali al-Sharif and Osama Ibrahim Hafiz, *al-Nusuh wa al-Tabyin fi Tashih Mafahim al-Muhtasibin*, 2002; Karam Muhammad Zuhdi, Najih Ibrahim Abdullah, Ali Muhammad Ali Sharif, Osama Ibrahim Hafiz, Hamdi Abd al-Rahman Abd al-Azim, Fuad Muhammad al-Dualibi, Asim Abd al-Majid Muhammad, and Muhammad Isam al-Din Dirbala, *Tafjirat al-Riyad: al-Ahkam wa al-Athar*, 2003; Karam Muhammad Zuhdi, Najih Ibrahim Abdullah, Ali Muhammad Ali Sharif, Osama Ibrahim Hafiz, Hamdi Abd al-Rahman Abd al-Azim, Fuad Muhammad al-Dualibi, Asim Abd al-Majid Muhammad, and Muhammad Isam al-Din Dirbala, *Istratijiyyat Tafjirat al-Qa'ida: Al-Akhta wa al-Akhtar*, 2004. For a detailed memoir detailing the activities of al-Jama'at al-Islamiyya, see Muntasir al-Zayyat, *al-Jama'at al-Islamiyya: Riwaya min al-Dakhil* (Cairo: Dar Misr al-Mahrusa, 2005).

48. Karam Muhammad Zuhdi, Najih Ibrahim Abdullah, Ali Muhammad Ali Sharif, Osama Ibrahim Hafiz, Hamdi Abd al-Rahman Abd al-Azim, Fuad Muhammad al-Dualibi, Asim Abd al-Majid Muhammad, and Muhammad Isam al-Din Dirbala, *Tafjirat al-Riyad: al-Ahkam wa al-Athar* (Cairo: Maktabat al-Turath al-Islami, 2003), p. 52.

49. Zuhdi et al., *Tafjirat al-Riyad*, p. 40.

50. Ibid., p. 116.

51. Public Law 107–245, October 21, 2002.

52. Public Law 105–338, October 31, 1998.

53. Public Law 108–175, December 12, 2003.

54. Zuhdi et al., *Tafjirat al-Riyad*, p. 12.

55. Al-Rifa'i and Qubaisi, *Amerka*, pp. 299–300.

56. Remarks by the President at the 20th Anniversary of the National Endowment for Democracy, US Chamber of Commerce, White House, November 6, 2003.

57. For an extensive discussion of the topic, see Al-Rifa'i and Qubaisi, *Amerka*.

58. Shimon Peres and Arye Naor, *The New Middle East* (New York: Henry Holt, 1993).

59. Al-Rifa'i and Qubaisi, *Amerka*, p. 256. See also Muhammad Hasanain Haykal, *Al-Imbaratoriyya al-Amerikiyya wa Ighara ala al-Iraq* (Cairo: Dar al-Shuruq, 2003), p. 290.

60. Al-Rifa'i and Qubaisi, *Amerka*, pp. 36, 152.

61. Ibid., p. 238.

62. http://tinyurl.com/5shao5f.

63. Ibid.

64. Transcript of Obama's speech to AIPAC, June 4, 2008, http://tinyurl.com/54js93.

65. Ibid.

66. Obama Tricks the Islamic World with Sweet Speech in AIPAC, http://tinyurl.com/6hls9e9.

67. "Hamas Un-'Endorses' Obama," June 4, 2008, http://tinyurl.com/5uvq8x.

68. President Barack H. Obama, Executive Order 13491, January 22, 2009.

69. Ibid.

70. President Barack H. Obama, Executive Order 13492, January 22, 2009.

71. Ibid.

72. President Barack H. Obama, Executive Order 13493, January 22, 2009.

73. President Obama's Cairo Speech Is a Foundation for Mutual Recognition and Positive Engagement, ISNA, http://tinyurl.com/4l6gxpx.

74. Khaled Hroub, Barack Obama, Muslims and Islamism, February 15, 2010, http://tinyurl.com/4nwrago.

75. Joe Klein, "A Meeting in Damascus," June 4, 2009, http://tinyurl.com/4ol8tb7.

76. Gihan Shahine, "Seeing Eye to Eye," June 4–11, 2009, http://tinyurl.com/4b4hek2.

77. Rohee Nahmias, "Nasrallah: Obama Fully Committed to Israel," November 11, 2009, http://tinyurl.com/yclw2qm.

78. The Goldstone Report found that Israel had illegally targeted civilian populations with phosphate bombs and other weapons during its assault on Gaza in the summer of 2009. These offenses amounted to war crimes.

79. "CAIR Calls President's Cairo Speech 'Comprehensive, Balanced and Forthright,'" June 4, 2009, http://tinyurl.com/6hpr4be.

80. Juan Cole, "Zawahiri: Obama is the anti-Malcom X," November 20, 2008, http://tinyurl.com/6ntwmr; bin Laden Statement, September 13, 2009, http://tinyurl.com/6gz8j7u.

81. "Mishaal: Washington Strives to Abort Palestinian Reconciliation," February 9, 2010, http://tinyurl.com/5rccbzj.

82. http://tinyurl.com/4nwrago.

CHAPTER 26

US RELATIONS WITH AL-QA'IDA

Heather S. Gregg

Describing US engagement with al-Qa'ida as "relations" may sound counterintuitive. Al-Qa'ida is not a state nor is it confined to one state, making traditional foreign relations impossible. Moreover, al-Qa'ida uses terrorism to gain publicity and further its goals. Typically, the US government's policy is not to negotiate with terrorists. However, US efforts to kill or capture key leaders, including Osama bin Laden's demise in 2011, and its attempts to undermine al-Qa'ida's ideology affirm this group as an entity that the United States is committed to confronting. Likewise, US actions affect al-Qa'ida's operations, its ideology, and its appeal in the Muslim world. Put simply, by fighting al-Qa'ida—and by al-Qa'ida responding to these actions—the United States has a relationship with the al-Qa'ida phenomenon.

US relations with al-Qa'ida are directly related to how it understands this adversary. Considerable attention has been paid to fighting al-Qa'ida as an organization through targeting its leadership, freezing its assets, and attempting to deny it sanctuary in Afghanistan and Pakistan. The US government has also seen the importance of undermining al-Qa'ida's message and reaching out to the Muslim world in an attempt to fight al-Qa'ida's appeal. However, actions taken to fight one aspect of al-Qa'ida, particularly using force to target its leadership and denying the organization sanctuary, may actually be helping al-Qa'ida and increasing its popularity. US relations with al-Qa'ida, therefore, need to include strategies that undermine the organization while delegitimating its message and reducing its appeal in the Muslim world. This is no small task.

DEFINING THE AL-QA'IDA PHENOMENON

Perhaps the greatest challenge for the United States in addressing the threat posed by al-Qa'ida is developing a comprehensive understanding of the phenomenon. Al-Qa'ida has at least three distinct manifestations: a terrorist organization, an ideology, and a social movement. Perhaps more confounding, these dimensions are not mutually exclusive. All work to reinforce one another as a phenomenon that inspires, directs, and takes action. Each of these aspects requires definition in order to better understand al-Qa'ida.

Prior to September 11, and particularly between 1996 and 2001, most analysts agree that al-Qa'ida was an organization; it had leaders and a hierarchical structure, and it was headquartered in Afghanistan.[1] Al-Qa'ida's leader, Osama bin Laden, was well-known to the world prior to the attacks in New York and Washington, DC. Bin Laden began to gain notoriety in the 1980s through his involvement with the Soviet-Afghan war. Tales of his courage, heroism, and miraculous survival against a better-armed adversary were recounted by ideologue Sheikh Azzam in *Al Jihad* magazine and through the Arab media.[2] After the Soviet withdrawal from Afghanistan, bin Laden articulated al-Qa'ida's vision by issuing statements through the Advice and Reform Committee, a London-based center that aimed to revive the Muslim world and challenge the Saudi royal family.[3] Bin Laden also gained notoriety through terrorist actions. The 1998 US embassy bombings in Africa and the 2000 attack on the USS *Cole* alerted the United States to bin Laden's potential as an international terrorist, placing him on the FBI's most wanted list.

Al-Qa'ida has also benefited from the leadership of Egyptian physician Ayman al-Zawahiri. The founder of a radical Islamist group in Egypt, Zawahiri brought to the organization knowledge on recruitment and structuring as well as coordinating and executing operations.[4] Zawahiri also added to al-Qa'ida's vision, writing his own statements, including *Knights Under the Prophet's Banner*, *Bitter Harvest*, and *Loyalty and Separation*.[5]

Aside from its visible leaders, al-Qa'ida also has an organizational structure that allows it to plan, train, and execute deadly attacks and project its force around the globe. During the Afghan-Soviet war, bin Laden, along with his mentor Sheikh Azzam, founded a safe house and training center for incoming mujahideen, the Beit al-Ansar, later to become the Maktab al-Khidamat (MAK), which sought to recruit individuals to aid in the war and keep records on international fighters that came through their training camps.[6] This organization evolved into al-Qa'ida (the "base") in 1986, which recruited, trained, and organized fighters for transnational jihad. The al-Qa'ida organization has an *emir*, bin Laden, a second in command, Zawahiri, a chief operations officer, an individual in charge of public relations ("Abu Reuters"), and other executives with specified tasks.[7] Bin Laden and his cohorts turned the recruitment and training for jihad into what Peter Bergen dubs "Holy War, Inc.," a multinational jihad corporation.[8]

Finally, prior to September 11, al-Qa'ida's central leadership had a location. Bin Laden spent time in the Sudan between 1992 and 1996, but it was al-Qa'ida's operational base in Afghanistan that allowed it to prosper as an organization and recruit, train, and plan operations. Policy analysts Daniel Benjamin and Steven Simon go so far as to argue: "In Afghanistan, al-Qa'ida was, in truth, a state. It controlled territory, maintained an army and waged war, forged alliances, taxed and spent and enforced a system of law."[9] Following the initiation of Operation Enduring Freedom in Afghanistan in October 2001, al-Qa'ida's statelike structure was disbanded, but its persistence as a functioning organization—although compromised—persists.

Perhaps more important than al-Qa'ida's organization and operational capabilities is its ideology, which will outlive its leaders and current cadre of supporters. Al-Qa'ida's ideology is powerful because it is the continuation of a narrative that has its antecedents in ideologues that stretch back to the 1920s, including Hassan al-Banna (the founder of the Muslim Brotherhood in 1928), Abu al-Ala'a Mawdudi (the founder of Jamaat-i-islami), Sayyid Qutb (author of *In the Shade of the Quran* and *Milestones*), Muhammad Abd al-Salam Faraj (author of *The Forgotten Obligation*), and Sheikh Abdullah Yusuf Azzam (the ideologue of the Afghan Jihad and bin Laden's mentor).

The foremost theme of al-Qa'ida's ideology is an urgent sense of threat, the perception that Islam is gravely endangered by internal and external enemies. Muslims have strayed from the true path of Islam, and corrupt Muslim leadership, seduced by the West, is to blame for this crisis. Bin Laden holds up Saudi Arabia as the premier example of wayward Muslim leadership and its effects on the *ummah*, the worldwide Muslim community. His first public statement, "An Open Letter to King Fahd," argues that the Saudi government has violated *tawhid*, the oneness of God, by creating laws that diverge from shari'a, Islamic law.[10] These ideas build on the arguments of Banna, Qutb, and Mawdudi, who all argue that Western ideologies have polluted the Muslim world and diverted it from its one, true ideology—Islam.[11] The model for the Islamic polity is the first Muslim community, the Prophet, his Companions, and the first four Caliphs, which governed the unified *ummah* and propagated the faith.[12] Ultimately an Islamic system should recognize *hakimiyah* and *tawhid*, the sovereignty and oneness of God, undivided by human innovation and ambition.

In addition to corrupt Muslim leadership threatening the *ummah*, an international conspiracy consisting, according to Zawahiri, of "the United Nations; the servile rulers of the Muslim peoples; multinational corporations; international news agencies and satellite media channels; international relief agencies and nongovernmental organizations, which are used as a cover for espionage, conspiracies, proselytizing and arms smuggling," is attacking Islam.[13] Despite the long list of perpetrators, the preeminent foreign threat is the United States, which has showed its intentions by spreading its morally corrupt culture and bankrupt ideology of democracy around the globe. America has attempted to achieve these objectives through a combination of economic domination, placing troops in the Muslim world—particularly in the noble sanctuary of Saudi Arabia—and its wars in Iraq and Afghanistan.[14]

Bin Laden and Zawahiri claim that in order for corrupt Muslim leaders to be overthrown, their international supporters—namely, the United States—must first be attacked and compelled to retreat.[15] According to bin Laden:

> The time has come for Muslim people to realize after these attacks [Desert Fox] that the states of the region do not have their own sovereignty. For our enemies disporting themselves in our seas and on our lands and in our airspace, striking without anyone's permission . . . but these other regimes, they no longer have any real power. They are either colluding with America and Britain or have lost the power to do anything against this barefaced occupation.[16]

Bin Laden asserts that Western powers—specifically the United States, Britain, and Israel—are preventing jihadis from toppling Muslim regimes. No change in the Muslim world—the "near enemy"—can come without attacking this "far" enemy first.

In order to realize the true path, the faithful must rise up to restore Islam to its rightful place as the foundation of society and government and to unify the worldwide Muslim community. Jihad is not only permissible but necessary for returning the Muslim world from its fallen state. In *Knights Under the Prophet's Banner*, Zawahiri contends that "no solution is possible without jihad."[17]

Once Muslim insurgents establish a foothold in the Muslim world through jihad, their influence will spread and win Muslims throughout the *ummah* to their cause, ultimately creating a united Muslim nation under the leadership of a restored caliphate. Zawahiri argues:

> Liberating the Muslim nation, confronting the enemies of Islam, and launching jihad against them require a Muslim authority, established on a Muslim land, that raises the banner of jihad and rallies the Muslims around it. Without achieving this goal our actions will mean nothing more than a mere and repeated disturbances that will not lead to the aspired goal, which is the restoration of the caliphate and the dismissal of the invaders from the land of Islam. This goal must remain the basic objective of the Islamic jihad movement, regardless of the sacrifices and the time involved.[18]

Zawahiri goes on to argue: "The jihad movement must follow a plan aimed at establishing an Islamic state it can defend on a territory in the Muslim world; from there, it will lead the struggle to restore the rightly guided caliphate after the Prophet's model."[19]

Al-Qa'ida's vision, therefore, is for a mass social movement, for the Muslim world to rise up and, through jihad, establish a unified and free *ummah* that is governed by a rightly guided caliph and, ultimately, by God. Zawahiri confirms this goal, stating: "In short, the jihad movement must enter the battle in midst of the community and lead it to the battle field. It must guard against isolating itself from its community in an elitist battle against the authorities."[20] The Terrorist Perspectives Project, which analyzes captured al-Qaʾida documents, further echoes that al-Qaʾidaʾs senior leadership sees itself as a social movement: "Al Qaida and its theological brethren believe that in order to realize a "restored" caliphate, they must unify the *ummah* under the banner of Salafi Jihadism. Central to that objective—almost its defining characteristic—is the creation and growth of a movement with a revolutionary vanguard, marching at its head."[21]

Critical to al-Qaʾidaʾs desire to be a social movement is its appeal to Muslims around the globe. Al-Qaʾida aims to be the vanguard of pure Islam and to facilitate the *ummah*ʾs reunion as one body that transcends race, ethnicity, and nationality. In order to achieve these ends, al-Qaʾida needs to be seen as legitimate and its jihad justified. One means for achieving this legitimacy is by provoking the United States into actions that appear to validate al-Qaʾidaʾs ideological claims that it is out to destroy Islam. Al-Qaʾida leadership has claimed that the wars in Afghanistan and Iraq demonstrate these hostile intentions and require all Muslims to rise up in defensive jihad against this aggression.[22]

Al-Qaʾida has inspired loosely affiliated groups around the globe to answer the call for jihad. Al-Qaʾida in Iraq emerged shortly following the initiation of Operation Iraqi Freedom in 2003. Also in 2003, the Algerian Salafist Group for Preaching and Combat (GSPC) forged an alliance with al-Qaʾida, becoming the al-Qaʾida Organization in the Islamic Maghreb. In 2009 jihadi groups in Yemen and Saudi Arabia merged to found al-Qaʾida in the Arabian Peninsula (AQAP), which includes the US-born Muslim cleric Anwar al-Awlaki. Alongside these emerging al-Qaʾida affiliates, specific attacks have been carried out under the banner of al-Qaʾida. The 2004 Madrid bombing, the 2008 London bombings, the November 2009 shooting attacks at Fort Hood, the foiled 2009 Christmas "underwear" bomber, the failed 2010 bombing attempt on Times Square in New York, and the 2010 intercepted printer cartridge bombs all claim to be inspired by al-Qaʾidaʾs ideology and, in the latter incidents, Awlakiʾs preaching.[23]

However, al-Qaʾida senior leadership has also expressed concern for affiliates that execute operations that turn average Muslims away from their cause. Communiqués between strategists reveal considerable frustration over foot soldiersʾ lack of strategic vision and their "thirst for martyrdom."[24] *Takfiri* violence—actions that target wayward Muslims—is an example of operations that do not sit well with the larger Muslim *ummah*. For example, a November 2005 series of suicide attacks on Western hotels in Amman, Jordan, killed over sixty people, mostly Muslims; the attacks prompted street protests condemning the acts.[25] Similarly, operations directed by al-Qaʾida in Iraq against Shias and uncooperative Sunnis provoked angry letters from senior al-Qaʾida leadership, demanding that the al-Qaʾida leader in Iraq, Abu Musab Zarqawi, stop targeting other Muslims.[26]

Each of these manifestations of the al-Qaʾida phenomenon—as an organization, an ideology, and a social movement—has presented challenges and opportunities for US relations with al-Qaʾida and its affiliate movements. As the following section will show, US actions toward al-Qa'ida have focused most heavily on defeating the organization, with less attention paid to its ideology and almost no attention given to al-Qa'ida's aims to create a social movement.

US RELATIONS WITH AL-QA'IDA: 1998–2011

US efforts to counter the al-Qa'ida phenomenon have focused primarily on dismantling the organization by capturing or killing its leaders, freezing its financial assets, and denying the organization sanctuary in Afghanistan. Targeting al-Qa'ida's leaders and assets has undoubtedly affected the organization's capabilities. However, this approach has also helped to feed al-Qa'ida's ideology and possibly strengthen its efforts to foment a social movement; therefore, the United States has done relatively little to undermine these aspects of the al-Qa'ida phenomenon.

Following the African embassy bombings in 1998, the 2000 USS *Cole* bombing, and the September 11 attacks, the Clinton and Bush administrations focused their efforts on destroying al-Qa'ida as an organization. In response to the 2008 African embassy bombings, the Clinton administration used missile strikes to target al-Qa'ida training camps in Afghanistan and an alleged chemical weapons facility in Sudan.[27] Within weeks of the September 11 attacks, the US government targeted bin Laden and al-Qa'ida's financial assets as a means of disrupting their terrorist capabilities. The Bush administration froze an estimated $138 billion in terrorist financial assets by the end of 2003. Some claimed the loss of capital had limited al-Qa'ida's capabilities, while others argued that it had little to no effect.[28]

In addition to freezing financial assets, the Bush administration targeted al-Qa'ida's leadership and key operatives. Within the first two years of September 11, the administration claimed to have killed or captured nearly twenty core members of the organization, including the believed number three in command, Muhammad Atef (killed in Afghanistan as part of OEF in 2001), his replacement Abu Zubaydah (captured in Pakistan in 2002), the putative architect of the September 11 attacks, Khaled Sheikh Muhammad (captured in Pakistan in 2003), and al-Nashiri, the operations chief and architect of the 1998 US embassy bombings in Africa and the 2000 attack on the USS *Cole* (captured in the Arabian Peninsula in 2002).[29] Efforts to kill or capture al-Qa'ida leaders have continued to be a central component of US operations. Under the Barack Obama administration, attacks in Pakistan have increased dramatically, killing senior leaders—including Osama bin Laden in 2011 (which occurred as the book was going to press)—and destroying safe houses.[30]

The United States has also focused on denying al-Qa'ida physical sanctuary. Operation Enduring Freedom (OEF) aimed to depose of the Taliban regime in Afghanistan and deny a safe haven to al-Qa'ida. Although OEF accomplished both objectives within weeks of the invasion, key leaders of al-Qa'ida have managed to hold some operational control over the organization in neighboring Pakistan, and its leaders have continued to issue public statements broadcast to the world. Al-

Qa'ida, therefore, has demonstrated that it is organizationally and operationally resilient.

US actions aimed at freezing assets, attacking the leadership, and denying the organization sanctuary have had an effect on al-Qa'ida, but the extent to which its command and control has been affected is debated. On one hand, the 2007 National Intelligence Estimate asserted that:

> We assess that greatly increased worldwide counterterrorism efforts over the past five years have constrained the ability of al-Qa'ida to attack the US Homeland again and have led terrorist groups to perceive the Homeland as a harder target to strike than on September 11th. Al-Qa'ida is and will remain the most serious terrorist threat to the Homeland, as its central leadership continues to plan high-impact plots, while pushing others in extremist Sunni communities to mimic its efforts and to supplement its capabilities.[31]

Similarly, former CIA analyst Bruce Riedel argues that "Bin Laden continues to influence its direction and provide general guidance and, on occasion, specific instructions. But overall the movement is more loosely structured, which leaves more room for independent and copycat terrorist operations."[32] Marc Sageman describes al-Qa'ida's organization, what he calls "al-Qa'ida central," as "degraded" from the result of OEF and attacks on its leadership.[33] And 2010 comments from CIA director Leon Panetta claim that, "It's pretty clear from all the intelligence we are getting that they [al-Qa'ida] are having a very difficult time putting together any kind of command and control, that they are scrambling. And that we really do have them on the run."[34]

However, attacks on al-Qa'ida's leadership and sanctuary have also had unintended consequences, some of which have aided and some of which have harmed US goals and interests. In the short term, the weakening of al-Qa'ida's leadership and reduction of command and control may have launched "loose cannons," semi-independent operators who carry out attacks without senior al-Qa'ida leadership's consent. These attacks have inflicted pain on those targeted, but they have also been controversial with Muslim populations. As previously mentioned, operators like Zarqawi in Iraq were undermining al-Qa'ida's appeal to local Muslims, and bigger operations, such as the 2008 Amman attacks, were appalling to Muslims around the globe. Although the short-term consequences of these operations are detrimental to the countries in which they occur, the long-term effects may be beneficial to US goals of undermining al-Qa'ida and its appeal. US intelligence forecasting in 2008 suggested that support for al-Qa'ida is declining, "having alienated Muslim supporters with indiscriminate killing and inattention to the practical problems of poverty, unemployment and education."[35]

However, attacking al-Qa'ida as an organization, using military means to target the leadership and deny sanctuary, may also be feeding al-Qa'ida's ideology.

Al-Qa'ida claims that the Western world, particularly the United States, is out to destroy Islam through military, economic, and cultural means. Polling data suggest that the wars in Afghanistan and Iraq have helped fuel perceptions that the United States is targeting the Muslim world, and that further US military action is possible.[36] Similarly, attacks on Muslim leadership in the tribal areas of Pakistan are also believed to be fueling anti-American sentiment and perceptions that these operations are killing mostly innocent civilians.[37] In other words, US operations aimed at destroying al-Qa'ida as an organization may be legitimating its ideological claims.[38]

In addition to, and independent from, US efforts to destroy al-Qa'ida's organization, the US government has also developed programs to fight al-Qa'ida's ideology, although these efforts have been less of a priority than attacking the organization. In the wake of September 11, the Bush administration hired Charlotte Beers, a New York–based advertising executive, to work on promoting a better image of the United States to the Muslim world. Under Beers's direction, the State Department produced documentaries on Muslims in America to be distributed abroad, and it launched Radio Sawa, an Arabic-language radio station broadcast throughout the Middle East. Beers resigned in March 2003 after her campaign was criticized for not understanding its target audience and achieving little to no visible results.[39]

In June 2007—nearly six years after September 11—the Strategic Communication and Public Diplomacy Policy Coordinating Center (PCC) of the State Department issued the *US National Strategy for Public Diplomacy and Strategic Communication,* which aims to set the agenda for an information campaign to counter al-Qa'ida and other anti-American extremist messages. The document stresses the importance of emphasizing the US values to the world through promoting "democratization . . . amplifying mainstream Muslim voices . . . isolating and discrediting terrorist leaders . . . delegitimizing terror . . . [and] demonstrating that the West is open to all religions and is not in conflict with any faith." The PCC further argues that "America must offer a positive vision of hope and opportunity that is rooted in our most basic values. These values include our deep belief in freedom, and the dignity and equality of every person."[40]

This document assumes that Western and US values are viewed as hope and liberty by the rest of the world, that the United States is "a light unto the nations." However, the desire to promote US values abroad often does not take seriously the extent to which US foreign policy actions and motives are suspect in the Muslim world. Al-Qa'ida claims that it has the true, authentic, and correct path for Muslims and that the West is out to undermine the faith through political, economic, and cultural means. In essence, the PCC plays into al-Qa'ida's game, where values and the Muslim way of life are being threatened by the imposition of foreign values. This approach, in other words, validates al-Qa'ida's claims. Describing the fight against al-Qa'ida in these terms creates a zero-sum environment for Muslims, where they have to choose between a country whose policies they find suspect and an organization with an extreme interpretation of Islam.

Beginning in 2009, the Obama administration made several ch;
oric with the aim of improving the US image abroad and possib
Qa'ida's message. The administration began describing military
al-Qa'ida and other threats as "overseas contingency operations,
the term "global war on terror." In June 2009, President Obama gave a spee-
Cairo that also aimed to change the rhetoric between the United States and the
Muslim world and introduce "a new beginning":

> I've come here to Cairo to seek a new beginning between the United States
> and Muslims around the world, one based on mutual interest and mutual
> respect, and one based upon the truth that America and Islam are not ex-
> clusive and need not be in competition. Instead, they overlap, and share
> common principles—principles of justice and progress; tolerance and the
> dignity of all human beings.[41]

The 2010 *National Security Strategy* continues to emphasize the importance of
US values, but argues that the United States should "lead by example" and work
to restore its image as a global leader. "Our moral leadership is grounded principally
in the power of our example—not through an effort to impose our system on other
peoples."[42] The Obama administration also established a new unit in the State Department aimed at countering Taliban and al-Qa'ida messaging in Afghanistan and
Pakistan.[43]

US efforts to counter al-Qa'ida's message, however, have received sharp criticism
from policy and academic circles, and debate continues over how to effectively
fight its ideology.[44] In 2009, Admiral Mike Mullen published an article in *Joint
Forces Quarterly* that is highly critical of US communications efforts, especially to
the Muslim world: "I would argue that most strategic communication problems
are not communication problems at all, they are policy and execution problems.
Each time we fail to live up to our values or don't follow up on a promise, we look
more and more like the arrogant Americans the enemy claims we are."[45] In addition
to receiving domestic criticism, US efforts to counter al-Qa'ida's message do not
appear to be resonating with Muslims around the globe. Pew polling data from
2010 suggests that Muslims throughout the world remain suspicious of US actions
and intentions.[46]

If programs to counter al-Qa'ida's ideology have proven ineffective, US efforts
to fight al-Qa'ida as a potential social movement have been virtually nonexistent.
The lack of attention paid to countering al-Qa'ida's goals of creating a social movement stem, in part, from a failure to understand al-Qa'ida's message. Al-Qa'ida
aims to inspire more than terrorist cells around the globe. Its ideology is a call for
mass participation to drive back domestic and international threats to the faith
and to (re)create a social and political system based on Islam.[47] It is a promise for
a consistent, pious, and authentic existence based on God's justice, free of Western
influences, which have polluted Muslim society, corrupted its leaders, wreaked

economic havoc, and threatened the community's very existence with war. In other words, al-Qa'ida's message promises a better way of life. Most of al-Qa'ida's message, as previously noted, is not new but builds on a persistent call for the return to the right path of Islam.

In the aftermath of September 11, the United States has attempted to improve the lives of average Muslims by spreading "human dignity," democracy, and open economies. The *National Security Strategy, 2006* echoed these priorities, claiming that US security extends from "promoting freedom, justice, and human dignity—working to end tyranny, to promote effective democracies, and to extend prosperity through free and fair trade and wise development policies" and "confronting the challenges of our time by leading a growing community of democracies."[48]

The assumption in promoting Western values, democracy, and an open economy is that these outcomes will create political space, individual liberty, and economic prosperity. In short, spreading democracy and open economies will produce a better life for recipients and subsequently US security will be enhanced. In practice, however, much of the Muslim world heard these promises after achieving independence from colonial rule. These ends were not delivered, however, which produced frustration and disillusionment.[49] Moreover, while Westerners may see democracy as a universal right, some citizens of non-Western countries view this system as an unwelcome imposition or even Christian proselytizing, since it emanates from the West.[50] Al-Qa'ida echoes this sentiment. Zawahiri argues that "in Islam, legislation comes from God; in a democracy, this capacity is given to the people. Therefore, this is a new religion, based on making the people into gods and giving them God's rights and attributes."[51]

The 2010–2011 Jasmine Revolution in Tunisia and Egypt's Purity Protests that ousted President Hosni Mubarak present, however, an interesting development for the prospects of democracy in Muslim states. In both countries, social movements employed peaceful protests to topple decades-long dictators, throwing into question al-Qa'ida's maxim that change can come only through jihad. Moreover, protesters in both countries called for free and fair elections, press freedoms, civil liberties, transparent rule of law, and national unity. Both countries, in other words, have called for the foundations of democracy.

Significantly, these developments occurred without US support or actions and, in fact, took Washington by surprise. The protests and demands for more democratic regimes came from within these countries and, therefore, can be embraced as authentic.

In the near term, these revolutions—and the subsequent protests they have sparked in nearby states—could undermine al-Qa'ida's message and appeal because they are borne out of fundamentally different means and goals. Expectations for political change that bring about greater liberties and a better way of life are, however, high throughout the region. If new governments fail to meet these expectations, disillusionment could become a breeding ground for alternative ideologies, including al-Qa'ida's.

STRATEGIES FOR FIGHTING
THE AL-QA'IDA PHENOMENON

In order to truly defeat the al-Qa'ida phenomenon, the United States needs to fight more than just the organization and its leadership. US efforts also need to include a rigorous program to undermine the ideology and reduce the popular appeal of al-Qa'ida's message. Moreover, these efforts need to be coordinated. The challenge for the United States in its fight against al-Qa'ida is to find a means to target the organization and other groups that claim a connection to al-Qa'ida in a way that does not validate their ideology and attract Muslims to its camp. This is a difficult task, but the United States has options for realizing a holistic approach.

First, killing al-Qa'ida's leaders is an important and effective tool for undermining the organization, but this approach comes with problematic side effects, including making martyrs of those killed and lending credence to al-Qa'ida's ideology. In any event, there are numerous al-Qa'ida cadres ready and willing to step into leadership positions. The United States, however, has other options for undermining the leadership. In particular, the United States could learn from its efforts to undermine the Kremlin and Politburo during the cold war. At the advent of the cold war, the Truman administration launched programs aimed at better understanding the power dynamics within the Communist Party—and the Kremlin in particular—with the hopes of exploiting weaknesses in the Soviet leadership. The Eisenhower administration launched a series of operations following the death of Josef Stalin that attempted to foment mistrust and discontent within the Politburo, including Operation Overload, Delay, and Cancellation. The United States also initiated Operation Engross, which encouraged high-level members of the Communist Party to defect and weaken the resolve of the leadership.[52]

Similarly today, the United States could create programs that seek to undermine al-Qa'ida's leadership by exploiting defectors and creating a sense of mistrust within its ranks. Just as jihadi war vets who return from battle are important for recruitment back in their home countries, so their defections are important for debunking the myths of the glory of jihad. Several prominent figures in the global jihad movement have renounced al-Qa'ida's ideology and operations. The Algerian Abdullah Anas was one of al-Qa'ida's first heroes of the Afghan-Soviet war and became a key player in al-Qa'ida's service bureau, the Maktab Al Khidamat. Following the war—and the assassination of Sheikh Azzam, his father-in-law—Anas had a falling-out with bin Laden, whom he accused of killing Azzam. Anas has since renounced al-Qa'ida and its goal of global jihad to change the Muslim world.[53] Following more than a decade in prison, members of the Egyptian Gama't Islamiyya drafted a series of books critiquing the jihadi approach, including al-Qa'ida's use of violence, and published them in a London-based Arabic newspaper.[54] In 2007, Dr. al-Fadl, a member of the Egyptian Islamic Jihad, followed with a similar renunciation of violence and critique of al-Qa'ida's theology and tactics.[55] These defectors are important for debunking heroic myths of al-Qa'ida and its leaders, the ideology, and for exposing fissures within the organization.

Furthermore, defectors and other sources describe tensions between different leaders in al-Qa'ida, especially the Egyptian members of the organization—headed by Zawahiri—and the Saudi constituents, led by bin Laden.[56] These persisting debates within the leadership provide valuable opportunities for the United States to exploit. The overall goal would be to undermine confidence within the organization, sow fear and mistrust, and evoke debate. This process may be slower than killing the leadership, but it could both undermine the organization and delegitimate its message.

The biggest threat to al-Qa'ida's ideology is a debate. Al-Qa'ida claims to have the one and only true interpretation of the faith and the correct path for realizing a unified *ummah*. Debate over the validity of these claims, in and of itself, introduces doubt into al-Qa'ida's claims. The United States can play an indirect role in fostering debate by providing information that exposes the inconsistencies of al-Qa'ida's message. For example, the West Point Combating Terrorism Center website posts reports that describe debates within al-Qa'ida over strategies and tactics, and it publishes primary documents captured from al-Qa'ida. These documents reveal critical debates within jihadi circles over the right to kill fellow Muslims and the progress that al-Qa'ida has made in realizing its vision. In 2008 Zawahiri denounced the works of CTC as Western propaganda, suggesting that he felt compelled to challenge their accusations.[57]

As for its aspirations to foment a social movement that will transform the Muslim world, al-Qa'ida may be its own worst enemy. Certain operations, especially those that cause Muslim casualties, appear to be turning the *ummah* against al-Qa'ida's cause. Furthermore, al-Qa'ida does not use social outreach as a means of caring for its constituents and calling people to their interpretation of the faith. Its lack of care for communities and average Muslims, compared with more moderate Islamist movements, will likely hinder its growth as a social movement. Finally, in the few places where al-Qa'ida has actually controlled territory and governed people, its rule was unpopular. This was especially true with al-Qa'ida in Iraq and its tenure as governor in Anbar province. Although al-Qa'ida was originally welcomed by the local population to fight Coalition Forces, its use of brutal measures to keep the population in line—including beheadings, forced marriages between foreign fighters and local girls, and the assassination of several prominent sheiks—prompted the Anbar Awakening, an alliance with Coalition Forces to oust al-Qa'ida from Iraq.[58] Its aspirations to spearhead a social movement, therefore, seem unlikely in the face of such examples.

The change in al-Qa'ida's command and control structure, caused in large part by US operations against the organization, appears to have helped set the stage for these self-destructive operations: a good thing for the United States. However, US operations against al-Qa'ida also appear to be garnering sympathy for the organization and fueling anti-American sentiment. This is true of not only

US conventional wars but also covert operations that target the leadership. Operations in 2010 against al-Qa'ida and the Taliban in the tribal areas of Pakistan angered the local population and prompted the Pakistani government to close its borders with Afghanistan, hindering the movement of fuel and other resources to US troops in the region.[59] The May 2011 targeted assassination of Osama bin Laden, while an important intelligence and operational victory and a boon to US morale, has not spelled the end of al-Qa'ida. Key leaders remain. As importantly, al-Qa-ida's message persists and threatens to inspire new leaders to mobilize new movements.

Ultimately the United States needs to develop a coordinated strategy that targets the many manifestations of al-Qa'ida. Developing such a strategy requires, first, a holistic understanding of what al-Qa'ida is and what it is trying to do. Academic and policy circles have made considerable strides in understanding the al-Qa'ida phenomenon since September 11. Likewise, it is important to better understand the aspirations of different Muslim populations. The 2010–2011 revolutions in Tunisia and Egypt demonstrate that democratic values and goals are not incompatible with Islam, and that the people want political and social changes that are in line with US values. However, these protests came from within, not from US efforts to promote democratic revolution. Muslims around the globe most likely remain mistrustful of US intentions, including US aspirations to spread democracy. For democracy to take hold and delegitimize al-Qa'ida's ideology, liberal principles need to be embraced as authentic. The US government should therefore resist the temptation to identify these changes as inspired by US policies or actions, which could compromise their authenticity.

Simultaneously working to defeat the al-Qa'ida leadership, its capabilities, its message, and its appeal in the Muslim world requires a coordinated effort. No one department in the US government owns the fight against al-Qa'ida. The Defense Department has led the first decade of efforts to destroy al-Qa'ida post–September 11, but other agencies have also played an important role in the battle, including the State Department, Justice Department, Treasury Department, CIA, and other government assets. The private sector and the arts may also have a role to play in fighting al-Qa'ida, as they did in fighting communism during the cold war.[60] Furthermore, because al-Qa'ida is an international phenomenon, reducing its threat and appeal will require working with other countries and building international alliances. Ultimately, a successful strategy to defeat al-Qa'ida requires, first, a comprehensive understanding of the phenomenon and, second, a coordinated interagency and international effort that fights the organization, delegitimizes its message, and positively engages Muslim populations.

Does the United States have the patience to do all of this? The forty-five-year cold war suggests that it does. Undermining ideology is difficult but not impossible. The United States fought a long cold war that, in part, aimed to undermine the appeal of communism around the globe, a goal that it achieved through persistent, concerted effort and an understanding of its adversary.

Notes

1. See, for example: *Jason Burke, Al Qa'ida: Casting a Shadow of Terror* (London: I. B. Taurus, 2003), pp. 10–13; and *Terrorist Perspectives Project: Strategic and Operational Views of Al Qaida and Associated Movements*, ed. Mark E. Stout et al. (Annapolis: Naval Institute Press, 2008), p. 32.

2. Peter L. Bergen, *The Osama bin Laden I Know* (New York: Free Press, 2006), p. 50.

3. Also known as the Advice and Reformation Committee. See *Messages to the World: The Statements of Osama bin Laden*, ed. Bruce Lawrence, transl. James Howarth (New York: Verso, 2005), p. 3; Peter L. Bergen, *Holy War, Inc.: Inside the Secret World of Osama bin Laden* (New York: Touchstone, 2002), pp. 91–92.

4. Lawrence Wright, *The Looming Tower: Al Qa'ida and the Road to 9–11* (New York: Knopf, 2007), pp. 37–59. See also Lawrence Wright, "The Man Behind bin Laden: How an Egyptian Doctor Became a Master of Terror," *New Yorker*, September 16, 2002.

5. For excerpts of Zawahiri's writings, see *Al Qa'ida in Its Own Words*, ed. Gilles Kepel and Jean-Pierre Milelli (Cambridge: Belknap, 2008), pp. 171–236.

6. Peter L. Bergen, *Holy War*, p. 51; Wright, *Looming Tower*, pp. 94–98; Anonymous, *Through Our Enemies' Eyes: Osama bin Laden, Radical Islam, and the Future of America* (Washington, DC: Brassey's, 2002), pp. 98–102.

7. "Cracks in the Foundation: Leadership Schisms in Al-Qaida from 1998–2006," Combating Terrorism Center at West Point, September 2007.

8. Taken from the title of Bergen's book.

9. Daniel Benjamin and Steven Simon, *The Age of Sacred Terror* (New York: Random House, 2002), p. 169.

10. Osama bin Laden, "Open Letter to bin Baz," *Messages to the World*, p. 8.

11. Brynjar Lia, *The Society of Muslim Brothers in Egypt* (Ithaca: Ithaca Press, 1998), esp. pp. 54–60; John L. Esposito, *Islamic Threat: Myth or Reality?* (New York: Oxford University Press, 1992), p. 121.

12. Charles J. Adams, "Mawdudi and the Islamic State," in *Voices of Resurgent Islam*, ed. John L. Esposito (New York: Oxford University Press, 1983), pp. 112–114.

13. Zawahiri, "Knights Under the Prophet's Banner," in *Al Qa'ida in Its Own Words*, p. 193.

14. See, for example, Osama bin Laden, "Jihad Against Jews and Crusaders," World Islamic Front Statement, February 23, 1998.

15. Fawas Gerges, *The Far Enemy: Why Jihad Went Global* (New York: Cambridge University Press, 2005), pp. 1–15.

16. Osama bin Laden, interview by Al Jazeera, 1998, in *Messages to the World*, p. 68.

17. Zawahiri, "Knights Under the Prophet's Banner," pp. 194–195.

18. Zawahiri, "Knights Under the Prophet's Banner," pts. 1–11.

19. Zawahiri, "Knights Under the Prophet's Banner," pp. 198–199.

20. Zawahiri, "Knights Under the Prophet's Banner," p. 196.

21. *Terrorist Perspectives Project*, p. 34.

22. *Terrorist Perspectives Project*, pp. 145–146.

23. See, for example, "People: Anwar al-Awlaki," *New York Times*, August 4, 2010.

24. *Terrorist Perspectives Project*, p. 48.

25. See, for example, "Dozens Held over Jordan Bombings," BBC News, November 11, 2005.

26. *Terrorist Perspectives Project*, pp. 21–22.

27. This was Operation Infinite Reach. See Wright, *Looming Tower*, pp. 281–286; and Bergen, *Holy War*, pp. 108–129.

28. One of the goals of the Patriot Act, which President Bush signed into law on October 26, 2002, is to target terrorist financing. See "Anti Money Laundering," US Commodities Futures Training Commission, October 25, 2010. See also Douglas Farah, "Al Qa'ida's Finances Ample, Say Probers," *Washington Post*, December 14, 2003.

29. For a list of captured al-Qa'ida operatives, see "Hunt for Al-Qaida: Al-Qaida Dead or Captured," MSNBC Online, November 18, 2010; "Fact Box: Major al Qa'ida Leaders Killed or Captured," Reuters, May 1, 2008; "Who's Who in al-Qa'ida," BBC Online, April 27, 2007.

30. Candace Rondeax, "Suspected US Missile Strike Kills at Least 20 in Pakistan," *Washington Post*, January 23, 2009; "CIA Steps Up Drone Attacks in Pakistan: WSJ," *The Express Tribune*, October 3, 2010; Rob Crilly, "Al Qa'ida Pakistan Operations Director Killed in Drone Attacks," *Telegraph*, September 28, 2010.

31. "The Terrorist Threat to US Homeland," National Intelligence Estimate, July 2007.

32. Bruce Riedel, "Al Qa'ida Fights Back," *Foreign Affairs*, May-June 2007, p. 24.

33. Marc Sageman, *Leaderless Jihad: Terror Networks in the Twenty-First Century* (Philadelphia: University of Pennsylvania Press, 2008), p. 126.

34. Joby Warrick and Peter Finn, "CIA Director Says Secret Attacks in Pakistan Have Hobbled Al-Qa'ida," *Washington Post*, March 18, 2010.

35. Scott Shane, "Global Forecast by American Intelligence Expects Al Qa'ida's Appeal to Falter," *New York Times*, November 20, 2008.

36. "America's Image Slips, but Allies Share US Concerns Over Iran, Hamas," Pew Global Attitudes Project, June 13, 2006.

37. "Poll: Pakistan Tribal Areas Oppose US Strikes," CBS News, October 1, 2010.

38. Heather S. Gregg, "Fighting Cosmic Warriors: Lessons from the First Seven Years of the Global War on Terror," *Studies in Conflict and Terrorism* 32, no. 3 (2009): 188–208.

39. Jane Perlez, "Muslim-as-Apple-Pie Videos Are Greeted with Skepticism, *New York Times*, October 30, 2002; Karen De Young, "Bush to Create Formal Office to Shape US Image Abroad," *Washington Post*, July 30, 2002; Alexandra Starr, "Charlotte Beers' Toughest Sell," *BusinessWeek* online, December 17, 2001.

40. "U.S National Strategy for Public Diplomacy and Strategic Communication," Strategic Communication and Public Diplomacy Policy Coordinating Committee, June 2007, p. 3.

41. "Remarks by the President [Obama] on a New Beginning: Cairo University, Cairo," The White House, June 4, 2009.

42. The White House, *National Security Strategy*, May 2010, quote from p. 10.

43. Thomas Shanker, "US Plans a Mission Against Taliban Propaganda," *New York Times*, August 15, 2009.

44. See, for example, Gregg, "Fighting the Jihad of the Pen," *Terrorism and Political Violence* 22, no. 2 (2010): 294–314.

45. Mike Mullen, "Strategic Communications: Getting Back to Basics," *Joint Forces Quarterly* 55 (2009).

46. Andrew Kohut, "Restoring America's Reputation in the World, *Pew Research Center Publications*, March 4, 2010.

47. There appears to be a rift in al-Qa'ida over means for achieving the new Islamic order. Zawahiri calls for an Islamic vanguard that will seize the state and impose new order from the top down, while other strategists, such as bin Laden and Naji, argue for individuals to rise up and fight to create the new order.

48. United States National Security Strategy, 2006, The White House, p. ii.

49. Esposito, *Islamic Threat*, pp. 67–76.

50. Mark Juergensmeyer, *The New Cold War: Religious Nationalism Confronts the Secular State* (Berkeley: University of California Press, 1993), esp. pp. 26–41.

51. Ayman al-Zawahiri, "Advice to Reject the Fatwa of Bin Baz," *Al Qa'ida in Its Own Words*, pp. 182–192, quote taken from p. 184. See also Wright, "The Man Behind Bin Laden."

52. Gregory Mitrovich, *Undermining the Kremlin: America's Strategy to Subvert the Soviet Bloc, 1947–1956* (Ithaca: Cornell University Press, 2000), p. 184. See also Heather S. Gregg, "Crafting a Better Grand Strategy to Fight the Global War on Terror: Lessons from the Early Years of the Cold War," *Foreign Policy Analysis*, July 2010, pp. 237–255. The success of these programs remains classified.

53. For more on Anas, see Wright, *Looming Tower*, pp. 134–135, 189; Bergen, *Osama Bin Laden*, pp. 104–105; Gerges, *The Far Enemy*, pp. 89, 137; Judith Miller, "After the Attacks: The Organizer; Bin Laden: Child of Privilege Who Champions Holy War," *New York Times*, September 14, 2001.

54. For more on Gamaat's books criticizing the use of violence and al-Qa'ida, see Chris Zambelis, "Egyptian Gama'a al-Islamiyya's Public Relations Campaign," *Terrorism Monitor*, September 12, 2006; Lisa Blaydes and Lawrence Rubin, "Ideological Reorientation and Counterterrorism: Confronting Militant Islam in Egypt," *Terrorism and Political Violence*, November 2008, pp. 1–37.

55. See also Lawrence Wright, "The Rebellion Within: Al Qa'ida Mastermind Questions Terrorism," *New Yorker*, June 2, 2008.

56. For more on fissures within the al-Qa'ida's leadership, see "Cracks in the Foundation: Leadership Schisms in Al-Qaida from 1998–2006," and "Harmony and Disharmony: Exploiting Al-Qaida's Organizational Vulnerabilities," Combating Terrorism Center at West Point, February 14, 2006.

57. "Passing Cars Can Be Heard in the Background in Al Zawahiri Video," CBS Internet Terrorism Monitor, November 28, 2008.

58. For more on the Awakening, see John A. McCary, "The Anbar Awakening: An Alliance of Incentives," *Washington Quarterly*, January 2009, pp. 43–59.

59. Dan Murphy, "Pakistan Keeps Khyber Pass Closed as US Strikes Drone On," *Christian Science Monitor*, October 5, 2010.

60. Scott Lucas, *Freedom's War: The American Crusade Against the Soviet Union* (New York: New York University Press, 1999), pp. 97–99; Liam Kennedy and Scott Lucas, "Enduring Freedom: Public Diplomacy and US Foreign Policy," *American Quarterly* 57, no. 2 (2005): 309–333, esp. p. 314.

CHAPTER 27

NEW US POLICIES FOR
A NEW MIDDLE EAST?

William B. Quandt

September 11, 2001, is one of those dates that Americans will remember and reflect on for a very long time. Did this unprecedented terrorist attack on the United States show the bankruptcy of years of US involvement in the Middle East? Many Americans seemed puzzled. "Why do they hate us so much?" became a common question. After all, don't we support peace and stability in the Middle East? Don't we promote economic development and democracy?

Paradoxically, the answer to why September 11 happened can be found not just in some of the obvious flaws in US policy in the Middle East—its support for repressive regimes, its failure to resolve the Israeli-Palestinian conflict, its sanctions against Iraq—but also must be understood, in part, as a result of the remarkable success of US policy over the preceding fifty years. Because the United States was the most powerful player in the Middle East, because so many regimes were beholden to it, Washington became the target of the grievances of all those who were unhappy with the existing order in the region. If a Saudi or an Egyptian wanted to overthrow the regimes in Riyadh or Cairo, he might try direct action against those targets. But such efforts have been thwarted quite successfully in recent years, in part because of support given to those regimes by the United States. Ironically, striking at the United States became the least dangerous means, or so it must have seemed to Osama bin Laden and his followers, to bring down the hated regimes that had done so much to weaken and corrupt Islamic political movements in the previous decade. Had all gone as planned, the United States would have reacted harshly and indiscriminately to the September 11 attacks, outraging Arab public opinion, delegitimizing pro-American regimes, and setting the stage for the eventual overthrow of the existing order.

But it seems unlikely to turn out that way. Just as Saddam Hussein in 1990 had calculated that Arab public opinion might shield him from the power of US retaliation, so must have Osama bin Laden counted on widespread support from angry Muslims throughout the region. And there was a great deal of anti-American sentiment around, both in 1990 and in 2001. But US power was not deterred, nor was it indiscriminate, and a surprisingly large number of Middle Eastern and Central Asian states ended up cooperating in the initial phase of the "war on terror."

President George W. Bush had come to office just nine months before the attacks of September 11, 2001, without a fully developed plan for the Middle East. But he did come to office with a team of policy advisers who had sharply defined views on the region. Some, like Vice President Dick Cheney and Secretary of State Colin Powell, were veterans of the George H. W. Bush administration, while others, like Secretary of Defense Donald Rumsfeld, had served in various capacities with presidents Ford and Reagan. In addition, a flock of so-called neoconservatives occupied secondary positions in the Defense Department and the White House. Many of them were identified with views calling for the transformation of the Middle East—overthrowing Saddam Hussein, fully backing Israel, and promoting the spread of democracy.

It took some time after 9/11 for President Bush to embark on an entirely new approach to dealing with the Middle East. Initially he seemed inclined to strike back at al-Qa'ida and topple the Taliban regime in Afghanistan, where Osama bin Laden had found refuge. That was accomplished fairly quickly and without great loss of life. But some in the Bush administration argued for a more ambitious policy of remaking the Middle East, starting with the removal of Saddam's regime. Sometime during 2002, President Bush made the fateful decision to embark on this strategy, arguing in public that Iraq possessed weapons of mass destruction and had ties to al-Qa'ida. Powell managed to slow down the rush to war, but only for a few months. In March 2003, the US-led invasion of Iraq began, and with it a new era for American policy in the Middle East. To appreciate how great a departure this policy was from traditional approaches, we need to look back a bit and then reflect on the likely consequences of this radical approach to remaking the Middle East.

Despite 9/11, one could argue that US policy in the Middle East from 1945 to 2000 had been remarkably successful *in terms of the standard definition of US national interests.* Although this is a contested view, I think it is reasonably accurate within the framework of stated US objectives in the Middle East.

The normal definition of US interests in the Middle East throughout the cold war era had consisted of essentially three points. One was to ensure that the Soviet Union, our global rival and adversary, did not succeed in extending hegemony into the Middle East. Given what we now know, that may never have been a likely prospect, but after World War II, with US-Soviet competition for influence in Iran and Turkey and the establishment of the Kremlin's domination in Eastern Europe, there was real concern that Soviet power would extend quickly into the Middle East and perhaps be very difficult to contain. For the entire post–World War II period up to 1990, the problem of how to deal with the Soviet Union was number one on the list of Middle East policymakers in Washington.

The second issue was oil. There were times when access to oil was taken for granted, but everyone understood that the Persian Gulf region was the single largest source of oil in the world; indeed it comprises two-thirds of the globe's proven oil reserves. We simply could not ignore the strategic significance of that fact.

Third was the special relationship between the United States and Israel. The relationship has not always been a comfortable one, but every president since Harry S Truman has felt a special commitment to Israel's security and well-being that has not been matched by a comparable commitment to any other single state in the region.

If one takes these three points as the definition of Washington's major interests in the region—containing the Soviet Union, oil, and Israel's security—we can then determine how successful US policy had been up until 9/11. Compared to our policy in Southeast Asia, for example, US policy in the Middle East had been a relative success, certainly in terms of costs, both human and economic. Calculating the human costs to the United States of pursuing our policies, with all the mistakes made over this entire fifty-five-year period, it is estimated that at most some 550 Americans lost their lives in Middle East–related violence up to 2001 (plus almost 3,000 more in the September 11 attacks). In Southeast Asia, the comparable number exceeded 50,000. This is not meant to minimize the importance of those losses in the Middle East, only to put them in perspective.

In economic terms, the cost of pursuing US policies in the Middle East is not so easy to calculate. For implementing Middle East policy between 1945 and 2000, Congress authorized, just in terms of budget outlays, expenditures of about $200–250 billion (in current dollars), which, of course, seems like a huge amount of money. This works out to somewhat more than $4 billion per year over this entire period. These numbers are inexact at best, but compared to the costs of supporting the North Atlantic Treaty Organization (NATO) or financing the war in Vietnam, the expense for US policy in the Middle East had been quite low until the Bush administration decided to intervene in Iraq.

With respect to the US interest in Middle East oil, it is probably no exaggeration to say that if the United States and its allies had not had access to that resource at low prices in the 1950s and early 1960s, the rebuilding of Europe and Japan along democratic lines as a bulwark against Soviet expansion would have been exponentially more costly. In a way, then, the Middle East did fit into the grand strategy of the United States during this era.

To appreciate how much changed with the invasion of Iraq, consider the costs to America of the first seven years of the war, from spring 2003 to spring 2010. In human terms, more than 4,500 Americans were killed and more than 35,000 wounded, many very seriously. The cost of the war was staggering when compared with costs up to that time, probably equaling all the expenditures for Middle East policy in the previous fifty years—well over $750 billion in direct costs. And the price of a barrel of oil, which had been relatively level in the mid-$20 range before the Iraq war, rose to $70 per barrel by the middle of the decade and remained there through 2010. Such an elevated price of oil ensured a vast flow of revenues to states like Iran, Saudi Arabia, Kuwait, and Libya, many of whom were hostile to US policy, and was comparable in effect on the US economy to a major tax hike, but with the revenues going to foreign governments instead of the US Treasury.

Prior to 9/11 and the Iraq adventure, the United States had relied on a series of policy instruments to pursue its goals in the Middle East: economic and military assistance, arms sales, covert interventions, military presence, diplomacy—particularly in the Arab-Israeli peace process beginning in 1967—but only rarely the direct use of US military forces, as in Lebanon in 1958 and 1982 and the war against Iraq in 1990–1991. During the cold war era, the US public seemed willing to support these policies, by and large. There were occasional debates and protests but never anything like the massive alienation from official policy that occurred as the costs of our involvement in Southeast Asia grew in the 1960s and 1970s. For the most part, Democrats and Republicans, year after year, were prepared to support the main thrust of US policy in pursuit of widely supported American national interests. Both President George H. W. Bush and President George W. Bush, the first in 1990–1991 and the second in 2001–2002, were able to count on extremely high levels of public support for their military responses to what seemed to be direct threats to US interests in the Middle East. It was only as the costs of the Iraq war—both economic and human—continued to grow in 2005–2006 and the perception set in that American objectives could not be easily achieved that public opinion began to turn decisively against the war.

The Gulf crisis and war of 1990–1991 looks very much like the end of one phase in US foreign policy—a kind of watershed between the cold war and the post–cold war eras. It occurred just as the Soviet Union was disintegrating, but when the United States was still fully mobilized following the intense military buildup under the Ronald Reagan administration in the 1980s. Oil was seen to be at risk. Washington's military strategy promised success with relatively few US casualties. The United States had Arab allies on its side to fight against another Arab regime, and it had other countries willing to help foot the bill. That is what made it possible to mobilize the 500,000 US troops to fight the war efficiently and successfully, and to sustain public support. But note, this was not the beginning of a new burst of enthusiasm for redrawing the map of the Middle East. Pax Americana was not on the minds of official Washington after settling accounts with Saddam Hussein in Kuwait. Instead, Saddam Hussein was allowed to remain in power, and the United States relied on sanctions, containment, and deterrence—tried-and-true policies from the cold war arsenal—to deal with the remaining threat from Iraq.

The apparent inertia in US Middle East policy after the cold war came to an end on September 11, 2001. The initial reaction of striking at al-Qaʾida and the

Taliban regime in Afghanistan was a standard "realist" response to a direct attack on the United States. It was only after the fall of the Taliban in late 2001 that the real debate got under way in the Bush administration about whether and how to refashion American policy in the Middle East. As it turned out, this supposedly conservative president, George W. Bush, opted for a remarkably ambitious policy consisting of several main themes: First, the war on terror would be pursued aggressively; second, the Saddam Hussein regime in Iraq would be overthrown and disarmed; third, pressure would be exerted on Iran and Syria to change their hostile foreign policies; fourth, the Israeli-Palestinian conflict would be placed on the back burner, and Israeli prime minister Ariel Sharon would be supported as he developed his own new approach to dealing with the Palestinians. In all of these initiatives, the United States would act according to its own definition of its interests. If others chose to participate in these initiatives, they would be welcome. But Bush would not waste much time or energy on multilateral diplomacy.

As time went on and the ostensible reason for invading Iraq became questionable—there were no weapons of mass destruction, and ties to al-Qa'ida were flimsy at best—the Bush administration developed a new rationale for its Middle East policy. Arguing that terrorism had its roots in the undemocratic nature of Middle East regimes—an intriguing and controversial proposition—the Bush administration declared that its goal was to fight terror by bringing democracy to the Middle East, starting with Afghanistan and Iraq. No longer would friendly dictators be coddled—or so the rhetoric implied. To say the least, this was a dramatic departure from anything that had come before. Could the United States really deliver on this ambitious new program for the Middle East? Let us look at the issues one by one, though they are all interconnected.

IRAQ

When George W. Bush was running for president in 2000, he could not possibly have imagined that Iraq would become the defining issue of his presidency—if he were, indeed, to win. Well, he did win—sort of—and Iraq did become the defining issue, at least in the eyes of most commentators in early 2006. How did this happen?

The decision to invade Iraq stemmed from the reaction to 9/11, the transformational views on the Middle East of the neoconservatives, and Rumsfeld's desire to disprove the Powell Doctrine, which held that the United States should use force only when it had a massive military advantage and a clear exit strategy. The decision to go to war in Iraq in March 2003 with about 150,000 US troops was also anchored in a remarkably optimistic view of what would likely occur. The military correctly understood that Iraq's army would not put up much of a fight, but the war planners also had a naive notion that they would be met by grateful Iraqis who would quickly transition to a pro-American democracy. Within months, in this view, most American troops would be on their way home. All that needed to be done was to remove Saddam and his top henchmen, install a government of pro-US Iraqi exiles

(Ahmed Chalabi, Ayad al-Alawi), and Iraq could then rely on its oil wealth to develop its economy and buttress its democratic leanings.

The war planning was faultless, as far as it went—which was to Baghdad and the fall of the regime. But it made little provision for what would happen after the war, and the political planning was even more incompetent. From the outset of the post-Saddam era, there were too few American troops to guarantee security, a problem compounded by the decision to disband the Iraqi army and to purge the government of most Ba'th party cadres. Instead of a functioning Iraqi state without Saddam, the Americans confronted chaos. Over the ensuing months, as a robust insurgency began to take hold in the Sunni areas of Iraq, Iraqi politics began to polarize along sectarian lines.

By mid-2004, Americans realized that they needed to put more of an Iraqi face on the day-to-day governing of Iraq. A provisional authority was created and elections were called for in January 2005. Those elections resulted in large-scale participation on the part of Kurds and Shi'as—the two groups that had suffered most under Saddam—but an almost total boycott by the Sunni Arab minority. The next months were spent fighting the insurgency, including a small but virulent element of foreign fighters aligned with al-Qa'ida who seemed intent on fomenting sectarian violence. In addition, work began on a constitution, which was ratified in the fall of 2005, again with Shi'a and Kurdish support but Sunni opposition (especially to its federal provisions, which could leave the Sunni areas without access to a fair share of central government oil revenues). With considerable effort, Sunnis were persuaded not to boycott the elections held in December 2005, elections that were supposed to set in place the first "permanent" democratic government of the country.

By the time these elections were held, American opinion was turning against the war, and many were losing faith that a US-imposed democracy could be established there. Instead, the new Iraq was beginning to look ungovernable, fragmented, sectarian, not very democratic, filled with religious zealots, and tilting ominously toward Iran. This was not exactly what the Americans had in mind when they sent troops into battle three years earlier.

The November 2006 congressional elections were something of a wake-up call for the Bush administration. Antiwar sentiment meant that Republicans did relatively poorly at the polls. Bush responded by making changes in personnel—Rumsfeld was replaced at Defense by Robert Gates—and policy. The new policy, which came to be known by the shorthand term "surge," was in fact a combination of several tactical adjustments that had the effect of changing the dynamic of the war, at least to some extent. First, in 2006–2007, American commanders on the ground, especially in the largely Sunni Anbar province, started to cut deals with insurgents, offering them money and political backing if they would turn against the al-Qa'ida extremists in Iraq. Second, Bush decided to send additional forces to Iraq, largely to enhance security in the Baghdad area. And then, under the direction of General David Petraeus, a counterinsurgency doctrine was adopted that placed emphasis on protecting the population without inflicting so many civilian casualties. By 2008 the violence was beginning to decline, although Iraq remained a very troubled country, and millions of Iraqis had fled their homes and were still reluctant or unable to return.

As a parting gift to the newly elected president, Barack Obama, the outgoing Bush administration negotiated a Status of Forces Agreement with the government of Nuri al-Maliki that called for a staged withdrawal of American forces, with all forces out of the country by the end of 2011. Obama, who had been a strong critic of both Bush and the war, ended up adopting the new policy and keeping much of the Bush team—Gates, Petraeus, and others—who had designed the surge. As of late 2010, American combat troops were largely gone from Iraq, American casualties were dramatically down, and Iraq had dropped off the American radar screen, despite the ongoing political, security, and strategic troubles that continued to flow from the historic decision taken by George W. Bush to remake the Middle East, starting with regime change in Iraq.

IRAN

If Iraq was the most obvious target of Bush's design to transform the Middle East, Iran was the most obvious unintended beneficiary. The demise of Saddam Hussein and the emergence of a Shi'a-dominated government—to say nothing of exploding oil prices—opened the way for Iran to act on its ambition to become a major regional power. Strangely, the Bush team had not seemed to anticipate this geostrategic shift and was not prepared to deal with it either by diplomacy or by force.

Toward the end of the Clinton administration, the United States was trying to improve relations with Iran. The two countries have been at odds with one another ever since the 1979 revolution. But the Clinton administration had sent a number of signals suggesting that better relations might soon be a possibility. The fact that the elected president of Iran, Muhammad Khatami, was an outspoken reformer also seemed to indicate that a thaw between Tehran and Washington might be imminent. But that was not to happen.

As early as January 2002, President Bush had gone on record labeling Iran as a charter member of the "axis of evil," along with Iraq and North Korea. The main complaints were that Iran supported terrorism, was hostile to Israel, and was pursuing a nuclear program that might have the potential to produce highly enriched uranium.

Among neoconservatives, there were some who felt that Iran was even more of a threat than Saddam's Iraq. But Bush's decision in early 2003 to invade Iraq put the Iran issue on hold, at least for the time being. No one in Washington wanted to face two simultaneous military confrontations in the Middle East, especially since Iran was a very large country, and there was no obvious casus belli.

One lesson from the crisis of 2003 was that the United States was much less likely to attack a country that had nuclear weapons, such as North Korea, than one that simply had a nuclear research program, like Iraq. Iran seemed to act on this lesson by accelerating its moves in the direction of an actual weapons capability, while constantly denying any such intent. Toward the end of 2003, Iran seemed interested in the possibility of discussing a "package deal" with the United States. The proposal was intriguing, but its provenance was a bit uncertain. The Bush administration chose to ignore it, however, and within a matter of years its proponents were no longer running Iranian foreign policy.

The Bush administration view of Iran was harsh—it belonged to an axis of evil. But rhetoric was not matched by direct threats to use force. Indeed, apart from maintaining sanctions on Iran, the United States reluctantly agreed to let a number of European states explore the possibility of working out a compromise with Iran that would allow Tehran to pursue its nuclear research without developing its own ability to enrich uranium to high levels. The talks dragged on inconclusively. Meanwhile, in 2005 and again in 2009, Iran elected a new hard-line president, Mahmoud Ahmadinejad, making any near-term reconciliation between the United States and Iran quite unlikely.

During the election campaign of 2008, Barack Obama sharply critiqued Bush for overemphasizing force and undervaluing diplomacy. In the Middle East context, he said that he would be inclined to engage with countries like Iran (and Syria). But the circumstances surrounding Ahmadinejad's reelection in 2009 made it difficult for Obama to act on this principle once he became president. In short order, he, like Bush, was talking of the need to tighten sanctions on Iran and insisted that all options, including force, remained on the table to prevent Iran from becoming a nuclear weapons state.

ISRAEL-PALESTINE

One might have thought that 9/11 would have convinced Americans to make an all-out effort to resolve the Israeli-Palestinian conflict. After all, one of the major sources of anti-Americanism in the region was the ongoing violence in Israel-Palestine and the perception in much of the Arab and Muslim world that the United States was unreservedly supporting Israel. But the Bush team was worried that pressure on Israel would be seen as bending to the demands of terrorists, and this was ruled out from the beginning. In addition, Bush seemed to have a good opinion of Israeli Prime Minister Sharon and a very dim one of PLO leader Yasser Arafat. Thus, in early 2002, when Arafat was believed to have lied to Bush about an apparent arms smuggling operation, Bush essentially ended official contact with Arafat. During the summer, the president gave an important speech in which he called for creation of a Palestinian state, existing side by side with Israel, but the call was coupled with a demand that Palestinians carry out far-reaching political reforms. In short, as long as Arafat was in charge, the United States would do little on the peace front.

In response to pressure from British Prime Minister Tony Blair, Bush did agree, shortly after the invasion of Iraq in spring 2003, to put forward a so-called Road Map for Israeli-Palestinian peace negotiations. Part of the goal was to hold out some hope to Arabs that the United States would use its influence to moderate Sharon's harsh policies at a time when Arab opinion was being agitated by the war in Iraq. The Road Map demanded that the Palestinians end their use of violence against Israel, called on Israel to stop building settlements, and laid out a series of steps that might result in a Palestinian state with provisional borders within a matter of years. Since there was no agreed mechanism for making any of the provisions of the Road Map actually occur, it quickly bogged down, with Palestinians saying they could not improve the security situation until Israel stopped erecting settlements and pulled back troops, and Israelis arguing that they would do no such thing until the attacks ceased.

Meanwhile, Arafat was becoming increasingly isolated—physically and politically. Sharon would have no dealings with him, and soon the Americans joined in shunning him. In fall 2004, Arafat's health took a sudden turn for the worse, and on November 11 he died in a Paris hospital. His successor, much to the satisfaction of American officials, was the relatively moderate Mahmoud Abbas (Abu Mazen), who was elected president in a relatively free election in January 2005.

Meanwhile, Sharon had begun to develop a strategy that would effectively bypass the Road Map. He proposed not negotiations but unilateral Israeli steps that would change realities on the ground. One part of the plan was the construction of a barrier between Israelis and Palestinians. It would follow the 1967 lines in some areas, while in others it would intrude into the West Bank in very disruptive ways for Palestinians. Many thought they could see the outline of Israel's de facto future borders in the route of the barrier. The second part of the strategy was to evacuate Israeli settlers—about 8,000 of them—from Gaza, leaving this area entirely in Palestinian hands but tightly surrounded by Israel. Optimists thought that Sharon's initiative, carried out successfully in mid-2005, might be followed by further unilateral moves that would bring about a reduction in the violence and a period of de facto peaceful coexistence between Israelis and Palestinians. Pessimists were more inclined to see the Gaza disengagement as a way of gaining time for consolidating Israel's position in crucial parts of the West Bank, while completing the construction of the barrier.

Bush's attitude toward all of this was a typical mixture of disengagement, support for Sharon, and occasional pronouncements about what the future shape of a peace agreement would look like. At his most expansive, Bush put forward a view that called for two states, Israel and Palestine, living side by side. Israel would not be expected to withdraw all the way to the 1967 lines, but those lines should serve as the main point of reference when final borders would be drawn up. In addition, Bush said explicitly that a Palestinian state should be democratic, contiguous, and economically viable. In a nod to Israeli sensitivities, he said that Palestinian refugees could not expect to return to homes in Israel proper. For some reason, he did not go on to say that they should receive generous compensation for their losses, although that would certainly be part of any full statement of the American position. Only on Jerusalem and its future was Bush notably silent. But even more important, beyond his words he seemed to have no strategy to make any of this happen. Indeed, up until the moment in early 2006 when Ariel Sharon suffered a massive stroke, Bush seemed to believe that the best stance for the United States was to hold back and let the parties work their way through their respective elections, scheduled for early in 2006, and then assess the new political realities that would face him. Such a restrained approach was called into question with the departure of Sharon from the political stage and the subsequent victory by Hamas in Palestinian parliamentary elections in late January 2006. In short, Bush began 2006 without a credible strategy for Israeli-Palestinian peace, just as events on the ground were casting a dark cloud over the future.

Israeli elections were held in March 2006. The party formed by Sharon before his stroke, Kadima, won, but with only 29 of the 120 seats in the Knesset. The new prime minister, Ehud Olmert, presided over a multiparty coalition of the center. In theory, this gave him room to engage in negotiations, but the harsh reality was that the Hamas victory made such negotiations unlikely. The Bush team, clearly surprised by the victory of the radical Hamas movement, laid down strict conditions for Hamas to meet if it were to be brought into the peace process. These included abandoning the use of force, recognizing Israel's right to exist, and accepting prior agreements reached between Israel and the PLO. This Hamas was not prepared to do, and the Bush team then set out, in collaboration with elements within the PLO, to oust them from power. But the effort failed in 2007, and instead Hamas seized full control of Gaza, leaving the Palestinian movement bifurcated—Abu Mazen in charge of the West Bank, with Gaza under Hamas control.

For reasons that remain a bit mysterious, the Bush administration, like Clinton in his last year, made a last-ditch effort to encourage Israeli-Palestinian peace talks. A formal conference was convened in Annapolis, Maryland, in November 2007, and Secretary of State Condoleezza Rice threw herself energetically into the diplomatic fray. Toward the end of 2008, Israeli Prime Minister Olmert, by then under a dark cloud generated by corruption charges, made an offer to Abu Mazen that went beyond what any Israeli government had previously considered. But it was a sign of how weak both Olmert and Abu Mazen were, and how ineffectual American mediation was, that this effort fizzled, literally going up in smoke in the last days of December 2008 as Israel invaded Gaza in order to stop rocket attacks by Hamas and, more importantly, to try to weaken the radical Palestinian movement.

Obama, who was much more outspoken as a candidate about the importance of Arab-Israeli peace for American national interests than Bush had ever been, inherited a very unpromising situation in the Holy Land. The Gaza war was over, but tensions ran high. Anti-Americanism was raging in much of the Arab and Muslim world. And when Israelis went to the polls in early 2009, they elected a divided Knesset that eventually gave its support to Benjamin Netanyahu, the hard-line Likud leader.

The new American administration took a surprisingly tough line with Netanyahu, calling on him to stop all settlement activity in the West Bank in order to create promising conditions for the resumption of negotiations. Netanyahu refused, and US-Israeli relations suffered an unusual turn for the worse. It took more than a year before the tension was eased, and during much of the latter part of 2010 Obama was preoccupied with getting Israelis and Palestinians back to the negotiating table. Whether or not he had a strategy for what to do after that was unclear, but in this arena, as in others, his actions were considerably more modest than his initial rhetoric led many of his supporters to expect.

DEMOCRACY

The last of the major themes of the Bush administration's Middle East policy was democratization. The policy was never fully elaborated, but the main idea was that the time had come for the United States to place more emphasis on political and economic reform in the region. There was definitely an audience for such views. Many Middle Easterners did want to see economic change, they did want to see more responsible and accountable governments, and they were fed up with the corruption of their own leaders. But there was always the dilemma for the United States of trying to impose its views, which may ultimately produce a negative nationalistic backlash. The issue of how best to encourage political reforms and democratization is not an easy one for any administration.

The Bush administration introduced the notion in 2005 that the United States has sacrificed democracy for stability in the Middle East and had achieved neither. This seemed to foreshadow a robust policy of democracy promotion, and for a brief moment there was indeed some enthusiasm in official Washington for pushing for free and fair elections in the Middle East. That enthusiasm waned quite suddenly when Hamas won the elections held in early 2006 in the Palestinian territories. By the time Barack Obama arrived at the White House, he and his advisers were determined to improve relations with the Muslim and Arab peoples, but priority for doing so was given to a responsible exit from Iraq, a return to serious Arab-Israeli peacemaking, and an attempt to engage with countries and movements that had previously been viewed with deep suspicion by the Bush administration. This did not mean that democracy and human rights were ignored. In his much-awaited speech in Cairo in mid 2009, Obama addressed these issues in a very general way, but democratization did not seem to top his regional agenda.

All that changed in early 2011. First Tunisia and then Egypt saw sustained popular uprisings that led to the overthrow of entrenched pro-American governments. While Obama generally welcomed the change in Tunisia, Egypt, a major strategic ally and the first Arab country to make peace with Israel, posed a more complex challenge. Some of Obama's advisers seemed to want to support Mubarak, or at least to slow the pace of change, while others wanted to be on "the right side of history." The president himself seemed at times ambivalent, but at the crucial moment when Mubarak seemed reluctant to go, Obama threw his weight on the side of change, clearly conveying to the Egyptian military that the United States favored a quick resolution of the crisis, and that Mubarak's insistence on hanging on was delaying that. On February 11, 2011, Mubarak resigned, and within a few hours Obama gave an eloquent speech aligning the United States with the democratic aspirations of the people in the Middle East. How exactly this would play itself out in the region was impossible to foresee, but at least the United States was rhetorically on the side of democratic change in the region. But unlike Bush, he would not seek to promote democracy by sending troops.

CONCLUSION

Above all, the Middle East region, as the dramatic events early in 2011 showed, is not ours to design. We have done best in protecting our interests when we have adopted realistic goals that we could pursue in cooperation with regional allies. As all administrations realized, this meant keeping access to the Gulf region, promoting some form of stability, and trying to both contain and, if possible, resolve the Arab-Israeli conflict. And now those guidelines must be amended to include support for democratic change. Despite many missteps, the United States did fairly well in protecting its core interests in the Middle East up until about 2000.

We will never know what course the Bush administration might have taken had it not been for 9/11. As a candidate, Bush had spoken of modest foreign policy goals and had eschewed nation building. But 9/11 changed all that and brought to the fore those who believed that the Middle East needed a total makeover, that the old goals of regional stability and Arab-Israeli peace were too limited—or even irrelevant—to the challenge of combating terror and Islamic radicalism. The new mind-set privileged unilateralism, the use of force, regime change, democracy promotion, with little attention paid to the costs that would be incurred.

Not surprisingly, the grand plan to remake the Middle East proved to be overly ambitious. The Iraq project will be debated by Americans for decades to come, much like Vietnam for an earlier generation. Was it worth it? Were there alternatives? Could we have made better choices? But as of 2011, most Americans look at Iraq as an expensive misadventure, one that we should be wary of repeating. And the Obama administration seems intent on carrying through with the withdrawal of American troops from this expensive and inconclusive venture. The remaining challenges, however, are daunting—Arab-Israeli peace, Iran's regional ambitions, nuclear proliferation, terrorism, the instability that may flow from popular protests against autocratic regimes. All of these will be extremely difficult for Obama, especially if he adheres to the formulas of the past. If there was ever a time for serious new thinking about how to address the foreign policy challenges facing the United States in the Middle East, early 2011 is the time. But without clear guidelines, and with deep partisan divides at home and a reelection bid on the horizon, it seems unlikely that Obama will find a bold new way of pursuing American interests in the region.

CHAPTER 28

THE UNITED STATES
AND THE ARAB SPRING

Threats and Opportunities in a Revolutionary Era

Mark L. Haas

In June 2009, President Barack Obama gave a major agenda-setting speech in Cairo, Egypt. The president asserted that the spread to Muslim-majority countries of democratic "governments that reflect the will of the people" would be a key outcome that would make these states "ultimately more stable, successful and secure." This development would also result in improved relations with the United States. Obama promised to "welcome all elected, peaceful governments—provided they govern with respect for all their people."[1] Given that the Middle East and North Africa at the time were widely deemed to be the least politically free regions in the world, no one expected Obama's hope for the spread of democracy at the expense of dictatorial regimes to be realized anytime soon.

Events that seemed revolutionary in every sense of the word ran counter to this expectation. Massive political protests against authoritarian governments began in Tunisia in December 2010. By 2013, protests in varying degrees of intensity, but all of major significance, had occurred in Algeria, Bahrain, Egypt, Jordan, Kuwait, Libya, Morocco, Syria, Sudan, Tunisia, and Yemen. By early 2012, dictators in Egypt, Libya, Tunisia, and Yemen had been forced from power, and competitive elections followed in the first three of these countries.

This chapter has three primary purposes. First, I summarize the major political consequences of the Arab Spring protests in North Africa and the Middle East. Second, I analyze how and why US leaders responded to these developments. Prominent in this analysis is a detailed examination of the threats and opportunities to US interests created by the uprisings. I conclude the chapter with a discussion of various policies the United States might adopt to best advance US security in a post–Arab Spring era.

I begin my analysis with an exploration of the Obama administration's reactions to the first set of Middle East mass protests that occurred during his presidency; these took place not in an Arab country but in Iran. The lessons learned from these demonstrations would have major effects on how Obama responded to the uprisings that occurred across the Arab world beginning in 2010.

OBAMA'S TRANSFORMATION:
FROM PERSIAN PROTESTS TO THE ARAB SPRING

Although Obama in his 2009 speech in Cairo had called for the spread of democracy in the Muslim world, his administration's reactions to the Arab Spring beginning in late 2010 were most likely not the same as they would have been nearly two years earlier. Obama came into office believing that the George W. Bush administration's "freedom agenda"—meaning the use or threat of force to help spread liberal regimes in the Middle East—had been a mistake.[2] He thought his predecessor's policies had resulted in a backlash against the United States that had left it isolated and reviled throughout much of the Islamic world. Thus to restore America's reputation, it was necessary to adopt less forceful and more accommodating actions.

Obama's dominant foreign policy inclinations—especially during his first year as president—reinforced the conclusions resulting from the perceived failings of the Bush administration. Obama's dominant view of international relations was that what united countries—even ideological rivals—was or should be more important to their interactions than what divided them. According to international relations scholar Henry Nau, Obama "has a coherent worldview that highlights 'shared' interests defined by interconnected material problems such as climate, energy, and nonproliferation and de-emphasizes 'sovereign' interests that separate countries along political and moral lines. He tacks away from topics that he believes divide nations—democracy, defense, markets, and unilateral leadership—and toward topics that he believes integrate them—stability, disarmament, regulations, and diplomacy."[3] If shared interests are more important to states' foreign policies than divisive ones, including disputes due to the effects of ideological differences, then policies of engagement should dominate America's relations with rivals, and democracy promotion as a means of advancing US security owing to the creation of shared values with others is not paramount. This perspective helps explain Obama's call for the spread of democracy in his Cairo speech as more of a human rights than a security issue.

To the Obama administration, in sum, the use of force in the service of the spread of democracy was both ineffective (as the Bush administration's policies had apparently demonstrated) and less necessary than some believed because the United States possessed important common interests with illiberal regimes, which could be more determinative of relations than ideological differences. Pragmatic economic and political considerations, most notably a weakened US economy due to the 2008 financial crisis and subsequent recession, as well as public opinion polls that showed the American public was strongly opposed to additional military interventions, reinforced the inclination against aggressive foreign policies. Obama succinctly expressed his views in his Cairo speech when he asserted that despite the benefits of democracy, "no system of government can or should be imposed upon one nation by any other."[4]

Occuring during his first year as president, the most important test case in the Middle East for Obama's beliefs in the power of engagement and his rejection of the use of force to alter others' regimes was Iran.[5] In 2009, the president made a number of important conciliatory gestures toward Iran that were designed to reduce hostilities. Two months after his inauguration, Obama made a videotaped message directed to the Iranians. In the message, the president took an unusual step for a high-ranking US official by referring to Iran as "the Islamic Republic of Iran," which was a nod to the legitimacy of the Iranian Islamist revolution. Obama offered the promise of a "new day" in US-Iranian relations, which would allow for "renewed exchanges among our people, and greater opportunities for partnership and commerce." The process of improving relations, the president said, "will not be advanced by threats. We seek instead engagement that is honest and grounded in mutual respect."[6] Most important for this chapter's purposes, the president offered little criticism of the major irregularities, likely involving fraud, in the June 2009 Iranian presidential elections and the subsequent violent crackdown on popular protests of the election results. Obama did call for the peaceful resolution of disputes, but he stated that he did not want to be seen as meddling in Iranian domestic affairs.[7] Obama also promised to continue to engage Iran despite the fraudulent elections and subsequent violence against those who protested them.[8]

Instead of supporting the Iranian protesters and the reformist political candidates they championed, Obama minimized the differences between Iranian political hard-liners and reformers. Obama officials claimed that the international policy differences between Iranian conservatives and reformers were slight. Consequently, the United States had little strategic interest in helping reformers augment their power. In a June 2009 interview, Obama stated that from a national security perspective, there was little difference for America if the hard-liner Mahmoud Ahmadinejad or the reformer Mir Hussein Mousavi won the 2009 presidential elections. "Either way," asserted Obama, the United States is "going to be dealing with an Iranian regime that has historically been hostile to the United States, that has caused some problems in the neighborhood and is pursuing nuclear weapons." Indeed, because Iranian reformers and conservatives were likely to pursue similar international policies toward America despite their domestic differences, in some ways it was better for the United States to have Iranian conservatives win the election. As a senior Obama official told the *Wall Street Journal*: "Had there been a transition to a new government [if Mousavi won], a new president wouldn't have emerged until August. In some respects, [Ahmadinejad's victory] might allow Iran to engage the international community quicker."[9]

Obama's engagement of the Iranian regime did not succeed in improving relations. To the contrary, Iran's most powerful leaders responded to Obama's overtures with contempt and threats. In reaction to Obama's videotaped message to Iran, Supreme Leader Khamenei claimed that there was no change in US-Iranian relations and that Obama had "insulted the Islamic Republic of Iran from the first day."[10] At the end of June 2009, after his reelection, President Ahmadinejad stated, "Without a doubt, Iran's new government will have a more decisive and firmer approach toward the West." "This time [Iran's] reply will be harsh" to make the West regret its "meddlesome stance" toward Iranian politics.[11] (This charge of meddling was made despite Obama's unwillingness to interfere in Iran's politics in support of the 2009 protestors.) By the fall of 2009, Khamenei and other ideological conservatives labeled Obama's outreach policies ones of "soft war" (i.e., efforts at ideological subversion) that were in some ways more dangerous than the Bush's administration's conventional threats.[12] These charges continued into 2010.[13]

Obama's engagement of the Iranian government not only failed with respect to Iran's hard-line leaders but also angered many of those Iranians who were sympathetic to the reform movement. Many Iranian reformers advocated that the Obama administration take more forceful actions against the Iranian government after Ahmadinejad's reelection in 2009. One reformist activist told the *Los Angeles Times* in September 2009 that he welcomed more international "pressure on Ahmadinejad's government. This is good for the Green wave [i.e., reformers] in Iran and the [domestic] rift will increase for sure if pressure builds up."[14] One of the slogans shouted in the streets of Tehran in massive demonstrations held in November 2009 was: "Obama: either with the murderers or with us."[15] The protestors, according to observers of the movement, "perceive that [Obama's] international engagement with Mr. Ahmadinejad has come at the expense of their human rights . . . Many in the Green Movement [believe] that experience has shown that Mr. Ahmadinejad is neither willing nor able to change course. Instead, they would like to see the international community exert pressure on the regime through a progressive set of smart, vigorous and targeted sanctions and more forceful advocacy of human rights."[16]

Obama's failures toward Iran in 2009 apparently had a significant impact on how he responded to the protest movements of the Arab Spring beginning in 2010. Two lessons from the experience with Iran were particularly important. First, the Iranian case demonstrated that many who are struggling for greater protection of their rights do not consider US support of their efforts to be "meddling" that taints their cause (as quoted above, for example, Iranian protestors welcomed greater US involvement in support of their efforts). As one Obama official stated after the Arab Spring uprisings began: "There was a feeling of 'we ain't gonna be behind the curve on this again'" (as the United States found itself in the Iranian protests of

2009). Another senior aide similarly explained that Obama in 2011 believed "that the [Arab Spring] protestors want to hear from the American president, but not just any American president. They want to hear from this American president." In other words, they wanted to hear from the first black president, who symbolized the possibility of change.[17]

The second lesson that Obama seems to have learned from his failed Iranian policies was that supporting democratic movements was important not only for improving others' basic rights (which is the outcome that Obama's Cairo speech emphasized) but also for America's security. Not only are societies that better protect basic human rights likely to be more stable and peaceful, at least in the long run (analyzed more extensively below), but ideological differences among political groups matter greatly in terms of the level of hostility that is likely to be directed at the United States. Contrary to Obama's assertion quoted earlier, there were important foreign policy differences between Iranian ideological hard-liners and more liberal reformers.[18] Ideological hard-liners were likely to be highly hostile to the United States even if being engaged, reformers much less so. Thus it was in America's security interests to see more liberal groups come to power in Muslim-majority countries.

This second lesson resulted in a new narrative at the time of the Arab Spring uprisings. As David Sanger of the *New York Times* wrote, "in his first two years in office, Mr. Obama said little about democratic transformations as a core goal . . . now [in 2011] he has begun speaking of them as a central part of the 'alternative narrative' to [that of ideological enemies, e.g.,] Al Qaeda's theology, or Iran's."[19] Or as Deputy National Security Advisor Benjamin J. Rhodes stated: "The president wanted to clearly and unequivocally embrace change in the region [the Middle East and North Africa]. It was necessary for him to step back and say that not only does he support the aspirations of the people we have seen in the streets, but supporting them is in our long-term interest."[20] According to Obama in a major policy speech given in May 2011, which laid out his administration's vision for US-Middle Eastern relations in light of the Arab Spring protests: "We must acknowledge that a strategy based solely upon the narrow pursuit of [material] interests . . . will only feed the suspicion [among the peoples of the Middle East] that has festered for years that the United States pursues our interests at their expense . . . [As a result,] a failure to change our approach threatens a deepening spiral of division between the United States and the Arab world . . . Our support for [universal liberal] principles is not a secondary interest. Today I want to make it clear that it is a top priority that must be translated into concrete actions, and supported by all of the diplomatic, economic and strategic tools at our disposal . . . It will be the policy of the United States to promote reform across the region, and to support transitions to democracy . . . The United States of America was founded on the belief that people should govern themselves. And now we cannot hesitate to stand squarely on the side of those who are reaching for their rights, knowing that their success will bring about a world that is more peaceful, more stable, and more just."[21]

Although President Obama's dedication to the export of liberalism is not as expansive and urgent as that claimed by President George W. Bush in his second inaugural address, the spread of liberal institutions and values remained an important US security interest that played a central role in shaping America's responses to the Arab Spring protests, at least in some key cases.[22]

US RESPONSES TO THE ARAB SPRING UPRISINGS

The Obama administration did not adopt a "one size fits all" set of policies toward countries that experienced mass political protests during the Arab Spring. The United States was quickest to support protestors and to work for regime change in states hostile to America, but much less consistent in this area toward countries that were US allies. What follows is a summary of the key developments in six countries: Tunisia, Egypt, Libya, Yemen (the four countries in which protests have thus far resulted in the removal of dictators from power, with the United States providing important support for demonstrators in these countries even though three of the governments—Tunisia, Egypt, and Yemen—were US allies); Bahrain, where protests have been effectively crushed with US acquiescence; and Syria, which has descended into brutal civil war. In Syria, the United States has provided the rebels some support, though little military aid, and not enough help to tip the balance in their favor (as was done, for example, in Libya). The Obama White House has been highly hesitant to take actions that might draw the United States deeper into the Syrian conflict. The goal in this section is not to provide a comprehensive recounting of developments in these six countries. Instead, I summarize key events in each of the states and US leaders' reactions to them. The principal focus in this section is on the early stages of the protests; more recent developments are discussed later in the chapter.

The Arab Spring began in Tunisia in December 2010 when a street vendor, Mohammed Bouazizi, set himself on fire outside a municipal building in the city of Sidi Bouzid to protest his lack of economic opportunity, harassment by the police, and the regime's high level of corruption. This act of defiance led to widespread popular protests throughout the country, which forced the dictatorial leader, Zine al-Abidine Ben Ali, who had ruled Tunisia for twenty-three years, to flee the state on January 14, 2011. After Ben Ali went into exile, power moved to Mohammed Ghannouchi, who had been Ben Ali's longest-serving prime minister. The continued power of one of Ben Ali's allies resulted in more mass protests, which ultimately led to Ghannouchi's resignation on February 27, 2011. An interim government that was largely free of Ben Ali's cronies promised to hold free elections, draft a constitution, and create a new democratic government. Elections for the National Constituent Assembly—which were the first free elections in the country's history—were held in October 2011, with the moderate Islamist party Ennahda winning a plurality of votes. The National Assembly drafted a constitution in December 2011, which, according to Human Rights Watch, possesses some favorable protections of human rights.[23] The government has scheduled voting for parliament and direct election of the president for June 2013.

The US response to the Tunisian demonstrations was cautious, no doubt largely because Ben Ali was considered an ally in US counterterrorism efforts. Moreover, because the uprisings in Tunisia were the first ones to occur in the region, US leaders, like most others, doubted the protestors could successfully overthrow their government. A week before Ben Ali fled to Saudi Arabia, Secretary of State Hillary Clinton emphasized the need for political reform in Tunisia and the protestors' right to assemble, but she also stressed that the United States was "not taking sides" between the government and the protestors.[24] Only after Ben Ali's ouster did Obama applaud "the courage and dignity of the Tunisian people" and called on the government to "hold free and fair elections in the near future."[25] The US government also pledged a modest amount ($32 million) to aid Tunisia's political transition to a democratic regime. In the 2011 State of the Union Address, Obama praised the revolution in Tunisia, "where the will of the people proved more powerful than the writ of a dictator," and he expressed support for the "democratic aspirations of all people."[26]

The US response was much more active in support of protestors in Egypt, even though Egypt had been a critical ally of the United States since the late 1970s. Mass protests began in Egypt on January 25, 2011, which was eleven days after the removal of Ben Ali in Tunisia. Over the next eighteen days, an estimated six million Egyptians took to the streets, making these protests the largest pro-democracy demonstrations in Arab history.[27] By January 29, which was only four days into the Egyptian demonstrations, the Obama administration decided that it would support a political transition in Egypt and that an emissary would be sent to Hosni Mubarak "to explain that, in the judgment of the United States, he could not survive the protests. The emissary [Frank Wisner, the former ambassador to Egypt] would tell Mubarak that his best option was to try to leave a positive legacy by steering the country toward a real democratic transformation."[28] On February 1, Obama publicly announced that the end of Mubarak's rule "must begin now."[29] The Americans also pressured the Egyptian military not to fire on the protestors, while reinforcing the message to the Egyptian armed forces that Mubarak had to go.[30] Obama decided to push for Mubarak's removal from power despite objections from key advisers (most notably Secretary of Defense Robert Gates, Chairman of the Joint Chiefs of Staff Mike Mullen, and Assistant Secretary of State for Near Eastern Affairs Jeffrey Feltman) and from international allies, most notably Saudi Arabia (more about the latter below).[31]

Mubarak was removed from office on February 11, and largely free and competitive parliamentary elections were held roughly ten months later. The Muslim Brotherhood won 45 percent of the seats in the lower house (the People's Assembly) and 58 percent of the contested seats in the upper house (the Shura Council). The more hard-line Salafi Islamists won 25 percent of the seats in both houses. Liberal parties came in a distant third.[32] Mohamed Morsi, a senior Muslim Brotherhood leader, was elected president in the summer of 2012. Despite the fact that an Islamist party dominated Egypt's elections, the Obama White House both recognized the elections as legitimate and promised to engage the new regime. This was a major change from the Bush administration, which had isolated Islamist parties even if they won competitive elections (most notably in the case of America's relations with Hamas, which won Palestinian parliamentary elections in Gaza in 2006).[33]

The Obama administration's response to demonstrations in Libya were the most forceful—literally—of any country involved in the Arab Spring uprisings. Mass protests began in Libya on February 15, four days after Mubarak's ouster. Unlike in Egypt, the Gadafi government responded to the demonstrations with brute force as it led a violent campaign to crush opponents of the regime, killing thousands in the first month of conflict.[34] Rather than ending the protests, the government's brutality fueled only more resentment and support for the rebels' cause, including mass defections from the military. By March, Libya was in a state of civil war, with the opposition controlling much of the eastern half of the country. On March 17, with Gadafi's forces advancing into opposition strongholds and a likely massacre imminent, the United Nations Security Council—led by France, Britain, and the United States—voted "to take all necessary measures to protect civilians under threat of attack in the country." Although the explicit objective of UN Resolution 1973 was to protect Libyan civilians from their government, in practice the resolution worked for regime change by tipping the military balance of power in favor of the opposition.[35] On March 19, NATO fighters began to bomb the Libyan military while simultaneously imposing a blockade on Libyan ports to prevent weapons from entering the country.[36] Tripoli fell into rebel hands in August 2011, and on October 20 Gadafi was captured and killed. Libya held parliamentary elections the following July. The leading party was the National Forces Alliance, which is a coalition headed by the relatively liberal politician Mahmoud Jibril (a former political science professor at the University of Pittsburgh). The Muslim Brotherhood's Justice and Construction Party came in second. Libya is currently governed by an interim constitution that declares the country a democratic one with protections for minority rights. Islamic law is established as the principal source of legislation. A permanent constitution is scheduled to be drafted in 2013.

Although the French had led the charge pushing for the United Nations to authorize the creation of a no-fly zone in Libya, the Obama administration played the key role in massively strengthening the resolution into granting permission for a full-scale military intervention. Gadafi was primarily using tanks, not planes, to crush the rebellion, so a no-fly zone would have been largely ineffective in stopping the regime.[37] The US military also played a critical part in the intervention, especially in the areas of reconnaissance, intelligence, heavy airlift, and refueling.

Yemen is the fourth and final country that has to this point experienced a leadership change resulting from popular protests. Demonstrations began in Yemen in January 2011, and they intensified over the next several months. The response to the protests by President Ali Abdullah Saleh, who had governed since 1978, was harsh, as government troops killed scores of protestors. As in Libya, this brutality both fueled animosity toward the regime and led to key political and military lead-ers defecting to the side of the demonstrators. In April, US leaders, who had long supported Saleh and viewed his government as a critical ally against the Yemini branch of al-Qa'ida, concluded that he was unlikely to implement the political re-forms necessary to calm domestic unrest. The Obama administration, as a result, concluded that Saleh must be eased out of power.[38] In November, Saleh accepted a proposal in which he would resign as president in exchange for immunity from prosecution for him and his family. In February 2012, Saleh's vice president, Abdrabbuh Mansour Hadi, was elected president in a one-candidate election in which he won an inconceivable 99.8 percent of the votes. US leaders nevertheless praised the election as a "democratic" one.[39]

America's reactions to protests in two countries, Bahrain and Syria, neither of which has experienced a change in leadership at the time of this writing (April 2013), are also worth exploring. The Bahraini case, even more than Yemen, shows the limits of US support of democratization in some allies; the Syrian case dem-onstrates the Obama administration's unwillingness to intervene militarily to bring about regime change in some enemy states due to perceived high costs associated with this action.

Prodemocracy protests began in Bahrain on February 14, 2011, to which the government responded with deadly force. The Bahraini regime not only killed dozens of activists but in March declared a state of emergency that resulted in Bahrain taking on the "likeness of a police state." The result was "mass arrests, mass firings of government workers [and] reports of torture . . . Emergency laws [gave] the security forces the right to search houses at will without a warrant and dissolve any organization, including legal political parties, deemed a danger to the state."[40] Bahrain received international support for this crackdown when Saudi Arabia and the United Arab Emirates (UAE), at the request of Bahrain's monarch, sent 2,000 troops into Bahrain to help suppress the demonstrators.[41]

The Obama administration's response to the crushing of protests for political reform in Bahrain, which houses the US Navy's Fifth Fleet, has been for the most part muted. In May 2011, Obama did state that "the only way forward is for the [Bahraini] government and opposition to engage in a dialogue, and you can't have a real dialogue when parts of the peaceful opposition are in jail." Senior US officials, including Secretary of Defense Gates and Assistant Secretary of State for Near East-ern Affairs Feltman, also visited Bahrain to encourage the ruling family to accelerate democratic reforms.[42] Unlike other Arab Spring countries, though, the adminis-tration did not condemn or sanction the Bahraini government or call for its re-moval.[43] It even continued to sell weapons to Bahrain, although items that are particularly good at crowd control—such as tear gas, tear gas launchers, and Humvees—were banned in the sales.[44]

Political protests in Syria began on March 15, 2011. A fierce governmental crackdown on demonstrators resulted in the galvanization of opposition forces, in-cluding soldiers who defected from the Syrian army. Syria has been engaged in civil war since the end of 2011, at the latest. It is estimated that by March 2013 this conflict resulted in more than 70,000 deaths, over a million refugees entering neighboring countries, and approximately 2 million internally displaced Syrians.[45]

During the early stages of the Syrian uprising, Obama left open the possibility that President Bashar al-Asad could remain in power if he adopted meaningful liberalization policies. On May 19, 2011, Obama stated that Asad "can lead the transition, or get out of the way."[46] Over the course of the summer, as Syrian brutality escalated, US policymakers grew increasingly critical of the Asad government in both word and deed, including meeting with opposition leaders in Syria and encouraging the European Union to increase sanctions against the regime. European sanctions against Syria would be more effective than US sanctions because European countries interacted with Syria on an economic level much more than did the United States; a quarter of Syria's trade in 2011 was with the EU.[47] Finally, on August 18, the United States officially called on Asad to go. President Obama stated the following: "The future of Syria must be determined by its people, but President Bashar al-Asad is standing in their way. We have consistently said that President Asad must lead a democratic transition or get out of the way. He has not led. For the sake of the Syrian people, the time has come for President Asad to step aside."[48] In a coordinated diplomatic onslaught, the leaders of Canada, France, Germany, the United Kingdom, and the European Union did the same.

The United States also took some measures designed to put stress on the Syrian government and help the resistance. It led the way in organizing a new series of punishing economic sanctions against Syria, primarily beginning in August 2011. Although the United States has not directly armed the rebels, it both acquiesced to US allies doing so—Turkey, Saudi Arabia, and Qatar—and provided $50 million worth of communications equipment and training to the opposition to help those inside Syria organize, avoid attacks, and stay in contact with the outside world. In conjunction with US allies' efforts to arm the rebels, the CIA has stationed operatives in southern Turkey to help decide which Syrian opposition groups should receive weapons. In December 2012, the Obama administration announced that it would formally recognize a coalition of Syrian opposition groups as that country's legitimate representative, which further isolated the Asad regime. In February 2013, the Americans pledged to provide food rations and medical supplies to the military wing of the Syrian opposition and $60 million to help the political wing deliver basic services such as sanitation and education in areas of Syria the opposition controls. Washington has provided nearly $400 million in humanitarian aid to help refugees outside Syria and displaced people inside it.[49]

As of April 2013, however, the White House has refused either to send US troops into Syria to help topple the Asad government or to arm directly Syrian opposition forces. The Obama administration, in short, has not been willing to do in Syria what it did in Libya: engage in direct military intervention to overthrow a noxious regime. A number of concerns have been central to this choice. The Obama White House fears being dragged into and therefore escalating a proxy conflict between Iran and Saudi Arabia (more about this below). Most important from the US point of view is the number of hard-line Islamist groups that are members of the Syrian opposition. If these groups become armed with the most advanced weaponry, these weapons could be used against America and its allies after the conflict with Syria ends.[50] It is one thing to try to overthrow a dictator like Asad by supporting democratic opposition forces. It is much riskier to try to overthrow one ideological enemy (Asad's secular authoritarian regime) by aiding and arming another (hard-line Islamists).

WHAT'S AT STAKE FOR THE UNITED STATES IN THE ARAB SPRING ERA?

As the analysis in the previous section demonstrates, US policies concerning countries experiencing mass political protests for more democratic freedoms have exhibited considerable variation, from active support of the protests in some cases to acquiescence of governmental crackdowns in others. Some analysts explain this variation as a by-product of a conflict between American values and interests. To this perspective, the support of democracy is an important normative objective that flows out of Americans' ideological beliefs, but US leaders will tend to support this objective only as long as the material costs are low.[51] Hence policymakers' willingness to turn a blind eye to governments' repression of democratic demonstrators, as was the case in Bahrain, or to the crackdown by Syrian government forces.

The "values versus interests" explanation of US actions during the Arab Spring is correct in that there are major costs associated with democracy promotion, especially in the Middle East and North Africa. This account, according to many, misses the critical fact that support of prodemocracy movements is not only an important US value but also potentially creates major security benefits for the United States. Instead of values *versus* interests, values *and* interests may exist synergistically with the spread of democracy advancing US security. The following analysis explains the potential costs to US interests that may be created by democratization in the Middle East and why US leaders have been reluctant to support protestors in key instances. Then an examination of the potential security benefits of the spread of democracy helps explain why the United States at times supported democratic activists even in illiberal allies, most notably in Egypt.

The Potential Costs for the United States of Democracy Promotion in the Arab World

The creation of more democratic regimes in the Middle East and North Africa can potentially threaten US interests for two major reasons, both of which can result from multiple pathways. The spread of democracy can: 1) result in the replacement of allies with regimes that are much more hostile to the United States; and 2) fuel sectarian and ideological conflict throughout the region. I explore each of these potential outcomes and the various linkages that could lead to them in turn.

Greater democracy in the Middle East and North Africa can potentially result in the estrangement or loss of US allies for three main reasons. First, states that replace authoritarian regimes with more democratic regimes may empower groups

that are more suspicious, even hostile, to the United States than are many authoritarian leaders. At a minimum, the creation of more democratic governments
means that public opinion will have a much greater impact on foreign policies than
is the case in authoritarian states. This development is potentially problematic for
US interests because the populace in many Muslim-majority countries often has
negative views of US policy. Since the September 2001 terrorist attacks in New
York, Washington, and Pennsylvania, numerous surveys reveal, as one expert on
the subject summarizes, that "the overwhelming majority of the Arab publics, even
(sometimes *especially*) in countries whose governments are particularly close allies
of the United States (Egypt, Jordan, Morocco, Saudi Arabia, and the United Arab
Emirates), identified the United States as one of the two most threatening states
to them, after Israel."[52] These negative sentiments were particularly strong toward
the George W. Bush administration, even though its leaders openly claimed to be
champions of freedom and democracy in the Arab world. Many Arabs who have
been surveyed doubted that the United States was genuinely committed to the advancement of their rights but was instead using the rhetoric of democracy promotion as an excuse to advance US material interests, such as eliminating Iraq's
weapons of mass destruction program, maintaining access to cheap oil, and better
protecting Israel.

Even more troubling for US interests are the negative views of the United States
that have remained strong even after the Arab Spring uprisings began and despite
US support for the demonstrators in a number of cases. A July 2011 Zogby International poll found that favorable attitudes among citizens of Morocco, Egypt,
Jordan, Saudi Arabia, and the UAE had dropped since Obama became president.
People in Egypt, Lebanon, and the UAE believed that the United States was a key
source of their problems since "US interference in the Arab world" is "very much"
an obstacle to peace and stability in the Middle East and North Africa. Despite
the Obama administration's push for Mubarak's ouster in response to popular
protests, nearly 40 percent of Egyptians in an April 2011 Pew poll believed that
the United States played a negative role in the successful uprisings in their country.[53] In a spring 2012 Pew survey, only 19 percent of Egyptians possessed favorable
views of the United States, which was lower than in 2008.[54]

A key implication of these polling data for our purposes is clear. The establishment of more democratic regimes in the Middle East and North Africa is likely to
lead, at least in the short run, to the diminishment of US influence because Arab
publics are more suspicious and opposed to the United States than were authoritarian allies such as Ben Ali and Mubarak, who have been ousted from power. Arab
public opinion is even more hostile toward Israel than toward the United States,
further complicating matters for US leaders, because they have repeatedly expressed
strong support for Israel. These points help explain why some enemies of the
United States, most notably Iran, have welcomed the Arab Spring uprisings even
though the spread of democracy may also pose an ideological challenge to Iran's illiberal Islamist theocracy.[55]

Despite the potential downside to US interests created by the enhanced power of Arab public opinion on policymaking, there are important areas of good news for the United States on this topic. Large majorities of Arabs who possess negative views of the United States do so not because of ideological antipathy but because of opposition to particular US policies in the region. Many Muslims are particularly critical of America's one-sided support of Israel in the Israeli-Palestinian conflict. Also, US-led military intervention in the region, such as in Afghanistan and Iraq, has generated an anti-US backlash, as has America's use of drone strikes to target enemies in Muslim-majority countries.[56] Instead of ideological antipathy, large percentages of people in Muslim-majority countries, especially among younger-age cohorts, feel an ideological attraction to the United States. In a spring 2012 survey, nearly 60 percent of Tunisians (this number was 72 percent for eighteen- to twenty-nine-year-olds) and 40 percent of Egyptians, Jordanians, and Lebanese said that they liked American ideas about democracy.[57]

The facts that majorities of people in many Muslim-majority countries possess negative opinions of the United States primarily because of its policies while many individuals hold positive views of US principles are important because they point to the potentially mutable nature of the negativity. America's policies are much more likely to change than are its institutional structures and ideological beliefs. If US actions on the issues most disliked by Muslims alter or are at least perceived in a more positive light, favorable attitudes toward the United States among Arab publics are likely to increase. The ideological attraction that many Muslims feel for the United States makes this development particularly likely.

To state the preceding analysis another way, US deployment of "hard" (primarily military) power and one-sided support of Israel has resulted in negative views of the United States that have in many cases overwhelmed the positive feelings created by America's considerable "soft power," or the attractiveness created by its widespread individual liberties and representative form of government. More accommodating policies in some areas (see some options in greater detail below) are likely to allow sympathy created by ideological attraction to dominate public opinion. If so, the empowerment of public sentiment due to the success of popular uprisings may not result in a significant diminishment of US influence and interests. To the contrary, this development may place US influence on a more stable foundation than when the United States relied almost exclusively on the favor of authoritarian leaders.[58]

A second way in which the spread of more democratic regimes in the Middle East and North Africa may reduce the number of US allies in the region is by facilitating the rise to power of Islamist parties. This second pathway is related but distinct from the previous one. The preceding analysis examined the views of public opinion *as a whole* across a number of Muslim-majority countries. This second pathway analyzes the preferences of the specific parties that are most likely, at least in the short run, to dominate decision making in newly democratic states.

Islamist parties have done very well in those countries that have had competitive elections after ousting a dictator from power. They dominated the elections in

Egypt and Tunisia and came in second in Libya. They are also among the most powerful opposition forces fighting the Asad government in Syria's civil war. On one level, these outcomes may seem surprising because democracy activists and liberals appeared to lead many of the Arab Spring uprisings. On another level, however, these outcomes were to be anticipated. Islamist parties, although persecuted in most secular authoritarian regimes, in many cases continued to operate. When dictatorial governments fell, Islamists had major institutional and organizational advantages—such as existing fund-raising and patronage networks, a brand name, and longtime members who were highly invested in the cause—in comparison with most liberal and secular groups, many of which have also been targeted by authoritarian regimes.

The growing political power of Islamist parties in the Arab Spring era is potentially detrimental to US interests if Islamists possess an ideological antipathy toward the United States. Previous analysis revealed how public opinion in many Muslim-majority countries is suspicious of the United States primarily because of its policies. Ideology-based hostility is much worse from the US perspective because it implies more enduring, immutable, and intense hostility.

Although some Islamist groups and parties—such as al-Qa'ida and its affiliates, many Wahhabists in the religious establishment in Saudi Arabia, and the ruling political factions in Iran—are highly antagonistic to the United States largely for ideological reasons[59], it is not clear that all Islamists share this hostility. Indeed, in many ways the most important domestic battles in postauthoritarian societies in the wake of the Arab Spring will not be between Islamists and secular liberals but among different types of Islamists.[60] All Islamists believe that the prescriptions in the Quran and the traditions of the Prophet Muhammad should have important political effects. Beyond this agreement, though, major differences exist. Three broad varieties of Islamist leaders are likely to vie for power: hard-liners (ideological conservatives), pragmatic conservatives, and liberal Islamists.[61] Hard-line Islamists, including all of the groups mentioned above, believe that a primary objective of government is the regulation of personal virtue based on a narrow and literal interpretation of the Quran and the traditions of the Prophet. This position most often requires that religious authorities exercise important input into political decision making and also that there be limits on popular sovereignty. To hard-line Islamists, majority preferences should not take precedence over Sharia, or Islamic law. Hard-liners also tend not to support equal rights for all groups, especially women and religious minorities.

Pragmatic conservatives share with their hard-line brethren the objectives of creating a state based on Islamic law. This goal, however, is subordinate to more pragmatic considerations, including creating modern, dynamic economies and fostering domestic and international peace. The *New York Times* summarizes this position by examining the Egyptian Muslim Brotherhood's 2011 platform for parliamentary elections: "Unlike the Salafis [(hard-line Islamists), the Muslim Brotherhood] has not proposed to regulate the content of arts or entertainment, women's work or dress, or even the religious content of public education. In fact, the party's platform calls for smaller government to limit corruption and liberalize the economy."[62] There was also a prominent group of pragmatic conservatives in Iran in the 1990s and 2000s that pushed for cooperation with the West on the nuclear issue as long as the external incentives (e.g., economic benefits if Iran stopped its nuclear weapons program) were sufficiently strong.[63]

Liberal Islamists, like other Islamists, base their political prescriptions on Islamic principles and tenets. The *content* of these prescriptions is, however, largely liberal. Liberal Islamists include leaders of the Ennahda Party in Tunisia, the Justice and Development Party in Turkey, Iranian reformers, and at least some components of the Egyptian Muslim Brotherhood. Leaders of these groups assert, for example, that God gave individuals free will, which makes religious compulsion immoral. Similarly, because humans' interpretations of the Quran and God's will are always imperfect, pluralism, tolerance, democracy, separation of powers, the protection of minority rights, and an evolving interpretation of scripture are all necessities.[64]

Policies toward the United States are likely to vary significantly among these three varieties of Islamists. Hard-line Islamists have been and are likely to continue to be intensely hostile to the United States. Hard-liners tend to view the United States as an inevitable enemy, whose interests and values are fundamentally opposed to Muslims. Although pragmatic conservatives share to some degree hard-line Islamists' ideological antipathy to the United States, cooperation is more probable because pragmatists are highly interested in reducing international hostilities, receiving international development assistance, and engaging in high levels of trade in order to develop their country both economically and politically. Cooperation between the United States and liberal Islamist parties is particularly likely to grow. Most important, the ideological barriers to close ties with the United States are not nearly as great for liberal Islamists as for conservative groups. To the contrary, because liberal Islamists are dedicated to many of the political institutions that are hallmarks of Western liberal regimes, leaders of these parties often advocate close ties with Western nations as a means of achieving their domestic goals. This was the case, for example, in two instances when liberal Islamists held significant political power in Middle Eastern countries before the Arab Spring uprisings began: Iranian reformers from 1997 to 2005 and the Justice and Development Party in Turkey beginning in 2003. These groups pushed for extensive cooperation with the United States as a key means of facilitating the realization of their domestic liberalizing objectives.[65] To the extent that these cases are representative of the policies of other liberal Islamist groups, the election of these parties in the wake of the Arab Spring may not be very harmful for US interests.

A third and final way in which the spread of democratic regimes in general and US support of these outcomes in particular may damage America's alliance relationships pertains to those illiberal allies of the United States that do not succumb to revolution. US support of democracy is likely to cause these countries to view the United States as a fickle friend that is setting a very bad precedent, detrimental to their core interests.

This development has already occurred in a critical case: US relations with Saudi Arabia. Saudi leaders, as two *New York Times* reporters summarized shortly after

Mubarak's fall, possessed "little patience with American messages about embracing what Mr. Obama calls 'universal values,' including peaceful protests."[66] One Arab official stated that King Abdullah's willingness to listen to the Obama administration "evaporated" after Mubarak was forced from power in February 2011.[67] Another prominent Saudi analyst with ties to Saudi leaders similarly claimed that a "tectonic shift has occurred in the U.S.-Saudi relationship." Although the United States and Saudi Arabia still have a number of major common interests, in the wake of the events of 2011 "Riyadh intends to pursue a much more assertive foreign policy, at times conflicting with American interests."[68] In keeping with this prediction, Saudi Arabia has become a champion of counterrevolution in neighboring kingdoms, which has made US leaders choose between supporting democracy promotion and a longtime ally that is one of the largest oil-producing countries in the world. The Americans in key cases opted for the latter. Thus, as discussed above, when the Bahraini government, with the help of Saudi troops, crushed political demonstrations beginning in March 2011, the Obama administration offered almost no criticism of the brutality. Saudi actions have highlighted the hypocrisy of US policies. At a minimum, this hypocrisy will most likely amplify the massive doubts among Muslims that the United States is not genuinely interested in advancing their rights. At a maximum, these actions will fuel Muslim animosity as US leaders will be viewed as supporters of governmental repression. In either case, US soft power will be damaged.

Even more harmful for US interests are Saudi and American leaders' different reactions to the Arab Spring protests, which have highlighted the ideological competition between the two countries. In those instances when the United States has pushed allied governments to implement political reforms, such as in Jordan and Morocco, the Saudis have advocated that governments take a tough line.[69] In attempts to gain influence in newly revolutionized states, the Saudis have reportedly funded hard-line Islamist groups, which are likely to be hostile to the United States.[70] In the wake of the Arab Spring, the Saudis have also sought closer relations with China, whose leaders have little sympathy for democratic uprisings.[71] All of these outcomes threaten America's interests.

In addition to losses or increased frictions with allies, a second way in which the Arab Spring protests could endanger US interests is by fueling or facilitating international conflict. Two different pathways lead to this outcome. First, the weakening or overthrow of authoritarian regimes may allow the eruption of sectarian or ideological hostilities that had been repressed. Political scientists have asserted that many societies tend to fluctuate between the opposing outcomes of tyranny and anarchy, meaning that overwhelming governmental power is sometimes necessary to maintain order among opposing societal groups. When the coercive power of a dictatorial regime is removed, factional disputes that had been forced into submission are now able to surface. It is mainly for this reason that al-Qa'ida's leaders have praised the Arab Spring uprisings. They understand that the overthrow of dictatorial regimes allows them much greater operational room to try to achieve their extremist ideological agenda.[72] As we know from revolutionary democratic transitions in Western history, these political transformations are anything but a smooth ride, with retrenchment back toward authoritarian tendencies often preceding true democratic transformation accompanied by the implantation of democratic institutions.

The more divided a society, the more governmental power must be exerted to prevent these divisions from devolving into violence. Many countries in the Middle East and North Africa are split by fierce divisions: ethnic (e.g., Kurds versus Arabs), religious (e.g., Sunni versus Shia Muslims), and ideological (e.g., various types of Islamists, liberals, and secular authoritarians). As authoritarian regimes weaken or are overthrown, these disputes are much more free to turn violent. This tendency is most powerfully on display in Syria at the time of this writing. The weakening of Bashar al-Asad's regime has allowed sectarian and ideological animosities to explode. The civil war in Syria is much more than a product of the Syrian people struggling to liberate themselves from a dictator. It is also a struggle both between Syria's Sunni Muslim majority and the minority Alawite Muslim sect (to which Asad belongs), who fear repression and reprisals if they lose their position of political dominance, as well as among extremist Islamists, moderate Islamists, and secular groups, all of whom are part of the opposition.

All four of the countries that ousted a dictator in 2011 are suffering, to varying degrees, from the effects of anarchy created by weak governments and powerful social divisions. In Yemen, the south is experiencing a surging independence movement, al-Qa'ida's local affiliate is waging a new campaign of terror based on widespread political assassinations, and sectarian violence between Shia and Sunnis is on the rise.[73] Libya's weak government is having difficulty maintaining either internal order or the security of its borders. Local and regional militias apparently are able to smuggle weapons in and out of the country. Dozens of militants who attacked an Algerian natural gas plant in January 2013 came from Libya. Most troubling from the US point of view is the power of extremist groups, which was demonstrated most clearly by the killing in Benghazi of the American ambassador Chris Stevens and three other Americans in an attack in September 2012.[74] As a by-product of the growing polarization between secular and religious forces in Tunisia, which culminated in the assassination of secular opposition leader Chokri Belaid on February 6, 2013, tens of thousands of protestors once again took to the streets. On February 17, Tunisia's prime minister, Hemadi Jebali, resigned in protest of his own party, Ennhada, as its members refused to support the creation of an apolitical, technocratic government, which was meant to transcend the ideological differences dividing the country.[75]

Egypt, too, continues to experience mass political protests against the policies of an Islamist-led government. The root source of the protests is not so much the laws that the Muslim Brotherhood has implemented. The new Egyptian constitution, for example, is a compromise between the demands of individual liberties and religious edicts. According to a scholar of Egyptian politics, Nathan Brown, "from a liberal democratic perspective, there is much to like in [the constitution, but] the document includes just as much that causes concern." The new constitution provides for democratic systems, religious freedom, and personal liberty, while also opening the door to implementing Islamic law at the expense of some freedoms.[76] At the core of the current mass protests, according to Gregory Gause, is "a test of strength for Islamists"—who have consistently tried to consolidate their power at the expense of political inclusion and power sharing—"and their more secular opponents."[77] Widespread protests succeeded in forcing President Morsi in December 2012 to annul most of a decree issued the preceding month that massively increased his power, though both sides remain defiant.[78]

The increased likelihood that weakened or overthrown authoritarian regimes will result in widespread violence as long-repressed societal disputes are free to surface is exacerbated by the fact that sectarian or ideological civil wars in one country frequently create powerful incentives for foreign powers to intervene on behalf of their religious, ethnic, or ideological brethren. These incentives not only amplify the intensity of the original conflict but also increase the odds of the violence spreading to other countries. In the latter case, civil wars can grow into regional conflicts.

Policymakers face incentives to intervene in sectarian or ideological battles in other countries because leaders' identities often have major effects on their international relations and national interests. Policymakers frequently view others with similar identities—for example, shared ethnicity or similar religious or ideological beliefs—to be natural allies and those with opposing identities to be likely enemies.[79] Given these views, leaders possess major security interests in seeing likeminded individuals come to power in other countries. Politicians in support of virtually all ideological beliefs—monarchical, liberal, fascist, communist, and religious fundamentalist—have all attempted to export, including by force, their defining ideological principles and institutions.[80]

When a state is vulnerable to regime change, as clearly occurs during periods of civil war, is precisely when foreign leaders confront very strong incentives to help their ideological or sectarian allies in the contested state. If state X that is dedicated to identity A (e.g., a particular ideology or ethnicity or set of religious beliefs) is susceptible to revolution to identity B, adherents to A and B in other countries will have a strong security interest in seeing their brethren emerge victorious in X.[81] Proponents of identity A in other states will fear that a revolution to identity B in state X will result in a reduction of their international influence (including the loss of a likely ally), as well as a probable gain in influence (including the creation of a likely ally) for proponents of identity B in other countries. The same calculations will create incentives for supporters of identity B abroad to aid revolutionary forces in state X. The fluidity of internal politics in domestically vulnerable states, in sum, will tend to push leaders in other countries to view outcomes as a security gain or a loss for either themselves or their rivals.

To put the preceding analysis another way, when states are vulnerable to revolution, representatives of rival identities in other countries are caught in "an identity security dilemma."[82] Successful regime change from identity A to identity B in state X will tend to make proponents of B in other countries more secure. The more B's identity spreads or is empowered, the fewer the enemies in the system. B's increase in security, though, will make proponents of identity A less secure. The greater the number of governments that are dedicated to identity B, the more proponents of A will feel surrounded by enemies. Given these anticipated outcomes resulting from a civil war in state X, proponents of identity A will confront powerful incentives to interfere in X to maintain the identity—and thus security—status quo, while B will be inclined to interfere to take advantage of a newly created opportunity to increase international influence and security at A's expense.

The incentives for leaders to support their ideological or sectarian brethren in foreign disputes are clearly at work in the Syrian civil war, which is to a certain degree a proxy conflict for the regional rivalry between Saudi Arabia and Iran. Iran has provided money, logistical support, and arms to the Asad regime, a longtime ally of Tehran that happens to be controlled by Alawites, an offshoot of Shiism. Saudi Arabia, Qatar, and the UAE, meanwhile, have helped arm Sunni opposition groups, with apparent favoritism toward more hard-line Islamist parties. These three Gulf nations clearly believe that the empowerment of Sunni Islamists will give them much more influence in Syria, and reduce that of Iran's, than a Syria controlled by the Asad government. Turkey and the United States have also provided some assistance to the Syrian opposition, though they clearly prefer more moderate and secular parties. Similar dynamics are occurring in Yemen, where Iran is believed to be taking advantage of retreating governmental power and arming rebellious Shiite tribes, while Saudi Arabia is supporting the Sunni-led government.[83]

In addition to allowing repressed sectarian and ideological disputes to erupt into violence, a second way in which the overthrow of authoritarian regimes could increase the likelihood of conflict has to do with the perils of democratizing regimes. As two authorities on this subject state, "history shows that the consolidation of democracy tends to promote peace and stability, but the initial stages of democratization can stimulate both international and civil wars."[84] The key to avoiding conflict in democratizing regimes is the existence of effective political, legal, and civic institutions that help states manage the demands of groups that had previously been excluded from the levers of power. An important component of this process is the implementation of effective power-sharing arrangements that mitigate the divisive effects created by ethnic and sectarian differences. These institutions include: separation of powers and checks and balances designed to help restrain governmental power and protect political pluralism and minority rights; strong civil society groups that are able to push back against governmental excesses; an apolitical military; an independent transparent judiciary that enforces the rule of law; and a free press. "When these institutions are deformed or weak, politicians are better able to resort to nationalist or sectarian appeals, tarring their opponents as enemies of the nation, in order to prevail in electoral competition. The use of such appeals generally heightens the prospect that democratization will stimulate hostilities at home and abroad."[85] Unfortunately, many Middle Eastern and North African states, with their stunted political development due to decades of dictatorial rule and political oppression, are lacking in precisely those institutions and values that make democratic transitions most likely to succeed without creating increased incentives for aggression. As Kenneth Pollack states, "Nowhere in the Middle East are there strong institutions *and* a political culture of democracy *and* the rule of law."[86]

The relationship between the increased risks of civil and international wars in the Middle East and North Africa in the wake of the Arab Spring uprisings and threats to US interests is obvious. The United States has a number of key interests in the region, including maintaining access to the region's oil and natural gas reserves; containing Iranian power and influence; minimizing the threat posed by terrorist networks, most notably al-Qa'ida and its affiliates; and protecting Israel. Widespread conflict caused by democratization due to both of the pathways discussed above threatens all of these interests.

Potential Benefits for the United States Created by the Arab Spring

Although the Arab Spring uprisings clearly create a number of major risks to US interests in the Middle East and North Africa, they also could result in major advantages. The success of the Arab Spring demonstrations either have already or are likely in the future to create three major sets of benefits for US interests. These revolts could: 1) weaken existing enemies of the United States; 2) empower key allies; 3) create a more stable foundation for the projection of US influence in coming decades. These potential benefits of the Arab Spring are the flip side of the potential disadvantages analyzed in the previous section. Although the Arab Spring protests may topple illiberal allies of the United States, they may also overthrow or weaken illiberal enemies. Whereas the Arab Spring may lead to more violence and conflict, especially in the short run, in the long run these revolts may create a firmer foundation for greater peace and stability.

There are two principal ways by which the Arab Spring revolts could weaken existing enemies of the United States. First, these uprisings could result in a major ideological challenge to US rivals, including al-Qa'ida and Iran. Leaders of al-Qa'ida and its affiliates have long claimed that only violence could overthrow dictatorial regimes in the Middle East and North Africa, and such defeats of "near enemies" were only possible if the power that propped them up—the "far enemy" of the United States—was first defeated and forced to withdraw from the region. The overthrow of the Ben Ali, Mubarak, and Gadafi dictatorships refute these claims. Ben Ali and Mubarak were ousted largely by peaceful protests, and the United States supported the demonstrators in both Egypt and especially Libya.

More important, the Arab Spring uprisings reveal a widespread repudiation of al-Qa'ida's extremist objectives. Stephen Grand, the director of the Project on US Relations with the Islamic World at the Brookings Institution, asserts that "more than anything else, the Arab Spring has been about a yearning for democracy."[87] These aspirations are in direct opposition to al-Qa'ida's ideological beliefs and political goals. Daniel Byman summarizes this opposition when he writes: "Movement toward a free press, free elections, and civil liberties throughout the Middle East will highlight the least appealing part of al-Qaeda's dogma: its hostility toward democracy and desire to build a theocratic caliphate . . . Al-Qaeda believes that democracy is blasphemous, arguing that it places man's word above God's . . . Al-Qaeda's message is clear: it will fight democracy as hard as it has fought dictatorship. That is not a message likely to resonate with most of those" participating in the Arab Spring demonstrations.[88]

This ideological tension with al-Qa'ida in the wake of successful Arab Spring protests is likely to exist even if Islamist groups (as long as they are of the pragmatic or liberal variety described earlier) are elected into power. Al-Qa'ida's leaders, for example, have for many years been deeply critical of the Egyptian Muslim Brotherhood for the latter's rejection of violence and willingness to participate in elections. This feud is unlikely to end given the Brotherhood's electoral victories in 2011 and 2012. To the contrary, we might expect the Brotherhood to support US counterterrorism efforts against al-Qa'ida and its offshoots because Brotherhood leaders also view the latter as a rival and threat.[89]

Iran is another enemy of the United States that might be significantly harmed by the Arab Spring. The civil war in Syria is likely to weaken, and potentially end, Iran's alliance with Syria. This coalition, which began in 1979, has been critical to the advancement of Iran's interests through the decades. Close ties with Syria have provided Iran a conduit by which it could project its influence into the Arab world, most notably into Lebanon and the Israeli-Palestinian conflict. (Most of the weapons that Iran provides Hizbollah in Lebanon flow through Syria.)

The great importance of the Syrian-Iranian alliance is revealed by the lengths to which Iranian leaders have gone to help prop up the Asad government despite its brutality in the Syrian civil war. The Iranians have provided Asad expansive aid, including weapons, money, and logistical training and support. Asad's fall would most likely mean the empowerment of Sunni groups in Syria. At a minimum, this change would mean less cooperation with Iran as Syrian foreign policies become more similar to those adopted by most Sunni-led Arab countries. At a maximum, a new regime in Syria could ally with Saudi Arabia, which, among Muslim-majority countries, is Iran's greatest competitor in the region. Saudi and Qatari leaders are clearly hoping for this last outcome; hence their arming of Syrian opposition groups, including more hard-line Islamist factions.

In addition to potentially undermining the Syrian-Iranian alliance, the Arab Spring protests also threaten Iran's interests by reducing its "soft power," which is the ability to influence others based on the attractiveness of one's beliefs, principles, and actions. Iranian leaders have long tried to gain support in the Arab world by attempting to exploit Arab populations' frustrations with the lack of freedom and opportunity in their countries.[90] To the extent that democratic revolutions succeed in the Middle East and North Africa, this opportunity for Iran is reduced because a key source of Arabs' frustrations—the oppressiveness of their governments—has been removed. Even worse from Iranian leaders' perspective is the issue of their crushing Iran's protest movement in 2009 and supporting the Asad government's brutality in the Syrian civil war, making clear that Iranian policymakers care little for people's rights. This issue has also weakened Hizbollah's standing in the region, as it, too, has strongly supported the Asad regime. US leaders have been quick to try to capitalize on these developments. As President Obama stated, Iran's support of Asad "speaks to the hypocrisy of the Iranian regime, which says it stands for the rights of protesters abroad, yet represses its own people at home. Let's remember that the first peaceful protests in the region were in the streets of Tehran."[91] Even leaders who are potentially more sympathetic to Iran have condemned it for its actions in Syria. Most notably, Egyptian President Morsi, while visiting Iran in a gathering of the 120-nation Nonaligned Movement, rebuked his host and all those who supported Asad instead of the forces for democracy in Syria.[92] The more the illiberalism and brutality of the Iranian regime is spotlighted, the less soft power it is likely to have, to the benefit of US interests in the region.

A second way in which the Arab Spring protests might benefit the United States is by empowering a key ally in the region, Turkey. Numerous public opinion polls and related data have documented that Turkey—especially in states like Tunisia, Egypt, and Libya that are trying to create new political systems after ousting authoritarian governments—is the most popular country in the Islamic world. One 2012 pubic option poll found that 80 percent of respondents had a favorable view of Turkey, and 60 percent considered Turkey's political system under the leadership of the Justice and Development Party (JDP) a model for their country.[93] Leading political parties in Tunisia and Egypt have explicitly modeled themselves on the JDP in Turkey.[94] The sources of this popularity and emulation are clearly based upon Turkey's ample soft power. The success of the JDP in creating a dynamic economy and advancing political rights while also protecting religious identities is a source of tremendous appeal throughout the Islamic world. Given these facts, the more that democratic revolutions succeed in the Middle East and North Africa, the more Turkey's influence is likely to grow. As one senior Turkish official stated in the fall of 2011, "What's happening in the Middle East is a big opportunity, a golden opportunity" for Turkey. Suat Kiniklioğlu, the JDP's deputy chairman of external affairs, similarly asserted that his government's reactions to the Arab Spring were designed "to make the most of the influence we have in a region that is embracing our leadership."[95]

The growth of Turkey's influence in the Middle East and North Africa, based on its soft power and the appeal of its secular Islamist democracy, benefits US interests in key ways, most notably by helping to curtail the spread of Iranian sway in the region. Iranian policymakers are aware that they are in a soft-power contest with Turkey to see which state has more allure throughout the Arab world. Iranian leaders, for example, derided Turkey's prime minister Recep Tayyip Erdoğan's calls for Egypt and Tunisia to adopt secularism in their new constitutions. The Iranians no doubt hoped to see these countries adopt more hard-line Islamist governments. Ayatollah Mahmood Hashemi Shahroudi, the former chief of Iran's judiciary, scornfully dismissed Turkey's efforts to spread democracy in the Middle East as an example of "liberal Islam" that was designed to try to counter Iran's regional influence.[96] Ali-Akbar Velayati, senior adviser to Supreme Leader Ali Khamenei, made similar statements, as did Yahya Safavi, the former commander of the Revolutionary Guards.[97] Iranian policymakers recognize that the more that Turkey is able to spread its ideological principles in those states made vulnerable by the Arab Spring, the more Iran's regional influence will be reduced.[98] Making matters worse for the Iranians, "privately, Iranian officials acknowledge that Ankara's soft-power strategy is more appealing in the long term . . . Turkey's comprehensive soft power in the region, including cultural affinity, economic ties, a balanced approach toward Israel, and the example of a democratic government that allows for the assertion of Islamic identity, presents Iran with a major challenge in any future competition for leadership in the region."[99] US leaders have recognized that the spread of Turkish influence in the Middle East and North Africa benefits US interests and have pushed Turkey to assert itself as an ideological model throughout the region.[100] The result has been a deepening of the alliance between the two countries, one that had been strained in previous years because of the 2003 US-led invasion of Iraq.

A final potential US advantage created by the spread of democracy in the Middle East and North Africa is that in the future this outcome could be a potent force for political stability. It is true, as discussed previously, that the overthrow of dictatorial regimes allows for greater opportunities for civil violence as factional disputes in this new environment are much more free to surface in the absence of governmental coercion. At the same time, however, the end of a dictatorial regime removes a major source of popular frustration and resentment, which in turn also reduces the ability of violent organizations like al-Qa'ida to recruit people to join their extremist cause. Both developments are important forces working for domestic peace. The Obama administration recognized these relationships even before the Arab Spring uprisings began. On August 12, 2010, Obama sent a five-page memorandum titled "Political Reform in the Middle East and North Africa" to senior members of his foreign policy team. The president noted that there was evidence in the Middle East and North Africa of "growing citizen discontent with the region's regimes . . . If present trends continue," allies there would "opt for repression rather than reform to manage domestic dissent . . . Increased repression could threaten the political and economic stability of some of our allies, leave us with fewer capable, credible partners who can support our regional priorities, and further alienate citizens in the region . . . Moreover, our regional and international credibility will be undermined if we are seen or perceived to be backing repressive regimes and ignoring the rights and aspirations of citizens."[101]

Related forces are at work at the international level. Although democratizing states are often a source of international conflict as documented above, established democratic regimes tend to be pacific, at least in terms of relations with one another. This relationship is known in the international relations literature as the "democratic peace." One prominent political scientist labels the tendency for established democratic states not to war with one another "the closest thing to an empirical law in international relations [that] we have."[102]

Based on the insights of the democratic peace thesis, the spread of stable democratic regimes could benefit the United States by removing ideology-based hostilities with illiberal enemies and ideology-based frictions with illiberal allies.[103] The establishment of stable democracies in the Middle East and North Africa thus creates a greater likelihood that cooperation between the United States and some countries in these regions will be based not only on shared material interests but also on shared values. The more this is the case, the more solid the foundation America's alliance relations will be.

The key to maximizing the likelihood of realizing these last domestic and international benefits created by the spread of democracy is for authoritarian regimes to transition to stable liberal democratic governments as quickly and painlessly as possible. The next section discusses some strategies US leaders could adopt to aid this process.

WHAT SHOULD THE UNITED STATES DO?

Given the major potential threats and opportunities to US interests created by the Arab Spring uprisings, what policies should US leaders adopt to minimize the costs and maximize the benefits? The first step in effective policymaking in response to the Arab Spring should be dispositional in nature, meaning that US leaders should approach decision making in the context of specific attitudes. Most important, the Americans should have both realistic expectations about what is possible in the region and humility about their ability to affect change in the desired direction. States in the Middle East and North Africa, even ones that have recently held reasonably competitive elections after overthrowing a dictator, are unlikely to become stable liberal democracies anytime soon. Many of the major problems and issues that led to the Arab Spring uprisings—including widespread "youth bulges" (disproportionate numbers of young people in a society and strongly associated with domestic violence) and very high levels of unemployment and corruption—are likely to remain potent forces of instability even after transitions to democracy have begun. The end of authoritarian regimes does eliminate some key sources of instability by reducing political repression and advancing the rule of law and transparency. The same development, though, could also increase the probability of continued civil violence by allowing social divisions and extremist groups more room to operate, hence the perils of democratizing states discussed earlier.

In addition to realistic expectations about the likelihood of transitions to stable democracies in the near future, humility should also inform US policymaking. American leaders should recognize that if they choose to intervene in Middle Eastern and North African politics, their ability to help create democratic regimes is modest. The US experience in Iraq after 2003 demonstrates this point. The United States invaded this country, occupied it for a decade, and spent hundreds of billions of dollars on development and reconstruction—none of which are likely to happen again in the foreseeable future. Many would argue Iraq is a much better place than when it was ruled by the iron fist of Saddam Hussein; however, even after all the American blood and treasure spent there, it remains, according to independent analyses, an "unfree" state marked by high levels of political corruption, sectarian disputes, and major threats to minority rights.[104]

A humble disposition would also help make US policymakers more aware of the potential pernicious effects of unintended consequences. The impossibility of anticipating all outcomes created by interventions should be a major source of caution and restraint. For example, the prevention of a massacre in Libya and the subsequent toppling of the brutal Gadafi regime was clearly a good thing. But the latter outcome also allowed thousands of weapons to disappear, many of which ended up in the hands of extremist Islamist groups who used them to take over northern Mali, which in turn led to military intervention by France in 2013 to counter this threat in its former colony.[105] Awareness of the potential negative effects of unintended consequences should help to avoid rash interventions while creating additional incentives for higher levels of preparedness to deal with unexpected contingencies if the United States and its allies should choose to intervene. For example, a larger NATO ground presence in Libya at the end of the intervention could have helped secure more of Gadafi's huge store of weapons before they fell into extremist groups' hands.

Finally, American policymakers must recognize, in a spirit of humility, that democratic institutions and values in the Islamic world are probably not going to replicate those found in the United States. Democracy is most likely to be successful when it grows organically out of a culture's traditions and values. In the Middle East and North Africa, this means that religion will probably have a much greater impact on political and social life than many in the United States would deem acceptable. Political Islamists of some variety may well be the key actors in many newly revolutionized countries for the foreseeable future. However, as argued above, this outcome is not necessarily detrimental to US interests, especially if liberal Islamists dominate decision making. In this scenario, the content of leaders' institutions and norms will be liberal, even if the foundations for them are religiously based.

Although US leaders should not be overly optimistic about either the probability of Middle Eastern and North African states smoothly transitioning to stable democracies or America's ability to move outcomes in this direction, they should not be overly pessimistic either. Because authoritarian regimes do not allow for the development of effective political and legal institutions, political parties, or civil institutions, many of the troubles that newly revolutionized countries in the Arab world are currently experiencing are neither surprising nor unusual. To the contrary, these challenges are very similar, according to political scientist Sheri Berman, to the early stages of democratic transitions in other countries worldwide, including those in Europe.[106] Violence and political paralysis after the ouster of a dictator, in short, by no means precludes an eventual successful evolution to stable democracy.

Furthermore, although the ability to export democracy is limited, this does not mean that the United States cannot be a valuable aid to the creation of key components of liberalization, including helping to create transparent, accountable, inclusive political and legal institutions as well as a thriving civil society. Many of the policies that could help to bring about these outcomes are not particularly expensive or risky.

Some of the Bush administration's less expensive policies, for example, may have played an important role in fomenting the Arab Spring uprisings by training various leaders of reform movements in the Middle East in such ventures as campaigning, organizing, and using media and social networking tools. These efforts took place even in authoritarian allies of the United States, including in Bahrain, Egypt, and Yemen.[107] US leaders can continue these programs and add to them in order to help create engaged, educated, cosmopolitan civil societies. According to Stephen Grand, "The United States should be encouraging 'brain circulation'—the flow of people and ideas in, out, and across the region. For example, Washington should continue to support greater Internet access and Internet freedom, and find more ways for Arab and American youth to connect via social and virtual media . . . The aim should be to help create a new generation of citizens who are more educated, more open to the world, and more connected to one another. If the past is any guide, this will be the best guarantor of democracy's long-term success."[108] To achieve these outcomes, US leaders could also push for extensive student, professional development, and cultural exchanges, as well as the creation in Muslim-majority countries of educational institutions that stress science and technology and the dangers of extremism.[109]

In terms of encouraging governments to adopt liberalizing reforms, Washington again is not without leverage. US leaders could threaten to take away or reduce economic or military support from allies (e.g., Egypt's roughly $2 billion a year in aid), or promise to provide additional aid every time a country meets a predetermined benchmark for reform. Some of the United States' greatest success stories in the past of fostering liberalism have been with allies (including South Korea, Taiwan, South Africa, and the Philippines), and the use of these "carrots and sticks" has been key to this process.[110]

Beyond these policies designed to stimulate reform are the much more risky and costly ones of direct military interventions, from arming insurgents in target states to the deployment of US forces. At the time of this writing, the United States and its allies are struggling with the costs created by both aggressive and half-hearted, cautious interventions. The overthrow of Gadafi's regime through assertive military intervention resulted in extremist groups acquiring large amounts of weaponry, which they have used against Western interests, most notably in Mali, Algeria, and Lebanon; some of the weapons have also reportedly been smuggled into Egypt, Gaza, Chad, and Syria.[111] The fear that an analogous outcome would take place in Syria has played a key role in the Obama administration's refusal to arm the Syrian rebels. However, by not doing so, some argue that Obama is not only refusing to tilt the balance against a brutal regime but may also be forgoing opportunities of gaining influence among the next generation of Syrian leaders (assuming Asad is ousted from power) and ensuring that moderate groups within the opposition remain more powerful than extremist ones. Unfortunately, there are few low-risk options when it comes to using force to help others liberate themselves from oppression.[112]

US efforts (especially the lower-risk options explored above) to encourage reform in the Middle East and North Africa are most likely to succeed when two conditions are met. First, the United States must push for a just solution to the Israeli-Palestinian conflict. As discussed above, America's one-sided support of Israel in this dispute is a central reason for its low popularity among many Muslims, which in turn is a major impediment to efforts to advance liberalization. Negative views push people to doubt the sincerity of US motives and make some loath to receive aid from the United States lest they be painted as stooges of an untrustworthy actor. Solving the Israeli-Palestinian conflict would reduce hostility and mistrust of the United States, thereby allowing the significant ideological affinity for it (highlighted earlier) to become more determinative of overall perceptions.

Second, the United States must try to reassure Saudi leaders that policies designed to stimulate reforms across the Middle East and North Africa do not endanger their core interests. As discussed, the Al Saud have viewed the Arab Spring uprisings as highly threatening to their security, and they have championed counterrevolution in a number of countries, even in some where the United States is actively pushing for reforms. As long as these policies continue, US efforts at democracy promotion will be much less effective. If, for example, the United States threatens to reduce aid from allies due to unacceptable domestic policies, the Saudis, in an effort to preserve the status quo, could use their vast oil wealth to offset losses created by the withdrawal of US financial support. Similarly, if the Americans promise additional aid to those countries that make important progress toward liberalization, the Saudis could promise more funding to maintain the status quo.

The good news for the United States is that it is not impossible to convince at least some key Saudi policymakers that reforms are in their self-interest. To the contrary, powerful leaders, including King Abdullah, have asserted a positive relationship between some liberalization—as long as it is controlled from above—and long-run domestic stability. In support of these claims, the Saudis have engaged in a number of important liberalizing reforms since the early 2000s, especially in the areas of education and women's rights.[113] The more Saudi leaders feel comfortable with political reforms at home, the less likely they will be to oppose liberalizing policies in other countries.

This chapter has described the considerable potential advantages and disadvantages for US security as a result of the Arab Spring uprisings. Some important dimensions of America's security architecture in the region are unlikely to change in the near future despite these revolutionary developments. The United States, for example, is likely to continue to rely on close relations with some authoritarian governments (especially those, like Saudi Arabia, that have been largely untouched by the Arab Spring) in order to best protect some of its core material interests. However, the Middle East and North Africa will almost certainly not return to the political status quo that held before the protests began. The powerful forces that led to the demonstrations, including a widespread yearning for democracy, will surely not abate. Given this reality, a central way for US leaders to maximize the likelihood of reaping the benefits created by the Arab Spring while minimizing the costs would be to help democratizing states transition quickly and smoothly to stable democratic regimes. This, of course, is easier said than done. The first step, though, is to recognize the advantages of achieving this outcome, which was one of this chapter's key goals.

NOTES

1. "Text: Obama's Speech in Cairo," *New York Times*, June 4, 2009.

2. Ryan Lizza, "The Consequentialist: How the Arab Spring Remade Obama's Foreign Policy," *The New Yorker*, May 2, 2011. The decision to invade Iraq in 2003 and try to democratize it is the most obvious example of Bush's freedom agenda at work. It also included hard-line policies toward Iran and Syria as part of an effort to provoke regime changes in these countries.

3. Henry R. Nau, "Obama's Foreign Policy," *Policy Review*, no. 160 (April and May, 2010).

4. "Obama's Speech in Cairo."

5. The following four paragraphs are drawn from Mark L. Haas, *The Clash of Ideologies: Middle Eastern Politics and American Security* (New York: Oxford University Press, 2012), pp. 118–119, 122, 285–286.

6. All quotations from Alan Cowell, "In a Video Appeal to Iran, Obama Offers a 'New Day,'" *New York Times*, March 21, 2009.

7. Helene Cooper and Robert F. Worth, "In Arab Spring, Obama Finds Sharp Test," *New York Times*, September 24, 2012. According to one report, some analysts at the White House were irate over a State Department official's request to Twitter to not perform a planned upgrade that would have temporarily shut down service in Iran. Iranian protestors were using Twitter to organize and get information to the international media. In the words of one former Obama administration official, advisers in the White House "were so mad that somebody had actually 'interfered' in Iranian politics, because they were doing their damnedest to not interfere . . . The core of it was we were still trying to engage the Iranian government and we did not want to do anything that made us side with the protesters" (quoted in Lizza, "The Consequentialist").

8. Mark Landler, "U.S. Officials to Continue to Engage Iran," *New York Times*, June 13, 2009.

9. Quotations from, respectively, Helene Cooper and Mark Landler, "For Obama, Pressure to Strike a Firmer Tone," *New York Times*, June 18, 2009, and Jay Solomon and Chip Cummins, "Iran's Election Results Stoke Global Debate," *Wall Street Journal*, June 15, 2009.

10. Quoted in "Iran's Supreme Leader Dismisses Obama Overtures," Associated Press, March 21, 2009.

11. Quoted in Thomas Erdbrink and William Branigin, "Iran's President Rebukes Obama," *Washington Post*, June 28, 2009.

12. Robert F. Worth, "Iran Expanding Effort to Stifle the Opposition," *New York Times*, November 24, 2009.

13. "Obama Offer is Denounced by Ayatollah," Associated Press, March 21, 2010.

14. Quoted in Jeffrey Fleishman and Ramin Mostaghim, "Disclosure of Secret Nuclear Plant Further Divides Iran's Hard-liners, Opposition," *Los Angeles Times*, September 27, 2009.

15. Quoted in Nazenin Ansari and Jonathan Paris, "The Message from the Streets in Tehran," *New York Times*, November 6, 2009.

16. Ibid. Egyptian protestors have offered similar criticism of Obama for his muted censure of some of the policies of the Muslim Brotherhood–led government after Hosni Mubarak's ouster. In a February 2013 open letter to Obama in *Al-Ahram Weekly*, Egyptian human rights activist Bahieddin Hassan wrote that the "stances of your administration have given political cover to the current authoritarian regime in Egypt and allowed it to fearlessly implement undemocratic policies and commit numerous acts of repression." http://www.jadaliyya.com/pages/index/10170/open-letter-to-president-obama

17. Both quotations from Cooper and Worth, "In Arab Spring, Obama Finds Sharp Test."

18. Haas, *The Clash of Ideologies*, ch. 2.

19. David Sanger, "Half a Doctrine Will Have to Do," *New York Times*, May 21, 2011.

20. Quoted in Sanger, "Half a Doctrine Will Have to Do."

21. "Obama's Mideast Speech," *New York Times*, May 19, 2011. Earlier in the year, Obama's secretary of state, Hillary Clinton, also asserted a synergy between America's ideological and security interests when she claimed that "without genuine progress [in the Middle East] toward open and accountable political systems, the gap between people and their governments will grow, and instability will only deepen. This is not simply a matter of idealism; it is a strategic necessity" (quoted in "Clinton: Mideast Must Reform Despite Risks," Associated Press, February 5, 2011).

22. The exportation of liberalism was the primary thrust of Bush's second inaugural: "For as long as whole regions of the world simmer in resentment and tyranny prone to ideologies that feed hatred and excuse murder, violence will gather and multiply in destructive power, and cross the most defended borders, and raise a mortal threat. There is only one force of history that can break the reign of hatred and resentment, and expose the pretensions of tyrants and reward the hopes of the decent and tolerant, and that is the force of human freedom. We are led, by events and common sense, to one conclusion: The survival of liberty in our land increasingly depends on the success of liberty in other lands. The best hope for peace in our world is the expansion of freedom in all the world. America's vital interests and our deepest beliefs are now one . . . So it is the policy of the United States to seek and support the growth of democratic movements and institutions in every nation and culture, with the ultimate goal of ending tyranny in our world."

23. Kenneth Jost, "Unrest in the Arab World," *CQ Researcher* 23, no. 5 (February 1, 2013), p. 124.

24. Kim Ghattas, "How Does the US View Tunisia's Revolt?" BBC News, January 16, 2011.

25. Quoted in Shadi Hamid, "Tunisia: Birthplace of the Revolution," in Kenneth M. Pollack et al., *The Arab Awakening: America and the Transformation of the Middle East* (Washington, DC: Brookings Institution Press, 2011), p. 115.

26. Quoted in Lizza, "The Consequentialist."

27. Shadi Hamid, "Egypt: The Prize," in Pollack et al., *The Arab Awakening*, p. 103.

28. Lizza, "The Consequentialist."

29. Quoted in Cooper and Worth, "In Arab Spring, Obama Finds Sharp Test."

30. Jeremy Pressman, "Same Old Story? Obama and the Arab Uprisings," in Mark L. Haas and David W. Lesch, eds., *The Arab Spring: Change and Resistance in the Middle East* (Boulder: Westview Press, 2013), p. 224.

31. Cooper and Worth, "In Arab Spring, Obama Finds Sharp Test." Regret over American inaction as Iran crushed protestors in 2009 apparently played a particularly important role in pushing some in the Obama administration to push for more assertive policies in support of the Egyptian demonstrators (Lizza, "The Consequentialist").

32. Bruce K. Rutherford, "Egypt: The Origins and Consequences of the January 25 Uprising," in Haas and Lesch, eds., *The Arab Spring*, p. 43.

33. On this change, see Pressman, "Same Old Story?" pp. 222, 230–231.

34. Akram Al-Turk, "Libya: From Revolt to State Building," in Pollack et al., *The Arab Awakening*, p. 120.

35. Russia abstained in the vote on this resolution. When the Western powers used it as cover for regime change in Libya as opposed to preventing mass killings only, Russian leaders felt duped, which subsequently hardened their position against a similar UN resolution when civilian deaths in Syria escalated.

36. Mary-Jane Deeb, "The Arab Spring: Libya's Second Revolution," in Haas and Lesch, eds., *The Arab Spring,"* p. 65.

37. Lizza, "The Consequentialist."

38. Laura Kasinof and David E. Sanger, "U.S. Shifts to Seek Removal of Yemen's Leader, An Ally," *New York Times*, April 3, 2011.

39. Quoted in Pressman, "Same Old Story?," p. 224.

40. Clifford Krauss, "Bahrain's Rulers Tighten Their Grip on Battered Opposition," *New York Times*, April 6, 2011.

41. Ethan Bronner and Michael Slackman, "Saudi Troops Enter Bahrain to Help Put Down Unrest," *New York Times*, March 14, 2011.

42. Michael S. Doran and Salman Shaikh, "Bahrain: Island of Troubles," in Pollack et al., *The Arab Awakening*, p. 193.

43. Pressman, "Same Old Story?," p. 224.

44. "U.S. Resumes Bahrain Arms Sales Despite Rights Concerns," Reuters, May 11, 2012.

45. Rick Gladstone and Anne Barnard, "U.N. Warns of Dire Rise in Refugees from Syria," *New York Times*, February 27, 2013.

46. Quoted in Pressman, "Same Old Story?," p. 226.

47. For a comprehensive analysis of US policies, objectives, and concerns toward Syria in this period, see David W. Lesch, *Syria: The Fall of the House of Assad* (New Haven, CT: Yale University Press, 2012). Part of my analysis in this section is drawn from this work.

48. CNN.com, "U.S., Europe call for Syrian leader al-Assad to step down," August 18, 2011, http://articles.cnn.com/2011-08-18/politics/us.syria_1_president-bashar-al-assad-president-assad-syrian-people?_s-PM;POLITICS.

49. On the preceding points, see Steven Lee Myers, "U.S. Joins Effort to Equip and Pay Rebels in Syria," *New York Times*, April 1, 2012; Eric Schmitt and Helene Cooper, "Stymied at U.N., U.S. Refines Plan to Remove Asad," *New York Times*, July 21, 2012; David E. Sanger and Eric Schmitt, "U.S. Weighs Bolder Effort to Intervene in Syria's Conflict," *New York Times*, November 28, 2012; Mark Landler and Michael R. Gordon, "Obama Says U.S. Will Recognize Syrian Rebels," *New York Times*, December 11, 2012; Michael R. Gordon, "U.S. Steps Up Aid to Syrian Opposition, Pledging $60 Million,"

New York Times, February 28, 2013; Michael R. Gordon, "Kerry Says Administration Backs Mideast Efforts to Arm Syrian Rebels," *New York Times*, March 5, 2013.

50. Mark Landler and Michael R. Gordon, "Obama Could Revisit Arming Syria Rebels as Asad Holds Firm," *New York Times*, February 18, 2013.

51. See, for example, David D. Kirkpatrick, "For the United States, Arab Spring Raises Questions of Values Versus Interests," *New York Times*, July 27, 2012.

52. Shibley Telhami, "Arab Public Opinion: What Do They Want?" in Pollack et al., *The Arab Awakening*, p. 15, emphasis in original.

53. Both sets of polling data from Telhami, "Arab Public Opinion," p. 18.

54. Richard Wike, "Wait, You Still Don't Like Us?," ForeignPolicy.com, September 19, 2012.

55. Reza Marashi and Trita Parsi, "The Gift and the Curse: Iran and the Arab Spring," in Haas and Lesch, eds., *The Arab Spring,"* pp. 133–151; Suzanne Maloney, "Iran: The Bogeyman," in Pollack et al., *The Arab Awakening*, pp. 258–261.

56. Wike, "Wait, You Still Don't Like Us?" See also Telhami, "Arab Public Opinion," p. 15.

57. Wike, "Wait, You Still Don't Like Us?"

58. Additional good news in this area for the United States is that liberalizing elites in other countries are sometimes more interested in close ties with it than public opinion would seem to allow. Liberalizing political groups have an interest in cooperation with the United States if this cooperation results in economic, security, or other benefits that facilitate the realization of their domestic objectives. (For evidence that supports these claims for liberalizing groups in Iran and Turkey, see Mark L. Haas "Missed Ideological Opportunities and George W. Bush's Middle Eastern Policies," *Security Studies* 21, no. 3 (September 2012), pp. 436–439; Haas, *The Clash of Ideologies*, ch. 4). It is true that US support of reformist groups in the Middle East and North Africa can hurt their cause by allowing them to be portrayed by rivals as "traitors" or "stooges" of foreigners (see Ronald R. Krebs, "Rethinking the Battle of Ideas: How the United States Can Help Muslim Moderates," *Orbis* 52, no. 2 (Spring 1988), pp. 332–346). However, groups that already possess some political power or have an already established base of domestic support are likely to be less worried about alienating nationalistic sentiments, which will allow them to court foreign support with greater impunity.

59. See Haas, *The Clash of Ideologies*, chs. 2 and 5.

60. The following three paragraphs are taken from Mark L. Haas and David W. Lesch, "Introduction," in Haas and Lesch, eds., *The Arab Spring*, pp. 5–6.

61. Anthony Shadid and David D. Kirkpatrick, "Activists in Arab World Vie to Define Islamic State," *New York Times*, September 21, 2011; Carrie Rosefsky Wickham, "The Muslim Brotherhood After Mubarak," *Foreign Affairs* online, February 3, 2011, http://www.foreignaffairs.com/articles/67348/carrie-rosefsky-wickham/the-muslim-brotherhood-after-mubarak

62. David D. Kirkpatrick, "Egypt's Vote Puts Emphasis on Split over Religious Rule," *New York Times*, December 11, 2011. See also Wickham, "The Muslim Brotherhood after Mubarak."

63. Haas, *The Clash of Ideologies*, pp. 91–92.

64. Stéphane Lacroix, "Between Islamists and Liberals: Saudi Arabia's New 'Islamo-Liberal' Reformists," *Middle East Journal* 58, no. 3 (Summer 2004), pp. 345–365; Rutherford, "Egypt."

65. Haas, *The Clash of Ideologies*, chs. 2 and 4.

66. David Sanger and Eric Schmitt, "U.S.-Saudi Tensions Intensify with Mideast Turmoil," *New York Times*, March 14, 2011.

67. Quoted in Cooper and Landler, "Interests of Saudi Arabia and Iran Collide."

68. Nawaf Obaid, "Amid the Arab Spring, a U.S.-Saudi Split," *Washington Post*, May 15, 2011.

69. Bruce O. Riedel, "Saudi Arabia: The Elephant in the Living Room," in Pollack et al., *The Arab Awakening*, p. 161; Samuel Helfont and Tally Helfont, "Jordan: Between the Arab Spring and the Gulf Cooperation Council," and Mehran Kamrava, "The Arab Spring and the Saudi-led Counterrevolution," both in *Orbis* 56, no. 1 (Winter 2012), pp. 82–95 and 96–104, respectively.

70. John R. Bradley, "Saudi Arabia's Invisible Hand in the Arab Spring," *Foreign Affairs* online, October 13, 2011.

71. Riedel, "Saudi Arabia," p. 163.

72. Daniel L. Byman, "Terrorism: Al-Qaeda and the Arab Spring," in Pollack et al., *The Arab Awakening*, pp. 76–77.

73. Robert F. Worth, "Yemen, Hailed as Model, Struggles for Stability," *New York Times*, February 18, 2013.

74. Steven Erlanger, "Two Years after Revolt, Libya Faces a Host of Problems," *New York Times*, February 12, 2013.

75. Kareem Fahim and Farah Samti, "Denied New Government, Tunisian Premier Resigns," *New York Times*, February 19, 2013.

76. Jost, "Unrest in the Arab World," p. 120. Brown's quotation is from this page.

77. F. Gregory Gause, III, "The Year the Arab Spring Went Bad," ForeignPolicy.com, December 31, 2012.

78. Stephanie McCrummen and Abigail Hauslohner, "Egyptian Opposition Remains Defiant after Morsi Annuls Decree," *Washington Post*, December 9, 2012.

79. See, for example, Haas, *The Clash of Ideologies*; John M. Owen, *The Clash of Ideas in World Politics: Transnational Networks, States, and Regime Change, 1510–2010* (Princeton, NJ: Princeton University Press, 2010).

80. For extensive analysis of regime promotion by multiple ideological groups over the last five hundred years, see Owen, *Clash of Ideas*. Owen finds that since 1510 states have used force on more than two hundred separate occasions to alter or preserve the ideological principles and institutions of another country. Instances of engagement policies designed to support specific ideological groups in other countries are much greater in number.

81. The following two paragraphs are drawn from Mark L. Haas, "Turkey and the Arab Spring: Ideological Promotion in a Revolutionary Era," in Haas and Lesch, eds., *The Arab Spring*, pp. 156–157.

82. The traditional security dilemma is a realist international relations concept that asserts that it is very difficult for one state to make itself feel safe without making a neighboring country feel less safe. When one state increases its military spending to enhance its security, others will feel more endangered.

83. C. J. Shivers and Robert F. Worth, "Seizure of Antiaircraft Missiles in Yemen Raises Fears That Iran is Arming Rebels There," *New York Times*, February 8, 2013.

84. Edward D. Mansfield and Jack Snyder, "Democratization and the Arab Spring," *International Interactions* 38, no. 5 (November 2012), p. 723.

85. Ibid.

86. Kenneth M. Pollack, "Democratizers? The Pursuit of Pluralism," in Pollack et al., *The Arab Awakening*, p. 90, emphasis in original.

87. Stephen R. Grand, "Democratization 101: Historical Lessons for the Arab Spring," in Pollack et al., *The Arab Awakening*, p. 21.

88. Byman, "Terrorism," pp. 77–78.

89. Byman, "Terrorism," pp. 80–81.

90. Marashi and Parsi, "The Gift and the Curse," p. 135.

91. Quoted in Marashi and Parsi, "The Gift and the Curse," p. 146.

92. "Egypt Leader Slams Syrian Regime During Iran Visit," Associated Press, August 30, 2012.

93. "Some See Turkey as a Useful Model for New Arab Regimes," Agence France Presse, February 5, 2012. For similar polling data, see "Erdogan Most Popular Leader by Far Among Arabs," Inter Press Service, November 21, 2011.

94. "Emerging Arab Islamists Look to 'Turkish Model,'" *Daily News Egypt*, December 4, 2011; Asef Bayat, "Arab Revolts: Islamists Aren't Coming!," *Insight Turkey* 13, no. 2 (2011): 12–13.

95. Both quotations are from Anthony Shadid, "In Riddle of Mideast Upheaval, Turkey Offers Itself as an Answer," *New York Times*, September 26, 2011. This analysis is drawn from Haas, "Turkey and the Arab Spring," pp. 164–165.

96. Quoted in Mustafa Akyol, "The Problem with 'Zero Problems,'" *New York Times*, November 15, 2011; Gonul Tol, "Ankara Is Trying to Have It Both Ways," *New York Times*, November 15, 2011.

97. "Senior Adviser to Iran's Supreme Leader Says Turkey's Secularism Not Suitable for Arab States," AlArabiya.net, December 13, 2011; "Paper looks into Regional Competition between Turkey, Iran," BBC Monitoring Europe, October 18, 2011.

98. Haas, "Turkey and the Arab Spring," p. 166.

99. Marashi and Parsi, "The Gift and the Curse," pp. 141–142.

100. Haas, "Turkey and the Arab Spring," p. 166.

101. Quoted in Lizza, "The Consequentialist."

102. Jack S. Levy, "Domestic Politics and War," *Journal of Interdisciplinary Research* 18 (1988), p. 654.

103. For an analysis of ideology-based frictions between the United States and Saudi Arabia after the end of the cold war, see Haas, *The Clash of Ideologies*, pp. 242–249, 271–272.

104. See, for example, the scoring by Freedom House at http://www.freedom house.org/country/iraq.

105. C. J. Shivers, "Looted Libyan Arms in Mali May have Shifted Conflict's Path," *New York Times*, February 7, 2013.

106. Sheri Berman, "The Promise of the Arab Spring," *Foreign Affairs* 92, no. 1 (January/February 2013), pp. 64–74.

107. See Ron Nixon, "U.S. Groups Helped Nurture Arab Uprisings," *New York Times*, April 14, 2011.

108. Grand, "Democratization 101," pp. 27–28.

109. A prime example of this last policy in action is the King Abdullah University of Science and Technology (KAUST), which was founded in Saudi Arabia in 2009. KAUST is the first of several new universities that are scheduled to be built in the kingdom, all of which will focus not on religious studies, but applied sciences. KAUST is

Saudi Arabia's first co-ed university, and others plan to be so as well. The Saudis contracted with leading US universities to provide curricular, research, and faculty-hiring help.

110. David Adesnik and Michael McFaul, "Engaging Autocratic Allies to Promote Democracy," *Washington Quarterly* 29, no. 2 (Spring 2006), pp. 7–26.

111. Shivers, "Looted Libyan Arms in Mali May have Shifted Conflict's Path."

112. For greater analysis on this issue, see David W. Lesch, "The Risks of Going into Syria," *Current History* (November 2012), pp. 299–304.

113. For details, see Haas, *The Clash of Ideologies*, pp. 260–264.

ABOUT THE EDITORS
AND CONTRIBUTORS

Ali R. Abootalebi is associate professor of Middle Eastern and international studies at the University of Wisconsin–Eau Claire. He is the author of *Islam and Democracy: State-Society Relations in Developing Countries, 1980–1994* (2000) and more than thirty articles on Iran and the Middle East.

Robert J. Allison chairs the History Department at Suffolk University in Boston. He is the author of *The Crescent Obscured: The United States and the Muslim World, 1776–1815* (2000) and *Stephen Decatur: American Naval Hero 1779–1820* (2005).

Jon B. Alterman is director of the Middle East program at the Center for Strategic and International Studies in Washington.

Henri J. Barkey is the Bernard and Bertha Cohen Professor of International Relations at Lehigh University. He previously served on the US State Department's Policy Planning Staff (1998–2000), working on issues related to the Eastern Mediterranean and the Middle East. Currently he is a nonresident senior associate at the Carnegie Endowment for International Peace. Among his recent publications are *Turkey's New Engagement in Iraq: Embracing Iraqi Kurdistan* (2010) and "Turkey's Moment of Inflection" (*Survival*, 2010).

Sir Sam Falle is a retired British diplomat. He served in Iran from 1949 to 1952, in Lebanon from 1952 to 1955, on the Middle East oil desk in London from 1955 to 1957, and in Iraq from 1957 to 1961. He was ambassador to Kuwait from 1969 to 1970, and he has also been ambassador to Sweden and high commissioner to Singapore and Nigeria. His remarkable autobiography is entitled *My Lucky Life, in War, Revolution, Peace, and Diplomacy* (1996).

Robert O. Freedman is the Peggy Meyerhoff Pearlstone Professor of Political Science Emeritus at Baltimore Hebrew University and visiting professor of political science at Johns Hopkins University, where he teaches courses on the Arab-Israeli conflict and Russian foreign policy. Among his publications are *Moscow and the Middle East* (1991), *Israel Under Rabin* (1995), and *The Middle East Enters the 21st Century* (2002).

Mark Gasiorowski is professor of political science and international studies at Louisiana State University. His books include *Mohammad Mossadeq and the 1953 Coup in Iran* (coeditor, 2004), *US Foreign Policy and the Shah: Building a Client State in Iran* (1991), and *Neither East nor West* (coeditor, 1990).

F. Gregory Gause III is professor of political science at the University of Vermont. Among his publications are *The International Relations of the Persian Gulf* (2010), *Oil Monarchies: Domestic and Security Challenges in the Arab Gulf States* (1994), and *Saudi-Yemeni Relations: Domestic Structures and Foreign Influence* (1990).

James Gelvin is professor of history at the University of California–Los Angeles. He is the author of *Divided Loyalties: Nationalism and Mass Politics in Syria at the Close of Empire* (1998), *The Modern Middle East: A History* (2004), and *The Israel-Palestine Conflict: One Hundred Years of War* (2005).

Fawaz A. Gerges is a professor of Middle Eastern politics and international relations at the London School of Economics and Political Science. He also holds the Emirates Chair of the Contemporary Middle East and is the director of the Middle East Centre at LSE. His publications include *The Far Enemy: Why Jihad Went Global* (2005), *America and Political Islam: Clash of Cultures or Clash of Interests?* (2000), and *The Superpowers and the Middle East: Regional and International Politics, 1955–1967* (1994).

Heather S. Gregg is an assistant professor at the Naval Postgraduate School. She is the author of several articles on al-Qa'ida and is a coeditor of *The Three Circles of War: Understanding the Dynamics of Conflict in Iraq* (2010).

Mark L. Haas is an associate professor of political science at Duquesne University in Pittsburgh. Among his publications are *Ideologies and American Security in the Middle East* (2012) and *The Ideological Origins of Great Power Politics, 1789–1989* (2005).

Yvonne Yazbeck Haddad is professor of the history of Islam and Christian-Muslim relations at the Center for Muslim-Christian Understanding at Georgetown University. She has published numerous books and articles on Islam, including *Contemporary Islam and the Challenge of History* (1982) and *The Islamic Impact* (1984).

Peter Hahn is professor of history and department chair at Ohio State University and executive director of the Society for Historians of American Foreign Relations. Among his books are *Missions Accomplished? The United States and Iraq Since World War I* (2011), *Historical Dictionary of US-Middle East Relations* (2007), and *Crisis and Crossfire: The United States and the Middle East Since 1945* (2005).

Rashid Khalidi is the Edward Said Professor of Arab Studies in the History Department at Columbia University. He was president of the Middle East Studies Association and advised the Palestinian delegation to the Madrid and Washington Arab-Israeli peace negotiations from October 1991 until June 1993. His books include *Sowing Crisis: American Dominance and the Cold War in the Middle East* (2009), *The Iron Cage: The Story of the Palestinian Struggle for Statehood* (2006), and *Resurrecting Empire: Western Footprints and America's Perilous Path in the Middle East* (2004).

Paul W. T. Kingston is associate professor of political science at the University of Toronto, Scarborough College. A specialist on Middle East development policy during the immediate post–World War II period, he is the author of *Debating Development: Britain and the Politics of Modernization in the Middle East, 1945–1958* (1996).

David W. Lesch is professor of Middle East history at Trinity University in San Antonio, Texas. Among his books are the following: *The Arab-Israeli Conflict: A History* (2008), *The New Lion of Damascus: Bashar al-Asad and Modern Syria* (2005), and *1979: The Year That Shaped the Modern Middle East* (2001).

Georgiy Mirsky is a distinguished scholar at the Institute of World Economy and International Relations in Moscow. He is the author of numerous books and articles in Russian and English, and he has advised Soviet and Russian leaders.

Malik Mufti is associate professor of political science at Tufts University. He is the author of *Sovereign Creations: Pan-Arabism and Political Order in Syria and Iraq* (1996), as well as articles on Turkey and Jordan in the *Middle East Journal* and *Comparative Political Studies*.

Elie Podeh is associate professor in the Department of Islam and Middle Eastern Studies at the Hebrew University of Jerusalem. Among his publications are *The Decline of Arab Unity: The Rise and Fall of the United Arab Republic* (1999), *The Arab-Israeli Conflict in Israeli History Textbooks, 1948–2000* (2002), and *The Politics of National Celebrations in the Arab World* (2011).

Shannon Powers is a doctoral candidate in political science at George Washington University with a specialization in the field of international affairs.

Jeremy Pressman is the Alan R. Bennett Honors Professor of political science at the University of Connecticut. He is the author of *Warring Friends* (2008) and coauthor of *Point of No Return: The Deadly Struggle for Middle East Peace* (1997).

William B. Quandt is the Edward R. Stettinius Professor of Politics at the University of Virginia. He served as a staff member on the National Security Council from 1972 to 1974 and participated in the negotiations that led to the Camp David Accords and the Egyptian-Israeli peace treaty from 1977 to 1979. Among his many books are *Peace Process: American Diplomacy and the Arab-Israeli Conflict Since 1967* (third edition, 2005) and *Camp David: Peacemaking and Politics* (1986).

Bernard Reich is professor of political science and international affairs at George Washington University. His books include *The United States and Israel: Influence in the Special Relationship* (1984), *Securing the Covenant: United States–Israel Relations After the Cold War* (1995), and *A Brief History of Israel* (second edition, 2008).

Gary Sick is the executive director of the Gulf/2000 project at Columbia University, a research and documentation program. He was the principal White House aide for Iran on the National Security Council staff at the time of the Iranian revolution and hostage crisis and is the author of two books on US Persian Gulf policy.

Janice Gross Stein is Belzberg Professor of Conflict Management and the director of the Munk Center for International Studies at the University of Toronto. She has published a number of articles and books on Middle East affairs and international relations, including *We All Lost the Cold War* (1984) and *Peace-Making in the Middle East: Problems and Prospects* (1985).

Marvin G. Weinbaum is professor emeritus of political science at the University of Illinois at Urbana-Champaign. From 1999 to 2003 he served as senior analyst on Pakistan and Afghanistan in the Bureau of Intelligence and Research at the US State Department. He is currently a scholar in residence at the Middle East Institute. Among his numerous publications are the following books: *Afghanistan and Pakistan: Resistance and Reconstruction* (1994) and *South Asia Approaches the Millennium: Reexamining National Security* (coeditor, 1995).

Steve A. Yetiv is University Professor of Political Science at Old Dominion University. He is the author of *Explaining Foreign Policy* (second edition, 2011), *Crude Awakenings* (2004), and *The Petroleum Triangle* (2011).

INDEX

CPSIA information can be obtained at www.ICGtesting.com
Printed in the USA
LVOW10s0953161115

462749LV00004B/7/P

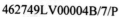